G. W. Anderson is Professor of Hebrew and
Old Testament Studies at the University of
Edinburgh.

TRADITION AND
INTERPRETATION

TRADITION AND INTERPRETATION

*Essays by Members of
the Society for
Old Testament Study*

EDITED BY

G. W. ANDERSON

CLARENDON PRESS • OXFORD
1979

Oxford University Press, Walton Street, Oxford OX2 6DP

OXFORD LONDON GLASGOW
NEW YORK TORONTO MELBOURNE WELLINGTON
NAIROBI DAR ES SALAAM CAPE TOWN
KUALA LUMPUR SINGAPORE JAKARTA HONG KONG TOKYO
DELHI BOMBAY CALCUTTA MADRAS KARACHI

*Published in the United States by
Oxford University Press, New York*

© *Oxford University Press 1979*

British Library Cataloguing in Publication Data
Tradition and interpretation.
 1. Bible. Old Testament – Criticism, interpretation, etc.
 I. Anderson, George Wishart II. Society for Old Testament Study
221   BS1171.2   78–40252

ISBN 0–19–826315–5

Typeset by CCC, printed and bound in Great Britain by William Clowes,
Beccles and London

PREFACE

THIS collection of essays is the successor of *The People and the Book* (1925), edited by A. S. Peake, *Record and Revelation* (1938), edited by H. Wheeler Robinson, and *The Old Testament and Modern Study* (1951), edited by H. H. Rowley. Like these earlier volumes, it seeks to give a general account of the present position in the various branches of Old Testament study. The essays are all by members of the Society for Old Testament Study, including two distinguished Honorary Members, Professor Henri Cazelles and Professor Walther Zimmerli.

Various difficulties have delayed the production of the volume, which is now published considerably later than was originally planned. In expressing his regrets and apologies for the protracted delay, the Editor wishes to put on record the fact that the bulk of the material was in his hands by the end of 1974.

Thanks are due to the Revd. A. Graeme Auld, M.A., B.D., PH.D., Lecturer in Hebrew and Old Testament Studies in the University of Edinburgh, and to Mlle Claudine M. Dauphin, M.A., PH.D., F.S.A.(Scot.), sometime Tweedie Fellow of the University of Edinburgh, who translated the essays by Professor Zimmerli and Professor Cazelles respectively, and to the Revd. Martin Reid, who compiled the Indexes.

The Society is indebted to the Oxford University Press for undertaking the publication of the volume. The Editor wishes to express his own appreciation of the help and patient consideration which he has received from the Publishers. He also wishes to record his gratitude to the Society for inviting him to edit this volume and to the contributors for their co-operation.

G. W. A.

CONTENTS

CONTRIBUTORS

P. R. Ackroyd, M.A., M.TH., PH.D., D.D., Samuel Davidson Professor of Old Testament Studies, University of London, King's College.

G. W. Anderson, M.A., D.D., TEOL.D., F.B.A., F.R.S.E., Professor of Hebrew and Old Testament Studies, University of Edinburgh.

J. Barr, M.A., D.D., F.B.A., Regius Professor of Hebrew, University of Oxford.

F. F. Bruce, M.A., D.D., F.B.A., formerly Rylands Professor of Biblical Criticism and Exegesis, Victoria University of Manchester.

H. Cazelles, PH.D., D.TH., Professeur d'Exégèse de l'Ancien Testament à la Faculté de Théologie, Directeur de la Section Biblique, Institut Catholique de Paris.

R. E. Clements, M.A., B.D., PH.D., Lecturer in Divinity, University of Cambridge, Fellow of Fitzwilliam College.

J. H. Eaton, M.A., Reader in Old Testament Studies, University of Birmingham.

J. A. Emerton, M.A., D.D., Regius Professor of Divinity, University of Cambridge, Fellow of St. John's College.

J. Gray, M.A., PH.D., D.D., Professor of Hebrew and Semitic Languages, University of Aberdeen.

W. McKane, M.A., B.D., PH.D., Professor of Hebrew and Semitic Languages, University of St. Andrews.

E. W. Nicholson, M.A., B.D., PH.D., D.D., Lecturer in Divinity, University of Cambridge, Dean of Pembroke College.

J. R. Porter, M.A., Professor of Theology, University of Exeter.

[1] B. J. Roberts, M.A., D.D., Professor Emeritus of Hebrew and Biblical Studies, University College of North Wales, Bangor.

W. Zimmerli, D.THEOL., D.D., Professor Emeritus für Altes Testament an der Universität Göttingen.

[1] Professor Roberts died on 11 August 1977.

ABBREVIATIONS

AASF	Annales Academiae Scientiarum Fennicae
AASOR	*Annual of the American Schools of Oriental Research*
AB	Analecta Biblica
AJSL	*American Journal of Semitic Languages and Literatures*
AncB	Anchor Bible
ANEP	J. B. Pritchard (ed.), *The Ancient Near East in Pictures Relating to the Old Testament*, 2nd edn., 1969.
ANET	J. B. Pritchard (ed.), *Ancient Near Eastern Texts Relating to the Old Testament*, 3rd edn., 1969
AnO	Analecta Orientalia
ANVAO	Avhandlinger utgitt av Det Norske Videnskaps-Akademi i Oslo
AOAT	Alter Orient und Altes Testament
AOTS	D. Winton Thomas (ed.), *Archaeology and Old Testament Study*, 1967
ASTI	*Annual of the Swedish Theological Institute*
ATANT	Abhandlungen zur Theologie des Alten und Neuen Testaments
ATD	Das Alte Testament Deutsch
ATh	Arbeiten zur Theologie
AUSS	Andrews University Seminary Studies
BA	*The Biblical Archaeologist*
BASOR	*Bulletin of the American Schools of Oriental Research*
BBB	Bonner Biblische Beiträge
BEvTh	Beiträge zur Evangelischen Theologie
BH	R. Kittel (ed.), *Biblia Hebraica*
BHS	K. Elliger and W. Rudolph (eds.), *Biblia Hebraica Stuttgartensia*
Bibl.	*Biblica*
BJRL	*Bulletin of the John Rylands Library*
BKAT	Biblischer Kommentar: Altes Testament
BOT	De Boeken van het Oude Testament
BSOAS	*Bulletin of the School of Oriental and African Studies*
BWANT	Beiträge zur Wissenschaft vom Alten und Neuen Testament

BWAT	Beiträge zur Wissenschaft vom Alten Testament
BZ	*Biblische Zeitschrift*
BZAW	Beihefte zur *Zeitschrift für die alttestamentliche Wissenschaft*
CAH	*Cambridge Ancient History*
CBQ	*Catholic Biblical Quarterly*
CHB	*Cambridge History of the Bible*
CRAIBL	*Comptes rendus de l'Académie des Inscriptions et Belles Lettres*
CTA	A. Herdner (ed.), *Corpus de tablettes en cunéiformes alphabétiques découvertes à Ras-Shamra-Ugarit de 1929 à 1939*, 1963
CTM	*Concordia Theological Monthly*
DOTT	D. Winton Thomas (ed.), *Documents from Old Testament Times*, 1958
EchtB	Echter Bibel
EJ	*Encyclopaedia Judaica*
ET	*Expository Times*
ETL	*Ephemerides Theologicae Lovanienses*
ETr	English Translation
EvTh	*Evangelische Theologie*
EVV	English Versions
FRLANT	Forschungen zur Religion und Literatur des Alten und Neuen Testaments
GSAT	*Gesammelte Studien zum Alten Testament*
HAT	Handbuch zum Alten Testament
HdO	*Handbuch der Orientalistik*
HibJ	*Hibbert Journal*
HTR	*Harvard Theological Review*
HUCA	*Hebrew Union College Annual*
IB	*The Interpreter's Bible*
ICC	The International Critical Commentary
IDB	*The Interpreter's Dictionary of the Bible*
IEJ	*Israel Exploration Journal*
JAOS	*Journal of the American Oriental Society*
JBL	*Journal of Biblical Literature*
JCS	*Journal of Cuneiform Studies*
JE	*Jewish Encyclopedia*

JEA	*Journal of Egyptian Archaeology*
JNES	*Journal of Near Eastern Studies*
JPOS	*Journal of the Palestine Oriental Society*
JQR	*Jewish Quarterly Review*
JSJ	*Journal for the Study of Judaism in the Persian, Hellenistic and Roman Periods*
JSS	*Journal of Semitic Studies*
JTC	*Journal for Theology and the Church*
JTS	*Journal of Theological Studies*
KAI	H. Donner and W. Röllig (eds.), *Kanaanäische und Aramäische Inschriften* i, 1962; ii, iii, 1964
KS	*Kleine Schriften*
LUÅ	Lunds Universitets Årsskrift
MT	Massoretic Text
NCB	New Century Bible
NEB	*New English Bible*
NedTT	*Nederlands Theologisch Tijdschrift*
NTT	*Norsk Teologisk Tidsskrift*
OA	*Oriens Antiquus*
Or	*Orientalia*
OTMS	H. H. Rowley (ed.), *The Old Testament and Modern Study*, 1951
OTS	*Oudtestamentische Studiën*
PEFQS	*Quarterly Statement of the Palestine Exploration Fund*
PEQ	*Palestine Exploration Quarterly*
PIW	S. Mowinckel, *The Psalms in Israel's Worship*, i, ii, 1962
PJB	*Palästina Jahrbuch des deutschen evangelischen Instituts für Altertumswissenschaft des Heiligen Landes zu Jerusalem*
POTT	D. J. Wiseman (ed.), *Peoples of Old Testament Times*, 1973
PRU	*Le Palais royal d'Ugarit*
QDAP	*Quarterly of the Department of Antiquities of Palestine*
RA	*Revue d'Assyriologie et d'Archéologie orientale*
RB	*Revue Biblique*
REJ	*Revue des Études Juives*

RGG	*Die Religion in Geschichte und Gegenwart.* Unless otherwise stated, references are to 3rd edn., 1957–65
RHR	*Revue de l'Histoire des Religions*
RSR	*Recherches de Science Religieuse*
RThPh	*Revue de Théologie et de Philosophie*
RV	*Revised Version*
SBT	Studies in Biblical Theology
SDB	L. Pirot, A. Robert, H. Cazelles, A. Feuillet (eds.), *Supplément au Dictionnaire de la Bible*, 1928–
SBU	*Svenskt Bibliskt Uppslagsverk*
SEÅ	*Svensk Exegetisk Årsbok*
SJk	*Schriften zur Judentumskunde*
SNVAO	Skrifter utgitt av Det Norske Videnskaps-Akademi i Oslo
SS	Studi Semitici
SSN	Studia Semitica Neerlandica
StTh	*Studia Theologica*
SVT	Supplements to Vetus Testamentum
TC	Torch Commentary
ThB	Theologische Bücherei
ThS	Theologische Studien
ThZ	*Theologische Zeitschrift*
TLZ	*Theologische Literaturzeitung*
TR	*Theologische Rundschau*
ÜGS	M. Noth, *Überlieferungsgeschichtliche Studien I*, 1943, 1967
UT	C. H. Gordon, *Ugaritic Textbook*, AnO xxxviii, 1965
UUÅ	Uppsala Universitets Årsskrift
VT	*Vetus Testamentum*
WMANT	Wissenschaftliche Monographien zum Alten und Neuen Testament
WO	*Die Welt des Orients*
WZ	*Wissenschaftliche Zeitschrift der Karl Marx-Universität Leipzig*
ZA	*Zeitschrift fur Assyriologie*
ZAW	*Zeitschrift für die alttestamentliche Wissenschaft*
ZDMG	*Zeitschrift der deutschen morgenländischen Gesellschaft*
ZThK	*Zeitschrift für Theologie und Kirche*

INTRODUCTION

CHANGING PERSPECTIVES IN
OLD TESTAMENT STUDY

WHEN the predecessor of this volume, *The Old Testament and Modern Study*, appeared in 1951, the task of renewing international communication and co-operation in Old Testament research after the difficulties of the war years was already well under way. An immense amount of work remained to be done on the new material which had become available in the years between the wars, of which the discoveries at Ras Shamra were the most important; and, shortly before the period covered by the present volume, the sensational finds at Qumran brought to light manuscript riches which opened up new perspectives both in the history of the text of the Old Testament and in the varieties of sectarian belief and practice in early Judaism. Discoveries apart, important developments in various fields of Old Testament research, which had been initiated before the outbreak of war and continued during the years of restricted communication between scholars, had now to be assessed and taken further.

The *cacoethes emendandi* which had distorted textual criticism of the Old Testament for two generations or more had begun to be replaced by an enhanced respect for the received Hebrew text. From sundry quarters, assaults had been made on some of the most widely accepted conclusions of source criticism, and, more constructively, important attempts had been made to use the techniques of form and tradition criticism to reconstruct the development and interrelations of the hypothetical written sources and to assess the extent and nature of oral tradition. Some scholars, indeed, assigned a dominant and creative role to oral tradition in certain types of literature, notably in some of the prophetic books, which, it was alleged, contained material which had been transmitted, expanded, arranged, and interpreted within circles of prophetic disciples. In the origin, formation, and content of the literature, much was attributed to the influence of cultic patterns, not only in the Psalms, where it was most natural to expect such influence to be operative, but in some parts of the prophetic literature and of the Pentateuch. In the study of Israelite religion, cultic practice, illuminated by increasing knowledge of that of Israel's neighbours, had come into the centre of the discussion; and, in this connection, the religious status and functions of the monarchy in Israel, or in Judah as distinct from Israel, had assumed a special though disputed importance. As, on the one hand, attempts to reconstruct Israel's religion in terms of a quasi-evolutionary development were opposed by theories of myth and ritual patterns and the like, so, on the other hand, there were those who held that the record of Israel's religious history could provide characteristic and distinctive material for a theological structure which was not predetermined by later dogmatic formulas but representative of the entire range of Israelite faith and worship. The stream of publications seeking to rehabilitate Old Testament Theology as a legitimate branch of scientific study had not yet reached full flood; but some Old Testament Theologies had already appeared, of which the massive tripartite work by W. Eichrodt was the most influential. Furthermore, ever since, in the 1920s, biblical study had felt the impact of the Barthian theology, attention had been paid, somewhat spasmodically, to the problems of Old Testament interpretation in ways which were designed to go beyond the conclusions of critical exegesis.

Thus, a generation ago, the situation in practically the entire field of Old Testament research was the very antithesis of stalemate. New materials were being interpreted and co-ordinated and new lines of inquiry were being pursued with intense interest and energy. In the period covered by the present volume, though there has been no flagging of either interest or energy, the emphases and perspectives have changed.

The new manuscript discoveries have made available to the textual critic a wealth of material such as would have seemed beyond all the bounds of likelihood. As often happens, however, wealth has brought its attendant problems. It is now clear that the history of the Hebrew text of the Old Testament was more complex than had been realized. It is unthinkable that any responsible textual scholar would today indulge in the uncritical reliance on the Versions or the undisciplined excesses of conjectural emendation which were once fashionable. Further, the involved history of the Septuagint and the other ancient Greek Versions and of their relation to the Hebrew textual tradition rules out of court the use of a Greek text to reconstruct a presumed original Hebrew without scrupulous regard to the character of that Greek text and its internal history and problems. In the approach to textual difficulties there is no simple rule of thumb. In each instance all the available facts must be accurately assessed and handled with critical judgement. This caution implies that the renewed confidence in the Massoretic Text, to which reference was made above, may have to be qualified but has not been undermined. The situation is to some extent reflected in the contrast between the third and subsequent editions of Kittel's *Biblia Hebraica* and the *Biblia Hebraica Stuttgartensia*. It is noteworthy, however, that recent translations of the Old Testament into English contain more departures from the MT than might have been expected from the current state of textual criticism.

In the philological field there has of late been a renewed concern about the application of sound method in the appropriation, for the elucidation of biblical Hebrew, of the store of philological material now available from many quarters, ranging from Ugarit in the north to the southern extremities of the Arabian peninsula and to Ethiopia. Imaginative exploitation of these resources can provide new meanings for old words, achieving for the text in translation a face-lift as startling as that which daring conjectural emendation contrives for the original. Due recognition of geographical and chronological gaps between the extra-biblical and the biblical material under discussion should induce an attitude of caution. Nevertheless, there has been, and will doubtless continue to be, a steady enrichment of our knowledge of Hebrew, derived from the cognate languages, an enrichment which is bound, subtly and indirectly, to extend to every other area of Old Testament study. Nor is it only from the broad field of comparative Semitic philology that such resources may be derived. The continuing history of Hebrew, especially in the Mishnaic period, has its own contribution to make. Considerable advances remain to be achieved in the understanding of the syntax of biblical poetry; but where the stimulus of new data has produced unduly daring hypotheses, there may well be a need for strategic retreat.

In no area has change been more rapid, more sensational, or more vividly brought to the attention of the public, than in archaeology; and in none is it harder to maintain a sense of balance and perspective and a recognition of the all-important distinction between fact and interpretation. This is not the place to attempt to summarize, even in the sketchiest way, the discoveries and developments which are described elsewhere in this volume. Two points, however, may be noted. The first is the increased refinement and precision in technique, by means of which more exact and reliable inferences may be drawn from the results of excavation. The most familiar example of this is the use of radiocarbon dating for the establishment of a more satisfactory chronology. The second point is the continuing debate concerning the correlation or conflict between archaeological evidence and the biblical records, a debate in which the problems of the patriarchal narratives and of the date and character of the settlement of the Israelites in Canaan have been specially prominent, and which has been associated particularly with the opposing views of Alt and Noth on the one hand and of the school of Albright on the other. It is obvious that enthusiasm for the corroboration by archaeology of biblical evidence may lead to hasty and tendentious conclusions. The problem of relating the two is intensified by the rapid accumulation of fresh archaeological material, so that constant reappraisal is necessary, and by the complex literary character of many of the biblical records. If it be argued that, to preserve scientific objectivity from the distorting influence of an apologetic interest, archaeology must maintain a certain detachment from the study of Old Testament history, it is nevertheless true that the Old Testament historian must take stock of the relevant results of archaeological research, though they may complicate some problems as well as helping to bring others nearer to solution.

Unlike its two predecessors, *The Old Testament and Modern Study* did not include any essay on the history of ancient Israel. The present volume includes two: one on the pre-exilic period, the other on its exilic and post-exilic sequel. This marks both a renewal of interest and also significant changes in approach. Particular attention has been devoted during the period covered by this volume to the nature, structure, and development of the ancient Israelite community. The much debated word 'Hebrew' is by some understood in sociological rather than ethnological terms. In the understanding of pre-monarchic Israel, Noth's hypothesis of an amphictyony has continued to exercise considerable influence, but has also been subjected to varied criticisms. In recent years, the history of individual tribes has been the subject of detailed research. Such investigations are inevitably intricate, because of the problems of disentangling sources, reconstructing the history of traditions, and settling the relevant topographical questions. At a somewhat later and more sophisticated stage in Israel's communal and political development, attention has been directed to the monarchy as a channel of foreign influence, the nature of the hierarchy of court officials, and the special character of the royal cities. A generation ago, various factors, such as the reaction against late dating of many of the documents, had led to a concentration of interest in pre-exilic Israel. There has now been a revival of research in the exilic and post-exilic periods. New archaeological material has enabled us to gain a clearer and more detailed picture of events and conditions during certain phases of those periods. In particular, new light on developments and personalities in the northern part of Palestine and on the history of the Samaritan textual tradition have contributed to a reappraisal of the so-called Samaritan Schism.

One of the most striking features of the revival of interest in post-exilic developments is the spate of books and articles devoted to the analysis and interpretation of the work of the Chronicler. The day is long past when it could be dismissed as simply an inaccurate and tendentious piece of history writing, providing little or no reliable information which was not already available elsewhere in the Old Testament. As a record of historical fact it is certainly not impeccable; but in important ways it supplements the books of Samuel and Kings and, perhaps even more important, it is a substantial corpus of Old Testament historiography, presenting a distinctive understanding of the religious character of Israel's life.

The character of Old Testament historiography in its ancient Near Eastern setting has during our period been a major preoccupation of students of Old Testament literature and thought. This fact is reflected in the title and approach of the essay in the present volume which deals with the historical books. In addition to the continuing work of source analysis, form criticism, and the like, much has been made of the element of theological interpretation in the historical compilations contained in the Old Testament. It has been claimed that Israel's faith in Yahweh's purposive action in history produced in Israel a kind of historical record to which there was no parallel among Israel's neighbours. This claim is closely linked with the contention that the saving acts of God in history constitute the substance of Old Testament Theology, and that, accordingly, history is in the Old Testament the supreme medium of revelation. As there has been a reaction against the latter view, so the former has been strenuously challenged. It has been pointed out that not only in Israel but elsewhere in the ancient Near East historical events were described in terms of divine action. This is an understandable and necessary corrective to a view which has sometimes been incautiously and even crudely formulated. However, even when all points of similarity with other records are admitted, the distinctive character of much of the historical material in the Old Testament cannot be denied, though it must be defined with caution.

Throughout most areas of Old Testament literature, form-critical techniques have continued to be applied with unabated zeal. Indeed, some of the most recent developments in the study of the Pentateuch might be taken to threaten a dissolution of the older pattern of source analysis, which, if it came about, would be an ironically inappropriate celebration of the centenary of the first publication of Wellhausen's masterpiece. Following on Noth's pioneering researches into the tradition history of the historical compilations (the Pentateuch, the Deuteronomistic Work, and the Chronistic Work), the older formulation of questions about the growth and structure of the Pentateuch or Hexateuch has had to give way to a more complex set of problems. Not the least perplexing of these is whether we must conclude that the Tetrateuch (Genesis–Numbers) is a truncated corpus, the climactic conclusion of which has been lost, or that elements of that conclusion are to be found in the Deuteronomistic history. At all events, the main lines of Noth's view concerning the latter work seem to be generally accepted.

Deuteronomy itself, the linchpin of the older Pentateuchal criticism, has become the subject of renewed attention. The range of its creative influence is seen as so extensive that it is not entirely out of place to speak of a pan-Deuteronomic phase in Old Testament study. One of the most important aspects of this development is the claim that there are signs in the prophetic corpus of a far-reaching Deuteronomic redaction. This approach to the prophetic literature has in part replaced the preoccupation with the respective roles of oral tradition and scribal transmission which obtained about a generation ago. In the study of the prophetic movement itself, there has been, and continues to be, much debate about the role and functions of the prophet. Guidelines to the debate are difficult to establish, because of the variety of prophetic types which appear to have existed in Israel; but discussion has in the main been concentrated on the relation of the prophets to the covenant and to the cult.

The widely accepted view that prophecy was the parent of Apocalyptic was vigorously challenged during our period by von Rad, who held that the apocalypses reveal much more clearly the influence of Wisdom. In spite of the validity of some of the points which he made, his argument, taken as a whole, lacks cogency and has failed to gain general assent. However different Apocalyptic may be from prophecy (and the differences are real and manifest), there can be little doubt that its true lineage is to be found in that quarter. As the relevant essays in the present volume indicate, much new work has been done in the study of both Apocalyptic and

Wisdom, particularly the latter, for which there is an abundance of comparable material extant from the surrounding cultures.

During our period, the study of the Psalms has continued to be dominated by the influence of Gunkel and Mowinckel and enriched by material from Ugarit. The application of form-critical methods has been extended and in some respects made more precise. Further attempts have been made to reconstruct the patterns of Israel's festal worship and to delineate the status and functions of cultic prophet and sacral king, though scepticism about the existence of such persons has not been wholly dispelled.

These latter questions do not, of course, belong solely to the study of the Psalms (though much of the relevant evidence is to be found there) but to the history and phenomenology of Israel's religion. Indeed, at the beginning of our period the concept of sacral kingship seemed to some to occupy a commanding position. Soon, however, the covenant concept (or concepts) attracted renewed attention in a wide-ranging and complex debate which is lucidly outlined in Professor Zimmerli's contribution to this volume. Views have varied so greatly in so short a time that it is difficult to maintain a clear perspective or to make a just assessment of theories which on the one hand make much of the parallels from suzerainty treaties or on the other assign the major impetus to Deuteronomy and the Deuteronomic school. It may be some time before a balanced and secure interpretation is possible; but the importance of achieving that is undeniable, since the concept(s) of covenant, together with that of kingship, are central in the Old Testament itself and also in its links with the New Testament.

The development of Old Testament Theology has been marked by sharp reaction against some of the views which were widely and confidently held at the beginning of our period, notably the alleged sharp antithesis between Hebrew and Greek modes of thought and, as has already been mentioned, the emphasis on the acts of God in history as constituting the substance of Old Testament Theology. The event of outstanding importance, however, has been the publication of von Rad's *Old Testament Theology*. Whereas

most of his twentieth-century predecessors had sought to
extract from the historical development of Israel's religion
those elements which are constant and representative and to
combine them in some more or less systematic presentation,
von Rad's treatment is based on the great compilations of
tradition and the major types of literature. Even if valid
criticisms may be levelled at his estimate of the historical
credo, his deliberate neglect of religious concepts, or his use of
typology, it remains true that his understanding of the nature,
the transmission, and the reinterpretation (sometimes the
radical reinterpretation) of the ancient traditions of Israel
gives vivid expression to the living relationship between
tradition and the continuing life of the community which
inherited and interpreted it. Without this awareness of the
interaction between tradition and interpretation the Old
Testament cannot be understood.

I

THE TEXTUAL TRANSMISSION OF THE OLD TESTAMENT

B. J. ROBERTS

By changing the traditional title, 'Textual Criticism' to 'Textual Transmission', the editor has recognized the change of character that has taken place in the topic during the past few years. In contrast to earlier attitudes the concern of the textualist now is to retain the Massoretic text wherever possible, not on grounds of dogma or a return to 'orthodoxy', but simply because of the misleading results produced by earlier approaches. Textual emendation is, of course, still a legitimate exercise, but it now demands acceptance of criteria reflecting a better understanding of the textual transmission.

I. NEW MATERIAL

During the past twenty-five years a substantial amount of new texts and material for textual study has become available, which needs to be surveyed before we embark on the actual topic of this essay. In order of priority, pride of place goes to the new critical editions of the text—this despite the current popularity of the Dead Sea Scrolls. The new texts are *Biblia Hebraica Stuttgartensia*[1] and the recent edition by the Hebrew University in Jerusalem, based on the *Aleppo Codex*.[2] The reason for the priority is that all other discoveries and hypotheses based on them are subservient to the basic Massoretic text which had become an authoritative text.

---

[1] The successor of *Biblia Hebraica*, 1937, and published by the Württembergische Bibelanstalt, Stuttgart, with *Liber Jesaiae*, ed. D. Winton Thomas as the first fascicle, 1968, now followed by several others. (Publication now complete: 1976. Ed.)

[2] See *The Book of Isaiah, Sample Edition*, by M. H. Goshen-Gottstein, 1965, and the Annual, *Textus*, the periodical produced for the *Hebrew University Bible Project*, ed. C. Rabin and later S. Talmon, 1960–9. See further, p. 15, n. 39.

Next came the Dead Sea Scrolls, which fall into two quite distinct groups, namely those from Qumran and those from Murabbaʿat and near-by sites not to be identified with Qumran. This sectarian provenance of Qumran texts puts them outside the main current of the Massoretic-type transmission, but the fact that they have a great deal in common with this transmission, together with their age, makes them highly significant.[3] On the other hand, the Murabbaʿat and related texts do belong to the Massoretic type, and give direct evidence about its early history—indeed they form the oldest extant specimens of this text.[4]

Third in the list are the texts and fragments of actual Massoretic remains from the Middle Ages. Among the complete texts are a series of what are technically known as Ben Asher texts, and mainly consist of the following: *The Cairo Codex of the Prophets* (A.D. 895), the *Aleppo Codex* (early tenth century A.D.), the *Leningrad Codex* (A.D. 1008), and a codex of the Pentateuch, *British Lib. Or. 4445*, (early tenth century A.D.). They will be discussed later in this survey. No less important for the period are manuscripts from a rival transmission, that of Ben Naphtali, which is represented by three *Erfurt Codices* now in Marburg and Tübingen. They belong, it is estimated, to the thirteenth and fourteenth centuries A.D., but a third manuscript is thought to belong to the period before A.D. 1100. Finally in this section, the *Petersburg Codex* of the Latter Prophets should be mentioned. It belongs to A.D. 916, was edited by H. L. Strack in 1876, and reissued, with a discussion of the background in 1971.[5]

---

[3] The relevant Qumran texts published to date are: *1Q Isa, The Dead Sea Scrolls of St. Mark's Monastery*, i. *The Isaiah Manuscript and the Habakkuk Commentary (1QpHab)*. ed. M. Burrows (with J. C. Trever and W. H. Brownlee), New Haven, 1950. *1Q Isb. The Dead Sea Scrolls of the Hebrew University*, ed. E. L. Sukenik, Jerusalem, 1955. *1Q fragments. Discoveries in the Judean Desert of Jordan*, i. *Qumran Cave 1*, ed. D. Barthélemy, O.P., and J. T. Milik, London, 1955; iii. *Les 'Petites Grottes' de Qumran. Cave 3*, 1962, ed. M. Baillet, J. T. Milik, R. de Vaux. iv. *The Psalm Scroll of Qumran, Cave 11*. ed. J. A. Sanders, 1967. See also J. A. Sanders, 'Palestinian Manuscripts, 1947–67'. *JBL* lxxxvi (1967), 431–40.

[4] Murrʾbbaʿat. Ditto, *Discoveries in the Judaean' Desert of Jordan*, ii. *Qumran—les grottes de Murabbaʿat*. Plates 56–73; Text, pp. 181–205, ed. P. Benoit, J. T. Milk, R. de Vaux, 1961.

[5] The reissue, with a Prolegomenon by P. Wernberg-Møller, is in the series The Library of Biblical Studies, ed. H. M. Orlinsky, published by Ktav Publishing

Finally, and sometimes sadly unproductive from the standpoint of the survey, the recent editions of printed Hebrew Bibles are mentioned.[6] The text of *Biblia Hebraica* (3rd edn., Stuttgart, 1937) was reproduced on numerous occasions, with corrections and additions—e.g. the addition in 1951 of variants from the Qumran Isaiah and Habakkuk scrolls. In 1958 a new text was edited by N. H. Snaith.[7] Hebrew Bibles from Jerusalem during recent years have had a mixed reception, though the eclectic text of the Qoren Bible is praised for its 'close scrutiny of previous editions, both manuscripts and printed, and masoretic lists'.[8] New materials from the Versions are best discussed in the appropriate section of the survey.

II. WRITING—EPIGRAPHY AND PALAEOGRAPHY

Although it strictly falls within the field of the archaeologist, it seems reasonable to include the topic of script transmission in the present survey, for it relates immediately to textual transmission. Again, since the script found on tablets (epigraphy) is the natural precursor (at least as far as archaeological discovery goes) of writing on papyrus or leather (palaeography), both are included here. Nevertheless, our main interest lies in the palaeography of the Dead Sea Scrolls as a source with direct relevance for the present survey, and one which provides a considerable body of evidence from the beginning of the Christian era.

But we must go farther back. In a symposium published in

House, New York. Among other important services rendered by the series are standard works dealing with the history of the Massora. It is a subject of growing significance, and will involve the student in a reassessment of many of the grammatical details of Hebrew. In the present context the following might be mentioned: S. Frensdorff, *Das Buch 'Ochlah w'Ochlah (Massora)*, Hanover, 1864, reissued by Ktav, New York, 1972; S. Frensdorff, *The Massorah Magna*, I, *Massoretic Dictionary*, Hanover and Leipzig, 1876, reissued with *Prolegomena* by G. E. Weil, New York, 1968.

[6] See H. M. Orlinsky, 'The Masoretic Text: A Critical Evaluation', Prolegomenon to C. D. Ginsburg, *Introduction to the Massoretico-Critical Edition of the Hebrew Bible* (London, 1897), New York, 1966, pp. i–xlv.

[7] Based on *B.Lib. Or. 2626–8*, and *Or. 2375* and *Shem Tob*. The edition will be discussed later.

[8] See H. M. Orlinsky, op. cit., p. xv.

1970,[9] Dr. Joseph Naveh shows how, from three alphabetic scripts, there developed in the eleventh century B.C. the linear form, the right-to-left direction, and the limitation of the alphabet to twenty-two consonants. The Hebrews took over this script from the Phoenicians until the ninth century, and then developed their own. The Aramaeans had also borrowed the same script in the eleventh or tenth century, and it is difficult to decide which script was used, e.g. for a tenth- or ninth-century inscription. This persisted, roughly, until the seventh century, when there are found some Aramaic forms infiltrating into Moabite-Hebrew writing; nevertheless jar-handles from Gibeon and a crude inscription from a cave at Beit Lei, near Lachish, show that in the sixth century B.C. the writing was still palaeo-Hebrew.

The change to the Aramaic script occurred, albeit without the complete disappearance of the older script, after the return from Exile, along with the introduction of Aramaic as an official language in the western parts of the Persian Empire. It is called Aramaic (after its origin) or 'square' (because of its shape), and was later recognized by the Rabbis as the only script suitable for the Scriptures. But the persistence of the archaic, Phoenician script is to be noted, because, along with some coins from the pre-Christian era, it figures quite prominently in manuscripts from Qumran and Murabba'at, as well as on coins from the Bar Cochba revolt in the second century A.D.

As a script form, the Phoenician retained its early features practically unchanged. A fragment of Leviticus in this script was claimed by S. A. Birnbaum[10] to belong to the fifth century B.C., though other renowned palaeographers argue for the third century. There are a number of other fragments with the same script from Cave 4, but not until their publication will it be possible, provided the reproduction is suitably clear, to scrutinize the letter-formations and so

[9] J. A. Sanders (ed.), *Near Eastern Archaeology in the Twentieth Century*, New York, 1970. See J. Naveh, 'The Scripts in Palestine and Transjordan in the Iron Age' (pp. 277-83); F. M. Cross, 'The Cave Inscriptions from Khirbet Beit Lei' (pp. 299-306).

[10] 'How Old are the Cave Manuscripts?' *VT* i (1951), 91-109. For a full treatment, see id., *The Qumran (Dead Sea) Scrolls and Palaeography, BASOR* Supplementary Studies, 13-14, 1952, and *The Hebrew Scripts*, London, 1954-7.

establish the point more convincingly. The enigma seems to be that, by comparison with other scripts, it is very unlikely that there had been no development if the script was in constant use; on the other hand a renaissance on 'nationalistic' grounds, in the third century B.C., would not explain the presence of the script in sectarian Qumran and the later opposition to it by the Rabbis. The problem is further complicated by the use of the Phoenician script for the Divine Name in some Greek manuscripts of the Septuagint during a long period from the second century B.C. until well into the Christian era.

The Aramaic script, of course, has received an immense accession of material through the scrolls, and it is well to remember that it was on palaeographical grounds that they were first identified. Dr. J. C. Trever (at the time a young scholar in the American School of Oriental Research in Jerusalem) saw the similarity of the script to the Nash Papyrus, dated in the first century B.C. (or, possibly, the following century). Subsequently all the Qumran and Murabba'at scripts were scrutinized, and various types[11] (on a chronological basis) and forms[12] (literary, official, and cursive) have been identified.

Finally, mention must be made of the two-volume study of the *Scribal Character of the Dead Sea Scrolls* [13] by Father M. Martin, S. J., which discusses in great detail a mass of linguistic and philological information based on Cave I material. One of the interesting questions raised by him is whether or not one might speak of a 'Qumran school of scribes' or something of the kind, but he concludes against it. Another problem is that of copying (was it 'from memory or from dictation') and the extent to which scribal errors can be attributed to either or both. There are abundant scribal errors in the scrolls and the scrutiny cannot but be instructive to the student of the actual Hebrew Massoretic text.

It is studies along these and similar lines that ultimately highlight the relevance of the biblical scrolls from the Dead

[11] See F. M. Cross, *Ancient Library of Qumran*, 2nd edn., New York, 1961, pp. 88–90.
[12] J. T. Milik, *Discoveries in the Judean Desert*, ii. 70 f.
[13] In the series Bibliothèque du Muséon, xliv, xlv, Louvain, 1958.

Sea region; they provide first-hand evidence of what happened in the actual transmission. Individual variant readings from them may or may not be relevant, but the activity of the scribes within the community is always relevant. Consequently the appeal to the Scrolls is for evidence of the significance of the archaic Phoenician script as well as the preponderance of the square Aramaic script, to show why it is now necessary to scrutinize the Hebrew text for possible errors on the basis of both scripts and not merely the latter. Secondly, the evidence of scribal activity gives some of the reasons for what later produced Massoretic activity within the orthodox transmission.

III. THE MASSORETIC TEXT

There has been a significant change in the attitude of scholars to the study of the Massora and its relationship to the text. The old view that the text was fixed in the second century A.D., and that it, and the accompanying Massora, were corrupted through the ages, has long been abandoned. Then came the view that the Massoretic text emerged in its final form in the Middle Ages, as the result of Massoretic activity in the academies, but now it is increasingly realized that the Massoretic text, in some form or other, indeed had an authoritative position at least in the time of the Bar Cochba revolt of A.D. 132–5 when copies of the scriptures used by the soldiers were as 'Massoretic' as any from a later time. Probably the best witness to it is the Murabba'at text of the Minor Prophets,[14] and its existence makes it difficult to accept the view that the Massoretic text was fixed only at the same time as the Canon at the Synod of Jamnia at the end of the first century A.D. Another indication of an early date for this text is found in the Qumran scroll *1QIsb*, the so-called 'second' Isaiah scroll. It is given a date *c.* A.D. 60, but its text is practically identical with the Massoretic.[15] Now, since the

---

[14] See *Discoveries in the Judaean Desert*, ii, col. viii. Also E. Würthwein, *Der Text des Alten Testaments*, 4th edn., Stuttgart, 1973, Table 16. This text is not to be confused with *Greek Text of the Minor Prophets* from the Dead Sea Scrolls.

[15] B. J. Roberts, 'The Second Isaiah Scroll from Qumran' (*1QIsb*), *BJRL* xlii (1959), 132–44.

text was current among the sectaries, it is highly unlikely that the Rabbis, a generation later, would select it for their 'fixed text'—such an idea flies in the face of any concept of sectarianism. A third pointer to the early existence of the Massoretic-type text comes again from Qumran. Most of the textual divergences in a large number of the scrolls are to be understood in relation to the Massoretic text, and not vice versa. And the conclusion is obvious, namely that the Massoretic-type text was in existence before Qumran. It should be noted, however, that other text-types also receive support from Qumran, and therefore it is misleading to think of Qumran texts as wholly reflecting orthodox Judaism.

One problem that is already evident concerns the use of the word Massoretic, and its sub-forms, especially pre-Massoretic, proto-Massoretic, and the like. Some scholars do not admit the existence of a pure Massoretic text until the 'Massoretes' had produced the vocalized and accented form of the Ben Asher text of the eleventh century, and the prefixes 'pre-' 'proto-', are used for earlier texts. But the simple meaning of the word Massora is 'tradition', and from the early days of Judaism the word is used with this meaning. Rabbi Akiba[16] in the early second century A.D. used the word in the sense of 'a hedge around the Law', i.e. a 'safeguard' in the textual sense as in every other. Moses 'received' (*māsar*) the Law from Sinai in the same way as one generation 'received' the traditional text from its predecessor. The Massoretic text was essentially a transmitted text-form, and there was always a 'safeguard' to the transmission. The Scribes (*sôpᵉrîm*)[17] counted the number of words and even letters in the various books, and noted the middle word and the middle consonant of the Torah and the Psalms; and they did it not from curiosity but to warn copyists about the spacing of the columns. Even in the Qumran scrolls there are signs used by scribes which are similar to those used by the Massoretes, and there are

---

[16] Mishna Pirke Aboth 1:1; 3:14.

[17] Kiddushin 30a. These are the Scribes of New Testament, and it is possible that the reticence of scholars to use the term Massorete for the earlier stages is due to the Rabbinic preference for *sôpᵉrîm*. It is also true that the term *Baʿalê ha-massōret* (masters of the Massora) does not occur until later in the story of the transmission. See A. Dotan, 'Masorah', Supplementary Article in *EJ*, Jerusalem, 1971, cols. 1401–1482.

Talmudic references to Massoretic annotations in the text which, at a later date, became part of actual Massoretic works. As a recent authority on the topic has explained,[18] divergent readings were banned from the copies which were earmarked for public worship and for official text transmission, whereas marginal comments and Massoretic annotation often became the bearers of traditional variations.[19]

Among Massoretic terms preserved in Rabbinic writings, the following stand out: *Puncta extraordinaria* (ten passages in the Pentateuch and five others listed in Siphre—third century A.D.); *tiḳḳûnê ha-sôpᵉrîm* and *ʿiṭṭûrê ha-sôpᵉrîm* (emendations and omissions of the Scribes respectively) and particularly the cases of *Ḳᵉrê* and *Ḳᵉṭîḇ* ('what is read' and 'what is written').[20] In order to see their role in the history of the transmission it is necessary first to outline another factor in the general history of Judaism, namely the growth of the divergent traditions in Judaism.

After the fall of Jerusalem in A.D. 70, Judaism struggled for survival in the two major centres of Jewish colonization, Galilee and Babylon, and the cultural-religious life was maintained in academies in these two areas, the Western and the Eastern. In Galilee the academy was set up in Tiberias after some unsuccessful attempts in other places, and in Babylon the academies of Sura, Nehardea, and later Pumbedita became renowned. Jewish oral tradition in the Mishna was codified and developed along separate lines in Palestine and Babylon, and so we have the two distinct Talmuds. Actually, individual developments went further, and each separate school or academy had its own 'Mishna'.[21] But our concern is that each school, or at least each region, Palestine and Babylon, had its own tradition of textual transmission,

---

[18] See S. Talmon, 'Aspects of the Textual Transmission of the Bible in the Light of Qumran Manuscripts', *Textus* iv (1964), 95–132; id., 'The Old Testament Text', in *CHB* i, *From the Beginnings to Jerome*, Cambridge, 1970, ed. P. R. Ackroyd and C. F. Evans.

[19] *CHB* i. p. 187.

[20] See e.g. R. Gordis, *The Biblical Text in the Making. A Study of Kethib-Qre.* Augmented edition with Prolegomenon by R. Gordis, New York, 1971. The author argues, from the study of the text and of Qumran, that these variations go back to the time before Rabbi Akiba.

[21] Cf. G. F. Moore, *Judaism in the First Centuries of the Christian Era*, i, Cambridge (Mass.), 1927, p. 24.

and especially its own Massora. It was the notable contribution of Paul Kahle in the present century that he produced manuscript evidence of the two transmissions, which he named the Western and the Eastern Massora.[22] The manuscripts are derived in the main from the Geniza (the lumber-room of a synagogue in which are deposited the disposable remnants of scribal material) of a synagogue in Old Cairo. The *Geniza Fragments*, as they are generally called, belong to the mid-ninth century A.D. and later, and since the late nineteenth century they have been dispersed, in fantastic numbers, in major libraries in Britain and elsewhere. It was here that Kahle discovered and interpreted examples of Babylonian and Palestinian Massoretic annotations and vocalizations. He traced the development in each transmission, and demonstrated the transition from *Einfach* (simple) to *Kompliziert* (complex) in Babylonian pointing, and from Palestinian to Tiberian pointing in Tiberias. In the course of time the Babylonian Massora and vocalization were absorbed into the Tiberian system, and were finally eliminated.

The story of this development, with details of Massoroth on the one hand, and vowel and accent marks on the other, is complicated, and will be over-simplified in the present account. But its main features must be outlined, and also its implication for the study of Hebrew grammar and linguistics—an aspect frequently not appreciated except by specialists. People who were taught their advanced Hebrew grammar by means of Gesenius–Kautzsch, for instance, should be disturbed to know that much of it is now antiquated and quite misleading. Its main thesis was that 'uniformity' or 'the striving after a certain uniformity' in vocalization is essential to the Massora, despite 'the inconsistencies which have crept in'.[23] The present view on the other hand, is that 'inconsistencies' were of the essence of the Massora, and form part of the Massoretic tradition.

---

[22] See his pioneering works, *Masoreten des Ostens*, BWAT xv, 1913; *Masoreten des Westens*, i. BWAT (N.F.) viii. 1927, ii, BWANT iii. 14, 1930; his introduction to *Biblia Hebraica*, 3rd edn., and numerous works culminating in *The Cairo Geniza*, 2nd edn., Oxford, 1959.
[23] *Gesenius' Hebrew Grammar as edited and enlarged by the late E. Kautzsch*, 2nd English edn. by A. E. Cowley, Oxford, 1910. See p. 38, Recent works, e.g. A.

This minor digression is permitted because of the need to deal with a seemingly unwelcome feature in recent editions of the Massoretic text, namely the inclusion of Massoretic notes on the margins of the pages.[24] The background is that, as far back as the actual transmission can be traced, there has been a Massora attached to each text-form. From the tenth century A.D. and later, however, Massoretic works were also independently transmitted, and contained lists of variants according to two identifiable Massoretic families, namely Ben Asher and Ben Naphtali.

Some examples of these lists occur among Geniza fragments, but in recent years interest has been shown in complete lists from an early period. The most important is that known as the *Book of Hilluphim* ('differences'), written by Mishael ben Uzziel, probably in the eleventh or twelfth century.[25] It is a comparatively complete list (about 800 readings in all) of the divergencies between Ben Asher and Ben Naphtali, and because it is earlier than any other list and consequently nearer the time when the actual Massoretic families were recording them, it has a special interest. There are, however, later examples—for instance, the *Aberdeen Codex*[26] from 1493 which is worth seeing for its sheer artistic value.

It is a matter of history that the outcome of the struggle between the two Tiberian families of Massoretes went in favour of Ben Asher, and from the time of the latest of the Ben Asher texts, the late ninth and early tenth centuries, the pride of almost every edition of the Hebrew text has been to be called a 'Ben Asher' text.[27]

Murtonen, *Materials for a non-Masoretic Grammar*, i, Helsinki, 1958, serve to indicate the scope a revision of Gesenius–Kautzsch would have to cover.

[24] See e.g. *BHS*, with the title-page reference, '*Masoram curavit* G. E. Weil', and the description in the Prolegomena by Professor Weil.

[25] L. Lipschütz, *Kitab al Khilaph. Mishael ben Uzziel's treatise on the differences between Ben Asher and Ben Naphtali*, i, Stuttgart, 1937; and in *Textus*, ii (1962); a further discussion by the same author in *Textus*, iv (1964), 1–29.

[26] *Aberdeen Codex No. 23*, ed. C. Roth, 1958. Fourteen plates illustrate the kind of material to be found in the Massoretic lists.

[27] In the Prolegomena to the Ktav reissue of Ginsburg's *Introduction* already mentioned, H. M. Orlinsky has argued with considerable verve and acuteness that there never has been 'the true Massoretic text'—not even Ben Asher. All the early edited texts and the manuscripts were 'a' Massoretic text, not 'the' Massoretic text. It might appear rather Irish, however, to give as the title of the article 'The Massoretic Text: A critical evaluation'!

Four manuscripts claim the distinction of being actual Ben Asher texts, namely: the *Cairo Codex of the Prophets* written in Tiberias in A.D. 895; the *British Library Codex* of the Pentateuch (*B.Lib. Or. 4445*), probably from the tenth century, which has the name Ben Asher frequently mentioned in the margins; the *Leningrad Codex* (*B19a*), copied in A.D. 1008, which forms the basic text of *Biblia Hebraica* (3rd edn., 1937) and of the present *Biblia Hebraica Stuttgartensia*; the *Aleppo Codex* (tenth century), for long lost to scholarly scrutiny, and reported destroyed in 1948, but now rediscovered and adopted for the Hebrew University projected edition of the Hebrew Bible. It is claimed to have been written by Aaron ben Asher, the most illustrious member of the Ben Asher family, and it is also believed that it received, as it were, its imprimatur by Maimonides in the twelfth century.

Only the last two contain the complete text of the Old Testament[28] and it is natural that they have been adopted for contemporary editions. The Leningrad text was the only one available in the 1930s, when Professor Kahle persuaded Kittel that only a true Ben Asher text could aspire to the prestige of an acceptable Massoretic text. On the other hand, the projected new edition of the Hebrew University does appear to have the edge on *Biblia Hebraica* by virtue of the authority the Aleppo codex has always enjoyed in Judaism, as witness Maimonides' commendation. In any case, it is important to note that each of these editions will also publish, and editorially discuss, the individual Massora of the codex.

This is probably a convenient place to mention the early Massoretic works transmitted independently of the texts. The earliest is attributed to the above-mentioned Aaron Ben Asher, and is known as *Dikdûkê ha-ṭeʿāmîm* ('rules of accents', i.e. for reading and chanting), but the history of its editing has been unfortunate. In 1879 it was edited by two leading nineteenth-century Massoretic scholars, S. Baer and H. L. Strack,[29] but, true to the canons of that age, the material was manipulated from the point of view of obtaining the 'correct' (according to the editor's standpoint) text of the Bible. In any

---

[28] Substantial parts of the *Aleppo Codex* have been lost.
[29] *Die Dikduke ha-ṭeʿamim des Ahron ben Mosche ben Ascher . . .*, Leipzig, 1897.

case, since the time of Baer, not only has the approach changed but also new material has become available, and a fresh edition of this important Massoretic work has now appeared,[30] and along with it a valuable introduction to the topic by the same author, Professor A. Dotan of Tel Aviv University.[31] Whether or not the Massora of the Ben Asher texts continued to claim the attention of scribes is a moot question, but in manuscripts from the fourteenth and fifteenth centuries we find that though it is still copied, it is rendered in ornamental and pictorial patterns, and it is likely that the change represents a stage when the Massora was little more than a calligraphic indulgence.[32]

Attention now turns, however, to the appearance of a Massoretic work which was complementary to the marginal Massora mentioned above. It is the *Massora Finalis*, and consists of lists of words, normally in alphabetical order, which occur in pairs, once without and once with the conjunction. It is known by its initial entry, *'Ochlâh we-Ochlâh*, and has survived in a number of manuscripts, including some of the Geniza fragments. The main source, however, is the copy produced by Jacob Ben Chayim for his *Second Rabbinic Bible* of 1524-5. It was published by S. Frensdorff in 1864.[33]

The reference to Jacob Ben Chayim's Bible introduces the next phase in the story of the transmission, when the text of this edition became virtually the *textus receptus* of the Massoretic Bible until its replacement by the Leningrad Codex for the Kittel *Biblia Hebraica* (3rd edn., 1937).[34] The general criticism of the Ben Chayim text is that its sources

---

[30] A. Dotan, *The Diqduqe Hatte'amim of Ahron ben Mosche ben Asher*, with a critical edition of the original text from new manuscripts, 1967.

[31] Cf. William Wickes, *Two Treatises on the Accentuation of the Old Testament: On Psalms, Proverbs and Job and on the Twenty-One Prose Books*, 1881, 1887, reprinted with Prolegomenon by Aron Dotan, Library of Biblical Studies, ed. H. M. Orlinsky, New York, 1970. Incidentally, in the second of the volumes *Twenty-one Prose Books*, Wickes was able to publish a facsimile of the *Aleppo Codex*—an unbelievable scoop, but, to add a touch of irony, Wickes insisted that the codex was a fabrication!

[32] A good example may be seen in the above-mentioned *Aberdeen Codex*, and also in illustrations published in a variety of encyclopedias, e.g. *JE* and *EJ*. They are highly photogenic.

[33] See above, p. 2, n. 5.

[34] Even the first two editions of *Biblia Hebraica* were based on the Ben Chayim text.

consisted of recent and unsatisfactory manuscripts, an observation that goes back to Ben Chayim himself. The last of the great Massoretic works brings us down to the present century, namely C. D. Ginsburg's massive *The Massorah Compiled from Manuscripts, Alphabetically and Lexically Arranged*, London, 1881–1905. It is in four volumes, folio, and is incomplete, for a fifth volume had been promised. But within a few years it became clear that any Massoretic work claiming to be 'compiled from manuscripts' was damned, because of the nature of the Massora. At the same time it is foolish to adopt an extreme position, and there is a great amount of extremely useful material in Ginsburg's *Massorah*, as indeed there is in Ginsburg's *Introduction*.[35]

Ginsburg also produced editions of the Massoretic text, notably the four-volume edition to celebrate the centenary of the British and Foreign Bible Society.[36] It has the text of Ben Chayim, but the apparatus criticus contains variants from some ninety manuscripts and printed Bibles. It does not seem to have been in common use except by specialists, for the Bible Society was recently handing out to students free copies of the Letteris text of 1866, and it was only by dint of classroom instruction that students in the 1930s adopted Kittel's *Biblia Hebraica*. In 1934 the Bible Society invited Dr. N. H. Snaith to prepare a replacement for the Letteris text, and it appeared in 1958.[37] The text is based on three manuscripts, *B.Lib. Or. 2626–8*, from 1482, *B.Lib. Or, 2375* from 1460–80, and the *Shem Tob* Bible from 1312. Use was also made of Norzi's text in *Minchat Shai*, 1742. That is, all the source material comes from a period later than the Ben Asher texts, but before Ben Chayim; but the significance is that Snaith can claim that the resultant text is practically identical with Ben Asher.[38] This is, indeed, a highly important conclusion, though in fact it merely underlines the unfortunate absence of the data to establish the claim, namely,

[35] *Introduction to the Massoretico-Critical Edition of the Hebrew Bible*, London, 1897, reissued, with a Prolegomenon by H. M. Orlinsky, New York, 1966.
[36] *The Old Testament, diligently revised according to the Massorah and the early editions, with the various readings from MSS and the ancient versions*, London, 1908, revised 1926.
[37] *Sepher Tora, Nebi'im u-Kethubim*, London, 1958.
[38] See N. H. Snaith, 'The Ben Asher Text', *Textus* ii (1962), 8–13.

annotations to the published text. It is one of the serious shortcomings of the Bible Society's editions of biblical texts that so many are published without an apparatus criticus, which is the very life-blood of edited texts.

IV. THE TEXTUAL CRITICISM OF THE MASSORETIC TEXT

Since the transmission of the Massoretic text was so obviously fixed and hedged around, the task of reconstructing an 'original' form is essentially different in nature from that of any other known textual transmission. At the same time, there are abundant and clear signs that at an early period the Hebrew transmission was far from uniform. There are duplicate texts which vary, Rabbinic writings which provide examples of mixed text-forms, the Qumran scrolls which often go their own way, and the text of the Septuagint and other versions vary from free-ranging paraphrase to literal renderings, especially in some of the Aramaic Targums. Furthermore, there has flourished over the centuries the discipline of Old Testament textual criticism, and nothing has happened in principle to change this aspect of the study of Holy Writ. For an adequate understanding it is necessary to be able to handle the apparatus criticus of the Old Testament in Hebrew.

In general terms, there are two main ways of constructing an apparatus criticus, and, quite conveniently, the two are well exemplified in the two major editions current today. They are *Biblia Hebraica Stuttgartensia* and the *Hebrew University Bible Project*.

The former, though in many ways similar to its predecessors, has the advantage of including a correctly understood Massora. The *Massora Parva* is entered down the margins, and it is the Massora of its actual basic text, *Leningrad B 19a*. True, the abbreviations are puzzling, and the reference back to the list in the Preface is tedious, but it is an essential part of the text. The *Massora Magna* of the text is to appear separately, in a forthcoming volume, and both are in the charge of Professor G. E. Weil, the person best equipped to deal with such a complex matter. Next, we have the apparatus criticus proper, produced by the editors of each individual book, and mainly intended to provide readings from the Versions and elsewhere which can be used for emendation. This, possibly, is the most controversial part of *BHS*—as it was of *BH*³. At least one might comment that it is surprising that since the 1937 edition, and even since the earlier appearances of *BH* in 1905 and in 1912, there has been no real modification in the way the readings have been chosen and presented. Nevertheless, *BHS* is the only edition available to most of us, and is indispensable.

The Hebrew University text is far more comprehensive and ambitious. Various aspects of the work are handled in the periodical *Textus*; and in the Sample Edition of chapters 2, 5, 11, and 51 of the Book of Isaiah, and the accompanying introductory chapter,³⁹ we are given an outline of the work. For the present purpose a comment from the Preface will indicate the main feature of the edition; it is that the apparatus criticus does not include a 'single suggestion for emendation of the Massoretic Text'. That is, the function of the apparatus is simply to present variants, and the choice of 'emendation', if any, is left to the student. Furthermore, a reading derived from one of the Versions is scrupulously offered as an 'inferred variant' because retranslation always bears a hazard.

On some matters of construction of the apparatus criticus one might have reservations, but the whole formation is instructive. There are four sections. In the first, the Versions claim pride of place, particularly, of course, the Septuagint, because they offer 'material' variants as opposed to the more incidental (if the word is not misunderstood) variants of the Massoretic transmission as such. The second section provides readings with a Hebrew provenance, namely the Scrolls and the Rabbinic literature. The former includes all kinds of Scroll readings, not only the biblical and the *pēsher* scrolls, but also quotations from non-biblical scrolls. How all this material and that from the Rabbinic sources (Mishna, Talmuds, Midrash) is to be compressed into one section defies every sense, but it has been done for these few chapters of Isaiah. Apparatus III is given over to the medieval biblical

³⁹ M. H. Goshen-Gottstein, *The Book of Isaiah: Sample Edition with Introduction*, Jerusalem, 1965; Parts I–II (Isaiah 1:1–22:10), 1975.

manuscripts, and here we find not only Ben Asher and Ben Naphtali variants, but also cases of vocalization variants, with Geniza fragments being accorded a prominent role. Apparatus IV is brief, consisting of minutiae of variants of spelling, vowels, and accents, which are entered on the left-hand margin of the text. The *Massora Parva* is along the right-hand margin and *Massora Magna* is at the top of the page. Obviously, when the edition ultimately appears, it will be an achievement of the highest order.

V. THE VERSIONS

It will be impossible even to touch on this subject with any sense of adequacy; consequently the reader should be warned that the topics dealt with here are those which appear to the writer as most pertinent for the present purpose. There is one major line of demarcation which should be mentioned at the outset, namely that those versions which derive from the Christian Church form a separate group from those with a synagogue background, because the whole story of the transmission is different. Thus, the Septuagint, the Old Latin, the Vulgate, and the so-called daughter-versions belong to the one group, and the Aramaic Targums and the Samaritan Pentateuch belong to the other. The Syriac Peshitta comes somewhere in between them.

The Christian Versions: The Septuagint

The recent acquisition which demands first attention is the fragment known as the *Minor Prophets in Greek*, which forms part of the Dead Sea Scrolls.[40] It comes from Murabba'at or thereabouts, and not Qumran—an important point for the relevance of its text. There are two views on its significance. It is agreed that, though it has many of the characteristics of the Septuagint, it is more closely related to the Massoretic text-type than is usual with this version. Consequently, it can

---

[40] The discovery was first described by Father D. Barthélemy in a general survey, 'Redécouverte d'un chaînon manquant de l'histoire de la Septante', *RB* ix (1953), 18–29; and subsequently a number of specialist articles have dealt with it. See particularly Barthélemy's treatment of the whole topic in *Les Devanciers d'Aquila*, SVT x, 1963.

belong to one of two text-forms. It may be a Greek text which was revised to bring it to a closer alignment with the Hebrew text, along the same lines as Aquila, Symmachus, and Theodotion in the second century A.D., and similar to the text quoted by Justin Martyr in the same period. This is the case put forward by Barthélemy and numerous supporters. The alternative view is argued by Kahle.[41] Consistent with his views on the early history of the Septuagint, to which we shall return, Kahle sees here an example of the 'popular', unofficial renderings of the Hebrew text into Greek in the 'pre-Septuagint' era. Of course, appeal to the date of the document is vital, and independent Greek palaeographers who are quite outside the pro- or anti-Kahle controversy, have placed the fragment between 50 B.C. and A.D. 50. Actually, the date could support either of the above views, but, what lies behind the debate is whether or not we have some vital evidence (possibly the only real evidence) of the existence of the Septuagint as a version earlier than the beginning of the Christian era.

The evidence for such a pre-Christian version of the Pentateuch is granted. Fragments of books of the Pentateuch, especially Deuteronomy, have been known for a long time,[42] and from Qumran Cave 4 we have a papyrus scroll with fragments of Leviticus, a leather scroll of portions of Leviticus, and another of Numbers—all from the second century B.C.[43] But, according to Kahle's hypothesis,[44] the Septuagint, apart from the Pentateuch, was produced by the early Church, and Greek renderings, like early pre-Christian Aramaic Targums, were 'popular' unofficial text-forms, which were ultimately (as were all Targums) brought into a uniform rendering. The controversy has raged for a long time and has involved a number of side-issues, but it seems to have abated since Kahle's death, unless the above-mentioned *Greek Minor Prophets* will rekindle it.

What is clear is that the Septuagint has always shown that

---

[41] See *The Cairo Geniza*, 2nd edn., pp. 226 f.

[42] Such as the *Rylands Papyrus* and the *Fouad Papyrus 226*.

[43] This reference, together with a great deal of the discussion of the contents of Cave 4 of Qumran depends on F. M. Cross's book, *The Ancient Library of Qumran and Modern Biblical Studies*. He is the best living authority on these texts, which, however, are as yet (1975) unpublished.

[44] See Kahle, *The Cairo Geniza*, 2nd edn., pp. 191–264.

its parent text, at least for some books, represented a text-form which differed from the present Massoretic text. This has long since been acknowledged for the books of Samuel and Jeremiah. Furthermore, Qumran Cave 4 has produced evidence for such a variant text for those same books. There are other fragments which show doublets, with both the Massoretic and the divergent parent of the Septuagint, e.g. Deut. 32:43. This, and other relevant material from Cave 4, will throw light on the problem when they become available; it is also possible, however, that the case has been over-exposed in current interpretations. We can only wait and see.

Meanwhile, further information is becoming available on the history of the Septuagint, and its related(?) Greek renderings of the second century A.D., the above-mentioned Aquila, Symmachus, and Theodotion, and some quotations in the writings of the early Church Fathers.[45]

The next step in the history of the Septuagint is the discovery of papyri from between the mid-second and fourth centuries A.D., such as the Chester Beatty manuscripts and more recently the Bodmer papyri. The former have been known for some years, the latter should really be more fully discussed. But they are very few (very different from the New Testament Bodmer) and in the main they support what was said about the Chester Beatty texts.

The appearance of Origen's *Hexapla*, A.D. 240-5, is as significant now as it ever was—possibly more so. The alignment of the Septuagint, begun in the second century A.D. with Aquila, Symmachus, and Theodotion (whatever is thought of the *Greek Minor Prophets*) came to a head in the six columns of Origen. He was first and foremost a Christian teacher, and, seemingly, the first Christian scholar in the accepted sense. He was convinced of the superiority of the Hebrew text of the Old Testament, but he was equally convinced of the inspiration of the Septuagint, the Bible of the Church. So, the reconstruction of the Septuagint in the

---

[45] See Barthélemy, *Les Devanciers d'Aquila*, where the above-mentioned *Greek Minor Prophets*, is studied against the background of the first century A.D. and the influence of Rabbinic Judaism. Relevant to the discussion, also, is the subsequent history of Justin, the columns of the Hexapla, and daughter-versions of the Septuagint.

Hexapla always lies at the head of the priorities for the Septuagint student, but the search is continually complicated by the discovery of unexpected material and the need for making allowances for new interpretations. Thus, the discovery (1895–6) and publication (1958)[46] of the Mercati fragments of some Psalms brought considerable rethinking, and recent publication[47] of specialist works have shown that the situation is still fluid in the study of the early transmission of the Septuagint: it is probably the most important side of the study of this version for us because of the interaction of the Hebrew text on its development. Before leaving the *Hexapla*, however, we must mention the *Syro-Hexapla*, a Syriac rendering which, in contrast to other copies, e.g. the above-mentioned Mercati fragments, retained the Aristarchean signs whereby Origen indicated the varying text-form of the Septuagint over against the Hebrew text.

The subsequent history of Origen's text, and its continuation in the recensions, is crucial. It was *c.* A.D. 400 that Jerome said that the Septuagint text was to be found in three recensions, those of Hesychius in Alexandria and Egypt, Lucian in Constantinople and Syria, and Origen, edited by Eusebius and Pamphilus, in Palestine; and it is to be presumed that this view obtained throughout Christendom at that time. Consequently, subsequent study of the Septuagint has been directed to the classification and reconstruction of these three recensions. But the situation is more complex, as witness, e.g., the conclusion that a further recension, the *Catena* group (a 'chain' of quotations) must be added to the Three.

The process of relating the recensions to the actual history of the text, however, is again confused by the probability, at least in the case of the Lucianic recension, that there had existed an earlier recension of this text, which had close affinities with the Antiochean transmission. Furthermore,

[46] J. Mercati, *Psalterii Hexapli Reliquiae. Pars Prima, Codex Rescriptus Bybliothecae Ambrosianae 039 SVP*, i, Vatican, 1958; ii, '*Osservazioni*'. *Commento critico al testo dei frammenti esaplari, Vatican, 1965.*

[47] e.g. I. Soisalon-Soininen, *Die Textformen der Septuaginta—Übersetzung des Richterbuches*, AASF B.72:1, Helsinki, 1951; Bo Johnson, *Die hexaplarische Rezension des I Samuelbuches der Septuaginta*, Lund 1963. See also reviews by W. G. Lambert in *VT* ii (1952), 184–9, and by S. P. Brock, *JTS* xv (1964), 112–17.

soon after the time when the recensions had become established, we are already in the period of the great codices— *Vaticanus* and *Sinaiticus* (both fourth century), *Alexandrinus* (fifth century), and some fifteen or sixteen others which form the majuscles, and hundreds of minuscles, all of which form part of the apparatus criticus of an edited text of the Septuagint. A significant generalization which may be allowed in this context (despite the above-mentioned dictum by Jerome) is that it is impossible to identify any of the recensions simply on the basis of the manuscript evidence of the codices.

Consequently, the chase after the growth of the Septuagint text is very much a matter for the Septuagint specialist,[48] and since the present survey deals primarily with the Version only from the standpoint of Old Testament study, we shall pass over the centuries of Septuagint transmission and simply describe current texts and editions as they are relevant to the Old Testament text as we understand it.

Four editions might be mentioned. The Swete edition[49] which consisted of *Codex Vaticanus* as a basic text with selected variants in the apparatus criticus. This was replaced by the much more ambitious Cambridge Septuagint[50] from 1906, for which the basic text was again *Codex Vaticanus*, but with the apparatus criticus more wide-ranging. It should be clear that the edition was not meant to be in any way representative of 'the original' Septuagint, but one which provided the student with a choice of variants which could help in reconstructing such a text. The early editors were A. E. Brooke, N. McLean, and H. St. J. Thackeray, joined later by T. W. Manson, but since his death the project seems to have folded up, after the publication of the Octateuch, King-

---

[48] The whole topic has been adequately dealt with in various scholarly works, two of which may be mentioned here. The first (and extremely thorough one) is by J. W. Wevers, 'Septuaginta-Forschungen. I. Ausgaben und Texte. II. Die Septuaginta als Übersetzungsurkunde', *TR* N.F. xxii (1954), 85–138, to which a sequel has appeared, again by Wevers, 'Septuaginta-Forschungen seit 1954', *TR* N.F. xxxvi (1968), 18–76. Another study, very comprehensive and invaluable for the student is S. Jellicoe, *The Septuagint and Modern Study*, Oxford, 1968.

[49] H. B. Swete, *The Old Testament in Greek*, i, 1st edn., Cambridge, 1887, 4th edn., 1909; ii, 1st edn., 1890, 3rd edn., 1907; iii, 1st edn., 1894, 4th edn., 1912.

[50] *The Old Testament in Greek*, Octateuch, Cambridge, 1906–17, The Later Historical Books, 1927–35, Esther, Judith, Tobit, 1940.

doms, Chronicles 1 and 2, Esdras, Esther, Judith, and Tobit. The other two are of German origin. The *Göttingen Edition*[51] is a highly significant product of Septuagint scholarship at its best. Its beginnings go back to the work of Paul de Lagarde (1827–91), who argued that by reconstructing the three recension texts he could regain the 'original' text (the *Ur-Septuaginta*, as it is universally known). Then there was established the *Göttingen Septuagint Institute*, led by A. Rahlfs (1865–1935), which showed Lagarde's theory to be untenable in that form; nevertheless, by dint of thorough scrutiny, and classification for each individual book, it appears that the resultant text approximates as near as possible to the 'original Septuagint'. In any case, as a storehouse of variants conveniently classified, the Göttingen Septuagint is an important work and cannot be bettered for the present purpose, short of producing an edition in which every possible reading is included lest anything be missed. The only *caveat* that must be entered against the Göttingen text is that an eclectic text is usually a hazardous one.

Finally, and probably the most useful one for the student, there is the text of Rahlfs[52] for which three of the great codices, *Vaticanus*, *Sinaiticus*, and *Alexandrinus* are collated, with occasional additional readings from other sources.

On the basis of one of these texts the student quickly comes to realize that the Septuagint is not only a text-critical tool but also a source for the historical reassessment of the Christian understanding of the Old Testament itself. The massive, sometimes seemingly impenetrable, apparatus criticus demonstrates it, and the study of the text itself proves it. In fact, the Septuagint is far greater than a source of textual variants, for it represents on the one hand a different attitude from the Hebrew to the textual authority of the Scriptures and, on the other, it indicates a different quality in the message of the

---

[51] *Septuaginta, Vetus Testamentum Graecum, auctoritate Societatis Litterarum Gottingensis editum*, Göttingen, 1931– . See also J. W. Wevers, *The Text History of the Greek Genesis*, Göttingen, 1974, and the announcement, in the issues of Genesis (Wevers) and 1 Esdras (Hanhart), of the Göttingen LXX, 1974, that each editor will issue special treatments in forthcoming volumes of *Mitteilungen des LXX-Unternehmens*.

[52] *Septuaginta. Id est Vetus Testamentum Graece iuxta LXX interpretes*. 2 vols., Stuttgart, 1935, and subsequent impressions.

Scriptures. The one is Jewish, the other Christian. The one is strictly hedged around, the other is free, sometimes to the point of embarrassment. After studying the intricate apparatus criticus of the Greek text and having seen its use in the apparatus of the Massoretic text, the student turns to the inspiration of the Septuagint text, with the help of a dictionary, or rather the concordance of Hatch and Redpath.[53] Here he finds how the Greek text represents a large number of Hebrew words with a wide range of meaning, and it becomes clear that the Version was never meant to be a crib for the Hebrew. It was, rather, a live rendering of the parent text, and contained much Greek philosophy and still more religious interpretation. It became the Bible of the early Church, but it is equally historically relevant that the Church was always moved to revise its Greek Bible according to the more authoritative (and 'better'—so Origen, Jerome, Luther, and others) Hebrew text. It would be sad if the Church today were to be deprived of one of its major paradoxes.

The Old Latin and the Vulgate

In theory, the Latin Versions as a whole are similar to the Greek texts in character and in function. Actually, the Old Latin are presumably based on Greek texts, and reflect the freedom of the Christian transmission, parallel to other daughter-versions of the Septuagint—the Coptic, Ethiopic, Armenian, and others, and provide evidence for the variety of text-forms current up to the fourth century A.D. and later. They also frequently demonstrate how Hebraisms came to be introduced into the Christian transmission, though they also provide indirect readings from the pre-Hexaplaric Greek text. They have elements in common with the early papyri of both Old and New Testaments, and witness to the early spread of Christianity in North Africa and Europe. Finally, and again in common with the New Testament, they are basic to our understanding of the Latin Fathers. Consequently, the Old Latin texts have great textual value, and

---

[53] E. Hatch and H. A. Redpath, *A Concordance to the Septuagint and the other Greek Versions of the Old Testament including the Apocryphal Books*, 2 vols., Oxford, 1897; with Supplements, 1900–6. See also E. Camilo dos Santos, *An Expanded Hebrew Index for the Hatch-Redpath Concordance to the Septuagint*, Jerusalem, 1975.

have been assembled quite diligently, from Paul Sabatier's work in the eighteenth century down to the latest collection by monks in the Monastery of Beuron.

But greater interest attaches to Jerome's version, the Vulgate, which was commissioned by Pope Damasus in A.D. 382 to provide the Church with a standard text and reduce the welter of chaotic Latin and Greek variant texts current in the Church. Jerome started on his work by cleaning up the Old Latin texts of the Psalter, and produced the *Psalterium Romanum*. He then issued the *Psalterium Gallicanum*, based on the Origen recension, and along with it he produced Job (still partially extant). Surviving portions of the Writings suggest he rendered the whole Bible in this way. But the actual Vulgate is the version he produced on the basis of what he called *Hebraica veritas*, the Hebrew text current in his day. He worked at it from *c.* A.D. 390 to 405, and though he translated on his own he consulted Rabbis and made use of as much technical help as possible. It was a daring step to take, and by taking it Jerome antagonized almost the whole of Christendom and prejudiced the survival of his Version. St. Augustine was probably the leading churchman of his time and he regarded the Septuagint as Holy Writ; how much more so did the local abbots and monks who felt that the new text was not only troublesome but dangerous. Little wonder, then, that from the outset the Vulgate text, where it was accepted at all, very quickly became impregnated with Old Latin readings.

We might, however, have expected the Vulgate to provide its share of variant readings for the Massoretic text, since it represented a text-form from a period centuries earlier than the first extant fragments from the Cairo Geniza and the Ben Asher texts. We might also have expected Rabbinic readings from Jerome's Hebrew advisers. But in vain. The vast majority of Vulgate variants support the Septuagint, and it is mainly in the rendering of Hebrew orthography (e.g. in proper names) that the Vulgate helps, and sometimes in grammar, when the evidence of the commentaries is useful.[54]

[54] In two papers in *Textus*, 'Divergent Hebrew Readings in Jerome's Isaiah', 1964, and 'Textual Gleanings from the Vulgate to Jeremiah', 1969, B. Kedar-Kopfstein gleans evidence for the textual significance of this Version, but does not find the

The Vulgate lacked any official recognition of superiority over the Old Latin, and the Council of Trent, in 1546, though giving it a status, did not displace the Septuagint. For current use, the appropriate edition is that by R. Weber.[55] A massive critical edition is being produced by the Benedictines,[56] based on a highly efficient scrutiny of classified manuscripts.

The Peshitta

The origins of the Syriac Version are in debate—some argue for a Jewish, others a Christian origin. But its transmission, as shown in extant manuscripts, is wholly Christian, and it is therefore listed among the Christian Versions in the present survey. At the same time it should be noted that it does not have the loose textual transmission of the Greek texts, and it may be regarded as reflecting the nature of the Eastern transmission rather than the Western.

Similarly, the influences which played on the Version indicate a dual provenance. On the one hand there are traces of old Targumic readings in some of the texts, and, according to some,[57] there are close affinities with the Hebrew text itself. On the other hand, the strongest influence of all is that left by the Septuagint, and it seems to be a working rule that where Septuagint and Peshitta agree against a Hebrew reading, the evidence should be understood as one against one. Yet again, it has been cogently argued that there are cases where Peshitta, Septuagint, and Targum all alike draw on a common tradition.[58]

The study of the Peshitta transmission is more difficult than many because it has lacked a critical edition, and despite

---

evidence conclusive. Cf. H. F. D. Sparks's comment in 'Jerome as a Bible Translator', *CHB* i, 525, that the Vulgate is 'a curious mixture' of literalness and latitude. Its purpose was to secure a rendering for the use of the Church, rather than a simple and direct translation.

[55] *Biblia Sacra iuxta Vulgatam Versionem*, 2 vols., Stuttgart, 1969. It is published by the Württembergische Bibelanstalt and takes its place alongside the other Bibles from that Bible House, *Biblia Hebraica* and *Septuaginta* (2nd edn. 1975).

[56] *Biblia Sacra iuxta latinam vulgatam versionem ad codicum fidem ... cura et studio Monachorum Abbatiae Pontificiae S. Hieronymi in urbe ordinis S. Benedicti edita*, Rome, 1926– .

[57] e.g. Kahle, *The Cairo Geniza*, 2nd edn., devotes a whole section of the book to show how Geniza material throws light on the translation.

[58] See E. R. Rowlands, 'Targum and Peshitta of Isaiah'. *VT* ix (1959), 178–91.

a large number of manuscripts, there has been no clear classification. Furthermore, the very fruitful source of Syriac Fathers has been neglected. The Walton Polyglot in 1657 included the Peshitta text, and in 1823 Samuel Lee produced an edition which was virtually the Walton text. A revision was produced in 1914.

How welcome, then, was the news in 1961 that the Peshitta Institute of the University of Leiden was undertaking the task of publishing lists of classified manuscripts under the direction of Professor P. A. H. de Boer and W. Baars, and that a new edition of the Peshitta was to be produced under its auspices. The sample edition, Song of Songs (J. A. Emerton), Tobit (J. C. H. Lebram), Ezra (R. J. Bidawid), was published in 1966, and in 1972 we had the first full edition of six books, mainly Apocrypha, with a general preface.[59]

The Jewish Versions: The Targums

For the background study of the Old Testament transmission in Judaism, the Aramaic Targums are probably more interesting than any other source, including even the Mishna and Talmuds, but their relationship with the Massoretic text is mixed. Some of them are represented in the Geniza fragments, and are supplied with a Massora, others have contacts with Qumran,[60] and lie outside the direct Massoretic transmission. There are extant Targumic texts of all Old Testament books except Daniel and Ezra–Nehemia.

The dividing line between two types of Targum should probably reflect their varying natures—official Targums which simply translate the Massoretic text, and free renderings which retain traditions of paraphrases, interpretation, and even folk-lore. The official Targums are those of Onkelos for the Pentateuch and Jonathan for the Prophets. Apparently, the Onkelos text was revised in Babylon in the fifth century, and even if it is not certain that Onkelos and Aquila are identical names, the two texts are very similar in character.

[59] *The Old Testament in Syriac according to the Peshitta Version*, Part iv, fasc. 6, Leiden, 1972; iv. 3, Apoc. Bar.-4 Esd., 1973; i. 1, Gen.-Exod., 1977.

[60] e.g. the Targum to Job; cf. J. van der Ploeg, *Le Targum de Job de la Grotte 11 de Qumran*, Amsterdam, 1962, which also describes the Targums in general. Whether or not the Genesis Apocryphon is a Targum is questionable.

Onkelos was later brought to Palestine, and there became the authoritative Targum.[61] Targum Jonathan of the Prophets has a similar history to that of Onkelos, and even has its Greek counterpart in Theodotion. The main difference is that, whereas Onkelos is a slavish rendering, Jonathan is more free and contains later accretions.

The second group of Targums is earlier, and has a varied history which makes reconstruction problematical. This probably accounts for the fact that there never has been an adequately assimilated text of this type of Targum, but the situation will soon be totally changed. In 1956 the discovery was announced of the Targum text of the Pentateuch, *Neofiti 1*, a Vatican manuscript from the sixteenth century.[62] When the text of the manuscript is fully published it will be possible to assess the significance of other fragments of Targums as well, especially the Palestinian Targum,[63] the Fragment Targum,[64] and Pseudo-Jonathan.[65]

Meanwhile, for the various Targums we must be satisfied with the current standard publications of A. Sperber, *The Bible in Aramaic*,[66] which gives Targum Onkelos for the Pentateuch, Jonathan for the Prophets (Former and Latter), and the Hagiographa drawn from various sources. There is also J. F. Stenning's Targum of Isaiah.[67]

[61] Cf. Kahle, *The Cairo Geniza*, pp. 191–3.

[62] A. Diez Macho, who discovered the manuscript and is responsible for editing the text, has written widely about it, but see particularly, 'Codex Neofiti 1' in *Christian News from Israel*, July 1962, and 'The recently discovered Palestinian Targum: its antiquity and relationship with the other Targums', *Congress Volume, Oxford 1959* SVT vii, 1960, pp. 222–45. The publication of the *editio princeps* started in 1968; *Neophyti 1, Targum Palestinense Ms de la Biblioteca Vaticana*, ed. A. Diez Macho.

[63] See Kahle, *The Cairo Geniza*, pp. 196–8.

[64] Ed. M. Ginsburger, *Das Fragmenten-Targum*, Berlin, 1899.

[65] Ed. M. Ginsburger, Berlin, 1903.

[66] i–iv, Leiden, 1959, 1962, 1968, 1973. The volume designated iv A deals with the Hagiographa, and shows some of the development in the nature of the Targum. Thus, Chronicles is a translation with additional Rabbinic interpretation in short passages, likewise Ruth, with slightly longer interpolations. Translations and interpretation are more fully fused in Song of Songs, Lamentations, and Ecclesiastes. Finally, the book of Esther is almost wholly interpretation. In volume ivB, *The Targum and the Hebrew Bible*, the author discusses philological material and the relationships with the parent Hebrew text.

[67] The first edition of this work, in 1949, received such critical comments that a 2nd edition was produced in 1953.

The Samaritan Pentatecuch

The reader will be surprised to find this version appearing last in the survey, for normally it appears at the head of the list—either as a form of the Massoretic text or as an independent version. True, the Samaritan text might be thought of as the oldest extant version, older than the Septuagint and Qumran. Its variations from the Massoretic text are legion, and might well be frequently significant. But its placing is deliberate, and reflects an inherent suspect element in the text in its present form. The edition normally used by scholars is von Gall,[68] admittedly an unsatisfactory, eclectic text. But the *coup de grâce* was delivered to the Samaritan text as a whole when there was published,[69] in 1959, a text that showed that the traditional '*Abisha*ʻ *Scroll*, generally assumed to be the Samaritan text *par excellence*, was nothing better than a mixture of divergent texts, the oldest of which was from the eleventh century A.D.

There is, however, one possibility for its rehabilitation. Some fragments from Qumran Cave 4 reflect the same text-type as the Samaritan, and when these texts are published, and, after collation with the published text of the '*Abisha*ʻ *Scroll*, are found to have common elements with the later texts, then once more there might be a sound basis for including the Samaritan text within the scheme of textual criticism.

Conclusion Wide-ranging, complicated, seemingly academic and unrewarding, the study of the text is still the Cinderella of biblical studies, and maybe the present essay has done but little to remedy the situation. But a few comments may indicate how the study is reacting to new standpoints. Firstly, textual errors are still to be found in the Massoretic text. Similar letters are confused in both archaic and square scripts, consonants have been transposed, cases of haplography, dittography, homoeoteleuton are still discovered. Recently, the existence of abbreviations has been established as a possible source of corruption, and the presence

---

[68] A. von Gall, *Der hebraische Pentateuch der Samaritaner*, i–v, Giessen, 1914–18 (reprint 1960).

[69] F. Perez Castro, *Séfer Abishaʻ*, Madrid, 1959.

of doublets has been established in the text and certainly in the Versions. But the great importance of the Versions in this context is to act as a check for the traditional use of this kind of error-spotting, and it is now tacitly understood that emendation of the text should not be encouraged unless there is support from the text itself or the Versions.

More seriously, it is becoming clear that all is not well with the editing of the texts. It is premature to comment on the Hebrew text of the Hebrew University, but the four chapters published in the above-mentioned *Sample Edition* show it to be highly ambitious, but also formidably massive and unwieldy. Many of the details are important, but it might well be that on second thoughts it is unnecessary to incorporate them all in the one edition. Could not the work be lightened by allocating some of the contents of the four-fold apparatus criticus to separate works? One feels sometimes that the edition will look like a huge mansion with the scaffolding still standing around it.

But it is *Biblia Hebraica* that gives cause for concern, even (or maybe especially) in the latest edition, *Stuttgartensia.* As a critical text Kittel's editions have enjoyed practically a monopoly during the whole of this century, but the principle underlying its apparatus criticus has remained largely unaltered. True, for the third edition, 1937, the variants were divided into two groups, but on the whole scholars felt that the division was often arbitrary. It will be remembered that when the edition first appeared some eminent reviewers, especially experts in Septuagint studies, made serious criticism about the lack of systematic, disciplined treatment of the Versions. A similar reaction might be expected to the present edition. When we realize that so much trouble has been taken with procuring a true Ben Asher text for the Hebrew, and that the notoriously complicated Massoretic notes are so carefully added, and that another additional volume of Massora is to be published, one is dismayed at the way the all-important apparatus criticus is cavalierly treated.

The task of producing an edited text should surely be entrusted to scholars (preferably a board of scholars) expert in the Versions and able to manipulate them, both as historical documents and in their relationship with the Massoretic text and its antecedents. One may hope that enough has been said in the present outline to show that when an editor offers a variant which is supported by Septuagint, Syriac, and Vulgate, it generally means that only one source offers the variant. It is true that there are fewer of these offences in books where the editor has been chosen not simply because of his prestige as an Old Testament exponent, but because he is a known textualist; but, even so, the apparatus has the appearance of a lay production. The editorial lay-out prevents full annotation, and there is serious unevenness between the various books. Critical editions of the Septuagint and New Testament text are scrupulously worked over by specialist boards; the Old Testament could also be vastly improved by a similar procedure.

BIBLIOGRAPHY

(*Works included in this list are within the academic reach of the student and interested layman*)

AP-THOMAS, D. R. *A Primer of Old Testament Text Criticism*, 2nd edn., London, 1964.

BH, ed. R. Kittel, 3rd edn., Stuttgart, 1937: 'Prolegomena', i, R. Kittel; ii, A. Alt, O. Eissfeldt; iii, P. Kahle.

BHS, fasc. 7, *Liber Jesaiae*, ed. D. Winton Thomas, Stuttgart, 1968: 'Prolegomena', i, K. Elliger, W. Rudolph; ii, G. E. Weil.

BROCK, S. P., FRITSCH, C. T., JELLICOE, S. *A Classified Bibliography of the Septuagint*, Leiden, 1973.

BROCKINGTON, L. H. *The Hebrew Text of the Old Testament. The Readings Adopted by the Translators of the New English Bible*, Oxford and Cambridge, 1973.

CHB, i. *From the Beginnings to Jerome*, ed. P. R. Ackroyd and C. F. Evans, Cambridge, 1970, arts. 'The Old Testament Text', by S. Talmon; 'Origen as Biblical Scholar', by M. F. Wiles; 'Jerome as Biblical Scholar', by H. F. D. Sparks.

—— ii. *The West from the Fathers to the Reformation*, ed. G. W. H. Lampe, 1969, art. 'The Old Testament Manuscripts, Text and Versions', by B. J. Roberts.

CROSS, F. M. *The Ancient Library of Qumran and Modern Biblical Studies*, 2nd edn., New York, 1961.

DRIVER, G. R. *Semitic Writing: From Pictograph to Alphabet*, 2nd edn., London, 1954; 3rd edn., 1976.

EISSFELDT, O. *The Old Testament. An Introduction*, ETr by P. R. Ackroyd, Oxford, 1965.

EJ, Jerusalem, 1971, Supplementary Vol. art. 'Masorah', by A. Dotan.

FLACK, E. E. and METZGER, B. M. *The Text, Canon and Principal Versions of the Bible*, Grand Rapids, 1956.

Hastings' Dictionary of the Bible, 2nd edn., ed. by F. C. Grant and H. H. Rowley, Edinburgh, 1963, arts. 'Greek Versions of OT' and 'Text and Versions of OT', by H. S. Gehman.

IDB, iv, arts. 'Septuagint', by J. W. Wevers; 'Writing', by R. J. Williams.

JELLICOE, S. *The Septuagint and Modern Study*, London, 1968.

KAHLE, P. E. *The Cairo Geniza*, 2nd edn., Oxford, 1959.

KENYON, F. G. *Our Bible and the Ancient Manuscripts*, 5th edn., revised by A. W. Adams, London, 1958.

—— *The Text of the Greek Bible*, 3rd edn., revised by A. W. Adams, London, 1975.

KLEIN, R. W. *Textual Criticism of the Old Testament. From the Septuagint to Qumran*, Philadelphia, 1974.

LEIMAN, S. Z. (ed.) *The Canon and Masorah of the Hebrew Bible. An Introductory Reader*. New York, 1974.

The New English Bible, Oxford and Cambridge, 1970: 'Introduction to the Old Testament' by G. R. Driver.

PRICE, I. M. *The Ancestry of Our English Bible*, 3rd edn., revised by W. A. Irwin and A. P. Wikgren, New York, 1956.

The Septuagint Version of the Old Testament and Apocrypha with an English Translation and with Various Readings and Critical Notes, Grand Rapids, 1972.

WALTERS, P. *The Text of the Septuagint. Its Corruptions and their Emendation*, ed. D. W. Gooding, Cambridge, 1973.

WEIL, G. *Initiation à la Massorah*, Leiden, 1964.

WÜRTHWEIN, E. *The Text of the Old Testament*, ETr of 1st edn., by P. R. Ackroyd, Oxford, 1957.

—— *Der Text des Alten Testaments. Eine Einführung in die Biblia Hebraica*, 4th edn., Stuttgart, 1973.

II

SEMITIC PHILOLOGY AND THE INTERPRETATION OF THE OLD TESTAMENT

THE language of the Old Testament has been intensively studied for the most part of two millennia, and every detail has been subjected to multiple scrutiny. Persons ignorant of the true state of affairs in the field often imagine that there can be little room for fresh research, since almost everything must already have been 'done'. Within such a subject, can anything really new arise? In fact, on the contrary, the pace of new research is increasing, and the years since 1951 have seen remarkable shifts in emphasis and understanding. The influences which have encouraged this series of changes may be categorized as: 1. increased knowledge of the related Semitic languages in general, especially of those of the ancient Near East, and also of some other languages which are pertinent; 2. a more intense application of this knowledge of other languages to the solution of problems within the text of the Hebrew Bible; 3. increased knowledge of the language traditions and manuscript traditions within Hebrew itself, and of the process of their transmission down to modern times; 4. new ways of understanding and studying language in general. These various elements cannot be entirely separated from one another, but this essay will follow roughly the sequence stated above.[1]

I. THE LANGUAGES RELATED TO HEBREW

That biblical Hebrew should be seen within the framework

---

[1] The writer is grateful to his colleague Mr. M. E. J. Richardson for helpful discussion of many points within this essay.

of the Semitic family of languages is in itself nothing new: 'comparative' study of this kind has been significant since early in the nineteenth century and in a more rudimentary form goes back to the medieval Jewish grammarians. From the nineteenth century onwards, 'comparative philology' (the term is somewhat misleading) has been *historical* in character and aims, and has sought to offer an exact statement of the detailed interrelation of languages that are 'related', in the sense of having a common previous origin or ancestor. It is thus the construction of a common scheme, historically stated, within which the material of related languages can be placed. To be historical in this sense entails an implication of prehistory: the relations which we can now see between Arabic, Hebrew, and Akkadian can in principle be traced back to relations which obtained at a time before any of our texts in any such language. Comparative study in this sense may aspire to reconstruct the earlier state of the entire language family, or to reconstruct the state of any particular language, such as Hebrew, at a time before the extant documents. Any such projections of the early or prehistoric state of the language will affect our understanding of its later and historical state. Elements can be explained, in one sense of the word 'explanation', if we know that from which they have grown.

Moreover, in spite of modern finds, very little Hebrew of the biblical period survives other than what can be found within the covers of the Bible itself. Thus, comparative-historical philology may be of importance to us, not only because it can reconstruct what the Hebrew language was like in (say) 1200 B.C., or what its ancestor language was like in 1800, but still more because it may suggest to us ways of understanding and interpreting the material of biblical texts themselves. Quite apart from reconstructions of the most ancient stages, the Bible itself is not always clear, and its language is full of difficulties, many of which have long been recognized. The tradition of meanings within Hebrew, which has come down to us through the centuries, may well not have been properly informed about many of these points. Many such problems may be cleared up through our knowledge of the related languages; and it is through comparative and historical philology that scholars have disciplined and controlled the application of that knowledge.

Basic comparative-historical methods were worked out in the nineteenth century, following largely in the track of Indo-European language studies, and the great synthesis of Brockelmann (*Grundriss*, 2 vols., Berlin, 1908 and 1913) has not yet been replaced. Indeed one may say that, in spite of the importance which comparative-historical work on the grand scale has for biblical study, rather less effort at synthetic comprehension has been recently made; the tendency has rather been towards the solution of individual problems through comparative philology than towards general comparative studies for their own sake. The work which since Brockelmann has become the handbook in general Semitics of the average Old Testament scholar is *An Introduction to the Comparative Grammar of the Semitic Languages: Phonology and Morphology*, edited by S. Moscati (Wiesbaden, 1964). Moscati had the collaboration of several specialists (A. Spitaler, E. Ullendorff, and W. von Soden, doubtless in the main for Arabic, Ethiopic and South Semitic, and Akkadian respectively) and was able to incorporate into the work insights gained from them. Though the work is brief, and intended for the use of students, and though it suffers somewhat from the composite mode of its origin, it is striking that it is the only main work of its genre to appear in our period. Essential reference elements like its tables of phonological correspondences are widely used, not least because by their inclusion of Ugaritic they make out of date the information of older works such as Brockelmann.

On the lexical side, an important advance was made with the appearance of the first fascicle of D. Cohen, *Dictionnaire des racines sémitiques* (Paris and The Hague, from 1970). By collecting the known Semitic roots and carefully classifying their exponents in the various languages, this work promises to bring some much needed discipline into an area where much arbitrariness has often prevailed. In the examination of particular areas within the Semitic vocabulary, such as the terms for domestic animals, foodstuffs, etc., the most important research has been that of P. Fronzaroli, 'Studi sul lessico comune semitico', Accademia Nazionale dei Lincei, *Rendi-*

conti, from 1964. Similarly, P. Marrassini writes on the vocabulary for military architecture in the Syrian area (Florence, 1971).

In basic structure and word-formation, study of the possible combinations of consonants in Semitic roots begins with the important article of J. H. Greenberg, 'The Patterning of Root Morphemes in Semitic', *Word*, vi (1950), 162–81. The idea that an earlier 'biliteralism' lies behind the triliteral root pattern characteristic of later Semitic was studied by, among others, S. Moscati, *Biblica*, xxviii (1947), 113–35, and G. J. Botterweck, *Der Triliterismus in Semitischen* (Bonn, 1952). Deep-ranging studies of structure are carried out by J. Kuryłowitz in his *L'Apophonie en sémitique* (Warsaw, 1961), revised and enlarged as *Studies in Semitic Grammar and Metrics* (London, 1973). Fundamental studies in phonology have come from J. Aro, A. F. L. Beeston, J. Cantineau, P. Fronzaroli, S. Moscati, K. Petráček, O. Rössler, R. Růžička, and E. Ullendorff, to pick out only some leading names.

There is not space to describe the development of studies in each of the various areas of Semitics, and only some essential indications will be offered. On the Assyriological side two great dictionaries are now making rapid progress, the *Chicago Assyrian Dictionary* and W. von Soden's *Akkadisches Handwörterbuch* (Wiesbaden); alongside them may be reckoned von Soden's *Grundriss der akkadischen Grammatik* (Rome, 1952; a new edition with supplement, 1969). A number of grammars of particular stages or groups of texts have also appeared. Erica Reiner's *A Linguistic Analysis of Akkadian* (The Hague, 1966) is one of the first full attempts to describe an ancient Semitic language in the terms and categories of modern linguistics. In general, Assyriology has become conscious of itself as a subject quite independent of Old Testament studies and not existing as an ancillary to them. But, seen from the Old Testament side, our knowledge of language, life, and letters in ancient Mesopotamia has become the most widely based and securely known foundation for knowledge and comparison, both through being set in the most relevant period (say, 2000 to 500 B.C.) and because the texts derive directly from that period and do not come down to us (as biblical texts do) by a long channel of transmission.

Moreover, some Akkadian texts exist in various versions, earlier and later, Assyrian and Babylonian, so that we can distinguish the earlier stages from the later and trace the changes in the texts and their language. But perhaps the most striking single area in which the influence of Akkadian linguistic phenomena on the understanding of biblical Hebrew can be seen is the study of the verb system.

The other Semitic language, alongside Hebrew, that was basic to traditional Oriental studies was Arabic; and, if its direct importance has somewhat fallen as that of Akkadian and Ugaritic has grown, Arabic still remains the Semitic language that is most fully known and most comprehensively evidenced of all. In all attempts to reconstruct the phonology of early Semitic the evidence of Arabic is of paramount importance; and its numerous dialects, many of which have been carefully studied, provide important analogies of the ways in which a Semitic language may in the course of time diverge from an original form. One example of such study within our period, by a scholar who is also a distinguished Hebraist, is the *Ancient West-Arabian* of C. Rabin (London, 1951). Although in its phonology Arabic comes perhaps closer to the proto-Semitic ancestor than any other extant Semitic language, there is reason to suppose that on the lexical side it has been rather innovative, producing many forms and meanings without good parallel in the more ancient cognate languages. The traditional Arabic dictionary (built upon the indigenous medieval lexicography) has often been a trap for the biblical scholar who has tried to derive from it meanings for rare Hebrew words; and biblical scholars must hope that haste will be made with the *Belegwörterbuch zur klassischen arabischen Sprache*, based upon the literary *Nachlass* of Th. Nöldeke, that has begun to appear under the editorship of J. Kraemer, M. Ullmann, *et al.* (Berlin, from 1952).

Incidentally, during the Middle Ages Arabic was important in another way, in that it was the mother tongue of many Jews and especially of most Jewish grammarians and lexicographers; and this in turn is important for the transmission of text and meanings during that time. The most distinguished authority on this is J. Blau: see for instance his *Grammar of Mediaeval Judaeo-Arabic* (Hebrew; Jerusalem, 1961), and his *The Emergence and Linguistic Background of Judaeo-Arabic* (Oxford, 1965).

The South Semitic field (South Arabian and the Ethiopian languages) has by contrast, and in spite of its intrinsic importance, remained the preserve of a minority of scholars. It is significant in that the South Arabian inscriptional material goes back to a time well before Islam and some of it is contemporary with events of the Old Testament, while both South Arabian and Ethiopic have many linguistic features in common with Hebrew; cf. E. Ullendorff's section on 'The contribution of Ethiopic to Old Testament lexicography' within his Schweich Lectures, *Ethiopia and the Bible* (London, 1968), pp. 125–30, and earlier in *VT* vi (1956), 190–8; also W. Leslau, *Ethiopic and South Arabic Contributions to the Hebrew Lexicon* (Berkeley, 1958). In ancient South Arabian the major development has been the appearance of A. F. L. Beeston's *A Descriptive Grammar of Epigraphic South Arabian* (London, 1962); and meanwhile many new texts have been published, not least by A. Jamme. In the modern South Arabian languages, Socotri etc., research by W. Leslau, T. M. Johnstone, and others should be mentioned.

In the judgement of most scholars, however, the area that comes closest to the Old Testament is North-West Semitic, and there has been very great interest in Ugaritic in particular. The inscriptional evidence from the Canaanite-Aramaic area has continued to build up, and the last decade has seen the publication of important new editions, along with dependent studies such as grammars and dictionaries. H. Donner and W. Röllig's *Kanaanäische und aramäische Inschriften* (3 vols., Wiesbaden, 1962–4, including a contribution by O. Rössler on the Numidian elements; new and corrected edition, 1966–1969), popularly known as *KAI*, is likely to be the standard textbook on the main inscriptions for some time to come. More recently J. C. L. Gibson's *Textbook of Syrian Semitic Inscriptions*: 1: *Hebrew and Moabite Inscriptions* (Oxford, 1971), 2. *Aramaic Inscriptions, including Inscriptions in the Dialect of Zenjirli* (Oxford, 1975), has been added. The *Dictionnaire des inscriptions sémitiques de l'ouest* by C.-F. Jean and J. Hoftijzer (Leiden, 1965) gives lexicographical coverage of the entire area, including Phoenician, Punic, Moabite,

Aramaic, Ya'udic, Nabataean, Palmyrene, and Hebrew inscriptional material. Grammars, on the other hand, have taken on only one or two of the dialects at a time. The most important are J. Friedrich's *Phönizisch-punische Grammatik* (Rome, 1951; new edition, supervised by W. Röllig, Rome, 1970)—which in its first edition included in an appendix a separate treatment of Ya'udic but has now omitted this, a sign of changing opinion about the placing of this dialect—and on the Aramaic side the very precise *Altaramäische Grammatik* of R. Degen (Wiesbaden, 1969). Re-editions of particular inscriptions include J. A. Fitzmyer's *The Aramaic Inscriptions of Sefire* (Rome, 1967).

Among the North-West Semitic languages the place of Aramaic is a special one. Though in its earlier forms it is known from inscriptions, just as Phoenician is, in its later stages it is known from extensive literary sources; it became the language of large groups of Jews, some parts of the Old Testament itself are written in it, it eventually replaced Hebrew as the main spoken language of Palestine and ruled also in the important Babylonian community of Jewry, and it became a major vehicle of Jewish tradition, as well as becoming in another form (called Syriac) the language of an important part of Christendom with an extensive literature. The older research in all branches of Aramaic was well surveyed by F. Rosenthal, *Die aramaistische Forschung seit Th. Nöldeke's Veröffentlichungen* (Leiden, 1939; reprint, 1964). For a more recent survey we may refer to the comprehensive article 'Aramaic' by E. Y. Kutscher in *EJ*, Jerusalem, 1972, iii, cols. 259–87, with extensive bibliography, and likewise to his article 'Aramaic' in *Current Trends in Linguistics*, vi (1971), 347–412.

The early Aramaic stage, known from inscriptional evidence, has already been mentioned; the names of workers like A. Dupont-Sommer, G. Garbini, and J. C. Greenfield may be added. A dictionary of this material was published by I. N. Vinnikov in *Palestinsky Sbornik* (1958–65).

In the important Persian period the basic Elephantine papyri (conveniently available in A. Cowley, *Aramaic Papyri of the Fifth Century B.C.*, Oxford, 1923; reprinted 1967) have now been supplemented, especially by E. G. Kraeling, *The*

Brooklyn Museum Aramaic Papyri (New Haven, 1953) and by G. R. Driver, *Aramaic Documents of the Fifth Century B.C.,* (Oxford, 1954; abridged edition, 1957). The most comprehensive study of the Jewish society of Elephantine is B. Porten's *Archives from Elephantine* (Berkeley, 1968).

Biblical Aramaic studies, working on the small corpus of material in Ezra and Daniel, plus other fragments, have also been well served. F. Rosenthal published *A Grammar of Biblical Aramaic* (Wiesbaden, 1961). The *Lexicon in veteris testamenti libros* of L. Koehler and W. Baumgartner, which had many weaknesses in its Hebrew part (see discussion below), was from the beginning very strong and thorough in its Aramaic part, prepared by Baumgartner (first edition completed, Leiden, 1953, with introduction on the problems of Aramaic lexicography on pp. xvi–xlix).

Passing to the wide field of post-biblical Jewish Aramaic, we note the stimulus provided by new editions of Targums (A. Sperber, *The Bible in Aramaic*, Leiden, from 1959) and the publication of other Targums newly discovered (the *MS. Neophyti I* to the Pentateuch, ed. A. Diez Macho, Madrid and Barcelona, from 1968, and the Job Targum, *Le Targum de Job*, ed. J. P. M. van der Ploeg and A. S. van der Woude along with B. Jongeling, Leiden, 1971); to this should be added the other Aramaic documents from Qumran, such as J. A. Fitzmyer's edition of *The Genesis Apocryphon of Qumran Cave I* (Rome, 1966). E. Y. Kutscher published many specific studies, e.g. his series on Galilean Aramaic in *Tarbiṣ*, 1950–2. The question of the linguistic situation in Palestine about the beginning of the era, and the shift from Hebrew to Aramaic, will be mentioned below.

Much of the work in Syriac has been interested in the literature and its content, generally theological, and is thus less directly relevant to our purpose. The basic reference works are still the grammar of Th. Nöldeke (ETr, London, 1904) and the *Lexicon Syriacum* of C. Brockelmann (Halle, 1928). Work on the early Syriac inscriptions, carried forward notably by J. B. Segal, has recently given us also H. J. W. Drijvers's *Old-Syriac (Edessean) Inscriptions* (Leiden, 1972). Segal's *The Diacritical Point and the Accents in Syriac* (London, 1953) parallels studies in the Massoretic techniques in Hebrew, to be mentioned later; and F. Rundgren's *Das altsyrische Verbalsystem* (Uppsala, 1960) parallels the many discussions of the verb systems.

In the Mesopotamian language Mandaic, major new works have included E. S. Drower and R. Macuch, *A Mandaic Dictionary* (Oxford, 1963), and R. Macuch, *Handbook of Classical and Modern Mandaic* (Berlin, 1965).

From these rather later outgrowths of Aramaic we turn, however, back to the second millennium and to studies in Ugaritic, which have formed a particularly energetic and intensive centre of study during the decades of our survey. Among significant publications of the basic material we must mention G. R. Driver's *Canaanite Myths and Legends* (Edinburgh, 1956); the latest of C. H. Gordon's series of handbooks in his *Ugaritic Textbook* (Rome, 1965; reprint with additions, 1967); and the definitive re-edition of the earlier texts in Mlle A. Herdner's *Corpus des tablettes en cunéiformes alphabétiques* (= *CTA*, Paris, 1963). Further important new texts have been published in volumes of the series *Palais royal d'Ugarit* (*PRU* ii, 1957; v, 1965) and *Ugaritica* (*Ugaritica* v, 1968). Important works of reference include: J. Aistleitner's *Wörterbuch der ugaritischen Sprache* (3rd edn., Berlin, 1967), in which O. Eissfeldt co-operated and which he saw through the press after Aistleitner's death; R. E. Whitaker's *A Concordance of the Ugaritic Literature* (Harvard, 1972); and the *Konkordanz der ugaritischen Textzählungen* of M. Dietrich and O. Loretz (Neukirchen, 1972), which provides cross-references for each text between the many different systems of numbering which have grown up independently of one another. S. Segert has written a grammar, *Ugaritsky Yazyk* (Moscow, 1965). Among periodicals and series we may note the appearance of *Ugarit-Forschungen* and the series Alter Orient und Altes Testament, the latter including many Ugaritic items, particularly the Ugarit bibliography currently in process of publication.[2]

Thus a very large work of analysis and interpretation of the Ugaritic material has now grown up, and it would be impossible to give a detailed impression of it here, or to

---

[2] M. Dietrich, O. Loretz, P.-R. Berger, J. Sandmartin, *Ugarit-Bibliographie 1928–1966*, AOAT xx. 1–4, Neukirchen–Vluyn, 1973.

mention particular names without being invidious. But there are two aspects which deserve some special mention.

Firstly, it remains a matter of debate into what place Ugaritic fits within the classification of the Semitic languages. While it clearly shares many features with the languages of the north-western group, such as Canaanite (Phoenician and Hebrew) and Aramaic, it has been observed that common features are strikingly shared by Ugaritic with other areas of Semitic also. As a second-millennium language, Ugaritic may fit better into a classification valid for the conditions of that period, rather than into a classification based on first-millennium language states. The question of the grouping and classification of the known languages and dialects is an interesting one but also a somewhat abstract one: it does not decide a great deal for anything else, and in particular it cannot be confidently used to force into a pattern evidence other than that which was used in setting up the classification in the first place.

Secondly, Ugaritic literature is notable for the large number of parallels with the Old Testament in style, in expression and in vocabulary grouping. Many studies of the linguistic and literary parallels between Ugaritic poetry and the Bible have been carried out, including elements like word-pairs and prosodic patterns. S. Gevirtz with his *Patterns in the Early Poetry of Israel* (Chicago, 1963) exemplifies this kind of work, and a large project for the collection of these materials, now in process of publication, is the *Ras Shamra Parallels* edited by L. R. Fisher (i, ii, AnO xlix, l, Rome, 1972, 1975). Relations of *content*, such as the information derived from Ugaritic sources about the mythology and religion of Syria–Palestine in the late second millennium, fall outside the scope of the present article, and the practical question concerning the use of Ugaritic material for new semantic interpretations of the Old Testament text will be considered below.

It is to the *ancient* languages of the Semitic family, naturally, that scholars mainly relate biblical Hebrew in their researches, and historical reconstruction will naturally begin from the earliest sources. But the modern languages should not be forgotten, even though they have in many cases substantially diverged from certain patterns characteristic of ancient

Semitic. Alongside their innovative elements, it is common for modern Semitic languages to conserve features which are ancient, and these conservative traits are often made to stand out when a modern language is written in a script that is essentially ancient (so, for instance, the script of modern Hebrew or Amharic). Moreover, modern linguistics have emphasized the central importance of *spoken* language; and in the study of the ancient languages themselves much freshness has been brought in by those scholars who also have considerable experience with modern Semitic languages (for example, M. Cohen, H. Polotsky). In general, then, studies in Amharic, in modern Hebrew, in modern Arabic dialects, and in neo-Syriac form an essential part of the scene of modern Semitics and cannot be ignored.

Moreover, it has long been recognized that the Semitic language family cannot be entirely isolated and that certain family resemblances can be discerned which stretch, geographically expressed, through large areas of northern Africa. This larger language grouping has generally been called 'Hamito-Semitic', although more recently other terms like 'Afro-Asiatic' have been proposed (see for example the essays collected in C. T. Hodge (ed.), *Afroasiatic*, The Hague, 1971). It includes the Cushitic languages, which abut upon the modern Semitic languages of Ethiopia; the Berber of North Africa; a group farther west and south, now being called 'Chadic', of which the best-known representative is Hausa; and, coming back closer to the Old Testament, the ancient Egyptian language. Central works in Hamito-Semitic linguistics have included: M. Cohen's *Essai comparatif sur le vocabulaire et la phonétique du chamito-sémitique* (Paris, 1947); I. M. Diakonoff's *Semito-Hamitic Languages: an Essay in Classification* (Moscow, 1965). Two particular studies which have sought to establish particular relations between one or more Semitic languages and one or more of the wider Hamito-Semitic family are: T. W. Thacker's *The Relationship of the Semitic and Egyptian Verbal Systems* (Oxford, 1954), which is rather stronger on the Egyptian side; and O. Rössler's studies, which have maintained that there is a special relationship between Akkadian and the language of the old Lybian inscriptions (or, conversely, that Lybian was a Semitic language): see articles such as *ZDMG* (c (1950), 461–514; *Orientalia* xx (1951), 101–7, 366–73; *ZA* l (N.F. xvi), (1952), 121–50.)

The practical importance, for detailed questions in the interpretation of the Old Testament, of Hamito-Semitic comparative linguistics should not be set too high. Some connoisseurs in this field remain rather pessimistic about the results attainable (cf. Polotsky, Ullendorff; see for instance Polotsky in *The World History of the Jewish People*, London, 1964, articles 'Semitics' and 'Egyptian', i. 99–111, 121–34, and especially 122 f., with Ullendorff in Hodge, *Afroasiatic*, p. 34.) Some have thought that relations such as those between Hamitic and Semitic are not genetic 'family' relationships but are the result of influence or contagion: 'some African languages became Hamitic when they were exposed to the impact of a strong Semitic superstratum' (G. Garbini, 'La semitistica: definizione e prospettive di una disciplina', 1965, reported by Ullendorff, ibid., p. 34).

Thus, to sum up, the inclusion of the Hamito-Semitic perspective alters the horizon within which Semitic problems are seen, and thus indirectly alters the aspect of studies in the language of the Hebrew Bible. But the effect of this is macrocosmic rather than microcosmic and only occasionally will this perspective affect the detailed questions of biblical philology.

Of the total Hamito-Semitic field, there is one portion which for historical and cultural reasons comes much closer than others to the Old Testament, and that is ancient Egyptian: comparisons of the verb system have already been mentioned, and to this must be added lexical loan-words from Egyptian within Hebrew, plus some personal names. The later form of the same language, Coptic, must not be forgotten, since its Greek writing-system permits an insight into the vocalization of Egyptian, even though in a late stage of that language tradition.

In general, then, in so far as linguistic study is intended to assist in the reconstruction of the prehistory and origins of the Hebrew language, account will have to be taken of the entire Hamito-Semitic problem, even if, at least at the present time, precision in the necessary phonological and lexical relationships is attainable only within the Semitic field. But for detailed problems, such as the understanding of this or that individual word, it is unlikely that these more remote linguistic relationships will furnish much light to the exegete.

Alongside the study of languages proper, the study of writing, its origin and development, has also been a centre of activity and progress, and it is not surprising that Semitists have had a prominent place in this, since all modern western writing systems are descended from Near Eastern origins. The work that has been most systematic and most influential has been I. J. Gelb's *A Study of Writing* (Chicago, 1952); its terminology and its reasoning are not always, however, very lucid. Other works have been G. R. Driver's Schweich Lectures, *Semitic Writing: from Pictograph to Alphabet* (London, 1948; 3rd edn. now published, 1976); M. Cohen's *La grande invention de l'écriture et son évolution* (Paris, 1958). The most recent major work, again by a Semitist, has been J. Friedrich's *Geschichte der Schrift* (Heidelberg, 1966).

The history of writing, seen from a practical aspect, is connected with the interpretation of ancient inscriptions and thereby with the history of grammar; on this side of the subject, influential work has been done by the school of W. F. Albright, as in F. M. Cross and D. N. Freedman's *Early Hebrew Orthography* (New Haven, 1952). Recent years have brought signs of some reaction against their position: see D. W. Goodwin, *Text-Restoration Methods in Contemporary U.S.A. Biblical Scholarship* (Naples, 1969) and L. A. Bange, *A Study of the Use of Vowel-Letters in Alphabetic Consonantal Writing* (Munich, 1971). On the presence or absence of word-division, whether by signs or by spaces, in various relevant scripts, the facts are summarized by A. R. Millard, '*Scriptio continua* in early Hebrew', *JSS* xv (1970), 2–15. Notable studies of particular scripts are those of M. Martin on the Dead Sea Scrolls (Louvain, 1958), of J. B. Peckham on late Phoenician (Harvard, 1968), and of J. Naveh on Aramaic (Jerusalem, 1970). Such studies shade into the work of manuscript studies, such as the interpretation of the Qumran finds, and later the understanding of vocalization systems and the work of the Massoretes.

Finally, not all relevant sources from the ancient Near East are linguistically Semitic. Relations with Egyptian have already been mentioned; and the place of Sumerian, Hittite, Hurrian, Elamite, and Old Persian texts must be remembered, for there may be important common literary or cultural elements even where the languages are not related within a common genetic family. On the further question, whether there existed a common culture area not only in the Near East but also in the Mediterranean basin, let it suffice here to indicate that such a view exists: see C. H. Gordon's *Before the Bible* (London, 1962) and M. C. Astour's *Hellenosemitica* (Leiden, 1965). Such a view could carry with it linguistic implications, e.g. in the search for common elements between the Semitic and the Indo-European language families; and we simply mention the theory that some of the Minoan writings from Crete are in a Semitic language. (On the wild claim that an inscription allegedly found in Brazil was genuinely 'Phoenician', see the opinions of J. Friedrich, C. H. Gordon and F. M. Cross in *Biblica* xxxvii (1968), 421–63). But, generally, in so far as biblical Hebrew has to be seen against a wider linguistic background, the major element in that background has been, and is likely to remain, the evidence of the Semitic languages rather than any other.

2. THE APPLICATION OF SEMITIC LINGUISTICS TO THE OLD TESTAMENT

Our knowledge of the Semitic languages impinges in several ways upon the more particular task of understanding the Hebrew Bible. First of all, as evidence from the ancient Near East expands, there is the task of interpreting this evidence; and this enlargement of evidence goes hand in hand with the expansion and refinement of linguistic study. Evidence thus interpreted may be relevant for the Old Testament through linguistic relations, or through cultural (social, historical, religious) content, or through both. In this article, however, our attention is devoted to the linguistic relations.

The study of biblical Hebrew, if pursued in isolation, would be a somewhat limited and limiting subject. The Bible constitutes a quite restricted corpus of texts, as has often been remarked, and this restriction has its consequence in the considerable numbers of *hapax legomena* and anomalous forms; see recently, for instance, E. Ullendorff, 'Is biblical Hebrew a language?', *BSOAS* xxxiv (1971), 241–55. Our awareness of the potentialities and limitations of Hebrew is suitably extended if we add to it the study of the Semitic family as a whole (or, indeed, if we add to the study of biblical Hebrew the study of later periods of the same language). Linguistic reconstruction in Hebrew can to some limited extent be carried out on the basis of extrapolation from the evidence of known data within Hebrew; but, on the whole, reconstruction, whether of Hebrew as it was within the biblical period but beyond the limits of our direct evidence, or of Hebrew as it was at a stage earlier than the extant texts, depends on hypotheses which rest upon the cognate Semitic evidence. Thus Semitic linguistics widens the horizon within which all study of the Hebrew Bible takes place.

On the other hand, knowledge of the multiplicity and variety existing within the Semitic group as a whole should not cause the student to lose sight of the individuality of Hebrew and to force its phenomena into those patterns which, from the point of view of what is known through comparative study, seem most convenient and most natural— and the same is true, after all, of Arabic or of Ugaritic or of any other language. The many gaps and unevennesses in our knowledge of ancient Hebrew do not constitute it a senseless labyrinth of unrelated threads, forming evidence which becomes meaningful only when reinterpreted from a comparative standpoint. Biblical Hebrew still forms a proper subject of study in its own right.

Moreover, the study of general Semitics also is a subject in its own right; the facts of the Semitic languages have to be studied and appreciated for themselves, and not cultivated in a merely utilitarian way as a tool for the provision of new interpretations of phenomena within Hebrew. With these general remarks about the relation between general Semitics and the particular problems of Hebrew we may turn to some more particular applications of Semitic linguistics to the Old Testament.

Information derived from one Semitic language or another, or from general Semitics, may be applied by the scholar to the resolving of particular difficulties within the Old Testament. This form of applied philology has been assiduously practised in the last decades. Where the Hebrew text appears difficult or unintelligible, its words (commonly the consonants of its words) are used as clues which lead the researcher to a word or form in a related language, of which the meaning is known. From this word in another language (say, Ugaritic) a projection is made of a Hebrew word or form, the existence of which is now postulated; and, if the meaning of this postulated word or form, gained from Ugaritic, fits the Hebrew passage and provides good sense, then the process is held to have led to a solution. In contrast with an older tendency, which was more conservative towards the meanings attached to Hebrew words but more willing to consider the text corrupt, this newer tendency is conservative towards the text, at least in its consonantal element, but semantically innovative: hundreds or even thousands of new Hebrew words, or new meanings for Hebrew words and forms, have been suggested. The method is not in principle novel, and had analogies already in the Middle Ages, when Jewish exegetes used meanings derived from Aramaic and Arabic; but its scale and its comprehensiveness, as seen in modern practice, are unexampled in the earlier history of the subject; it rests on the systematic and historical principles worked out in the nineteenth century and unknown to the medieval scholars, and it gains from the general prestige of comparative philology in modern times.

Among the scholars who have produced large numbers of new philological explanations of Hebrew words we may mention N. H. Tur-Sinai, especially in his commentary on Job (English form, *The Book of Job*, Jerusalem, 1957); G. R. Driver, in a long series of philological notes in various journals, notably *JTS*; and most recently M. J. Dahood, in a long series of publications, including many articles in *Biblica* and the commentary on the Psalms in the Anchor Bible series (i–iii, New York, 1966, 1968, 1970). Dahood's proposals purport to rest mainly upon a basis in Ugaritic and Phoenician; and they seem to suggest a view that Ugaritic,

Phoenician, and Hebrew were all slightly-differentiated dialects within one great linguistic and cultural complex, this complex having continuity with the Old Testament on the linguistic, the literary, and the religious-theological levels. His proposals up to 1967 are usefully indexed in E. R. Martinez, *Hebrew-Ugaritic Index to the Writings of Mitchell J. Dahood* (Rome, 1967). Driver's suggestions, by contrast, derive from a much wider spread within the Semitic field, notably from Arabic but also from many other areas, and are independent of the cultural implications entailed for Syria–Palestine by Dahood's ideas.

The new meanings thus discovered for Hebrew words have come before the public with remarkably little delay through the medium of popular translations of the Bible. It is no secret that the Old Testament of the *New English Bible* (Oxford and Cambridge, 1970) contains hundreds of these new interpretations, often closely allied to those already published by G. R. Driver; and Dahood's interpretations in the Psalms have likewise been made public property through the Anchor Bible series (though this particular characteristic does not obtain for the series in general). It is of course right that the public should have access to the latest results of linguistic research and exegesis; but it is in our era for the first time that hypotheses of linguistic research have been laid before the public, in a form that seemed to bespeak some definitiveness, before they had even become known to the world of competent scholarship, much less been approved and accepted by it.

An analysis and evaluation of this method of discovering new meanings for Hebrew words and forms has been published by the present writer (J. Barr, *Comparative Philology and the Text of the Old Testament*, Oxford, 1968, supplemented by other articles, such as 'Philology and Exegesis'[3]), and only certain points can be summarized here.

Firstly, two components of method may be usefully distinguished. The first is the stage of devising possible solutions to difficulties on the basis of information from

---

[3] In C. Brekelmans (ed.), *Questions disputées d'Ancien Testament. Méthode et théologie. XXIIIᵉ session des Journées Bibliques de Louvain*, Bibliotheca Ephemeridum Theologicarum Lovaniensium, XXXIII, Louvain, 1974, pp. 39–61.

cognate languages; the second is the stage of considering these
possibilities, in order to see whether they will stand up to
critical examination. For the first stage the equipment
required includes a knowledge of the standard phonological
correspondences (e.g. that Hebrew *š* will normally correspond
with either *th* or *s* in Arabic), a knowledge of meanings in
cognate languages (accessible through a dictionary), and some
experience of the potential of philological suggestions.

Thus at 1 Sam. 1:5, MT *mānâh 'aḥaṭ 'appāyim kî* . . ., the
'appāyim has long been considered anomalous and has
commonly been emended into the (not very similar) *'epes* (so
even *NEB*). Can any alternative suggestion be derived from
our knowledge of other Semitic languages? Ugaritic has
several adverb forms like *'phn, 'pn, 'pnk*, meaning something
like 'then', 'thereafter', 'also', and perhaps related to the simpler
'p. This might suggest that a similar adverb form might be
detected here in Hebrew, without any emendation; and it
might be a parallel extension of the common Hebrew adverb
'ap, and have like it the sense 'but', which fits the context and
indeed gives the same sense as the emendation *'epes* 'except',
fitting in also with the LXX (πλήν). The idea of such a
solution can in fact be produced very easily; and an
experienced scholar, faced with a difficulty in the Hebrew
text, may set out in his mind three or four such philological
suggestions for consideration.

But the second component is the stage of considering
whether such proposals will hold water. This, though it may
be considered more 'negative' in contrast with the 'positive'
first component, is a much more complicated, lengthier and
more sophisticated procedure, for the number of considerations to be taken into account is much greater. Many of the
philological proposals which have been published must be
considered to have gone little beyond the first stage: they are
suggestions put forward, along with some evidence which
may favour them. Comparatively seldom are they fully
researched investigations which take into account all the
circumstances, favourable and unfavourable. Purely quanti-
tatively one might suggest a rule that, if one is to demonstrate
that a Hebrew word had a meaning not hitherto known for it,
the demonstration should require an article of twenty or

thirty pages for each word, in order that the various levels of evidence should be taken into account. The fact that many philological proposals have been propounded in notes of three or four lines tells against their being accepted as more than possibilities for consideration.

Secondly, the current pursuit of new philological explanations is (not necessarily, but commonly in fact) carried on in neglect of other forms of modern scholarship which are equally valid. Textual criticism, for instance, has sometimes been pushed aside. When this is so, we find a blind veneration for the signs on paper combined with the pragmatic necessities of the philological method (for, if there is no consonantal skeleton to start from, there is no means of knowing what words in other Semitic languages should be taken into account). It is pseudo-historical to accept the consonantal component of the text and blithely to ignore the vocalization. For it is true that the vowel pointing was added at a historically later stage; but this applies only to the graphic registration of the transmission. The 'original text' of many passages was the phonetic text, of which, through the nature of the script, the consonantal element (along with *some* vowels, through *matres lectionis*) was first marked in writing, the remaining vowel component being preserved in oral tradition until at a later stage it also was marked with written signs. This does not mean that the vocalization is 'correct': it only means that it is evidence of much greater age than the registration of it by the Massoretes, and that it cannot be merely ignored or dismissed without specific reasons. In any case, the philological approach has not consistently sustained the Massoretic text, and variant readings and even conjectural emendations have been sporadically accepted. But it is not sufficient that textual considerations should be accepted only after every philological possibility has been exhausted; on the contrary, no justice can be done to the work of textual criticism unless it is accepted as an equal partner in the task of interpretation from the beginning.

The same is the case with literary source-criticism: the 'difficulties' to which modern philological solutions have been offered are sometimes difficulties which can be solved by other means also. Thus the difficulty in *wayyiqqaḥ* (Num.

16:1), which has led to the suggestion of another Hebrew word, different from *lāqaḥ* 'take' and meaning 'was insolent, was defiant, rebelled (followed by *NEB*), is a difficulty only if the source-critical analysis of the passage (as set out, for instance, by S. R. Driver in his *Introduction*, 1891, p. 59) is ignored: for by that analysis 'took' belonged to one source, which said that 'Korah took men of the children of Israel', while another source related that 'Dathan and Abiram arose before Moses'. If the source-division is accepted, then there is no reason to seek another explanation. Thus in general the recent vogue of philological explanation, in spite of its modernity, is often a conservative tendency in relation to other forms of analysis which have been used in modern Old Testament scholarship.

Thirdly, although the entire procedure of philological solution of particular problems in Hebrew logically rests and depends upon comparative Semitic philology, it is by no means sure that it is actually supported by that discipline. On the contrary, there is reason to believe that the impulse to produce quick identifications for words in the Hebrew Bible on the basis of other Semitic languages has actually harmed the edifice of Semitic philology and neglected elements which are essential to it. Thus to look critically at the prevailing fashion is not to undermine the edifice of philology; it is rather to reassert the standards of that discipline as against hasty applications of it. The study of cognate languages like Ugaritic is harmed and distorted if these are seen primarily as quarries from which may be hewn fresh pieces of evidence about meanings in Hebrew; the study of any language is distorted if it is not seen *for itself*, as a linguistic system differing from others and having its own individuality. Ugaritic, or Arabic, or Akkadian, deserve to be studied and assessed on their own merits, as Hebrew does.

To sum up, there is no question that the *method* as a method, the method of seeking solutions for biblical-Hebrew texts in the linguistic evidence of the cognate languages, is basically justified by comparative-philological method; but then so also is the criticism of the method. Such criticism can be regarded as the systematic carrying out of what we have seen to be the second component within the method itself; and it is on such criticism that probable future success for the method depends. There is every reason to expect that over coming decades a steady progress will be made in new identifications of Hebrew forms and meanings on the basis of cognate materials; but this will be so only if suggestions are carefully and critically examined, and if the uncertainties and limitations of the method are seen and admitted.

If this is not done, it is likely that the method will by its own excesses provoke the same sort of sceptical reaction as arose against the excess of conjectural emendation. Plausible as may be the claim that the method 'in fact works', the fact remains that, of all the philological solutions that have been propounded in the present century, only a small proportion are convincing and only a small proportion are likely ever to be accepted by a majority of competent scholars. If this is so, it is not because there is something 'wrong' with the philological approach to such questions; it may well be, rather, that there are too many gaps in our knowledge for any method to provide the answer to every difficulty, and that an imbalance between innovative ingenuity and the resources for conclusive demonstration has resulted. The pragmatic demand, that if the text is unintelligible something 'must be done', carries little force: if the essentials for decisions about meaning are not known, then nothing can be 'done' beyond the careful delimitation of the extent of our knowledge.

3. STUDIES OF HEBREW ITSELF

We now pass to a review of important recent work done on the linguistics of biblical Hebrew itself. The review will follow roughly the following order: beginning with general surveys and major works of reference, it will pass to special studies, especially in the function of morphological categories, and then to syntactical questions; from there it will return to questions of phonology and pronunciation traditions, which will then lead us to connections with post-biblical Hebrew and the transmission of the text. But it is impossible to isolate these various matters, since any grammatical discussion involves several of these dimensions at once.

In general, it is remarkable how little has been done to

produce massive surveys of the Hebrew language which might match those achieved by earlier generations. For the Hebrew of all periods see the survey of C. Rabin in *Current Trends in Linguistics*, vi (1971), 304–46, divided into six periods; also the article 'Hebrew Language' in *EJ*, Jerusalem, 1972, xvi, cols. 1559–1662, by several authors and divided into several periods (the article 'Hebrew Grammar' in viii, cols. 77–175, by U. Ornan is modern and universal in scope and is not divided according to period). But even within the biblical period new major treatises have not been forthcoming: in English, for instance, A. E. Cowley's edition of Gesenius–Kautzsch (Oxford, 1910) remains unreplaced as a reference grammar for the facts of the Massoretic Text; and the more modern and critical grammars of G. Bergsträsser (Leipzig, 1918; never completed) and H. Bauer and P. Leander (Halle, 1922) have neither been translated into English nor replaced. It may be that the increasing impact of comparative philological material from many sources, and of new evidence within the Hebrew tradition itself, has made it difficult to attempt such imposing works of synthesis in our era.

Similarly, Hebrew lexicography has been slow to surpass, or even to equal, the achievements of Brown–Driver–Briggs and of Gesenius–Buhl at the beginning of the century, and these two dictionaries still remain basic because of their reliability and good judgement. A new project, directed by L. Koehler and W. Baumgartner, began to appear in 1948 and was completed in its first edition in 1953; its Aramaic section has already been mentioned above and was the more highly esteemed. On the Hebrew side the work was less than a complete success. It was praiseworthy that both German and English were used in all entries, but this cut down the space available, and the English was often very peculiar; and many doubts were felt about the accuracy of the printing and transliteration of oriental scripts. A second edition provided corrections but not much more. In 1967 a completely reworked third edition began to appear, under the editorship of Baumgartner himself, and one fascicle, about one-third of the entire work, was published. This shows many signs of greatly surpassing the previous editions (cf. review by the writer, *JSS* xiii (1968), 260–7). Professor Baumgartner in turn unhappily died before the project could be completed, but it is understood that the continuation of the project is in able hands.[4] The new edition, unlike the earlier ones, uses German only and not English.

Other projects for new major dictionaries are on the way in Germany and in England. Students have been served by the short and simple dictionaries of G. Fohrer (Berlin, 1971; English, London, 1973) and W. L. Holladay (Leiden, 1971), the latter being an abridgement of Koehler–Baumgartner. The relations between the handling of biblical and that of post-biblical Hebrew in lexicography will be mentioned below. On the general problems of Hebrew lexicography see the writer's article in the Proceedings of the Colloquium on Semitic Lexicography held at Florence, April 1972,[5] along with other articles in the same volume, on the lexicography of other Semitic languages and of the Semitic family as a whole.

The Hebrew dictionary of the future will have to deal in greater degree with the following problems:

(a) It will have to accommodate the mass of suggestions made on the basis of cognate languages. Here it will have to strike a happy mean between the two extremes of registering (more 'subjectively') only those words and meanings which the editor himself considers to be 'right', and (more 'objectively') registering every form and interpretation that anyone has put forward, however probable and improbable. To deal with this problem the writer has suggested a notation of four grades of probability (see *JSS* xiii (1968), 261 f.).

(b) It will have to have a policy about the importance and prominence to be accorded to etymological/comparative information. Past dictionaries appear to have dealt with this on an *ad hoc* basis, sometimes giving more information and fuller discussions, sometimes less information and no alternative possibilities, and sometimes ordering the sequence of the Hebrew entry according to order of distance from the putative etymological guidance, sometimes not. A more

---

[4] A second fascicle appeared in 1974. Baumgartner's colleague E. Y. Kutscher had died in 1974. The continuation of the work was undertaken by B. Hartmann, Ph. Reymond, and J. J. Stamm.

[5] P. Fronzaroli (ed.), *Studies on Semitic Lexicography*, Quaderni di Semitistica ii, Florence, 1973.

consistent policy, following the example of modern dictionaries in Akkadian and other languages, will be necessary.

(c) Because of the increasing interest in semantics, greater
thought will have to be given to the ways in which the ranges
and varieties of meanings can be methodically arranged,
suitably displayed and economically stated. In the past it has
seemed sufficient if an English gloss (e.g. that *yāšaḇ* means
'sit') is provided, along with short notes about the circumstances on a rather *ad hoc* basis. Where several meanings or
departments of meaning have to be distinguished, many
different schemes of classification and sequence have been
used: a classification controlled by the etymology, one
controlled by the chronology of uses within Hebrew, one
controlled by the distinction between direct and transferred
or metaphorical senses, one controlled by statistical frequen-
cies, and so on. We can expect that selection among these
principles will have to be made more explicit in the future.
Since meanings are not really stated by glosses in another
language such as English, and actually reside in the differences
from other words in Hebrew, and since much emphasis has
recently been laid on word-pairs and vocabulary groupings,
ways for displaying the relationships of groups of words will
have to take a larger place, in comparison with the traditional
one-word entry.

Among works of reference the concordance should not be
neglected. The traditional work of S. Mandelkern is well
organized for the checking of detailed word-forms and thus
for textual and Massoretic research, but not for modern
semantic study: 'my father' comes in a different entry from
'the father' or 'his fathers', and so on. A new concordance,
using a more purely semantic mode of organization, and
separating out major cases (with nouns, whether used as
subject, as object, or otherwise) but not the simpler formal
and morphological differences, was published by G. Lisowsky
(Stuttgart, 1958).

We now turn therefore to studies in the functions of
morphological categories. One of the most active areas of
discussion has been the verb system of Hebrew and its
peculiar interrelation of the types *ḳaṭal/yiḳṭol* and
weḳaṭal/wayyiḳṭol—a situation which as a whole can scarcely

be paralleled elsewhere, unless in dialects themselves very close to Hebrew, though various individual items can be paralleled in other Semitic languages. One major question has been how far these tenses (I use this as an empty traditional label for these types; the term does not imply anything about their function) mark the time of actions, the 'aspect' (as complete, incomplete, etc.), or the kind of action (*Aktionsart*, as habitual, continual, once-for-all, etc.). Most modern studies of the Hebrew tenses have been strongly comparative in character, relating the phenomena especially to types like the Akkadian permansive and the Egyptian 'old perfective'. An influential study was G. R. Driver's *Problems of the Hebrew Verbal System* (Edinburgh, 1936).

In 1951 an essay by F. R. Blake, *A Resurvey of the Hebrew Tenses* (Rome), undertook to get rid of 'the unrealistic and fanciful explanations of syntactic facts arising out of the usually accepted "aspect theory"' (p. vii)—the 'aspect theory' being here represented by the older work of S. R. Driver, *Hebrew Tenses* (3rd edn., 1892). Following H. Bauer (1910), Blake argued that the imperfect was *originally* omnitemporal but that in essence throughout the main biblical period 'the perfect and imperfect are opposed to one another as past and present-progressive past-future-modal respectively' (p. 72). But in the same year C. Brockelmann published an essay, 'Die "Tempora" des Semitischen', *Zeitschrift für Phonetik* v (1951), 133–54, which maintained that the tenses indicated subjective aspects, the perfect simply stating that an event had occurred, the imperfect depicting it in its course. An aspect theory of a subtle and complicated type, with a considerable theoretical introduction, is put forward by F. Rundgren in his *Das althebräische Verbum: Abriss der Aspektlehre* (Uppsala, 1961); cf. his related work on Syriac, already mentioned. A close study of a particular corpus, with care to note the literary context in each case, is that of D. Michel, *Tempora und Satzstellung in den Psalmen* (Bonn, 1960); in his judgement the perfect indicates an action which is seen as independent, as taking place in and for itself; the imperfect indicates an action seen as relative, as deriving its meaning from something outside of itself (p. 254). The question is examined again by P. Kustár, *Aspekt im*

Hebräischen (Theologische Dissertationen, ed. B. Reicke, ix,
Basel, 1972); in his view aspect is subjective and has nothing
to do with time or with the external character of actions: the
perfect marks actions which are regarded as 'determining'
(others) and the imperfect those which are regarded as
'determined' (by others). This is connected by the writer with
the Hebrew way of thinking. With J. A. Hughes, *JNES* xxix
(1970), 12–24, we are back in distinctions of real time, with an
argument that the cases which appear not to fit with a time-
marking function can be explained through syntactical
collocation with certain particles or sentence-types. Incidentally, K. Aartun in his *Zur Frage altarabischer Tempora* (Oslo,
1963) similarly concludes that the tense opposition in classical
Arabic is of temporal character. We thus see that the question
of verb tense and aspect continues to excite much discussion
and research, partly because a solution of the question would
make more clear the exact connotation of many passages, and
partly because the whole question is felt to bear upon the
understanding of the special character of the Semitic
languages and/or of that elusive entity, 'Hebrew thought'.

Among works on the verb system one of the most striking
has certainly been E. Jenni's *Das hebräische Pi'el* (Zurich,
1968). This attempts to give a comprehensive and rigorous
statement of the function of the *pi'el*, and the analogy of the
Akkadian D-stem has had considerable influence. According
to Jenni, the traditional term 'intensive' applied to the *pi'el* is
quite wrong. The *pi'el* has a quite unitary meaning, which
stands in opposition to all other stems: where the basic sense
of the verb is intransitive, the *pi'el* is factitive, and where the
basic sense is transitive, the *pi'el* is resultative. The sense of
these terms is carefully defined by Jenni in his closely
reasoned book, and his view is worked out on the basis of a
complete collection of examples throughout the entire
Hebrew Bible. A contrast and complement will be provided
when W. T. Claassen's 'The Hiph'il Verbal Theme in biblical
Hebrew' (doctoral thesis, Stellenbosch, 1971) is published, for
it both examines another verb theme and offers a detailed
critical examination of Jenni's work.

It would be impossible, however, to survey here all the
contributions made to the various departments of Hebrew

language study. In the field of syntax the main work has been the *Hebräische Syntax* of the veteran C. Brockelmann, published at Neukirchen in 1956, the year of the writer's death. Apart from particular points, the book does not represent any outstanding advance in the subject. In general there continue to be complaints that syntax is neglected in grammatical presentations of Hebrew (and of other Semitic languages); if this is so, it is probably the result of the old-fashioned philological structure adopted, under which phonology and morphology dominate the scene and absorb the description of syntactic elements, leaving over only fragments for the department of syntax. A work that is informed by a more modern kind of linguistics and uses a strictly controlled (if somewhat mechanical) 'tagmemic' technique, is F. I. Andersen's *The Hebrew Verbless Clause in the Pentateuch* (Nashville and New York, 1970); cf. also the lengthy review of the same by J. Hoftijzer, 'The nominal Clause reconsidered', *VT* xxiii (1973), 446–510. In the same context may be mentioned Hoftijzer's painstaking study of the particle *'eṭ*, *OTS* xiv (1965), 1–99.

Throughout the period surveyed in this article the study of biblical Hebrew, if stimulated on the one hand by work in other Semitic languages and in general Semitics, has on the other hand been revitalized by fresh knowledge of *later* Hebrew and of the conditions in which the text and language of the Bible were transmitted. Until recent decades the omnipresence of the Massoretic text, and the lack of substantial amounts of really early manuscript material, had restricted the possibilities for work on post-biblical grammatical development. Now, while studies on materials like the Hebrew Sirach, stimulated by new manuscript discoveries, continue to expand, the major example lies in the Dead Sea Scrolls. There spellings of the personal pronoun 'he' as *hw'h* (Massoretic *hw'*) suggest a different (disyllabic?) pronunciation; and writings of verb imperfects such as *ydwršhw* 'he shall assess him' seem to suggest a pattern like *yᵉḏoreš* (Massoretic *yiḏrōš*; the example is from 1QS vi. 14). Among the many studies published since the Qumran finds, a very solid example is E. Y. Kutscher's *The Language and Linguistic Background of the Isaiah Scroll* (Hebrew; Jerusalem, 1959), but a long list of other workers could be added, such as F. M. Cross, J. Fitzmyer, M. Goshen-Gottstein, R. Meyer, C. Rabin, J. A. Sanders, S. Segert, and P. Wernberg-Møller. Useful working instruments are K. G. Kuhn's *Konkordanz zu den Qumrantexten* (Göttingen, 1960), and the bibliographies of C. Burchard (Berlin, 1957 and 1965), W. S. LaSor (Pasadena, 1958), B. Jongeling (Leiden, 1971), and, for works in Hebrew, M. Yizhar (Harvard, 1967).

Study in this later period involves not only the new-found documents like the Scrolls but also Rabbinic Hebrew. Though it is as long ago as 1927 that M. H. Segal published his *Grammar of Mishnaic Hebrew* (Oxford), biblical studies have continued to be somewhat isolated from study of the Hebrew of later times; but there are signs that this situation is changing. The view, long widely current, and accepted especially in New Testament studies, that in the first century Hebrew was no longer a spoken language and Aramaic therefore the only living Semitic language of Palestine, and that Mishnaic Hebrew was an artificial language having no real continuity with biblical Hebrew, is now on the way to abandonment. Apart from H. Birkeland's *The Language of Jesus* (Oslo, 1954), something of a *tour de force* which sought to show that Jesus had spoken Hebrew and not Aramaic, see for a survey of recent arguments J. A. Emerton in *JTS* xii (1961), 189–202; xxiv (1973), 1–23; J. Barr, *BJRL* liii (1970–1971), 9–29; and literature cited in these articles. In all work on later Hebrew, Israeli scholarship is particularly distinguished; see *inter alia* the surveys of the total history of Hebrew, already cited above (p. 52).

Among distinguished workers the name of E. Y. Kutscher must again be mentioned. His work on Mishnaic Hebrew brought some important corrections to the idea of M. H. Segal: Segal, according to Kutscher, though right in his main contentions, had underestimated the degree of Aramaic influence on Mishnaic Hebrew, because the later manuscripts had assimilated Mishnaic diction to biblical patterns; see for instance his 'Mišnisches Hebräisch' in *Rocznik Orientalisticzny* xxviii (1964), 35–48.

In lexicography, in the third edition of the Baumgartner dictionary, already described above, Kutscher reworked the information about post-biblical Hebrew, marking with the symbols mhe.[1] and mhe.[2] the distinction between two periods, roughly the Tannaitic and the Amoraic respectively: see, in addition to the preface to the dictionary itself, Kutscher's article in SVT xvi, 1967, pp. 158–75. Much is to be expected also from the large-scale computerized lexicographical project sponsored by the Academy of the Hebrew Language, Jerusalem, and directed by Z. Ben-Hayyim. This, while leaving biblical Hebrew aside for separate treatment, will organize all later Hebrew literature under several periods and will be able to produce lexica of individual texts or periods; see the Hebrew pamphlet, *The Historical Dictionary of the Hebrew Language* (Academy of the Hebrew Language, Jerusalem, 1969).

Major research has also been done into the Massoretic and pre-Massoretic pointing systems and the pronunciation traditions underlying them, and the variant systems and pronunciations such as the Samaritan. Much attention has been given to the various Jewish pronunciations of Hebrew and the liturgical reading traditions, especially of communities like the Yemenites, understood and analysed at the last moment, before they are likely to disappear for ever. S. Morag's work is particularly important; see his 'Pronunciations of Hebrew', *EJ* xiii, cols. 1120–45 and bibliography on col. 1145, and on the pointing systems themselves his *The Vocalization Systems of Arabic, Hebrew and Aramaic* (The Hague, 1962). The Massoretic writing system is studied also by G. M. Schramm, *The Graphemes of Tiberian Hebrew* (Berkeley, 1964), and by scholars like J. C. L. Gibson (e.g. *Archivum Linguisticum* xvii (1969), 131–60). Among studies of pointing systems other than the Tiberian we may mention the work of P. Kahle (*The Cairo Geniza*, 2nd edn., Oxford, 1959, and many other works) and, following him, studies by M. Dietrich (Leiden, 1966), A. Diez-Macho, A. Murtonen, and E. J. Revell (*Hebrew Texts with Palestinian Vocalization*, Toronto, 1970); but in this we come close to the material of textual rather than linguistic study.

On the language traditions of the Samaritans the work of Z. Ben-Hayyim, *The Literary and Oral Tradition of Hebrew and Aramaic amongst the Samaritans* (Hebrew, i–iv, Jerusalem,

1957–67) and R. Macuch's imposing *Grammatik des samaritanischen Hebräisch* (Berlin, 1969) are central; cf. also the studies of A. Murtonen.

Another source which has been much used for the reconstruction of Hebrew in the early centuries A.D. has been the transliterations found in Origen's *Hexapla* and in Jerome. A. Sperber drew heavily on this source in the series of monographs later republished in his *A Historical Grammar of Biblical Hebrew* (Leiden, 1966), a work of great compass if of doubtful reliability. A series of patient studies has come from E. Brønno (recently *Die Aussprache der hebräischen Laryngale nach Zeugnissen des Hieronymus*, Aarhus, 1970), and on Jerome see also J. Barr in *JSS* xii (1967), 1–36, and *BJRL* xlix (1966–67), 281–302. On the original purpose of the Second Column of the Hexapla see J. A. Emerton's discussion in *JTS* vii (1956), 79–87, with summary of earlier views.

The understanding of Hebrew personal names is something in which progress cannot be made without comparative attention to the structure of personal names in other Semitic languages, as was already recognized by M. Noth in his handbook *Die israelitischen Personennamen im Rahmen der gemeinsemitischen Namengebung* (Stuttgart, 1928), a work which has still not been replaced. Corpora of names continue to be published, such as the names from Amorite sources (H. B. Huffmon, Baltimore, 1965), from Ugarit (F. Gröndahl, Rome, 1967), from Palmyra (J. K. Stark, Oxford, 1971), and from Phoenician and Punic sources (F. L. Benz, Rome, 1972). On Hebrew names themselves the major specialist is J. J. Stamm of Bern, see for instance his article 'Hebräische Frauennamen', SVT xvi, 1967, pp. 301–39, and his other studies, going back to his earlier work on Akkadian names (1939).

Not all the personal names of the Bible are of Hebrew origin, and the place names are still less so; and it is fitting to conclude this section with the reminder that biblical Hebrew contains so-called 'loan-words', words adopted from another language. These are not words inherited by Hebrew from its Semitic ancestor language by direct descent, but adopted from another language, sometimes Semitic and sometimes not. Sometimes the date and the circumstances of the adoptions can be known, and sometimes the borrowings can be classified in respect of subject (e.g. many adoptions from Akkadian in administration, and later many from Greek in matters of law). One study published, that of M. Ellenbogen, *Foreign Words in the Old Testament: their Origin and Etymology* (London, 1962), is a simple preliminary list with annotations. Some scholars have looked systematically for words derived from remoter sources, cf. C. Rabin's studies of words that may derive from Hittite (*Orientalia* xxxii (1963) 113–39) and even from the Dravidian languages of south India. But the language which is likely to have had the greatest influence on Hebrew in this respect is Aramaic, and M. Wagner has collected many examples in his *Die lexikalischen und grammatikalischen Aramaismen im alttestamentlichen Hebräisch* (Berlin, 1966); but many identifications continue to be disputed.

4. NEW WAYS OF LOOKING AT LANGUAGE

Finally, we turn to consider the general ideas about language which form the background to Old Testament studies. Older work, as has been seen, was mostly comparative-historical in its orientation, or at least intended to be so: in fact this often meant a bias towards origins rather than effects, towards hypothetical reconstruction rather than description of functions as they were within the biblical period, towards seeing Hebrew in terms of parallels with other languages rather than seeing it for what it was in itself. A newer approach to language has grown up over the last century or so but has come into prominence more recently. It puts the emphasis elsewhere: it affirms the importance of both synchronic and diachronic axes in description; it sees a language, or a department of a language such as its phonology, more as a system of elements functioning at one time; and it explains not by tracing back individual elements to an earlier stage or 'origin' but by stating the interrelation of elements within a system. To know that from which something has grown is not, after all, to explain it; it is at most one kind of explanation, and a very partial one at that. The older approach is sometimes called *philology*, the newer *linguistics*, though this use of terms is not strictly observed.

The two are not opposed in principle: rather, what used to be called philology can now take its place as a perspective within historical linguistics, or as the department of linguistics concerned with ancient texts and with the reconstruction of the stages (like proto-Semitic) antecedent to extant ancient texts. All that must be affirmed is that the attitudes and interests of the older philology should be somewhat complemented and corrected through the wider scope of the newer linguistics. This is not surprising, since the questions from which the newer linguistics arose are often questions thrown up by the desire to be rigorous in explanation within the framework of the older philology. No one would suppose that W. von Soden was deficient in the *akribeia* of historical philology; it is all the more impressive that he wrote in 1965: 'the times are long past, in which linguistic science was almost uniquely dominated by the historical-genetic view of language worked out by Indo-European studies' (*JSS* x (1965), 161).

But within Semitic language studies, as yet, the frontiers between the different approaches are far from clear-cut. Perhaps three classes can be roughly distinguished: (a) studies which belong entirely to the older comparative-historical approach, working with the identification of discrete elements and showing a strong bias towards origins, e.g. in lexical questions towards etymology; (b) studies which use a good deal of modern-looking terminology ('system', 'syntagmeme', 'phonemic', and so on) but which in way of thinking are not essentially different from the former class; (c) studies which are really integrated in spirit and in way of thinking with modern linguistics.

The contrast varies between the scholarship of different lands and cultures. Much Anglo-Saxon Hebrew scholarship has until very recent times been entirely comparative-historical; American structuralism made little impact on biblical study. Scandinavian, French, Italian, Slavonic, and some Israeli scholarship has been much closer in spirit to modern linguistics. German Old Testament scholarship, as expressed in the many commentaries and monographs produced, has in most of our period been historically careful and exact but linguistically traditional and unadventurous. Very recent developments, such as the extension of structur-

alism from the strictly linguistic realm and over wider fields
of study, or the rise of techniques such as 'text-linguistics',
promise to bring biblical linguistics back into a closer contact
with literary appreciation and form-critical studies, from
which many philologists of the older vintage were rather
alienated. 'Transformational' linguistics of the Chomskyan
type might also mean some relationship with logic.

One area which is particularly dependent on the advance
of linguistic methods of analysis, and which is in any case of
growing importance, is the study of semantics. Here, if
difficulty has been caused on the one side by the older
philology, with its reliance on etymology and its tendency to
suppose that a correct translation was also an account of the
meaning of a word, on the other side difficulty has come from
the tradition of theological interpretation, with its tendency
to read a word as a sign for a theological concept. Today we
can maintain that there must be a linguistic account of
meanings that is semantically deep but is yet different in level
from the registration of theological concepts. For some
examination of the problems see J. Barr, *The Semantics of
Biblical Language* (London, 1961), with a survey of the
ensuing discussion in J. Barr, *Biblical Words for Time* (2nd
edn., London, 1969), pp. 170–207. A recent exploration, taking
the words for salvation as centre, is J. F. A. Sawyer, *Semantics
in Biblical Research* (London, 1972). Earlier exercises in the
analysis of semantic fields included colours (P. Fronzaroli,
Studi ... Pisani, Brescia, 1969), 'folly' and 'rich and poor' (T.
Donald, *VT* xiii (1963), 285–92; *Oriens Antiquus* iii (1964), 27–
41), and 'image, likeness' (J. Barr, *BJRL* li (1968–9), 11–26).

Some effect of the semantic discussion from the 1960s
onward can be seen in the planning and execution of the two
dictionaries now in process of publication which are concerned with the theology of the Old Testament, the *Theologisches Wörterbuch zum Alten Testament* of G. J. Botterweck
and H. Ringgren (Stuttgart, since 1970) and the *Theologisches
Handwörterbuch zum Alten Testament* of E. Jenni and C.
Westermann (Zurich, since 1971). In both cases the editors
have shown a proper desire to observe sound linguistic
methods and not to allow linguistic evidence to be misused in
the interests of theological results.

To sum up, then, it may be expected that the comparative and historical emphasis, through which Semitic language studies have impinged upon the study of the Old Testament, will continue and indeed be strengthened; but it will do its work within a different framework of thinking about language. This will mean the opening up of questions of new kinds and the reopening of some that have been neglected; it will mean the restudy of questions about Hebrew in itself, which have often been neglected in favour of comparative observations; it will mean also the rethinking of what it is to study language historically. But it can be expected with assurance that the moving currents of linguistic study will guide us towards new trends in the general interpretation of the Old Testament.

III

RECENT ARCHAEOLOGICAL DISCOVERIES AND THEIR BEARING ON THE OLD TESTAMENT

J GRAY

IN this chapter one is conscious of the necessity of selection and the consequent limitation. To say nothing of the formative cultures of earlier periods, we shall not be able to discuss major texts with the fullness they deserve, important data of archaeology as they are, not only for the dating of associated strata as direct evidence for historical and cultural conditions in relevant periods and areas, but as relating directly to the Old Testament in content, literary form, and language.

Thus for instance the administrative correspondence from Mari in the Middle Bronze Age elucidates the impingement of semi-nomad tribal confederacies on the settled land[1] as a more aggressive movement than Alt and Noth envisaged for the penetration of the fathers of Israel until their eventual local clashes with the Canaanites.[2] Certain aspects of prophecy which are familiar from Israel are also illustrated,[3] though the comparison reveals significant differences, the large perspective of the consistent purpose of God in history

---

[1] J. R. Kupper, *Les Nomades en Mésopotamie au temps des rois de Mari,* Paris, 1957; M. Weippert, *The Settlement of the Israelite Tribes in Palestine,* SBT, 2nd series, xxi, 1971 (ETr). Actually the Mari texts refer both to transhumance by the nomads, whose seasonal rights were recognized and who had villages for seasonal occupation, and to more hostile encounters with the forces of Mari.

[2] A. Alt, 'The Settlement of the Israelites in Palestine', *Essays on Old Testament History and Religion,* ETr Oxford, 1966, pp. 175–221; 'Erwägungen über die Landnahme der Israeliten in Palästina', *PJB* xxxv (1939), 8–63 = *KS* i, Munich, 1953, pp. 126–75. M. Noth, *The History of Israel,* ETr London, 2nd edn., 1960, pp. 68 ff.

[3] W. von Soden in *WO* i (1950), 396–403; A. Malamat in *SVT* xv, 1966, pp. 202–27. H. B. Huffmon in *BA* xxxi (1968), 101–24.

characteristic of the great prophets of Israel being so far without parallel.[4]

The literary form and also much of the content of casuistic law in the Book of the Covenant (Exod. 20:22–3, 33) is illustrated in the Mesopotamian codes of Urnammu,[5] Lipit-Ishtar,[6] Eshnunna,[7] and Hammurabi of Babylon[8] in the Middle Bronze Age, the Hittite code in the Late Bronze Age,[9] and the Assyrian laws from the twelfth century.[10] In all probability there was a similar legal convention in Canaan which Israel adapted in the Book of the Covenant, as Alt proposed,[11] but so far the lack of anything like a law code is one of the great disappointments in archaeology, particularly at Ras Shamra. Here again the affinity with the biblical material highlights the distinctive nature of the latter, there being no parallel to the categorical religious and social obligations of the covenant as creative of a sacral community.

Absolute covenant obligations, however, are illustrated in Hittite vassal treaties from the archives at Boghazköi[12] and Ras Shamra,[13] which have made such a vital contribution to our appreciation of the presentation of the covenant obligations in the Old Testament.[14]

[4] M. Noth, *The Laws in the Pentateuch*, Edinburgh, 1966 (ETr), pp. 179–93.

[5] *ANET*, pp. 523–25.

[6] Ibid., pp. 159–61.

[7] Ibid., pp. 161–3.

[8] Ibid., pp. 163–80; G. R. Driver and J. C. Miles, *The Babylonian Laws*, i, Oxford, 1952.

[9] *ANET*, pp. 188–97.

[10] Ibid., pp. 180–8. G. R. Driver and J. C. Miles, *The Assyrian Laws*, Oxford, 1935.

[11] A. Alt, 'The Origins of Israelite Law', *Essays on Old Testament History and Religion*, pp. 103–71.

[12] V. Korošec, *Hethitische Staatsverträge, ein Beitrag zu ihrer juristischen Wertung*, Leipziger Rechtswissenschaftliche Studien, lx, 1931.

[13] J. Nougayrol, *PRU* iv, 1956, pp. 48–52, 85 f., 88 f.

[14] For the studies of Mendenhall, Baltzer, and McCarthy, see below, Ch. IV, pp. 111, 114, 118; Ch. XII, pp. 373 ff.; Ch. XIII, pp. 395 f. K. A. Kitchen (*Ancient Orient and Old Testament*, London, 1966, pp. 92–102) has demonstrated in detail that vassal treaties after the thirteenth century do not display the same consistency in form as those of the earlier period, so that Mendenhall's argument for a Mosaic date for the Decalogue still stands. We consider it possible that the form of the obligations of the covenant in the oldest Israelite tradition was influenced by the vassal-treaty form known in Canaan, possibly in the city state of Shechem, which was associated with the covenant in the first phase of the history of the sacral community of Israel in Canaan, but we consider that it more probably reflects the conditions in the Empire of David and Solomon.

Liturgical and sapiential texts from Mesopotamia have contributed significantly to the debate on the form and scope of the Book of Job,[15] and the discovery of an Akkadian text on the worthy sufferer at Ras Shamra[16] indicates that the theme was known in the west and, perhaps in a popular form surviving in the Prologue and Epilogue of the extant Book of Job, was used for edification by the sages of Israel in the early monarchy, a period in which the influence of cosmopolitan Wisdom teaching appears to have been extensive in Israel.

Mesopotamian and Egyptian love poetry too, both in form and imagery, have helped to elucidate the Song of Songs,[17] as has the liturgy of the Canaanite fertility cult, exemplified in certain texts from Ras Shamra.[18]

As providing a substantial cross-section of the literature of Canaan on the eve of the settlement of Israel, the Ras Shamra texts are of inestimable value for the study of the Old Testament. With Amorite features in the Mari texts[19] from the eighteenth century and the Canaanite glosses on the Amarna Tablets and the Phoenician inscriptions from the Early Iron Age, they provide the basis for the historical study of Hebrew ($s^{e}pat\ k^{e}na^{c}an$ of Isa. 19:18), which is now rounded out in the non-biblical texts from Qumran and the correspondence of the colleagues of Simon bar Cochba from the Wadi

---

[15] *ANET*, pp. 589–91, 596–600, 601–4; W. G. Lambert, *Babylonian Wisdom Literature*, Oxford, 1960, pp. 21–62; Lambert, op. cit., pp. 63–91. J. Nougayrol in *RB* lix (1952), 239–50; J. J. van Dijk, *La Sagesse suméro-accadienne. Recherches sur les genres littéraires des textes sapientaux*, Leiden, 1953; J. Nougayrol, *Ugaritica* v (1968), 273–300. For comparative study of those texts with reference to Job, J. J. Stamm, *Das Leiden des Unschuldigen in Babylon und Israel*, ATANT x, 1946; J. Gray in *ZAW* lxxxii (1970), 251–69.

[16] J. Nougayrol, *loc. cit.*

[17] W. G. Lambert in *JSS* iv (1959), 1–15; F. Dornseiff in *ZDMG* xv (1936), 589–601; S. Schott, *Altägyptische Liebeslieder, eingeleitet und übertragen*, Zürich, 1950; A. Hermann, *Altägyptische Liebesdichtung*, Wiesbaden, 1959, suggesting that the lyrics he cites may have been related to the cult of the fertility goddess Hathor. G. Gerleman stresses the conventional roles of the lovers, with Egyptian parallels, *Ruth, Das Hohelied*, BKAT xviii, 1965, pp. 59 ff.

[18] e.g. *UT* 52 = *CTA* 23; *UT* 132 = *CTA* 11; *CRAIBL* 1960 (1961), pp. 180–6. T. J. Meek in *AJSL* xxix (1922–3), 1–14; W. Wittekindt, *Das Hohe Lied und seine Beziehungen zum Ištar Kult*, Hanover, 1927; H. Schmökel in *ZAW* lxiv (1952), 148–55; id., *Heilige Hochzeit und Hoheslied*, Wiesbaden, 1956.

[19] Specific Amorite peculiarities are studied by H. B. Huffmon in the grammatical structure of theophoric names: *Amorite Personal Names in the Mari Texts: a Structural and Lexical Study*, Baltimore, 1965.

Murabba'at[20] and the Nahal Heber.[21] No commentary on the Old Testament is up to date without reckoning with Ugaritic vocabulary, grammar, and, in poetic books, prosody, which occasionally prompts the emendation of a corrupt passage, but more often obviates emendation of the consonantal MT, as M. J. Dahood's studies in Proverbs, Job, Ecclesiastes, and Psalms[22] have clearly shown. The Ras Shamra texts have elucidated the administration of a feudal monarchy, with obvious relevance to the biblical data on Solomon's administration,[23] while the legends of Krt and Aqht contribute to the debate on the nature of the monarchy in Israel, not only by what they assert, but significantly by what they omit.[24]

The Baal fragments are vital to the debate on the Enthronement Psalms in the Old Testament, constituting locally and in time an important link between these texts and the Babylonian *enūma eliš*, with its theme of the conflict of Marduk with Tiamat (salt water), his victory, kingship, and ordered creation. In the Ras Shamra fragments on the subject of Baal's acquisition of kingship in conflict with Sea and Ocean Current (cf. Ps. 93),[25] the building of his 'house' as befitted a king (cf. Isa. 2:1–4; Mic. 4:1–3), his feast of housewarming to his colleagues (cf. Isa. 25:6; Zeph. 1:7 f.; and Solomon's feast at the dedication of the Temple, 1 Kgs. 8:62 ff.), and his final conflict with Mot (Death, Sterility), we

[20] P. Benoit, J. T. Milik, and R. de Vaux, *Discoveries in the Judaean Desert:* ii, *Les Grottes de Murabba'at*, Oxford, 1961.

[21] Y. Yadin, *The Finds from the Bar-Kokhba Period in the Cave of the Letters*, Jerusalem, 1963; *Bar-Kokhba: The Rediscovery of the Legendary Hero of the Last Jewish Revolt against Imperial Rome*, London, 1971.

[22] *Canaanite and Phoenician Influence in Qoheleth*, Rome, 1952; 'Northwest Semitic Philology and Job', *The Bible in Current Catholic Thought*, ed. J. L. McKenzie, New York, 1962, pp. 55–74; *Proverbs and Northwest Semitic Philology*, Rome, 1963; *Psalms*, 3 vols., AncB, New York, 1962, 1966, 1970.

[23] J. Gray, *The Legacy of Canaan*, SVT v, 1965, pp. 222–5. The immediate prototype of Solomon's administration, however, was almost certainly Egyptian bureaucracy; see E. W. Heaton, *Solomon's New Men*, London, 1974, pp. 74 ff.

[24] In a fresh study of the most recent evidence in the royal legends of Ugarit and in the administrative texts, 'Sacral Kingship in Ugarit', *Ugaritica* vi (1969), 289–302, the writer can find nothing to support Engnell's views of the king as representative of the dying and rising god in the Canaanite fertility cult (*Studies in Divine Kingship*, 2nd edn., Oxford, 1967).

[25] *UT* 129, 137, 68 = *CTA* 2, iii, i, iv.

notice an association of motifs strikingly reproduced in the
Enthronement Psalms and other texts on the Kingship of
God in the Old Testament, in which we should include those
on the Day of Yahweh. More particularly, we claim, the Baal
myth of Ras Shamra supports Mowinckel's thesis of the
original *Sitz im Leben* of Enthronement Psalms in the liturgy
of the autumn festival, if, as we are prepared to demonstrate,
the Baal fragments are a unity and related to the autumn
festival. It is important to establish the unity of these
fragments, since the leading motifs of the Enthronement
Psalms are those of the Ugaritic fragments describing the
conflict of Baal and Sea, while the others establish the
association with the autumn festival. This, fortunately, may
be done through the motif of the house befitting the divine
king. In his review article, 'Sabbatical Cycle or Seasonal
Pattern? Reflections on a New Book (A. S. Kapelrud, *Baal in
the Ras Shamra Texts*, 1952)', *Or* xxii (1953), 79 ff., C. H.
Gordon relates the Baal text to a septennial rather than to an
annual occasion, by what we regard as a somewhat literalistic
interpretation of the culminating passage. We should agree
with J. C. de Moor[26] that even if the text in its literary form
were composed for a septennial occasion, that was still the
occasion of the autumn festival, the liturgy of which as an
annual festival it largely comprises. The references to this
season at the apogee of Baal's power as effective King are very
impressive, with undoubted analogy to the epiphany of
Yahweh as King in thunder (e.g. Ps. 29) and the autumn rain
(e.g. Ps. 68).

The historical records of Assyria and Babylon and the
much more scanty Egyptian and Aramaic material in the
first half of the first millennium B.C. are understandably
relevant to the Books of Kings. Certain events, conditions,
places, and personalities are directly referred to, and in other
cases the evidence is more general. The factual accounts of
the Assyrians, however, which from a purely historical point
of view are more complete and objective than Kings, serve to
emphasize the literary character of Kings not as pure history

---

[26] *The Seasonal Pattern in the Ugaritic Myth of Ba'lu according to the Version of
Ilimilku*, AOAT xvi, 1971.

but as a theological interpretation of history, using sources selectively, as the compiler is constantly reminding his readers. The same of course applies to the whole Deutero-nomistic History. Thus in considering the relevance of archaeological findings to the Israelite 'Conquest' in Joshua and Judges we must consider the sources according to the nature of each rather than the representation in the final compilation.

In the use of Assyrian material, however, we must heed the caution of A. T. Olmstead in 1916,[27] that earlier annals were incorporated in résumé in later annals on the occasion of some notable event or in monumental inscriptions. The annals then are of direct relevance only for contemporary events, and earlier events are apt to be summarized often according to a geographical arrangement and are often telescoped, something we must be prepared for also in Kings. A notable instance is the claim by Sargon II to have taken Samaria, in which H. Tadmor has argued[28] that events of 723–722, 720, and 716 have been telescoped in Sargon's Khorsabad Annals,[29] his Display Inscription,[30] and his Nimrud Prisms.[31]

The Babylonian Chronicle,[32] in its sustained interest in consecutive history, with synchronisms with contemporary events from 626 to 556 B.C., may illustrate the form of the synchronistic history of Israel and Judah, which was probably one of the sources of Kings. Its value in reconstructing the general situation in the Near East in the decline and fall of Assyria, despite Egyptian support, the Neo-Babylonian ascendancy, the rise of the Medes, and particularly the fall of Jerusalem in March 597 B.C., is too well known for the Chronicle to be more than mentioned here.

[27] A. T. ·Olmstead, *Assyrian Historiography: a Source Study*, University of Missouri Studies, Social Science Series iii, 1916.

[28] *JCS* xii (1958), 22–40, 77–100.

[29] *ANET*, pp. 284 f.

[30] Ibid.

[31] C. J. Gadd, 'Inscribed Prisms of Sargon II from Nimrud', *Iraq* xvi (1954), 173–201.

[32] The Chronicle is of course fragmentary, published in its various fragments by Gadd, *The Fall of Nineveh*, London, 1923; S. Smith, *Babylonian Historical Texts*, London, 1924, and D. J. Wiseman, *Chronicles of Chaldaean Kings 626–556 B.C. in the British Museum*, London, 1956.

The biblical and non-biblical texts from Qumran, Wadi Murabba'at, Nahal Heber, and Masada, with their relevance to the transmission of the MT and to the history of the Hasmonean period and the two great Jewish revolts, and the relevance of Qumran texts for the rise of sects, especially the Essenes, and the background of eschatological expectation in the inter-testamental period, are subjects which, regrettably, we must leave for discussion elsewhere. Similarly we can do no more than note the supplementation to the knowledge of the development of calligraphy and orthography during the growth and transmission of the Old Testament especially from the Samaritan ostraca, which Yadin now dates on archaeological evidence between 750 and 722 B.C.,[33] the Murabba'at palimpsest,[34] the Yabneh-yam letter from the time of Josiah,[35] the Adon Papyrus (Aramaic), probably from between 604 and 586,[36] the Elephantine Papyri from 459 to 398,[37] and the Aramaic papyri from the Wadi Daliyeh dating between 365 and 357 B.C.[38] Among the ever increasing epigraphic data, the 200 ostraca from Tell Arad have a peculiar significance,[39] coming from various strata at one site between the tenth and the sixth centuries B.C.

The present generation of archaeologists in Palestine entered upon their work with an enormous amount of material from such sites as Megiddo, Bethshan, Lachish, Jericho, Tell Beit Mirsim, and sites excavated by Petrie on

[33] Y. Yadin in *Studies in the Bible*, Scripta Hierosolymitana viii, 1960, 1–17. The date is accepted by F. M. Cross on palaeographic grounds in *BASOR* clxv (1962), 35.

[34] J. T. Milik, *Discoveries in the Judaean Desert* ii. *Les Grottes de Murabba'at*, Oxford, 1961, pp. 93–100, Pl. XXVIII. Cross, *Ancient Library of Qumran*, New York, 1958, p. 14, n. 22. Milik adduces evidence for the occupation of the cave where the papyrus was discovered in the eighth or seventh century B.C., to which date he assigns the original papyrus in the reign of Uzziah, whose occupation of the desert he cites (2 Chr. 26: 1, 7, 10, cf. 2 Kgs, 14:22). Cross seems to be nearer the mark in regarding the occupation of the cave as by Jewish refugees in Sennacherib's campaign in 701 B.C.

[35] J. Naveh in *IEJ* x (1960), 129–39, Pl. 17.

[36] A. Dupont-Sommer in *Semitica* i (1948), 43–68; H. L. Ginsberg in *BASOR* cxi (1948), 24–7.

[37] A. E. Cowley, *Aramaic Papyri of the Fifth Century B.C.*, Oxford, 1923; E. G. Kraeling, *The Brooklyn Museum Aramaic Papyri*, New Haven and London, 1953; G. R. Driver in *ZAW* lxvii (1949–50), 232.

[38] F. M. Cross in *New Directions in Biblical Archaeology*, ed. D. N. Freedman and J. C. Greenfield, New York, 1969, pp. 41–62.

[39] Y. Aharoni in *BA* xxxi (1968), 2–32, and in *IEJ* xvi (1966), 1–7.

the Wadi Ghazzeh. The conclusions of the late R. P. Hugues Vincent, C. S. Fisher, and W. F. Albright on the sequence of strata and interrelation of cultures based on the development of tools, weapons, and ornaments, and especially the variations in pottery pioneered by Petrie at Tell el-Hesi, stand in the main, but have been refined to a remarkable degree. A much more professional approach at all levels is now taken to archaeology, not only in the field, but as a recognized academic discipline.

Field-work is now much more meticulous and not on the broad surface as between the two World Wars, but in sections, where intervening balks are left as a record of stratification until conclusions can be cross-checked and confirmed. Thus from a relatively limited area a conspectus of cultural development may be obtained, leaving undisturbed areas for future excavation. Modern science may also be employed. The mine-detector was used in the caves in the Nahal Heber, where caches of Roman bronze vessels were detected with other remains including letters from the revolt of Bar Cochba,[40] and in 1964 in the Princeton excavations at Hebron P. C. Hammond used a proton magnetometer capable of detecting not only metal but burnt structures. The amount of radio-activity in wood, leather, and the linen covering of scrolls may be determined to fix the date at which the matter was living or growing with a margin of error of 200 years either way.

The progress of archaeological method may be illustrated from Gezer. Between 1902 and 1909 R. A. S. Macalister, with no European staff, trenched certain sections over the whole width of the *tell* to bedrock. Stratification was observed though rather broadly considered, as evidenced by the classification of the pottery as Pre-Semitic, First, Second, Third, and Fourth Semitic, Hellenistic, Roman, Byzantine.[41] Trenches were filled in with the debris of the excavation, so that none of Macalister's conclusions could be checked or revised except by the excavation of an untouched area or an arduous critical review of his publication. The latter was undertaken for a doctoral thesis by G. E. Wright under

[40] Yadin, *The Finds from the Bar Kokhba Period*, pp. 115 ff.
[41] R. A. S. Macalister, *The Excavation of Gezer*, 3 vols., London, 1912.

Albright's direction, and Wright excavated at Gezer in 1964–5. Meanwhile Yadin, who in seminar work in the University of Jerusalem had been revising earlier excavation reports, including Gezer, revised Macalister's plans of a complex in the wall which he had interpreted as a 'Maccabaean castle', with the result that Yadin was able, particularly after the recovery of a Solomonic gateway at Hazor, to demonstrate that the six-chambered gate associated with a casemate city-wall at Hazor, Gezer, and also Megiddo had been built to the same plan and dimensions by the same military engineer,[42] a striking corroboration of the account of Solomon's fortifications in 1 Kgs. 9: 15. The most recent phase is the excavation of Gezer since 1966 by the Hebrew Union College supported by the Harvard Semitic Museum under the direction of W. G. Dever. In contrast to Macalister's single-handed effort, Dever was assisted by a large staff, many of them trained both in seminar and field-work under G. E. Wright and his staff at Shechem. Though not all were experienced, they were all more inducted into the historical background and the technical problems of archaeology than most of the enlightened amateurs who assisted directors between the two World Wars, and the director provided for lectures in archaeological method and the history of Palestine on the field.

Work proceeded with all the meticulous method now generally applied in Palestine, with all the refinements possible through detailed knowledge of pottery types. Perhaps the most important result has been the new understanding of the inner wall with glacis of earth and plaster (the latter dismissed by Macalister as builder's debris) and the outer, retaining wall as from *c.* 1600 B.C.,[43] contemporary with the putative 'high place' with its ten massive standing stones. Delicate sectional excavation under those stones has demonstrated that they were erected simultaneously, and therefore were not, as has been suggested,[44] memorials of conspicuous

[42] Yadin in *IEJ* viii (1958), 80–6; *Hazor. The Head of all Those Kingdoms* (Schweich Lectures), London, 1972, pp. 147–64; also in *BA* xxii (1960), 62–8; Aharoni in *BASOR* cliv (1959), 35–9.

[43] W. G. Dever in *BA* xxx (1967), 56 f.

[44] e.g. by the writer, *The Canaanites*, London, 1964, pp. 66–8, on the analogy of standing stones from one of the Late Bronze sanctuaries at Hazor.

ancestors, but rather tokens of parties to a covenant, possibly of ten cities,[45] with a possible analogy in the twelve stones of Gilgal (Josh. 4:1–8). Yadin's conclusion on the Solomonic gate has similarly been confirmed, and the destruction of the City (Stratum 7 in Field II) c. 950 B.C.,[46] like the contemporary destruction of Beth-shemesh II, Tell Mor, and Ashdod,[47] may reasonably be related to the expedition of the Pharaoh mentioned in 1 Kgs. 9:15 f.

The Pharaoh in question was probably Siamun of the XXIst Dynasty, who is depicted in a sculpture from Tanis[48] slaying a foreign enemy, whose double-headed axe suggests perhaps the Philistines. This reassertion of Egyptian influence in the coastal plain may have been motivated by Israel's reputation among the Philistines, the marriage of Solomon and the cession of Gezer reflecting a concordat on the respective spheres of Israelite and Egyptian influence, the latter being secured by the Philistines in their original pro-Egyptian role, as under Ramesses III. The explanation of the destruction of Gezer before its cession to Solomon may be that the Pharaoh felt his influence better secured by the great fortress of Ekron (Tell el-Muqanna'), a new foundation of the Iron Age, associated from the first with the Philistines.[49]

The relation of phases of occupation and recession to biblical statements, even when controlled by a discriminating appreciation of the historical character of the latter, requires some justification. This is done not by a junta of biblical literalists, but by professional archaeologists and biblical scholars, and is subject to criticism in the international forum of learned journals. In the last analysis, of course, the correspondence between archaeological data and the events in Scripture cannot be absolute. Archaeology is competent only to date its evidence; and that must stand up to professional criticism. Where statements are made in the

[45] Dever in *PEQ* cv (1973), 68–70.

[46] Dever in *BA* xxx (1967), 60.

[47] At least the fortress in Area A, D. N. Freedman in *BA* xxvi (1963), 139.

[48] P. Montet, *L'Égypte et la Bible*, Neuchâtel, 1959, fig. 5.

[49] J. Naveh proposed this location in *IEJ* viii (1958), 87–100, 165–70. His conclusion, based on a regional survey of the district, is confirmed by a survey by G. E. Wright and a team from the Hebrew Union College Biblical and Archaeological School; see *BA* xxix (1966), 76.

records of Israel and Judah from genuinely historical sources, either directly concerning sites excavated or concerning the affairs of small kingdoms, the repercussions of which were likely to be felt throughout the land, the correspondence between archaeology and Scripture is likely to be close.

The ceramic sequence, which is the main key to dating, now commands general agreement, and is corroborated moreover by certain material where dating is more precise. Thus the first systematic fortification of the ruined site of Hazor in the tenth century agrees with the memory of the dereliction of the place in Josh. 11:13 in the early monarchy and its fortification by Solomon (1 Kgs. 9:15), so that here and in similar fortifications at Megiddo and Gezer we have a point of reference for the related material in Solomon's reign. Another piece of datable evidence is the fragment of the stele of Sheshonk I at Megiddo,[50] taken in conjunction with his Karnak inscription describing his campaign in Palestine,[51] which 1 Kgs. 14:25 notices in the fifth year of Rehoboam (930–914 B.C.); and so associated artefacts from Megiddo are a clue to the date of those associated with the destruction of other sites mentioned in Sheshonk's itinerary, such as Arad. Omri's fortification of the acropolis of Samaria with associated pottery corresponding to that in the recession of occupation at the old capital Tirzah, Tell el-Far'a (1 Kgs. 16:23)[52] gives a valuable fixed point in 880 B.C. In the eighth century fragments of a monumental inscription of Sargon II found in the stratum succeeding the destruction of the first stratum of Iron Age II at Ashdod[53] gives a date between 712 B.C., when Sargon records the fall of Ashdod,[54] and his death in 705 B.C., to permit further precision in dating the related artefacts. The artefacts found in conjunction with Sargon's stele corroborate the date of the fall of Lachish, the reduction of which in 701, laconically noted in 2 Kgs. 18:14, is so graphically depicted on reliefs from Sennacherib's palace at Nineveh,[55]

[50] *ANET*, pp. 242 ff.
[51] Read *boustrophedon*, as Mazar noticed in *Volume du Congrès, Strasbourg 1956*, SVT iv, 1957, pp. 57–66.
[52] R. de Vaux, 'Tirzah', *AOTS*, pp. 377, 381.
[53] Freedman in *BA* xxvi (1963), 137 f.
[54] In an inscription of his eleventh year, *ANET*, p. 286.
[55] *ANEP*, figs. 371–4.

amplified by the remains of about 1500 bodies dumped with refuse into pits in the area adjoining the citadel.[56] The neighbouring Tell Beit Mirsim also suffered destruction at this time. Lachish was rebuilt on the burnt brick debris of the Assyrian destruction. This stratum is surely that begun by Manasseh's occupation as an Assyrian vassal who evidently merited the restoration of the frontier fortresses (cf. 2 Chr. 33:13 f.) including Lachish, which Sennacherib had stripped from Judah. The destruction of the final Jewish occupation at Lachish may reasonably be dated by the ostraca found in the charred debris in one of the chambers of the gate,[57] one of which mentions Lachish and Azekah, which Jeremiah mentions (Jer. 34:7) with Jerusalem as the last bastions of the kingdom in 586 B.C. The fall of Lachish synchronized with the destruction of Tell Beit Mirsim, Tell el-Hesi (Eglon), Beth-shemesh, Beth-sur, Arad, Engedi, Ramat Rahel (Beth-hakkerem), and Tell el-Ful (Gibeah). The ostracon from Yabneh-yam[58] registering the complaint of a peasant against the military officer Hosha'yah similarly dates its context. The script gives a date in the eighth or seventh century, which in modern palaeography can be more accurate than sceptics allow. The proto-Hebraic character and the language, indistinguishable from classical Hebrew, and even the note on the Sabbath or the reference to the distraining of a cloak as a token of liability (cf. Exod. 22:25 f.; Deut. 24:10–13; Amos. 2:8), do not of themselves prove that Yabneh-yam was in Jewish hands at that time. But the theophoric name Hosha'yah settles the question. The region was not in the control of Judah after the time of David until the time of Uzziah (766–740 B.C.) according to 2 Chr. 26:6[59] and certainly the time of Josiah (640–609 B.C.) after the decline of Assyria after 629 B.C.[60]

[56] O. Tufnell, *Lachish III. The Iron Age*, Oxford, 1953, pp. 55 ff., 62–4.

[57] J. L. Starkey, *Lachish I*, Oxford, 1938, pp. 11–14; H. Torczyner (now Tur-Sinai), ibid., pp. 15 ff.

[58] See above, p. 71, n. 35.

[59] This passage mentions the destruction of Gath, Yabneh, and Ashdod and the building of certain unnamed places near Ashdod. The limitation of this activity to that part of the coastal plain most accessible to Judah is an argument for the genuineness of the passage.

[60] So Naveh, op. cit.; F. M. Cross in *BASOR* clxv (1962), 34–6, 42; S. Talmon in *BASOR* clxxvi (1964), 27–38.

The sequence of pottery and other artefacts, increasingly well defined by such synchronisms, indicates that jar-handles stamped 'belonging to the king' and designated 'Hebron', 'Ziph', 'Socoh', or '*mmšt*' (i.e. possibly *mamšelet*, 'government', or fiscal headquarters at Jerusalem) and limited to the kingdom of Judah[61] relate to the reigns of Hezekiah, Manasseh, and possibly Josiah. The stamps are distinguished by their designs, a four-winged scarab, a double-winged scarab, and a rosette, which roughly coincide respectively with the periods of Hezekiah, Manasseh, and Josiah.[62] Since, however, the vessels might have been used after the fiscal system they represented had lapsed, they do not necessarily date a stratum except as a *terminus post quem*, though the relative frequency may indicate a contemporary date. If the above dating is correct, the first type of jar-handle would amplify the statement of 2 Chr. 32:28 that Hezekiah built 'barns for the harvests of corn, new wine, and oil', Hebron, Ziph, Socoh, and Jerusalem being the receiving centres for the produce. The relative limitation of the realm here suggested casts some light on the curtailment of Hezekiah's realm which Sennacherib records.[63]

The increased precision in the dating of pottery also facilitated Avigad's dating of the newly discovered monarchic city-wall on the south-west hill of Jerusalem[64] (see below, pp. 91 f.) and Aharoni's dating of the citadel at Ramat Rahel (eighth or seventh century B.C.) and the later palace (*c.* 600 B.C.),[65] which was destroyed in 597 or 586 B.C.

Since Judah was denuded of her leading citizens and lost political status under Babylon (586–539 B.C.) there are no significant remains from that time. The Persian period (539–

---

[61] The jar-handles are now attested from Tell en-Nasbeh in the north to Khirbet Gharreh 11 miles east of Beersheba in the south and from Jericho to Gezer; Aharoni, *The Land of the Bible*, p. 344.

[62] Aharoni, op. cit., pp. 340–6; P. Welten, *Die Konigs-stempel. Ein Beitrag zur Miltarpolitik Judas unter Hiskia und Josia*, Abhandlungen des Deutschen Palästina-vereins, Wiesbaden, 1969. Welten suggests that the stamps refer to royal potteries at crown estates and that they were distributed to centres for provisioning of the fortresses of the kingdom in time of emergency.

[63] But not the Old Testament.

[64] N. Avigad in *IEJ* xx (1970), 1–8, 129–140.

[65] Aharoni, 'Beth-haccerem', *AOTS*, mainly on the evidence of jar-handle stamps.

332 B.C.) is better attested, with distinctive pottery, now being recognized, thanks to deposits dated by coins, which now make their first appearance in Palestine, as in the deposit of pottery with coins not later than 335 B.C. and papyrus documents discovered by the indefatigable Ta'amira in the cave of Abu Sinjil in the Wadi Daliyeh,[66] some 12 miles north-north-west of Jericho. Apart from their relevance to the pottery, those documents, belonging to refugees from Samaria in the beginning of the Greek occupation, have a direct bearing on the relations of Jews and Samaritans. According to Josephus (*Ant.* XI vii 2), Sanballat the governor of Samaria in the time of Darius III (338–331 B.C.) gave his daughter in marriage to Manasseh the brother of Jaddua the Jewish High Priest. Manasseh was asked to divorce the lady, and, refusing, withdrew to his father-in-law, who built a temple on Gerizim[67] and installed him as priest. If this is correct surely this would finally occasion the Samaritan schism. One of the new documents dated 354 B.C. names Hananiyah the son of Sanballat as governor (*pḥt*)[68] of Samaria. This Sanballat was probably the grandson of Sanballat the contemporary of Nehemiah and on the principle of papponymy it would be feasible that Hananiyah had a son Sanballat governor of Samaria in the reign of Darius III. The date of the Samaritan schism is not conclusively settled, but Josephus' statement is now a degree more credible.

Refinements in the interpretation of artefacts have occasioned the revision of certain conclusions of archaeologists affecting the Old Testament. Thus Dr. Kenyon put an end to the dispute over the fall of Late Bronze Age Jericho in *c.* 1225

[66] See above, p. 71, n. 38.

[67] The Hellenistic pottery from the second and third centuries B.C. and Iron Age sherds found by R. J. Bull in his excavation of the Roman Temple to Olympian Zeus on Tell er Ra's on Mount Gerizim in 1966 may indicate the location of this temple, *BASOR* cxc (1968), 13, 18.

[68] Cf. the plural *paḥᵃwôt* ('governors'), Ezra 8:36; Neh. 2:7, 9 and *pḥt* with the same meaning, the title of Bigvai the governor of YEHUD in the Elephantine papyri; cf. *pḥw* on jar-handle stamps from the Persian period at Ramat Rahel, Aharoni, op. cit., pp. 174–6. The last two stamps *yhwd/yhwʿzr/pḥw* and *lʾḥzy/pḥw* indicate that the governor of YEHUD was Jewish like Zerubbabel (Hag. 1:1) and Nehemiah; cf. the small silver coin from Beth-sur stamped with the name Hezekiah and *yhwd*, O. R. Sellers, *The Citadel of Beth Sur*, 1933, 73, taken in conjunction with Josephus' mention of the High Priest Hezekiah as an able statesman at the end of the Persian period and the beginning of the Greek period (*Ap.* i. 187–9).

(so Vincent) or *c.* 1400 (so Garstang) by demonstrating that what was claimed to be the Late Bronze city-wall was actually Early Bronze and that ceramic evidence from tombs, and from what of the *tell* had not been eroded, indicated *c.* 1350 B.C. as the end of Bronze Age Jericho. What Albright had claimed as a Philistine redoubt at Tell el-Ful (Gibeah of Saul)[69] before it became the fortress of Saul has been demonstrated by L. A. Sinclair to date somewhat later and so to have been probably the work of Saul[70] on the evidence mainly of collar-rimmed *pithoi* current in the pre-fortress period but absent in the period of the fortress, this pottery not being attested at Megiddo after the destruction of Stratum VI (*c.* 1100 B.C.)[71] and appearing at other sites in the tenth and ninth centuries, e.g. Samaria[72] and Tell Qasileh (Stratum VIII) vestigially.[73] This and similar ceramic evidence for new village settlements in the hill country of Palestine attest a very significant phase in the settlement of the country in which Israel was directly involved, which would lead ultimately to the political unification of a land immemorially divided into a number of city-states. Such evidence rather than the destruction of various Bronze Age cities Aharoni has rightly appraised as evidence of the occupation by those who were to emerge as Israel, the power which effected the unification under David.[74]

A more precise division in the Iron Age in the Hebrew Monarchy is now proposed by Aharoni and Ruth Amiran,[75] viz. Iron II, 1000–840 B.C., Iron III, 840–586 B.C.; cf. G. E. Wright, who dates the beginning of the last phase *c.* 815, when Palestine was less under the cultural influence of Phoenicia than in the time of David, Solomon, and the House of Omri and its Judaean allies, and reflected rather the culture of her Aramean neighbours in inland Syria.[76] However that

[69] Albright, *The Archaeology of Palestine*, Harmondsworth, 1949, pp. 118 f.

[70] L. A. Sinclair, *An Archaeological Study of Gibeah, (Tell el-Ful)*, AASOR xxxiv–xxxv (1960), 16–18.

[71] Perhaps even a quarter of a century later, according to Sinclair's revised evidence accepted by Albright, Sinclair, op. cit., p. 17, n. 3.

[72] K. M. Kenyon, *Samaria–Sebaste* iii, London, 1957, fig. 1:16.

[73] Maisler (now Mazar), *IEJ* i (1951), 199, fig. 10c.

[74] Aharoni, *The Land of the Bible*, pp. 217 ff.

[75] Aharoni and R. Amiran, *IEJ* viii, (1958), 171 ff.

[76] G. E. Wright, *BASOR* clv (1959), 13–29.

may be, this precision in pottery of the later Iron Age is an important clue to the development of the Negeb. This area, explored by Sir Leonard Woolley and T. E. Lawrence, was dramatically opened up by the regional surveys of Nelson Glueck between 1932 and 1947[77] and by his excavation of Tell el-Kheleifeh (Ezion-geber, later Elath) half a mile from the north shore of the Gulf of Aqaba.[78] Here the casemate wall with six-chambered gateway enclosing what Glueck later admitted was a storehouse and not a smelter[79] was certainly from the time of Solomon, who engaged on merchant ventures in the Red Sea (1 Kgs. 9:26). Its destruction agrees with the raid of Sheshonk in the fifth year of Rehoboam (1 Kgs. 14:25), which, penetrating so deep into the Negeb, could hardly have omitted Ezion-geber though it is not actually mentioned in Sheshonk's Karnak inscription. The development of Ezion-geber, in which Solomon's enclosure was itself enclosed by a solid wall, a revetment, and a four-chambered gateway,[80] marks a new phase of the development of the Negeb in the Jewish monarchy in the ninth century at the earliest. This may perhaps be associated with Jehoshaphat,[81] who built fortresses and store-cities in Judah (2 Chr. 17:12 f.) and endeavoured unsuccessfully to revive Solomon's sea trade (1 Kgs. 22:47 f.). A period of recession probably coincides with the Edomite revival (2 Kgs. 8:20–2), and the third period of settlement with Judah's revival under Uzziah (766–740 B.C.), who built fortifications in the desert (2 Chr. 26:10), perhaps including Ezion-geber, where a seal of Jotham may indicate his son as his representative[82] or the steward of Jotham as regent or king.[83]

Those clearly demarcated phases of the history of Tell el-Kheleifeh from the time of Solomon supplement the ceramic

---

[77] Published in *AASOR* xiv, 1934; xv, 1935; xviii–xix, 1939; xxv–xxviii, 1951; and more popularly in *Rivers in the Desert*, London, 1959.

[78] Glueck in *BASOR* lxxi (1938), 3–18; lxxv (1939), 8–22; lxxix (1940), 2–18.

[79] Glueck in *BA* xxviii (1965), 73 ff., after B. Rothenberg in *PEQ* xciv (1962), 45–56, supported by the metallurgist B. H. McLeod and the chemist Y. Bar Ilan.

[80] Glueck, op. cit., 82 ff., fig. 9. Glueck compared the gate to the post-Solomonic gate of Megiddo *IVA*, op. cit. 84.

[81] So Glueck, op. cit. 84.

[82] So Aharoni, *The Land of the Bible*, p. 314.

[83] This explanation is preferred by Glueck, op. cit. 86.

evidence for the development of the Negeb under Jehoshaphat and Uzziah. In this period the roads through the Negeb were controlled by a network of fortresses,[84] the chief of which are at Khirbet Gharreh *c.* 13 miles east of Beersheba, Khirbet Ghazzeh *c.* 11 miles east-south-east of Khirbet Gharreh and Tell Arad on the way to the Arabah by the Scorpion Pass, and at Ain Qedeirat in the oasis of Qadesh on the direct way to Ezion-geber,[85] which evidently date from the time of Uzziah.[86] Greater precision in those phases of fortification has been introduced by the full-scale excavation of Tell Arad.[87]

In view of this correspondence between the phases of occupation and recession of sites in the Monarchy with statements from historical sources in Kings and Chronicles, may we expect the same correspondence between statements in Joshua and Judges and archaeological findings at Jericho, Ai, Bethel, sites in the south-west in the district of Kiriath-sepher, or Debir, such as Tell Beit Mirsim and Tell ed-Duweir (Lachish), Tell el-Hesi (Eglon), and other sites in this region, and Hazor in the north? This is really a question of source-analysis as Alt, Noth,[88] and more recently M. Weippert[89] have emphasized, in contrast to the stress on the priority of archaeological facts made by Albright,[90] Wright,[91] and, with more caution, by Bright.[92]

In Josh. 1–8 the fact that everything is concentrated about Gilgal, the central sanctuary of the sacral confederacy, or on the road pilgrims travelled there past Ai (et-Tell), and is so

[84] Aharoni in *IEJ* viii (1958), 26–38.

[85] First noticed by Woolley and Lawrence and later explored more thoroughly by M. Dothan, *IEJ* xv (1965), 134–51, who determined the rectangular plan of the fortress with casemate walls and eight towers, which he dates tentatively to the ninth century B.C.

[86] Aharoni dates the square forts with casemate walls in the tenth century and those with casemate walls and eight towers at the corners and in the middle of each wall not earlier than the ninth century B.C., *IEJ* xvii (1967), 1–11.

[87] Aharoni and R. Amiran, *IEJ* xiv (1964), 131–47.

[88] See above, p. 65, n. 2.

[89] Op. cit., pp. 132 ff.

[90] *BASOR* lviii (1935), 10–18; lxviii (1937), 22–6; lxxiv (1939), 11–23; *The Biblical Period from Abraham to Ezra*, New York, 1963, pp. 24–34.

[91] *JNES* v (1946), 105–14; *Biblical Archaeology*, 2nd edn., London, 1962, pp. 69–85.

[92] *A History of Israel*, 2nd edn., London, 1972, pp. 126–35.

largely composed of aetiological traditions which helped to actualize the occupation of the Promised Land for worshippers, though it does not exclude a historical origin, obscures it. It is no longer an objective historical tradition which Josh. 1–8 presents, but a tradition shaped by the liturgy of Gilgal with no direct correspondence to archaeological data. In any case the fall of Late Bronze Jericho, dated by Dr. Kenyon, so far as erosion permits a decision, c. 1350 B.C.,[93] cannot be relevant to the same catastrophic situation as the destruction of Tell Beit Mirsim, Lachish, Hazor, and other sites c. 1225 B.C., or indeed even to the destruction of Late Bronze Bethel, for which the lowest date proposed is 1250 B.C.,[94] while Ai was derelict between c. 2500 and 1100 B.C.[95] If the destruction of Jericho was associated with elements in Israel it may be rather with an earlier confederacy of Benjamin, Reuben, which was evidently once west of Jordan,[96] and Gad, with its central sanctuary at Gilgal.[97]

Without repeating the arguments in the long-standing controversy between Alt and Albright and their followers, we notice that Aharoni has put his finger on the crux of the problem in noticing the progressive development of the doubtless historical local tradition[98] of the occupation of Hebron and Kiriath-sepher, or Debir, by the Kenizzites Caleb and Othniel (Josh. 15:13–19; Judg. 1:12–15) to the attribution of the exploit to Judah (Judg. 1:10 f.), then finally to all Israel under Joshua (Josh. 10:36–9). We may note a similar development in Josh. 10. In the battle with the king of Jerusalem and his Amorite allies occasioned by the alliance between the Israelites and Gibeonites and the pursuit, significantly limited, 'to Azekah' (Josh. 10:1–11) there is doubtless a sound local historical tradition, in which Joshua

[93] K. M. Kenyon, *Digging up Jericho*, London, 1957, pp. 63 ff.

[94] Wright, *JNES* v (1946), 108.

[95] J. Marquet-Krause, *Syria* xvi (1935), 326, confirmed by excavations in 1964, where Early Bronze deposits were found immediately under Iron Age buildings; see J. A. Callaway in *BASOR* clxxviii (1965), 13–40.

[96] 'The Stone of Bohan the son of Reuben' was the tribal boundary of Judah (Josh. 15:6) and Benjamin (Josh. 18:17) and the clan Carmi, located here (Josh. 7:18), was reckoned both to Judah (Josh. 7:1) and Reuben (Gen. 46:9; Exod. 6:14; Num. 26:6; 1 Chr. 5:3).

[97] K. Möhlenbrink, *ZAW* xv (1938), 246 ff.

[98] Aharoni, *The Land of the Bible*, p. 197, n. 64.

was properly at home,[99] though this has no archaeological support beyond the general evidence of new village settlements in the hill country in the Early Iron Age. *Pace* G. E. Wright,[100] it is more than doubtful if the destruction of Lachish (*c.* 1220 B.C.),[101] Tell Beit Mirsim (*c.* 1225 B.C.),[102] and other Late Bronze settlements in the south-west such as Eglon (Tell el-Hesi),[103] Askalon,[104] and Ashdod[105] is relevant to the tradition in Josh. 10:1–11, which has undergone secondary development. In the return of 'Joshua and all Israel' to Gilgal (Josh. 10:15) we detect the incorporation of the local tradition in Josh. 10:1–11 in the secondary one of a holy war of the sacral confederacy derived from the cult at Gilgal. The description of the Makkedah incident (Josh. 10:16–27), with its obvious character as topographic aetiology, coming after the return to Gilgal, is surely an accretion, and the sweeping conquest of the south-west (Josh. 10:33 ff.) has been developed from the Makkedah incident by local association. If there is any connection between the fall of Late Bronze Lachish and Tell el-Hesi and the Israelite occupation that may rather be the result of the expansion of Judah from Bethlehem down the Wadi Nattif and the Wadi es-Sant and the southern Shephelah, or of the Kenizzites from Hebron and Kiryath-sepher or possibly of both together. Moreover, in his Hamadah stele Merneptah attests Bedouin aggression from Palestine as far as the Delta.[106] The destruction of Late Bronze Askalon and Ashdod could be the result of such raids,

[99] So Alt, 'Josua', *KS* i. 189 ff.

[100] Op. cit.

[101] J. L. Starkey, *PEFQS*, 1935, p. 239 (the destruction of the Fosse temple); O. Tufnell, *Lachish III, The Iron Age*, p. 46, suggests on the basis of a scarab with a legend familiar on those of Ramesses III that the city may have been destroyed 'a decade or so after rather than before 1200 B.C.'. Albright, however, points out that the titulary on the scarab was used also by Ramesses II.

[102] Albright, *AASOR*, xvii (1938), 78 ff.

[103] F. J. Bliss, *A Mound of Many Cities*, 1898, pp. 71 ff., 147. Work has been resumed at Tell el-hesi under L. E. Toombs in 1970 and Toombs and J. E. Worrell in 1971.

[104] W. J. Phythian-Adams, *PEFQS*, 1921, p. 163; 1923, p. 60, reports as the result of sounding at Askalon that there was evidence of destruction either in the fourteenth century or *c.* 1200.

[105] See above, p. 74, n. 47.

[106] Breasted, *Ancient Records of Egypt* iii (1906–7), 606; A. Youssuf, *Annales du Service des antiquités de l'Égypte* lviii (1964), 273–80.

but in view of Merneptah's claim that he took Ashkelon and Gezer, devastating the former, in 1220 B.C.,[107] it is more likely that he was responsible for the destruction of Ashdod and Ashkelon. Merneptah's mention of Israel in the same inscription, with the determinative for 'people', indicates that a sacral confederacy so designated was already established in Palestine, though the mention of Israel after Yanoam indicates a location in south Galilee,[108] where perhaps the central sanctuary of the sacral confederacy was at Tabor.

The incidental mention of the fall of Bethel to 'the house of Joseph' (Judg. 1:22–26), significantly not all Israel, merits serious consideration and might be associated with the destruction of Bethel in the first half of the thirteenth century B.C. and its resettlement, like others in the hill country at this time, on a poorer scale with new and cruder pottery and building.

The tradition of the destruction of Arad (Judg. 1:16 f.), Tell Arad excavated by Aharoni and Ruth Amiran between 1962 and 1967 and in 1971, must be analysed with the same caution before the relevance of archaeological evidence is assessed. According to Judg. 1:16 f. Arad was settled by the Kenites and Judah after destruction, hence the name Hormah, understood as 'put to the ban'; cf. Num. 21:1–3, where 'the place'[109] was called Hormah; cf. the banning of Zephath[110] in the Negeb of Arad (Judg. 1:17). The destruction of Arad is not supported by excavations at Tell Arad, which was unoccupied from *c.* 2500 to the eleventh century B.C.[111] This suggests to Aharoni that Canaanite, or Late Bronze, Arad may have been elsewhere in the neighbourhood.[112] The apparent discrepancy, however, between Judg. 1:16 f. and the archaeological data is possibly owing to the name Hormah attached to Arad. This might have meant 'sanctuary' (cf.

[107] *ANET*, p. 378.

[108] Yanoam is mentioned also in an account of campaigns of Seti I from his base at Bethshan, *ANET*, p. 253.

[109] It is uncertain from the context whether 'the place' refers to Arad or the district, being mentioned after the statement of the destruction of the local allies of the king of Arad 'and their cities'.

[110] This may be a common noun 'watchpost', and may refer to Arad or a part of it.

[111] Aharoni, 'The Negeb', *AOTS*, p. 392.

[112] viz. Tell Milh *c.* 8 miles south-west of Arad or Tell Mashash *c.* 3 miles further in the same direction; Aharoni, op. cit., p. 389.

Arabic *ḥaram*), denoting possibly an original Kenite sanctuary[113] prior to the tenth century Israelite temple discovered
at Tell Arad.[114] In the banning (*ḥērem*) of Arad we may
suspect aetiology owing to the influence of the tradition of the
holy war which the Deuteronomistic Historian incorporated
in his account of the 'conquest' under the influence of the
Gilgal tradition, which he endorsed in Josh. 2–8. The
association of Judah with the Kenites from the base at 'the
City of Palm Trees' (Judg. 1:16), by which the Deuteronomist
understood Jericho (Deut. 34:3; Judg. 3:13; cf. 2 Chron.
28:15), also indicates the Deuteronomistic association of the
Arad tradition with that of Gilgal. We may thus reduce the
Scriptural tradition to its historical nucleus, the occupation of
Arad and district by the Kenites, who were traditionally
confederate with Israel.[115] This is neither proved nor
contradicted by the excavation of Tell Arad, though the
Israelite temple may indicate an earlier sanctuary (*ḥormâh*) of
the Kenites.[116]

In his critical assessment of archaeological evidence[117]
Noth significantly admittted only the data from Hazor as
relevant to the account of the 'conquest' in Josh. 11:1–11. This
passage, without any element of aetiology or sacral tradition,
is purely historical, apart from its association with Joshua and
all Israel. How then do archaeological discoveries at Hazor
relate to it? The destruction of the city, both citadel and lower
city with its late Bronze Age temples, attested by the
excavation of Yadin and his colleagues was certainly the work
of an enemy *c.* 1225 B.C. It is unlikely that it was the result of
Merneptah's campaign in Palestine, since it is unmentioned
by him in his hymn of victory, and there was no local rival
strong enough to overthrow Hazor, with its hegemony in
Galilee (Josh. 11:1 f., 10). After the destruction of the Late

---

[113] Aharoni, op. cit., p. 401; *JNES* xxiv (1965), 297–303.

[114] Aharoni, op. cit., 395–7.

[115] Cf. Exod. 18, where we regard the Midianites as Kenites, the former denoting
local origin and the latter being a vocational designation; 1 Sam. 15:6; 2 Sam. 30:30.

[116] This need not have been a built shrine, but rather a precinct, the conception of
which is illustrated by the walled hilltop above Bir Rekhmeh; Glueck, *Rivers in the
Desert*, pp. 83 f.; Aharoni in B. Rothenberg *et al.*, *God's Wilderness*, London, 1961, p.
139.

[117] Noth in *Congress Volume, Oxford, 1959*, SVT vii (1960), 262–82.

Bronze city there were only two levels of occupation of the citadel in the Early Iron Age (*c.* 1200–950 B.C.) before its rebuilding under Solomon.[118] These Yadin considers as settlements of semi-nomads, the remains consisting of storage pits, hearths, and the stone foundations for huts or windbreaks for tents. Is it possible that the squatters who occupied the citadel of Hazor were responsible for its destruction? Aharoni has maintained that the occupation of a city does not necessarily register the whole situation of the country, and so he insists that excavation should be accompanied by a more extensive regional survey.[119] Such a survey undertaken by him in Upper Galilee revealed that the Early Iron Age pottery at Hazor had no affinities with that of the new settlements of the period in the centre and south of Palestine, but was paralleled in new village settlements in east Galilee northwards from the great central plain.[120]

The settlement of east Galilee up to the point at which Hazor and her allies vainly attempted to stem the penetration was not likely to be suddenly achieved, and this movement may be connected with the *'prw* whom Seti I mentions in his stele at Bethshan as active in the mountains of Yarmuth[121] (Remeth in Isaachar, Josh. 19:21?). This would give a date some time after 1313 B.C. for the beginnings of their settlement in the uplands of Lower Galilee south of Meirun, giving almost a century for the clearance of scrub and the thick settlement which Aharoni attests, until they eventually expanded to menace the Canaanite settlements on the plateau of Upper Galilee. The second last of the destructions of Bronze Age Hazor may be associated with Seti's Campaigns. This would account for the movement of those recognized later as Naphtali, independent of the Israelites of the south, as the ceramic evidence suggests. The deposit of bronze weapons and a figurine of Canaanite type at what was evidently a cult

---

[118] Yadin, 'Hazor', *AOTS*, p. 254; *Hazor*, London, 1975, pp. 252–7.

[119] Aharoni, *The Land of the Bible*, pp. 91 ff. Notable recent regional surveys are the work of Naveh and Kaplan in the Shephelah and coastal plain around Jaffa, Wright and colleagues in the same region, the modern survey of the Negeb since its inception by Rothenberg, Aharoni, and others in the Six Day War, and Aharoni's own important survey of Upper Galilee, *Antiquity and Survival* ii. 142–50.

[120] Aharoni, *Antiquity and Survival*, ii. 142 ff.

[121] *ANET*, p. 255.

place in the Early Iron settlement at Hazor[122] does not suggest a militant group fired by its new Covenant allegiance to Yahweh, with the religious obligations familiar from the categorical demands in the Book of the Covenant and the original form of the Decalogue, the core around which the sacral confederacy was to develop. In this connection it may be recalled that the local members of that confederacy, Naphtali, were regarded as one of the concubine tribes (Gen. 30:8).

Thus, in our assessment of the relevance of the archaeological data to the biblical account of the settlement of Israel in Palestine, such correspondence as there may be is with local traditions and historical sources delimited by literary criticism, as Alt and Noth emphasized, rather than with the Deuteronomistic compilation.

We cannot always find such spectacular evidence as at Hazor. Generally the indication of a new element in the land is the settlement of hitherto unpopulated areas attested by new pottery types of the Early Iron Age. The destruction of Late Bronze cities over about a century and a half (e.g. Jericho c. 1350, Tell Beit Mirsim etc., c. 1225 B.C.) denotes more complex causes than the invasion of Israel as represented in Josh. 1:1–11. The tradition of the symbiosis of Jacob with the people of Shechem and the inclusion of Canaanite settlements like Tirzah and Shechem in the family of Manasseh (Josh. 17:2–4 cf. Num. 26:28–34; 27:1) accords with the fact that excavations at Shechem and Tirzah (Tell el-Far'a) attest no destruction of the Late Bronze strata that would correspond with the settlement in the Early Iron Age.[123] This could support Alt's view that the penetration of Israel was effected by the gradual settlement of the less populous hills by seasonal immigrants, who only latterly came into conflict with the inhabitants of the plains, as Judges describes.[124]

If archaeology does not confirm the final tradition of the Deuteronomistic History in Joshua, it at least alerts us to the significance of sources, some of which it may confirm. A case in point is that of the town lists in the tribal divisions in Josh.

---

[122] Yadin in *AOTS*, p. 256; *Hazor*, pp. 132–4.
[123] Wright, *Shechem*, pp. 101 f.; de Vaux, 'Tirzah', *AOTS*, pp. 376 f.
[124] See above, p. 65, nn. 1, 2.

13–19. As is well known, Alt considered that the town lists as distinct from the tribal boundaries were taken from fiscal lists in administrative records of the Davidic monarchy.[125] To be sure, he thought of administrative divisions in Josiah's reign, which might be admitted for the districts claimed for Judah in the Philistine plain and immediately north of Jerusalem. But it is now demonstrated that the wilderness settlements of Middin, Secacah, Nibshan, and the City of Salt (Josh. 15:61 f.), the last being the Iron Age settlement discovered by de Vaux at Khirbet Qumran,[126] and the others in the plain el-Buqei'a,[127] were not settled before the ninth century B.C.,[128] which may corroborate the statement of 2 Chr. 17:12–19 on Jehoshaphat's store-cities. This town-list in Joshua therefore cannot antedate the ninth century B.C. Neither is it the ideal reconstruction of P, since the tribal boundaries show many odd projections and indentations (e.g. Josh. 15:5; 16:7) in contrast to Ezekiel's reconstruction with the new Israel (Ezek. 48:1–29), and the tribal boundaries of Simeon, Dan, and Issachar are lacking. Alt's theory of the use of administrative lists from the Davidic monarchy in the lists of the settlements in the tribal districts in Josh. 13–19 is corroborated by archaeology, though in the wilderness settlements the source is later than Alt proposed.

A notable instance of a problem raised by archaeology and solved by source and form criticism is the account of Sennacherib's invasion of Judah (2 Kgs. 18:13–19:37; cf. Isa. 36–37). 2 Kgs. 18:13–16, agrees with Sennacherib's account[129] that Hezekiah surrendered unconditionally and was laid under heavy tribute. But in 2 Kgs. 18:17 ff. there is no mention of tribute. It has therefore been claimed that 2 Kgs. 18:13–16 and 18:17 ff. refer to two different campaigns.[130]

---

[125] Alt, 'Das System der Stammesgrenzen im Buche Josua', *KS* i. 132–202.

[126] De Vaux, *Archaeology and the Dead Sea Scrolls*, 2nd edn., London, 1973, pp. 1–3.

[127] Respectively, Khirbet Abu Tabaq, Khirbet es-Samra, and Khirbet el-Maqari.

[128] So J. T. Milik and F. M. Cross, *BASOR* cxlii (1956), 5–17; Cross and G. E. Wright, *JBL* lxxv (1956), 223–6.

[129] *ANET*, pp. 287 f.

[130] H. Winckler, *Alttestamentliche Untersuchungen*, Leipzig, 1892, pp. 28 ff.; R. W. Rogers in *Wellhausen Festschrift*, Giessen, 1914, pp. 319 ff.; Albright in *JQR* xxiv (1934), 370 f., and, in the light of evidence adduced from the Sudan (see below, p. 89, n. 132), *BASOR* cxxx (1953), 8–11; E. W. Nicholson in *VT* xiii (1963), 280–9; R. de

No Assyrian record mentions any campaign of Sennacherib to the west after 701 B.C., though for the next decade he was preoccupied with Babylon and Elam and in 691 B.C. sustained a serious defeat which might well have encouraged rebellion in Palestine. Superficially, the alleged second Assyrian campaign in Hezekiah's reign is supported by association with the campaign of the Sudanese Tirhakah in 2 Kgs. 19:9; but since by cross-reference to the dates of the death and installation of Apis bulls Tirhakah is demonstrated to have reigned as sole king from 684 to 664,[131] such a campaign must have occurred after the death of Hezekiah. Admittedly, Tirhakah states in his stele from Kawa that he came to the court of his brother six years before his accession as sole king;[132] but he emphasizes his extreme immaturity, so that he would hardly have commanded an expedition (as 2 Kgs. 19:9 states) before Hezekiah's death in 689. Thus, on the evidence of the Apis stelae, Tirhakah was not even in Egypt proper in 701 B.C., though his father Piankhi (740–10) had founded a Sudanese dynasty there. There was, however, an Egyptian expedition defeated at Eltekeh, as Sennacherib claims, in which Sudanese forces were recognized. The most likely explanation is that in 2 Kgs. 19:9 the reference to 'the king of the Sudan' is accurate, but that 'Tirhakah' is an inaccuracy,[133] which is the solution that we prefer.

The inaccuracy of the reference to Tirhakah in 2 Kgs. 19:9 may further be explained by appreciating that, while 2 Kgs. 18:13–16 is a historical digest of events of 701 B.C., the parallel passages in 2 Kgs. 18:17–19:7 and 19:9–20 are of a different literary character. The former is historical narrative about the good King Hezekiah and the prophet Isaiah in the style of prophetic anecdote as background to the prophet's

Vaux in *RB* lxxiii (1966), 498–500; Bright, op. cit., pp. 284 f., 296–308. The present writer also accepted this view in the 1st edn. of his *I & II Kings*, pp. 599–632, but revoked it in the 2nd edn., pp. 660 f.

[131] P. van der Meer, *The Chronology of Ancient Western Asia and Egypt*, 2nd edn., Leiden, 1955, pp. 81 f.

[132] M. L. Macadam, *The Temples of Kawa I. The Inscriptions*, 1949, v. 15.

[133] So Noth, *History*, 2nd edn., p. 268; H. H. Rowley, 'Hezekiah's Reform and Rebellion', in *Men of God*, London, 1963, pp. 98 ff. For an earlier discussion of this problem, see W. O. E. Oesterley and T. H. Robinson, *A History of Israel* i, Oxford, 1932, pp. 397, 409 f.

mission.[134] The latter has a definite theological interest and is an edifying legend of the good King Hezekiah. In such a context, then, as 2 Kgs. 19:9–20, composed freely at some remove from 701 B.C., we may understand the anachronistic mention of Tirhakah, the most famous Pharaoh of the Sudanese dynasty.

That is not to say, however, that 2 Kgs. 18:17–19:7, to which 2 Kgs. 19:9–20 is secondary,[135] was entirely divorced from history. The approach of the Rabshakeh is formally paralleled by that of the delegation of Tiglath-pileser III to the rebel king of Babylon, who heard the demands and arguments of the Assyrians, and their attempts to split the opposition, behind his barred gates.[136]

Source and also form criticism are also relevant to the correspondence we have noted between statements in Chronicles and archaeological data. Such references are not indiscriminate. Only the passages which have no religious motivation are so emphasized, their historical value being warranted by the Chronicler's references to records of the monarchy, on which the Deuteronomistic Historian in Kings also drew selectively. It is with the historical sources, strictly determined, that we must expect such correspondence as there may be with archaeological data. The net result of such a study is that the historical information that Chronicles provides beyond Kings merits serious consideration.[137]

Discoveries in Jerusalem have a peculiar interest, with

---

[134] So G. Fohrer, *Das Buch Jesaja* ii (Zürich, 1967), 159, who, however, characterizes the whole as an 'edifying legend' or 'prophetic midrash'. A more accurate form-critical analysis is that of B. S. Childs, *Isaiah and the Assyrian Crisis*, SBT, 2nd series, 3, 1967.

[135] Summarizing as it does the arguments of the Rabshakeh in 18:19–21, 23 f., 22, 35, 31–32a, 30, 32b–35.

[136] H. W. F. Saggs in *Iraq* xvii (1955), 21–56, 126–60. There is no reason to doubt the truth of the tradition in 2 Kgs. 18:17 ff. that Hezekiah did not submit at the summons of the Rabshakeh, but neither is there any reason to suppose that the delegation did not succeed in preventing him joining the Egyptians and other rebels, and in fact Sennacherib does not mention Hezekiah in the battle of Eltekeh. Indeed he claims that his action against Jerusalem was essentially one of containing the enemy (*ANET*, p. 288) and preventing his linking up with his allies rather than an attempt to reduce the city.

[137] On historical sources used by the Chronicler, see A. M. Brunet, *RB* lx (1953), 451–508; lxi (1954), 349–86; W. Rudolph, *Chronikbücher*, HAT xxi, Tübingen, 1955, pp. x–xiii.

some problems solved and others stubbornly defying solution. (Mazar's spectacular exposure of the southern and south-western faces of the *temenos* of Herod's Temple and their adjuncts[138] belongs to a later phase of the city's history than that which immediately concerns us.) Outstanding among the certainties is the discovery in 1961 that the city taken and occupied by David on the south-eastern hill extended to almost the depth of the Kidron Valley, thus including the famous shaft to the tunnel from the spring of Gihon. The buttress and terrace work on the steep eastern slope is feasibly the *millô* (lit. 'filling') mentioned several times in the building and repair work of the Davidic kings. The same expedition uncovered a seventh-century wall, replacing the old eastern wall; and this is probably the work ascribed to Manasseh in 2 Chr. 33:14. Possible evidence of the northern wall of David's city and its predecessor is a fragment of wall on the saddle between the south-eastern hill and the Temple hill, with tenth- or ninth-century pottery to the north and early monarchic and Late Bronze pottery to the south. Solomon's fortification to the north, however, will probably remain an unsolved problem because of the Muslim sacred area. Since the ancient wall round the south-western hill, south of the Turkish Citadel to Birket el-Hamra, is now demonstrated to be from the time of Herod Agrippa I,[139] the problem of the defence of the Pool of Siloam is still outstanding.

Repeated excavations on the western hill have revealed that it was occupied in the early monarchy,[140] though not necessarily fortified. Avigad discovered on the high ground west of the southern corner of Herod's *temenos* a wall over 20 feet thick from the end of this period,[141] which is surely Hezekiah's wall (the 'other wall without' of 2 Chron. 32:5) enclosing the Mishneh, which was already occupied, probably by the official class (2 Kgs. 22:14). Since only 35 metres of this

---

[138] *The Excavations in the Old City of Jerusalem near the Temple Mount*, Jerusalem, 1971.

[139] K. M. Kenyon in *PEQ* xciv (1962), 84.

[140] Kenyon (Armenian Quarter, Muristan), ibid. 72–89; xcv (1963), 7–21; xcvi (1964), 7–18; xcvii (1965), 9–20; xcviii (1966), 73–88; C. N. Johns (Citadel), *QDAP* xiv (1950), 139–47; D. Broshi (House of Caiaphas), *Archaeological News* (Hebrew), xl (1971), 14; lv (1973), 122; R. Amiran and A. Eitan (Citadel), *IEJ* xx (1970), 9–17.

[141] *IEJ* xx (1970), 1–8, 129–34, Pl. 29; xxii (1972) 193–200.

wall is known, running north-east and south-west, it is premature to hazard a further reconstruction of the monarchic wall from here to the north-western corner of the city at the Tower of Hananeel (Jer. 31:38; Zech. 14:10; Neh. 12:39) or southwards. The direction of this wall to the south-west, however, suggests that it ran south then south-east to enclose the Pool of Siloam.[142] Admittedly no trace of such a wall west of the Pool of Siloam has been detected, and it seems hardly feasible strategically, but the description of Hezekiah's pool 'between the two walls' (Isa. 22:11) indicates something of the sort. Dr. Kenyon's discovery that the wall round the south-western hill that crosses the central valley is from A.D. 40 to A.D. 44 does not exclude an earlier wall at the mouth of the central valley, where indeed she attests seventh-century debris under Agrippa's wall.

In a review of Avigad's discoveries, Avi-Yonah[143] concludes from the fact that Israelite remains of the seventh century are succeeded immediately by Hellenistic artefacts that the western part of the city was not reoccupied under Nehemiah. This would tally with the reduction of the city in the east, where Dr. Kenyon demonstrated that the so-called 'Jebusite buttress' was Hasmonean work on the line of Nehemiah's wall. Such a limited area would accord with the dereliction of Jerusalem (Neh. 7:4), which Nehemiah endeavoured to remedy by the inducement of Jews from the country districts to settle in the city (Neh. 7:11). This is an interesting possibility and would reopen the whole question of the location of the gates of the city. Such a restriction to the south-east and Temple hill, however, would not admit of 1,000 cubits between the Valley Gate in the western wall of the south-eastern hill and the Dung Gate south of that (Neh. 3:13). Actually, Nehemiah's restoration of the walls of Jerusalem was not simply dictated by the exigencies of the situation, but had a token significance. The restriction of the fortifications to the crest of the south-eastern hill was imposed by practical difficulties, and it is much more likely that elsewhere Nehemiah built on the ruined wall of the last city.

Excavation in the Hellenistic strata of the old Jewish

[142] *IEJ* xx (1970), 134 f.
[143] *IEJ* xxi (1971), 168 f.

Quarter of Jerusalem may yet have something concrete to contribute to a solution of the problem of the Hasmonean palace here and possibly also to that of the location of the *akra*, or Seleucid citadel. This, on the varying interpretations of the fragmentary evidence in Josephus, *BJ* V, iv, 1 and 1 Macc, 1:33–6; 12:35; 14:37, is variously held to be the south-eastern hill as a cantonment for the Seleucid garrison and their Jewish collaborators[144] or a citadel on the south-western hill,[145] which, of course, need not exclude the south-eastern hill as a cantonment, which in any case would be important as commanding access to water at Gihon, which would be less vulnerable than the conduits from the Wadi Urtas.[146]

In the intensive archaeological activity in modern Israel the field is full of surprises. Thus Beersheba is well known as the conventional southern limit of the settled occupation in Judah. Now excavations by the University of Tel Aviv have revealed a settlement in the twelfth or eleventh century B.C. like the hitherto unoccupied hill-country further north. The fortification of the place coincides with the early monarchy, with glacis, solid walls, four-chambered gateway, and tower, similar to the fortification discovered by A. Biran at Dan (Tell el-Qadi).[147] Care for water-conservation in the dry south, familiar in Nabatean times, is illustrated in a deep-built stone conduit covered in stone slabs (reminiscent of the early monarchic canal from the spring of Gihon round the south-eastern hill at Jerusalem), which gathered the rain-water from the surface in Beersheba to pond it in a large open reservoir outside the gate.

The evidence of the religious life of Israelite Beersheba, if and when it is all assembled, will be found to be rather revealing, contrasting strongly with evidence of the cult of

---

[144] So J. Simons, *Jerusalem in the Old Testament*, Leiden, 1952, pp. 144–357.

[145] So F. M. Abel, *RB* xxv (1926), 520 ff., and L. H. Vincent, *RB* xlii (1934), 205 ff.; *Jérusalem de l'Ancien Testament* i. 7 ff., 17–21.

[146] On the basis of affinity in certain sections with the conduit round the east side of the south-eastern hill from Gihon to the Old Pool (Birket el-Hamra), Vincent (op. cit. i. 309) considered that this was the work of Solomon. The pool at Birket es-Sultan which caught its overflow was considered by him to be the Dragon Well of Neh. 2:13, so called because of the serpentine course of the conduit.

[147] A. Biran, *IEJ* xix (1969), 121 f., noting the affinity with the gate of Carchemish (eleventh to ninth century B.C.).

Yahweh at neighbouring Arad.[148] In the open area within the gate an incense altar evokes comparison with the cult-installation at the gate of Jerusalem mentioned in Josiah's reformation (2 Kgs. 23:8) and those inside the gate of Tirzah, which persisted from the Late Bronze Age throughout the Israelite period[149] and may be associated with some ritual admitting the stranger (*gēr*) to the security of the community, perhaps suggesting the particular significance of 'the stranger within thy gates'. There is nothing 'unorthodox' in this. Amulets, however, including the falcon of Egyptian Horus and Hathor figurines indicate aberrations which the prophets deplored.

The Israelite settlement evidently did not resume after destruction by the Assyrians in 701 B.C., and, like Ezion-geber[150] Beersheba was eventually settled by Edomites, attested in theophoric compounds of Kos in Aramaic ostraca, which now amount to forty, of economic content. This record is continued by the Edomite names and Aramaic inscriptions in the Phoenician-type tombs at Tell es-Sandahannah (Marissa). Thus the collapse of the state of Judah began the Edomite occupation of southern Palestine, Idumea of the Books of the Maccabees, Josephus, and the New Testament, whence Herod the Great came eventually to the throne in Jerusalem.

BIBLIOGRAPHY

AHARONI, Y. *The Land of the Bible*, London, 1966.
ALBRIGHT, W. F. *The Archaeology of Palestine*, Harmondsworth, 1949.
   Archaeology and the Religion of Israel, 5th edn., Baltimore, 1969.
ALT, A. *Kleine Schriften zur Geschichte des Volkes Israel*, i, ii, Munich, 1953, iii, 1959.
—— *Essays on Old Testament History and Religion*, ETr, Oxford, 1966.
AVI-YONAH, M. (ed.) *Encyclopaedia of Archaeological Excavations in the Holy Land*, i, ii, Oxford, 1975, 1976.
BARDTKE, H. *Bibel, Spaten und Geschichte*, Leipzig, 1967.

[148] Aharoni, 'The Negeb', *AOTS*, pp. 395-7.
[149] De Vaux, 'Tirzah', *AOTS*, p. 377.
[150] Glueck, *Rivers in the Desert*, p. 168.

BARROIS, A. G. *Manuel d' archéologie biblique*, i, ii, Paris, 1939, 1953.

BOTTÉRO, J. (ed.) *Le Problème des Habiru à la 4ᵉ rencontre assyriologique internationale*, Paris, 1954.

BRIGHT, J. *A History of Israel*, 2nd edn., London, 1972.

EISSFELDT, O. 'Palestine in the Time of the Nineteenth Dynasty (*a*) The Exodus and Wanderings', *CAH*, rev. edn., ii, Ch. xxvi (*a*).

—— 'The Hebrew Kingdom', *CAH*, rev. edn., ii, Ch. xxxiv.

FRANKEN, H. J. 'Palestine in the Time of the Nineteenth Dynasty. (*b*) Archaeological Evidence', *CAH* rev. edn., ii, Ch. xxvi (*b*).

FREEDMAN, D. N. and GREENFIELD, J. C. (eds.) *New Directions in Biblical Archaeology*, New York, 1969 (1971).

GLUECK, N. *The Other Side of the Jordan*, 2nd edn., Cambridge, Mass., 1970.

—— *Rivers in the Desert*, London, 1959.

GRAY, J. *The Legacy of Canaan*, SVT V, 2nd edn., Leiden, 1965.

KENYON, K. M. *Archaeology in the Holy Land*, London, 1960.

—— *Jerusalem*. London, 1967.

—— *Royal Cities of the Old Testament*, London, 1971.

KUPPER, J. R. 'Northern Mesopotamia and Syria', *CAH*, rev. edn., ii, Ch. i.

MAZAR, B. *The Excavations in the Old City of Jerusalem Near the Temple Mount*, Jerusalem, 1971.

NOTH, M. *The History of Israel*, ETr, 2nd edn., London, 1960

SANDERS, J. A. (ed.) *Essays in Honor of Nelson Glueck: Near Eastern Archaeology in the Twentieth Century*, New York, 1970.

SIMONS, J. *Jerusalem in the Old Testament*, Leiden, 1952.

DE VAUX, R. *Ancient Israel, Its Life and Institutions*, ETr., London, 1961.

—— *Archaeology and the Dead Sea Scrolls*, 2nd edn., London, 1973.

—— *Histoire ancienne d' Israël: Des origines à l' installation en Canaan*, Paris, 1971; *La Période des Juges*, 1973.

VINCENT, L. H., and STÈVE, A. M. *Jérusalem de l' Ancien Testament*, i–iii, Paris, 1954, 1956.

YADIN, Y. *Hazor, The Rediscovery of a Great Citadel of the Bible*, London, 1975.

—— (ed.) *Jerusalem Revealed. Archaeology in the Holy City 1968–1974*, Jerusalem, 1975.

Also *ANEP, ANET, AOTS, DOTT* (see list of abbreviations).

IV

PENTATEUCHAL PROBLEMS

R. E. CLEMENTS

In reviewing the position of Pentateuchal studies in 1951 C. R. North[1] was able to look back over a period in which the literary-critical analyses, which had dominated research for more than half a century, were being subjected to increasing scrutiny. Several scholars had come to argue that a fuller recognition of the role of oral tradition and a thorough application of the methods of tradition-history removed the necessity for positing documentary sources underlying our extant books. Instead they were suggesting that such documents could be better understood as strata, or tradition-complexes, which represented the residual collections of material of varying ages which had been handed down largely orally, and only in part in written form. Thus the three major streams of Pentateuchal material: JE, D, and P represented source strata which had only secondarily become documents. In association with such a view went the claim that these sources were in some measure overlapping, and contained parallel traditions, each of which could be regarded as preserving both pre- and post-exilic material. The most urgent of such claimants was I. Engnell,[2] but varying degrees of support for such views were to be found also in J. Pedersen[3] and A. Bentzen.[4] C. R. North brought the work of M. Noth into relation with discussion of these issues, since his study of

---

[1] C. R. North, 'Pentateuchal Criticism', *OTMS*, pp. 48 ff.

[2] I. Engnell, *Gamla Testamentet. En traditionshistorisk inledning* i, Stockholm, 1945, 211 ff. Cf. also his studies in *Critical Essays on the Old Testament*, translated and edited by J. T. Willis, London, 1970, 'The Traditio-Historical Method in Old Testament Research', pp. 3–11, and 'The Pentateuch', pp. 50–67.

[3] J. Pedersen, 'Die Auffassung vom Alten Testament', *ZAW* xlix (1931), 161–81, and also *Israel. Its Life and Culture* iii–iv, London–Copenhagen, 1940, 725–27.

[4] A. Bentzen, *Introduction to the Old Testament*, 2nd edn. Copenhagen, 1952, especially pp. 19–24.

the history of the Pentateuchal traditions[5] devoted new and extensive attention to the processes of redaction and transmission which underly the formation of the written documents, and also since his isolation of the Deuteronomic material into a separate category enabled him to deal primarily with the Tetrateuchal traditions of Genesis to Numbers. In spite of some similarities, however, it is apparent in retrospect that the degree of overlap between the work of these Scandinavian scholars and that of M. Noth is not great, and in the ensuing years it is the work of the latter scholar which has dominated the main areas of research. The claims of Engnell and others, that we can either discount, or radically revise, our traditional literary-critical analyses have gone by default for lack of any convincing supporting evidence. Suggestions regarding the far-reaching implications of a lengthy period of oral transmission, implying in some cases the great antiquity of material contained in relatively late literary sources, have proved of limited value. The role of oral tradition has not been, and cannot be, discounted, but the contrast between oral or written traditions has shown itself to be a false one. Both methods of transmission were undoubtedly current in Israel at early and late stages in the development of the Pentateuch. The question of how specific material was handed on was determined by the nature of the material itself, by the facilities available and the circumstances prevailing at the time of its transmission. That some traditions in Israel were written down early, and that major collections of traditions were incorporated into written documents, which were then edited and combined to form more extended documents, appears certain. Thus the methods of critical analysis familiar as literary criticism, remain indispensable to the study of the Pentateuch. Furthermore no detailed and convincing alternative has been able to replace the basic recognition that the major sources JE, D, and P at one time existed as separate documents. Short of this, argument about the method by which the material contained in these documents was transmitted in Israel can only be of secondary

---

[5] M. Noth, *Überlieferungsgeschichte des Pentateuch*, Stuttgart, 1948; ETr by Bernhard W. Anderson, *A History of Pentateuchal Traditions*, Englewood Cliffs, 1972.

interest. Where the importance of recognizing the role of oral tradition has proved most influential has been in counteracting a tendency to over-refinement in dividing up the major sources into subsidiary ones. Thus the division of such sources as J and P into a host of lesser documents has become much less prominent, not because the reasons for doing so were false, but because of the wider recognition that all the major documentary sources were composed with the help of materials which were older than the authors of the sources themselves. This does not mean that these sources are mere collections—repositories of tradition that had accumulated in a particular circle of tradents over an extensive period—but that the authors who composed them made use of material which had already acquired a well-defined form. Questions of the age, nature, and origin of the narrative, legal, and cultic materials which have been used in the composition of the major sources have faced scholars with a multiplicity of problems which have not been amenable to simple, or monochrome, solutions. Nevertheless the stamp which the particular authors of the documentary sources have left upon the material has proved an important key to understanding their significance. When this is coupled with the interest in questions of how the sources have been combined together into larger complexes, and how eventually our Pentateuch was formed, it is evident that the range of Pentateuchal research has greatly broadened. The traditio-historical method initiated by H. Gunkel[6] has provided a basis for a considerable programme of further study which has not yet been exhausted. The question of identifying the scope of the source documents implies also an investigation of the character and history of the materials from which they have been composed, and leads on further to a study of the redactional processes which have brought about their combination and supplementation until they have reached the

---

[6] The significant studies of H. Gunkel's *gattungsgeschichtliche* method have served to illustrate this; W. Klatt, *Hermann Gunkel. Zu seiner Theologie der Religionsgeschichte und zur Entstehung der formgeschichtlichen Methode* FRLANT c, Göttingen, 1969, and K. Koch, *Was ist Formgeschichte? Neue Wege der Bibelexegese*, Neukirchen–Vluyn, 1964, ETr by S. M. Cupitt as *The Growth of the Biblical Tradition*, London, 1969.

form which they now possess.[7] Thus the analysis of the Pentateuch into its literary sources is only one step towards the investigation of the problems of its origin and meaning. We can therefore separate our examination of recent Pentateuchal research into three main areas of study, roughly corresponding to the three major critical aspects of approach comprising literary criticism, tradition criticism, and redaction criticism. The first concerns the identification of the major documentary sources, the second deals with the history of the traditions which have been used in these documents, and the third concerns the processes of editing and redaction by which these major documentary sources have been woven together into their present form. We should note, however, that there is inescapably a degree of overlap of all three aspects of study in examining the stages of the growth of the Pentateuch.

As we have noted, the analysis of the Pentateuch into its constituent literary sources has remained a primary feature of study, so that fresh insights and methods of approach must be regarded as supplementing, rather than replacing, it. Both literary criticism, and recognition of the documents it has discovered, remain indispensable, even though more recent insights have meant that their identification has not dominated Old Testament research to the extent that it once did. Overarching all recent Pentateuchal studies has been the work of M. Noth, who has provided the most comprehensive and detailed treatment of the traditio-historical and redaction-critical problems of the Pentateuch. Further exposition of his basic conclusions are to be found in his commentaries on the books of Exodus, Leviticus, and Numbers,[8] and in his studies of the Deuteronomist's and Chronicler's histories.[9]

Whilst in Noth's work the problems of literary criticism

---

[7] W. Klatt op. cit., p. 12, n. 6, suggests that 'Form Criticism' may be regarded as an over-all title, and 'Type (*Gattungs*) Criticism', 'Tradition Criticism', and 'Redaction Criticism' as aspects of it.

[8] M. Noth, *Das zweite Buch Mose. Exodus* ATD v, Göttingen, 1959. ETr by J. Bowden, *Exodus* (Old Testament Library), London, 1962; *Das dritte Buch Mose. Leviticus* ATD vi, Göttingen, 1962. ETr by J. E. Anderson, *Leviticus* (Old Testament Library), London, 1965; *Das vierte Buch Mose. Numeri* ATD vii, Göttingen, 1966. ETr by J. D. Martin, *Numbers* (Old Testament Library), London, 1968.

[9] *ÜGS.*

fall rather into the background, they are not regarded as entirely settled. Two of the four classical documentary sources raise literary problems which are particularly difficult to resolve, namely E and P. As regards the former, the problem arises from the fact that E material is preserved only in a fragmentary way, which Noth, along with others, regards as due to E's having contained much parallel material to that found in J, which was passed over when the redactor of JE used J as his groundwork. That the extant material which is usually ascribed to E contains several duplicates, with certain variations, of stories preserved also in J is accounted for by Noth on the hypothesis that underlying both sources lies a common *Grundlage* (G) of which both J and E were developments. So Noth is able to reckon with a continuous epic narrative E, comparable in scope and character to J, but of which we now have only very disconnected fragments. This point of literary criticism is taken up by S. Mowinckel in some detail, and the alternative case presented that what is usually called JE can better be regarded as J^v (J variatus).[10] By this Mowinckel means that this source arose from the supplementation of J by other material, which had for the most part circulated orally, so that there never was a separate document E. JE, or J^v as Mowinckel prefers to designate it, did not arise from the redaction of two separate documents, but from the supplementation of J by individual traditions, some of which were variants of narratives already to be found in J. The crux of the problem here lies with the answer to the question of whether or not we can find in the E material any indication that it once constituted a coherent narrative document, or whether it is merely a collection of separate, and only loosely related, traditions. Here the characteristic features of style, vocabulary, and theological outlook which are familiar to literary critics require to be examined further to see whether they constitute more than the chance similarities of comparable material and indicate the planned work of an author. A resolute attempt to answer this question in the affirmative, and thereby to exclude Mowinckel's contention,

[10] S. Mowinckel, *Erwägungen zur Pentateuchquellenfrage*, Oslo, 1964, pp. 59–118. Cf. especially p. 112 'A source E, as understood by the traditional source criticism, cannot be demonstrated, to say nothing of a "North-Israelite saga document, the Elohist source" (Procksch).'

has been made by H. W. Wolff in his Inaugural Address at Heidelberg.[11] Wolff seeks to single out certain basic religious themes found in E and to show that they constitute evidence of a consciously planned work. In many respects the material adduced by Wolff appears meagre, but in view of the very fragmentary way in which E material has survived at all, this is no doubt as much as we can expect. Furthermore, the stylistic and theological connections within the E material are none the less more than we can account for as the unconscious reflection of material preserved orally, and the very consistency of the pattern of E's variation from J suggests a continuous narrative form. All in all therefore we must certainly reckon with the presence of pre-Deuteronomic Pentateuchal material which exists alongside the narrative of J. Most of this is usually ascribed to a roughly parallel documentary source E, and this would still appear to be the most likely explanation of its origin. However, if we reject Mowinckel's counter-explanation of the origin of the E material in its full form, we may nevertheless regard it as a possible explanation of some of that material. It would certainly appear to be too rigid a feature of earlier literary criticism that it was inclined to assign all the pre-Deuteronomic Pentateuchal material that is not J to E. This is to allow too little room for the work of redactors and supplementers, who may readily have filled out the original J narrative from independent traditions, preserved orally. Here, as also in a number of other respects, the difficulty of distinguishing between the presence of a separate documentary source and the work of an editor represents a serious problem in Pentateuchal research. Certainly if Mowinckel's claim were to be upheld, it would rule out Noth's hypothesis regarding G, but in any case there is great difficulty in defining the scope of G and arriving at any conclusion as to whether or not it once existed as a separate document.[12]

[11] H. W. Wolff, 'Zur Thematik der elohistischen Fragmente im Pentateuch', *EvTh* xxix (1969), 59–72, reprinted in *GSAT*, 2nd edn., Munich 1973, pp. 402–17.

[12] M. Noth, *Pentateuchal Traditions*, p. 39, comments: 'whether this *Grundlage* was written or oral can hardly be answered with any certainty; but then, traditio-historically this is not of great consequence.' However, it is perhaps worth noting that if this G is regarded as an oral source, then Noth's view differs very little from that of earlier critics, who had consistently recognized a basis of common material between J and E.

Alongside the problem posed by E we may note briefly the claims of O. Eissfeldt[13] and G. Fohrer[14] to find traces of another early source, older than either J or E, which they label respectively L (for *Laienquelle*) and N (*Nomadenquelle*). This concerns material which is otherwise usually ascribed to J and which is believed to show evidence of a common cultural and theological outlook. However the existence of such a further literary source must be seriously doubted, not because these common features in parts of the material are not to be found, but because it appears unnecessary to conclude that their presence constitutes evidence of a further documentary source. On any reckoning the J and E authors were also collectors of earlier material, and we cannot assume that all the blocks of material which betray common characteristics once existed separately in an independent document. It is one of the merits of tradition criticism that it recognizes that this is not always so. This also means that Fohrer's further attempt to distinguish a G^1, underlying his source N, from a G^2 underlying his JE, appears more refined and precise than the evidence warrants.[15]

So far as the P document is concerned, Engnell's attempt, following an earlier suggestion by P. Volz,[16] to dismiss this, and to speak rather of a P work extending from Genesis to Numbers,[17] must be rejected. Such a view regards P not as an independent author, but as the collector and redactor of the material now preserved in these books, apart from some later additions. Engnell does not deny that there is early (JE) and late (P) material to be found here, but rather that what is usually called P did not exist as a separate narrative with a purpose and character of its own. The issue here raises the important consideration which we have already noted in connection with E, that there is a difference between the work of an author and that of a redactor, and that it is

---

[13] O. Eissfeldt, *Einleitung in das alte Testament*, 3rd edn., Tübingen, 1964, ETr by P. R. Ackroyd, *The Old Testament, an Introduction*, Oxford, 1965, pp. 194–9.

[14] E. Sellin–G. Fohrer, *Einleitung in das Alte Testament*, Heidelberg, 1965. ETr by D. Green, *Introduction to the Old Testament*, London, 1970, pp. 159–64.

[15] G. Fohrer, *Introduction to the Old Testament*, pp. 148, 164.

[16] In P. Volz–W. Rudolph, *Der Elohist als Erzähler. Ein Irrweg der Pentateuchkritik?* BZAW lxiii, Giessen, 1933, pp. 135 ff.

[17] I. Engnell, *Gamla Testamentet*, pp. 211–13.

necessary to look for valid criteria by which to distinguish them. In this direction S. Mowinckel has come to the defence of the view that P once existed as an independent narrative by showing that where J^v (JE) and P have parallel accounts, the inclusion of the P sections makes no sense at all unless it is to preserve what was already extant in an independent narrative.[18] Hence Mowinckel, in company with M. Noth, upholds the usually accepted view that there was once an independent P narrative, and this must certainly be regarded as correct over against the attempt to reduce P to the status of an editor.

On the question of the identification of P material, however, M. Noth has introduced some important fresh considerations which affect the over-all picture.[19] The first of these is that P is essentially a work of narrative history, so that the inclusion in it of large collections of laws and cultic regulations must be accounted for by recognizing that these have been introduced subsequently. This becomes most evident in the book of Leviticus, where Noth finds virtually no evidence of the original P narrative, admitting it only in Lev. 8–10.[20] Even the Holiness Code (Lev. 17–26), which almost all earlier critics had regarded as having been taken up in virtually its present form by P, Noth regards as a subsequent insertion into this narrative source. The issue here is probably not as serious in its implications as may at first appear, for on any reckoning the lists of laws and regulations in question must be seen as collections which grew up over a long period within their own cultic context. This is certainly true, for example, of the Manual of Sacrifice preserved in Lev. 1–7. Whether the original P author incorporated this into his narrative, or whether this was done by a later redactor, scarcely affects the dating of the material it contains, and belongs rather to the many difficult problems relating to the history of the redaction of the Pentateuch. Noth is perhaps too rigid in insisting that the narrative character of P precludes our finding within it extensive lists of cultic laws, for, as Mowinckel points out, it

[18] S. Mowinckel, op. cit., pp. 16–18.
[19] M. Noth, *Pentateuchal Traditions*, pp. 8–19.
[20] Id., *Pentateuchal Traditions*, pp. 8 f.; cf. *Leviticus*, pp. 12–14.

is plausible enough from the general interests of P that he should have planned to introduce such lists at appropriate places in his story.[21] Nevertheless the position is firmly assured that P must be regarded as a narrative history, for which JE provided the major source, and which once existed independently.

The second of Noth's major revisions of earlier views about P is his contention that this document cannot be traced beyond the end of the book of Numbers into Joshua.[22] This conclusion relates to Noth's recovery of the structure and scope of the Deuteronomistic History, and belongs together with his rejection of the attempts to trace the continuation of J into Joshua. In both cases Noth's contentions and conclusions have been attacked by S. Mowinckel, who is otherwise generally in support of Noth's views regarding the Deuteronomistic History. In the case of J, Noth agrees with von Rad that this source must once have continued its story to tell of Israel's occupation of the land.[23] However, as a result of the redaction into the combined JEP narrative and the linking of this with the book of Deuteronomy, the original J occupation narrative was broken off and has not survived. Mowinckel differs from Noth on this latter point, for he believes that we do possess fragments of this narrative, primarily in Judg. 1, but also secondarily in Josh. 15:13–19, 63; 16:10 and 17:11–13, where use has been made of this old J occupation narrative.[24] This material has been incorporated into the Deuteronomistic History, and, whilst Noth admits the feasibility of ascribing it to J, he argues that we are not justified in doing so since we lack any firm evidence for such an identification.[25]

So far as the Priestly Document is concerned, Noth argues, against the majority of earlier critics, that this source did not continue beyond the book of Numbers to tell of the

[21] S. Mowinckel, op. cit., pp. 24–6.
[22] M. Noth, *Pentateuchal Traditions*, pp. 9 f.; *ÜGS*, pp. 182–90; *Das Buch Josua*, pp. 10 f.
[23] Id., *Pentateuchal Traditions*, p. 16; *ÜGS*, pp. 180, 210. Cf. G. von Rad, *The Form-Critical Problem of the Hexateuch*, p. 51.
[24] S. Mowinckel, *Tetrateuch–Pentateuch–Hexateuch*, BZAW xc, Berlin, 1964, pp. 9–33.
[25] M. Noth, *Pentateuchal Traditions*, p. 33, n. 127.

occupation.[26] In fact, according to Noth, several of the later chapters of Numbers were only secondarily added to P.[27]

On this point Mowinckel differs most sharply from Noth, and argues that the lists of tribal cities and boundaries to be found in Josh. 13–19 were incorporated into P[28] and that Josh. 12 is essentially the Priestly occupation narrative. Here too the degree of divergence between the two scholars is not as sharp as may first appear. It is important for Noth's understanding of the Deuteronomistic History that he recognizes that these chapters in the book of Joshua did not originally form a part of it, but have been incorporated subsequently.[29] He notes, too, some degree of affinity with P, so that any conclusions on this point are of relevance for our understanding of P and its scope, but do not significantly affect the interpretation of the Deuteronomistic History. The openness of the issue should be noted, but in general it is probably true, as Noth mentions, that any really decisive evidence to identify these chapters as from P is lacking. That P should have completed his story of Israel's origins without following the earlier sources in recounting the occupation of the land is perfectly credible. Whereas J's narrative is markedly truncated by the breaking off of its narrative of the occupation of the land, this is not true of P. Where the former's theme of promise and fulfilment centres on the gift of the land, the promise theme in P is directed towards the cultus and the divine revelation of its institutions at Sinai. W. Zimmerli has shown that the covenant theology of P shows a considerable shift from that found in JE.[30]

The question of the date of P has continued to occupy attention, and there has been widespread acceptance of the recognition that lists of cultic laws and rules of varying antiquity were incorporated into it by either the original author or a later editor. This makes readily explicable the fact

[26] Id., *Pentateuchal Traditions*, p. 6; *ÜGS*, pp. 182–90; *Das Buch Josua*, p. 16.

[27] Id., *ÜGS*, pp. 190–206.

[28] S. Mowinckel, *Zur Frage nach dokumentarischen Quellen in Josua 13–19*, ANVAO, ii. 1, Oslo, 1946; *Tetrateuch–Pentateuch–Hexateuch*, pp. 51–76.

[29] M. Noth, *ÜGS*, pp. 45 ff., 183 f.

[30] W. Zimmerli, 'Sinaibund und Abrahambund. Ein Beitrag zum Verständnis der Priesterschrift', *ThZ* x (1960), 268–80. = *Gottes Offenbarung. Gesammelte Aufsätze*, Munich, 1963, pp. 205–16.

that these partly reflect a pre-exilic situation. What is not shown by this, however, is that the P narrative history is of such early origin, and this can confidently be rejected, since this source reflects so much of the theological world of the sixth century B.C. M. Noth has suggested that it may have been composed by the time of the rededication of the Jerusalem temple in 516 B.C.,[31] and the same tendency towards a sixth-century date, rather than a later one, is adopted by A. S. Kapelrud.[32] The connections with the theological ideas and outlook of the exilic prophets Ezekiel and Deutero-Isaiah are sufficiently strong to make such a view probable. In contrast with this, J. G. Vink has argued for an early-fourth-century date for P, by attempting a revival of the earlier view that it is to be identified with Ezra's law book of Neh. 8.[33] However, many steps in Vink's thesis appear dubious and insecure, and his reliance for his assessment of the character of P upon contested material from the book of Joshua undermines the strength of his claim. Over all, therefore, there is much to favour a date in the last quarter of the sixth century B.C.[34]

If the problems of literary criticism have focused most sharply on the sources E and P, this is not similarly true of tradition criticism. Here all of the major sources have continued to receive fresh attention, because the insights of this method have opened up a wide range of possibilities regarding the interpretation and dating of material. However the Yahwist source in particular has attracted very special interest because of its historical primacy in the development of the Pentateuchal tradition. A study of the form and

[31] M. Noth, *Pentateuchal Traditions*, p. 243, n. 636, 'I would not be able to adduce any decisive argument against the view that P may have been composed in the so-called Babylonian Exile; yet I can give no positive argument for it either.' Cf. also his *Exodus*, p. 17.

[32] A. S. Kapelrud, 'The Date of the Priestly Code', *ASTI* iii (1964), 58–64.

[33] J. G. Vink, 'The Date and Origin of the Priestly Code in the Old Testament', *OTS* xi (1969), 1–144.

[34] J. Hempel, 'Priesterkodex', in Pauly–Wissowa, *Realencyclopädie der klass. Altertumswissenschaft*, xxii. 2, Stuttgart, 1954, cols. 1943–67, suggests a late-seventh-century date for P, *c.* 610 B.C. (cols. 1965 f.). S. R. Külling, *Zur Datierung der 'Genesis P-Stücke', namentlich des Kapitels Genesis XVII*, Kampen, 1964, would place it very much earlier still, but on arguments regarding the history of covenant forms which are scarcely acceptable.

character of J must unquestionably stand in the forefront of any traditio-historical approach into the origins of the Pentateuch, since this is the earliest documentary source. It established an outline sketch of Israel's origins which has acquired a classical permanence. All the subsequent sources, as well as various prophets and psalmists, inherited a picture of the beginnings of Israel which was fundamentally dependent upon that provided by J. How then did this picture of the rise of Israel come into being? That J possessed any kind of official annals or records of the events he recounts must be entirely ruled out. Rather he was dependent upon a varied mass of traditions which had survived orally within Israel, and which were associated with a whole miscellany of tribal feelings, geographical observations, and cultic practices which were current among its members.

In efforts to reach an understanding of how J arrived at his outline scheme of the rise of Israel, two major studies have been presented linked respectively with the names of G. von Rad and M. Noth. Since that by Noth refers to, and seeks to build upon, that by von Rad, it is appropriate to consider this latter first.

Von Rad's *Das formgeschichtliche Problem des Hexateuch* was first published in 1938 as an investigation into the structure and character of J.[35] Central to the thesis is the claim that before J was composed a brief outline sketch of Israel's origins was current in cultic celebrations as a confessional recital affirmed by lay Israelite worshippers. Examples of this primitive 'credo' are to be found in Deut. 6:20–4; 26:5b–9 and Josh. 24:2b–13, where in each case the original brief summary has been incorporated into a later literary context. For the original setting of these summaries in Israel's worship von Rad pointed to the Festival of Weeks

[35] BWANT iv. 26, Stuttgart, 1938 = *GSAT*, Munich, 1958, pp. 9–86. ETr. by E. W. T. Dicken, *The Problem of the Hexateuch and Other Essays*, Edinburgh–London, 1965, pp. 1–78. The conclusions of this foundational essay are presupposed in the same author's commentary on Genesis, *Das Erste Buch Mose. Genesis*, ATD ii–iv, Göttingen, 1956; ETr by J. H. Marks. 2nd edn., London, 1963, esp. pp. 13 ff. They further provide a basic starting-point for von Rad's theology of the Old Testament: *Theologie des Alten Testaments* i. *Die Theologie der geschichtlichen Überlieferungen Israels*, Munich, 1957; ETr by D. M. G. Stalker, *Old Testament Theology*, i. *The Theology of Israel's Historical Traditions*, Edinburgh–London, 1962.

in Gilgal. Since these confessional summaries contained no reference to the making of a covenant on Mount Sinai, von Rad drew the conclusion that the tradition of such a covenant had only entered into the outline of the special saving events of Israel's birth at a relatively late stage. This did not, of course, imply that the tradition itself was not of considerable antiquity, and von Rad pointed to the celebration of Ingathering at Shechem as its original setting.

Von Rad's thesis has been the subject of extensive further examination, and has enjoyed considerable support, in many cases from scholars who wish to modify some of its primary conclusions. It has also elicited strong opposition, chiefly on the ground that no firm evidence exists to show that such credos did circulate in Israel at a period sufficiently early for them to have provided an outline history for the J author to have used. Von Rad's case rests entirely on the claim that the historical summaries referred to once circulated independently, and are very much older than their present literary settings which are admitted to be late. However the summaries cited from the book of Deuteronomy would appear rather to be Deuteronomic, or perhaps only secondarily Deuteronomic, compositions outlining Israel's history, based on an already established tradition of events.[36] The summary in Josh. 24:2b–13 is certainly post-exilic, in keeping with the fact that the chapter in which it is set is a very late supplement to the Deuteronomistic History.[37] Hence an early date for the currency of such summaries cannot be said to have been established at all.[38] Overall, in spite of the popularity which it has enjoyed, von Rad's claim regarding the currency of this cultic 'credo' as the basis of J's outline cannot be upheld. It has also been opposed on the further grounds that its separation

---

[36] So L. Rost, 'Das kleine geschichtliche Credo', *Das kleine Credo und andere Studien zum Alten Testament,* Heidelberg, 1965, pp. 11–25; N Lohfink, 'Zum kleinen geschichtlichen Credo, Dtn. 26, 5–9', *Theologie und Philosophie* xlvi (1971), 19–39; C. H. W. Brekelmans, 'Het "historische credo" van Israël', *Tijdschrift voor Theologie* iii (1963), 1–11.

[37] Cf. M. Noth, *Das Buch Josua,* pp. 135 ff.; *ÜGS,* pp. 9 n. 1, 181.

[38] The whole thesis of the early currency of such a credo is strongly opposed by Th. C. Vriezen, 'The Credo in the Old Testament', *Studies in the Psalms* (Die Ou Testamentiese Werkgemeenschap in Suid Afrika), ed. A. H. van Zyl, Potchefstrom, 1963, pp. 5–17.

of the traditions of Exodus and Sinai is historically unconvincing and contradicts important aspects of both traditions.
Criticism on this score has come from a number of scholars,
among whom we may note A. Weiser, who posits the early
currency of such a 'credo', but as a kind of liturgical
introduction to a covenant festival.[39] However the problem
here is really part of the wider problem regarding the whole
sequence and connection of events as presented in the J
narrative, which can be better considered in relation to Noth's
attempts to deal with the question of the growth of the
historical tradition underlying J.

Noth's views on this issue start from the recognition that J's
historical outline is formulated around five main themes:
the promise to the patriarchs, the deliverance from Egypt, the
wandering in the wilderness, the revelation at Sinai, and the
occupation of the land.[40] Of these themes the last, the
occupation of the land, appears only in an abbreviated form,
since the J material concerning it has not survived in the
tradition and P has omitted it. The theme of the wandering
in the wilderness has been split up into two phases by the
insertion of the account of the revelation at Sinai. Apart from
these provisional considerations, the presence of these five
themes corresponds in all essentials to five scenes, or chapters,
in the unfolding story. By the time that the author of J wrote
his narrative these five themes had grown together to establish
the basic outline of events with which we are now familiar.[41]
During this process of 'growing together' each theme acted as
a magnet, drawing together a great variety of tribal and local
traditions to form them into a coherent whole.

Fundamental to this presentation by the Yahwist of the
foundations of Israelite history is the conviction that all Israel
is one, so that the present 'all Israel' orientation imposes a
unity and chronological sequence upon the narratives which

[39] A. Weiser, *Einleitung in das Alte Testament*, 5th edn., Göttingen, 1963; ETr of
the 4th German ed., by D. M. Barton, *Introduction to the Old Testament*, London,
1961, pp. 87–99.
[40] M. Noth, *Pentateuchal Traditions*, pp. 46–62.
[41] Ibid., p. 46, 'These themes were not added to one another all at once in order to
form the basis for the further expansion of the Pentateuchal-tradition, but rather
were joined together step by step in a definite sequence which can still be determined
in general.'

in their separate existence they did not possess. Traditions of a local, or purely tribal, significance have been incorporated into a larger narrative context which gives them a national reference. Admittedly there were links of various kinds between the separate traditions, established by geographical or tribal connections, but in general the unity which now exists between the traditions is one that has been acquired in the process of transmission, rather than one that was originally latent in the interconnection of the events themselves. In this respect the five themes play a large part in Noth's analysis for they function both as editorial categories within the J story and also as pointers to the history of the transmission of the individual traditions. For the assertion that each of the five themes was originally unrelated to the others, and that only one, that of the Exodus, was primary, Noth points to the conclusions of von Rad, and also to earlier studies by E. Meyer[42] and K. Galling.[43] The figure of Moses, who appears in several themes, must at one time have been at home in only one of them, and have been secondarily introduced into others as veneration for him as a religious leader of Israel grew.

Clearly Noth is right in his contention that the present unified picture to be found in J of a history of all Israel is an artificial production. Nevertheless this thoroughgoing separation of the five themes has appeared unacceptable to many scholars, most especially because of its cutting apart of the Exodus and Sinai events, and also because it reduces the person and work of Moses to very small proportions.

So far as the first point is concerned, A. Weiser, whilst accepting the view that brief summaries of Yahweh's saving history towards Israel were current at an early stage in Israel's cult, explained the absence in them of any reference to the revelation at Mount Sinai as a consequence of the fact that the entire cultic celebration in which the summary was recited was a re-enactment of the Sinai event.[44] Thus an explicit reference to it in the summary would have been superfluous, and out of place in recalling what Yahweh had

---

[42] E. Meyer, *Die Israeliten und ihre Nachbarstämme*, Halle, 1906, pp. 73 ff.

[43] K. Galling, *Die Erwählungstraditionen Israels*, BZAW xlviii, Giessen, 1928.

[44] A. Weiser, op. cit., pp. 87 ff.

done for Israel, since elsewhere in the liturgy reference was made to the law of Sinai as Israel's response to this. Essentially the same point is made by Weiser's pupil, W. Beyerlin,[45] who sought to reinforce his argument by appealing to the hypothesis put forward by G. E. Mendenhall that the Decalogue of Exod. 20:2–17 displays a form borrowed from that of Near Eastern suzerainty treaties.[46] In these a 'historical prologue' formed a separate part of the treaty document from that of the stipulations, to which Beyerlin finds parallels in the preamble and laws of the Decalogue. In so far as Beyerlin is able to show a direct historical connection between the Exodus and Sinai events, he does so by appealing to the view of H. Gressmann that the Israelites who came out of Egypt established themselves at Kadesh, from where a pilgrimage journey was made to Mount Sinai, the mountain of the god who was regarded as Israel's deliverer from Egyptian slavery.[47] There was therefore an original historical link between the Exodus deliverance, the wilderness wandering, and the Sinai revelation, which provided a nucleus of events around which the themes grew up. M. L. Newman[48] has similarly argued for the importance of what took place at Kadesh as an explanation of the connection between the Exodus, wilderness, and Sinai themes, which he further develops in an attempt to explain the differences between the J and E accounts of what happened at Sinai.

Clearly the problem posed by the five themes, and the hypothesis of their original separation from each other, is a very difficult one. It is undoubtedly true that the broad sweep of J's narrative has drawn upon a great variety of traditions, drawn from many sources, which it has combined into a unity. Nevertheless, is it true that each of the five themes was built up around a kernel of events which were originally

---

[45] W. Beyerlin, *Herkunft und Geschichte der ältesten Sinaitraditionen*, Tübingen, 1961; ETr by S. Rudman, *Origins and History of the Oldest Sinaitic Traditions*, Oxford, 1965.

[46] G. E. Mendenhall, 'Covenant Forms in Israelite Traditions', *BA* xvii (1954), 50–76; 'Ancient Oriental and Biblical Law', *BA* xvii (1954), 26–46.

[47] W. Beyerlin, op. cit., pp. 145 ff.

[48] M. L. Newman, *The People of the Covenant*, London, 1965. On the whole problem see especially the study by E. W. Nicholson, *Exodus and Sinai in History and Tradition*, Oxford, 1973.

unrelated to each other? Noth himself can do little more than adumbrate this as a hypothesis. Yet, as S. Herrmann points out, what begins as a working hypothesis is soon regarded as an established foundation.[49] A number of relevant points may be made which go some way towards undermining the validity of the insistence upon separating the themes, or more specifically the events to which they witness, from each other. The rejection of von Rad's hypothesis regarding the early currency in Israel's cult of confessional recitals of saving events removes the major reason for regarding the theme of the revelation at Sinai as separate from the other four themes and especially from that of the Exodus. Further, the remaining three themes: the promise to the patriarchs, the wandering in the wilderness, and the occupation of the land scarcely derive from single events, but are more in the nature of editorial categories by which very varied incidents and traditions have been grouped together. As several scholars have noted, links between elements contained in the individual themes lie embedded in the material itself quite apart from the narrative framework which now binds the separate themes into a whole.[50] As Noth admits, this merely reflects the fact that the combination of the themes has not taken place all at once, but is the result of a long process of growing together. Nevertheless there can be no *a priori* objection in principle on literary or traditio-historical grounds to a historical connection having existed between events which appear in separate themes.

On the positive side we may note certain factors which favour the view that some original historical interconnection does link the Exodus and Sinai themes together, and thereby serves to provide a historical datum of unity between the five themes. These are, first, the importance of the use of the divine name Yahweh for the God of the Exodus and the God

[49] S. Herrmann, 'Mose', *EvTh* xxviii (1968), especially 318 ff. Cf. also the same author's *Israels Aufenthalt in Ägypten*, Stuttgarter Bibelstudien xl, Stuttgart, 1970; ETr by M. Kohl, *Israel in Egypt*, SBT, 2nd series, xxvii, London, 1973, pp. 42 f., and his *Geschichte Israels in alttestamentlicher Zeit*, Münich, 1973, pp. 54 ff.; ETr by John Bowden, *A History of Israel in Old Testament Times*, London, 1975, pp. 31 ff.

[50] So H. Gese, 'Bemerkungen zur Sinaitradition', *ZAW* lxxix (1967), 137–54. Cf. further the works of Beyerlin, Newman, and Herrmann already cited, besides G. Widengren, 'What do we know about Moses?', *Proclamation and Presence. Old Testament Essays in Honour of G. Henton Davies*, ed. J. I. Durham and J. R. Porter, London, 1970, pp. 42 ff., and E. Osswald, 'Mose', *RGG* iv, cols. 1151–5.

of Sinai. Secondly the importance of the figure of Moses in relation to four of the themes means that it is very unsatisfactory to eliminate him from any, or all, of them. Thirdly the role played by Kadesh in the content and transmission of a number of tradition elements points to a geographical location at which a historical interconnection of 'theme' events becomes perfectly credible.

There do appear therefore to be serious considerations which weigh against acceptance of Noth's sharp separation of the five main Pentateuchal themes. These serve to show why many scholars have felt such a separation to be too radical a conclusion to draw from a historical, if not a literary, point of view. Nevertheless the problem of the themes is only one feature of Noth's wide ranging examination of the growth of the Pentateuchal traditions, which stands alone in recent scholarship for its comprehensive treatment of the material. While disagreement may be felt with certain of its points it undoubtedly represents the most thorough statement of the problems and a very cautious and balanced attempt to solve them. Certainly the complexity of the problems rules out of court conservative attempts to overthrow the basic insights of literary criticism and tradition-history in the interests of a return to a very uncritical position.[51]

No comparable comprehensive treatment of Pentateuchal problems, using the insights of tradition-history and redaction criticism, has appeared to rival the work of M. Noth, although a number of detailed studies on parts of the tradition have appeared. Some of these have a bearing on questions of method which reach beyond the specific passages studied. R. Kilian's study of the Abraham traditions seeks to reach back to the basic elements which have been preserved in the J and E narratives.[51a] We may class with it studies of the tradition of a divine covenant with Abraham reported in Gen. 15,[52]

[51] As for instance is attempted by M. H. Segal, *The Pentateuch. Its Composition and Its Authorship and Other Biblical Studies,* Jerusalem, 1967, and U. Cassuto, *The Documentary Hypothesis and the Composition of the Pentateuch,* ETr from the Hebrew by I. Abrahams, Jerusalem, 1961.

[51a] R. Kilian, *Die vorpriestlichen Abrahamsüberlieferungen literarkritisch und traditionsgeschichtlich untersucht;* BBB xxiv, Bonn, 1966.

[52] Cf. N. Lohfink, *Die Landverheissung als Eid. Eine Studie zu Gn. 15* Stuttgarter Bibelstudien, xxviii, Stuttgart, 1967; R. E. Clements, *Abraham and David. Genesis XV and Its Meaning for Israelite Tradition* (SBT, 2nd series, 5), London, 1967.

which provides a central focus of the J history. For the character and purpose of J's redaction of these traditions, and their place within the epic portrait he provides of Israel's origins, we may point to the important essay by H. W. Wolff,[53] alongside the works of von Rad and Noth to which we have already referred.

It is, however, the Sinai tradition of Exod. 19–34 which has occupied the greatest interest of scholars in attempts to probe behind the finished narratives of J and E in order to reach an original kernel of tradition which lies at its centre.

The studies of this tradition by W. Beyerlin and M. L. Newman, to which we have referred, readily accept that the Decalogue of Exod. 20:2–17, in a form closely similar to that which it now possesses, is of Mosaic origin, and derives from the original event of covenant-making on Sinai. Mendenhall's thesis[54] that this Decalogue represents a distinctive Israelite religious adaptation of the form of international suzerainty treaties has been thought by a number of scholars to strengthen this claim. However, in spite of the widespread popularity and support which such a view has enjoyed, it must be rejected as unproven.[55] Too many features of the treaty form are absent from the Decalogue and the form can only be reconstructed in the Old Testament by drawing on widely diverse passages. In general the contention that the Decalogue of Exod. 20:2–17 represents an original kernel of the tradition of the event at Sinai has been widely assumed but scarcely demonstrated. In consequence a number of studies of the problems concerning the Sinai tradition have used it as a given datum for demonstrating its central core, without adequate attention to the literary-critical and form-critical problems which such a view entails. All too readily A. Alt's view of a cultic origin and transmission of apodictic law,[56] such as is found in the Decalogue, has been regarded as easily fitting in with belief in its Mosaic origin, and even

[53] H. W. Wolff. 'Das Kerygma des Jahwisten', *EvTh* xxiv (1964), 73–98 = *GSAT*, 2nd edn., Munich, 1973, pp. 345–73.

[54] Cf. above, p. 111 n. 46.

[55] For some criticisms see D. J. McCarthy, *Old Testament Covenant. A Survey of Current Opinions,* Oxford, 1972, pp. 15 ff.

[56] A. Alt, 'Die Ursprünge des Israelitischen Rechts', *KS* i (Munich, 1953), 278–332; ETr by R. A. Wilson, 'The Origins of Israelite Law', *Essays on Old Testament History and Religion,* Oxford, 1966, pp. 79–132.

with the derivation of the form of these demands from the stipulations of suzerainty treaties. Such claims greatly exceed, and in some cases contradict, Alt's own explanation of the origin of this apodictic form. However, even this latter claim has been strongly contested by E. Gerstenberger, who argues that the apodictic form originated in the moral instruction given in the context of the family life of the clan, and is thereby related to the old clan wisdom of Israel.[57] Over all therefore we can see that attempts to solve the problem of the origin of the Sinai tradition on the basis of theories about the form and structure of the Decalogue of Exod. 20:2-17 have foundered through over-concentration on form-critical theories and a lack of attention to certain theological and literary-critical observations which earlier critics had rightly stressed. The whole question of the time at which the Decalogue was introduced into its present position in the Pentateuchal narrative remains open to further examination, and it can by no means be readily assumed that it was already incorporated into the combined JE. In a late study, O. Eissfeldt[58] reaffirms the view that it was incorporated into the Elohist source, and thence into the combined JE; but such a view has increasingly come under criticism and has met with rejection.[59] Noteworthy in this regard is a fresh and interesting work on the J and E accounts of the Sinai theophany by E. Zenger in which he ascribes the incorporation of both the Decalogue (Exod. 20:2-17) and the Book of the Covenant (Exod. 20:22-23:19) to the work of a late, post-exilic redactor.[60]

Among the individual themes of the Pentateuch that of the Sinai revelation has enjoyed most attention, although others have not been neglected. In particular we may note that the view that the Exodus tradition recounted in Exod. 1-15 grew up as a narrative development of the Passover liturgy, a view

[57] E. Gerstenberger, *Herkunft und Geschichte des 'apodiktischen Rechts'*, WMANT xx, Neukirchen–Vluyn, 1965.

[58] O. Eissfeldt, *Die Komposition der Sinai-Erzählung. Exodus 19–34*, Berlin, 1966; abbreviated in *KS* iv (Tübingen, 1968), 231–7.

[59] E. Nielsen, *The Ten Commandments in New Perspective*, SBT, 2nd series, vii, London, 1968, p. 55; M. Noth, *Exodus*, pp. 154 f.; S. Mowinckel, *Erwägungen zur Pentateuchquellenfrage*, p. 32.

[60] E. Zenger, *Die Sinaitheophanie. Untersuchungen zum Jahwistischen und Elohistischen Geschichtswerk*, Forschung zur Bibel iii, Würzburg, 1971.

which J. Pedersen advocated[61] and which M. Noth[62] still regarded as plausible, has been strongly attacked and rejected by G. Fohrer.[63] Fohrer's objections are forceful and pertinent, and serve greatly to undermine the assumption that we must look to the early Israelite cultus for the development of historical 'confessions', or narratives, which underly the emergence of historiography in ancient Israel. From more than one direction hypotheses regarding the cultic transmission of legal and historical traditions in the Pentateuch have been subjected to strong criticism, so that they cannot now readily be upheld without fresh examination.

Traditio-historical research into the Pentateuch has understandably concentrated on the problems relating to the growth of the historical tradition as it is found in the J and E sources, since these provided an outline of events which has remained fundamental to all subsequent presentations of Israel's origins. However the method has been applied extensively to the other source documents of the Pentateuch, since each of them incorporated material of varying degrees of antiquity, which has meant that we must see their authors as also in some measure collectors. Such a recognition of the preservation of older material in literary sources of a relatively late date has opened up the possibility of regarding differing traditions as the result of parallel developments, rather than as the result of a series of historical changes in a central tradition. Certainly Wellhausen's concern to show the proper chronological sequence and development of the religious ideas and cultic institutions referred to in the various sources reckoned on a unilinear progression, with little allowance for the overlap of different traditions preserved concurrently in different places, or among different communities, of Israel.

On the basis of such insights, the ideas and cultic traditions in the books of Deuteronomy, the Holiness Code (Lev. 17–

---

[61] J. Pedersen, 'Passahfest und Passahlegende', *ZAW* lii (1934), 161–75; cf. *Israel III–IV*, pp. 728–37.

[62] M. Noth, *Pentateuchal Traditions*, pp. 65–71. Noth restricts Pedersen's thesis to Exod. 1–13 only.

[63] G. Fohrer, *Überlieferung und Geschichte des Exodus*, BZAW xci, Berlin, 1964. Cf. his *Introduction to the Old Testament*, p. 117, and S. Mowinckel, 'Die vermeintliche "Passahlegende". Ex. 1–15 in Bezug auf die Frage: Literarkritik und Traditionskritik', *StTh* v (1951), 66–88.

26), and the Priestly Document have all been subjected to very extensive traditio-historical analyses. They have been studied either as independent wholes or in specific parts, in an endeavour to trace the original location and significance of the material which they contain. Such work has in fact been so extensive that it is impossible to summarize all its conclusions, or to attempt to bring them into any kind of consensus. All these analyses have recognized that older traditions are preserved in the extant documents; some have concentrated on seeking to uncover the earlier setting of these traditions, while others have given greater attention to the problem of understanding the redactional interests and aims which have resulted in these extended documentary sources.

The problems of the date and provenance of the book of Deuteronomy have enjoyed particular attention, resulting for brief periods in the appearance of a scholarly consensus, only for this to be broken up again by new suggestions and new insights. So far as the provenance of the book is concerned, von Rad's suggestion has enjoyed wide popularity that we must look for the authors of the work to Levites from the Northern Kingdom who had been dispossessed and who had moved south after the annexation of that kingdom by Assyria in 721 B.C.[64] This thesis has been taken up and developed by J. Lindblom[65] with whom O. Eissfeldt expressed agreement,[66] and in a modified way by G. E. Wright.[67] Wright has sought to extend the scope of this view by seeing such northern Levites as the custodians of a range of cultic, political, and legal traditions which ultimately derive from Israel's pre-monarchic organization as an amphictyony. The association of Deuteronomy with the Northern Kingdom ultimately goes back to the suggestions of C. F. Burney[68] and A. C. Welch,[69]

[64] Von Rad, *Deuteronomium-Studien* FRLANT lviii, Göttingen, 1947 = *GSAT* ii, Munich, 1973, pp. 109–53. ETr by D. M. G. Stalker, *Studies in Deuteronomy*, SBT ix, London, 1953.

[65] J. Lindblom, *Erwägungen zur Herkunft der Josianischen Tempelurkunde*, Lund, 1971.

[66] Cf. Eissfeldt's appendix to Lindblom's monograph, pp. 76–9.

[67] G. E. Wright, 'Deuteronomy', *IB* ii. 309–537.

[68] C. F. Burney, *The Book of Judges*, London, 1918, p. xlvi n.

[69] A. C. Welch, *The Code of Deuteronomy. A New Theory of its Origin*, London, 1923.

which have enjoyed a continuing measure of support.[70] However such a contention has recently been so modified and criticized as to lose much of its weight.[71] Even the assumption that the authors of the work are Levites, or a special order of lay Levites as Lindblom contends, has lost support in the growing recognition of many affinities between Deuteronomy and the ideas and didactic techniques associated with wisdom.[72] In a prominent way also the distinctive covenant theology of Deuteronomy has attracted comparisons with Near Eastern vassal treaties which Mendenhall has brought into the discussion of Israel's covenant forms and ideas.[73] In this, as in other of its manifestations, the comparisons between these ancient vassal treaties and Old Testament covenant narratives have undoubtedly been much overpressed, so that it still appears doubtful whether they can clarify the question of the provenance of Deuteronomy.

So far as the Holiness Code (Lev. 17–26) is concerned, a number of significant treatments have been published along traditio-historical lines, and by way of comparison with other cultic and legal material of the Pentateuch and the Reconstruction Programme of Ezekiel.[74] Studies of blocks of cultic material in the Priestly Document have also proceeded on the assumption that much early material of pre-exilic origin is to be found in its instructions for sacrifice,[75] its account of the Tent of Meeting,[76] and its accounts of priestly investiture.[77] So far as information concerning Israel's cultic history is

[70] Cf. especially A. Alt, 'Die Heimat des Deuteronomiums', *KS* ii (Munich, 1953), 250–75.

[71] Cf. N. Lohfink, 'Die Bundesurkunde des Königs Josias', *Biblica* xliv (1963), 261–88, 461–98.

[72] See especially M. Weinfeldt, *Deuteronomy and the Deuteronomic School*, Oxford, 1972, pp. 244 ff.

[73] So especially D. J. McCarthy, *Treaty and Covenant*, AB xxi, Rome, 1963. Mention may also be made of the very conservative work in this direction by M. G. Kline, *Treaty of the Great King. The Covenant Structure of Deuteronomy*, Grand Rapids, 1963.

[74] H. Graf Reventlow, *Das Heiligkeitsgesetz formgeschichtlich untersucht*, Neu-kirchen–Vluyn, 1961; R. Kilian, *Literarkritische und Formgeschichtliche Untersuchung des Heiligkeitsgesetz*, BBB xix, Bonn, 1963.

[75] R. Rendtorff, *Studien zur Geschichte des Opfers in Alten Israel*, WMANT xxiv, Neukirchen–Vluyn, 1967.

[76] M. Görg, *Das Zelt der Begegnung*, BBB xxvii, Bonn, 1967.

[77] K. H. Walkenhorst, *Der Sinai im liturgischen Verständnis der Deuteronomistischen und Priesterlichen Tradition*, BBB xxxiii, Bonn, 1969.

concerned, the basic assumptions in this proceeding are certainly correct, however much uncertainty remains on details, although it is still exceedingly difficult to arrive at anything more than very general conclusions as regards questions of date and chronological sequence.

Where new insights in method have appeared, and where new and unexpected problems have emerged, is in the field of redaction criticism, which represents a more recent development of techniques of study built upon the foundations of H. Gunkel's method of *Gattungsgeschichte*.

We have already referred to the attempt to revise the interpretation of P by regarding it as the comprehensive redaction of the Tetrateuch of Genesis to Numbers, rather than as an independent literary source. The failure of this attempt should not, however, lead us to ignore the fact that the unnamed men to whom we refer as the redactors of the Pentateuch also acted as its interpreters, and contributed to its growth and meaning. Indeed the final form given to it is the result of the activities of a number of redactors working in the post-exilic era, whose understanding of the material they were transmitting saw in it a normative, or classical, significance which resulted in its use as a scriptural canon.[78] The theological problems of the Old Testament canon therefore are closely related to the redactional processes through which the Pentateuch has passed.

At all periods of its growth the Pentateuch presents us with problems which are essentially those which come under the scrutiny of redaction criticism. The J author himself, precisely because he collected and used older traditions which once possessed a local or tribal setting, acted as a redactor and interpreter of these traditions. This leads us to a concern with examining how J's adoption and use of this material affected its meaning. We may also reflect that at an early period in the growth of the Pentateuch the J and E narratives were combined together. While the fact of this redaction at the hands of a writer or school whom we can label R^JE has been posited by almost all critics, his purpose and contribution have not always been adequately considered. That his

[78] This point has been heavily stressed by J. A. Sanders, *Torah and Canon*, Philadelphia, 1973.

intention was simply to preserve what might otherwise be lost is an inadequate assessment of such a literary proceeding. E. Zenger has made the justifiable criticism that critics have too often concluded that they have found separate documentary sources when what they have in reality been faced with is the work of a redactor, or even of a series of redactors.[79] It is not surprising therefore to find in several recent studies, including that by E. Zenger himself on the Sinai tradition, that the work of more than one such redactor is regarded as evident. The result is that less of the Pentateuch is accounted for by an ascription to the accepted J, E, D, and P source documents than has been the case in the past.[80] This does not mean a return to the obsolete 'fragment hypothesis' of H. Hupfeld, but is the result of a growing awareness of the various levels of interpretation which lie locked within the Pentateuch and of the ways in which redactors as well as authors have contributed to these. In view of the studies by which traditio-historical criticism has demonstrated that each of the major sources represents a collection and re-presentation of earlier material, the dividing line between an 'author' and a 'redactor' becomes an increasingly difficult one to draw with any precision.

In this area it is noteworthy that uncertainties have multiplied, and the difficulties in asserting the precise dates, or in some cases even the precise sequence, of the processes of redaction have become strongly evident. In consequence marked disagreements have appeared which are more easily noted than resolved. Whereas earlier literary critics have reckoned with an extensive Deuteronomistic redaction of the combined JE source, such a view has become subject to criticism in the light of M. Noth's researches. His claim that the original law book of Deuteronomy was incorporated into the Deuteronomistic History and only came to be joined on to the combined JEP narrative of Genesis to Numbers at a comparatively late stage makes the question of such a Deuteronomistic revision appear problematical.[81] Although

---

[79] E. Zenger, *Die Sinaitheophanie*, p. 47.

[80] Cf. the ascriptions by Zenger in his synopsis of Exod. 19–34, op. cit., pp. 164–205.

[81] Noth, *ÜGS*, p. 13, 'In the books of Genesis–Numbers any trace of a "Deuteronomic redaction" is lacking, such as is generally recognized ... There are individual passages at which the text has been expanded in the Deuteronomic style.'

he still reckons with some measure of Deuteronomistic supplementation in Genesis to Numbers, this does not amount to a full scale redaction. On this point S. Mowinckel is also in substantial agreement with Noth.[82] The problem raised here concerning the presence of Deuteronomistic material in these books has been taken up by C. H. W. Brekelmans in an essay[83] in which he notes the Deuteron-omistic character of passages which many critics have assigned to such a redactor, but argues that they are in fact pre-Deuteronomic in their origin, and belong to the layer of E material which otherwise shows a number of affinities with Deuteronomic ideas.

In marked contrast with such an attempt to minimize the amount of material in the Tetrateuch assigned to a Deuter-onomistic redactor we find a scholar such as W. Fuss greatly magnifying it and reckoning in Exod. 3–17 with a complex interweaving of JE and Deuteronomistic material.[84] More plausibly, and in closer agreement with Noth, Zenger has pleaded for a recognition of the work of two Deuteronomistic redactional stages in the growth of the narrative of the Sinai theophany.[85] The detailed arguments call for a very critical scrutiny, and there is no doubt need for closer definition of what features of an editor's work entitle him to be regarded as Deuteronomic or as Deuteronomistic. Nevertheless it is significant that, in contrast to Noth's caution regarding a Deuteronomistic redaction of JE, other scholars have shown a willingness to ascribe more material to the work of such redactors, so that the need to define more exactly the stages of the growth of the Pentateuch has emerged with it.[86] No

[82] S. Mowinckel, *Erwägungen zur Pentateuchquellenfrage*, p. 47.

[83] C. H. W. Brekelmans. 'Die sogenannten deuteronomistischen Elemente in Genesis bis Numeri. Ein Beitrag zur Vorgeschichte des Deuteronomiums', *Volume du Congrès. Genève, 1965*, SVT xv, 1966, pp. 90–6.

[84] W. Fuss, *Die deuteronomistische Pentateuchredaktion in Ex. 3–17* BZAW cxxvi, Berlin–New York, 1972.

[85] Zenger, op. cit., pp. 164 f.

[86] Noth, *Pentateuchal Traditions*, p. 250, 'The question still remains as to whether the combination of the sources—even though the purpose of this was simply to augment the tradition-material through addition—actually did not give rise to something new, which transcended the individual sources and their particular content and put them in a peculiar light, beyond the conscious intentions of the redactors.'

longer can it be readily assumed that the Decalogue of Exod. 20:2–17 and the Book of the Covenant of Exod. 20:22–23:19 were included in E, or that H was incorporated by P into his narrative. Other possibilities in the formation of the Pentateuch must be reckoned with, and more importance must be attached to understanding the way in which the over-all unity came into being. It has often been remarked that the redactors who gave the Pentateuch its present form contributed as significantly to its creation as the authors of the various source documents which literary analysis has rediscovered. Each author or redactor introduced his own layer of meaning and interpretation. Nevertheless, so far as illuminating the role of the redactors is concerned, it has proved much more difficult in practice to show the nature and scope of their work, than it has been to show what the authors of the individual source documents were seeking to achieve.

BIBLIOGRAPHY

BENTZEN, A. *Introduction to the Old Testament*, 2nd edn., Copenhagen, 1952.

BEYERLIN, W. *Origins and History of the Oldest Sinaitic Traditions*, Oxford, 1965, ETr by S. Rudman of *Herkunft und Geschichte der ältesten Sinaitraditionen*, Tübingen, 1961.

BREKELMANS, C. H. W. 'Het "historische Credo" van Israel', *Tijdschrift voor Theologie* iii (1963), 1–10.

—— 'Die sogenannten deuteronomistischen Elemente in Genesis bis Numeri. Ein Beitrag zur Vorgeschichte des Deuteronomiums", *Volume du Congrès. Genève, 1965*, SVT xv, 1966, pp. 90–6.

CAZELLES, H. 'Positions actuelles dans l'exégèse du Pentateuque', *Ephemerides Theologicae Lovanienses* xliv. 1 (1968), 55–78.

—— 'Pentateuque', *SDB* vii, Paris, 1964, cols. 687–858.

CHILDS, B. S. *Exodus. A Commentary*, London, 1974.

COATS, G. W. *Rebellion in the Wilderness. The Murmuring Motif in the Wilderness Traditions of the Old Testament*, New York, Nashville, 1968.

EISSFELDT, O. *The Old Testament. An Introduction*, Oxford, 1965, ETr by P. R. Ackroyd of *Einleitung in das Alte Testament*, 3rd edn., Tubingen, 1964.

—— *Die Komposition der Sinai-Erzählung Ex. 19–34*, Sitzungsberichte der Sächsischen Akademie der Wissenschaften zu Leipzig. Philologisch-historische Klasse 113, 1, Berlin, 1966. Abbrev. in *KS* iv, Tübingen, 1968, pp. 231–7.

—— 'Erwägungen zur Pentateuchquellenfrage', *KS* iv, 259–63.

—— 'Deuteronomium und Hexateuch', *KS* iv 238–58.

ELLIS, P. F. *The Yahwist; the Bible's First Theologian*, London, 1969.

ENGNELL, I. *Gamla Testamentet. En traditionshistorisk inledning* i, Stockholm, 1945.

—— 'Pentateuch', *Critical Essays on the Old Testament*, ETr and ed. by J. T. Willis, London, 1970, pp. 50–67.

FOHRER, G. *Introduction to the Old Testament*, London, 1970, ETr by D. Green of E. Sellin–G. Fohrer, *Einleitung in das Alte Testament*, Heidelberg, 1965.

—— *Überlieferung und Geschichte des Exodus*, BZAW xci, Berlin, 1964.

FUSS, W. *Die deuteronomistische Pentateuchredaktion in Ex. 3–17*, BZAW cxxvi, Berlin–New York, 1972.

GESE, H. 'Bemerkungen zur Sinaitradition', *ZAW* lxxix (1967), 137–54 = *Vom Sinai zum Zion, Alttestamentliche Beiträge zur biblischen Theologie*, BEvTh lxiv (1974), 31–48.

HEMPEL, J. 'Priesterkodex', Pauly-Wissowa *Realencyclopädie der klassischen Altentumswissenschaft*, xxii 2, Stuttgart, 1954, cols. 1943–67.

KAISER, O. *Einleitung in das Alte Testament*, Gütersloh, 1969, ETr by J. Sturdy, *Introduction to the Old Testament*, Oxford, 1975.

KAPELRUD, A. S. 'The Date of the Priestly Code', *ASTI* iii, 1964, pp. 58–64.

LOERSCH, S. *Das Deuteronomium und seine Deutungen*, Stuttgarter bibelstudien xxii, Stuttgart, 1967.

LOHFINK, N. 'Zum kleinen geschichtlichen Credo, Dtn. 26, 5–9', *Theologie und Philosophie* xlvi (1971), 19–39.

McEVENUE, S. E. *The Narrative Style of the Priestly Writer*, AB l, 1971.

MOWINCKEL, S. *Erwägungen zur Pentateuchquellenfrage*, Oslo, 1964.

—— *Tetrateuch–Pentateuch–Hexateuch. Die Berichte über die Landnahme in den drei altisraelitischen Geschichtswerken*, BZAW xc, 1964.

NICHOLSON, E. W. *Exodus and Sinai in History and Tradition*, Oxford, 1973.

NOTH, M. *A History of Pentateuchal Traditions*, Englewood Cliffs, 1972, ETr by B. W. Anderson of *Überlieferungsgeschichte des Pentateuch*, Stuttgart, 1948.

—— *ÜGS*, Halle, 1943, reprinted Tübingen, 1957.

PLÖGER, O. 'Pentateuch', *RGG* v, cols. 211–17.

VON RAD, G. 'The Form-Critical Problem of the Hexateuch', *The Problem of the Hexateuch and Other Essays*, Edinburgh–London, 1965, pp. 1–78, ETr by E. W. T. Dicken of *Das formgeschichtliche Problem des Hexateuch*, BWANT iv. 26, 1938.

ROST, L. 'Zum geschichtlichen Ort der Pentateuchquellen', *Das kleine Credo und andere studien zum Alten Testament*, Heidelberg, 1965, pp. 1–10.

—— 'Das kleine geschichtliche Credo', ibid., pp. 11–25.

SANDERS, J. A. *Torah and Canon*, Philadelphia, 1973.

VINK, J. G. 'The Date and Origin of the Priestly Code in the Old Testament', *OTS* xv (1969), 1–144.

VRIEZEN, TH. C. 'The Credo in the Old Testament', *Studies in the Psalms* (Die Ou Testamentiese Werkgemeenschap in Suid Afrika), ed. A. H. van Zyl, Potchefstroom, 1963, pp. 5–17.

WALKENHORST, K. H. *Der Sinai im liturgischen Verständnis der Deuteronomistischen und Priesterlichen Tradition,* BBB xxxiii, 1969.

WEISER, A. *Introduction to the Old Testament,* London, 1961, ETr by D. M. Barton of *Einleitung in das Alte Testament,* 4th edn., Göttingen, 1957.

WOLFF, H. W. 'Zur Thematik der elohistischen Fragmente im Pentateuch', *GSAT,* 2nd edn., Munich, 1973, pp. 402–17.

—— 'Das Kerygma des Jahwisten', ibid., pp. 345–73.

V

OLD TESTAMENT HISTORIOGRAPHY

J. R. PORTER

BEFORE attempting an evaluation of some modern critical approaches to the main historiographical works of the Old Testament, something must briefly be said about the significance of history and history-writing among the Israelites, a topic which has provoked a lively debate in recent years. This question has two aspects. On the one hand, there is the hermeneutical problem, which focuses on the concept of revelation and how far it is true to claim 'that Biblical theology is *the confessional recital of the redemptive acts of God* in a particular history, because history is the chief medium of revelation'.[1] Since this primarily concerns Old Testament theology it will not be further considered here, although to some degree it overlaps with the second aspect of the question.[2]

For, on the other hand, it has generally been claimed that, in the context of the ancient Near Eastern world, Israel had a unique concept of history and that Hebrew historical

---

[1] G. Ernest Wright, *God who Acts. Biblical Theology as Recital,* SBT viii, London, 1952, p.13.

[2] For some recent discussions of history as a hermeneutical question with particular reference to the Old Testament, cf. G. von Rad, 'Typologische Auslegung des Alten Testaments', *EvTh* xii (1952), 6 ff., ETr in C. Westermann (ed.), *Essays on Old Testament Interpretation,* London, 1963, pp. 1 ff.; Eric Voegelin, *Order and History*: i, *Israel and Revelation,* Louisiana and Oxford, 1956; C. A. Simpson, 'Old Testament Historiography and Revelation', *HibJ* lvi (1957/8), 319 ff.; 'An Inquiry into the Biblical Theology of History', *JTS* N.S. xii (1961), 1 ff.; Brevard S. Childs, *Memory and Tradition in Israel,* SBT xxxvii, London, 1962, pp. 81 ff.; R. Rendtorff, 'Geschichte und Wort im Alten Testament', *EvTh* xxii (1962), 626 ff.; F. Mildenberger, *Gottes Tat im Wort,* Gütersloh, 1964; J. Barr, *Old and New in Interpretation. A Study of the Two Testaments,* London, 1966, pp. 65 ff.; G. E. Wright, 'Reflections concerning Old Testament Theology', *Studia Biblica et Semitica Prof. Dr. Th. C Vriezen dedicata,* 1966, pp. 376 ff.; *The Old Testament and Theology,* 1969, pp. 39ff.; Georg Fohrer, *Theologische Grundstrukturen des Alten Testaments,* 1972, pp. 42 ff.; F. Hesse, 'Bewährt sich eine "Theologie der Heilstatsachen" am Alten Testament?', *ZAW* lxxxi (1969), 1–18.

literature is without any genuine parallel, at least before the emergence of Greek historiography.[3] Indeed, Mowinckel considers it 'a well known fact' that historiography, in the proper sense of the term, developed only in Israel among the peoples of the ancient Near East[4] and it has been denied that the Mesopotamian view of the universe could have any place for history as a concept.[5] That world-view was fundamentally static, based on the experience of the divine in nature, rather than in events, while, in a polytheistic religion, the intervention of the gods in human affairs could not be conceived in the consistent and purposive manner that was possible for Hebrew monotheism.[6] As a result, Mesopotamian civilization had only a cyclic conception of history,[7] in contrast to the Israelite idea of history as the working out of a divine plan, leading to an ultimate goal.[8] These generally held views have recently been strongly contested in an important book by Bertil Albrektson.[9] He concludes that the Old Testament idea of historical events as divine revelation is not distinctive but forms part of the common theology of the ancient Near East: he recognizes, however, that the Hebrews produced historiography on a level unknown in their environment, although he is unable to explain precisely why this should be so.[10]

Albrektson's work has not been without its critics, largely on the grounds that he has been too selective in his treatment of the Old Testament evidence.[11] It seems likely that the truth in this matter lies between the two extremes and that a

[3] For a short statement of this position, cf. J. A. Montgomery, *The Books of Kings*, ICC, 1951, pp. 24–30.

[4] Cf. S. Mowinckel, 'Israelite Historiography', *ASTI*, ii (1963), 4–26; the statement quoted occurs on p. 8.

[5] Cf. W. G. Lambert, 'Destiny and Divine Intervention', *OTS* xvii (1972), 70, 72.

[6] Cf. E. A. Speiser, 'The Biblical Idea of History in its Common Near Eastern Setting', *IEJ* vii (1957), 203. The same point is made by Lambert, op. cit. 65.

[7] Cf. E. A. Speiser, 'Ancient Mesopotamia', in R. C. Dentan (ed.), *The Idea of History in the Ancient Near East*, New Haven and London, 1955, pp. 55 f.; A. K. Grayson and W. S. Lambert, 'Akkadian Prophecies', *JCS* xviii (1964), 10.

[8] Cf. M. Burrows, 'Ancient Israel', in Dentan (ed.), op. cit., p. 127; S. Mowinckel, *He That Cometh*, Oxford, 1956, p. 151.

[9] Cf. Bertil Albrektson, *History and the Gods. An Essay on the Idea of Historical Events as Divine Manifestations in the Ancient Near East and in Israel*, Lund, 1967.

[10] Op. cit., p. 114.

[11] Cf. e.g. the important review of Albrektson's book by W. G. Lambert, *Or* xxxix (1970), 170–7.

great deal depends on the way in which the question is approached. It is at least debatable how far it is possible to reconstruct anything like a common theology of the ancient Near East which would have a great deal of meaning[12] and we have to recognize that there are similarities and differences, not simply between Israel and the rest of the ancient world, but also between the various religions and cultures of that world, not least in their appreciation and creation of history.[13] Similarly, there are dangers in a simple comparison of the comparatively clear and coherent picture of Israelite religion and its development which the Old Testament presents with the much more limited and disparate evidence available for the other religions of the ancient Near East.[14] These, and related, considerations make it very difficult to assess how far an apparently identical concept has in fact the same significance and importance in the religion of Israel as it has in a different religious structure.

On the other hand, Israel formed part of the ancient Near Eastern world and it seems clear that many of the elements which help to make up the viewpoint and structure of Israelite historiography find their parallels in the surrounding civiliz-ations, suggesting that Israel was heir to already established ideas of history and practices of history-writing. In the first place, this would seem to be the case with respect to concepts of motivation and purpose to explain the actual development of events.[15] From a very early period in the ancient Near

[12] Recent discussion here has centred largely on the problem of 'patternism', but the issue is wider than that. Cf. H. Frankfort, *The Problem of Similarity in Ancient Near Eastern Religions*, Oxford, 1951; S. H. Hooke, 'Myth and Ritual: Past and Present', in S. H. Hooke (ed.), *Myth, Ritual, and Kingship*, Oxford, 1958, pp. 1 ff.; I. Engnell, 'Methodological Aspects of Old Testament Study', SVT vii (1960), 17 ff.

[13] e.g. it is widely recognized that something akin to Hebrew historical composition can be found among the literature of the Hittite empire, cf. M. Noth, 'Geschichts-schreibung. I. Im AT', *RGG* ii, 1958, col. 1499, whereas it has been claimed that the ancient Egyptians did not develop a philosophy of history, cf. L. Bull, 'Ancient Egypt', Dentan (ed.), op. cit., pp. 32 f., although this is probably too extreme a view, cf. G. Goossens, 'La philosophie de l'histoire dans l'Ancien Orient', in. J. Coppens, A. Descamps, É. Massaux (eds.), *Sacra Pagina* i (1959), 244 ff., especially 247 f.

[14] For the problems involved in a systematic presentation of Mesopotamian religion, cf. A. L. Oppenheim, *Ancient Mesopotamia*, Chicago, 1964, pp. 172 ff. Similar difficulties arise in the case of other ancient Near Eastern religions.

[15] Cf. in particular the important article by H. Gese, 'Geschichtliches Denken im Alten Orient und im Alten Testament', *ZThK* lv (1958), 137 ff., ETr, 'The Idea of History in the Ancient Near East and the Old Testament', *JTC* i (1965), 49 ff.

East, we find the ability to systematize and interpret history from a particular viewpoint, to see it as leading up to the present and to discern a development in it. In however rudimentary a manner, this is the case even with the well-known Sumerian King List which is written from the standpoint that the country had always had only one centre of kingship and which, at least in its standard form, is conscious of a marked change in the historical process between the ante- and post-diluvian eras: before the Flood, the transfer of kingship was not the result of defeat in battle and the kings reigned for extremely long periods, which did not happen after it.[16] Again from a very early period, we find an awareness of what Gese has called 'the connection between act and consequence',[17] expressed particularly in the view that national disaster is the result of the ruler's transgression of divine law which causes the god directly to punish the community.[18] Here attention may be called to the position of the king, whose wrongdoing brings disaster to his country, and to the fact that that wrongdoing, in a number of instances, consisted of offences against the cult of the central temple in Babylon, behind which would seem to lie the Mesopotamian view that the temple was the embodiment of a covenant between the god and king and people,[19] a relationship which would be broken if the temple was abused in any way. However, such offences were not confined to the cultic sphere[20] and they could be committed, with the same

[16] Thus the Sumerian King List is much closer in character to the Pentateuch than Lambert supposes, *OTS* xvii (1972), 71.

[17] Cf. H. Gese, *Lehre und Wirklichkeit in der alten Weisheit*, Tübingen, 1958, pp. 42 ff., 65 ff., although his attempt to pinpoint the emergence of this idea in the ancient Near East is questionable.

[18] For examples, we may cite the Sumerian 'Curse on Agade', cf. S. N. Kramer, *History Begins at Sumer*, Indian Hills, 1956, pp. 305 ff., and A. Falkenstein, 'Fluch über Akkade', *ZA* lvii (1965), 43 ff.; the so-called Weidner Chronicle, cf. E. A. Speiser, 'Ancient Mesopotamia', in Dentan (ed.), op. cit., pp. 59 f.; the 'Sargon Chronicle', cf. *ANET*, 2nd edn., 1955, pp. 266 f. For a Hittite example, cf. the Plague Prayers of Mursilis II, discussed with reference to an Old Testament parallel by A. Malamat, 'Doctrines of Causality in Hittite and Biblical Historiography: a Parallel', *VT* v (1955), 1 ff.

[19] Cf. E. A. Speiser, op. cit., p. 47.

[20] They could involve the breaking of an oath or of a treaty, or such things as slander and false accusation.

consequences, by the whole people as well as simply by the king.[21] We find, too, the idea of deities who stand in a special relationship to a people, a city, or individuals, and who are conceived of as taking purposive action on their behalf, as in the choice and guidance of a king or the defeat of enemies. In this connection, we may note the interweaving of myth and legend[22] with more strictly historical material, as in the Sumerian King List, and the concept of development or transition from one to the other, as in the *enūma eliš*, features which can be seen in Genesis[23] but also, if to a lesser degree, in later Israelite historical writings.[24] Also, in some ancient Near Eastern texts, there are attempts to schematize the past as a pattern of alternating periods of good and ill fortune: another attempt to explain historical events is that they are determined by divine prophecies which in due course are fulfilled.[25] Significant, too, is the emergence of history-writing

---

[21] Cf. the crime attributed to the inhabitants of Babylon in one of Esarhaddon's inscriptions, published by R. Borger, *Die Inschriften Asarhaddons Königs von Assyrien*, Graz, 1956, p. 13.

[22] The definitions of various literary types which modern Introductions to the Old Testament, as, for example, those of Eissfeldt or Fohrer, attempt to draw, are of doubtful value. It is no doubt possible to distinguish such types on grounds of *form*— e.g. genealogies, annals—but it is much more difficult to do so on grounds of *content*— i.e. to distinguish between myth, saga, and various kinds of legend, etc. These terms are not really applicable to the ancient Near East, not least because the languages have no corresponding expressions for them, and, in this context create more problems than they solve—note, for example, the continuing debate as to the exact nature of the Ugaritic texts. Indeed, they can only be used on the basis of very limited definitions, as in O. Eissfeldt's statement, 'if a narrative is concerned with the world of the gods, or if gods are to a considerable extent involved in it, we may speak of a myth', *The Old Testament. An Introduction*, ETr, 1965, p. 33, which is a very inadequate description of myth. It is only fair to add, however, that Eissfeldt himself is aware of the difficulty of applying this and similar terms to the Old Testament.

[23] Cf. G. Widengren, 'Myth and History in Israelite-Jewish Thought' in S. Diamond (ed.), *Culture in History. Essays in Honor of Paul Radin*, New York, 1960, pp. 484 f.

[24] Thus there are pronounced mythical and legendary elements in Joshua and Judges and even in 1 & 2 Samuel: they are much less prominent in the Books of Kings.

[25] Cf. e.g. the text on p. 70 in J. B. Pritchard (ed.), *The Ancient Near East. Supplementary Texts and Pictures Relating to the Old Testament*, Princeton, 1969. This is a narrative, contained in a letter, of how Sennacherib received a divine promise that he would conquer several countries. The writer notes that he in fact conquered Egypt and goes on to state that Sennacherib's grandson will complete the promised victories.

suaded by this kind of argumentation.

employed for didactic purposes, for instruction and edification, as in the so-called *narū* literature.[26]

All these ancient Near Eastern ideas, interpretations, and
understandings of history clearly find their parallels as
elements in the conceptual world of Old Testament historiography. In the second place, and similarly, it is equally clear
that the formal literary types in which the nations of the
ancient world expressed their interest in, and concern for, the
past are also to be found as a major part of the material from
which the Old Testament history-writings were constructed.
As examples may be mentioned royal annals, accounts of the
building and adornment of temples,[27] the synchronistic
chronicle form,[28] accounts of dreams and visions,[29] genealogical lists,[30] lists of officials, legends of former heroes, poems
recounting events in the past, letters, biographical texts, the
Novelle type of literature,[31] even the autobiographical form
characteristic of royal inscriptions,[32] and many others.

However, it is perhaps just when we consider the character
of these ancient Near Eastern materials and the use made of
similar types in the Old Testament, that we may find a clue
to the distinctive character of Hebrew historiography, and
this along two lines. In the first place, in the cultures
surrounding Israel, these literary forms are found almost
entirely as separate units. In this sense it would be true to say
that they are the raw materials of history, rather than history
proper, although many of them are genuine historiography,

[26] Cf. H. Gese, *ZThK* lv (1958), 137, *JTC* i (1965), 58; H. W F. Saggs, *The Greatness that was Babylon*, London, 1962, pp. 427 ff.

[27] Cf. A. S. Kapelrud, 'Temple Building, a Task for Gods and Kings', *Or* xxxii (1963), 56 ff.

[28] Cf. A. Jepsen, *Die Quellen des Königbuches*, Halle, 1953, pp. 30 ff.

[29] Cf. E. L. Ehrlich, *Der Traum im Alten Testament*, BZAW lxxiii, 1953; *Les Songes et leur interpretation*, Sources Orientales, ii, 1959, especially pp. 81 ff., 99 ff.

[30] Cf. L. Bull, 'Ancient Egypt', in Dentan (ed.), op. cit., pp. 9 ff.

[31] Cf. S. Herrmann, 'Die Königsnovelle in Ägypten und in Israel. Ein Beitrag zur Gattungsgeschichte in den Geschichtsbüchern des Alten Testaments', *WZ* iii (1953), 51 ff.

[32] It is commonly stated that such royal autobiographical reports are entirely lacking in the Old Testament, cf. O. Eissfeldt, op. cit., p. 51. Nevertheless such passages as the 'last words of David', 2 Sam. 23:1–7; 2 Sam. 7:18 ff.; 1 Kgs. 3:6 ff.; 1 Kgs. 5:2 ff. may at least betray the influence of this kind of material. We may note too how a number of psalms are in fact made into royal autobiographies by the addition of historical introductions and also 2 Sam. 23, cf. F. F. Bruce, 'The Earliest Old Testament Interpretation', *OTS*, xvii (1972), 44 ff.

in so far as they present interpretations and understanding of history and an awareness of direction within it. By contrast, in the Old Testament, all these elements, as far as the Pentateuch and the Former Prophets are concerned, are embedded in a chronologically added narrative. It is this that provides their setting, it is only in this framework that they have eventually been preserved, and it is the narrative which is intended to determine their significance. Nowhere else in the ancient Near East is there to be found anything strictly comparable to this collecting and arranging of traditions and documents as successive elements in larger corpora and, ultimately, into a single corpus. A second consideration may throw some light on the possible reasons for this difference. What is really lacking in the history-writing of the ancient Near East, in marked contrast to the Old Testament, is the presence of authentic narrative, reflecting the customs, relationships, and, particularly, the speech of real life and what may be called ordinary people. As Eissfeldt has perceptively stated, 'the really characteristic sagas for Israel are those of the tribe and people.'[33] In Mesopotamia, different peoples at different times were assimilated and submerged their identity in one dominant and long-established culture, that of Sumer and Akkad,[34] and a somewhat similar situation prevailed in Egypt. By contrast, 'Israel' was constituted by the gradual union, over a long period of time, of different groups, each of whom had its own history and its own traditions which it brought with it. There was always a consciousness of successive stages of development in the growth of 'Israel' and so too the common Israelite tradition first came into being by preserving and incorporating the ancient traditions of the different groups into a unified literary whole, as the nation had itself become such a whole. These factors determined the character and the development of Old Testament historiography, the actual history of the emergence of 'Israel' rather than a unique understanding of history on the part of the Hebrew people.[35]

[33] Op. cit., p. 40.

[34] Cf. H. Gese, *ZThK* lv (1958), 128–9, 140–1, *JTC* i (1965), 50–1, 61.

[35] In this connection, it is worth calling attention to the fact that, in many respects, the Israelite tradition of historiography is closer to that of the pre-Islamic Arabs than

THE DEUTERONOMIC HISTORICAL WORK

The main impetus for the concern of much recent Old Testament scholarship with the so-called Deuteronomic history book has been provided by Martin Noth in his *Überlieferungsgeschichtliche Studien I*, first published in 1943, with its suggestive sub-title 'die sammelnden und bearbeitenden Geschichtswerke im Alten Testament'.[36] Leaving aside the question of Noth's traditio-historical approach to the Old Testament material,[37] discussion of his views has perhaps centred mainly on two of his particular contentions. First, there is his claim that the Deuteronomic history is 'a single work written by a Judean historian who may conveniently be called the Deuteronomist',[38] active in Judah some time after 561 B.C. Secondly, Noth holds that Josh.–2 Kgs. forms an independent work, with the book of Deuteronomy added to it as a kind of paradigmatic prologue, originally quite distinct from the complex Genesis–Numbers, and that there is no trace of the compositional activity of the Pentateuchal, or rather Tetrateuchal, sources in what is to be seen as the original Deuteronomic history.[39] A consideration of these two positions may form a convenient starting-point for the present examination.

---

it is to that of the ancient Near East and, again, it may be suspected that this is because of the generally similar social structure and historical development of these two peoples, as compared with Egypt or Mesopotamia. Thus we find that the pre-Islamic literary deposit consists very largely of narratives about the past of various tribes and that a connected history of the Arabs had come into existence precisely to provide a common national tradition for originally independent groups. For a preliminary discussion of the question, cf. J. R. Porter, 'Pre-Islamic Arabic Historical Tradition and the Early Historical Narratives of the Old Testament', *JBL* lxxxvii (1968), 17–26.

[36] Cf. also, M. Noth, 'Zur deuteronomistischen Geschichtsauffassung', *Proc. XXII Congress of Orientalists, Istanbul, 1951*, ii (1957), 558 f. The application of Noth's theories to the actual texts of the Old Testament are to be seen in his commmentaries, *Das Buch Josua*, HAT, 2nd edn., Tübingen, 1953, and his unfinished *Könige*, BKAT, Neukirchen-Vluyn, 1968.

[37] Cf. for this, B. W. Anderson's introduction to his translation of Noth's *Überlieferungsgeschichte des Pentateuch, A History of Pentateuchal Traditions*, Englewood Cliffs, 1972, pp. i–xii.

[38] W. F. Albright, *Prolegomenon* to C. F. Burney, *Judges and Kings*, New York, 1970, p. 1.

[39] Cf. also I. Engnell, *Gamla Testamentet* i, Stockholm, 1945; 'Moseböckerna', *SBU*, 2nd edn., ii, Stockholm, 1963, col. 161, ETr, *Critical Essays on the Old Testament*, London, 1970, pp. 61 ff.

Noth was led to his conclusion that this history work was the composition of a single individual because he saw it as expressing 'une thèse historique et théologique bien précise'[40] to interpret the catastrophe which the writer himself had experienced,[41] and thus it is those scholars who point most strongly to a clearly defined outlook and purpose in the Deuteronomic history who have been most sympathetic to Noth's postulate of one particular author.[42] It is important to realize, however, that for Noth the individuality of the author's understanding of events lies in its unrelieved pessimism: the fall of Jerusalem was the ultimate catastrophe, the final and irreversible divine answer to Israel's repeated apostasy, and no hope for the future was conceivable.[43] There has been much discussion as to whether in fact such is the outlook of the Deuteronomist. E. Janssen has called attention to the element of instruction and edification, which is so strongly marked in the Deuteronomic work and which would lose its point if those addressed had no real possibility of heeding it in the future.[44] Von Rad rejects Noth's wholly negative view of 2 Kgs. 25:27–30, seeing in these verses at least the possibility that Yahweh can take up again the promise of the Nathan prophecy[45] and he claims that the real theme of the Deuteronomic work is a messianic one,[46] a view further developed by Carlson.[47] Von Rad also notes the significance of the term šûḇ in certain key passages of the Deuteronomic history and concludes that what the Deuteronomist hoped for, as a response to the disaster of 587 B.C., was a return to Yahweh, with all the possibilities for a restoration

[40] G. Minette de Tillesse, 'Sections "tu" et sections "vous" dans le Deutéronome' *VT* xii (1962), 31.

[41] *ÜGS*, p. 110.

[42] Cf. e.g. P. R. Ackroyd, *Exile and Restoration*, London, 1968, pp. 62–83, especially pp. 63 f.

[43] Cf. M. Noth, op. cit., pp. 108 f.

[44] Cf. E. Janssen, *Juda in der Exilszeit*, FRLANT, N.F., li (1956), 65 n. 2.

[45] Cf. G. von Rad, *Theologie des Alten Testaments*, i, 2nd edn., Munich, 1958, 341, ETr, *Old Testament Theology*, i (Edinburgh, 1962), 343. Cf. Janssen, op. cit., p. 76; A. van den Born, *Koningen uit de grondtekst vertaald en uitgelegd*, BOT, Roermond and Maaseik, 1958, pp. 12 ff.

[46] Op. cit., p. 342, ETr, p. 344. Cf. also K. Baltzer, 'Das Ende des Staates Juda und die Messias–Frage', R. Rendtorff and K. Koch (eds.), *Studien zur Theologie der alttestamentlichen Überlieferungen*, Neukirchen, 1961, pp. 33–43.

[47] Cf. R. A. Carlson, *David, the Chosen King*, Stockholm, 1964, pp. 30 ff., 263–7.

of the national life which that would entail:[48] H. W. Wolff developed this view,[49] although he does not think that the notice of the release of Jehoiachin contains any echo of the Nathan prophecy or, in contrast to Carlson, any hope of a renewed monarchy.[50]

These various criticisms tend to emphasize the fact that, even if we are to think of a single final author of the Deuteronomic work, he was yet one who represented a long and well-established theological tradition of homiletic teaching and interpretation, not least in respect of the nation's history.[51] We are then led on to ask whether the Deuteronomic history may not rather be a collective rather than an individual work, the product of the 'D-group', who gave it its final redaction during the exile. It is usual to dismiss the question of group or individual authorship as being of comparatively little importance, on the ground that, in either case, the work displays so striking 'a consistency of ideology and composition'[52] that it can be treated as a unity. But once we begin to think of a Deuteronomic circle or school, it is natural to speculate how in fact it operated, to wonder whether particular individuals or groups within it may not have been responsible for the editing of different sections within the Deuteronomic work and whether, in that case, they all had a virtually identical method of working and theological viewpoint. Clearly, it is reasonable to speak of books such as Leviticus and Numbers as works of the Priestly school, in contrast to works of the Deuteronomic school, but, equally clearly, they reveal the contributions of differing epochs, groups, and standpoints within a general over-all redactional outlook, nor have Leviticus and Numbers both been edited in exactly the

[48] Cf. von Rad, op. cit., p. 344, ETr, p. 346.

[49] Cf. H. W. Wolff, 'Das Kerygma des deuteronomistischen Geschichtswerks', *ZAW* lxxiii (1961), 315 ff., reprinted in his *GSAT*, Munich, 1964, pp. 315 ff. A somewhat similar view of the message of the Deuteronomic work is given by E. W. Nicholson, *Deuteronomy and Tradition*, Oxford, 1967, pp. 123 f. Cf. also P. Diepold, *Israels Land*, BWANT xcv, 1972.

[50] Op. cit., p. 174, *GSAT*, p. 311.

[51] Cf. H. W. Hertzberg, *Die Bücher Josua, Richter, Ruth*, ATD, Göttingen, 1953, pp. 8 f.; Ackroyd, op. cit., pp. 63 f.

[52] Carlson, op. cit., p. 30. Cf. also his comment, p. 30, n. 1, on the oscillation between individual and collective views of the composition of the Deuteronomic work in the writings of a number of scholars.

same way.[53] It is therefore possible to ask whether similar considerations do not apply to the postulate of a Deuteronomic school, especially if we think of its activity extending over a long period of time, for this is one of the strongest arguments in favour of the Deuteronomic history being a collective work.[54] Here various points are involved. One is the problem whether the book of Deuteronomy, at least in its original form, ever existed as a written document previous to the composition of the Deuteronomic history and so provided the impetus for the development of the Deuteronomic school in succeeding years. This problem is again bound up with the question whether Deuteronomy is to be identified with Josiah's law-book[55] or whether it is to be viewed as a post-exilic work, not really separable from the complex Joshua-2 Kings, as has been the general opinion of Scandinavian scholars since Pedersen. Again, in view of the emphasis on oral tradition and the traditio-historical approach in modern Old Testament study, it may be that we should distinguish between a Deuteronomic school which collected, preserved, and, in the course of transmission, inevitably shaped ancient traditions (in which case one could even think of a 'Deuteronomistic trend' originating very far back in Israel's history[56]) and a more narrowly defined 'D-group' which was responsible for the final, written redaction of the Deuteronomic history in the exilic age.[57] The debate would then be

---

[53] Cf. e.g. K. Elliger, *Leviticus*, ATD, Göttingen, 1966, pp. 9 ff. and the introduction to Noth's *Das vierte Buch Mose, Numeri*, ATD, Göttingen, 1966, ETr, *Numbers*, London, 1968. For an examination of the distinctive editorial processes of Numbers, cf. the unpublished Oxford dissertation of J. Sandys-Wunsch, 'The Purpose of the Book of Numbers in Relation to the Rest of the Pentateuch and Post-exilic Judaism', 1961.

[54] Cf. J. A. Soggin, *Josué*, Neuchâtel, 1970, p. 12, ETr, *Joshua*, London, 1972, p. 5. Cf. also A. Rofé, 'The Strata of the Law about the Centralization of Worship in Deuteronomy and the History of the Deuteronomic Movement', *Congress Volume, Uppsala 1971*, SVT xxii, 1972, pp. 221-6.

[55] For the most recent defence of this view, cf. Nicholson, op. cit., pp. 1-17, and, for a recent criticism, cf. N. Lohfink, 'Die Bundesurkunde des Königs Josias. Eine Frage an die Deuteronomiumsforschung', *Biblica* xliv (1963), 261-88, 461-98. Cf. also J. Lindblom, *Erwägungen zur Herkunft der Josianischen Tempelurkunde*, Lund, 1971.

[56] Cf. E. Nielsen, *Oral Tradition*, SBT xi, London, 1954, pp. 56 f.

[57] Carlson, op. cit., p. 29. This, of course, does not exclude the view that the period of Josiah gave a special impetus to the development of the Deuteronomic tradition school, as Carlson himself notes.

concerned with whether any of the previously existing sources, which, as all would agree, are used in the Deuteronomic history, had assumed the form of Deuteronomistically edited complexes, whether oral or written, before the final redaction and collection; and it can be claimed that evidence in support of this contention may be found in different theological outlooks and methods of composition in different sections of the work.

Thus, von Rad has claimed that the Deuteronomic editing of the book of Judges and of the book of Kings are so different from each other that they could not represent a single piece of work: he also calls attention to the absence of any Deuteronomic interpretation between 1 Sam. 12 and 1 Kgs. 3, with the implication that this section has received again a different kind of treatment within the Deuteronomic history.[58] Von Rad also believes that there is not only a chronological and literary distinction between Deuteronomy and the Deuteronomic history work (or, at least, between it and 1 and 2 Kings) but also a difference in viewpoint with regard to the monarchy and the use, in the latter, of specifically Jerusalemite traditions.[59] Again, it has often been suggested that there were two successive editions of the material now comprising the two books of Kings, one pre-exilic, the other post-exilic[60] and evidence has been adduced for such a double edition of the whole of the Deuteronomic history.[61] These and similar considerations have led some scholars to deny that there ever was a Deuteronomic work as a unified literary or theological entity. Thus Fohrer believes that we should think only of a series of books, each produced in a different way, so that, in Judges, an existing work has been subjected to thorough Deuteronomic editing, while, in the books of Kings, all the material was selected and arranged by the Deuteronomic author who at the same time composed the interpretative

[58] Cf. von Rad, op. cit., pp. 344 f., ETr, pp. 346 f.; cf. also p. 332, ETr, p. 334.

[59] Cf. von Rad, op. cit., p. 334, n. 5, ETr, p. 336, n. 5; pp. 336 ff., ETr, pp. 337 ff.

[60] Cf. e.g. J Gray, *I & II Kings*, 2nd edn., London, 1970, pp. 6–9.

[61] Cf. Eissfeldt, op. cit., p. 280; J Gray, *Joshua, Judges and Ruth*, NCB, London, 1967, pp. 7 f.; F. M. Cross, 'The Structure of the Deuteronomic History', *Perspectives in Jewish Learning* iii Chicago, 1968, 9–24; W. Dietrich, *Prophetie und Geschichte. Eine redaktionsgeschichtliche Untersuchung zum deuteronomistischen Geschichtswerk*, FRLANT cviii, 1972.

framework, and, in the books of Samuel, there is only very slight Deuteronomic influence.[62]

That there are divergent editorial and compositional procedures in different sections of the Deuteronomic history can hardly be denied and this may point to the activity of various groups within a general Deuteronomic school, but it does not necessarily imply that there is not an over-all conception and interpretation of the course of Israel's history, the idea of a law of retribution,[63] marking the entire work, although this may well not be as precise and pervasive as many critics have supposed. A crucial point here is the use of earlier sources in the Deuteronomic history work, about which something more must be said later. Following Noth,[64] the great majority of scholars have agreed that earlier material is largely reproduced faithfully in the form in which this was known to the Deuteronomists,[65] although they have selected and, on occasion, rearranged this material to make it exemplify the lesson they wished to convey and made that lesson explicit by means of occasional comments, extended homiletic passages, and summaries. In this connection, insufficient attention has usually been paid to the fact that the Deuteronomic history came into existence at a time when the whole foundation of Israelite society was gravely threatened, for in such periods there is a strong tendency to reassert and preserve in writing the ancient national traditions.[66] This would be especially imperative immediately after the Exile, when many documents must have been destroyed[67] and even the transmission of oral traditions would have been in danger of being broken in the prevailing disruption.[68] Once this

---

[62] Cf. G. Fohrer, *Introduction to the Old Testament*, ETr, 1968, pp. 194 f.

[63] Cf. B. Albrektson, op. cit., p. 82.

[64] Cf. Noth, op. cit., pp. 95 ff.

[65] Cf. A. Soggin, op. cit., pp. 12 f., ETr, pp. 5 f.

[66] Cf. E. Nielsen, op. cit., pp. 60 f.

[67] Cf. S. Mowinckel, *ASTI* ii (1963), 22 f.

[68] For example, the destruction of the Temple may have prompted the writing down of the homiletic historical retrospects which are so marked a feature of the Deuteronomic work and which may have had their origin as sermons in the cult. Cf. A. Weiser, *Einleitung in das Alte Testament*, 6th edn., Göttingen, 1966, p. 121, ETr, *Introduction to the Old Testament*, London, 1961, p. 130; *Die Psalmen*, ATD, Göttingen, 1950, pp. 22 ff., pp. 33 f., ETr, *The Psalms*, 1959, pp. 42 ff., pp. 59 f. Cf. also A. Lauha, *Die Geschichtsmotive in den alttestamentlichen Psalmen*, AASF B lvi. l, Helsinki, 1945.

character of the circle behind the Deuteronomic history as collectors is grasped, it can be postulated that much of the old material will have been reproduced simply for its own sake and that it cannot be expected to display a consistent outlook or one that always accords with the main outlook of the Deuteronomic redaction. In this case, we can give full weight both to the arguments in favour of a unified ideological outlook and to those mentioned above which appear to throw doubt on this, by realizing that the different types of material they had received compelled the Deuteronomic editors to treat it in different ways.[69] On the one hand, all the passages which have been brought forward to suggest a double Deuteronomic recension can plausibly be attributed to earlier sources and the Deuteronomic sections which appear to contradict them can be viewed as 'neutralizing'[70] expansions.[71] On the other hand, when von Rad asks why the same *Generationsschema* as is found in Judges is not used in Kings, since the editor of the latter had at his disposal copious material dealing with political successes and reverses, the answer may well be that the editorial process was in each case determined by the available material. In Judges, probably all that the editor had at his disposal was a number of unconnected sagas of the heroic and successful exploits of various Israelite leaders: he was thus free to construct a 'philosophy of history', exemplifying the law of retribution, by linking them together by his scheme of apostasy, oppression, repentance, deliverance. In the case of the period covered by Kings, however, he knew from his sources that divine judgement, in the shape of subjugation to foreign enemies, had only come upon Israel and Judah after several hundred years, and thus he had to present his theory of retribution in history in a quite different way. We do not necessarily require to postulate either different editors or

---

[69] Cf. J. R. Porter, 'Some Considerations on the Structure of the Book of Judges', *Proceedings of the Oxford Society of Historical Theology*, 1950–1, pp. 27 ff.

[70] The word is Eissfeldt's, cf. op. cit., pp. 222 f., 240, 255, 266.

[71] Thus e.g. 1 Kgs. 11:36 and 2 Kgs. 22:20 belong to sources used by the Deuteronomic writers, while passages which suggest the permanence of the house of David, such as 1 Kgs. 8:25 and 9:5 are quotations from the terms of the Davidic covenant and are immediately 'neutralized' by 1 Kgs, 8:31 ff. and 9:6 ff. On these two latter sections, cf. M. Noth, *Könige*, pp. 174, 195 f.

different ideological outlooks. Not dissimilar considerations apply to the comparative absence of specific Deuteronomic editing in at least large parts of the books of Samuel, and here various alternative explanations are possible. The Deuteronomic school may have taken over one or more already existing traditional complexes about David and incorporated them virtually without change at the appropriate point in its history. Carlson objects to this view, which he thinks does not allow for the Deuteronomists' principle of carefully selecting their material as seen elsewhere in their work, but, while it seems very likely that the Deuteronomic circle had a considerable amount of material to select from for their composition of 1 and 2 Kings,[72] we cannot know how much was available to them with regard to David and his reign. The Deuteronomic school may in any case have found in the already existing shape of the material sufficient exemplification of its theory of retribution in the story of Saul and the various episodes of the so-called 'Succession History'. Perhaps, however, we should think of the section 1 Sam. 13–2 Kgs. 3 as a Deuteronomic creation, but one produced not by rewriting or by the addition of editorial reflections, but by placing the old material in a new setting and giving it a new significance 'through compositional technique and association'.[73] It should be noted that such a view implies a different redactional procedure from what is found elsewhere in the Deuteronomic history and would therefore again suggest that the editing of the work was not uniform.

The problem of a possible difference in theological viewpoint between Deuteronomy itself and the Deuteronomic history is a rather more complicated one. Working with the same premises as von Rad, Nicholson has tried to show that the Jerusalemite traditions about the Davidic monarchy and the Temple which the Deuteronomic circle took over were radically modified by that circle under the influence of the

[72] But cf. the cautions of S. Mowinckel, op. cit., pp. 22 f.

[73] Carlson, op. cit., p. 22, cf. also pp. 24 f. and the working out of this view throughout the whole of Carlson's book. For a similar approach to the material concerning Saul in 1 Samuel, cf. the unpublished Exeter dissertation by H. S. Wentz, 'The Monarchy of Saul: Antecedents, "Deuteronomic" Interpretation, and Ideology', 1971. But cf. J. H. Grønbaek, *Die Geschichte vom Aufstieg Davids (1. Sam. 15–2. Sam. 5). Tradition und Komposition*, Copenhagen, 1971.

basic theological concepts presented in the book of Deuteronomy.[74] It is doubtful whether, even from his own
standpoint, he is entirely successful in overcoming the
difficulties raised by von Rad, for the Deuteronomic work
clearly reproduces the promises of the David covenant in 2
Sam. 7, which, as has been seen, plays a very important part
in determining the outlook of the Deuteronomic history,
while Nicholson takes too negative and polemical a view of
the so-called 'name theology', the purpose of which is certainly
to affirm a real presence of Yahweh in his Temple and which
is not a Deuteronomic creation but probably derives from
liturgical usage.[75] However, it may be queried how far the
supposition accepted by both von Rad and Nicholson, of a
clear distinction and tension between amphictyonic and
Mosaic traditions, represented in Deuteronomy, and Jerusalem and Davidic traditions, can really be sustained. The
theory that there ever was an organized Israelite amphictyony,
which alone could originate any supposed amphictyonic
traditions, has increasingly come under heavy critical fire,[76]
and, in any event, it is wrong to put too deep a gulf between
Israel's pre-monarchical and monarchical traditions, for the
Davidic monarchy was able to focus the former on itself
without apparent difficulty.[77] Given the fact that the setting
of Deuteronomy is the period before the introduction of the
monarchy, we should not expect to find a great deal about
kingship in it, but the 'law of king' in Deut. 17:14 f. does not
represent a polemic against the monarchy[78] and displays
exactly the same attitude of critical acceptance as is seen in

[74] Cf. Nicholson, op. cit., pp. 107–14. Cf. also N. Poulssen, *König und Tempel im
Glaubenszeugnis des Alten Testaments*, Stuttgart, 1967.

[75] Cf. R. de Vaux, '"Le lieu que Yahvé a choisi pour y établir son nom"', in F. Maas
(ed.), *Das ferne und nahe Wort*, BZAW cv, 1967, especially pp. 220, 225 ff.

[76] Cf. R. de Vaux, 'La Thèse de l'"Amphictyonie Israëlite"', *HTR* lxiv (1971), 415
ff., especially the literature cited p. 417, n. 10. Cf. also R. Smend, *Jahwekrieg und
Stämmebund*, FRLANT lxxxiv, 1963; A. D. H. Mayes, *Israel in the Period of the
Judges*, London, 1974.

[77] Cf. J. R. Porter, *Moses and Monarchy*, Oxford, 1963, especially pp. 26 ff.

[78] Cf. A. Caquot, 'Remarques sur la "loi royale" du Deutéronome', *Semitica* ix
(1959), 21–33; O. Bächli, *Israel und die Völker. Eine Studie zum Deuteronomium*,
ATANT xli, 1962, pp. 187 ff.; J. R. Porter, 'The Succession of Joshua', in J. I.
Durham and J. R. Porter (ed.), *Proclamation and Presence*, London, 1970, p. 112,
n. 31.

the Deuteronomic history's picture of the establishment of that institution.[79] Once again, whether we are to think of an already written corpus of laws, comprising the original form of Deuteronomy, which was taken over and expanded by the Deuteronomic circle in its historical work, or whether Deuteronomy was created by that circle, as part of the composition of that history, probably from material preserved by oral transmission, it seems justified to see an essential unity in the general ideological and theological position of the two complexes.

By way of summary of this discussion of the nature of the composition of the Deuteronomic work, it may perhaps be said that none of the various theories which have been surveyed need be regarded as mutually exclusive. Under the influence of Noth, the concern of the Deuteronomic school has probably been seen too exclusively as that of expounding a very precise understanding of the course of Israel's history, although this is indeed an essential element in its achievement; and this remains true even when the hortatory purpose of the Deuteronomic work, with its message for an Israel at a crisis of its existence, is equally strongly emphasized. Due weight must also be given to the Deuteronomists' aim of collecting and preserving the traditions and other material of which they were aware, and their essential faithfulness in reproducing and transmitting what they had received. This means both that the inculcation of a particular theological understanding of history or of a contemporary message need not always be at the forefront in every part of the Deuteronomic work and also that the way in which that understanding and message were conveyed was in many cases determined by the nature of the pre-existing material. In this way, we could hold that the Deuteronomic history always contained those not inconsiderable sections which Noth felt obliged to regard as later additions, because they did not fit in with what he considered to be the author's purpose and method. Even allowing for these factors, it would seem most likely that the differences in editorial procedure in various parts of the work

[79] Cf. H. J. Boecker, *Die Beurteilung der Anfänge der Königtums in den deuteronomistischen Abschnitten des 1 Samuelbuches. Ein Beitrag zum Problem des 'deuteronomistischen Geschichtswerks'*, WMANT xxxi, 1969.

are the result of the activity of different groups within a broader Deuteronomic circle which was active from the period of Josiah down at least to some time after 561 B.C., or, if Deuteronomy is to be included, well before Josiah. If the thesis of a first pre-exilic Deuteronomic recension of the history were to be accepted, then the Deuteronomic work would be basically pre-exilic, for it would have included the major part of the existing material, since the first edition, whether we date it shortly before 609 B.C.[80] or shortly before 597 B.C.,[81] would include the greater part of the Deuteronomic history, the second edition being a continuation and rounding off, with occasional additions, using the same editorial technique. However, as has been seen, the whole tenor of the Deuteronomic work, with respect both to its aspect as a collection and as preaching, seems better fitted to an exilic situation, and thus we may perhaps think of a specific 'D-group', or even individual author, responsible for the existing, final redaction of the Deuteronomic history during the exilic period, as the culmination of the long-established Deuteronomic school.

A further word should perhaps be added at this point about the *Sitz im Leben* of the people responsible for the Deuteronomic work. There has been a good deal of discussion as to whether the history was written down in Palestine or in Babylonia. Recently, most scholars have tended to adopt the former alternative but the arguments used to support this view are totally inconclusive,[82] if we bear in mind that the Deuteronomic history is the end-product of the lengthy activity of a Deuteronomic circle in Judah and that it reproduces a great deal of earlier material. The other alternative has never been without its advocates[83] and it has recently been persuasively defended by Soggin.[84] However,

---

[80] Cf. Eissfeldt, op. cit., p. 285; Fohrer, op. cit., p. 248.

[81] Cf. Gray, I & II Kings, p. 753.

[82] The arguments of Noth and Janssen are conveniently summarized by Ackroyd, op. cit., pp. 65 ff.

[83] Cf. e.g. E. Sellin and L. Rost, *Einleitung in das Alte Testament*, Heidelberg, 1950, pp. 93 f., 96 f.

[84] Cf. Soggin, 'Deuteronomistische Geschichtsauslegung während des babylonischen Exils', *Oikonomia. Festschrift O. Cullmann*, Hamburg, 1967, pp. 14 ff.; *Josué*, p. 162, ETr, p. 219. Cf. Nicholson, *Preaching to the Exiles*, Oxford, 1970.

his views really rest upon an attempt to identify the particular group to which the Deuteronomic hortatory passages are addressed and when we note that, precisely in these passages, 'all Israel' is in view, it may be wondered whether the Deuteronomists' horizon can be limited to either Palestine or Babylon. We must conclude that there is simply no evidence for deciding the issue. More important is the question of the kind of people who may be supposed to have constituted the Deuteronomic circle, and on this matter three broad views at present appear to hold the field. First, there is the claim that the marked homiletic style in the Deuteronomic work has its home in the cult and thus that the members of the Deuteronomic school formed part of the cultic personnel, whether they are to be identified with the country Levites[85] or were part of the Jerusalem priesthood.[86] But there are serious objections, among others, to thinking of such Levites as having access to the rich and varied material to be found in the Deuteronomic history[87] nor do the concerns of that history square very well with the concerns of the Jerusalem priesthood as these appear elsewhere in the Old Testament. Secondly, there is the long-held opinion that the Deuteronomic circle was essentially a prophetic group,[88] though this view must be carefully distinguished from the more cautious position which sees the Deuteronomists as influenced by, and the successors of, the eighth-century prophets, but not necessarily prophets themselves.[89] Unfortunately, there is little evidence of any direct influence on the Deuteronomic work of the actual oracles and messages of the great prophets, which we should surely expect to find were the connection so intimate. The only one of them mentioned at all in the Deuteronomic history is Isaiah, and then only in a prophetic

[85] A. Bentzen, *Die Josianische Reform und ihre Voraussetzungen*, Copenhagen, 1926, pp. 95 ff. As is well known, von Rad in his *Deuteronomiumstudien*, Göttingen, 1947, ETr, *Studies in Deuteronomy*, 1953, attributed Deuteronomy to these Levites. He has not explicitly discussed their possible role in the composition of the Deuteronomic work.

[86] Cf. L. Köhler, *Der Hebräische Mensch*, Tübingen, 1953, p. 165, ETr, *Hebrew Man*, London, 1956, p. 169.

[87] Cf. Bächli, op. cit., pp. 183 f.

[88] Cf. most recently, Nicholson, op. cit., pp. 114 ff.

[89] Cf. Ackroyd, 'The Vitality of the Word of God in the Old Testament', *ASTI*, i (1962), 12, following Köhler, op. cit., p. 164, ETr, p. 168.

legend, in which he appears, not as a preacher but as a foreteller and wonder-worker.[90] Attention has been drawn to the importance of the scheme of 'prophecy and fulfilment' in the Deuteronomic work, but it is noteworthy that almost all the prophetic oracles quoted come from a prophetic adaptation of historical narrative or from cycles of prophetic legends which were already available for the Deuteronomists' use. We may also ask why the prophetic books show no trace of having been formed and transmitted by the Deuteronomic circle,[90a] apart from Jeremiah who is the exception that proves the rule, since he was probably closely identified with the Deuteronomic movement.[91] Thirdly, the view has recently been propounded by M. Weinfeld that Deuteronomy, the Deuteronomic history, and the prose sermons in Jeremiah are all the product of official scribal circles in Jerusalem, the 'wise men' of the court and the public service.[92] These leading men would best have been in a position to have access to the vast reservoir of literary material which lies behind the Deuteronomic work and, although Weinfeld somewhat neglects the importance of oral tradition, not the least value of his book is its demonstration of the close links between the Deuteronomic material and the language, thought, and culture of the contemporary ancient Near East, a milieu with which the scribes would be in particularly close contact. A somewhat similar, if more one-sided and less clearly worked-out view, was put forward by Bächli, who sought to discover who could be responsible for combining all the wide range of interests covered in Deuteronomy and concluded that this could only be the Davidic king and that, therefore, the Deuteronomic school was to be identified with a circle in Jerusalem closely connected with the monarchy.[93] Such a thesis as Weinfeld's has the advantage of accounting most

[90] Cf. Y. Kaufmann, *The Religion of Israel*, ETr, London, 1961, p. 158.

[90a] But cf. p. 171 below. [Ed.]

[91] Cf. H. H. Rowley, 'Jeremiah and Deuteronomy', *Studies in Old Testament Prophecy*, 1950, pp. 172 ff.; H. Cazelles, 'Jérémie et le Deutéronome', *RSR* xxxviii (1951), 28 ff.; W. Rudolph, *Jeremia*, 2nd edn., HAT, Göttingen, 1958, pp. 73 f. The literature on this problem is now extensive. For recent discussions, cf. H. Weippert, *Die Prosareden des Jeremiabuches*, BZAW cxxxii, 1973; W. L. Holladay, 'A fresh Look at "Source B" and "Source C" in Jeremiah', *VT* xxv (1975), 394–412.

[92] Cf. M. Weinfeld, *Deuteronomy and the Deuteronomic School*, Oxford, 1972.

[93] Cf. Bächli, op. cit., pp. 181 ff.

satisfactorily for the sophisticated literary activity of the Deuteronomic school and also for the breadth of its concerns, which other views of the nature of the Deuteronomic circle are in danger of unduly limiting.

The foregoing discussion is not without significance for the second question raised by Noth's work, his contention that there is no trace of any continuation of the so-called Pentateuchal sources in Joshua and the succeeding books of the Deuteronomic history. No doubt this is much less of a burning issue than it was when Noth first wrote. On the one hand, there is now much less certainty about the precise nature, or even the existence, of the sources of the Pentateuch and there has been a strong reaction against the attempts of the older literary criticism to define documents or strata there of ever increasing complexity. On the other hand, the newer approaches to the criticism of the Old Testament such as the aetiological,[94] the form-critical,[95] and the traditio-historical,[96] have led, as will be seen later, to a greater concern with small, and originally independent, units of tradition and to a recognition that the development of larger complexes has often come about by processes which literary criticism[97] alone is too blunt a tool to uncover. In any case, from the standpoint of the present inquiry, the question really falls under a consideration of the source material which was available to the Deuteronomic historians and the way in which they may be supposed to have used it. Therefore, in dealing with the possible presence of Pentateuchal elements within the Deuteronomic work, it will not be necessary to discuss in

[94] Cf. J. Bright, *Israel in Recent History Writing*, SBT xix, 1956, pp. 91–110; J. Fichtner, 'Die etymologische Ätiologie in den Namengebungen der geschichtlichen Bücher des Alten Testaments', *VT* vi (1956), 372–96; M. Noth, 'Der Beitrag der Archäologie zur Geschichte Israels', SVT vii, 1960, pp. 278–82; I. L. Seeligmann, 'Aetiological Elements in Biblical Historiography' (Hebrew), *Zion* xxvi (1961), 141–169; B. S. Childs, 'A Study of the Formula "Until This Day"', *JBL* lxxii (1963), 279–292; C. Westermann, *Forschung am Alten Testament*, Munich, 1964, pp. 29–47; B. O. Long, *The Problem of Etiological Narrative in the Old Testament*, BZAW cviii, 1968; F. W. Golka, *Die Ätiologien im Alten Testament* (Dissertation, Heidelberg), 1972.

[95] Cf. K. Koch, *Was ist Formgeschichte? Neue Wege der Bibelexegese*, 2nd edn., 1967, ETr, *The Growth of the Biblical Tradition*, 1969; G. M. Tucker, *Form Criticism of the Old Testament*, Philadelphia, 1971; J. H. Hayes (ed.), *Old Testament Form Criticism*, San Antonio, 1974.

[96] Cf. W. E. Rast, *Tradition History and the Old Testament*, Philadelphia, 1972.

[97] Cf. N. Habel, *Literary Criticism of the Old Testament*, Philadelphia, 1971.

detail the supposed various strands in the Pentateuch which are non-Deuteronomic, because it would be generally agreed that these had been combined into a single narrative, which may for convenience be called JE, before they were incorporated in the Deuteronomic history or the Deuteronomic editions of the various books. The scholars who have attempted to discover such a narrative running through Joshua–2 Kings[98] employ various arguments to demonstrate its existence. One, which, in theory at least, should be the most decisive, is that of stylistic connections between blocks of materials in Joshua–2 Kings and the combined pre-Deuteronomic narrative of the Pentateuch.[99] But JE, as it is reconstructed, has nothing like so distinctive a vocabulary and style as is the case with material of Deuteronomic origin, and most of its supposedly characteristic words and phrases, as given, for example, in the table in C. A. Simpson's *The Early Traditions of Israel*, pp. 403–9, seem to be no more than part of the common vocabulary of biblical Hebrew. The linguistic evidence is not incompatible with the thesis that JE can be recognized in the Deuteronomic work, but it proves no more than that the Deuteronomic editors have made use of already existing material. A second argument is the presence of doublets in a number of the narratives in the Deuteronomic history, similar to the phenomena to be found in the Pentateuch,[100] but the difficulty here is to demonstrate the hypothesis that these belong to two or more relatively homogeneous works of considerable extent, even if one or other of them is recognized as having affinities with pre-Deuteronomic Pentateuchal material.[101] Again, attempts have been made to show a pre-Deuteronomic narrative in Joshua–2 Kings by assigning to it a clear standpoint and purpose, whether this was to present the course of Israel's history as leading up to the establishment of the Davidic

[98] Cf. G. Hölscher, *Geschichtsschreibung in Israel*, Lund, 1952; O. Eissfeldt, *Geschichtsschreibung im Alten Testament*, Berlin, 1948; *Die ältesten Traditionen Israels*, BZAW lxxi, 1952; *Introduction*, pp. 242–301; C. A. Simpson, *The Early Traditions of Israel*, 1948; *Composition of the Book of Judges*, 1957.

[99] Eissfeldt, *Introduction*, p. 250.

[100] Cf. e.g. Eissfeldt, op. cit., pp. 252 f.

[101] Cf. F. Langlamet, *Gilgal et les récits de la traversée du Jourdain*, Paris, 1969, especially p. 104. He speaks of material 'dans la ligne des traditions J', op. cit., p. 103.

monarchy or with some other object.[102] But this is almost
inevitably to argue in a circle, by ascribing passages to such a
narrative on the ground that they exemplify its standpoint
and then to use the passages to develop that standpoint, and
it clearly makes a great difference to our assessment of such
a hypothetical document whether we see it as reaching its
conclusion with the conquest of the Promised Land or the
death of Solomon or some later period, and about this there
is no agreement. The most plausible contention along these
lines is that the JE, and also the P, source in the Pentateuch
must have included an account of the taking possession of the
land long ago promised to the patriarchs and that it is
plausible to expect to find this continuation in the present
book of Joshua, which has the conquest of Palestine as its
theme. For this reason, the main weight of scholarly opinion
has tended to favour the view that the Pentateuchal sources
are continued in the book of Joshua,[103] thus making it
possible perhaps to speak of a Hexateuch, while being much
more sceptical about any further continuation, for undoubtedly evidence for these sources becomes much more tenuous
the further one proceeds in the Deuteronomic history.[104] But,
when the objective evidence of the texts is as doubtful as we
have seen it to be, other hypotheses will remain equally
plausible: it may be that, for example, the Yahwistic account
of the conquest has simply disappeared, as Noth believes, or
that in fact the Yahwist's purpose and outlook excluded his
producing a Conquest narrative.[105] Once again, it is not
unreasonable to call attention to material in the book of
Joshua which may have affinities with the early Pentateuchal
narrative,[106] but it is another matter to demonstrate that it
formed part of a lengthy preceding history work. The case for
a continuation of the P source in Joshua is even less

---

[102] For the most recent of such attempts, cf. H. Schulte, *Die Entstehung der
Geschichtsschreibung im Alten Israel*, BZAW cxxviii, 1972.

[103] Cf. S. Mowinckel, *Tetrateuch–Pentateuch–Hexateuch*, BZAW xc, 1964; G. von
Rad, *Theologie*, i. 295, ETr, i. 296.

[104] Cf. Eissfeldt, op. cit., pp. 298 f.

[105] Cf. H. W. Wolff, 'The Kerygma of the Yahwist', *Interpretation* xx (1966), 129–
58, especially 133; P. F. Ellis, *The Yahwist*, London, 1969, pp. 29 ff.

[106] Cf. F. Langlamet, 'Josué, II, et les traditions de l'Hexateuque', *RB* lxxviii
(1971), 5–17, 161–83, 321–54.

convincing. Apart from the fact that the concerns of P may well not have required any account of the occupation of Canaan or of Israel's life in the land, recent studies have shown that Josh. 13–21, on which the case for P in Joshua must largely rest and which were therefore excluded by Noth from his Deuteronomic history, can hardly be considered a P composition, and that they are most likely to be official lists of various periods which the Deuteronomists incorporated in their work.[107]

It would appear that investigation of the possible continuation of the Pentateuchal sources in any part of Joshua–2 Kings has come to something of a dead end and it is not surprising that recent scholarship has devoted more attention to isolating in these books blocks of traditional material which would have been used either by a lengthy 'Pentateuchal' narrative or directly by the Deuteronomic circle. Many of such studies have been concerned with the *Sitz im Leben* of small independent local traditions and these investigations are too numerous to permit of a review here, but in any event, in most cases at least, it is likely that these traditions were not available directly to the Deuteronomists but had already been worked up into larger complexes. It is thus some of these pre-Deuteronomic 'compositions' which fall to be considered at this point and it is noteworthy how strongly the creative role of the sanctuaries and their cult is now emphasized in the development of these units. In Joshua, leaving aside the passages, such as Josh. 1 and 23, which appear to be straight Deuteronomic compositions,[108] it is possible to distinguish three such sources. The first is the collection of local traditions and aetiological tales in Josh. 1–12:24. Noth, who first clearly discerned this unit, called attention to the place of the Gilgal sanctuary in the assembling of this material,[109] but, since his

[107] Cf. F. M. Cross and G. E. Wright, 'The Boundary and Province Lists of the Kingdom of Judah', *JBL* lxxv (1956), 202–26; Z. Kallai-Kleinmann, 'The Town Lists of Judah, Simeon, Benjamin and Dan', *VT* viii (1958), 134–60; 'Note on the Town Lists of Judah, Simeon, Benjamin and Dan', *VT* xi (1961), 223–7; Y. Aharoni, 'The Province List of Judah', *VT* ix (1959), 225–46; B. Mazar, 'The Cities of the Priests and the Levites', SVT vii, 1960, pp. 193–205.

[108] Although, even here, the Deuteronomic presentation may often reflect much older patterns of thought and practice, cf. e.g. J. R. Porter in *Proclamation and Presence*, pp. 105 ff.

[109] Cf. Noth, *Josua*, pp. 11 ff.

work, a number of studies have shown how the cult there played a much more active part in the shaping of this complex than Noth realized.[110] Even here, however, the Deuteronomic editors may have played an important part in giving this section its present form, not just by the addition of brief comments, but in presenting it, within the over-all structure of their history, in a new light.[111] Secondly, the various lists in Josh. 13–21 were probably brought together in one collection for official purposes,[112] but were given a narrative shaping in the Deuteronomic history, while thirdly Josh. 24 is generally recognized as a distinct Shechemite sanctuary tradition, although again considerably expanded by the Deuteronomic circle.[113] In Judges, the most important source is a collection of cycles of ancient Israelite heroes,[114] each of which has been formed from a combination of tribal[115] and cultic and sanctuary[116] traditions. But this was not a mere random collection but already an interpretative composition when it was known to the Deuteronomic school: the framework, which provides the interpretation and is usually considered to be Deuteronomic, may well be much older[117] and its context is probably the rite of the renewal of the

[110] Cf. H. J. Kraus, 'Gilgal—ein Beitrag zur Kultusgeschichte Israels', *VT* i (1951), 181 f.; *Gottesdienst in Israel*, 1962, pp. 183 ff., ETr, 1966, pp. 156 ff.; J. A. Soggin, 'Gilgal, Passah und Landnahme', SVT 15 (1966), pp. 265 ff.; J. A. Wilcoxen, 'Narrative Structure and Cult Legend: a study of Joshua 1–6' in J. C. Rylaarsdam (ed.), *Transitions in Biblical Scholarship*, Chicago, 1968, pp. 69 ff.; J. R. Porter, 'The Background of Joshua III–V', *SEÅ* xxxvi (1971), 5 ff. Cf. also the criticisms of Kraus's views by Nicholson, *Exodus and Sinai in History and Tradition*, Oxford, 1973, p. 28, n. 76.

[111] For possible examples of this, cf. Kraus, *VT* i (1951), 198 ff.; Porter, op. cit., p. 132.

[112] Cf. Noth op. cit., p. 10.

[113] The literature on Josh. 24 is extensive; for a bibliography, cf. Soggin, *Josué*, p. 163, ETr, pp. 222 f.

[114] Cf. W. Richter, *Traditionsgeschichtliche Untersuchungen zum Richterbuch*, BBB xviii, 1963.

[115] Cf. E. Täubler, *Biblische Studien. Die Epoche der Richter*, Tübingen, 1958.

[116] Cf. G. von Rad, *Der heilige Krieg im alten Israel*, ATANT xx, 1951; C. A. Keller, 'Über einige alttestamentliche Heiligtumslegenden', *ZAW* lxvii (1956), 154–162; W. Beyerlin, 'Geschichte und heilsgeschichtliche Traditionsbildung im Alten Testament (Richter vi–viii)', *VT* xiii (1963), 1–25; H.-P. Müller, 'Die kultische Darstellung der Theophanie', *VT* xiv (1964), 183–91.

[117] Cf. W. Richter, *Die Bearbeitungen des 'Retterbuches' in der deuteronomischen Epoche*, BBB xxi, 1964, though his thesis that a *Retterbuch* ever existed apart from the 'framework' is more dubious.

Covenant at the sanctuary.[118] If this is so, it overcomes the problem of the difference in the 'Deuteronomic' editorial technique, discussed earlier, between Judges and 1 and 2 Kings, and provides an excellent example of how the Deuteronomic circle was able to use older material which fitted in perfectly with its own theological viewpoint, while not deriving directly from it. It is generally agreed that at least the material concerning David in 1 and 2 Samuel consists of various collections of traditions about him which have been incorporated in the Deuteronomic history, and the question of the use made of it by the Deuteronomists has to some extent been discussed earlier, but there are two important sections about which perhaps a further word needs to be said. The first is the story of Saul and the foundation of the monarchy in 1 Sam. 7–12. Critical opinion has usually been divided between the view that the two basic accounts of the introduction of kingship represent two of the early Pentateuchal sources[119] and Noth's view that, while the 'favourable' picture of the monarchy is older material, the 'unfavourable' one is the actual work of the Deuteronomic editors.[120] Recent studies, however, have strongly suggested that both these views are over-simplifications, that the supposed anti-monarchical source is itself built up of a variety of traditions, which do not always reflect exactly the same point of view, so that it cannot be considered to be entirely Deuteronomic,[121] and that the differences in these chapters largely reflect a number of traditions, probably preserved at different sanctuaries.[122] Again, we do not meet here a confrontation of clear-cut ideologies, and the Deuteronomic circle was able to take over the whole complex, with very little adaptation, because it could be made to answer to that circle's acceptance of the monarchy while, as in such a passage as

[118] Cf. W. Beyerlin, 'Gattung und Herkunft des Rahmens im Richterbuch', E. Würthwein and O. Kaiser (ed.), *Tradition und Situation*, Göttingen, 1963, pp. 1–29.

[119] Cf. Eissfeldt, op. cit., pp. 271 ff.

[120] Cf. M. Noth, *ÜGS*, pp. 54 ff.

[121] Cf. A. Weiser, *Samuel. Seine geschichtliche Aufgabe und religiöse Bedeutung*, FRLANT lxxxi, 1962; M. H. Segal, *The Pentateuch and other Biblical Studies*, Jerusalem, 1967, pp. 203 ff.

[122] Thus Hertzberg sees traditions from Mizpah and Gilgal in these chapters, cf. op. cit. e.g. pp. 130 ff.

I Sam. 8:11-17, also making clear the limitations which, from the Deuteronomic point of view, had to be imposed upon it. The second section is 2 Sam. 9-20 with 1 Kgs. 1-2, which, since the classic work of L. Rost in 1926, has been viewed by most scholars as a well defined and closely-knit unit, a genuine work of history,[123] written by a contemporary of the events described, with the clear purpose of describing and legitimizing Solomon's accession to the throne. This view has been questioned for more than one reason. Rost's conception of the extent of the work has been doubted (so Mowinckel believes that 1 Kgs. 1-2 have no organic connection with 2 Sam. 9-20,[124] which destroys Rost's whole thesis of the purpose of the 'Succession' history) and the original unity of the supposed composition can be cogently argued against.[125] The various traditions in the Succession Document need not be sharply distinguished in character from the other traditions about David in 1 and 2 Samuel and the possibility remains open that, throughout, their order and arrangement, not least in the Succession story, betray the interest of the Deuteronomic redactors.[126] From a different point of view, it has been claimed that the Succession narrative is not history at all, but a piece of wisdom propaganda to support Solomon's regime, comparable in character to the Egyptian *Novelle* type of literature.[127] It is implausible to view this narrative as a product of wisdom circles,[128] and indeed the idea of wisdom as a definite 'category' is in danger of becoming something of a King Charles's head in modern Old Testament criticism, but in any case this theory is open to the same objection as

---

[123] For von Rad, this work marks the real beginning of Israelite historiography, cf. his 'The Beginnings of Historical Writing in Ancient Israel', *The Problem of the Hexateuch and Other Essays*, Edinburgh, 1965, pp. 166-205.

[124] Cf. S. Mowinckel in *ASTI* ii (1963), 11.

[125] Cf. J. Blenkinsopp, 'Theme and Motif in the Succession History (2 Sam. XI 2 ff.) and the Yahwist Corpus', SVT xv, 1965, pp. 44-57; W. Brueggemann, 'David and his Theologian', *CBQ* xxx (1968), 156-81; J. W. Flanagan, 'Court History or Succession Document? A Study of 2 Samuel 9-20 and 1 Kings 1-2', *JBL* xci (1972), 172-91; E. Würthwein, *Die Erzählung von der Thronfolge Davids—theologische oder politische Geschichtsschreibung?*, Zürich, 1974.

[126] Cf. R. A. Carlson, op. cit., pp. 131-9.

[127] Cf. R. N. Whybray, *The Succession Narrative*, SBT, 2nd series, ix, 1968.

[128] Cf. J. L. Crenshaw, 'Method in Determining Wisdom Influence upon "Historical" Literature', *JBL* lxxxviii (1969), 137-40.

Rost's, that it depends on the thesis of a definite document with a consciously polemical purpose. Finally, little need be said here about the sources employed by the Deuteronomic history in 1 and 2 Kings, as these have been widely recognized and frequently discussed.[129] In these books, the Deuteronomic circle had a rich variety of material, from a variety of backgrounds, upon which to draw and so was able to select, arrange, and systematize more obviously and clearly than is the case in other parts of its history. Two points, however, may be noted. It has been suggested that the main structural work in 1 and 2 Kings is not Deuteronomic but is in fact a Jerusalemite priestly redaction of a synchronistic chronicle of Israel and Judah, which incorporated what are generally recognized as excerpts from the royal annals of both states.[130] But, as Weinfeld has pointed out,[131] the linguistic evidence does not support the thesis that there is any extensive history book in 1 and 2 Kings other than the Deuteronomic work. Secondly, there has perhaps been an over-emphasis on the reliance upon, and reproduction of, written texts and official documents by the Deuteronomistic historians in 1 and 2 Kings and we must bear in mind Mowinckel's suggestion[132] that they may have made much greater use of orally transmitted complexes, even when these were of considerable extent, than has generally been allowed for.

THE CHRONISTIC HISTORICAL WORK

Similar problems, with regard to such matters as the unity of the work, its treatment of its sources and the question of its over-all purpose and background, to those that arise in connection with the Deuteronomic history, confront us in the historical work of the 'Chronicler'. Perhaps the first problem which needs to be discussed is precisely what is to be included in the Chronicler's history, for the answer to be given to this will have considerable bearing on our assessment of the aim and the setting of the whole work. It has generally been taken

---

[129] They are well surveyed in Gray, *I & II Kings*, pp. 14–35.
[130] Cf. A. Jepsen, *Die Quellen des Königbuches*, 2nd edn., Halle, 1956.
[131] Cf. Weinfeld, op. cit., p. 8, n. 2.
[132] Mowinckel, op. cit., pp. 17–21.

for granted that the original form of the Chronistic history included at least some of the material in the existing books of Ezra and Nehemiah, particularly that dealing with Ezra,[133] and the importance of this assumption is that, if justified, we are able to see 'the central moment of the Chronicler's activity as coming after that of Ezra, so that the whole of the previous history is summed up in the most recent and, to the Chronicler's theology, in many ways most significant moment'.[134] However, the reasons for such a view appear on examination to be somewhat slight. The fact that the conclusion of 2 Chronicles agrees verbally with the opening of Ezra is no indication that a division of an originally single composition was made at this point:[135] 2 Chr. 36:20 f. forms a perfectly satisfactory conclusion to the Chronicler's history[136] and it would be generally agreed that 2 Chr. 36:22 f. have been added later at some stage, probably copied from the opening of Ezra, in order to give the book a 'happy ending'. Nor are Chronicles and Ezra–Nehemiah perhaps as closely related in language and theology[137] as has usually been supposed. Recently, S. Japhat has examined in detail the linguistic and stylistic resemblances of the two complexes and claims that, as a result, the books could not have been written or compiled by the same author and that a certain period of time must separate the two.[138] Similarly, there are considerable theological differences between Chronicles and at least the material dealing with Ezra and Nehemiah, notably the prominence of the Davidic tradition in the former compared with the Exodus tradition in the latter,[139] and, although the extent of the differences has been questioned,[140] it still remains substantial. This not to deny a real relationship

[133] Cf. e.g. L. H. Brockington, *Ezra, Nehemiah and Esther*, NCB, London, 1969, p. 8.

[134] Ackroyd, 'History and Theology in the Writings of the Chronicler', *CTM* xxviii (1967), 504.

[135] Cf. Eissfeldt, op. cit., pp. 530 f.

[136] Cf. Ackroyd, 'The Interpretation of the Exile and Restoration', *Canadian Journal of Theology*, xiv (1968), 4 f.; *Exile and Restoration*, pp. 239 ff.

[137] Cf. J. M. Myers, *I Chronicles*, AncB, New York, 1965, p. XVIII.

[138] Cf. S. Japhat, 'The supposed common authorship of Chronicles and Ezra–Nehemiah investigated anew', *VT* xviii (1968), 330–71.

[139] Cf. D. N. Freedman, 'The Chronicler's Purpose', *CBQ* xxiii (1961), 436–42.

[140] Cf. Ackroyd in *CTM* xxviii (1967), 511.

between Chronicles and Ezra–Nehemiah, but, in view of the above considerations, it would seem more desirable to think of a Chronistic school whose activity, in a way similar to that of the Deuteronomic school, extended over a period from about 515 B.C. to some time after the work of Ezra or Nehemiah, whichever was the later. The collection and interpretation of various kinds of material by this school crystallized into a number of literary productions at different epochs, reflecting the particular needs and interests of such periods, within a general concern for the reconstruction of the national life, especially in its religious and cultic aspects, after the return from the exile. In what follows we shall, therefore, examine Chronicles separately from Ezra–Nehemiah.

A characteristic of much recent work on Chronicles, in contrast to earlier scholarship, has been a new appreciation of the value and significance of the theological outlook of the book and an attempted delineation of a clear and definite outlook and purpose in the presentation and ordering of its material.[141] In this respect, it could be thought of as a parallel work to the Deuteronomic history, with which of course it has close connections, theological as much as literary. As compared with the Deuteronomists, however, the Chronicler has no regular editorial framework in which he makes plain his interpretation of the older material he is using.[142] His outlook must be largely deduced from the way in which he treats this older material and by attempting to discover those passages in the work which may be considered to represent

---

[141] Cf. G. von Rad, *Das Geschichtsbild des chronistischen Werkes*, BWANT lv, 1930; *Theologie*, i, pp. 344 ff., ETr, pp. 347 ff.; W. Rudolph, 'Problems of the Books of Chronicles', *VT* iv (1954), 404 ff.; *Chronikbücher*, HAT, Tübingen, 1955, pp. xviii–xxiv; A. M. Brunet, 'Le Chroniste et ses sources', *RB* lx (1953), 481–508, *RB* lxi (1954) 349–86; 'La Théologie du Chroniste, théocratie et messianisme', J. Coppens, A. Descamps, É Massaux, *Sacra Pagina*, i (1959), 384–97; R. North, 'Theology of the Chronicler', *JBL* 82 (1963), 369–81; J. M. Myers, 'The Kerygma of the Chronicler. History and Theology in the Service of Religion', *Interpretation* xx (1966), 259–73. Cf. the works of Ackroyd cited earlier and also his *The Age of the Chronicler*, 1970; 'The Theology of the Chronicler', *Lexington Theological Quarterly*, viii (1973), 101–116; *I & II Chronicles, Ezra, Nehemiah*, TC, London, 1973, pp. 27 ff. Cf. also P. Welten, *Geschichte und Geschichtsdarstellung in den Chronikbüchern*, WMANT xlii, 1973.

[142] But cf. G. von Rad, 'Das levitische Predigt in den Büchern der Chronik', *GSAT*, 1958, pp. 248–61, ETr, in *The Problem of the Hexateuch*, pp. 267–80.

the Chronicler's own composition, and hence the question of the sources and their extent becomes a particularly crucial question. Thus, the Chronistic history has often been described as covering the period from Creation to Ezra, or at least to the Exile,[143] but this view can only be upheld if, in contrast to many scholars, 1 Chr. 1–9 are taken to be an original part of the work, although it could still be maintained that, in any discussion of the outlook of Chronicles, the work must be taken as it stands, even if its present form is the product of a 'second Chronicler' who has redacted the whole.[144] The argument is not substantially altered, if, with the majority of scholars, we think that the Chronicler did have a brief introduction beginning with the Creation but that it has been so extensively interpolated that only a fraction of what we now have can be attributed to him.[145] In any event, when one looks at these chapters without preconceptions, it is difficult to believe that they represent a carefully worked out introduction to the Chronicler's historical work,[146] still less a sort of paradigm of his whole theological outlook.[147] Again, if we should think of large additions to the material about David in 1 Chr. 10–29,[148] including the greater part of what is there said about the ordering of the priests, Levites, and temple-singers, it may be asked whether too much emphasis has not often been placed on the original 'Chronicler's' great interest in the cult-personnel and on the possibility of his having himself been a Levitical singer. Further the question of the Chronicler's treatment of what is clearly his main source, the material which is parallel to that found in the books of Samuel and Kings, can now be seen to be considerably more complicated than has often been

[143] Cf. Ackroyd in *CTM* xxviii (1967), 509.

[144] Cf. K. Galling, *Die Bücher der Chronik, Esra, Nehemia*, ATD, Göttingen, 1954, pp. 10 ff. Cf. the criticisms of S. Mowinckel, 'Erwägungen zum chronistischen Geschichtswerk', *TLZ* lxxxv (1960), 1–8.

[145] Cf. Rudolph, *Chronikbücher*, pp. I ff.; *VT* iv (1954), 402, but cf. the curious inconsistency in his comment on Welch's views on 404.

[146] Myers, *I Chronicles*, p. xli, refers to them as 'a file prefixed to the Chronicler's work', and, although the term is no doubt anachronistic, it is a fair description of their character.

[147] Cf. Ackroyd, *I & II Chronicles*, pp. 30 f.

[148] Cf. J. Botterweck, 'Zur Eigenart der chronistischen Davidgeschichte', *Festschrift Viktor Christian*, 1956, pp. 12–31.

supposed. It has commonly been held that he had these books before him virtually in their present form and that much can be deduced about his outlook and method of working from the deliberate changes in wording and order which he makes in these sources.[149] But, on the one hand, evidence from Qumran now makes it very likely that the text of Samuel–Kings which the Chronicler had before him was of an old Palestinian type, different in many respects from that represented in the Massoretic tradition[150] and W. E. Lemke, after a careful discussion, has concluded that detailed comparisons of the Massoretic texts of Chronicles and Samuel–Kings are methodologically unsound.[151] While this would not exclude the view that, even when the Chronicler reproduces material already in his sources, he makes use of it in a particular way,[152] yet it suggests a greater degree of caution in reconstructing a definite ideology for the Chronicler than has often been shown and it may go some way to explain the often noted phenomenon that sometimes the Chronicler appears to reproduce the existing text of Samuel–Kings almost verbatim, while on other occasions he departs considerably from it.[153] On the other hand, we have seriously to reckon with the possibility that the Chronicler only knew the material of Samuel–Kings, at least as far as concerns the kings of Israel and Judah after David, in a form that is much more than a mere variant textual tradition, namely as the 'midrash of the book of the kings',[154] referred to in 2 Chr. 24:27. If this is so, once more we cannot be certain how much

---

[149] Cf. Brunet, op. cit.; J. Schildenberger, *Literarische Arten der Geschichtsschreibung im Alten Testament*, Zürich, 1964, pp. 43 ff.; T. Willi, *Die Chronik als Auslegung. Untersuchungen zur literarischen Gestaltung der historischen Überlieferung Israels*, FRLANT cvi 1972, pp. 48–244.

[150] Cf. F. M. Cross, *The Ancient Library of Qumran*, 2nd edn., New York, 1961, pp. 188–91; 'The History of the Biblical Text in the Light of Discoveries in the Judaean Desert', *HTR* lvii (1964), 281–99.

[151] Cf. W.E. Lemke, 'The Synoptic Problem in the Chronicler's History', *HTR* lviii (1965), pp. 349–63, especially 362 f.

[152] Cf. Ackroyd's comments on Lemke's conclusions, in *CTM* xxviii (1967), 507, n. 25.

[153] Cf. the view that the Chronicler used a *Vorlage* of the present books of Samuel and Kings, e.g. M. Rehm, *Die Bücher der Chronik*, EchtB, 2nd edn., Würzburg, 1956, p. 275.

[154] For the meaning of this expression, cf. Eissfeldt, op. cit., p. 534; Myers, *II Chronicles*, p. 79.

of what may seem at first sight to represent the distinctive standpoint of an individual 'Chronicler' has not in fact come to him as the result of a process of reflection upon, and embellishment of, the Deuteronomic work, in an already well established tradition. Even those sections in 1 and 2 Chronicles where we can strongly suspect the composition of an individual author may yet rest on this continuing process of oral tradition which had not in this case so far crystallized into written shape, as had happened with the midrash and the various books concerned with prophets.[155]

From all this it would seem best to conclude that the Chronistic historical work, and in this respect we may include Ezra and Nehemiah, is again primarily the product of a school or circle active over a considerable period and that the collection and preservation of earlier material, both oral and written, was not the least of its concerns. This school had links, and the work it produced has links, with both the Deuteronomic and the Priestly School, but, in view of the specific interests of the Chronistic history, its kernel is to be sought among the cult personnel of the Jerusalem Temple, probably, though by no means as certainly as is sometimes supposed, among the ancestors of those who became the post-exilic Levites, and thus had its beginnings in the period of the monarchy. However, it certainly appears that a key point in the development of this circle came with the composition of 1 and 2 Chronicles, quite probably, in its original form, so far as that can be discovered, the work of a single author. It may be agreed that this author had a definite purpose in view, which was to set before his contemporaries the true standards for the ordering of the national and religious life, by showing how those standards had once been established in the people's history and how history had shown that departure from those standards inevitably brought disaster.[156] Can the contempor-

---

[155] Cf. Mowinckel in *ASTI* ii (1963), 23. For an example of the Chronicler's working with various materials, cf. Ackroyd, 'Historians and Prophets', *SEÅ* xxxiii (1968), 33 ff.

[156] Ackroyd's description of the Chronicler's work as 'dehistoricizing', in *CTM* xxviii (1967), 509 f., in criticizing the views of H. G. Guthrie, *Wisdom and Canon. Meanings of the Law and the Prophets*, Evanston, 1966, depends on too modern a view of 'history', which does not correspond to the concept of historiography in the ancient world. Cf. also R. Mosis, *Untersuchungen zur Theologie des Chronistischen Geschichtswerkes*, Freiburg, 1973.

ary situation to which the Chronicler was addressing himself
be more precisely discovered? That he has in view a
community which could look to the possibility of a renewed
existence is suggested by the frequent examples he gives of
how divine retribution can be tempered by repentance and
divine grace, here going beyond the Deuteronomic outlook
which he basically shares. But of crucial importance here is
the central place in his work of Jerusalem, the Temple, and
especially David who, in the Chronicler's presentation, is on
the human level responsible for the other two. It is usual to
say either that the Chronicler was writing in the fourth
century B.C. when the prospect of a Davidic monarchy had
disappeared, and so for him the significance of David was as
the founder of the holy city and the holy place with its
worship, the twin pillars of the restored community's life, and
as a type of divine grace;[157] or that for him the figure of
David is already assuming a messianic and eschatological
character as part of a future hope.[158] But a fourth-century
date for the original Chronicler largely rests on what we have
seen to be the questionable assumption that he wrote after
Ezra and Nehemiah,[159] and in any case we still have to ask
why, if he merely wanted a convenient cult founder, the
Chronicler in effect transferred the arrangements for the
Temple to David from Solomon, whom he knew to be its
actual builder and of whom he takes a very favourable
view:[160] the most likely answer would seem to be that David
was recognized as the embodiment of the sacral Judean
monarchy. Along the same line of argument, it is often stated
that the Chronicler is presenting the ideal of a theocracy.[161]
In one sense, this is no doubt true, but only in the sense that
the theocratic ideal was normative for Israel,[162] and if it is

[157] So Ackroyd, op. cit., pp. 512 f.

[158] Cf. particularly, W. F. Stinespring, 'Eschatology in Chronicles', *JBL* lxxx
(1961), 209–19.

[159] This date for the Chronicler has often been supported by the contention that
his work is in part a polemic against the Samaritans. Apart from the question of the
relationship of the books of Ezra and Nehemiah to his history, this is doubtful on
other grounds, cf. R. J. Coggins, 'The Old Testament and Samaritan Origins', *ASTI*
vi (1968), 45 f.; 'The Interpretation of Ezra IV. 4', *JTS*, N.S. xvi (1965), 124–7.

[160] Cf. R. L. Braun, 'Solomonic Apologetic in Chronicles', *JBL* 92 (1973), 503–16.

[161] Cf. Rudolph, *Chronikbücher*, p. XXIII.

[162] Cf. T. C. Vriezen, *Theologie des Alten Testaments in Grundzügen*, 1965, p. 187

supposed to mean that the Chronicler was pointing to the temple-state of the post-exilic period, it must be observed that, in the Chronicler's history, the king is head alike of the nation and the cult, with the high priest playing only a very subsidiary role. Nor is it very easy to point to anything clearly messianic or eschatological, in the proper meaning of those terms, in 1 and 2 Chronicles.[163] It seems safest, therefore, to adopt in broad outline the position of Freedman as best accounting for all the characteristic features of the first and basic redaction of Chronicles, which would place it much earlier than has usually been done, perhaps around 515 B.C. The impetus for the writing of the work was the rebuilding of the Temple and it is influenced by the Davidic hopes also to be found in the prophecies of Haggai and Zechariah, a relationship which may, in part at least, account for the considerable place of prophets and the reference to prophetic sources in the Chronicler's history.[164] Such a hypothesis, of course, as has been seen, does not exclude the view that 1 and 2 Chronicles received more or less extensive additions at later dates, although the evidence brought forward for these is far from conclusive.[165]

Some of the issues in connection with the books of Ezra and Nehemiah have been briefly touched upon in our discussion of their relationship with 1 and 2 Chronicles. The main question concerns the growth of the materials in these works into their present form and in recent years a good deal of attention has been devoted to the background and development of the traditions on which these works are built. We may take first the matter which deals explicitly with Ezra

(cf. ETr, *An Outline of Old Testament Theology*, 2nd edn., Oxford, 1970, p. 368), although he is incorrect in contrasting this absolutely with the institution of kingship.

[163] Cf. A. Caquot, 'Peut on parler de messianisme dans l'oeuvre du Chroniste?', *RThPh* xcix (1966), 110–20. For the necessity of a careful definition, with regard to the Old Testament, of the terms in question, cf. J. P. M. van der Ploeg, 'Eschatology in the Old Testament', *OTS*, xvii (1972), 89–99.

[164] Compare e.g. Zech. 1:4–6 with 2 Chr. 36:15 f. Cf. J. D. Newsome, 'Toward a New Understanding of the Chronicler and his Purposes', *JBL* xciv (1975), 201–17.

[165] Particularly the claim that amplifications were made as late as the Maccabean period, cf. Noth, *ÜGS*, p. 155; Ackroyd, 'Criteria for Maccabean Dating of Old Testament Literature', *VT* iii (1952), 126 f.; P. Winter, 'Twenty-six priestly courses', *VT* vi (1956), 216; A. Jaubert, 'Le calendrier des Jubilés et les jours liturgiques de la semaine', *VT* vii (1957), 47.

and Nehemiah, and here, in addition to various official lists and records, it has long been recognized that there are two main 'literary' units at the base of the existing compositions, the so-called Memoirs of Nehemiah and of Ezra. Much debate has centred on whether the original history work of the Chronicler included accounts of both Ezra and Nehemiah[166] or whether the Nehemiah material was added later,[167] although in each case later additions, and even a later recension, have to be allowed for. A great deal of this discussion can perhaps be by-passed if, as we have seen good grounds for believing, the Chronicler's work, in its basic form, appeared before the activity of these two men and thus would not have dealt with them, and we do better to try to explain the development of the Ezra and Nehemiah material less in terms of the production of definite literary compositions and more by the collection and growth of the traditions about these men, much of this taking place through oral transmission.[168] The whole process may indeed have been part of a continuing Chronistic circle, which we have postulated as the setting for the Chronicler's activity and for which the rebuilding of the Temple would have provided a new home and impetus, and this would account for the links which undoubtedly exist between 1 and 2 Chronicles and Ezra and Nehemiah, while freeing us from over hypothetical speculations about a number of redactions of, or additions to, already existing compositions. In a doubtless over-simplified way, we can, however, possibly reconstruct certain stages in this development, centring on material about the two great historical figures of Ezra and Nehemiah. If Nehemiah preceded Ezra, we may postulate the writing of a *Denkschrift* about him on the model of similar contemporary Near Eastern royal inscriptions and other texts.[169] This would

---

[166] Cf. U. Kellermann, *Nehemia. Quellen, Überlieferung und Geschichte*, BZAW cii, 1967; In der Smitten, 'Die Gründe für die Aufnahme der Nehemiaschrift in das chronistische Geschichtswerk', *BZ* NF xvi (1972), 207–21; *Esra. Quellen, Überlieferung und Geschichte*, Assen, 1973.

[167] Cf. Mowinckel, *Studien zu dem Buche Ezra–Nehemia I. Die Nachchronische Redaktion des Buches. Die Listen*, Oslo, 1964, pp. 29–47.

[168] Cf. A. S. Kapelrud, *The Question of Authorship in the Ezra–Narrative. A Lexical Investigation*, Oslo, 1944.

[169] Cf. Mowinckel, *Studien zu dem Buche Ezra–Nehemia II. Die Nehemia–Denkschrift*, Oslo, 1964.

have been followed by an edificatory history of Ezra, designed to show him as the source of the basic institutions which were to order the life of post-exilic Israel[170] and this, along with other sources, included a *Denkschrift* of a similar type to that of Nehemiah, whether this is considered to be an originally independent production, incorporated by the historian in his work, or whether it is his own composition modelled on the Nehemiah material.[171] The present complex Ezra–Nehemiah would then be the result of a development by which the material about these two men was brought together, enriched by further traditions which had grown up about each of them, especially perhaps Nehemiah, and, in the process, with the traditions concerning the one influencing the traditions concerning the other.[172] In view of the lack of any indication in Ezra–Nehemiah that Persian rule has come to an end, we should probably date the final product about the middle of the fourth century B.C.

The case is somewhat different with the narrative in Ezra 1–6. Not only can this be considered as a direct continuation of 2 Chronicles, but it has closer linguistic affinities with, and is closer in its compositional technique to, the work of the Chronicler than other parts of Ezra–Nehemiah. Thus it has generally been viewed as the Chronicler's own writing and discussion has largely centred on the problem of the curiously unhistorical way in which he presents his material. But if the Artaxerxes correspondence in Ezra 4:11 f. is genuine, then the narrative cannot be earlier than Artaxerxes I and we have seen that it is likely that the Chronistic work was originally completed well before then. Although Ezra 1–6 has affinities with the Chronistic work, notably in the concern with the Temple, and specifically with the arrangements for the cultus, which, as in 1 Chronicles, precede the building of the Temple, and with genealogies, yet these chapters have their particular interests, especially in the desire to show the encouragement

---

[170] Cf. Mowinckel, *Studien zu dem Buche Ezra–Nehemia III. Die Ezrageschichte und das Gesetz Moses*, Oslo, 1965, especially p. 98.

[171] Cf. S. Mowinckel, '"Ich" und "Er" in der Ezrageschichte', in A. Kuschke (ed.), *Verbannung und Heimkehr*, Tübingen, 1961, pp. 211–33, although we need not follow him in his view that the author of the Ezra history deliberately intended to supersede Nehemiah.

[172] Cf. Ackroyd, *I & II Chronicles*, p. 26.

and goodwill of the Persian authorities for the restoration of
the exiles and the Temple. In fact, Ezra 1–6 is a very carefully
constructed unit which arranges the material the author had
at his disposal to present a clear picture of the course of
events, namely that the exiles returned at the earliest possible
moment, that they were eager to revive the cult and rebuild
the Temple immediately upon their return and were only
prevented from doing so by outside interference, and that
national restoration was the definite policy of the Persian
kings. We should then perhaps think of these chapters as an
originally independent work, written shortly before the time
of Nehemiah, as a continuation of the Chronistic work but
also probably as a corrective to the Davidic expectations
which appear to lie behind Haggai and Zechariah and which,
as has been seen, may well have been shared by the Chronicler
himself.[173]

[173] It is not possible here to discuss the later development of the Ezra tradition,
especially the question of 1 Esdras. The approach sketched above might suggest that
it is in an independent work, consisting of a different selection of the available
traditions from that in Ezra–Nehemiah, cf. Rudolph, *Esra und Nehemia samt 3 Esra*,
1949, p. xiv, although this is far from certain, cf. Mowinckel, *Studien zu dem Buche
Ezra–Nehemia* i, 7–28. For a recent review of the problems, cf. K. F. Pohlmann,
*Studien zum dritten Esra. Ein Beitrag zur Frage nach dem ursprünglichen Schluss des
chronistischen Geschichtswerkes*, 1970.

VI

PROPHECY AND THE PROPHETIC LITERATURE

W. MCKANE

CONSIDERATIONS of 'tradition and interpretation' exert their influence in many directions in the recent study of prophecy and the prophetic literature. One aspect of this is the diminishment of separability between prophecy, on the one hand, and prophetic literature, on the other, a manifestation of which is the persuasion that the prophetic message is the key to the understanding of prophecy and the only legitimate avenue of approach open to the investigator.[1] There has been a lessening of interest in questions about the origins of Israelite prophecy and in the direct study of the constituents of the prophetic experience, and a tendency to approach through the forms of the prophetic literature.[2] Hence it is argued that what we are told about Hosea's marriage in chapters 1 and 3 is oriented towards the prophet's message rather than towards biography,[3] that the same is true of the so-called Baruch biography (Jer. 19:1–20:6; 26–9; 36–45; 51:59–64),[4] and that descriptions of the visionary experiences of Ezekiel, together with the unusual physical and psychical effects to which he is subject (3:25 f.; 24:27; 33:22), are set in the framework of his proclamation and do not exist in their own right as accounts of his prophetic experiences. The stylized or generalized form in which the experiences of Ezekiel are reported makes the transition from kerygma to

---

[1] C. Westermann, *Basic Forms of Prophetic Speech*, London, 1967, pp. 63, 86 (ETr of *Grundformen prophetischer Rede*, BEvTh xxxi, 2nd edn., 1964).

[2] R. E. Clements, *Prophecy and Covenant*, SBT xi, 1955, pp. 25, 128.

[3] Cf. H. H. Rowley, 'The Marriage of Hosea', *Men of God*, London, 1963, pp. 66–97.

[4] Clements, *Prophecy and Tradition*, Oxford, 1975, pp. 31–3; G. Wanke, *Untersuchungen zur sogenannten Baruchschrift*, BZAW cxxii, 1971.

biography difficult to achieve.[5] The coolness towards the direct investigation of prophetic experience is not so much motivated by antipathy to these areas of study as it is by doubts whether the prophetic literature can answer the questions which are raised by these investigations, and whether consequently it is an area where agnosticism may have to prevail.

Another factor is the departure from the older view of the prophet as a specially gifted person of marked individuality who stands apart from public expressions of religion and its institutions, and there is a relation between the preoccupation with the cultic dimension of prophecy and the interest in traditional and public forms of religious expression which prophets are said to use. Moreover, the degree of dependence on these forms of religious expression with a cultic function which is posited reduces the impression of the privacy of prophetic experience which had made its mark on earlier scholarship, and if it does not reduce the degree of originality which can be attributed to prophetic preaching, it at least establishes a new kind of originality.

A host of questions are raised by this approach and fine critical decisions have to be made all along the line. Within the areas of form criticism and history of tradition there is much scope for nicety of appreciation when the nature of a prophet's dependence on forms and complexes of tradition is under consideration. The assumption that there is an indissolubility of form and setting, on which the transition from form-critical observations to conclusions about the cultic functions of prophets sometimes rests, appears particularly fragile.[6] The emphasis on the cultic anchorage of prophecy need not, however, necessarily set out from form-critical assumptions. It may rather be the consequence of a reconstruction of the history of Israelite prophecy and an appreciation of its nature on the basis of the biblical sources,[7] or it may, as in Engnell,[8] coexist with a scepticism about form-critical

---

[5] W. Zimmerli, *Ezechiel* BKAT XIII/1, Neukirchen, 1969, pp. 27 f., 30, 43 f., 572 f.; cf. H. Wildberger, *Jesaja* BKAT X./1, 1968, p. 238.

[6] G. Fohrer, 'Bemerkungen zum neueren Verständnis der Propheten', *Studien zur alttestamentlichen Prophetie (1949–1965)*, BZAW xcix, 1967, pp. 20 ff.

[7] A. R. Johnson, *The Cultic Prophet in Ancient Israel*, Cardiff, 2nd edn., 1962.

[8] I. Engnell, 'Profetia och Tradition', *SEÅ* xii (1947), 120.

procedures and be part of a comprehensive phenomenology of Old Testament religion dominated by the Jerusalem cult and sacral kingship.

These developments have not won unanimous approval and they have provoked significant reactions. They have, however, in their more moderate manifestations, commanded an impressive measure of support in the more recent study of prophecy and the prophetic literature. The older form of genetic inquiry in which a nomadic (*kāhin*) component and a Canaanite (*nābî*) component were thought to enter into the constitution of Israelite prophecy is not greatly in evidence,[9] but references to the activities of prophets at Mari have provided a new source of comparison and have revealed that prophets there, envisaged as 'messengers' of a god, intervened in important political and military issues.[10] The older antithesis between the canonical prophets and their predecessors in terms of enthusiasm and rationality[11] or spirit and word[12] has given place to a new antithesis based on a conviction that the canonical prophets are distinctive in view of their attachment to normative Jerusalem Yahwism.[13] The earlier antithesis had necessarily introduced a pejorative evaluation of the kind of ecstasy which is corporate, is induced by exercises, and is evidenced in the Northern Kingdom from the times of Samuel and Saul and in the stories of Elijah and Elisha. There are those, on the other hand, who would posit an important degree of continuity between guilds of prophets and the canonical prophets and who would regard these manifestations in the Northern Kingdom as affording significant support for their view that Israelite prophecy is a corporate and public phenomenon and that this holds also for those pre-exilic prophets who have left behind literature

[9] See, however, Fohrer, 'Die Propheten des alten Testaments im Blickfeld neuer Forschung', op. cit., p. 1.

[10] Westermann, 'Die Mari-Briefe und die Prophetie in Israel', *Forschung am alten Testament*, Munich, 1964, pp. 171–8.

[11] A. Jepsen, *Nabi. Soziologische Studien zur alttestamentlichen Literatur und Religionsgeschichte*, Munich, 1934, pp. 26 f.

[12] S. Mowinckel, 'The Spirit and the Word in the Pre-exilic reforming Prophets', *JBL* liii (1934), 199–227.

[13] Engnell, 'Prophets and Prophetism in the Old Testament', *Critical Essays on the Old Testament*, London, 1970, pp. 171 ff.; E. Nielsen, *Oral Tradition*, SBT xi, 1954, pp. 53 f.

bearing their names, some of whom were centred in Jerusalem (Isaiah, Jeremiah, Ezekiel), and one of whom (Jeremiah) certainly had relations with temple prophets.

A new kind of genetic interest focused on the prophetic office and associated with form criticism envisages the canonical prophet as discharging functions within the cult which are precisely regulated by a pre-existing covenant structure and are concerned with the exposition or 'actualizing' of divine law. The prophet is seen as an intermediary[14] between the worshipping community and Yahweh with well-defined functions which he exercises within the presuppositions of covenant theology and sacral law. Hence he is concerned with blessing and cursing[15] (Amos 1:3–2:16; 4:6–11; 9:13–15), with accusation and indictment[16] (Amos 5:12; Isa. 1:17, 23, 26; 5:23; 10:1 f.; Mic. 3:1, 9), with monitoring the behaviour of individuals by an 'actualization' of the Code of Holiness[17] (Lev. 17–26); he is an intercessor in a more exact sense who utters laments on behalf of the community.[18] He may be viewed as holding an office which descends in unbroken succession from an amphictyonic context, whether that of law-speaker or minor judge[19] or advocate (Reventlow) or watcher (Reventlow). The objectives of such an approach may be more limited than indicated above and may concentrate on the elucidation of the prophetic message. The argument then is that the element of 'lawsuit' in the prophetic preaching (Isa. 1:2 f., 10–20; Mic. 6:1–5) is to be related to an Israelite renewal of the covenant ceremony, the ultimate model of which is the vassal treaty.[20]

The distribution of emphasis in the recent study of prophecy as outlined above is somewhat contradicted by the lengthy discussion of the nature of prophetic experience in

[14] H. G. Reventlow, 'Prophetenamt und Mittleramt', *ZThK* lviii (1961), 269–84.

[15] A. Bentzen, 'The Ritual Background of Amos i 2–ii 16', *OTS* viii (1950), 85–99.

[16] E. Würthwein, 'Der Ursprung der prophetischen Gerichtsrede', *ZThK* xlix (1952), 1–15.

[17] H. G. Reventlow, *Wächter über Israel. Ezechiel und seine Tradition*, BZAW lxxxii, 1962.

[18] H. G. Reventlow, *Liturgie und prophetisches Ich bei Jeremia*, Gütersloh, 1963.

[19] H. J. Kraus, *Die prophetische Verkündigung des Rechts in Israel*, ThS li, 1957.

[20] G. E. Wright, 'The Law-Suit of God: A Form-Critical Study of Deuteronomy 32', *Israel's Prophetic Heritage (Muilenburg Festschrift)* ed. B. W. Anderson and W. Harrelson, New York and London, 1962, pp. 26–67.

Lindblom, where an attempt is made to set the Israelite prophet in the context of a wide-ranging treatment of mysticism.[21] The prophet speaks for Yahweh, but he has not obliterated the distinction between himself and Yahweh. The form of his message indicates an abnormal concentration of consciousness, an intensity of apperception or an absorption, which may be described as a quiet ecstasy. This, however, must be assessed as an attempt by Lindblom to delineate the psychological state of the prophet at the moment when he speaks for Yahweh rather than as a contribution to a theological evaluation of his utterance, since he does not suppose that the content of the utterance derives from the unusual psychological state which he describes. When he characterizes the Old Testament prophet as a kind of mystic, he is seeking to explain the form rather than the content of the message: the circumstance that the prophet identifies his own utterance with Yahweh's utterance is indicative of a special psychological condition. Hence only the psychological ground of the form of the message and not its theological validity is covered by this concept of ecstasy.

Lindblom's concern to carry the study of prophecy beyond the form-critical or exegetical limits which have been largely accepted is laudable. The contention that the study of prophecy can be most fruitfully conducted when it is organized as a study of the forms of the prophetic literature demands respect,[22] but the assertion that if the prophets are 'messengers' they cannot be ecstatics[23] is an unacceptable form-critical positivism or perhaps even a confusion of modes of literary description with psychological or theological categories. It is important to remember that 'message' is a model or analogy and that a message from God is different from any other kind of message. If it is established that a prophetic utterance has the form of word of God, that is, Yahweh is represented as speaking, this is a valid form-critical observation, but it is a mistake to suppose that in itself it is a contribution to the psychology or theology of prophecy. It is not a theological appraisal of 'word of God'; it does not

[21] J. Lindblom, *Prophecy in Ancient Israel*, Oxford, 1962, pp. 1–219.
[22] Clements, *Prophecy and Tradition*, pp. 24 ff.
[23] Westermann, *Basic Forms*, p. 63.

elucidate the truth of a prophetic utterance or the character of the prophet's inspiration.

It may be that these are insoluble questions and that agnosticism is the best stance in the face of them. At any rate the reaction of Fohrer[24] to the claim that prophecy can only be investigated exegetically by attending to the forms of the prophetic message is resolutely negative. He holds the contrary proposition, namely, that the mysterious essence of the prophetic awareness does not come to expression in public utterance; in one way or another words will always fail to disclose the secret, for they are imperfect media which cannot communicate the quintessence of the prophetic endowment. Here we find a link with the older view of the privacy and uniqueness of the prophetic experience, but as a dissuasive against the attempt to contain prophecy in public literary forms and functions this would seem to be something of a counsel of desperation. Its practical implications are that the essential prophet is hidden in a great silence which cannot be penetrated. The divorce of inner, ineffable experience from public, linguistic expression is very difficult to entertain. Does such experience have a substantial, independent existence apart from its verbalization? Is there much point in appealing to the existence of experience beyond its public expression?

The form-critical emphasis in the study of prophecy is related to the conviction that the only legitimate approach is an exegetical one. The deepest reason for Fohrer's antipathy to this method arises from his concept of *Botschaft* which contradicts the idea that a prophet can only be known through his message. Fohrer's use of *Botschaft* establishes a dichotomy between the prophetic experience, with which is associated ineffable, revelatory words, and the clothing of these words in literary forms. Apart from this, however, the presupposition that prophets make use of pre-existing forms with a high degree of verbal fixity is unacceptable to him.[25] There is, perhaps, something ultimately unsatisfactory in the reduction of prophetic speech to stereotypes and in the denial that it has

---

[24] Fohrer, 'Die Propheten des alten Testaments im Blickfeld neuer Forschung', op. cit., pp. 8 f.; 'Bemerkungen zum neueren Verständnis der Propheten', ibid., pp. 27 f.

[25] 'Bemerkungen' ibid., pp. 20 ff.

anything of the momentous character of a new creation. Even if it is necessarily an amalgam of traditional linguistic resources, it has elements of freeness and eclecticism to which a thoroughgoing form criticism does not do justice.

Fohrer is particularly impressed with this point over against those who concentrate on the cult as the source of prophetic forms, since the areas of life from which a prophet borrows are envisaged by him in much wider terms and this inhibits any ready association of form and setting in determining the prophet's functions. Thus he argues that the use of cultic forms does not establish that a prophet is discharging cultic functions any more than his use of the messenger form shows that he was an official at a royal court or his use of forensic forms shows that he was a jurist. This involves the denial that the messenger model[26] or the lawsuit model is cultic, but the main direction of the argument is towards a *reductio ad absurdum*: the prophet cannot have been cultic official, a royal messenger, jurist, wise man, and so on.

Against the contention that prophetic speech is not formed on the model of pre-existing stereotypes there is the reply of Westermann that forms are a community possession which furnish the prophet with a necessary *point d'appui* for the communication of his message.[27] The question, however, is whether a prophet like Deutero-Isaiah whose destiny is to proclaim words of hope and salvation to his people at a time when their fate seems to hang in the balance will form his words with such a deliberate and self-conscious dependence on prototypes as Westermann represents. To illustrate this we may take two of these alleged models, the individual lament and the communal lament. These are linked by Westermann with the promise of salvation and the proclamation of salvation respectively, as they appear in Deutero-Isaiah. In respect of the individual lament, Westermann is building on the work of Begrich[28] and the passage which is

[26] Ibid., p. 20.

[27] Westermann, 'Sprache und Struktur der Prophetie Deutero-jesajas', *Forschung am Alten Testament*, pp. 109 f.

[28] J. Begrich, 'Das priesterliche Heilsorakel', *ZAW* lii (1934), 81–92. *GSAT*, 1964, pp. 217–31.

thought to be most significant for establishing a connection between lament or plea and the reassuring oracle 'Do not be afraid' is Lam. 3:57. Hence oracles of salvation in Deutero-Isaiah which begin with the words 'Do not be afraid' (41:8–13, 14–16; 43:1–4, 5–9; 44:1–5; 51:7–8; 54:4–8) are to be understood as formed on the model of reassuring answers to individual laments, and motifs of such laments are to be found within these promises of salvation as a kind of dark contrast.[29] With regard to the proclamation of salvation this is said to be associated with a motif of the communal lament (drought—the poor seeking water and finding none) in 41:17–20, while in 49:14–26 elements of communal lament (vv. 14, 21, 24) are detected in the context of proclamation of salvation. Further, it is urged that in 51:9–52:6 proclamation of salvation (51:9, 17; 52:1) is set in the context of communal lament.[30]

It is the schematic and precise character of this account which raises doubts. Does a prophet employ models so deliberately? Is it probable that Deutero-Isaiah would reserve the model of the individual lament for a future promise of salvation and that of the communal lament for an announcement of present salvation with the degree of self-consciousness which the account presupposes? He does not create his words *ex nihilo* and he is familiar with the vocabulary and imagery of the Psalms, but his indebtedness is more subtle and the influences do not operate so near the surface of his consciousness. He has many resources for the expression of his message at his command, but these assist the freedom of his utterance rather than inclining him towards a calculated conformity to models.

We have noted[31] that one of the most influential ways of describing the indebtedness of the prophets to tradition has hinged on 'covenant', envisaged as a cultic ceremony with a literary structure. Clements[32] doubts whether the prophetic preaching is set in so elaborate a framework and sees it rather as the product of more general theological presuppositions,

---

[29] Westermann, op. cit., pp. 117–20.
[30] Ibid., pp. 120–2.
[31] Above, p. 166.
[32] *Prophecy and Tradition*, pp. 8–23, 41–57.

relating to an election doctrine and what this implies for Yahweh's people, together with an *ad hoc* use of a wide range of forms, motifs, and imagery. On the other hand, he conceives the prophetic literature as a second Deuteronomistic corpus which matches the Deuteronomistic history, and he attributes the covenant theology which appears in the prophetic literature to a Deuteronomistic redaction. This redaction has a comprehensive and systematic theological character and its concept of the model prophet appears in Deut. 18:15. It is represented in the prophetic literature by the terminology of covenant (*berît*) in Hos. 8:1 and by the idea without the terminology in Amos 2:4. Other examples of this covenant redaction are the references to Judah in the books of Hosea and Amos (Hos. 1:7; 4:15; 5:5; 6:11; 8:14; 10:11; Amos 2:4), the allusion to the Davidic king in Hos. 3:5, and the hopeful Messianic conclusion of the book of Amos (9:11–15). The last two are examples of Deuteronomistic promise added to original prophecies of doom.[33] The redaction effects a symbiosis of law and prophecy, of the prophetic word and the *tôrâh* which was given at Sinai, and it conceives the prophet as one who calls the people to repentance in relation to the demands of this *tôrâh* (2 Kgs. 17:13 f.; Jer. 11:1–8).

The significance of this contention is that it displays as redaction-history features in the prophetic literature which have been thought to throw light on the roots of prophecy and the sources of the prophetic message. The prophets, according to this view, contribute to the finished Deuteronomic covenant theology, but their preaching does not presuppose an extant covenant theology. If we are not to look for a precise covenant theology and its associated literary structures (as evidenced in the book of Deuteronomy) before the seventh century B.C., we can no longer say that cultic renewals of the covenant provide a model for the eighth century prophets, and the quest after extra-Israelite covenant models in vassal treaties loses something of its point. In any case the opinion may be ventured on the matter of Assyrian

---

[33] Cf. U. Kellermann, 'Der Amosschluss als Stimme deuteronomistischer Heilshoffnung', *EvTh* xxix (1969), 169–83; I. Willi-Plein, *Vorformen der Schriftexegese innerhalb des Alten Testaments*, BZAW cxxiii, 1971, pp. 60 ff., argues against the presence of Deuteronomistic redaction in the eighth-century prophets.

and Hittite vassal treaties that their significance in the field of Old Testament religion has been over-estimated, although the thesis that these sophisticated political instruments were appropriated as theological models deserves more serious consideration when it is worked out in the context of the late monarchy in connection with the developed concept of covenant evidenced in Deuteronomy.[34]

The reservations which have been expressed about Westermann's use of form criticism should not be understood as a demonstration that prophetic preaching never involves a deliberate use of cultic forms or traditional motifs. An illustration of this is provided by three passages in Jeremiah which can be interpreted as a use of cultic forms with a calculated reversal of the concluding oracle of reassurance. Thus Jer. 12:1–5 can be related to the individual lament and 14:1–10, 14:17–15:2 to the communal lament, and in each case the concluding oracle portends the reverse of šālôm (12:5; 14:10; 15:1–2). Again there is much to be said for the argument that the use made by Isaiah (2:12–17) and Amos (5:18–20) of the 'Day of Yahweh' motif involves a deliberate reversal of what was both joyful cultic experience and future hope.[35] There is also Mowinckel's view[36] that Amos 1:3–2:16 is a complex unity created out of elements which were originally independent of each other: the oracles against foreign nations are combined with words of indictment and threat against Israel (the words against Judah are formally homogeneous with the oracles against the foreign nations, whether or not they are original). Related to this view of Amos 1:3–2:16 is the supposition of Würthwein[37] that 2:6 marks the transition of Amos from salvation prophecy to doom prophecy. Other examples of traditional motifs which are reversed are noted by Fohrer:[38] Rock and Stone referring to Yahweh on which men will stumble and fall (Isa. 8:14); 'He who dwells in Zion' as a threat that Jerusalem will fall (Is.

[34] Cf. D. J. McCarthy, *Old Testament Covenant: A Survey of Current Opinions*, Oxford, 1972.

[35] Clements, *Prophecy and Covenant*, pp. 107, 109; cf. Mowinckel, *PIW* i, 189–91; ii. 226.

[36] S. Mowinckel, *Prophecy and Tradition*, ANVAO II, 1946, 3, 1947, pp. 56 f.

[37] E. Würthwein, 'Amos-Studien', *ZAW* lxii (1949/50), 10–52.

[38] G. Fohrer, 'Prophetie und Geschichte', op. cit., pp. 285 f.

8:18); the reply which is given to 'How long?' in Isa. 6:11–13.
Of these passages Jer. 14:1–10 and 14:17–15:2 are especially
notable, since they furnish a valuable indication that one
ought not to rebound too violently from the contention of
Reventlow and others that the canonical prophet *qua* cult
prophet is an intermediary. If it is a mistake to contain the
canonical prophet within the categories of cult prophecy, a
too severe disengagement of him from the cult may also
produce distortion. Mowinckel[39] has argued from the Psalms
that the cult prophet is an intercessor, and a verse like Jer.
15:1 shows that it was a fundamental deprivation for Jeremiah
to be denied the exercise of this office. The interdict on
intercession and the conflict with Hananiah (chapter 28)
show at once the extent to which Jeremiah was a cultic
prophet and the great gulf which had been placed between
him and cultic prophets by his prophetic destiny. A reasonable
interpretation of this is that a prophet believed that he was
endowed to win *šālôm* for his people from Yahweh and that
Hananiah exercised his office within this framework; but the
utterance of *šālôm* was denied to Jeremiah and he was set
apart for a more mysterious and lonely vocation.

This contrast of *šālôm* and doom can be related to a
widespread phenomenon in the prophetic literature, the
oracles against foreign nations (Amos 1:3–2:3; Isa. 13–23; Jer.
46–51; Ezek. 25–32; Nahum; Joel 4; Obadiah; Zeph. 3:8–20),
in so far as these can be interpreted as indirect assurances of
šālôm to Israel.[40] Thus the Amos passage has been elucidated
as an execration of enemies designed to guarantee victory for
Israel.[41] Mowinckel[42] has ventured the opinion that the pre-
exilic prophets were, for the most part, prophets of doom and
that when we find promises of *šālôm* in this literature we have
to reckon with a subsequent development of the original units
and with influence from the ideology of a Jerusalem Enthronement Festival. Mowinckel's treatment of Isa. 29:1–8

---

[39] Mowinckel, *Psalmenstudien III: Kultprophetie und prophetische Psalmen*,
SNVAO II, 1922, 1, 1923.
[40] Cf. S. Erlandsson, *The Burden of Babylon: A Study of Isaiah 13:2–14:23*, Lund,
1970, pp. 65 f.
[41] Above, p. 166, n. 15; Würthwein in *ZThK* xlix (1952), 11–16.
[42] *Prophecy and Tradition*, pp. 74 ff.

is particularly interesting, because the elements which he separates from the original unit are the promise contained in v. 8 and the threats against enemies in vv. 5a and 7. Further evidence that a guarantee of safety by Yahweh to Jerusalem in the face of the threats of the assembled nations was part of a Zion and Davidic ideology can be gathered from certain psalms (2:9–11; 46:8–10; 48:4–8; 76:1–6) and other psalms have been thought to point to the king's role as a leader in war[43] (20:6–8; 21:8–13). In the account of the defeat of the nations in Zeph. 3:8–20 there is a mingling of motifs (worship of Yahweh and defeat by Yahweh) with the emphasis on defeat, along with a marked Zion orientation, all of which is perhaps attributable to a cultic, ideological matrix. The same is true of Joel 4:1–3, 9–21, and a comparison of this with Isa. 2:1–4 (Mic. 4:1–4), especially Joel 4:10 with Isa. 2:4 (Mic. 4:3), suggests that the ideological kernel of the Isaiah/Micah passage may be defeat and submission. This has been developed in the direction of the homage offered by the nations to Yahweh enthroned on Zion and their enlightenment through his *tôrâh*, and has been wrested back in the Joel passage towards the motif of war against the assembled nations and their defeat by Yahweh who roars from Zion and is a refuge for his people (4:16).

There are other separate literary-critical considerations which would tend to separate the oracles against foreign nations from the prophets under whose names they appear. Thus Mowinckel[44] has described the entry at Jer. 45:1 as Baruch's signature which indicates that the book up to this point has been his work and that the conclusion has been reached. Hence he argues that the foreign oracles in chapters 46–51 constitute a separate collection which, for the most part, is not attributable to Jeremiah. With regard to Ezekiel, Zimmerli[45] maintains that the oracles against foreign nations interrupt an original connection between 24:27 and 33:21 ff.

The oracles against foreign nations have important con-

---

[43] The attempt to connect oracles against foreign nations with the procedures of 'Holy War' has been made by R. Bach, *Die Aufforderungen zur Flucht und zum Kampf im alttestamentlichen Prophetenspruch*, WMANT ix, 1962.

[44] Op. cit., p. 61.

[45] *Ezechiel* i, 111.

nections with *šalôm* prophecy, the ideological constitution of which has been sketched above, but too narrow an explanation of their entire range should be avoided, since other prophetic concerns are expressed through them. In Amos 1:3–2:3 there is a strong sense of moral outrage at the contempt which is being shown for Yahweh's order, which is not obviously associated with political animus or military threat. These oracles may also have to be related to the negative attitude adopted by the pre-exilic prophets to foreign alliances and to the whole complex of power politics and its corresponding ethos (Isa. 30:1–5; 31:1–3; cf. Jer. 46; Ezek. 29–32). They condemn the crimes which are committed as a consequence of consuming political and military ambitions and expend their satire and invective on foreign countries and their potentates whose *hubris* is an intolerable affront to Yahweh's order (Isa. 14:12 ff.; 16:6; 23:6–12; Jer. 48:28–33; Ezek. 26–8; 31:1 ff.; 32:1–16).

This sets the stage for a discussion of the relations between the prophets and political wisdom in terms of conflict,[46] whereas other scholars have sought rather to establish the dependence of prophets on forms of the wisdom literature. The degree of demonstration which is possible does not justify the conclusion that any of the prophets had special relations with wisdom or with circles of wise men.[47] Old Testament proverbial wisdom as it appears in the book of Proverbs has a broad community base rather than a special professional direction, and proverbial language should, for the most part, be regarded as a general possession of society rather than the trademark of a special class. It is not surprising that the prophets should have valued the concreteness and pithiness of the proverbial elements in the language which they spoke.

Among the considerations which Wolff[48] adduces to show that there is a special relation between Amos and wisdom, the firmest formal indication is the numerical saying (Amos 1:3–2:16). The function of the numerical saying is not altogether

[46] I have discussed this in *Prophets and Wise Men*, SBT xliv, 1965, pp. 65–93.

[47] As is argued for Isaiah by J. W. Whedbee, *Isaiah and Wisdom*, Nashville and New York, 1971.

[48] H. W. Wolff, *Amos' geistige Heimat*, WMANT xviii, 1964.

clear, but it is used in Proverbs and we know that it existed as
a convention of ancient Canaanite poetry. It would appear to
have had a wider distribution than wisdom literature and not
to have been confined to a didactic function.[49]

Nearer the middle ground of criticism it seems doubtful to
me whether progress can be made with the general problem
of the relation of the canonical prophets to the cult, if it is
discussed simply in terms of the texts around which the battle
has hitherto raged (Amos 5:21–27; Hos. 6:6; Mic. 6:6–8; Isa.
1:11–17; Jer. 7:22–8). The final answer depends on whether
these prophets knew themselves to be presiding over the
dissolution of existing political and ecclesiastical institutions
or whether rather they were intent on restoring the fabric of
Yahweh's community. In other words we may ask whether
the prophets are principally to be envisaged as preachers of
repentance (Buber and Fohrer) or whether their preaching is
better described as eschatological (von Rad). A serious source
of confusion is the tendency to equate eschatological proclamation with promise of restoration and reconstruction, and
so it is urged that there are more evidences of eschatology in
the exilic and post-exilic prophets than in their pre-exilic
counterparts.[50]

But a consideration of the propriety of using the word
'eschatological' in relation to the pre-exilic prophets should
not only be directed towards the constructive aspects of their
message, which may or may not be original to them,[51] but
also towards the elements of doom in their proclamation.
Whether or not they have an eschatology depends also on the
extent to which they were preachers of doom. Clements[52] has

[49] See especially W. M. W. Roth, *Numerical Sayings in the Old Testament*, SVT
xiii, 1965; cf. W. McKane, *Proverbs: A New Approach*, London, 1970, pp. 654–6.

[50] Clements, *Prophecy and Covenant*, pp. 105 ff.; G. Fohrer, 'Bermerkungen', op.
cit., p. 28.

[51] Cf. Isa. 7:14 ff.; 9:1–7; 11:1–10; Mic. 5:1–5; Hos. 3:4 f.; Amos. 9:11 ff.; Jer. 23:5
f.; 31:31–40; Ezek. 34:23 f.; 37. For Amos and Hosea, see above p. 171. Mowinckel,
Prophecy and Tradition, pp. 78 f., is inclined to conclude that Amos was entirely a
prophet of doom. Fohrer, op. cit., p. 26, supposes that the note of salvation is original
in Hosea, Jeremiah, and Ezekiel, but not in Amos, Micah, and Isaiah.

[52] Op. cit., pp. 39 f., 106; J. Jeremias, *Kultprophetie und Gerichtsverkündigung in der
späten Königszeit Israels*, WMANT xxxv, 1970, distinguishes between 'unattached'
prophets and cult prophets like Habakkuk and Nahum. The latter proclaim
judgement against Israelites but not a total judgement against Israel.

concluded that doom is the predominant note of the message of the pre-exilic prophets and von Rad[53] has organized his treatment of the theology of the prophetic traditions on the assumption that the prophets proclaim the coming dissolution of the old salvation-history. Whether this does not attach a too absolute unconditionality to prophetic threats is a matter for discussion, but von Rad is right in this respect, that the dissolution of the old no less than the descrying of the new is part of eschatology and that the degree of absoluteness with which the pre-exilic prophets envisaged disintegration and the termination of existing embodiments of salvation has a bearing on whether or not they were eschatological preachers.

M. Buber's[54] contention is that the prophets are not only preachers of repentance (turning) where they are explicitly so, but that there is always an implicit conditionality attaching to threats of doom which are expressed unconditionally. This offends against the principle that we must respect the forms of the prophetic proclamation in our attempts to discern prophetic attitudes, and it has the disadvantage of resting on an assumption which cannot be tested. Buber does not believe that a prophet who simply proclaims doom is ultimately credible and he holds that such a representation encroaches on the freedom of the individual to repent and the power of God to renew. Any assumption of an institutional rot which is so fundamental that it leaves individuals at the mercy of impending dissolution is a surrender of human freedom to impersonal structures. It represents for Buber an incipient dualism and is connected in his mind with apocalyptic, since he supposes that there is a threat of dualism whenever the wedge of apocalyptic has been inserted into the prophetic message.[55]

The line between prophecy and apocalyptic cannot be

[53] G. von Rad, *Old Testament Theology*, ii. *The Theology of Israel's Prophetic Traditions*, Edinburgh, 1956, ETr of *Theologie des Alten Testaments* ii. *Die Theologie der prophetischen Überlieferungen Israels*, Munich, 1960.

[54] 'The Faith of Judaism', *Israel and The World: Essays in a Time of Crisis*, 2nd edn., New York, 1963, pp. 19–21.

[55] M. Buber, 'The Faith of Judaism', op. cit., pp. 13–27; 'The Power of the Spirit', ibid., pp. 173–82; 'Prophecy, Apocalyptic and Historical Hour', *Pointing the Way*, New York, 1957, pp. 192–207. The view that the prophets are preachers of repentance is also represented by G. Fohrer, 'Bemerkungen', op. cit., pp. 28 ff.; 'Prophetie und Geschichte', ibid., pp. 279 ff.

drawn with quite the sharpness which Buber attempts. That there is a graduation between prophecy and apocalyptic is evident from a consideration of exilic and post-exilic prophecy. The relative detachment of the prophecies of Deutero-Isaiah from national particularities and the widening of horizons, which is seen by Westermann[56] as the attaining of a higher spiritual level of prophecy, has both its positive and negative aspects. When the contrast between the present state of Judah in exile and the glorious future which is portrayed becomes very stark, as in Deutero-Isaiah, a step has already been taken from prophecy to apocalyptic.[57] The path from exile to restoration has taken on supra-historical characteristics and the bridge between the present and the future is not really a historical one. This disengagement from historical particularities and political calculations, which from Westermann's point of view represents a further elevation of prophecy, may from another point of view be seen as a loss of touch with the actualities of the present.

At any rate the intense eschatological expectation of Deutero-Isaiah still lives on in Haggai, Zechariah, and Malachi, and they too, like the prophet of the Exile, focus their hopes on Zion. Hence their concern with a right cult is not merely ritual punctiliousness, but is related to their conviction that the eschatological glory portrayed by Deutero-Isaiah will radiate from Zion and that it will not eventuate until the Temple has been purged of all impurity (Hag. 1:7 ff.; Zech. 2:14–16; 8:3; Mal. 1:6 ff.; 2:1 ff.; 3:1 ff.). There is in these prophets, from Ezekiel on, impressive evidence of concentration of interest in the Jerusalem Temple which accords at least a measure of validity to what has been said about the connections between the canonical prophets and the Jerusalem cult.[58] It has been noted that in Isa. 55:1–5 the promise to David has been extended to all the survivors of Israel and that this represents a 'democratizing' of the Davidic hope,[59] but hopes of restoration which focus on the Davidic

---

[56] 'Sprache und Struktur der Prophetie Deutero-jesajas', op. cit., pp. 169 f.; *Isaiah 40–66*, London, 1969, p. 16.

[57] Cf. Fohrer, 'Prophetie und Geschichte', op. cit., pp. 282 f.

[58] Above p. 165, n. 13.

[59] O. Eissfeldt, 'The Promises of Grace to David in Isaiah 55:1–5', *Israel's Prophetic Heritage*, 196 ff.

king are still influential in Haggai and Zechariah (Hag. 1:12 ff.; 2:23; Zech. 3 ff.; 6:9–15), although a priestly figure exercising leadership is set alongside Zerubbabel, the Davidic Messiah.[60]

With regard to the Servant passages in Deutero-Isaiah (42:1–9; 49:1–13; 50:4–9; 52:13–53:12), a basic question involving 'tradition and interpretation' is whether we are to relate the Servant to Davidic theology (Engnell)[61] or whether we are to place him in a prophetic succession, although these are not necessarily exclusive alternatives, since it can be argued (Westermann[62]) that the characteristics of the Servant differ from Song to Song and that he is portrayed now as king, now as prophet. In fact, however, the prophetic, mediatorial role of the Servant is the one on which Westermann lays greatest emphasis, and Bentzen, whose investigation is differently oriented, reaches the conclusion that the prophetic features of the Servant are more prominent than the elements of a royal ideology.[63] Buber's tendency is also to locate the Servant in a prophetic succession, although he also envisages him as a kind of anti-type of the political Messiah of the pre-exilic prophecy, where the role of the Davidic king is related to the effective discharge of kingship.[64] According to Engnell, the Servant's mission corresponds to a scheme of suffering, death, and resurrection, the source of which is a Jerusalem New Year Festival, where the Davidic king as the incarnation of Yahweh participated in a ritual drama possessing such a pattern. It is arguable that the Servant is in important respects a prophetic figure and that his appearance represents a further development of the thought already present in the call narratives of Isaiah, Jeremiah, and Ezekiel (Isa. 6; Jer. 1; Ezek. 1 ff.), namely, that the prophetic vocation is sorrowful and demanding and that the prophet has to endure in the face of opposition and rejection. We may see in Deutero-Isaiah the affirmation that

---

[60] Cf. P. R. Ackroyd, *Exile and Restoration*, London, 1968, pp. 103–217.

[61] Engnell, 'The Ebed Yahweh Songs and the Suffering Messiah in "Deutero-Isaiah"', *BJRL* xxxi (1948), 54–93.

[62] *Isaiah 40–66*, pp. 20 f.

[63] A. Bentzen, *King and Messiah*, 2nd edn., Oxford, 1970, pp. 48–80.

[64] M. Buber, *The Prophetic Faith*, New York, 1949, pp. 217–35; *Two Types of Faith*, London, 1951, pp. 105 ff.

such prophetic suffering is not merely sublime or tragic, but that there is contained in it a source of healing for the prophet's community.

When 'tradition and interpretation' are related to prophecy the Janus-like aspect of tradition should not be overlooked. Tradition looks in two directions, backwards to the sources of prophetic utterance and forwards to the final shape of the prophetic books. The first of these orientations has occupied us up till now; the inquiry has been about the prophet's vocabulary and imagery, the extent to which he borrows traditional forms, and whether or not he approximates to antecedent cultic functions or offices. The second area of study is connected with the transmission of prophetic words and the accretions which they may acquire in the course of transmission. This involves a consideration of the role of oral tradition and of the contributions which may be attributable to traditionists or circles of prophetic disciples. It also raises the issue of redaction in a broader sense, where the subsequent subsuming of prophetic literature under a comprehensive, theological scheme is invoked in order to account for the final shape of the prophetic books.[65]

The protest[66] against the tendency of earlier literary criticism to make a sharp distinction between primary and secondary material in the prophetic books is justifiable in so far as it was once thought that when material had been classified as secondary a less serious exegetical duty remained in respect of it, and that the main energies of the exegete could be concentrated on what were believed to be the *ipsissima verba* of the prophets. The concern and application of the critic should be maintained over the whole field, beginning with the sources and presuppositions of prophetic speech and ending with a consideration of the final shape of the prophetic books.

Associated with the emphasis on oral tradition is a view of the transmission of the prophet's words which involves transformation and supplementation. This may take the form of the reapplication of words to new situations and is

---

[65] Above, pp. 171 ff.
[66] Nielsen, *Oral Tradition*, pp. 15 f.; Engnell, *Critical Essays*, pp. 168 f.

sometimes referred to as 'actualization'.[67] Conclusions which
are drawn from a consideration of the oral transmission of
prophetic books accord well with what we can reasonably
assume to have been the circumstances of prophetic communication. This would seem to have consisted of messages
directed with great intensity of conviction towards burning
issues and to have been fulfilled in oral delivery. In agreement
with this is the impression that the prophetic books are, in
large part, built up into their existing structures from what
are essentially short units of speech, and that they do not
possess a high degree of coherence.[68] They are not the kind
of literary works which follow from the master plan of a
single creative mind.

We have, however, to take into account the concept of
'liturgy' which is used both by Mowinckel[69] and Engnell[70]
and which owes something to Gunkel. It is clear that what
both these scholars have in mind in the first instance is a
literary entity which is more complex and coherent and
which has more evidence of artistic finish than the prophetic
unit of speech. For these two kinds of prophetic literature
Engnell uses the terms *dīwān* and liturgy: *dīwān* is indicative
of the aggregation of units into complexes by oral processes,
although it refers also to content. These pieces consist
characteristically of words and sayings of a prophet and
traditions concerning his life and actions, and examples of
dīwān given by Engnell are Hosea, Amos, Micah, and proto-
Isaiah. On the other hand there is a kind of prophetic
literature which contains so much evidence of artistic shape
that it should be regarded as a written production from the
outset.[71] Such pieces are the work of individual masters and
have affiliations with the style and conventions of Canaanite
cult poetry.

The transition from a literary concept of liturgy to cultic
considerations takes place in so far as it is thought that the

[67] Cf. C. Stuhlmueller, 'The Influence of Oral Tradition upon Exegesis and the
Senses of Scripture', *CBQ* xx (1958), 299–326, especially the analysis of Isa. 7–12, pp.
316 f.
[68] *Prophecy and Tradition*, pp. 40 f., 55 f.
[69] Ibid., pp. 56 ff.
[70] *Critical Essays*, pp. 166 ff.; *SEÅ* xii (1947), 105 ff.
[71] Ibid., pp. 113 f.

artistic shape of the liturgy is determined by a pattern of ritual,[72] and then two alternative conclusions are possible. Either the liturgy is the 'myth' of a pattern of rites, in which case we have cult prophecy and a cultic prophet; or the liturgy is formed on the model of such a myth, and then the literary structure is determined by a pattern of rites and is described as an imitation of cult prophecy. According to Engnell,[73] Joel and Habakkuk are actual cult poetry, Nahum is probably an imitation,[74] and Deutero-Isaiah certainly an imitation. Mowinckel[75] would seem to envisage only imitations: he says that in Isa. 33 the world of ideas associated with the Enthronement Festival has been converted into prophecy, and although he affirms that Habakkuk derives its shape from the connected parts of a cultic festival of lamentation and prayer, he supposes that this arrangement is secondary.

The difference between Mowinckel and Engnell can be further explored by having regard to what is implied by Mowinckel's statement that a prophetic unit of speech is essentially simple and has a single 'point'.[76] The effect of this is that he lays down stringent conditions for the acceptance of original complex unities and argues that such connections as are postulated between parts of an assumed original whole must be not only possible but necessary. He is resistant to the acceptance of liturgies where they offend against his form-critical dictum that the prophetic unit of speech has a single point. Thus if the point is threat and if threat is followed by promise, he appraises this not as an original complex of threat and promise, but as a unit of proclamation with a single point (threat) to which promise has been secondarily added.[77] This

---

[72] Cf. S. Mowinckel, op. cit., pp. 56 f. He observes that the source of the structure of a liturgy would normally be the pattern of 'a many-sided cultic situation'. He does, however, envisage liturgies which are not formed on cultic models (see above, p. 172 on Amos 1:3–2:16).

[73] *Critical Essays*, p. 167.

[74] This is also the view of H. Schulz, *Das Buch Nahum*, BZAW cxxix, 1973, pp. 133 f.

[75] Op. cit., pp. 56 f.   [76] Ibid., pp. 55 f.

[77] Ibid., pp. 74 f., 83, 86 f. Examples given by Mowinckel include the following: Hos. 2:4–25, vv. 16–25 are promise, vv. 20–5 prose; Isa. 28:1–6, vv. 5–6 are promise; Isa. 31:1–9, vv. 4–9 are promise; Isa. 32:9–20, vv. 9–14, 19 are threat and vv. 15, 18 and 20 are promise. The connection between v. 14 and v. 19 is broken by the insertion of

amounts to a distinction between primary and secondary which is unacceptable to Engnell who holds that the judgement-salvation pattern is original to the pre-exilic prophets and is inherited by them from the cult.[78] The concept of liturgy influences Mowinckel here in so far as he thinks that the element of promise in the prophetic literature, both as an addition to individual units and as a more far-reaching principle of structure (the threat–promise sequence in the ordering of oracles), is modelled on the threat–promise pattern of the Enthronement Festival (Pss. 46; 48).[79]

The clearest distinction between Mowinckel and Engnell in relation to 'liturgy' is seen in the differing criticisms which they offer of Deutero-Isaiah. Mowinckel's approach is essentially a form-critical one and he divides the book into fifty units,[80] acknowledging that the pattern of the Enthronement Festival exercises a structural influence. He supposes that both here and in Joel[81] 'the total picture of the coming of Yahweh and salvation of Israel that is hovering in the mind of the prophet in its broad outline has been taken from the Enthronement Festival.'[82] He denies, however, that Deutero-Isaiah is a liturgy in the more stringent sense which Engnell intends, namely, that the book has a massive unity of structure which is supplied by the myth and ritual pattern of the Enthronement Festival.[83]

If we take 'liturgy' in its primary literary sense, we may say that the same issues are raised by Muilenburg's view of Deutero-Isaiah as the product of a unitary literary design.[84] Westermann's criticism[85] of Muilenburg concentrates on two points, that literary continuity and consistency are not important considerations in relation to the proclamation of

promise in vv. 15–18. Mowinckel (ibid., p. 56) does, however, identify Isa. 48:1–11 and 55:6–13 as authentic liturgies which display 'an imaginative unity of threat and promise'.

[78] *SEÅ*, xii (1947), 108 f.
[79] Op. cit., pp. 77 f.
[80] Ibid., pp. 59 f.
[81] Ibid., pp. 82 f.
[82] Ibid., p. 104, n. 49.
[83] 'Till frågan om 'Ebed-Jahve-sångerna', *SEÅ* x (1945), 41.
[84] J. Muilenburg, 'The Book of Isaiah, Chapters 40–66', *IB* v. 1956, pp. 381 ff.
[85] 'Sprache und Struktur', *Forschung am Alten Testament*, pp. 106 ff.

the prophetic message and that the 'forms' are a community possession and a necessary bridge of communication. Westermann[86] would seem, however, subsequently to have moved nearer to Muilenburg's position, since he now envisages the prophet himself as being responsible for the over-all arrangement of chapters 40–55 and further ascribes two different kinds of activity to him: he is both a preacher and an author. His preaching is preserved in the short oracles of chapters 40–45, while the longer poems which are characteristic of the remaining chapters (46–55) may have been literary productions from the outset.

There is a certain incompatibility between the assertion that oral tradition is reliable and the insistence that it subjects the material with which it is exercised to a process of continuous organic change.[87] On the one hand, there is a concern to establish that in a culture different from ours and not dominated by written learning the memory is capable of great feats of retentiveness. On the other hand, there is a tendency to say that the effect of the on-going growth of the tradition is to obscure its earlier stages. These assertions do not hang together: if the first is true, there is no reason why the *ipsissima verba* should not be preserved by the processes of oral tradition, but it is the second which is more fundamental to Engnell's concept of oral tradition, and he tends to say that the *ipsissima verba* are irrecoverable,[88] although some tension in his thinking is discernible.[89]

In relation to the material which he describes as *dīwān*, Engnell, with his concept of tradition as a living, creative process within a circle of prophetic disciples,[90] can only locate writing at the point of fixation, where the formative process comes to an end and a final, canonical status is accorded to the

---

[86] *Isaiah 40–66*, p. 28.

[87] This point is noted by A. H. J. Gunneweg, *Mündliche und schriftliche Tradition der vorexilischen Prophetenbücher als Problem der neueren Prophetenforschung*, FRLANT lv, 1959, pp. 69 f.; J. Lindblom, *Prophecy in Ancient Israel*, pp. 220 ff., 235, concentrates on the aspect of reliability and exactness.

[88] *SEÅ* xii (1947), 118 f.

[89] Cf. 'The Traditio-Historical Method in Old Testament Research', *Critical Essays*, p. 8; 'Prophets and Prophetism in the Old Testament', ibid., p. 169.

[90] Engnell, ibid., p. 168; J. Lindblom, op. cit., p. 235.

material.[91] Hence both he and Nielsen[92] are concerned to establish that one cannot draw general conclusions from the special circumstances which led Jeremiah to have written down in a scroll a record of twenty-three years of proclamation (Jer. 36). Mowinckel's argument,[93] in which the evidence from Jeremiah plays an important part, is given a special orientation by Gunneweg[94] who characterizes the concurrent oral and written transmission as popular and official transmission respectively. The setting of the popular, oral transmission is the home and that of the official, written transmission is the cult. Stratification (that is, the recovery of the history of the tradition) is possible in respect of the written transmission, even although it has been subject to transformation, but it is not possible in respect of the oral transmission. It is difficult to believe that prophetic preaching, which in important respects was anti-cultic, would have been recorded by cultic agencies, but Gunneweg does focus attention on a genuine problem. The flaw in Mowinckel's argument, according to Gunneweg,[95] is that if a creative, transforming function is accorded to the oral transmission of prophetic words within a circle of disciples, and if a distinction is made between a pre-canonical formative stage and a post-canonical, static situation,[96] written transmission is appropriate to the latter, but does not seem to have a function in connection with the former.

We have to recognize that any distinction between primary and secondary material such as is made by Lindlom[97] introduces a concept of tradition which is incompatible with what is implied by 'traditionists' or 'circles of disciples' in

---

[91] 'The Traditio-Historical Method' op. cit., p. 6; 'Prophets and Prophetism', ibid., pp. 163 f. The same view is found in H. S. Nyberg, *Studien zum Hoseabuche*, UUÅ (1935:6), 1935, p. 8; also in E. Nielsen, *Oral Tradition*, p. 39.

[92] 'Prophets and Prophetism', p. 164; E. Nielsen, op. cit., pp. 66 f. Lindblom, on the other hand, says: 'What is true of the book of Jeremiah may possibly, *mutatis mutandis*, though not necessarily, have been true of other prophetic books (op. cit., p. 239).

[93] *Prophecy and Tradition*, pp. 60 ff.

[94] Op. cit., pp. 31 f.

[95] Ibid., p. 68.

[96] Mowinckel, 'Oppkomsten av profetlitteraturen', *NTT* xlii (1943), 92 ff.

[97] Op. cit., pp. 236, 239, n. 26.

Engnell's usage,[98] where, for example, Deutero-Isaiah is both a traditionist and a prophet in his own right. The emphasis on the unity of the tradition is such that any qualitative distinction between the contribution of the master and that of his disciples is precluded. Disciples are also prophets and so the tradition is indivisible, and a prophetic book is the record of the on-going life of a prophetic community.

The correct response to this debate is perhaps a refusal to adopt too ideological a stance and a resolve to proceed in a more empirical way. The older literary critics were not mistaken in their view that prophetic literature which is metrically formed constitutes a special category, and it still seems reasonable to entertain higher expectations of the preservation of the *ipsissima verba* in respect of poetry than in respect of prose in the prophetic books.[99] Birkeland's[100] 'smelting-oven' image, which implies the irrecoverability of the *ipsissima verba*, may be apposite to the Deuteronomic prose of Jeremiah, but not to the poetry of that book. One may venture a literary and theological value judgement that there is more evidence of prophetic vitality in the poetry of the book of Jeremiah than in the Deuteronomistic sermons. Not that all the poetry in the book is on the same level, for there is a marked difference in literary power and theological profundity between the poetry of the opening chapters and that of the oracles against foreign nations (chapters 46–51).

At any rate the ideal of recovering the *ipsissima verba* of a master prophet and of understanding his proclamation in relation to the historical situation which conditioned it is guided by a sound theological instinct.[101] That the words of pre-exilic prophets were actualized by men of exilic and post-exilic times is interesting and important and such redaction history is part of the exegesis of the prophetic books.[102] We

[98] Cf. *The Call of Isaiah, An Exegetical and Comparative Study*, UUÅ (1949:4), 1949, pp. 22 f.

[99] The importance of poetry in this connection is noted by Lindblom, op. cit., p. 235; Mowinckel, *Prophecy and Tradition*, p. 21; Gunneweg, op. cit., pp. 72 f.; W. Zimmerli, *Ezechiel* i, pp. 104* ff.

[100] H. Birkeland, *Zum hebräischen Traditionswesen. Die Komposition der prophetischen Bücher*. ANVAO II, 1938, i. 23.

[101] Cf. Mowinckel, op. cit., pp. 53, 84 f., 86, 88.

[102] Cf. E. W. Nicholson, *Preaching to the Exiles. A Study of the Prose Tradition in the Book of Jeremiah*, Oxford, 1970.

may be mistaken, however, if we suppose that these men of later times recaptured for themselves or can recapture for us the sharpness and hardness of a prophet's word as it sounded during his own times. Zimmerli[103] has indicated the kind of literary and theological losses which are associated with actualization. Imagery can lose its sharpness and its original force, as, for example, the images which relate to the journey home in Deutero-Isaiah do in the Jerusalem context of Trito-Isaiah. Language which was bold and striking when fully integrated into its original framework of meaning may be reduced to the rather flabby language which is the coin of conventional piety.

Jesus said to his contemporaries that their forefathers had killed the prophets and that they had built tombs for them (Luke 11:47 f.). When we say that the witness of the pre-exilic prophets was accepted and developed by pious men of later times, we should not forget that they believed themselves to stand on the other side of the judgement which the pre-exilic prophets had proclaimed and that this was more comfortable than standing under that judgement. If we are to recover the challenge of the words of these prophets, we have to understand them against the circumstances of their times, and so there are high theological reasons for not resiling from the task of recovering their *ipsissima verba*.

BIBLIOGRAPHY

(Works mentioned in the body of the essay are not listed here)

CHILDS, B. S. *Isaiah and the Assyrian Crisis*, SBT 2nd series, iii, 1967.
CRENSHAW, J. L. *Prophetic Conflict. Its Effect upon Israelite Religion*, BZAW 124, 1971.
EICHRODT, W. *Ezekiel*, London, 1970; ETr of *Der Prophet Hesekiel*, ATD xxiii/2, Göttingen, 1959, 1966.
GOTTWALD H. K. *All the Kingdoms of the Earth. Israelite Prophecy and International Relations in the Ancient Near East*, New York, 1964.
HAMMERSHAIMB, E. *Some Aspects of Old Testament Prophecy from Isaiah to Malachi*. Publications de la Société des Sciences et des Lettres d'Aarhus, Série de Théologie 4, 1966.

[103] W. Zimmerli, 'Zur Sprache Tritojesajas', *Gottes Offenbarung. Gesammelte Aufsätze zum Alten Testament*, Munich, 1963, pp. 217–33.

HENRY, M. L. *Prophet und Tradition. Versuch einer Problemstellung*, BZAW cxvi, 1969.

HERRMAN, S. *Die prophetischen Heilserwartungen im Alten Testament, Ursprung und Gestaltwandel*, BWANT v. 5. 1965.

HILLERS, D. R. *Treaty Curses and the Old Testament Prophets*, Biblica et Orientalia xvi, 1964.

JANZEN, W. *Mourning Cry and Woe Oracle*, BZAW cxxv, 1972.

KAISER, O. *Isaiah 1–12; Isaiah 13–39*, London, 1972, 1974; ETr of *Der Prophet Jesaja Kapitel 1–12; Der Prophet Jesaja Kapitel 13–39*, ATD xvii, xviii, Göttingen, 1963, 1973.

PERLITT, L. *Bundestheologie im Alten Testament*, WMANT xxxvi, 1969.

PORTEOUS, N. W. *Living the Mystery. Collected Essays*, Oxford, 1967.

REVENTLOW, H. G. *Das Amt des Propheten bei Amos*, FRLANT lxxx, 1962.

RICHTER, W. *Die sogenannten vorprophetischen Berufungsberichte. Eine literaturwissenschaftliche Studie zu I Sam. 9.1–10, 16, Ex. 3f. und Ri. 6.11b–17.* FRLANT ci, 1970.

SCOTT, R. B. Y. *The Relevance of the Prophets, An Introduction to the Old Testament Prophets and their Message*, revised edn., New York, 1968.

VOLLMER, J. *Geschichtliche Rückblicke und Motive in der Prophetie des Amos, Hosea and Jesaja*, BZAW cxix, 1971.

VON WALDOW, E. *Der traditionsgeschichtliche Hintergrund der prophetischen Gerichtsreden*, BZAW lxxxv, 1963.

WEIPPERT H. *Die Prosareden des Jeremiabuches*, BZAW cxxxii, 1973.

WEVERS, J. W. *Ezekiel*, NCB, London, 1969.

WHYBRAY, R. N. *The Heavenly Counsellor in Isaiah xl 13–14. A Study of the Sources of the Theology of Deutero-Isaiah.* The Society for Old Testament Study Monograph Series i, 1971.

WOLFF, H. W. *Hosea* BKAT XIV/1, 2nd edn., Neukirchen, 1965. *Joel und Amos*, BKAT XIV/2, 1969.

ZIMMERLI, W. *The Law and the Prophets*, London, 1965.

VII

APOCALYPTIC

E. W. NICHOLSON

In none of the previous volumes in this series was apocalyptic singled out for special treatment. In *The People and the Book*,[1] apart from a few incidental references, it is but briefly brought in, in the chapter on 'The Value and Significance of the Old Testament in Relation to the New'. In *Record and Revelation*[2] it is again only briefly dealt with in the chapters on 'The Literature of Israel' and 'The Old Testament and Christianity', whilst in the later volume, *The Old Testament and Modern Study*, [3] it is barely mentioned.

The reason for the absence of any treatment of apocalyptic in this latter volume is not so much that apocalyptic had been neglected by Old Testament scholars. In the period there surveyed much work had been done, though it cannot be said to have matched the formidable output on apocalyptic and its related literature by R. H. Charles and others in earlier decades of this century. In particular H. H. Rowley, the editor of that volume, had himself contributed much in this field and had published his well known work *The Relevance of Apocalyptic* in 1944, and produced a second edition of it in 1947, which went into a second printing in 1950.[4] But notwithstanding this and other contributions, apocalyptic was at that time greatly overshadowed by other fresh trends in Old Testament studies. It was the discussion of these trends which formed the basis and purpose of that volume and which Rowley adumbrated in his introduction to it, an

[1] Ed. A. S. Peake, Oxford, 1925.

[2] Ed. H. Wheeler Robinson, Oxford, 1938.

[3] Ed. H. H. Rowley, Oxford, 1951.

[4] Three further impressions of the 2nd edition appeared subsequently and a 3rd edition was published in 1963. References in the ensuing pages of this essay are to this 3rd edition.

introduction which itself makes no mention whatsoever of apocalyptic.

Since the publication of that volume, however, there has taken place a renewed and increasing interest in apocalyptic and this not only among Old Testament scholars but also among New Testament scholars and systematic theologians.[5] It is with the contribution of Old Testament scholars to this renaissance of interest in apocalyptic that this essay is concerned. Its purpose is to provide a survey of recent research into the main problems in the study of the origins and early development of apocalyptic, that is, of apocalyptic as it is found in the Old Testament.[6] It has not been possible within the space here allowed to discuss questions which arise in the study of later apocalyptic writings, including material from Qumran.

The study of Old Testament apocalyptic has centred on two main problems. When and among which circles did it originate in Israel? To what extent was it a native Israelite development dependent for the source of its dominant characteristics upon Israelite traditions, and to what extent did foreign religious ideas provide such a source?

These two problems involve several questions. To what extent had essential characteristics of apocalyptic developed in the centuries before the composition of the book of Daniel? If apocalyptic or 'proto-apocalyptic' developments did take place during these centuries, what circumstances may have given rise to them? Closely related to these questions is the further question: can apocalyptic be said to be rooted in and a development of prophecy? Or was Israel's wisdom tradition the ground from which it sprang? Can essential characteristics of apocalyptic such as its eschatology, determinism, dualism, and its marked mythological element be accounted for in terms of traditions and beliefs held and transmitted in Israel from early times, or were some of them or aspects of them

[5] See K. Koch, *Ratlos vor der Apokalyptik*, Gütersloh, 1970; ETr by M. Kohl, *The Rediscovery of Apocalyptic*, London, 1972.

[6] The period here surveyed is roughly the past twenty-five years. For a detailed survey of the study of apocalyptic before this see J. M. Schmidt, *Die jüdische Apokalyptik: Die Geschichte ihrer Erforschung von den Anfängen bis zu den Textfunden von Qumran*, Neukirchen, 1969.

derived from outside Israel, for example, from Babylonian or Persian religion and mythology?

Of these questions, the one which has received most attention is that of the role of prophecy in the origins and development of apocalyptic. Almost all students of the subject are agreed that prophecy contributed significantly to the emergence of apocalyptic. Some have maintained that all the essential characteristics of apocalyptic were inherited from prophecy, whilst not a few have claimed that some prophetic writings from the exilic and post-exilic periods are to be classified as apocalyptic. The investigation of the extent to which apocalyptic is indebted to prophecy has, therefore, inevitable implications, according to some scholars far reaching implications, for the discussion of the other questions mentioned in the previous paragraph. In view of this, the purpose of this essay will be best served by focusing attention on the ways in which and the extent to which apocalyptic has been considered to be the heir of prophecy.

In his well-known work already referred to, *The Relevance of Apocalyptic*, H. H. Rowley described apocalyptic as 'the child of prophecy, yet diverse from prophecy'. Apocalyptic has a character and purpose if its own which arose from the circumstances which gave it birth in the Maccabean period when Daniel, the first and greatest apocalyptic work, was composed. Nevertheless, the way had been prepared for the author of Daniel. Rowley affirmed the influence of foreign ideas, especially from Persia, in the emergence of apocalyptic, but stressed above all the contribution of prophetic eschatology. The belief in the coming 'day of Yahweh' as a day of universal judgement is already implied in the preaching of Amos and finds full expression in Zeph. 1:14 ff. Yet there was also in pre-exilic prophecy the vision of a new order beyond this judgement. Familiar is the teaching of Isaiah about the salvation of a 'remnant' and his vision of the transformation of nature itself (11:6 ff.) and of the establishment of peace and concord among men and nations who would find their unity in allegiance to Yahweh (2:2 ff. = Mic. 4:1 ff.). Taken together these elements 'yield a picture of divine judgement on the nations, but of deliverance and vindication for the righteous Remnant, leading to the Golden Age of justice and peace and

infinite bliss' (p. 24)—a picture characteristic of the eschatological hopes of the apocalyptic writers.

Rowley found a combination of these elements in various
post-exilic prophetic writings: in Isa. 24-7, though he agrees
with various scholars that these chapters are not to be
classified as an apocalypse,[7] as also in the book of Joel and in
Zech. 9-14: 'To all of these writers history was moving swiftly
towards a great climax, and the birth of a new age which
should belong to the faithful Remnant of Israel. From this it
was but a short step to the treatment of these themes by the
apocalyptists' (p.26). Rowley also pointed to the prophetic
promises of a future ideal Davidic king as the basis for the
Messianic hope of later apocalyptic, and to the figure of Gog
in Ezek. 38-9, who is the embodiment of the forces of evil to
be overcome by God 'in the latter days' and is thus the
forerunner of the 'Little Horn' of Dan. 7 and the prototype of
the Antichrist of the Christian tradition.

Essentially the same view of the origins of apocalyptic has
been advanced by D. S. Russell in his major work *The Method
and Message of Jewish Apocalyptic*.[8] The sources from which
the apocalyptists drew were widespread and manifold and
included both native and foreign elements. But the 'tap root'
of apocalyptic was prophecy, especially post-exilic prophecy.
In the latter, the future hopes expressed by the pre-exilic
prophets, in particular their proclamation of the coming 'day
of Yahweh', were developed into eschatology. This eschatology, together with other features distinctive of apocalyptic,
find expression in Ezek. 38-9; Zech. 1-8; 9-14; Joel 3; and Isa.
24-7. None of these prophetic writings can be termed
apocalyptic but they contain the 'stuff' of which apocalyptic
is made: an emphasis on divine transcendence, a development
of angelology, fantastic symbolism, cosmic imagery, foreign
mythology, the reinterpretation of prophecy, the visionary
form of inspiration, a distinct literary form, cataclysm and
judgement, the 'day of Yahweh', the destruction of the
gentiles, the coming of the golden age, the messianic deliverer,
and the resurrection of the dead. 'When at last the historical

[7] e.g. J. Lindblom, *Die Jesaja-Apokalypse, Jes. 24-27*, LUÅ., N.F.I, xxxiv, 3, Lund
and Leipzig, 1938.
[8] London, 1964.

conditions for growth were right, these seeds rapidly grew into full flower in the colourful and diverse literature of Jewish apocalyptic' (p. 91).

Though both Rowley and Russell draw special attention to eschatology in the connections they find between apocalyptic and prophecy, both stress that apocalyptic cannot simply be identified as eschatology. Whilst not disagreeing with this, other recent scholars have, however, laid much greater emphasis upon eschatology as the central creative element in the emergence and development of apocalyptic.

Of these scholars, attention may first of all be drawn to S. Mowinckel and in particular to his monumental work *He That Cometh*.[9] It is well known that Mowinckel denies that the pre-exilic prophets had an eschatology in the proper sense of the word:

Eschatology is a doctrine or a complex of ideas about "the last things", which is more or less organically coherent and developed. Every eschatology includes in some form or other a dualistic conception of the course of history, and implies that the present state of things and the present world order will suddenly come to an end and be superseded by another of an essentially different kind (p. 125).

In the time of the pre-exilic prophets no such doctrine existed. These prophets announced the destruction of Israel by Assyria or Babylon in fulfilment of Yahweh's judgement upon his people and as part of the working out of his purposes in history. But in all this nothing implies the end of the present world order. Isaiah, for example, announced the survival of a 'remnant' which would live on in history; Jeremiah has much to say about the future restoration of the exiles to their homeland where the everyday tasks of living would be resumed. In the books which bear the names of these pre-exilic prophets, eschatological passages, in the proper sense of the word, belong to the later strata and come from the age of post-exilic Judaism.[10]

[9] References here are to the English translation by G. W. Anderson, Oxford, 1956, from *Han som kommer*, Copenhagen, 1951.

[10] Against Mowinckel's view see L. Černý, *The Day of Yahweh and Some Relevant Problems*, Prague, 1948, esp. pp. 67 ff., 80 ff., and the remarks of B. Vawter, 'Apocalyptic: Its Relation to Prophecy', *CBQ* xxii (1960), 33–46.

A development towards eschatology took place in the preaching of Deutero-Isaiah who presented Israel's restoration as a drama of cosmic dimensions:

Behind the conflict of Cyrus with the Chaldeans and Babylon the prophet sees the victorious conflict of Yahweh with His adversaries. These enemies are not only human beings and earthly powers; for behind the latter stand the heathen deities and all creation's evil, cosmic forces, which are embodied in the adversaries of Cyrus and of Yahweh, the oppressors of Israel (p. 139).

The terms in which Deutero-Isaiah described what was about to happen, that is, the imminent victory of Cyrus over Babylon and the ensuing return of the exiles to Zion, are those of Yahweh's cosmic conflict, victory, and enthronement which together had formed the centre of the autumnal festival in the Jerusalem Temple in the pre-exilic period. In short, Deutero-Isaiah depicted the future in terms of Yahweh's kingly rule. But he did so in a way that made 'the object of the future hope ... something absolute and definitive, which, being absolute, becomes "the wholly Other", different from everything hitherto experienced on earth' (p. 261). The nature of the future hope as conceived of by the prophet was such that it could only be expressed in mythical terms, metaphors, and colours, with the result that, notwithstanding the earthly setting of the realization of that hope, the future state is lifted up into the transcendent, mythical sphere.

Yet Deutero-Isaiah's message, according to Mowinckel, fell short of eschatology. The prophet was limited by his presuppositions; he remained a Jew, affected by Jewish nationalism. Yahweh, though the universal God, was still primarily the God of Israel and his kingdom was still conceived of as a kingdom of this world. Nevertheless, Deutero-Isaiah pointed the way to eschatology. What was lacking, Mowinckel maintains, was a dualistic understanding of the world and history, for dualism was unfamiliar to the ancient Israelite. The Jewish future hope became eschatology in the proper sense of the word when it was linked, in the Hellenistic period and under Persian influence, to a dualistic view of the world. As a result of this, together with other developments which took place in post-exilic Judaism, a 'new eschatology came into existence, dualistic, cosmic, universalistic, transcendental, and individualistic' (p. 271).

But though the addition of Persian dualism was decisive in transforming the future hope of restoration into eschatology, of importance also was the work of circles of prophetic disciples in the post-exilic period who engaged in theological, exegetical, and speculative learning based upon the old prophetic sayings and books:

The latest phase of prophecy was, in large measure, an inspired revision, amplification, and interpretation of the earlier prophecy. It was spiritual learning or "wisdom" ... Out of this wisdom (combined with elements of all kinds of ancient oriental learning on cosmography, astrology, angelology, and medical magic) there finally arose apocalyptic, which may be defined as inspired learning or revealed theology, with eschatology as its centre (p. 266).

Observations and conclusions similar to some of those arrived at by Mowinckel have been advanced in several other recent works on apocalyptic. The importance he attaches to the preaching of Deutero-Isaiah and to this prophet's use of myth has been prominent. The contribution of prophetic circles in post-exilic Judaism has also been investigated, whilst apocalyptic's indebtedness to wisdom has been greatly emphasized, most notably by G. von Rad, as we shall see later. But the importance accorded by Mowinckel, as by many other scholars both past and present, to Persian influences in the development of apocalyptic has recently been vigorously challenged. In addition, against Mowinckel, as also against both Rowley and Russell, other recent works have contended for a much earlier origin of apocalyptic than they allow. Of these recent works, particular attention is here drawn to the contributions of S. B. Frost, O. Plöger, and P. D. Hanson.[11]

No one has more emphasized the relationship between

[11] Other recent contributions advocating a similar point of view are J. Bloch, *On the Apocalyptic in Judaism, JQR* Monograph Series ii, 1952, who argues that 'many of the later prophetic writings [from Ezekiel onwards] assume the character of apocalyptic' (p. 28); B. Vawter, op. cit., who, following Bloch, argues that there 'seems to be no reason to deny that much of Ezekiel is apocalyptic' (p. 41); F. M. Cross, 'New Directions in the Study of Apocalyptic', *JTC* vi (1969), 157–65: 'The origins of apocalyptic must be searched for as early as the sixth century BCE' (p. 161); R. North, 'Prophecy to Apocalyptic via Zechariah', SVT xxii, 1972, pp. 47–71; S. Amsler, 'Zacharie et l'origine de l'apocalyptique', ibid, pp. 227–231.

apocalyptic and prophecy than S. B. Frost in his work *Old Testament Apocalyptic: Its Origins and Growth*.[12] Whereas, for example, Rowley's assessment of that relationship points to an interval between prophecy and apocalyptic, the former preparing the way for the latter, the latter when the time was ripe taking up features and characteristics of the former. Frost argues that the first apocalyptist was a prophet and that it was at the hands of a prophet and not of the author of Daniel that apocalyptic first achieved its basic form.

Frost defines apocalyptic as the fusion of myth and eschatology and he believes that this fusion was first effected in the exilic period. In the pre-exilic period myth and eschatology were quite unrelated to each other. For myth is concerned with maintaining and perpetuating the created and ordered cosmos, the *status quo* of the annual cycle of nature and society. Eschatology on the other hand presupposed Israel's consciousness of a divine mission in history; fundamental to eschatology was the concept of 'teleological' history which was alien to a mythological, cyclic understanding of life.

Frost finds what he terms 'realised eschatology' in the work of the Yahwist in the mid-tenth century B.C.: what Yahweh had promised of old was now seen to have been fulfilled in the achievements of the nation under David. When, however, after the Disruption, political disaster befell Israel 'futuristic eschatology' was born. The 'day of Yahweh', whether this concept originated in the cultic or military sphere, now became the basis of popular hope that Yahweh would intervene to re-establish the pre-eminence of his people among the nations. But at the hands of Amos and Isaiah this popular hope was inverted: Yahweh would come, not to vindicate his people but to judge them because of their rebellion against him. In the preaching of Zephaniah 'the day of Yahweh' reached universalistic dimensions: the whole world was to come under God's judgement (Zeph. 3:8). But with this came also the promise that out of this judgement would come a chastened remnant (3:11-13).

[12] London 1952. Cf. also his article 'Eschatology and Myth', *VT* ii (1952), 70–80; 'Apocalyptic and History', *The Bible in Modern Scholarship*, ed. J. P. Hyatt, London, 1966, pp. 98–113.

Frost argues that this eschatology was transformed in the exilic period when it was fused with myth and that the consequent presentation of eschatology in the language of myth gave birth to apocalyptic. The creator of this fusion and thus the 'father of apocalyptic' was a prophet who lived among the exiles and who worked over the prophecies of Ezekiel and gave the book of Ezekiel its present form. Frost, at this point following the view of Herntrich on the composition of this book,[13] designates this anonymous prophet 'Babylonian Ezekiel' to distinguish him from Ezekiel proper whose ministry, it is believed, took place in Judah.

According to Frost, this exilic prophet adopted an at that time new Babylonian type of literary expression and by employing it became the first exemplar of the abundant imagery and strange symbolism of apocalyptic. More important, however, was his use of the language of myth to express his eschatology. Here special attention is drawn, not for the first time in the study of apocalyptic, to Ezek. 38–9. By the end of chapter 37 Israel's historical foes are subdued and the nation is again living in prosperity in the homeland. At this point, Frost suggests, we would expect chapters 40–8 with their plans for the new community and its cult to follow immediately. 'But Babylonian Ezekiel hestitates. The Golden Age cannot come quite so easily as that. Israel's enemies are Yahweh's enemies, but Yahweh has yet other antagonists to overthrow ... there is a larger battlefield, a greater foe who sums up all that is inimical to Yahweh and His people' (p. 88). Evil is now seen to be a supra-mundane force and Yahweh's conflict with it and victory over it can thus be portrayed only at the supra-mundane level. For this purpose, Frost argues, there was at hand in Babylon the old Semitic cosmological myth centring on the conflict between the creator-god and the chaos monster. 'At the back of the Jewish mind itself there were possibly folk-memories of similar myths. Contact with the Assyro-Babylonian cults before and especially during the Exile quickened those memories and the myths became a religious force in Jewry again ... As Yahweh slew Tiamat of old, so shall He conquer her—the Dragon—Evil—afresh!' (pp. 88 f.). Hence chapters 38–9

[13] V. Herntrich, *Ezechielprobleme*, BZAW lxi, 1932.

describe the coming and the defeat of the mythical figure Gog from the north symbolizing all that is anti-Yahweh.

With this anonymous prophet at whose hands the ground-plan of apocalyptic was thus laid there began, according to Frost, several centuries of anonymous apocalyptic. Into this category he places the visions of Zech. 1–8, the last two chapters of Joel (EVV 2:28–3:21), various apocalyptic insertions in Isa. 1–39 (he designates these insertions 'Extra-Isaiah') but excluding Isa. 24–7 (see below), and so-called Deutero-Zechariah (Zech. 8–14). The period of this anonymous apocalyptic lasted to the second century B.C.

Frost then classifies certain other writings as pseudony-mous apocalyptic. First in this category is the so-called 'Isaiah Apocalypse' the author of which is designated 'Pseudo-Isaiah'[14] and whose work he dates in the mid-third century B.C. This category also includes, it is maintained, books 1 and 4 of Enoch, Daniel, and books 2 and 5 of Enoch. Frost places great emphasis upon the work of 'Pseudo-Isaiah' and argues that at this author's hands apocalyptic finally achieved its characteristic form: ' ... it is one of the outstandingly important books of the whole Bible, since, on the one hand, processes long maturing come here to their fruition and, on the other, shapes and forms are here decided for the whole of the apocalyptic literature yet to come' (p. 157).

Many would accept Frost's view that Ezek. 38–9 is an apocalyptic passage dating from the sixth century B.C. and that the other prophetic writings from the post-exilic period to which he draws attention are similarly to be classified as apocalyptic. But a serious question-mark must be placed against his definition of apocalyptic. His contention, with which many would agree, that myth and eschatology are irreconcilable, renders it difficult to see how he can define

---

[14] Frost argues that it was this author who first adopted pseudonymity which was to become a characteristic of later apocalyptic writings. Of this, Rowley, op. cit., p. 24, n. 1, correctly says that 'there is no evidence that these chapters were inserted by their author in the Book of Isaiah, any more than Isa. 40–6 were inserted by their authors in the book, and no evidence that the author attached the name of Isaiah to these chapters before they were added to the book.' It may also be asked why, for example, on Frost's own understanding of the composition of Ezekiel, the author of Ezek. 38–9 ('Babylonian Ezekiel') should be regarded as anonymous rather than pseudonymous.

apocalyptic as a 'fusion of myth and eschatology'. If they were irreconcilable in the pre-exilic period it is hard to see how the exile could have altered this. It seems clear, however, that what Frost means is that from the exile onwards the language and some of the themes of myth, not myth as such, were employed in formulating eschatology.[15] But if apocalyptic were defined as eschatology described in the language of myth that would mean that it originated earlier than the exile, since such language is already found in pre-exilic eschatological passages.[16] Few scholars, however, including Frost himself, would wish to argue for such an early origin of apocalyptic. Nevertheless, the evidence is that during the exile and later the use of the language and themes of myth to describe eschatology became more intensive and several scholars have argued that this contributed vitally towards the emergence of apocalyptic.

A different setting and religio-historical background for the origins and emergence of apocalyptic has been advanced by O. Plöger in his monograph *Theocracy and Eschatology*.[17] He accepts the commonly held view that apocalyptic is related to prophecy and that the main connection between them is eschatology. Apocalyptic is not to be defined as eschatology, but eschatology was nevertheless the driving force in the origins and development of apocalyptic. Apocalyptic 'represents a world-view in an eschatological key' (p.27).

Plöger makes the basis for his discussion the existence of two groups referred to in 1 Macc. 2 as standing together in opposition to Antiochus Epiphanes. There were the Maccabees and their followers at whose hands military insurrection and the attempt to rebuild a Jewish kingdom were undertaken. There was also a group referred to as the Hasidim, the 'Pious', whose steadfast faith and loyalty to the Law are praised.

---

[15] See J. Barr, 'The Meaning of "Mythology" in Relation to the Old Testament', *VT* ix (1959), 9–10

[16] For example, the description of Yahweh's coming in judgement in Mic. 1:3 f. is couched in the language of myth. Concerning Frost's view J. Barr, op. cit., p. 10, asks pertinently: 'Can we really draw so sharp a distinction in nature between the fire which ate up *tehom rabbah* in Amos and the prophecies of the Golden Age?' Similarly, the description in Isa. 8:7 f. of the coming onslaught of Assyria upon Judah employs the mythic theme of the 'many waters'.

[17] ETr, by S. Rudman, Oxford, 1968 from the 2nd edn. of *Theokratie und Eschatologie*, WMANT ii, Neukirchen, 1962

Though the latter were at one time persuaded to engage in the military activity against Antiochus, they subsequently withdrew and reverted to a role of passive resistance. Plöger finds the passive but loyal attitude displayed by the book of Daniel to agree well with the outlook of the Hasidim discernible in 1 Macc. and suggests that the book of Daniel gave expression to the views of these Hasidim.

Notwithstanding their common opposition to Antiochus, these two groups were sharply divided in their evaluation of the events of the day. For those who stand behind the book of Daniel the onset of the *eschaton* was at hand. The real nature of what was happening and its significance are outlined in Dan. 12:1-3. As against this theocentric and eschatological understanding of the events of the day, the evaluation of them in 1 Macc. represents the view that, critical though the period was, it was one period of time among others and that with loyal and courageous faith its tribulations would be overcome. In other words, this understanding of the events of the time was, in contrast to that represented in the book of Daniel, non-eschatological.

It is Plöger's contention that neither of these two attitudes, the dualistic-eschatological of the group represented by the book of Daniel and the non-eschatological represented by the aims of the Maccabean movement, was new. Both had already behind them a considerable period of development which took place within the context of the post-exilic community established by the work of Ezra and Nehemiah. This community was a theocracy, as distinct from the old constitution of Israel as a nation, and the theological basis of it is reflected in P and in the work of the Chronicler. In P, world history is traced only as far as the establishment of the cultic community at Sinai. This marked the culmination of God's dealings with his creation and after this there was no prospect or necessity for any fundamental change. In such an understanding of history and of Israel there is no place for eschatology. The Chronicler confirmed this understanding of Israel but in view of the controversy with the Samaritans took the story futher than P to the point where the community existing in his days had been freshly constituted. To those who held that Israel's election found fulfilment in the

establishment of the theocratic community, prophetic eschatology could no longer be maintained in the traditional sense;
it had lost its point. Thus, as far as the authors of P and the
Chronicler were concerned, the 'goal of earlier eschatological
expectation, the winding-up of the nation on the lines of the
plan of Yahweh proclaimed by the prophets, was in principle
already attained in a community founded exclusively on cult
and law; the only justification for the maintenance of
eschatological hopes was that they confirmed what was, in
effect, already the case' (pp. 43 f.).

'But hope', Plöger continues, 'waiting upon God, is an
integral part of faith, and when faith is limited to the purely
cultic sphere, without a vital relationship to historical events,
it cannot find full expression. Israel was only able to express
its deepest religious experiences when it found itself *in statu
promissionis*' (p.44). Hence he argues that within the post-
exilic theocratic community there emerged conventicles
which were still convinced of the contemporary validity of
the prophetic word and it is to them that he attributes the
development of eschatology into the dualistic-eschatology of
apocalyptic.

The basic cleavage between such eschatologically orientated conventicles and the representatives of a theocracy such
as came into existence in the post-exilic period need not have
led to outward division as long as no particular occasion arose.
But the tendency for an opposition group to regard itself as an
independent community alongside or even replacing the
larger community would have increased. Plöger sees such a
development to have taken place during the period from the
foundation of the new community in the fifth century B.C. up
to the religious conflict under Antiochus Epiphanes when a
specific occasion brought it to a head. During this period and
especially during the last century or so of it, continued and
increasing indifference and probably even hostility to eschatology on the one side gave rise to a corresponding sharpening
of the eschatological point of view on the other. It was in such
a situation that prophetic eschatology was developed into the
apocalyptic view of the future. Plöger sees the culmination of
this development in Daniel, but finds such texts as the Isaiah
Apocalypse, Trito-Zechariah (Zech. 12–14) and Joel 3–4

(EVV 2:28–3:21) as evidence of its earlier stages in the post-exilic period.

Plöger affirms the view that foreign religious ideas of a pre-eminently eschatological nature played an important role in the development of apocalyptic. The conventicles which nourished and were concerned with maintaining prophetic eschatology would have been receptive to such new ideas, recognizing in cosmic-dualism views very pertinent to their own situation. Initially, it is suggested, such foreign ideas would have been taken up on a limited scale, but the unsympathetic attitude of the official community would have led to more and more borrowing of the new ideas on the part of the eschatological groups.

Plöger's thesis that apocalyptic originated among eschatologically orientated groups which emerged in opposition to the theological outlook of the theocratic community of post-exilic Judaism has found recent support in the work of P. D. Hanson.[18] At the same time Hanson's over-all understanding of the origin and development of apocalyptic differs in a number of major respects from that of Plöger and indeed from the others whose works we have so far briefly surveyed in this essay. He shares with them the view that apocalyptic developed out of prophecy and he sees this development to have taken place in the post-exilic period. But he denies that foreign religious ideas were at all operative in this development, maintaining that influences from Persian dualism and from Hellenism were late and came only after the essential character of apocalyptic was fully developed. Apocalyptic was a native product of post-exilic Judaism, emerged as the result of an unbroken pattern out of pre-exilic and exilic prophecy, and depended for the source of its main ideas and characteristics on traditions and beliefs long since at home in Israel, some of which were inherited from the nation's Canaanite environment.

[18] P. D. Hanson, 'Jewish Apocalyptic against its Near Eastern Environment', RB lxxviii (1971), 31–58; 'Old Testament Apocalyptic Reexamined', *Interpretation*, xxv (1971), 454–79. Cf. also his 'Zechariah 9 and the Recapitulation of an Ancient Ritual Pattern' *JBL* xcii (1973), 37–59. For our present purposes the first of these articles provides a sufficient indication of Hanson's views and references here will be limited to it.

In defining apocalyptic Hanson rejects those definitions of it which list features gleaned from the whole range of apocalyptic literature.[19] Such definitions are both confusing and misleading, for no single apocalyptic book comes close to embodying them all. He also rejects any attempt to define apocalyptic as a literary *Gattung*, since the apocalyptists employed many old literary *Gattungen* and transformed them. His own definition proceeds from the view that 'apocalyptic is the mode assumed by prophetic eschatology once it had been transferred to a new and radically altered setting in the post-Exilic community' (*RB* lxxviii (1971), 34). He defines prophetic eschatology as 'the announcement to the nation of the divine plans for Israel and the world which the prophet, with his insight into Yahweh's Divine Council, has witnessed unfolding within the Covenant Relationship between Yahweh and Israel, which plans the prophet proceeds to translate into the terms of plain history, real politics and human instrumentality' (p. 35). Apocalyptic he defines as

the disclosure (usually esoteric in nature) to the elect of the prophetic vision of Yahweh's sovereignty (including his future dealings with his people, the inner secrets of the cosmos, etc.) which vision the visionaries have ceased to translate into the terms of plain history, real politics and human instrumentality because of a pessimistic view of reality growing out of the bleak post-Exilic conditions in which the visionary group found itself, conditions seemingly unsuitable to them as a context for the envisioned restoration of Yahweh's people (p. 35).

The basis of these definitions lies in the distinction which Hanson believes to have been drawn in Israelite religion between the cosmic realm of Yahweh and his Divine Council on the one hand and the realm of the real world of man and his history on the other.[20] Because of her experiences in history in which she saw the hand of Yahweh at work in her election, Israel came to understand human history as an arena

---

[19] e.g., D. S. Russell, op. cit., p. 105.

[20] Hanson (*RB* lxxviii (1971), 36 ff.) contrasts this with other ancient Near Eastern religions which centred solely on myth and afforded no place for the development of a concept of history.

of divine activity alongside the divine activity in the cosmic realm.

This distinction gave rise in Israelite religion to a tension between 'vision' and 'reality', that is, between myth and history. Hanson argues that it was the unique contribution of prophetic Yahwism that 'it held these two elements together in a radical and very creative tension, for it viewed Yahweh as a Being whose power encompassed the cosmos, but nevertheless it insisted on interpreting his actions as occurring within the events of plain history' (p. 36). As against this, the apocalyptists became disillusioned with history and hence presented their message for the future 'in a manner of growing indifference to and independence of the contingencies of the politico-historical realm, thereby leaving the language increasingly in the idiom of the cosmic realm of the Divine Warrior and his Council' (p. 35).

Though there are some exceptions among the sayings of the pre-exilic prophets, Hanson finds that in general these prophets maintained a delicate balance between 'vision' and 'reality'; cosmic vision was translated into history and hence myth was forced to retreat and was held in check before a more 'secularized', 'humanistic' view of religion. In the theology of the Deuteronomic historian, however, this delicate balance was lost and by means of a dogmatic principle, the law of the centralization of the cult, this historian was able to present the ups and downs of the nation's history with precision: 'vision' was unnecessary and was thus eliminated. But the disasters befell the nation—the death of Josiah, the Exile, and continued subjugation to foreign dominion— shattered faith in this Deuteronomic theodicy and historiography.

It was Deutero-Isaiah who saved prophetic Yahwism from succumbing to the crisis brought about by the events of the early sixth century B.C. This he did by reintroducing the cosmic vision and applying it to his message of Yahweh's imminent restoration of his people. But the prophet maintained the delicate balance achieved by his predecessors between myth and history (e.g. in Isa. 51:9–11 the myth of Yahweh's cosmic victory over the Chaos Monster is applied to the historical realm). Futhermore there was now to be a cosmic change throughout nature inaugurated by Yahweh's new act on his people's behalf. This gave rise in the prophet's thinking to a division of history into two periods: the past which was now to be forgotten and the future 'new thing' to be brought about by Yahweh (Isa. 43:18–19).

Hanson argues that Deutero-Isaiah's marked use of myth was fraught with dangers and that within the circle of his disciples in the post-exilic period the balance achieved by their master between 'vision' and 'reality' collapsed at the expense of the latter. It was within this circle that apocalyptic was born. Thus Isa. 56–66 is of special significance for the investigation of the origins of apocalyptic as also are the Isaiah Apocalypse and Zech. 9–14. The late dates usually furnished for these compositions are rejected by Hanson, for there is no necessity to understand the dualism and eschatology found in them to have derived from Zoroastrianism. On the contrary, the mythic dualism influencing these compositions comes 'not from late Persian sources, but is part of the recrudescence of ancient Near Eastern (especially Canaanite) mythic motifs which throughout the monarchic period were nourished in the Jerusalem court and which were drawn into prophecy by Second Isaiah' (p. 50). The background to these compositions is the sixth century B.C.

It will be sufficient for our purposes to note briefly Hanson's observations concerning Isa. 56–66 and the setting which he believes these chapters to presuppose. He finds evidence here of a schism in the early post-exilic community, his conclusion in this respect being similar to Plöger's. Hanson sees the root of this schism to be a struggle between two contending parties for control of the restoration cult, the one a prophetic group and the other the 'normative *golah* group' led by the Zadokites. The former found themselves being pushed aside and their plans for restoration being crushed by the latter more powerful, hierocratic group. This accounts for the polemical element which Hanson sees as the most outstanding trait in Isa. 56–66. At the same time it also offers an explanation of the pronounced visionary nature of the oracles in these chapters. Behind such oracles can be discerned

the post-Exilic situation in which the oppressed and discouraged visionists were coming to recognize in myth a new way to conceive of the restoration hope, which historical circumstances had crushed so harshly, by looking to a deliverance raised above historical realities to a blissful realm in which they were freed from the weighty vocation of serving within the political order, freed from the necessity of interpreting divine activity in relation to the real events of human history (p. 52).

It is this mythic conception of Yahweh's future actions which forms the centre of apocalyptic and from three examples chosen from Third Isaiah (chapters 59, 65, 66) Hanson argues that the essential elements of apocalyptic are all nascent in this late-sixth-century-B.C. material: (1) the belief that the present order is dominated by evil and cannot be redeemed; (2) catastrophic judgement is imminent in which Yahweh's enemies will be destroyed and his faithful servants delivered; (3) beyond this judgement there would come a new era, a paradise inaugurated by Yahweh for his faithful (p. 54).

We may note briefly here some other recent contributions which lend support to Hanson's thesis or individual features of it. F. M. Cross has advanced an understanding of the origins of apocalyptic closely similar to Hanson's and emphasizes in particular that a recrudescence in post-exilic Judaism of old mythic themes stemming ultimately from ancient Canaanite sources played a vital role: 'It has become vividly clear that the primary source of mythic material informing Jewish apocalyptic was *old* Canaanite mythic lore . . . many apocalyptic traditions go back through earliest Israel to Canaanite sources so that more continuities with the old biblical community must be recognized rather than fewer.'[21] As an example of how fruitful this approach to the origins of the mythic themes and motifs of apocalyptic can be we may cite J. A. Emerton's cogently argued view that the tradition underlying the 'son of man' imagery in Dan. 7 and later apocalyptic texts derives ultimately from Canaanite myth and ritual [22] Such a view renders it unnecessary to look, for

---

[21] F. M. Cross, op. cit., p. 165, n. 23. Cf. also his 'The Divine Warrior in Israel's Early Cult', *Biblical Motifs*, ed. A. Altmann, Cambridge Mass., 1966, pp. 11–30; 'The Song of the Sea and Canaanite Myth', *JTC* v (1968) 1–25.

[22] J. A. Emerton, 'The Origin of the Son of Man Imagery', *JTS*, N.S. ix (1958), 225–42.

example, to Zoroastrianism for the origin of this imagery, as many scholars have suggested. Finally, serious doubt has been cast on the view, advocated by a number of scholars, that Zoroastrian eschatology was a formative influence in the emergence of apocalyptic. For whilst not denying influences from Zoroastrianism in post-exilic Judaism, R. C. Zaehner in his major work *The Dawn and Twilight of Zoroastrianism*[23] writes that 'we have no evidence as to what eschatological ideas the Zoroastrians had in the last four centuries before Christ' (p. 57). This lends support to those scholars who claimed that the eschatology of apocalyptic originated as a native Jewish development without recourse to foreign ideas.

The widely accepted view, some representatives of which we have seen in the foregoing pages, that the roots of apocalyptic lie in prophecy, has not gone unchallenged and in recent years has been firmly rejected by no less a scholar than the late G. von Rad. In the first edition of his *Old Testament Theology*[24] he advanced the view that Israel's wisdom tradition was the ground from which apocalyptic developed,[25] allowing at the same time for influences from Persian sources. In the fourth German edition of this work he reaffirmed this view, expanding his earlier treatment of it and placing it on a broader basis.[26] In his later book, *Wisdom in Israel*,[27] he dealt further with the origins of apocalyptic particularly in an excursus under the title 'The Divine Determination of Times'.[28]

As the title of this excursus itself indicates, von Rad believes that the key to the understanding of the origin of apocalyptic is its determinism, the belief that history from its beginnings to its culmination has been divinely predetermined. The historical summaries contained in apocalyptic writings served to demonstrate God's total sovereignty over history but most of all to indicate to the observer, by means of the division of

[23] London, 1961.
[24] ETr of vol. ii by D. M. G. Stalker, Edinburgh and London, 1965, from *Theologie des Alten Testaments*, ii, Munich, 1960.
[25] Another recent attempt to connect the origins of apocalyptic with wisdom is H.-P. Müller, 'Mantische Weisheit und Apokalyptik', SVT xxii, 1972, pp. 268–93.
[26] Munich, 1965.
[27] ETr by J. D. Martin, London, 1972, from *Weisheit in Israel*, Neukirchen, 1970.
[28] *Wisdom in Israel*, pp. 263–83.

history into periods, his own place in history and that the end
of the world's first age and the dawn of the new age were
imminent. But though this understanding of history was
pronouncedly eschatological, von Rad rejects any suggestion
that this points to Israel's prophetic tradition as the matrix
from which apocalyptic originated. On the contrary, the
apocalyptic view of history is incompatible with that of the
prophets. The prophetic message was founded upon the
saving history, Israel's election traditions; for the prophets
history was the arena of the saving acts of Yahweh and they
looked for the establishing of a new relationship between
Israel and Yahweh in history. In apocalyptic, by contrast, the
salvation event has been moved to the *eschaton* and is not
prepared for by events within history: 'Rather, the end erupts
abruptly into a world of history which is growing darker and
darker, and the benefits of salvation which have long been
pre-existent in the heavenly world ... make their appearance.'[29] Apocalyptic's view of history has, therefore, no
'confessional' character; it is not interested in those acts of
God on which salvation was based and in the light of which
earlier accounts of Israel's history had been written. There is,
therefore, an unbridgeable gulf between these two views of
history which renders it impossible to understand apocalyptic's view of history to have developed from that of prophecy.

The origin of apocalyptic's deterministic concept of history
is Israel's wisdom tradition. Thus, for example, Eccles. 6:10
is cited by von Rad as unambiguously deterministic and he
believes that this book contains many further examples. We
are also referred to a number of passages in Ecclesiasticus
which also, it is argued, speak clearly of a divine predetermination of history (e.g. 23:20; 33:7–15; 39:25, 30). Even the
expectation of a great culmination of history is already found
in Ecclesiasticus: 'Rouse your anger, pour out your wrath,
overthrow the adversary, destroy the enemy, hasten the end,
establish the time' (36:7–8).[30]

Von Rad believes that a number of other features of
apocalyptic literature confirm his thesis. The 'enormous
accumulation' of knowledge concerning the development of

[29] op. cit., p. 273.
[30] Ibid., p. 279.

civilization, the heavenly bodies, the calendar, meteorology and geography, contained, for example, in Ethiopic Enoch (chapters 8; 72–9) is taken as characteristic of the 'really encyclopedic "science"' to be found in wisdom literature. The presentation of history in apocalyptic, a presentation which is devoid of interest in the salvation history, is already exemplified in Ecclus. 44–50. Daniel, Enoch, and Ezra are described as belonging to the 'wise', whilst the interpretation of dreams, so prominent in Daniel, is also traditionally a function of the wise men, as, for example, the Joseph stories indicate. The book of Daniel ends with 'an apotheosis of the Wisdom teachers' (Dan. 12:3).

Von Rad also suggests that the presence in apocalyptic of ideas from Irano-Chaldean syncretism may have been due to 'the branching out of wisdom in the direction of widely varied intellectual spheres', adding that it 'would not have been the first time that Israelite wisdom had laid itself open to foreign intellectual material.'[31]

Von Rad's attempt to find the traditio-historical basis of apocalyptic in Israel's wisdom tradition has not carried conviction.[32] In particular he has scarcely succeeded in demonstrating how the radical eschatological nature of apocalyptic could have been derived from wisdom which was so lacking in eschatological perspective.[33] His understanding of Ecclus. 36:7–8, which he believes is evidence that Sirach held a doctrine of the culmination of history, must be rejected. For when one reads what follows (vv 9–17) it becomes clear that the author is here concerned not with the culmination of world history but with the nationalistic aim of the vindication of 'the tribes of Jacob' over against their oppressors. We note also that Sirach refers specifically to the promises of the prophets from whom, it is reasonable to suppose, he got his confidence in what God would perform on behalf of his people (16).

[31] Ibid., p. 279.

[32] A detailed critique of von Rad's views has been published by P. von der Osten-Sacken, *Die Apokalyptik in ihrem Verhältnis zu Prophetie und Weisheit*, Munich, 1969.

[33] Cf. P. Vielhauer's essay on apocalyptic in *Neutestamentliche Apokryphen*, ii, ed. E. Hennecke and W. Schneemelcher, Tübingen, 1964, ETr ed. by R. McL. Wilson, *New Testament Apocrypha*, ii, London, 1965.

Nor is it reasonable to dismiss with little or no discussion those passages in exilic and post-exilic prophetic literature which display some of the features familiar in apocalyptic literature. It is true that the apocalyptists were conscious that prophecy had ceased in Israel. But there is more than sufficient evidence to indicate that they regarded themselves as the interpreters of the prophets; Dan. 9 provides but one lucid example of this.[34]

In addition, von Rad's argument that the determinism of apocalyptic is already found in wisdom writings such as Ecclesiasticus does not bear scrutiny. For example, a passage such as Ecclus. 33:7-15 cannot seriously be regarded as exemplifying a determinism such as is characteristic of apocalyptic. This passage is concerned with man and his lot as part of a predetermined natural order. As such it reflects nothing more than that understanding of the finitude of man and creation which is already found in Ecclesiastes (especially ch. 6). But it has nothing to say of the predetermination of world history as such.[35] Much closer to the idea of the divine predetermination of history are surely, for example, the frequent statements in Deutero-Isaiah which refer to Yahweh's predetermination and foreknowledge of the events of history (e.g. Isa. 41:4, 21 ff., 25 ff.; 42:9; 44:7-8; etc.).[36]

We can agree with von Rad that apocalyptic's pessimistic understanding of history is removed from the concept of history to be found in the preaching of the prophets. The radical eschatology of apocalyptic brought with it the view that history was the aeon of evil.[37] But such a change in the understanding of history is readily explained as the result of the bleak transformation of Israel's lot from the exilic period

[34] Cf. J. Schreiner, *Alttestamentliche-jüdische Apokalyptik*, Munich, 1969, pp. 166 ff.

[35] Cf. P. von der Osten-Sacken, op. cit., pp. 53 ff.

[36] P. von der Osten-Sacken, ibid., pp. 18 ff., has argued that various aspects and concepts in Deutero-Isaiah have found expression in Daniel.

[37] Against D. Rössler, *Gesetz und Geschichte*, WMANT iii, 1960, who argues that a theology of history was of central importance to the apocalyptists who, it is maintained, in their schematic presentations of history sought to portray the entire course of history from the beginning to the *eschaton* as the working out of the divine election of Israel. For criticisms of Rössler's work see, e.g., P. Vielhauer, op. cit.; W, R. Murdock, 'History and Revelation in Jewish Apocalyptic', *Interpretation* xxi (1967), 167-87; H. D. Betz, 'The Concept of Apocalyptic in the Theology of the Pannenberg Group', *JTC* vi (1969), 192-207. On the concept of history in apocalyptic, see also M. Noth's important essay 'Das Geschichtsverständnis der alttestamentlichen

onwards, as Hanson, for example, has argued. It is worth recalling Rowley's dictum, referred to earlier, that 'apocalyptic is the child of prophecy, yet diverse from prophecy'. To argue that apocalyptic has its roots in prophecy, even to argue that it originated among prophetic circles, does not mean that it is identical with prophecy. There was clearly development and this development entailed the transformation of prophetic ideas as well as the absorption of concepts from other spheres, including wisdom.

We must now sum up. The majority of recent contributions to the investigation of the origins of apocalyptic have affirmed the view that it has its roots in prophecy. Though some scholars maintain that Daniel is the first apocalyptic work properly speaking, the general trend has been to find the origins of apocalyptic in a much earlier period, several scholars arguing that it emerged as early as the sixth century B.C. The contention that passages and whole sections of literature deriving from the exilic and post-exilic period and now embedded in prophetic books are to be classified as apocalyptic points to the possibility that groups of prophetic disciples were those among whom apocalyptic had its beginnings. That in the course of its development apocalyptic absorbed ideas from wisdom as well as from many other diverse spheres of knowledge has not been disputed. But the majority of scholars have rejected the view that wisdom and not prophecy was the ground from which apocalyptic sprang. Most scholars still allow, with varying degrees of emphasis, that influences from foreign sources, especially from Persia, contributed to the development of apocalyptic. We have noted, however, that the extent of such influences has more recently been severely questioned and it has been contended that the formative elements in the emergence of apocalyptic derived from traditions, ideas, and mythic themes long since at home in Israel and in some instances inherited ultimately from Canaanite sources. To this extent the case for regarding apocalyptic in its essentials as a native Israelite development has emerged strongly in recent research.

Apokalyptik' originally published in 1954 and now contained in his *GSAT*, 1960, pp. 248–73, ETr by D. R. Ap-Thomas in *The Laws in the Pentateuch and Other Essays*, Edinburgh and London, 1966, pp. 194–214.

BIBLIOGRAPHY

AMSLER, S. 'Zacharie et l'origine de l'apocalyptique', SVT xxii, 1972, pp. 227–31.

BARR, J. 'The Meaning of "Mythology" in Relation to the Old Testament', *VT* ix (1959), 1–10.

BETZ, H. D. 'The Concept of Apocalyptic in the Theology of the Pannenberg Group', *JTC* vi (1969), 192–207.

BLOCH, J. *On the Apocalyptic in Judaism*, *JQR* Monograph Series ii, 1952.

ČERNÝ, L. *The Day of Yahweh and Some Relevant Problems*, Prague, 1948.

CROSS, F. M. 'The Divine Warrior in Israel's Early Cult', *Biblical Motifs*, ed. A. Altmann, Cambridge, Mass., 1966, pp. 11–30.

—— 'The Song of the Sea and Canaanite Myth', *JTC* v (1968), 1–25.

—— 'New Directions in the Study of Apocalyptic', *JTC* (1969), 157–65.

EMERTON, J. A. 'The Origin of the Son of Man Imagery', *JTS* N.S. ix (1958), 225–42.

FROST, S. B. *Old Testament Apocalyptic: Its Origins and Growth*, London, 1952.

—— 'Eschatology and Myth', *VT* ii (1952), 70–80.

—— 'Apocalyptic and History', *The Bible in Modern Scholarship*, ed. J. P. Hyatt, London, 1966, pp. 98–113.

HANSON, P. D. 'Jewish Apocalyptic against its Near Eastern Environment', *RB* lxxviii (1971), 31–58.

—— 'Old Testament Apocalyptic Reexamined', *Interpretation*, xxv (1971), 454–79.

—— 'Zechariah 9 and the Recapitulation of an Ancient Ritual Pattern', *JBL* xcii (1973), 37–59.

—— *The Dawn of Apocalyptic: The Historical and Sociological Roots of Jewish Apocalyptic*, Philadelphia, 1975. (This work appeared too late to be used in the above essay.)

HERNTRICH, V. *Ezechielprobleme*, BZAW lxi, Giessen 1932.

KOCH, K. *Ratlos vor der Apokalyptik*, Gütersloh, 1970; ETr M.Kohl, *The Rediscovery of Apocalyptic*, London, 1972.

LINDBLOM, J. *Die Jesaja-Apokalypse, Jes. 24–27*, LUÅ, N.F.1, xxxiv, 3, Lund and Leipzig, 1938.

MOWINCKEL, S. *Han som kommer*, Copenhagen, 1951; ETr by G. W. Anderson, *He That Cometh*, Oxford, 1956.

MÜLLER, H.-P. 'Mantische Weisheit und Apokalyptik', SVT xxii, 1972, pp. 268–93.

MURDOCK, W. R. 'History and Revelation in Jewish Apocalyptic', *Interpretation*, xxi (1967), 167–187.

NORTH, R. 'Prophecy to Apocalyptic via Zechariah', SVT xxii, 1972, pp. 47–71.

NOTH, M. 'Das Geschichtsverständnis der alttestamentlichen Apokalyptik', now in his *GSAT*, 1960, pp. 248–73; ETr by D. R. Ap-Thomas in *The Laws in the Pentateuch and Other Essays*, Edinburgh and London, 1966, pp. 194–214.

VON DER OSTEN-SACKEN, P. *Die Apokalyptik in ihrem Verhältnis zu Prophetie und Weisheit*, Munich, 1969.

PEAKE, A. S. *The People and the Book*, Oxford, 1925.

PLÖGER, O. *Theokratie und Eschatologie*, WMANT ii, 2nd edn., Neukirchen, 1962; ETr by S. Rudman, *Theocracy and Eschatology*, Oxford, 1968.

VON RAD, G. *Theologie des Alten Testaments*, ii, Munich, 1960; ETr by D. M. G. Stalker, *Old Testament Theology*, ii, Edinburgh and London, 1965. The 4th German edition was published in Munich, 1965, and contains an expanded treatment of the chapter on apocalyptic in the 1st edition.

—— *Weisheit in Israel*, Neukirchen, 1970; ETr by J. D. Martin, *Wisdom in Israel*, London. 1972.

ROBINSON, H. W. *Record and Revelation*, Oxford, 1938.

RÖSSLER, D. *Gesetz und Geschichte*, WMANT iii, 1960, 2nd edn., 1962.

ROWLEY, H. H. *The Relevance of Apocalyptic*, 1st edn., London, 1944, 2nd edn., 1947, 3rd edn., 1963.

—— (ed.) *The Old Testament and Modern Study*, Oxford, 1951.

RUSSELL, D. S. *The Method and Message of Jewish Apocalyptic*, London, 1964.

SCHMIDT, J. M. *Die jüdische Apokalyptik: Die Geschichte ihrer Erforschung von den Anfängen bis zu den Textfunden von Qumran*, Neukirchen, 1969.

SCHREINER, J. *Alttestamentlich-Jüdische Apokalyptik*, Munich, 1969.

VAWTER, B. 'Apocalyptic: Its Relation to Prophecy', *CBQ* xxii (1960), 33–46.

VIELHAUER, P. Essay on apocalyptic in *Neutestamentliche Apokryphen*, ii, ed. E. Hennecke and W. Schneemelcher, Tübingen, 1964; ETr, ed. R. McL. Wilson, *New Testament Apocrypha*, ii, London, 1965.

ZAEHNER, R. C. *The Dawn and Twilight of Zoroastrianism*, London, 1961.

VIII

WISDOM

J. A. EMERTON

THE wisdom literature has moved towards the centre of interest of Old Testament scholars during the past quarter of a century. The following survey will, of necessity, be selective and will ignore much work, including some important work, concerned with the wisdom literature, such as studies of language, text, and versions, and it will be impossible even to list the relevant commentaries. The Apocrypha too will be almost entirely left out of consideration, notwithstanding the valuable work that has been done on Ecclesiasticus and the Wisdom of Solomon. I have, rather, chosen several questions in modern scholarly work on the wisdom literature of the Hebrew canon of the Old Testament, and sought to give some account of the principal developments.[1] The subjects that have received most attention include the literary forms of Israelite wisdom, its sociological background, the understanding of life in the book of Proverbs, and the relation of the wisdom literature of Israel to that of other peoples of the ancient Near East. A list of the books and articles to which reference is made will be found at the end.

I. NON-ISRAELITE WISDOM LITERATURE

Throughout the period of scholarship with which this book is concerned, work on non-Israelite wisdom literature has continued, and it has formed the background to developments in the study of the Old Testament. It is not the purpose of the present essay to survey recent study of wisdom in the ancient Near East in general, but it is necessary to mention some of it briefly.

---

[1] See also the surveys by Murphy (1967), and Scott (1970), and, for § II, Gemser (1962).

Perhaps the most important fresh ground that has been broken is in the study of Sumerian texts, and a valuable collection of material has been published by E. I. Gordon, a pupil of the pioneer scholar S. N. Kramer. Mention may also be made of the studies of Sumerian and Akkadian texts by J. J. A. van Dijk and W. G. Lambert. Wisdom texts in Akkadian have been discovered at Ras Shamra and published in *Ugaritica V*, Paris 1968, but none in the Ugaritic language has yet come to light.

The wisdom literature of Egypt has been of greatest interest to Old Testament scholars. To mention only two Egyptian texts, the publication of the Instruction of 'Onchsheshonqy has led B. Gemser (1960) and W. McKane (1970) to investigate its bearing on the Bible; and the priority of the Wisdom of Amenemope to Prov. 22:17–24:22 has been rendered even more probable than before by evidence about the Egyptian work's date (J. M. Plumley, p. 173) and by the refutation (R. J. Williams) of the theory that it is based on a Semitic original. To turn to a more general question, there has been a move in the last quarter of a century away from the tendency to see in Egyptian wisdom literature a merely secular utilitarianism and eudaemonism, and a religious understanding has been championed by such scholars as H. Frankfort and H. Brunner. The concept of *ma'at* has attracted much attention (see Brunner, pp. 93 ff.). The word can be translated 'truth', 'justice', or 'order' (Frankfort, p. 54); and it is used of 'a divine order, established at the time of creation; this order is manifest in nature in the normalcy of phenomena; it is manifest in society as justice; and it is manifest in an individual's life as truth' (p. 63). *Ma'at* is also sometimes thought of as a goddess. The way of life commended by Egyptian teachers of wisdom was to act according to this order, and the order was believed to be present in the universe as the result of the divine will.

II. THE WISDOM LITERATURE'S UNDERSTANDING OF THE WORLD, AND ITS BEARING ON OLD TESTAMENT THEOLOGY

Old Testament scholars have long been aware that the

wisdom literature of Israel raises theological problems. It was once generally believed that the older Israelite wisdom was utilitarian and eudaemonistic, rather than religious, and it is still understood in that way by such scholars as McKane, Würthwein, and Zimmerli. How was such a prudential, anthropocentric view of life, borrowed from foreign peoples, to be related to belief about Yahweh's election of Israel, his deliverance of the nation from slavery in Egypt, his revelation on Mount Sinai and the making of the covenant, and his saving acts in history? The difficulty was not removed by the presence in the Old Testament of a doctrine of retribution, whereby God punished or rewarded men according to their deserts.

The existence of a doctrine of divine retribution or requital (*Vergeltung*) was denied by K. Koch in 1955, and he later reaffirmed his thesis in answer to criticisms made by Reventlow. According to Koch, the suffering of the wicked was not regarded as a punishment meted out by Yahweh. Rather, the Israelites believed that there was an inner connection between an act and its consequences—indeed, they did not distinguish between the two. He finds a number of examples of that kind of thinking in Proverbs, such as 26:27: 'Whoso diggeth a pit shall fall therein: And he that rolleth a stone, it shall return upon him' (*RV*). It is not that Yahweh makes the punishment fit the crime: the very act of digging a pit or rolling a stone carries within itself the consequence of disaster for the person who performs it (cf. also 25:19; 26:28; 28:1, 10, 16b, 17, 18, 25b; 29:6, 23, 25). Yahweh is sometimes involved in the action: he watches over the connection between a deed and its consequence, enforces and hastens it, and brings it to completion; but what he does should not be described as *Vergeltung*, for that is too juridical a term, and it suggests that the consequence is something from outside a man and strange to his being (p. 32). The verbs *šillēm* and *hēšîḇ*, of which Yahweh is sometimes the subject, mean 'to make complete' and 'to turn back', respectively, not 'to requite', and *pāḳaḏ* has a similar meaning. However, it is doubtful whether Koch succeeds in fitting Yahweh's activity into a scheme of thought in which divine intervention would be superfluous, or whether it is possible to deny to Yahweh any initiative that goes beyond offering a helping hand to a sequence of events that would take place anyhow.

Koch notes that it had earlier been argued by Fahlgren[2] (whose book I have not seen) that, since Hebrew has a number of words denoting both a deed and its consequence (r^c, $r\check{s}^c$, $h\underline{t}^\prime t$, $p\check{s}^c$, $^c wn$, hms, $sdkh$), the Israelites, who had a 'synthetic understanding of life', did not distinguish between the two. Koch does not hesitate to follow Fahlgren in drawing from such lexical facts conclusions about the failure of Israelites to make a distinction between two types of concept. Finally, according to Koch, although the Israelite view of the world that underlies the belief in a connection between an act and its consequence has affinities with that of other peoples of the ancient Near East, it differs from them in that they were influenced by magic, whereas it was monotheism that caused the Israelite form of the belief to develop.

H. Gese begins with Egyptian wisdom literature, and he opposes the eudaemonistic understanding of its ethos and expounds it as living according to *ma'at*. He then turns to the Old Testament, and especially to the older collections incorporated in Proverbs (chapters 10–29). Here, too, he does not understand wisdom in a utilitarian way. Yahweh has ordered the world, and the wise man seeks to live according to the divinely established order even though he cannot always understand it, and the sages' teaching has behind it the authority of that order. Gese agrees with Koch that there was believed to be a connection between an act and its consequence and that such a way of thinking is not 'primitive', for it presupposes order in the world. He differs from Koch in two ways. First, he maintains that the Israelite view of life that he has described does not differ fundamentally from those of Mesopotamia and Egypt. Secondly, he finds in some verses in Proverbs (10:22; 16:1, 9, 33; 20:24; 21:1, 30, 31; 25:2) teaching that contrasts sharply with it. God is portrayed in them as free to act independently of the order in the universe, and Gese sees here evidence of the specifically Israelite faith in Yahweh. In 21:31, for example, we read: 'The horse is

---

[2] K. Hj. Fahlgren, *ṣ^edāḳā, nahestehende und entgegengesetzte Begriffe im Alten Testament*, Uppsala, 1932.

prepared against the day of battle: But victory is of the LORD'
(RV). The new outlook that such verses represent may have
had an influence on other sayings, where the old connection
between a deed and its consequence is found. The question is
then raised whether, after all, it may be legitimate to speak of
a doctrine of *Vergeltung* in the Old Testament. Thus, Gese
believes that, though most of the older Israelite teaching was
essentially similar to that of other nations in the ancient Near
East, the scheme is sometimes shattered by the free (and, it
must be said, somewhat irrational) grace of God.

U. Skladny's monograph on the oldest collections of sayings
in Proverbs agrees with much that has been said by Koch and
Gese. Men are to live according to Yahweh's ordering of the
world, and there is a connection between an act and its
consequence. However, he claims that differences of outlook
are found in the different collections, and he makes two new
contributions to the discussion. First, the collections in Prov.
10–15 and 28–9 contain a belief in a connection not so much
between a particular action and its consequence as between a
man's way of living and his destiny (e.g. 14:14a; 15:32a).
Secondly, he criticizes Gese's theory that certain passages
teach a doctrine of intervention by Yahweh that contradicts
the older doctrine, for he finds no contradiction in 10:22 and
25:2, and he offers a different explanation of the other verses.
They contain a new idea, but it does not break the connection
between an act and its consequence. For that, there would
need to be a statement that God grants wellbeing to the sinner
and trouble to one who has done good. What we find is divine
intervention, not between an act and its consequence, but
between the making of a human plan and its translation into
action. Skladny's explanation is satisfactory for most of the
sayings, but not perhaps for 21:31.

H. H. Schmid looks in turn at the literatures of Egypt,
Mesopotamia, and Israel, and seeks to expound their
understanding of wisdom, and to show how it was modified
according to the needs of particular historical situations[3] and
how a crisis arose when wisdom became an inflexible system.
Israelite wisdom, which was not secular in its origins any

---

[3] That does not, however, imply that the wisdom writers were interested in history.

more than that of Egypt, tended to become both more explicitly theological and more anthropological. Gese's claim that an outlook peculiar to Israel is found in certain passages ascribing a special initiative to Yahweh is contested on the ground that similar statements are made about God's activity in Egypt and Mesopotamia. Nor can monotheism in wisdom literature be regarded as distinctively Israelite, for a tendency to speak simply of 'God' is found outside Israel. However, Israelite wisdom literature is distinctive in laying stress on people rather than deeds: men are divided into two groups, contrasted with each other as good and bad. Schmid also places Job and Ecclesiastes in the context of a crisis in the wisdom literature comparable to the crises in Egypt and Mesopotamia.

W. Zimmerli, who published an article on the structure of Old Testament wisdom in 1933, returns in his commentary on Ecclesiastes in 1962 and in a paper published a year later to the question of the contrast between the Old Testament wisdom literature and faith in Yahweh the God of Israel.[4] Although he modifies his outlook in some ways (such as recognizing a religious element in Egyptian wisdom literature), his position remains essentially unchanged. There is a contrast between the tradition of the covenant and of Israel's historical confrontation with Yahweh on the one hand, and the very different outlook of wisdom on the other. In the wisdom literature, God is viewed as one who acts according to the order discerned by the wise men, rather than as one who acts freely. The outlook of wisdom is challenged in Ecclesiastes and its limits are seen, for the writer reasserts the freedom of God to act as he wills.

No recent writer has made a greater contribution to the understanding of Israelite wisdom literature than G. von Rad in his book of 1970, for which he had prepared the way in the first volume of his *Old Testament Theology*, and in his theory that Solomon's reign saw a change in some men's understanding of Yahweh's working in human life (see § III below). Before the monarchy, men had a 'sacral' view of life, and the old sagas told of Yahweh's direct intervention in striking

---

[4] The same problem is discussed by Würthwein.

ways in Israel's history. In the 'enlightened' intellectual climate of Solomon's age, however, such a naive understanding of Yahweh's activity became impossible for many men, especially for men influenced by wisdom.[5] Their view of life had become 'secular', and they knew that events happened as a result of cause and effect—yet they believed that God's providence worked in a hidden way through ordinary events. Against this background, von Rad expounds the older wisdom of Israel, which owed much to foreign influences and yet must be interpreted in its distinctively Israelite context. Although Yahweh is not mentioned in many of the early wisdom sayings, their teaching should not be regarded as utilitarian or eudaemonistic, and certainly not as hostile to Yahwism. The wise men believed that there was order in the universe (including a connection between an action and its consequence) and that it was possible for men to discover the order and to live according to it. There was no conflict with faith in Yahweh, for he was believed to have created and to sustain the order. Old wisdom was not a rigid system, and it was always open to revision in the light of experience and included a sense of the limits to men's understanding of the world. Nevertheless, although the wise men were Israelites and Yahwists, the wisdom literature said nothing of Yahweh's activity in history on behalf of his people.

In later times, there was a more theological exposition of wisdom in Prov. 1–9 and Job 28 and, later still, in Ecclesiasticus. The later texts did not introduce ideas contrary to the older wisdom, but made explicit and developed what was already implicit. Wisdom is personified in Proverbs, but it is not hypostatized, and it is to be understood as an attribute of the universe, not of Yahweh. Wisdom herself, the wisdom placed by God in his creation, approaches men and seeks to win them to herself. The description of this figure is probably dependent, in von Rad's opinion, on the Egyptian figure of *Ma'at* (see § V below), but it has been adapted to the Israelite situation. The world is said to praise God, as in certain psalms of the Hymn category (e.g. Pss. 19:2; 145:10).

[5] While Scott (1955) regards 1 Kgs. 5:9–14 (EVV 4:29–34); 10:1–10, 13, 23 f., as legendary in character, he does not deny that the 'beginnings of a wisdom *literature* were . . . associated with Solomon's court' (1970, p. 33).

Challenges to the wise men's understanding of the world
are found in Job and Ecclesiastes. Job questions the older
wisdom represented by his comforters, and the divine answer
from the whirlwind draws attention to the limitations of
man's knowledge, and creation is again made to bear witness
to Yahweh. Ecclesiastes is more radical. Though God is in
control of the world and there is a proper time for everything,
the author questions the connection between an act and its
consequences and maintains that man cannot understand
God's workings. Von Rad rejects Zimmerli's claim that
Qoheleth is the guardian of the old faith in Yahweh
reasserting itself against confidence in human theorizing.

III. THE WISDOM LITERATURE
AND OTHER PARTS OF THE
OLD TESTAMENT

In the period under discussion, some scholars have claimed
to find the influence of wisdom in an increasing number of
places in the Old Testament that are not normally reckoned
to belong to the wisdom literature. Such influence is usually
traced either to professional scribes and those associated with
them,[6] or to so-called 'clan wisdom' (*Sippenweisheit*). The
question of the relation between wisdom and apocalyptic will
not be discussed here, but will be left to the chapter by E. W.
Nicholson. Nor will there be an examination of S. Mowinckel's attempt to find in the wisdom psalms[7] evidence of the
work of scribes in the post-exilic period, for such ideas were
worked out as early as 1937 by his pupil H. L. Jansen.

G. von Rad finds affinities with the wisdom literature in
parts of the Pentateuch and the historical writings.[8] As was
seen in § II, he holds that a change from a 'sacral' to a 'secular'
outlook on life took place in Solomon's reign, and a belief
arose that Yahweh acts in a hidden way. Such a belief can be

---

[6] The theory that there was a professional class of wise men in Israel has been
subjected to a searching criticism by Whybray (1974), who thinks rather of 'an
educated class . . . of well-to-do citizens who were accustomed to read for edification
and for pleasure' (p. 69). His book was published after the present chapter had been
written, and it is impossible to discuss it more fully here.

[7] See also Murphy (1963) on the wisdom psalms.

[8] See his commentary on Genesis, and his articles of 1944 and 1953.

seen in the Succession Narrative in 2 Sam. 6–20 and 1 Kgs. 1–2,[9] where Yahweh's working is concealed in the course of ordinary human events (2 Sam. 11:27; 12:24; 17:14), and a similar outlook is reflected in the story of Joseph, which has close affinities with wisdom literature. The story of Joseph is a continuous narrative of some length written with great artistic skill. Joseph is portrayed as patient, restrained, and prudent, according to the ideal of the wise man who stands before kings (Prov. 22:29). As in some sayings in Proverbs (16:9; 19:21; 20:24), God's providence works through ordinary events (Gen. 45:8; 50:20). So closely does the story of Joseph reflect the outlook of wisdom that it can, in von Rad's opinion, be said to belong to the wisdom literature.

The Deuteronomic writings are examined by M. Weinfeld, who attributes them to scribal circles, to men who held public office in the period between the reign of Hezekiah, when Prov. 25:1 refers to their activity and Isaiah speaks of scribes (5:21; 29:14), and the fall of Judah. The word *sōp̄ēr* came to be used of someone whose work was, not only clerical, political, and didactic, but also religious. The Deuteronomic writings thus originated among scribes who belonged to the court, in contrast to the Priestly Document, which came from priests in the temple, and which Weinfeld, following Y. Kaufmann, dates in the pre-exilic period. The case for a connection between Deuteronomy and the wisdom literature is argued at length by Weinfeld. For example, Torah is identified with wisdom (Deut. 4:6), and wisdom and wise men are given a prominent place in Deuteronomy, sometimes in contrast to related earlier sources of the Pentateuch (e.g. Deut. 1:13–17, and Exod. 18:21 and Num. 11:16–30; Deut. 16:19, and Exod. 23:8). There are similarities of language and subject matter in, for instance, laws against moving a landmark (Deut. 19:14; 27:17; Prov. 22:28; 23:10), and against false weights (Deut. 25:13–16; Prov. 11:1; 20:10, 23). The wisdom literature is unlikely to be dependent on Deuteronomy, because some of the resemblances are also found in non-Israelite wisdom literature, and 'the material [in the wisdom literature] supposedly drawn from the book of Deuteronomy does not

[9] See also Whybray (1968).

contain the slightest suggestion of the religio-national concept that lay at the core of the deuteronomic teaching' (1972, p. 261). Further, Deuteronomy's humanitarian outlook is due to the influence of wisdom. Whether or not the details of his hypothesis are convincing, Weinfeld has built up a strong case for the influence of the wise men on Deuteronomy.

The concept of clan wisdom,[10] rather than scribal wisdom, is employed by E. Gerstenberger (1965) in his argument that apodictic law goes back to the clan or great family in the rules given to a family by its head. Examples can be found in the commands of Jonadab the son of Rechab to his followers (Jer. 35), and in Lev. 18 which is intended for the greater family. Similarly, Proverbs contains some teaching ostensibly given by a father to his son, and also various prohibitions (e.g. 22:22).

J. Fichtner discusses the relationship between the prophets and wisdom. Certain of the resemblances, such as some ethical requirements and a critical attitude towards the cult, are due to dependence on a common tradition in Israel or even the ancient Near East in general. Further, he claims, there is no sign of the influence of wisdom on Amos, Hosea, and Micah, who all come from the country. Isaiah is different. On the one hand, he attacks the wise men of Judah and other countries, particularly the statesmen who rely on their own wisdom (e.g. 3:1–3; 5:21; 19:11 f.; 29:14; 30:1 ff.). On the other, his prophecies show affinity with wisdom in, for example, the parables of 5:1 ff.; 28:23 ff., play on words, and the use of words like *ḥākām, bînâh, yāʿaṣ,* and *daʿaṯ.* Fichtner concludes that Isaiah was probably a wise man before his call to become a prophet.[11] After Isaiah, though there is little evidence for a connection between most prophets and wisdom, there are attacks on foreign wise men, and traces of the influence of wisdom can be found in Habakkuk, Jeremiah, and Deutero-Isaiah.

Like Fichtner, W. McKane (1965) sees a contrast between

[10] J. P. Audet believes that the origins of both wisdom and law are to be found in family life in pre-urban civilization.

[11] J. W. Whedbee's discussion of the problem leads him to doubt whether Isaiah had been a wise man, but he agrees that there was 'a vital connection between Isaiah and wisdom' (p. 151).

the prophets and the wise men. The former looked to the word of Yahweh for guidance, the latter to their own hard-headed, empirical judgement. McKane agrees with those who hold that wisdom was particularly connected with the class of officials, scribes, and statesmen, and he rejects von Rad's opinion that early Israelite wisdom had a religious character. Isaiah and the other prophets opposed the worldly-wise policies of the statesmen of Judah, and claimed that wisdom and power belonged to Yahweh alone. That claim implied a more positive attitude towards wisdom, and sapiential words were reinterpreted in terms of Yahweh's requirements from men (e.g. Hos. 4:6; Jer. 3:15). The wise men too changed their attitude, and came to regard God's law as wisdom. McKane agrees with Weinfeld in finding scribal influence in Deuteronomy: in 4:5 f., for instance, 'the vocabulary of old wisdom is reinterpreted in terms of Deuteronomic piety' (p. 107). Jeremiah, however, objects (8:8 f.) to the wise men's activity as apologists for the Torah, because it 'was essentially bogus and did not constitute an authentic response to the *dābār* of Yahweh' (p. 112).

The relation of the prophets in general to wisdom is discussed by J. Lindblom. He concludes that they knew of wisdom and valued it, but were hostile to it when it 'is opposed to the divine word through the prophets' (p. 204); and also that the influence of wisdom can be detected in the ideas and style of the prophets. In Amos, for example, there are sayings concerned with numbers (1:3, etc.; 4:8; 5:3; 6:5—an error for 6:9?), and a similar phenomenon can be found in the wisdom literature (e.g. Prov. 6:16; 30:15 ff.).

S. Terrien goes much farther than Lindblom in his interpretation of Amos and finds evidence for 'an acquaintance with the language and speech habits' of the wise men (p. 109), and he advances the 'conjecture' that 'the prophet received from the sapiential circles some of his ideas' (p. 114). His evidence includes, not only the numerical sayings, but also the belief that the underworld is within Yahweh's sphere of activity (9:2; cf. Prov. 15:11; Job. 26:6), the appeal to common sense, the rhetorical question, the use of the words *sôḏ* and *nᵉḵōḥâh*, the wording of 1:11 (cf. Job 16:9; 18:4), and the reference to Isaac (7:9, 16) and Beersheba (5:5; 8:14), which suggests to Terrien a connection with Edom, and so with Edomite wisdom. Similarly, Amos' knowledge about astronomy, geography, history, and the social customs of foreign nations, his lack of interest in idolatry, his belief that God rules all peoples and that ritual is less important than morality, his interpretation of history, and the presence in his teaching of 'the seed of a moralistic conception of salvation' (p. 115), all bear witness to the influence of wisdom.

H. W. Wolff's monograph works out more fully the arguments for Amos' dependence on wisdom. Thus, he argues that the *Mahnreden* (admonitions) in 4:4 f.; 5:4–6, 14 f. (with a command followed by a reason, and sometimes with an antithesis), and the passages beginning with *hôy*, 'woe', in 5:18; 6:1 (and probably the original form of 2:7; 5:7; 6:3–6, 13) are rooted in wisdom. In this he is influenced by his pupil Gerstenberger, and he thinks that what influenced Amos was the wisdom of the clan, not of the court and the school.

The arguments of Terrien and Wolff are examined by J. L. Crenshaw (1967), and most are rejected for one reason or another (e.g. some relevant passages in Amos are secondary; some similarities may be based on no more than a common experience of life). However, he accepts some of them, and also advances a new argument. He draws attention to the similarities between the doxologies in Amos 4:13; 5:6, 8, 10; 9:5 f. and Job 5:8–10, 14, 17; 9:5–9; he believes them to be secondary in Amos, but he argues that the resemblance 'possibly indicates that the language of Amos was influenced by the wisdom tradition sufficiently to encourage later redactors among the sages to insert portions of a hymn to Yahweh as creator' (p. 49). Despite the fact that Crenshaw notes some similarities in the Psalter, he does not discuss whether the passages in Job can be treated simply as characteristic of wisdom or whether they are themselves derived from psalms.

The influence of wisdom on Amos is also recognized by H. J. Hermisson, but he denies that it is the wisdom of the clan, and, indeed, challenges the theory that such wisdom can be found in the Old Testament. He questions the commonly accepted opinion that the book of Proverbs contains a number of popular proverbs, and argues that the contents are entirely, or almost entirely, the work of learned men. In particular, he subjects to a critical examination the theory advanced by O. Eissfeldt, *Der Maschal im Alten Testament*, BZAW xxiv, 1913, who finds in the Old Testament outside the wisdom literature some sayings that he believes to be popular proverbs (e.g. 1 Sam. 10:12; 24:14). Out of such popular proverbs, Eissfeldt thinks, were developed wisdom sayings in poetic parallelism and more polished literary form, and some traces of the originals can still be detected in Proverbs (e.g. 10:6b, 11b). Hermisson questions, on grounds of form and content, whether sayings such as those disentangled by Eissfeldt from their present form in Proverbs are true popular proverbs. In his opinion, the wisdom literature of the Old Testament reflects the world of the educated and wise. Although the Old Testament evidence is slight,[12] he argues that Israel, like Egypt and Mesopotamia, must have had some schools for the training of priests, and others for officials and probably also for the children of the upper classes. The collections of sayings in Proverbs have their setting in life in the schools, where they were used in teaching, and in the wider circle of readers who had been educated in them. It was for such readers that the Yahwist wrote, drawing on old traditions that originally had nothing to do with wisdom, and also the author of the Succession Narrative. Similarly, the traditions now found in Deuteronomy have passed through the hands of wise men, probably in Jerusalem. After the Exile, the traditions of the Temple and scribal schools flowed together.

How, then, are the affinities between wisdom and the teaching of some of the prophets to be explained? Hermisson thinks that Isaiah was an educated man, but he does not claim that Amos had been to school in Jerusalem. However, there were probably schools in other towns in Judah, and Hermisson cautiously suggests that the influence of wisdom on Amos is to be explained as the result of contact between him and such a school. Hermisson thus accounts for the affinities between the wisdom literature and other parts of the Old Testament by postulating the influence of men educated in schools.

E. Gerstenberger (1969) seeks to refute Hermisson's thesis.

[12] Whybray (1974), pp. 31 ff., shows how slight it is.

He maintains that Hermisson excludes in advance the possibility of finding popular proverbs, that his arguments are unconvincing, and that his attempt to find a setting in life is unsatisfactory. Not all Gerstenberger's criticisms are valid, but he raises some questions that will need further discussion by scholars.

Now that wisdom is being detected in many parts of the Old Testament, J. L. Crenshaw's attempt to find sound criteria is welcome. He points out the need, first, to define what is meant by 'wisdom', and to beware of 'a definition that is so comprehensive that it becomes unusable' (p. 131). Secondly, 'wisdom influence can only be proved by a stylistic or ideological peculiarity found primarily in wisdom literature' (p. 132). Thirdly, resemblances to wisdom literature in other parts of the Old Testament must be carefully examined to see whether there has been any change of meaning. Fourthly, ideas alien to wisdom must not be overlooked. Fifthly, the history of wisdom must, as far as possible, be taken into consideration. In the light of his principles he studies the attempts of G. von Rad, R. N. Whybray, and S. Talmon to find wisdom in, respectively, the story of Joseph, the Succession Narrative, and Esther. In the story of Joseph, for example, in Gen. 37, 39–50, he sees no clear 'stylistic and ideological peculiarities' (p. 136) as evidence for wisdom, and he argues that it conflicts in some places with the outlook of wisdom (cf. McKane, 1965, p. 49, and Redford, pp. 100–5). For instance, Joseph has not been trained in a school, and he is chosen by Pharaoh for his 'spiritualistic' qualifications; similarly, Joseph's relationships with his family and his inability to control his emotions do not exemplify the qualities expected in a wise man. Some of the arguments advanced by Crenshaw (and Redford) are challenged by G. W. Coats, who believes that the 'kernel' of the story, in Gen. 39–41 (where there is no mention of Joseph's emotions or his relationship with his brothers), is a 'political legend' concerned with the character and way of acting to be expected in an administrator, and that its author had been influenced by wisdom. The influence of wisdom in the story as a whole, which is a 'novella', is less evident, but the author may have lived in the 'enlightened' age of Solomon.

IV. LITERARY PROBLEMS IN PROVERBS

The four collections that are usually reckoned to be the oldest parts of Proverbs (A 10–15; B 16:1–22:16; C 25–7; D 28–9) are examined by U. Skladny from the point of view of both form and subject matter (attitude to Yahweh and to the king, social background, interest in agriculture, contrast between the righteous or wise and the wicked or foolish, doctrine of retribution). He dates them all before the Exile and argues (probably on insufficient grounds) that the relative chronological order is ADBC.

The subject of W. Richter's investigation is the literary form known as *Mahnspruch* (admonition), specially in Prov. 22:17–24:22. That part of Proverbs is not, he argues, a unity, and it is only the oldest part of it that is based on the Egyptian Wisdom of Amenemope. It is wrong to think that its literary form was simply borrowed from Egypt, for it already existed in Israel. Richter examines the form, both in Proverbs and elsewhere in the Old Testament, and distinguishes between two types of prohibition: the *Vetitiv* (*'al* with the jussive), which is accompanied by a reason and which is characteristic of the *Mahnspruch*; and the *Prohibitiv* (*lō'* with the imperfect), which is accompanied only secondarily by a reason. The former belongs to the school and reflects its outlook on life.

R. N. Whybray (1965) discusses the composition of Prov. 1–9, and argues, with the help of the ordinary methods of literary criticism, that the chapters are not a unity but are made up of ten discourses, each beginning with a similar formula (1:8; 2:1; 3:1, 21; 4:1,10, 20; 5:1; 6:20; 7:1), to which other material was added later. He compares the original discourses with Egyptian wisdom teaching. With the help of the same methods, he divides the later material into two classes, of which the first has been attached directly to the discourses and the second to the first. The reason why the discourses were thought to need supplementation was that, because of their Egyptian inspiration, their 'underlying ethos ... remained alien' (p. 93). The first additions were made to bring the discourses nearer the traditions of Yahwism and to give the teacher's words the authority, though not directly of Yahweh, at least of wisdom. However, 'no explicit mention is made ... of the connexion of this wisdom with God' (p. 92), because 'it was not yet possible to state the relation between Yahweh and wisdom unequivocally' (p. 94). The second additions seek to remedy the omission in the first by establishing a close connection between Yahweh and wisdom, and they were made in the Persian period. In contrast, the first additions reflect 'the period of the great pre-exilic prophets' (p. 105), and Whybray thus dates most of Prov. 1–9 before the Exile in opposition to the prevailing scholarly opinion that it is later.

Another challenge to the hypothesis of the post-exilic origin of Prov. 1–9 is offered by C. Kayatz, who notes two reasons for the commonly accepted view. First, it is claimed that the longer units, composed of a number of consecutive verses, represent a later stage of development than the verses complete in themselves in most of the rest of Proverbs. Secondly, the more religious character is thought to be evidence of a long period of development. Kayatz is sceptical about theories that postulate development along a single line, and she points out that longer units are found already in Egyptian wisdom texts.

In a massive work on Proverbs (1970), W. McKane combines a translation and detailed commentary on the text with a study of its literary forms in the light of other literatures of the ancient Near East. Apart from the poems and numerical sayings of Prov. 30; 31:10–31, which he considers on their own, he distinguishes between two types of literature in the book: the Instruction genre in 1–9; 22:17–24:22; 31:1–9; and the Sentence literature in the rest of the book. Whereas the Sentence literature is made up of wisdom sentences that are essentially self-contained and independent of one another, the Instruction consists of longer units. The indicative is characteristic of the former, but the latter gives commands and also reasons for what is commanded. McKane maintains that 'the Instruction is a separate genre whose syntactical structure can be described' (p. 5), and that it is found outside Israel. In order to demonstrate its international character, he examines in detail a number of wisdom writings from Egypt and Mesopotamia, and demonstrates the similarities. The Israelites thus made use of an international genre, and the

Instruction type of literature cannot be described as the end of an inner-Israelite evolution from the short wisdom sentence to the longer literary unit: it 'is not constituted by an agglomeration of wisdom sentences' (p. 5). The argument from form that Prov. 1–9 is post-exilic must, therefore, be rejected, whatever may be said in favour of a late date on the basis of subject matter. McKane's thesis, which he had worked out independently, is thus in essential agreement with that of Kayatz. He also agrees with Whybray's judgement that Proverbs 1–9 contains an instruction composed under Egyptian influence, and that it has been worked over and expanded from a Yahwistic point of view. He does not follow Whybray, however, in seeking, by means of literary critical methods, to separate the original Instruction from later additions (pp. 279 f.)

McKane's analysis of the Sentence literature of Proverbs leads him to challenge some recent theories. He classifies the material into three groups concerned with : A 'the education of the individual for a successful and harmonious life'; B 'the harmful effects on the life of the community of various manifestations of anti-social behaviour'; C 'a moralism which derives from Yahwistic piety' (p. 11). He argues that class C represents a reinterpretation of class A; and, if he is right, two consequences follow. First, Skladny's comparative dating of collections in Proverbs must be challenged, because the proportions of class A to class C material in the collections are not what would be expected. Secondly, there is reason to question the theory that Israelite wisdom was religious from the beginning. McKane rightly contends that his 'account of the relation of class C sentences to the class A sentences cannot adequately be refuted by entering objections of a very general character' (p. 16). The fact that wisdom had a religious nature outside Israel does not prove that it must always have been religious within Israel. McKane continues to maintain the theory advanced in his earlier book that it was only 'in the late pre-exilic period' that 'the wise men, who stood in an international tradition of wisdom, were beginning to come to terms with Yahwism' (p. 19).

Scott (1972) agrees with McKane's 'distinction between sayings with or without religious content and terminology' and carries it farther by analysing the sayings according to their aim and social background. He also challenges Skladny's arrangement of the collections in chronological sequence— indeed, he maintains that there 'is no firm evidence that the sentence proverbs in chapters x-xxii 16 (or, x-xv, xvi-xxii 16), xxv-xxvii, xxviii-xxix once existed as independent "collections"' (p. 164).

V. THE PERSONIFIED FIGURE OF WISDOM

A controversial problem of Prov. 1–9 is that of the origin and meaning of the personified figure of Wisdom in 1:20–33; 8:1–9:6. Some scholars stress its affinities with other parts of the Old Testament. Thus, while P. A. H. de Boer does not deny the possibility of foreign influence, he believes that the figure should be understood primarily in terms of the counsellor, who was familiar in Israelite life. Others postulate a non-Israelite origin and attach more importance to it, and two such theories will now be considered.

First, in an article discussing the general question of Canaanite and Phoenician sources of Israelite wisdom, W. F Albright argues that 'chapters viii-ix are full of Canaanite words and expressions, and may go back to Phoenician sources more directly than any other material in Proverbs' (p. 7). He here develops further a thesis that he earlier put forward in a book where he mentions the connection in Ugaritic texts between El and wisdom (*ḥkmt*), and the reference to wisdom in lines 94 f. of the Aramaic text of Aḥiqar from Elephantine, and speaks of a 'Canaanite-Aramaean origin'.[13] Albright's argument is far from satisfactory. Some of his alleged 'Canaanitisms' in language are unconvincing; and, even where there are linguistic affinities with Ugaritic or Phoenician, it is unnecessary to suppose that Prov. 8–9 is dependent on a Canaanite text. Hebrew is closely related to Ugaritic and Phoenician and shares much lexical and grammatical common ground with them, and such linguistic resemblances as are genuine are explicable in terms

---

[13] *From the Stone Age to Christianity*, 2nd edn., Baltimore, 1946, pp. 282–4. The Aramaic text is found in A. Cowley, *Aramaic Papyri of the Fifth Century B.C.*, Oxford, 1923, p. 215.

of that relationship without postulating dependence on a text. Nor does his appeal to the mythological background add much strength to his case. Quite apart from questionable details of his argument (such as his belief that 8:24 alludes to the dragon myth), similarities in ideas can be explained as examples of general Israelite beliefs held in common with, and doubtless ultimately borrowed from, peoples in and near Palestine. The Rephaim, for example, who are mentioned in 9:18, are spoken of elsewhere in the Old Testament and were part of the general Israelite belief about the underworld. As far as Ugaritic and Aramaic references to wisdom are concerned, there is no evidence for personification in the former, and an Aramaic document from a fifth-century Jewish colony in Egypt is of doubtful value as evidence for earlier 'Canaanite-Aramaean' ideas—and the expression 'Canaanite-Aramaean' itself needs further definition. Such criticisms of Albright's theory have been made by Whybray (1965) and McKane (1970).

Secondly, an Egyptian origin has been favoured by several scholars. In view of the interest recently shown in *Ma'at*, it was to be expected that a connection with the figure of wisdom would be suggested. The same passage in the Aramaic sayings of Aḥiqar from Elephantine that Albright regards as evidence for a 'Canaanite-Aramaean' origin is thought by H. Donner to point to Egyptian influence. He notes that *Ma'at* was regarded as both an abstract quality and a goddess, was believed to be highly regarded by the gods, and was of great importance for the wisdom literature. The Jewish colony living in Egypt were probably influenced by Egyptian ways of thought, and the idea of personified Wisdom, which had thus come into existence among Jews in Egypt, was the source of the personification in Proverbs.

C. Kayatz examines the literary form of Proverbs 8, particularly the way in which Wisdom speaks of herself in the first person. She compares texts in which Egyptian gods and goddesses speak and, although she cites no text in which *Ma'at* speaks in such a way, she argues that there are resemblances between *Ma'at* and Wisdom. *Ma'at* is pictured as a goddess: she is a daughter of Atum, and Prov. 8:30–31 (reading *'āmûn*, 'darling', instead of *'āmôn*) describes Wisdom as a child with Yahweh. Attention is drawn to other similarities—even the comparison of Wisdom to a necklace in Prov.1:9; 3:22. It is thus claimed that Prov. 8 owes much to Egyptian influence, although Kayatz recognizes that there are also differences and believes that the influence should not be understood to mean a direct taking over of the figure of *Ma'at*. Kayatz's theory about the Egyptian background of the portrayal of Wisdom is accepted by von Rad, but he is more interested in the place of Wisdom in Israelite thought, and his understanding of its significance was sketched above in § II.

Whybray's theory of the two stages by which the original discourses in Prov. 1–9 were supplemented has implications for his understanding of the personified figure of Wisdom. He attributes 1:20–33; 8:1–21, 32–6; 9:1–6 (and the personi-fication of Folly in 9:13–18) to the first addition. He believes that 'the figure of the goddess of love *Ištar-Astarte*' (p. 92) has had some influence, but he attaches little importance to it and maintains that it must be seen as merely one of several influences. The author's poetical imagination was also at work, and he drew on material in the discourses, and also sought to provide a counter-attraction to the 'strange woman' of earlier chapters. At the second stage, 8:13a, 22–31, 35b were added. They did not have a mythological origin, though they may have been dependent on a lost account of creation, and they were not intended 'to bridge the gulf between God and man ... but to bridge another gap—that between the wisdom tradition and the main Israelite religious tradition—by emphasizing that all wisdom comes from God' (p. 104).

VI. THE BOOK OF JOB

Although it is impossible to examine here most of what has been written recently about the book of Job, attention will be drawn briefly to some works involving a discussion of its literary form.

C. Westermann analyses in detail the various literary forms used in Job, such as those belonging to the psalms and to the courts of law. He maintains that the book should not be understood as a discussion of the intellectual problem of suffering such as might be expected in the wisdom literature, but that its theme is rather the existential question, 'Why do I suffer?', and that a most important element in it is the Lament. His careful study of the literary character and meaning of Job is valuable, but it needs to be read in the light of Fohrer's critical review.

H. Gese thinks that the existence of the Babylonian poem about a righteous sufferer (*ludlul bēl nēmeḳi*) and of related Sumerian texts makes it possible to speak of a distinct category (*Gattung*) of literature, which includes first an account of the suffering; secondly a lamentation; and thirdly the divine response in healing the sufferer. The scheme presupposes a connection between an act and its consequence, contrary to the beliefs of the earlier Sumerian cult, and its origin is to be sought among the Sumerian wise men. Gese believes that the popular story about Job, which was the basis of the present book, belongs to that category. The later writer, who used the old story but substituted his own poem for the middle section, thus took over the old scheme, but he changed it in such a way as to present ideas that contradicted those of tradition. The connection between an act and its consequence is broken, and Yahweh appears as one who is not bound by it. The poet consciously takes the same step that was taken, perhaps unconsciously, by those who added to Proverbs the sayings about Yahweh's freedom and power. Gese's interpretation of Job is thus related to his understanding of Proverbs, which was considered in § II. It remains interesting and stimulating, even though the amount of material available may not suffice to justify him in postulating the existence of a distinct literary category.

Finally, von Rad (1955) suggests that Job 38 may be dependent on a document like the list of various phenomena in the Egyptian Onomasticon of Amenope; and a similar kind of learning is found in the questions asked in Papyrus Anastasi I. Other Jewish works that perhaps have the same background are Ps. 148, Ecclus. 43, and the Song of the Three Holy Children.

BIBLIOGRAPHY

(SVT iii = NOTH, M., and THOMAS, D. W. (eds.), *Wisdom in Israel and in the Ancient Near East* (Rowley *Festschrift*), Leiden, 1955).

ALBRIGHT, W. F. 'Some Canaanite-Phoenician sources of Hebrew wisdom', SVT iii, pp. 1–15.

AUDET, J. P. 'Origines comparées de la double tradition de la loi et de la sagesse dans le Proche-Orient ancien', *Proceedings of the 25th International Congress of Orientalists at Moscow 1960*, i (1962), 352–7.

DE BOER, P. A. H. 'The counsellor', SVT iii, pp. 42–71.

BRUNNER, H. 'Die Weisheitsliteratur', in B. SPULER (ed.), *Handbuch der Orientalistik*, i. 2, Leiden, 1952, 90–110.

COATS, G. W. 'The Joseph Story and Ancient Wisdom: a Reappraisal', *CBQ* xxxv (1973), 285–97.

CRENSHAW, J. L. 'The Influence of the Wise upon Amos', *ZAW* lxxix (1967), 42–52.

—— 'Method in Determining Wisdom Influence upon "Historical" Literature', *JBL* lxxxviii (1969), 129–42.

VAN DIJK, J. J. A. *La Sagesse suméro-accadienne*, Leiden, 1953.

DONNER, H. 'Die religionsgeschichtlichen Ursprünge von Prov. Sal. 8, 1', *Zeitschrift für ägyptische Sprache und Altertumskunde*, lxxxii (1958), 8–18.

FICHTNER, J. 'Jesaja unter den Weisen', TLZ lxxiv (1949), 75–80, reprinted in *Gottes Weisheit*, Stuttgart, 1965, pp. 18–26.

—— 'Jahwes Plan in der Botschaft des Jesaja', *ZAW* lxiii (1951), 16–33, reprinted in *Gottes Weisheit*, pp. 27–43.

FOHRER, G. Review of Westermann in *VT* vii (1957), 107–11.

FRANKFORT, H. *Ancient Egyptian Religion. An Interpretation*, New York, 1948.

GEMSER, B. 'The Instructions of 'Onchsheshonqy and Biblical Wisdom Literature', *Congress Volume, Oxford 1959*, SVT vii (1960), pp. 102–28.

—— 'The Spiritual Structure of Biblical Aphoristic Wisdom', *Homiletica en Biblica*, xxi (1962), 3–10, reprinted in A. VAN SELMS and A. S. VAN DER WOUDE (ed.), *Adhuc loquitur*, Leiden, 1968, pp. 138–49.

GERSTENBERGER, E. *Wesen und Herkunft des 'apodiktischen Rechts'*, WMANT xx, Neukirchen, 1965.

—— 'Zur alttestamentlichen Weisheit', *Verkündigung und Forschung*, xiv. 1 (1969), 28–44.

GESE, H. *Lehre und Wirklichkeit in der alten Weisheit*, Tübingen, 1958.

GORDON, E. I. *Sumerian Proverbs*, Philadelphia, 1959.

HERMISSON, H. J. *Studien zur israelitischen Spruchweisheit*, WMANT xxviii, 1968.

JANSEN, H. L. *Die spätjudische Psalmendichtung, ihr Entstehungskreis und ihr 'Sitz im Leben'*, Oslo, 1937.

KAYATZ, C. *Studien zu Proverbien 1–9*, WMANT xxii, 1966.

KOCH, K. 'Gibt es ein Vergeltungsdogma im Alten Testament?', *Zeitschrift für Theologie und Kirche*, lii (1955), 1–42.

—— 'Der Spruch "Sein Blut bleibe auf seinem Haupt" und die israelitische Auffassung vom vergossenen Blut', *VT* xii (1962), 396–416.

LAMBERT, W. G. *Babylonian Wisdom Literature*, Oxford, 1960.

LINDBLOM, J. 'Wisdom in the Old Testament Prophets', SVT iii, pp. 192–204.

McKane, W. *Prophets and Wise Men*, SBT xliv, 1965.

—— *Proverbs. A New Approach*, London, 1970.

Mowinckel, S. 'Psalms and Wisdom', SVT iii, pp. 205–24.

Murphy R. E. 'A Consideration of the Classification "Wisdom Psalms",' *Congress Volume. Bonn 1962*, SVT ix, 1963, pp. 56–67.

—— 'Assumptions and Problems in Old Testament Wisdom Research', *CBQ* xxix (1967), 407–18.

Plumley, J. M. 'The teaching of Amenemope', *DOTT*, pp. 172–86.

von Rad, G. 'Der Anfang der Geschichtsschreibung im alten Israel', *Archiv für Kulturgeschichte* xxxii (1944), 1–42, reprinted in *GSAT*, Munich, 1958, pp. 148–88; ETr, 'The Beginnings of Historical Writing in Ancient Israel', in *The Problem of the Hexateuch and Other Essays*, Edinburgh, 1966, pp. 166–204.

—— 'Josephsgeschichte und ältere Chokma', *Congress Volume. Copenhagen 1953*, SVT i (1953), pp. 120–7, reprinted in *GSAT*, pp. 272–80; ETr, 'The Joseph Narrative and Ancient Wisdom', *Problem*, pp. 292–300.

—— 'Hiob xxxviii und die altägyptische Weisheit', SVT iii, pp. 293–301; reprinted in *GSAT*, pp. 262–71; ETr, '*Job* xxxviii and Ancient Egyptian Wisdom', *Problem*, pp. 281–91.

—— *Theologie des Alten Testaments*, i, Munich, 1957; ETr, *Old Testament Theology*, i, Edinburgh, 1962.

—— *Weisheit in Israel*, Neukirchen, 1970; ETr, *Wisdom in Israel*, London, 1972.

Redford, D. B. *A Study of the Biblical Story of Joseph*, SVT xx, 1970.

Reventlow, H. Graf 'Sein Blut komme über sein Haupt', *VT* x. (1960), 311–27.

Richter, W. *Recht und Ethos, Versuch einer Ortung des weisheitlichen Mahnspruches*, Munich, 1966.

Schmid, H. H. *Wesen und Geschichte der Weisheit. Eine Untersuchung zur altorientalischen und israelitischen Weisheitsliteratur*, BZAW ci, 1966.

Scott, R. B. Y. 'Solomon and the Beginnings of Wisdom in Israel', SVT iii, pp. 262–79.

—— 'The Study of the Wisdom Literature', *Interpretation*, xxiv (1970), 20–45.

—— 'Wise and Foolish, Righteous and Wicked', in *Studies in the Religion of Ancient Israel*, SVT xxiii, 1972, pp. 146–65.

Skladny, U. *Die ältesten Spruchsammlungen in Israel*, Göttingen, 1962.

Talmon, S. '"Wisdom" in the book of Esther', *VT* xiii (1963), 419–55.

Terrien, S. 'Amos and Wisdom', in B. W. Anderson and W. Harrelson (ed.), *Israel's Prophetic Heritage*, New York and London, 1962, pp. 108–15.

Weinfeld, M. 'The Origin of the Humanism in Deuteromomy', *JBL* lxxx (1961), 241–7.

—— *Deuteronomy and the Deuteronomic School*, Oxford, 1972.

Westermann, C. *Der Aufbau des Buches Hiob*, Tübingen, 1956.

Whedbee, J. W. *Isaiah and Wisdom*, Nashville, 1971.

Whybray, R. N. *Wisdom in Proverbs*, SBT xlv, London, 1965.

—— *The Succession Narrative*, SBT, 2nd series, ix, London, 1968.

—— *The Intellectual Tradition in the Old Testament*, BZAW cxxxv, 1974.

WILLIAMS, R. J. 'The Alleged Semitic Original of the Wisdom of Amenemope', *JEA* xlvii (1961), 100–6.

WOLFF, H. W. *Amos' geistige Heimat*, WMANT xviii, Neukirchen, 1964.

WÜRTHWEIN, E. *Die Weisheit Ägyptens und das Alte Testament*, Marburg, 1960, reprinted in *Wort und Existenz*, Göttingen, 1970, pp. 197–216.

ZIMMERLI, W. 'Zur Struktur der alttestamentlichen Weisheit', *ZAW* li (1935), 177–204.

—— Commentary on Ecclesiastes in H. RINGGREN and W. ZIMMERLI, *Sprüche/Prediger*, ATD xvi/1, Göttingen, 1962.

—— 'Ort und Grenze der Weisheit im Rahmen der alttestamentlichen Theologie', in *Les Sagesses du Proche-Orient ancien*, Paris, 1963, pp. 121–36, reprinted in *Gottes Offenbarung*, Munich, 1963, pp. 300–15; an abridged ETr appeared as 'The Place and Limit of Wisdom in the Framework of the Old Testament Theology', *Scottish Journal of Theology*, xvii (1964), 146–58.

IX

THE PSALMS AND ISRAELITE
WORSHIP

J. H. EATON

I. INTRODUCTION

(a) The nature of the task—difficulties and principles

THE study of the Psalms in relation to Israelite worship has
been very fruitful; it has rediscovered the vitality of many
texts and done much to change our whole view of Israelite
religion. Nevertheless, it has given rise to some difficult and
controversial questions.

Of the various sources of difficulty, we may mention first
the poetic style of the Psalms. This gives rise to many
ambiguities when the original human context has been lost.
Thus it is often doubtful whether a verb refers to past, present,
or future, or whether it describes a fact or expresses a wish.
Increasing knowledge of other Semitic languages has contributed much to the discussion of syntax and vocabulary, but
has also created many new uncertainties. The stimulating
commentary of M. Dahood well illustrates this, abounding in
novel and controversial renderings.

Another difficulty is to specify what we mean by a psalm's
'original' meaning or use. Ancient compositions so often
appear as new permutations of older stock rather than as
original creations. If one sentence reflects a rite of mythological
import, should we take it as evidence of the psalm's setting in
Israelite worship, or might it be a fragment from pre-Israelite
times, re-used with an altered intention? Are royal concepts
evidence of a king's psalm, or have they been reapplied to
commoners? Presumably, the most likely explanation of the
parts of a psalm will be that which leads to a good explanation
of the whole. 'Original' will refer to the meaning and use
which belonged to the psalm when it was constituted in its

wholeness. This wholeness will be seen in substantially the present form, though in some details the many centuries of further transmission may have left their traces. There is obviously scope here for differences of emphasis among scholars.

The most obvious difficulty, however, is that little coherent information about the rites of the Temple was preserved, especially for the period of the Davidic monarchy, 1000–586 B.C., which was decisive for the growth of psalmody. In post-exilic times conditions at the Temple were much altered. The calendar had been changed at the end of the monarchy to accord with Babylonian practice—in the year 604 according to E. Auerbach.[1] The contributions of prophets, which had formerly enhanced the drama of worship (below, p. 260), grew less, as huge accumulations of teachings were fixed and honoured in holy books. Above all, the sacred monarchy itself had disappeared, and therewith a constituent element of the earlier religion at the Temple. Admittedly, traditions from later times may have roots in the earlier period, traditions such as rabbinic statements about the usage of certain psalms at festivals, or similar information in the psalm-headings of the LXX, and other references to worship in the later biblical and rabbinic sources (see *PIW* i, pp. 2 ff.). But such information needs to be used cautiously with other lines of evidence if it is to throw light on the royal period.

Earlier references to worship, such as are found in Samuel and Kings, usually give us only glimpses of the rites. Some of these narratives, however, may yield more than is at first apparent, for the story of a particular occasion may reflect regular practices of commemoration. Thus the introduction of the ark of the covenant by David into Jerusalem (2 Sam. 6) and by Solomon into the Temple (1 Kgs. 8) may well give us impressions of an annual ceremony at the autumnal festival (8:2), a context for which Ps. 132 is admirably suited (cf. its use by Solomon according to 2 Chr. 6:41 f.). The whole curious story of the ark's loss and recovery in 1 Sam. 4–6; 2 Sam. 6 has seemed to some scholars to be related to a New Year ritual, particularly as Ps. 78:61 ff. gives a remarkably

---

[1] *VT* ix (1959), 113–21.

mythological version of the story. The argument here is much harder to establish, but suggestive treatments have been given by A. Bentzen (*JBL*, 1948) and J. R. Porter (*JTS*, 1954).[2]

In the psalms themselves there are many indications of accompanying rites: processions (as in 24, 48, 68, 118, 132), movements in or about the temple (5, 26, 138), sacrifice (5, 66, 116), music and dancing (57, 68, 81, 149, 150), mourning (42–3, 102); see further *PIW* i, 5 ff. But in themselves these do not yield an adequate view of the ceremonies or of psalmody's role in them.

Another disputed area is the application of knowledge about foreign worship to the study of Israelite practices. There are striking resemblances between the cultures of Israel and her neighbours, just as there are striking differences. In some ways, too, the primitive peoples of our own time may be closer to the thinking and practice of ancient Israel than are we. Fruitful comparison can obviously be made, and the often strident objections will hardly be justified, provided two conditions are observed. Firstly, one must be clear that the foreign element for comparison is firmly attested, and is not just a synthesis of items from different areas; one needs to know its own context in some detail. Secondly, one must not force the foreign idea into the Hebrew text; the act of comparison serves only to give us better eyesight to read across the many centuries what is actually in the psalm.

(b) Progress earlier in this century

The basis for fruitful research in our subject was laid early in the century by the great German scholar Hermann Gunkel (1862–1932), and his work has continued to shape the discussion since 1950. Of the various forms in which he presented his work, one slight and therefore perhaps misleading piece is now available in English, his article on Psalms in *RGG* (2nd edn.). But his two major volumes, recently reprinted, have never been translated: *Die Psalmen*, his great commentary of 1929, and *Einleitung in die Psalmen*, which surveys and classifies all psalmic materials, completed

---

[2] Here, and elsewhere in this essay where full bibliographical details are not given, reference may be made to the bibliography.

for posthumous publication by J. Begrich in 1933. Fortunately, an excellent account of Gunkel's work was given by A. R. Johnson in *OTMS*.

A decisive emphasis of Gunkel was on the importance of traditional language and ideas for the ancient poets—patterns of thought and expression that had been created for particular situations in society, even if, as Gunkel thought, they came to be used more widely. In accordance with such patterns he sorted the psalms and related materials into types or classes (Hymns, Royal Psalms, Laments of the Community, Laments of the Individual, Thanksgivings of the Individual etc.; see *OTMS*, pp. 166–81, and more briefly my *Psalms*, pp. 17–18). In this grouping much becomes apparent concerning the relation of the psalms to situations in worship, and much can be learnt about the structure of a psalm and the function of each part. But the psalms will not yield all their secrets to this systematic classification. Along with their custom-bound character, they still have much individual freshness and variation.

The development of Gunkel's perceptions was begun early by the gifted Norwegian, Sigmund Mowinckel (1884–1965). We shall be able to look at his views in some detail below, since not only have they continued to be much discussed, but Mowinckel himself was able to continue his prolific work for most of our period.

There were many other scholars, of course, who made useful contributions in the first half of the century, and a few of these must enter the discussion below.

II. YAHWEH'S FESTAL EPIPHANY

The first type of psalm listed and examined by Gunkel was the hymn or song of praise to God. He had no difficulty in showing that the situation which gave rise to this form of composition, and which long continued to be its main purpose, was the official worship at the Temple; he mentions especially the chief annual festivals and special victory celebrations (*Einleitung*, pp. 88 f.). In these festal praises he saw the high point of the 'most beautiful and profound days of Israel, on which she became conscious of the majesty, power, and grace of her God with full rapture and in deepest humility' (p. 68). He lists in the first place Pss. 8, 19, 29, 33, 65, 67, 68, 96, 98, 100, 103, 104, 105, 111, 113, 114, 117, 135, 136, 145–50 (p. 32).

He recognized further that there were two smaller groups which were to be attached to the hymns and which, we may add, have a peculiarly dramatic character. These were his Songs of Zion (he lists 46, 48, 76, 84, 87, 122, p. 32, but it is especially 46, 48, 76 which are relevant here) and his Songs of (Yahweh's) Throne-ascension (he lists 47, 93, 97, 99, p. 32; the customary translation 'enthronement' is too passive for *Thronbesteigung*). Here there is vivid proclamation and celebration of Yahweh's defeat of all his enemies, his assumption of his kingly power over all, and the perfecting of universal conditions; the Songs of Zion idealize the role of Zion as the place of the manifestation, while the Throne-ascension psalms stress the inauguration of the divine reign with the announcement *YHWH mālāḵ*, which Gunkel renders 'Yahweh has become King' (*Einleitung*, p. 94). Gunkel believed such psalms to be eschatological, referring to the future and final triumph of God's kingdom. He thought the decisive contribution came from prophets, who composed such celebratory songs as examples of what would be sung 'in that Day' (Isa. 26:1; 27:2–3; Jer. 31:23); then the psalmists had brought similar compositions into festal worship, in effect inviting the congregation to anticipate the future glory with full confidence. He was ready to admit that the prophets had drawn on concepts from older ceremonies; one influence might have been the model of human enthronements, and another (here, as will be explained, he responds to Mowinckel's theories) might have been a festival of God's Throne-ascension, introduced through Babylonian influence in the late monarchy (pp. 94–116). In spite of these complicated qualifications, however, he continued to maintain that the essence of the extant psalms is a depiction of God's future and final intervention, and that this derives, in all its tremendous scope and power, from the great prophets.

It was in connection with these dramatic hymns that Mowinckel made his most important development of Gunkel's insights. In *Psalmenstudien* ii he argued that these psalms were not songs about the future borrowed from prophecy, but were the very stuff of the ancient festal worship. He argued that this worship, like that of other early peoples, included dramatic rites to represent God's defeat of harmful forces and the renewal of his saving work. In particular, God made new the great acts of supremacy by which he had first created the living order. As God had asserted sovereign power as Creator in the beginning, so now on the festal day the psalms envisaged and proclaimed that he 'became King' (47:9/8; 93:1; 96:10; 97:1; 99:1; etc.). In accordance with the nature of such ritual all the world over, ancient and fundamental salvation appeared afresh. Renewal touched all aspects of present life that had classic form in the past: creation, covenant, national liberation, and settlement.

Working from this basic proposition that the dramatic hymns conveyed a present experience in worship, Mowinckel found that a large amount of material in the Old Testament appeared in a fresh light, a discovery which agreed with his estimate of the importance of festivals in early religion. Materials in the histories (2 Sam. 6; 1 Kgs. 8; 12; Neh. 8:10 etc.), prophets (Zech. 14:16–19; Hos, 7:5; Isa. 40–55 etc.), Pentateuch (Lev. 23:39; Num. 23:21 etc.), and in rabbinic sources combined with many psalms to fill out the picture of the rites and show that they were part of the annual observances which covered the transition to the agricultural new year about October. (Not read by Mowinckel until his own publication was ready, a small book by P. Volz, *Das Neujahrsfest Jahwes*, Tübingen, 1912, had reached a similar position.) In the post-exilic calendar we find a New Year's Day (i Tishri), a Day of Atonement (10 Tishri), and the feast of Booths (15–22 Tishri). In the pre-exilic calendar, thought Mowinckel, the week of Booths would have contained the essential New Year themes, though preceded by preparatory days concerned especially with expiation.

He argued that a considerable number of psalms belonged to the rites of this festival. To the aforementioned Songs of Zion and Songs of Yahweh's Throne-ascension, he added psalms which Gunkel had classified elsewhere. He was guided by the appropriateness of the contents, by clear affinities which often reach across Gunkel's divisions, by information in Jewish tradition, and by the perception that the rites had various phases and so would bring together psalms of different form within a complex of movements. Thus, for example, Ps. 95 consists of a section resembling the Songs of Yahweh's Throne-ascension (vv. 1–7a) and a prophetic section which mediates a speech of God (7b–11). Mowinckel saw no difficulty in using this to reconstruct the festal celebration of Yahweh's kingship, especially as its form is the same as that of Ps. 81, which by tradition and contents is a New Year psalm. In such fashion he gathered the following in *Psalmenstudien* ii as evidence for the rites and ideas of the festival: (a) Pss. 47, 93, 95–100, (b) 8, 15, 24, 29, 33, 46, 48, 50, 66A, 75, 76, 81, 82, 84, 87, 118, 132, 149, Exod. 15:1–18, (c) Pss. 65, 67, 85, 120–134. He later made good the omission of 68.

The drama of the festival centred on the manifestation of Yahweh as supreme. This supremacy, expressed in terms of 'kingship', was first and foremost shown by the work of creation, which was poetically imagined as a warrior's victory over a chaos personified as raging waters or dragons. The opposition to Yahweh in the festal drama might further involve the foreign gods or lesser beings of heaven. From Israel's history, also, were drawn figures which symbolized oppression or chaos and whose subjugation was celebrated in the festival, such as the Egypt of the Exodus or the kings of aggressive nations. All such were included in the demonstration of Yahweh's saving power. He was shown to be their conqueror and to execute judgement upon them. The way would thus be clear, if Yahweh so willed, for a time of good conditions in Nature and society, a time of salvation, of peace and plenty in the fellowship of God.

Such a prospect of ideal conditions under the realized kingship of God is, of course, very similar to eschatology, the hope of a future new age put forward by the prophets and developed by the apocalyptic movement. Mowinckel explained the resemblance thus: what was originally experienced as the meaning of the festival later gave content to a distinct and far-reaching hope for the future. The prospect of the New Year became the prospect of a new age or world. Given Israel's sense of her historical election and destiny, this was, in Mowinckel's view, a natural transition in times of protracted disappointment. For he reckoned that the festival had always had a concern for the future, if only for the fortunes of the coming year; in the ceremonies the past was renewed in order to affect the future. Yahweh's advent at the festival aroused hopeful expectations, and prophets who functioned in worship encouraged this mood with oracles (cf. § V below).

During four decades of further research and debate, Mowinckel did not alter the essentials of the views I have just sketched. Among his further expositions, the following deserve mention. In *Religion und Kultus* he set forth his views on the nature of cult in religion, and he related primitive to more developed forms. In *Zum israelitischen Neujahr* he defended his connection of his psalms with an annual celebration, as against theories linking them with daily sunrise or weekly Sabbath; he also re-examined the timing of the festival in the different periods and its character as a New Year observance. His Norwegian translation and annotation of the Psalms in *Det Gamle Testamente* showed his ability to give a good account of the whole Psalter; condensed in form, the work yet constitutes one of the most valuable interpretations of the whole. In *He That Cometh*, Oxford, 1956, he developed his views on the transition from cult through prophecy to eschatology, ending with the Son of Man. With this, the work of the great veteran at last began to make its proper impact on the English-speaking world, a process much aided by the appearance of *The Psalms in Israel's Worship* in 1962. In the latter work, he gave his views on the festival within a comprehensive treatment of the Psalms; he dealt with common misrepresentations of his work and gave extra emphasis to Israel's relating of salvation to the realm of history. His original presentation in *Psalmenstudien* ii, however, retains its value as a clear and attractive presentation of his thesis as such, and its reprinting with a new foreword by the author in 1961 was welcome.

In seeking to evaluate Mowinckel's theory, many still echo Gunkel's reactions (*Einleitung*, pp. 100 ff.). While Gunkel there accepts some of the theory, he cannot attribute as much creative power to the institutions and experience of public worship as does Mowinckel. He still maintains that the Songs of Yahweh's Throne-ascension incorporate a vision of future perfection which only the great prophets, Second Isaiah in particular, can have originated. As mentioned above, he concludes that a New Year festival of Yahweh's kingship had been introduced in Jerusalem in the late monarchy in reaction to the New Year festival of Babylon; elements from this worship were used by the prophets (e.g. Zeph. 3:14–15; Isa. 52:7–12), but recreated in an eschatological sense; post-exilic worship then celebrated Yahweh as King in the eschatological spirit of the prophets and from that worship come the extant psalms of Yahweh's Throne-ascension.

This tortuous proposal by Gunkel at least draws attention to the question of the relation of prophecy to the cult. But if we could only see prophecy as to a great extent an aspect of the cult, albeit a dynamic and sometimes radical aspect, its contributions and debts could be understood as continuous from ancient times, and we need not resort to the rather artificial zig-zags of influence imagined by Gunkel. His post-exilic dating of the Songs of Yahweh's Throne-ascension (especially 47 and 93) is very questionable. And in holding that the festival of Yahweh's kingship was such a late and minor introduction in the royal period, he has not reckoned with the ideology of the Davidic dynasty from its outset, whereby the Davidic ruler is the agent of God's kingship. Mowinckel's views, by contrast, leave the way open to a full appreciation of this point, to an early dating of much of the material, and to the possible tracing of characteristic elements to pre-Davidic Jerusalem.

In 1951 H.-J. Kraus attempted another solution of these problems (*Die Königsherrschaft Gottes im A.T.*). He was clearly anxious to secure for the dramatic psalms cultic contexts based on the commemoration of history to the exclusion of Nature-mythology. Thus, while he affirmed the dramatic translation 'Yahweh has become King!', he understood his theme and its materials to refer to the salvation of the Return from the Exile. He did not accept a pre-exilic celebration of Yahweh's kingship, even in the limited form eventually allowed by Gunkel. The theme, he claimed, was first launched in Israel by Second Isaiah, and its already cultic traits were due to the prophet's knowledge of the Babylonian festival. Post-exilic worship at Jerusalem had then followed Second Isaiah and created the Songs of Yahweh's Throne-ascension to celebrate ultimate salvation which had begun to dawn with the Return. As regards the pre-exilic worship, Kraus chose a few texts and fragments of texts to argue that the feast of Booths was introduced by a procession of the king with the ark (2 Sam. 6–7; 1 Kgs. 8; Ps. 132, etc.), his point being that this was commemorative of the oracles given at the foundation of David's dynasty in Jerusalem. Kraus called this piece of ceremonial 'the royal Zion festival', a representation of the historical election of David and Jerusalem. With this reconstruction, then, he sought to do justice to Mowinckel's success in rediscovering the importance and liveliness of Israelite festal worship, while avoiding what he saw as the danger of deriving the Bible from the rituals of Nature-mythology. According to this first attempt of Kraus, the post-exilic festival proclaimed Yahweh as having now 'become King' in relation to his developing work through history; the eternal Lord had appeared in the crisis of history to effect his sovereignty, superseding the Davidic kingship; the theme of creation was added to the celebration, as already in Second Isaiah, to stress Yahweh's universal power.

This theory shares the weaknesses already noted for Gunkel's (cf. *PIW* ii, 230 f.); above all, the celebration of Yahweh's kingship and many of its texts are surely not later than the monarchy based on such theology. Kraus himself soon realized this. In his major commentary, *Psalmen*, and in the revision of his useful *Gottesdienst*, he tries a new way of safeguarding his anti-mythological view of Israelite worship. He now clearly sees that worship of Yahweh as King–Creator in Jerusalem's autumn festival goes back to the early kings and has links with pre-Israelite tradition. But he modifies his position on the central proclamation, favouring the translation 'Yahweh is King' (after D. Michel in *VT*, 1956); it is a formula calling the congregation to prostrate themselves before the eternal King in Zion. In abandoning his earlier arguments in favour of 'Yahweh has become King', he is obviously concerned as ever to avoid any notion that Yahweh's power waxes and wanes with the cycle of Nature and ritual. But he admits that Ps. 47 does not fit his new explanation and he has great difficulty in accounting for its celebration of Yahweh's assumption of kingship as a dramatic event (*Psalmen,* pp. 204, 352). One may feel that Kraus increases the difficulties of interpretation by applying theological presuppositions. The whole range of texts must be considered and they must be allowed to speak for themselves. It may then appear that Israelite worship could enter into a rich use of drama and symbol in the service of characteristically biblical theology. It is especially important to allow that in the rapture of worship ultimate or fundamental realities are experienced as present *events.*

This last point, often made by Mowinckel, has been carefully considered by A. Weiser in his commentary. He is sympathetic to a dramatic interpretation of the rites provided due stress is given to the essentially Israelite inheritance, especially the manifestation of Yahweh over his Ark to renew his covenant. The worshippers there and then, Weiser explains, acclaim Yahweh as having now 'become King' in a scene of throne-ascension. Believing in Yahweh as Lord from all eternity, they yet experience this ascension as an event

'under the overwhelming impression of the presence of God. Time sinks into insignificance before God; to the eyes of faith the God-who-was is present as the God-who-is-to-come. It is at this point that the faithful experience the intersection of history and eschatology; and this is why the psalm (47) praises God's advent to kingship over the world as a recently accomplished event and calls upon the congregation to acclaim the King with enthusiastic shouts of joy' (*Psalms,* pp. 377 f.)

Before and during the monarchy, the feast of Yahweh was thus in essence 'a *sacred action,* a "cultic drama", in the course of which the fundamental events in the history of man's salvation were re-enacted ... [as] a new "event"'. The decisive part of the action is that of God who asserts his presence and conveys his word; to this is joined the action of the worshippers who respond with praises and prayers (pp. 28 f.). Above all, it is the making of the covenant on Mount Sinai which is thus re-experienced (p. 29).

Weiser's interpretation of such cultic experience is helpful, if rather too uniform in pressing everything into the tradition of the Sinai covenant, which in fact is not so prominent. Depictions of Yahweh appearing with storm or earthquake, for example, need not be linked directly with the Sinai revelation and indeed agree with the imagery of theophanies in the neighbouring cultures, as Lipiński shows in a substantial contribution of his own, *La Royauté de Yahwé*. Lipiński offers a copious survey of recent work on Yahweh's kingship and an elaborate discussion of three psalms in particular, 93, 97, 99. A valuable feature is his adducing of foreign parallels for many expressions. He re-examines at length and confirms the translation 'Yahweh has become King' as primarily a proclamation that Yahweh, triumphing over enemies, has acceded to the kingship. The conception, he argues, arose in very early times under influence from cults of Baal and El. For Israel, he thinks, it was first an expression of Yahweh's historical victories, and it is only in the monarchy period that a liturgical application is clearly established. He reconstructs the dramatic ceremonies of the autumn festival in pre-exilic Jerusalem, much in the tradition of Mowinckel: Yahweh's victory over his enemies is enacted at Gihon, followed by the carrying of the good tidings to Zion and a triumphant procession up to the Temple. Yahweh entered with his symbol, the Ark, while a priest proclaimed before it 'Yahweh has become King!'. Yahweh's self-manifestation as King in the Temple was signified to the faithful by clouds of incense.

While Lipiński places Ps. 93 simply in this setting, in other Songs of Yahweh's Throne-ascension he purports to find a long history of adaptation. Thus he thinks of Ps. 47 as made up from two pre-monarchy psalms, while 96 is said to contain reference to the end of the Exile, and 97 to events of 164 B.C. He is still clear, however, that 96 and 97 do not depend on Second Isaiah, while the prophet does depend on the treatment of Yahweh's kingship in liturgy. We can agree with Lipiński that these psalms are not entirely homogeneous, but Lipiński's distribution of them from before the monarchy down to 164 B.C. seems to have very little basis.

Some scholars have stood further apart from the tradition

of Mowinckel. C. Westermann, while keenly interested in the analysis of literary forms, was fearful lest the Israelite cult be seen as operating in a vacuum, rather than in constant relation to historical experience (*The Praise of God in the Psalms,* London, 1966, p. 21). He preferred the old view of psalm-singing as a form of worship accumulating from spontaneous reactions to national and personal events, and he defended the derivation of the Songs of Yahweh's Throne-ascension from Second Isaiah (pp. 146 f.). More recently, however, as in his *Isaiah 40–66,* his work is notable for the richness it ascribes to the pre-exilic psalmody of worship as the source of much in Second Isaiah, though he avoids specific discussion of the festival and the celebration of kingship.

While the discussion that has been traced above is far from closed, it will be seen that common ground has been found by several major authors, confirming Mowinckel's positive approach to pre-exilic festal rites: such worship is seen as an experience of dramatic encounter with Yahweh, who came with quickening grace and demonstration of his supremacy; it was of great significance for Israelite religion and all that flowed from that religion. At the same time, much effort has been made to show that the worship kept an 'Israelite' character, in that the sense of history was not lost in a maze of mythological ritual.

III. THE DAVIDIC KING IN THE FESTIVAL

In the kingdoms of the Near East it was natural for the ceremonies which fully inaugurated or renewed a king's reign to be part of a New Year festival. Government on earth was understood to be an expression of the order which came from heaven and which also quickened all Nature. The season for celebrating the life-giving rule of the deity was thus also the right time to install the man he chose to be his executive on earth, and it was the right time to hold the royal anniversaries or jubilees which strengthened his position.

A number of psalms have come to be seen as examples of the same basic connection of ideas and rites in the Davidic kingdom. Gunkel had put together nine complete psalms as his Royal Psalms used for ceremonies of the pre-exilic kings

(2, 18, 20, 21, 45, 72, 101, 110, 132), and of these he linked 2, 21, 72, 101, and 110 with the king's enthronement or its anniversary, and 132 with the anniversary of the royal sanctuary or palace. H. Schmidt (*Die Thronfahrt Jahwes*, Tübingen, 1927), accepting Mowinckel's view of the autumnal festival as including a dramatic celebration of God's kingship, expounded royal texts (Pss. 132; 89:1–3, 6–19; 1 Sam. 2:1–10; Pss. 2; 21; 110) within that setting: year by year on the first day of the festival, both Yahweh and the Davidic ruler symbolically defeated enemies and re-entered upon their reign (cf. 110:1). Mowinckel himself was notably restrained in use of the Royal Psalms for the reconstruction of the festival. However, he granted the likelihood that the king's enthronement was recelebrated annually in connection with the New Year festival (*PIW* i, 60, 66) and thus that 2, 72, 101, 110, as well as 132, 75, 118, would have a place there. Kraus, in his first account of the opening of the festival (above, p. 247), also took several Royal Psalms to be from annual rites celebrating Yahweh's covenant with the dynasty (132, 2, 72, 101; indirect evidence in 78:65–72 and 89:4, 5, 20–38). In his *Worship in Israel* (p. 222) he agrees that a new king's enthronement would be enacted in his first autumnal festival and adduces especially Ps. 110. He is reluctant to speak of regular renewals of the enthronement itself (p. 224), while still maintaining that there was an annual celebration of the royal covenant with other psalms (pp. 183 ff., cf. *Psalmen*, pp. LII f.).

The position thus far is widely agreed. The evidence for it is reasonably good. It may be summarized thus: (i) Kingship in the Near East was bound up with the deity's rule and hence with chief festivals. (ii) There is specific evidence in the neighbouring countries, especially Egypt, for the location of enthronement and its renewals in New Year festivals. (iii) Davidic ideology was also bound up with the deity's kingship and the Temple. (iv) There are strong clues that the autumnal festival had a fundamental significance for the Davidic ideology. Mention can be made especially of 1 Kgs. 12:25–33, of Ps. 132 taken with 2 Sam. 6 and 1 Kgs. 8, and of the system of dating by regnal years, which presupposes a constant starting date for new reigns; further, the new king's period of waiting until his enthronement in the festival seems to be denoted as the 'prelude of the reign' (*rēšît mamleket* N., Jer. 26.1, etc.) as in Mesopotamia. Certainly, a notion of 'making new' a kingship in grand cultic ceremony was known in Israel (1 Sam. 11.14). (v) Royal Psalms (2, 110, 72) strongly project Yahweh's kingship through the enthronement of the Davidic king; through this enthronement Yahweh asserts world-wide power.

It can thus be reasonably concluded that the meaning of the Davidic kingship was expressed by the custom of enthroning kings during their first autumnal festival and by recelebrating aspects of this ordination in the annual recurrences of the festival; Pss. 2, 21, 72, 101, 110, 132 will be some of the Royal Psalms which come from such rites.

Now what is striking about these texts is their vividly dramatic character. A classical story is re-enacted (132). Scenes of universal rebellion are projected 'live' (2). Symbolic demonstrations of the conquest of rebels are implied (2; 110). Words are launched from different angles: the king speaks to the nations (2); God speaks to the king (110; cf. 2 and 132); the king speaks to God (101; 132); a minister utters blessings and prayers over the king (21; 72). These texts, no less than those of Yahweh's kingship and care of Zion (above, p. 242), must have belonged to dramatic rites. The king was shown in active confrontation with the world-wide foes of Yahweh's rule.

But was his triumph then represented without more ado? Or was it shown to be reached only by way of tribulation? This latter possibility appears from Ps. 101, recently re-examined by O. Kaiser (*ZAW*, 1962). He points out that the plaintive prayer of the king, 'Oh when wilt thou come to me' (v. 2), joins with the elegiac rhythm of vv. 2–8 in pointing to a setting of ordeal. The king pleads his loyalty to Yahweh's requirements in a way that at this point resembles the Babylonian king's professions during his humiliation in the New Year ritual (*ANET*, p. 334).

The most serious attention to this question has been given by A. R. Johnson. First, in 1935, he contributed an essay to *The Labyrinth*, with a view of the autumnal festival rather like that of Mowinckel, but following H. Schmidt in drawing more royal texts into the reconstruction. A distinctive contribution was to link Pss. 89 (in entirety), 18, and 118 to a ritual humiliation of the king. Within the larger celebration of Yahweh's original work (as king-like Creator who mastered chaos), Johnson found a ritual sequence which conveyed Yahweh's work to revitalize society for the new year. This sequence of sacred drama showed Yahweh's defeat of the forces of darkness and death, which in the form of the kings of the nations had attacked his city (Ps. 48 etc.). Since the struggle was thus projected on the earthly plane, it was natural that Jerusalem's ruler, the Davidic king, should lead the defenders. Through 89, 18, 118, 2, 110 Johnson traced the symbolic confrontation: at first Yahweh allows his king, in a lesson of dependence, to succumb to the enemies, only to rescue him and crown him again with glory.

In his *Sacral Kingship in Ancient Israel* (1955, slightly revised in 1967) Johnson gives a fuller treatment; the king's ordeal is further shown in Ps. 101 and his vindication in Ps. 21. He now explains the significance of the sequence in a different way. Its main point, he thinks, was eschatological; that is, it was not the annual revitalizing of society but a disclosure of ultimate reality. It showed how the final triumph of the divine kingdom could come through the perfect service of a representative of David's house. Rather like the words and symbols of the prophets, it portrayed the ideal not as a far-off dream but with the impact of urgent challenge and encouragement. Johnson has certainly pondered deeply on the implications of these texts, which on any view have an amazing theological reach. He concludes (2nd edn., pp. 143 ff.) that this worship brings in particular

before each reigning member of the house of David the vision that he may yet be instrumental in preparing the way for the conclusive demonstration of Yahweh's sovereign power and his determination to secure an ordered world ... [he is] reminded that it is the responsibility of the true Messiah to put an end to everything which disturbs the right relationship between the various members of society ... In short, this great act of worship looks forward to the day when the crisis will have been reached in the persistent struggle between the forces of light and the forces of darkness, i.e. the day when the true Messiah of the House of David, by his own dependence upon the holy Spirit and his own filial devotion to the Godhead, will have justified the decisive intervention of Yahweh, and final victory (i.e. man's full 'salvation' or his enjoyment of perfect freedom) will thus be assured.

Thus Johnson has found another way of expounding the eschatological aspect of the worship, of which Gunkel, Mowinckel, Weiser, and Kraus, in their own ways, were conscious. It may be felt that his later work underestimates the intention of the rites to be revitalizing sacraments, legitimizing and empowering the work of reigning kings. But he has certainly helped us to appreciate the visionary power of pre-exilic worship. His reference of Pss. 89, 18, 118 to scenes of ritual humiliation is still considered by many to be unnecessary or improbable (so *PIW* ii. 253 ff. and Ward in *VT*, 1961). My own view, however, is that it gains support from further exploration of the Psalter's resources (below, pp. 259, 270 f.)

Mention must also be made of another type of interpretation of the royal rites, where a strong influence from polytheism is assumed. Some scholars thus take ritual experience of the king to represent the passion of a god who goes to the underworld and returns in triumph, an expression of the withering and renewal in Nature (cf. Engnell, *Critical Essays*, pp. 180 ff.). Re-enthronement would here be followed by union with the representative of a goddess, a divine marriage to promote the fruitfulness of land and people. G. W. Ahlström argues for such a cult in his *Psalm 89*; he thinks the king takes the role, not of Yahweh, but of a divine son or 'young god', whose name is to be found in the word 'David'. He follows G. Widengren in finding affinities between the psalm and Mesopotamian laments about the dethronement of the god Tammuz. Widengren has also related Ps. 88 to the descent to the underworld. In his *Sakrales Königtum*, which contains many interesting points, he brings together some evidence of a worship of Yahweh as a fertility god with a consort. This is not surprising, since the Old Testament tells of a constant and sometimes losing struggle against such a cult, as also against sun-god rituals, such as feature in the reconstructions of J. Morgenstern (*HUCA*, 1964). But such worship does not appear to be the mainspring of our psalms and one can hardly look here for their central interpretation. Some advocates of this type of theory have given justification to authors critical of most work on the psalms in royal ritual, though the hostility of R. de Fraine (*L'Aspect religieux de la royauté israélite*, Rome, 1954) and K.-H. Bernhardt (*Das Problem der altorientalischen Königsideologie*, SVT viii, 1961) is too undiscriminating, as also is the scepticism of G. Fohrer (*History of Israelite Religion*, London, 1973), and to a lesser extent R. de Vaux (*Ancient Israel*, London, 1961).

IV. PSALMS OF THE 'INDIVIDUAL'

So far we have seen that many psalms come from the great national and royal ceremonies. But what of the individual who prays in a private capacity, pouring out his heart in entreaty or in praise and thanksgiving?

The sixty or so psalms in which an individual speaker is prominent ('I' rather than 'we') were in former centuries generally regarded as utterances of David. But in the last century, when criticism came to regard the psalms as the expression of a religion much later than David, other explanations of the 'I' were sought. Many held it to be a collective, a personification of the nation or a pious party within it (Smend in *ZAW*, 1888). But E. Balla's argument for a truly individual speaker (*Das Ich der Psalmen*, FRLANT xvi, 1912) was vigorously endorsed by Gunkel, who had placed 'I' and 'we' psalms (laments and thanksgivings, but not hymns) in separate classes. While affirming that the types of the psalms of the Individual had first taken shape in the cult (as prayers and testimonies with personal offerings in the Temple), he considered that much of the extant material, especially the laments, expressed a private piety that had developed away from the institutions of the Temple. Thus he regarded it as a great error to interpret these psalms in a collective or national sense, for this was to misrepresent the heart-felt anguish and devotion of the single soul before God.

Since Gunkel, one line of development has accepted his argument for the truly singular 'I', but not his view of a divorce from the cult, which has seemed untrue to his own insights into the relation of literary form and social setting.

Accordingly, there have been several attempts to find a cultic setting where the laments could have been used by individuals. First Mowinckel had made a proposal in *Psalmenstudien* i, which he was soon to change considerably. His suggestion was that they were prayers provided in the Temple to go with purificatory rites; they enabled the individual to counter the malicious wishes and witchcraft of enemies and hence regain healing and good fortune. Then H. Schmidt (*Das Gebet der Angeklagten*) put forward another explanation for some twenty laments, which several current commentaries have adopted. He suggested a setting in the juridical processes of the Temple. The psalm would be a prayer for vindication by someone whose case could not be settled by ordinary courts and who was being held in custody at the temple, until the deity pronounced a verdict through rites of divination or ordeal (cf. 1 Kgs. 8:31–2). The linking of psalmody with ordeal trials, however, is pure speculation. Further, the varied psalms which Schmidt adduces (e.g. 4, 5, 7, 17, 26, 31, 57, 142) do not clearly conform to such a setting and are treated rather arbitrarily by Schmidt. Gunkel justly pronounced against the theory (*Einleitung* pp. 252 f.).

Another interesting attempt has been made recently by L. Delekat (*Asylie und Schutzorakel*). For most of the Laments of the Individual he proposes a setting in the procedures of asylum for fugitives at the Temple. Here too the individuals in need are awaiting God's verdict, in this case as to whether they can stay, or at least go with a safe-conduct, while their pursuers (cruel creditors, landlords, etc.) are waiting outside to pounce upon them if the verdict is unfavourable. The laments, Delekat believes, were not originally psalms for singing, but inscriptions deposited in the sanctuary on memorial stones or scrolls, to which happy acknowledgments could be added after a favourable verdict.

However, we may doubt whether the laments can be so sharply separated in origin from the other psalms, which were evidently designed to be sung with music. Personally dedicated inscriptions would have a different character, less poetic and with some specific references to people and circumstances. The asylum customs in Israel are not known to have covered the cases reconstructed by Delekat. The psalms do not so evidently centre on the need for asylum. And the expositions of particular psalms given by Delekat often seem fanciful and bizarre.

A recent contribution by W. Beyerlin (*Die Rettung der Bedrängten*) offers in effect a refinement of Schmidt's theory. He selects Pss. 3, 4, 5, 7, 11, 17, 23, 26, 27, 57, 63 as the most likely texts from ritual trials and suggests that their diversity is due to their belonging to different stages of the proceedings. It is valuable to have the case thus reassessed and remodelled in the light of recent work by so thorough a scholar. However, the result is no more convincing than in Schmidt's own presentation. The difficulties remain. Our information about cultic trials says nothing about psalmody. The psalms in question do not refer with any clarity to such a special situation, and indeed refer to quite other matters (e.g. warfare in Ps. 3). Nothing in tradition points to such a use. The selected psalms, diverse in themselves, do not stand out as a group from other psalms of conflict and entreaty.

Kraus has wrestled with these problems in his commentary and in his handbook on worship. He connects the 'I' psalms with individuals in various plights, including sickness and the cultic trials proposed by Schmidt. But he is inclined to consider the circumstances impenetrable, since traditional language has been used, which projects only archetypal patterns of suffering.

Only in the rarest cases were these songs the worshippers' own creation. Either they derived from the previously formed resources of worship—from adopted formulations that had been shaped by the cultic traditions, or they were a composition of the priestly circles, set prayers which the individual recited after the minister (my translation from *Gottesdienst*, p. 254; cf. *Worship*, p. 220).

Granted that the language is governed by tradition and that the circumstances are rarely particularized by the psalms, one may doubt whether the numerous modern treatments like that of Kraus have found the key. What is the value of insisting on the cultic situation proper to each class of psalm (cf. Kraus, *Psalmen*, p. XXXVIII) if this situation can only be explained as such an obscure medley? The situation of an ordeal trial, for example, should after all be quite other than that of prayer and sacrifice presented on behalf of an invalid. And it may be doubted whether the power and point of so many psalms could have been achieved by a putting together of traditional formulations in so impersonal a manner.

There has, however, been another line of development in the interpretation of these psalms. The fundamental contribution here was that of H. Birkeland in 1933 (*Die Feinde des Individuums*), which he defended anew in 1955 (*The Evildoers in the Book of Psalms*, ANVAO ii (1955), 2). He argues that the worshipper is Israel's leader, usually a king; the situation is the service of intercession which would be held in a particular crisis—for example when invasion was threatened or begun, or when a foreign overlord found fault with his vassal. The circumstances would thus be various and sometimes complex, but the role of the leader is a unifying factor in the situation of all such psalms. Birkeland was able to present a strong case, doing justice to the similarities between these psalms and those classed as national or royal, and also to the contents of the texts, which have mention of enemy nations and battle and use much royal ideology. His view is also closer to the traditional association of the Psalms with King David. From what we have learnt about the religious nature of ancient kingship, it would not be surprising if the Psalter bequeathed to us by the state Temple was so largely a royal collection. Birkeland's view also strikes a better balance between the individual and communal references in these psalms, and thereby between their formulaic style and their urgent personal focus. (This focus would remain, even if the actual composition and recitation of the psalms were commonly accomplished by specialists on the king's behalf.) The essential position of Birkeland was adopted by Mowinckel in *Det Gamle Testamente* and *PIW*. Mowinckel's earlier emphasis on the witchcraft of the enemies could still have some truth in it, since cursing rituals and the like were used in warfare (Num. 22–4).

The explanation of these psalms as royal has appealed to some scholars working from a different angle. Engnell, with his stress on the importance of annual rites (the king's combat with cosmic evil, his passion and exaltation, p. 254 above), was inclined to identify the suffering figure of these psalms with the king in ritual role. Ps. 22, for example, he regarded as one of the most central and typical of the royal passion psalms (*Critical Essays*, p. 122). Though he never accomplished a thorough treatment of the matter, his views stimulated A. Bentzen to revise the opinions he had expressed in his weighty Danish commentary of 1939 and to move towards a royal interpretation of many of these psalms. His consequent treatments in *Det sakrale kongedømme*, and *King and Messiah* are valuable reflections of his developing thought and contain many points of interest, but are presented in a rather sketchy manner. Another brief but helpful contribution from Scandinavia is H. Ringgren's *The Messiah in the Old Testament*, which relates the pattern of suffering in Pss. 18, 22, 49, 71, 88, 116, 118, Isa, 38 to the royal office in a suitably cautious manner. More bold is M.Bič in *Numen*, Supp. iv, who argues that Pss. 1–41 are an ancient liturgical sequence, the 'I' being the king in ritual role.

These contributions have been presented in a manner more stimulating than convincing. But at least they suggest how Birkeland's thesis might be improved if it took more account of the influence of the festal rites and their theology of kingship. From this point of view, my own conclusions (*Kingship and the Psalms*) involve accepting fifty-four of the psalms of the Individual as additional royal psalms. I take most of them to have been composed in particular crises, though sometimes giving valuable reflection of concepts from the great rites (especially 9–10, 40, 71); in about ten the king looks for help through a manifestation of the deity (17, 63, and perhaps 3, 4, 16, 57, 139) or through oracle or augury (5, 27, 143). A smaller number I take to have been created purely for the great rituals, especially 51 (which may belong to the annual Day of Atonement), 91 and 121 (which convey God's basic promise of protection to his king), 75 (where the king warns rebels), 22 (which shows him in rites of suffering succeeded by deliverance), 23 (his subsequent testimony), and 118 (where he looks back on his symbolic chastisement and deliverance, as he enters the Temple gloriously 'by the name of Yahweh'). From these extra resources for royal worship (to which we must add Ps. 144 in its entirety), I find confirmation that the king's office was indeed portrayed in the autumnal festival through a dramatic sequence of humiliation and glorification (cf. above, pp. 252 f.)

V. ORACLES IN THE PSALMS

Here is yet another aspect of psalm research which has helped to transform our view of Old Testament religion, although its implications are still insufficiently heeded. And once again we are indebted above all to Mowinckel, who in 1922 brought the matter to light and to life in a hundred fluent pages (*Psalmenstudien* iii; also *PIW* ii, ch. 12). Having taken a sympathetic view of the Temple's ceremonies as the actual setting of most psalms, he readily accepted the numerous passages where God is directly quoted or heard as products of real prophetic activity within the system of worship, and not some late literary embellishment. After portraying the prophetic ministers who functioned in worship and suggesting how free inspiration could have place alongside set forms, he expounded the following as oracular psalms: 2, 12, 14, 20, 21, 45, 50, 60, 72, 75, 81, 82, 87, 89, 91, 95, 108, 110, 132. Further, he agreed with Gunkel that many of the laments will have been answered by an encouraging oracle, not preserved in the text of the psalm, but giving rise to a concluding statement of relief by the psalmist (e.g. 13, 22); such oracles, Mowinckel suggested, were not recorded because they had a fixed wording.

Now such a large contribution of the prophetic ministries in the Psalms should tell us much about the dynamic nature of Israelite worship. Worship was experienced as a confrontation between the self-revealing deity and the assembly or individual. Whatever might be said or done from the human side was outweighed by the action and words of the divine party to the meeting. There and then he acted and spoke with power. While fixed ceremonies helped to express his presence, the participation of his prophets, responsive to fresh inspiration, marked his freedom. As a living and personal encounter requires, he might show pleasure or anger, speak comfort or criticism, decree blessing or disaster. Thus there was scope in Israelite worship for suspense, trepidation, awe, delight. No wonder the varied moods of the worshippers are so vividly reflected in the Psalms—sorrow, fear, indignation, ecstasy, jubilation.

The prophetic element in the Psalms should throw light on the nature and origin of the ministries which produced the prophetic books. Following Mowinckel, G. von Rad made good use of Pss. 50 and 81 for tracing the stern communication of God's will in the great festivals (*Problem of the Hexateuch*, pp. 22–5). E. Würthwein has since made helpful contributions. He argues that the great prophets' portrayal of God speaking to his people in a judgement scene derives its formal characteristics from a cultic enactment, where Yahweh confronted his covenanted people as in Ps. 50 and spoke admonition through a cultic minister (*ZThK*, 1952); Yahweh's advent in judgement is to be traced back to the cult with the aid of Pss. 68, 76, 82, 96–8. In another article (in *Tradition und Situation*) he examines the prophets' rejection of sacrifice (Amos 5; Isa. 1, etc.) and argues with the aid of Pss. 40, 50, 51, 69 etc. that the language derives from the cultic situation where prophets would pronounce whether or not Yahweh was pleased to accept the particular sacrifices offered on that occasion.

Evidence outside the Psalms for the existence of cultic prophets was carefully examined and affirmed by Johnson in *The Cultic Prophet*. His still awaited publication of its natural sequel, examining the cultic prophet in psalmody, will surely be another milestone in psalm research.

VI. THE POST-EXILIC PERIOD

Our discussion so far has shown how recent scholarship, in the main, regards the ceremonies in the Temple under the kings as decisive for the composition of the Psalms. In that setting, patterns of psalmody were established and many of the present psalms were already in use. Whereas it had once seemed a challenging task to identify psalms which could be pre-exilic, it is the establishment of post-exilic authorship which has become the more hazardous undertaking.

The question is treated by Mowinckel in *PIW* (ii, ch. 18 etc.). He sees the main period of composition as extending from about 1000–400 B.C. He thinks the Exile, though disrupting the specifically royal rites, did not occasion a new era of psalmody. The old styles continued to be followed. In a tentative fashion, however, he allows for a few psalms of rather different purpose and style having crept into the Psalter in its late stages of collection. He thinks especially of Pss. 1, 19B, 34, 37, 49, (73), 78, 105, 106, 111, 112, (119), 127. Such were compositions of the late collectors, he suggests, learned sages and experts in the sacred traditions, the type of man seen somewhat later in Ben Sirach. They will have composed psalms in their 'schools' to edify their disciples, or sometimes offered them as personal thanksgivings in the Temple. Such psalms often have the character of teaching, they use the old proverb forms, and make much of Yahweh's law. They are not totally divorced from the communal religion, not direct expressions of a purely private piety. But their atmosphere is the piety of the study circle rather than the public or royal worship. The setting, he thinks, would be akin to the devotions of the Therapeutai vividly described by Philo, where old and new hymns were sung by individuals in a gathering which had just heard a discourse on Scripture (*PIW* ii., p. 122).

The tentative nature of Mowinckel's identification of such psalms is significant. For the lateness of the psalms in question is far from certain. It is likely that the Wisdom schools were active in the vicinity of the Temple from Solomon's time; Wisdom style can hardly be a proof of lateness. Glorification of Yahweh's 'law', 'word', 'command', etc., could have arisen early, in view of the great importance of covenantal law in early Israelite religion. Indeed, some of the psalms in question have been linked to earlier times by recent writers.

There has, however, been one school of thought, strong among French Catholics, which has continued the late nineteenth century predilection for dating most of the extant psalms in the Persian period or later, the logic of Gunkel and Mowinckel being little regarded. Often the psalmists are imagined as scribes fitting together quotations from old literature. A convenient account of this school, in which we can number E. Podechard, A. Robert, R. Tournay, A. Deissler, and P. Bonnard, is given by J. Coppens (in *Le Psautier*, ed. R. de Langhe, pp. 28 ff.); as he indicates on pp. 60 ff., the reasoning for this account of the Psalter is not very cogent.

Although it is hard to find firm ground for relating the final selection and arrangement of the psalms to Jewish lectionary usage in Temple and synagogue, a contribution has been made by A. Arens (*Die Psalmen im Gottesdienst*), including a brief survey and criticism of modern work, while M. D. Goulder of Birmingham has an extensive study in preparation.

The Qumran discoveries have contributed some interesting data for the use of the Psalms shortly before Christ. More than thirty psalm texts have come to light, including a relatively well-preserved scroll that contains, with additional matter, all or parts of forty psalms from Books iv–v, but with striking 'novelties' of sequence and refrains. Debate continues as to whether these differences indicate new arrangements made for the liturgical requirements of a sect, or whether they are products of a fluidity in the older transmission of the Psalter (cf. J. A. Sanders, *The Dead Sea Psalms Scroll*, New York, 1967).

VII. CONCLUSION—THE SIGNIFICANCE OF THE AUTUMN FESTIVAL

A conclusion for the foregoing discussion may best be given in accordance with my own judgements expressed there, rather than in pursuit of an elusive consensus. In my view then, the core of the Psalter was composed for national and royal worship at the Temple. In particular, two situations occasioned abundant growth of psalmody: the chief annual festal season about October, and the fortuitous crises that often beset the kings in their national or personal capacity. It is the former situation, the great festival, which fostered the most remarkable contribution of psalmody to Israelite religion, and I therefore now turn to an interpretation of its main elements.

Although the sequence of the celebrations cannot be reconstructed with confidence, a good deal can be said about the liturgical ingredients. The abundance of psalms which are claimed to reveal these ingredients should not be a stumbling-block. There are other Old Testament books, such as Proverbs and Deuteronomy, in which one particular tradition is dominant. As regards the Psalter, therefore, it is surely reasonable to accept that the principal festival of the state Temple in the royal period has made a decisive contribution to the corpus of cultic songs preserved in that Temple. Nor is the decision between pre-exilic and post-exilic dating of great moment, once the main shape of the tradition is accepted as of pre-exilic origin. As Westermann and Lipiński stress in their recent works, the tenacity of forms means that psalms of later date can often illustrate the ancient tradition.

The timing of 'the festival of Yahweh', the autumnal festival in royal Jerusalem, is not known precisely; we may think of a complex of holy days that were the antecedents of the eventual Jewish New Year's Day (1 Tishri), Day of Atonement (10 Tishri), and week of Booths (15–22 Tishri). But we can well grasp the natural significance of the chosen season. After the annual summer drought under the burning sun (May to October), it was a time for keen anticipation of the somewhat uncertain winter rains, vital for the new cycle of growth. The development of historical and eschatological themes in the liturgy never obliterated this seasonal importance of the festival as a seeking of rain and life from the Creator–King, who alone governed the forces of Nature (cf. Zech. 14:17). The worshippers believed that, if Yahweh had pleasure in them, he came in the festival and 'crowned the year of his goodness' (Ps. 65:12/11), that is, he ordained a new year that would be characterized by his rich provision of life.

Like all the other institutions of worship, the festival was considered an appointment of Yahweh himself (Ps. 81). *The summons to attend* was therefore sent far and wide by his chief officer, the Davidic king (1 Kgs. 8:1), who must also have over-all responsibility for its conduct and provisions, often taking the lead in worship (1 Kgs. 8; 2 Sam. 6, etc.).

The journey to the festival was already part of the holy experience of the worshippers. Pss. 84 and 122 take rich account of this, though they seem more like pieces used in the Temple ceremonies than songs for the journey (cf. Isa. 30:29). Both psalms reveal much of the festal experience. From 122 we learn how the traveller to the festival rejoices over

Jerusalem as the place where Yahweh dwells and meets his whole society; Jerusalem is seen as the embodiment of unity and communion; here divine order is given through the Davidic kings; the worshipper's supplication rises up for the *šālôm* of this heart of the nation and the world, that is, for its material as well as spiritual provision. In 84 we see how the yearning need of the pilgrims is matched by faith in Yahweh's festal epiphany and rich provision; their thoughts put the rains high among the life-gifts sought from Yahweh, and prayer rises also for Yahweh's anointed king. Like the festival itself, the pilgrimage had universal implications. The Creator–King appeared in Zion as God of all, and pilgrimage to his worship was therefore seen as an ideal for all nations (47; 65; 76; 87, etc.).

Penitential and purificatory observances will have taken place at an early stage of the holy season; the rites of the post-exilic Day of Atonement (Lev. 16) indeed seem to be of great antiquity. Apart from the requirements of physical readiness for contact with the divine, the festal teaching of moral standards (Pss. 15, 24) had to be matched by opportunities for confession and forgiveness. Ps. 65 shows that the pilgrims from among all mankind converging at Zion to praise the Creator could look for atonement of their sins, enabling them to abide in his near presence and know his mighty work for the new year of growth. Forgiveness is prominent among the festal blessings also in 103 and 85; it is basic to renewal and provision for the coming days. As the post-exilic High Priest would later lead the annual ceremonies of atonement, so the king will have led the pre-exilic equivalents; his work in this respect may be reflected in 51; 102, 130, where the singer's person is bound up in royal fashion with the welfare of all Israel.

An essential feature of the worship was the understanding that the activity in the festival was primarily that of God rather than of men. There and then God acted to make new in the experience of the worshippers his work of salvation, the salvation which upheld the world of life and goodness. His deeds of creation and redemption were signified afresh in the liturgical movements and words. *His supremacy, pictured as kingship, was therefore presented dramatically and dynamically.*

In the ritual context, where eternal and archetypal ideals strike suddenly upon the present imperfect world, Yahweh overpowers chaos, takes his kingship effectively, and sends out the right order of creation and life. The triumphant proclamation 'Yahweh has begun to reign!' or 'Yahweh now reigns!' (93; 96; 97; 99, etc.) matches the excitement of this liturgical event and awakens the response of awed prostration, clapping, dancing, and exultant music (47 etc.). So far as the evidence of the Psalms goes, this dramatic experience did not presuppose that Yahweh in weakness was seasonally deprived of his kingship before so resuming it. As in the later eschatological scheme (cf. Rev. 11:17), thought was concentrated on the end of a period of need or disorder, as God now took his power and effected his kingship. So he is hailed as newly revealed in proven supremacy; he overpowers the chaos forces in all their forms—raging waters (Ps. 93), the water-monsters Rahab and Leviathan (89:74), the presumptuous kings and nations of the earth (46; 48; 76); with revelation of his dread divinity, he dominates and disposes of the heavenly beings or lesser gods of the nations (29; 82; 89; 95; 96; 97).

The rituals which expressed this dramatic assertion of Yahweh's supremacy may have included symbolic gestures of destruction such as are found in the Hebrew prophets (Jer. 19; Ezek. 5 etc.) and in the Egyptian New Year festivals (cf. Pss. 2:9; 68:3/2). But the best attested rites in demonstration of the triumph are the processions; such is the case also in Babylon, where the New Year procession of the gods to an outlying shrine actualized the primeval march to battle against the chaos powers (Lambert, *Iraq*, 1963). One or more processions of Yahweh showed forth his defeat of his enemies, his securing of the cosmos, his preparation of rain and growth, and his salvation of the oppressed. Thus in Pss. 68; 24; 47 we see his procession of triumphal return into his Temple, a ritual actualization of all that his kingship meant. There was a vivid belief in his own presence in the procession, and no doubt the portable Ark served as a pointer to this presence (cf. 68:2/1; 24:7; 132). News of the victory was carried by messengers (68:12/11), and perhaps also by release of birds as in Egypt (68:14/13; Lipiński, *Royauté*, p. 446), and jubilantly celebrated by dancing musicians in the column (68:26/25; cf. 2 Sam. 6).

The throngs of worshippers watched and heard intently (68:25/24; cf. 46:9/8; 48:9/8; 84:8/7), eagerly drinking in the revelation of salvation, as Yahweh's kingship was conveyed in terms of his scattering evil forces (68), his fixing life's foundations (24), his leading in of his Exodus-redeemed to possess the land (68; 47), his deliverance of the needy (68), his ascension to his throne-centre in his Temple (47), and his inauguration of his reign of salvation over all (47; 68). At the gates of his holy place liturgical dialogue sounded out, conveying with tremendous emphasis the significance of the moment, namely that Yahweh the Creator–King of proven supremacy now enters his residence (24:7–10). His ascension to his throne-residence is accompanied by a crescendo of trumpets, rhythmic cries and clapping; the music of praise expresses an ecstasy of jubilation (47). The procession of triumph and ascension to the Temple are as it were reflections of a progress transcending earth and heaven. The humble local route and holy stations were symbolic of Yahweh's progress in the clouds (68:5/4, 34/33), 'on high' (68:18–19/17–18; cf. 7:8/7), through the eternal gates of his heavenly palace (24:7), to his seat above the heavenly ocean (29:10; 2:4). The humble worshippers were the counterparts of the heavenly hosts (29, etc.); the little hill of Zion and its Temple were the sacramental forms of the divine mountain passing into the heavens and of the divine residence above it (48:3/2 etc.).

The main procession of Yahweh as King into Zion culminated with his ascension to his 'house' and throne-residence, represented from Solomon's time by the Temple into which the ark was borne. *Yahweh's occupying of his throne in Zion* brings the theme of his epiphany as newly reigning King to fullest expression. Psalms like 93; 96–9 now proclaim the good news of his reign, convey the sense of his manifestation in royal splendour and salvation, and lead the acclamations of homage from all creatures and elements of Nature.

The Creator–King is seated, not in repose, but in active rule; his rectifying acts of kingship (his 'judgements', etc.) continue to go forth with all the divine might of word and deed (cf. 9:5–12/4–11). There are some accounts to settle, *judgements to be pronounced* (cf. 76:9–10/8–9). Thus Yahweh as King in Zion deals with wicked heavenly beings (82; cf. 96:4–5; 97:9), nations (9–10; 96; 98), presumptuous men (75), sinners in Israel (50). The Jerusalem worship here inherits an element from the worship of the tribal league of Israel. Accordingly, *the manifest God has a living encounter with his covenanted people,* renewing their bond with him and speaking words of admonition and promise through his prophets (95; 81; 50; 85). As the triumphal advent of Yahweh into Zion had suggested the renewal of the Exodus invasion (68; cf. 114; 66:1–12; Exod. 15), so the consequent utterances of the God of the covenant from Mount Zion corresponded to his utterances from Mount Sinai after the Exodus triumph.

The ceremonies of the festival are in part *a sacrament of growth,* whereby the Creator, if he is favourable, conveys his blessings of fertility (65; 126–8; Zech. 14:17 etc.). The acclamation of Yahweh resident and reigning in Zion included confidence that he could provide the sorely needed winter rains and resulting nourishment. Newly robed in glory, the manifest King is praised as having subjugated the ocean and uttered the sure decrees which give life to the world, beginning with the divine life-power which radiates from his Temple (93;29). The primeval victory of kingship is recalled, whereby Yahweh clove the ocean-monsters and then created the sweet-water sources, day and night, sun, moon, stars, the firm edges of the earth, summer, and winter (cf. 74; 104). The hymns to the Creator–King who thus gives life to all the world must dwell on his universal role and power, and all species (angels, mankind, heaven, earth, sea, animals, trees, etc.) are envisaged as joining in a community of praise and joy at his work (98; 148; 150, etc.).

With the ceremonies of God's advent into Zion as King, *attention is naturally focused on Zion itself.* This sacramental form of his residence, which can comprise both city and Temple, is made new and replenished with his life-power through his re-entry. The procession evidenced in Ps. 132 repeats the first entry of Yahweh and his Ark, and so establishes afresh the basic function of Zion. It may be that phraseology about the 'building up' of the walls (51:20/18) and city (147:2) and restoration of the gate-bars (147:13) originates in the festal ideas rather than (as often assumed) in post-exilic circumstances of reconstruction, for the theme is also found in Babylonian festal prayers (*ANET*, pp. 390 f.). Following the throne-ascension of her King, Zion is newly acclaimed as holy (93), secure (48), blessed with life-sources (46), unique in beauty and exaltation (48; 87) and destined to gather in all peoples as Yahweh's worshippers (87; 76). Indeed, her personification as mother (87; 149:2; 147:12 f.), the celebration of her beauty (50; 48; Lam. 2:15) and of Yahweh's love and desire for her (132:13; 87:2) points to her role as the queen and bride taken in the festival by Yahweh the King and Husband, especially as this conception appears also in prophetic materials of liturgical character (Zeph. 3:14–18; Isa. 62:4–5). The theme has similarity with the idea of the personified people as Yahweh's wife in Hosea and Jeremiah; comparison may also be made with the 'sacred marriage' of the god and his spouse in New Year festivals of the type best evidenced in Sumeria. The Hebrew of Pss. 65:10/9 and 46:5/4 indeed seems to see Yahweh's festal advent as a conjugal visitation, fertilizing land or city.

The divine action to prepare the new season of growth is expressed in 65, as we have seen, as the 'crowning' of a new year. Here and in many other expressions there is *consciousness of standing on the threshold of a new period*; God has newly begun his reign; it is the dawn of salvation, the dawn even of a new world. The hymns therefore call for the tribute of a 'new song' (33; 96; 98; 149), responding to the 'good news' of Yahweh's victory and royal ascension (96:2–3; 68:12/11; cf. 40:10/9).

The essence of all the festal themes that have so far been mentioned is the sacramental assertion of God's power and grace, envisaged in terms of his kingship. The festal presentation of that kingship must, in the nature of the case, include a presentation of the Davidic role, publicly showing afresh God's covenant with his royal Servant, reminding him of his duties, replenishing him with grace. In this setting the Davidic king will have received his first enthronement, and in subsequent years aspects of the enthronement ritual were probably repeated to exhibit and renew his association with Yahweh's kingship (§ III above).

The festal ceremonies for the Davidic office clearly took a form no less dramatic than those celebrating Yahweh's kingship. The texts show several parties active in a succession of scenes. While the texts cannot be reordered with any certainty, the main lines of the sacred drama can be envisaged: Yahweh chooses his royal Servant, allows him to be humiliated awhile under the assaults of evil adversaries, then delivers and exalts him in confirmation of his office.

Thus the king, as the anointed and elect minister of Yahweh, first faces a world-wide conspiracy against Yahweh's reign, prepares for battle, and warns the rebels of Yahweh's judgement (2; 20; 75). Soon the king has to implore Yahweh to save him from the attacks of the death-powers, so that health and plenty may be secured for his society and he may accomplish the festal celebration of Yahweh (144). But his ordeal is not so easily ended. The enemies seem to triumph. As his humiliation is represented by deprival of his symbols of office, he calls upon Yahweh with all the might of inspired supplication, holding up Yahweh's earlier promises, his own office of witness to Yahweh's faithfulness (89), and his determination to rule as Yahweh wills (101). In lamenting cadences his theme is 'Oh when wilt thou come to me?' (101:2). From yet further depths of symbolic suffering he has to cry, his lament pathetically depicting the horrors of death and putting before Yahweh the mockery of the wicked over the man supposed to be Yahweh's protégé (22A).

At last he is rescued and restored to splendour in the midst of the great festal assembly; he leads a sacrificial feast and celebrates the new manifestation of Yahweh's kingship (22B), singing testimony to the Shepherd who has proved mightier than the gruesome shepherd of the valley of death (23; cf. 49:15/14). In token of salvation he is led up the sacred way through the Temple gates and around the altar in the court (118). His songs of thanksgiving look back on his rescue, telling how Yahweh rode on a cherub from heaven to snatch him from the grip of the underworld (18), or how by invocation of the name 'Yahweh' he vanquished his foes (118).

He has been utterly humiliated, a worm, not a man (22); he has been like a stone scorned and thrown aside by the builders (118). But now, because Yahweh accepts humility and faith, he is raised as head of the nations (18), the chief stone which holds together the structure of society (118).

Yahweh's oracle invites him to sit beside him on Mount Zion and bestows on him royal and eternal priesthood and authority over all men (110). He is thus established in the circle of the glory and shelter of the Most High God, attended by his protecting angels (91; 121). Through him Yahweh's justice will go forth, and health and fertility to all society (72). His offering of himself has been more pleasing to Yahweh than any animal sacrifices; he has Yahweh's law in his heart and carries a scroll of Yahweh's covenant (40A). He addresses the world with testimony and teachings and above all with the good news that Yahweh has triumphed, come as King, saved his Anointed, and established his rule of kindly order and plenty (40A; 22B; 18; cf. 9; 89).

In years of great adversity, such festal proclamation of salvation could stand in sharp contrast to the actual conditions of society. It seems that the contrast did in fact prompt *special intercessions in this context*. Hence we have psalms which combine echoes of the glorious proclamations and recitals with sharp complaints precisely about conditions which belie God's kingship (9–10; 40; 44; 94; cf. 74).

No doubt many other things took place in the festival which are not well reflected in the Psalter. Pilgrims often had private needs and would consult holy men (cf. 2 Kgs. 4:23), ask for blessings (1 Sam. 1), make personal vows or payment of vows with testimony (cf. Ps. 107). Other ceremonies were remembered in Jewish tradition, such as the use of torches, green branches, booths, and ritual pouring out of water. Nevertheless, as we have seen, the Psalms give us abundant material for the central experiences of the festival, understood to spring from the action of Yahweh himself. Such encounter with the deity brought *encounter with the ideal*, an experience which both touched present circumstances with reviving grace and also transcended them. The transcending vision was bequeathed by the pre-exilic festival to later centuries, a vision of God's ultimate perfecting action, the new reign of

God and his Anointed, an action still to come yet never far
away, its brightness already sending shafts into this needy
world.

BIBLIOGRAPHY

AHLSTRÖM, G. W. *Psalm 89: eine Liturgie aus dem Ritual des leidenden
  Königs*, Lund, 1959.
ANDERSON, A. A. *The Book of Psalms*, 2 vols., NCB, London, 1972.
ANDERSON, G. W. 'Psalms' in *Peake's Commentary on the Bible*, 2nd edn.,
  London and Edinburgh, 1962.
ARENS, A. *Die Psalmen im Gottesdienst des Alten Bundes*, Trier, 1961.
BENTZEN, A. 'The cultic use of the story of the Ark in Samuel', *JBL* lxvii
  (1948), 37–53.
—— *King and Messiah*, London 1955, Oxford 1970.
BEYERLIN, W. *Die Rettung der Bedrängten in den Feindpsalmen der
  Einzelnen*, FRLANT xcix, Göttingen, 1970.
BIČ, M. 'Das erste Buch des Psalters: eine Thronbesteigungsfestliturgie',
  Numen Supp. iv, 1959, pp. 316–32.
CLINES, D. J. A. 'Psalm Research since 1955: I. The Psalms and the Cult',
  Tyndale Bulletin xviii (1967), 103–26.
CRÜSEMANN, F. *Studien zur Formgeschichte von Hymnus und Danklied in
  Israel*, WMANT xxxii, Neukirchen, 1969.
CULLEY, R. C. *Oral formulaic language in the biblical psalms*, Toronto, 1967.
DAHOOD, M. *Psalms: Introduction, Translation and Notes*, 3 vols., AncB,
  New York, 1966–70.
DELEKAT, L. *Asylie und Schutzorakel am Zionheiligtum*, Leiden, 1967.
EATON, J. H. *Psalms: Introduction and Commentary*, TC London, 1967.
—— *Kingship and the Psalms*, SBT, 2nd series, xxxii, London, 1976.
ENGNELL, I. *Studies in Divine Kingship in the Ancient Near East*, Uppsala
  1943, 2nd edn., Oxford, 1967.
—— *Critical Essays on the Old Testament*, London, 1970.
GERSTENBERGER, E. 'Psalms' in *Old Testament Form Criticism*, ed. J. H.
  Hayes, San Antonio, 1974, pp. 179–224.
GUNKEL, H. *The Psalms: A Form-critical Introduction* (ETr of article in
  RGG, 2nd edn.), Philadelphia, 1967.
JOHNSON, A. R. *The Cultic Prophet in Ancient Israel*, Cardiff, 1944, 2nd edn.,
  1962.
—— 'The Psalms' in *OTMS*, pp. 162–209.
—— *Sacral Kingship in Ancient Israel*, Cardiff, 1955, 2nd edn., 1967.
KAISER, O. 'Erwägungen zu Ps. 101', *ZAW* lxxiv (1962), 195–205.
KRAUS, H.-J. *Psalmen* 2 vols., BKAT, Neukirchen, 1960, 5th edn., with
  corrections and bibliographical supplement, 1972. (See note at end.)
—— *Worship in Israel*, Oxford, 1966, ETr of *Gottesdienst in Israel*, 2nd edn.,
  Munich, 1962.

KÜHLEWEIN, J. *Geschichte in den Psalmen*, Stuttgart, 1973.

LAMBERT, W. G. 'The Great Battle of the Mesopotamian Religious Year; the Conflict in the akītu-house' (a summary), *Iraq* xxv (1963), 189 f.

LIPIŃSKI, E. *La Royauté de Yahwé dans la poésie et le culte de l'ancien Israël*, Brussels, 1965, 2nd edn., 1968.

—— *La Liturgie pénitentielle dans la Bible*, Paris, 1969.

MICHEL, D. 'Studien zu den sogenannten Thronbesteigungspsalmen', *VT* vi (1956), 40–68.

MORGENSTERN, J. 'The Cultic Setting of the Enthronement Psalms', *HUCA* xxxv (1964), 1–42.

MOWINCKEL, S. *Psalmenstudien* i–vi, 1921–4, reprint with new foreword, Amsterdam, 1961.

—— *Zum israelitischen Neujahr und zur Deutung der Thronbesteigungspsalmen*, ANVAO 11, 1952, 2.

—— *Religion und Kultus*, Göttingen, 1953.

—— *Det Gamle Testamente IV. 1, Salmeboken*, Oslo, 1955,

—— *The Psalms in Israel's Worship*, ETr, 2 vols., Oxford, 1962.

PORTER, J. R. 'The interpretation of 2 Sam. 6 and Ps. 132', *JTS*, N.S., v (1954), 247–61.

VON RAD, G. *The Problem of the Hexateuch and other Essays*, ETr Edinburgh, 1966.

ROBERTS, J. J. M. 'The Davidic Origin of the Zion Tradition', *JBL* xcii (1973), 329–44.

SCHMIDT, H. *Das Gebet der Angeklagten im Alten Testament*, BZAW xlix, 1928.

STAMM, J. 'Ein Vierteljahrhundert Psalmenforschung', *TR* xxiii (1955), 1–68.

WARD, J. M. 'The Literary Form and Background of Ps. 89', *VT* xi (1961), 321–39.

WEISER, A. *Die Psalmen*, ATD xiv/xv, 7th edn. Göttingen, 1966; ETr of 5th edn., *The Psalms: A Commentary*, London, 1962.

WESTERMANN, C. *Das Buch Jesaja Kapitel 40–66*, ATD xix, Göttingen, 1966; ETr, *Isaiah 40–66: A Commentary*, London, 1969.

WIDENGREN, G. *Sakrales Königtum im Alten Testament und im Judentum*, Stuttgart, 1955.

WÜRTHWEIN, E. 'Der Ursprung der prophetischen Gerichtsrede', *ZThK* xlix (1952), 1–15.

—— 'Kultpolemik oder Kultbescheid?', in *Tradition und Situation*, ed. E. Würthwein and O. Kaiser, Göttingen, 1963, pp. 115–30.

Note. The 5th edn., 1978, of KRAUS, *Psalmen*, was not used above. Its revisions are relevant only to pp. 257 f., Kraus having re-expressed his position.

X

THE HISTORY OF ISRAEL IN THE PRE-EXILIC PERIOD

H. CAZELLES

THE history of pre-exilic Israel is clearly divided into two periods, separated by the establishment of the monarchy. It is with the monarchy, its state, its administration, and its schools, its foreign relations and internal conflicts that Old Testament historiography is established.[1] With the monarchy, the Israelite state begins to appear in international politics and in its documents; the Assyrian Annals and the lists of officers who gave their name to the year (*limmū*), by mentioning its important events, allow necessary cross-checks with a relatively firm chronological framework.

The period prior to the monarchy is much more difficult to study, for biblical historiography was extremely selective in recording the data given by tribal traditions and local documents. The historiographers selected the data and gave their own interpretations according to their own syntheses. Modern historians consider these syntheses differently and disagree about most problems. The documents brought to light archaeologically help only indirectly and possible cross-checks are not always clear.[2] It is impossible to deny a historical basis to the traditions gathered together by the Yahwistic and Elohistic synthesis in the Pentateuch, or to the cycles preserved by the books of Judges, of Samuel, and of Kings; the recognized authority of these texts and the history of the people could not then be explained. These data,

[1] R. C. Dentan, *The Idea of History in the Ancient Near East*, New Haven and London, 1955.

[2] See G. E. Wright, *Biblical Archaeology*, London, 1957; J. Bright, *Early Israel in Recent History Writing*, SBT xix, 1960; and the critical observations made by M. Noth in 'Der Beitrag der Archäologie zur Geschichte Israels', *Congress Volume, Oxford 1959*, SVT vii, 1960, pp. 262–82.

however, appear in texts dependent upon cultural and religious factors, which are not always easy to determine. All the scenes which are described, seem to be based on some event, but the nature and sequence of these events must always be discussed according to the data and the sociological problems of the ancient Orient. If we agree that the Yahwist aimed at showing the constitution of Israel unified around the Judean dynasty and its problems, many points are then clarified, in relation to ethnic and archaeological data.[3] But he had to unify elements which were originally dissociated.

I. TOWARDS THE DAVIDIC MONARCHY

1. The Tribes

The most ancient sociological reality is the tribe, which, however, does not exclude the family nucleus. Historians agree in holding that tribal autonomy was originally considerable. This autonomy appears clearly in the studies made of the semi-nomadic tribes of the Near East,[4] as well as in the Mari texts[5] and biblical texts such as Judges 1. The tribe has relations with the cities, but wishes to retain freedom of movement and appears extremely touchy in its relationship with the rulers of these cities.

The Israelite tribe was composed of 'houses' (*bayit*) or of 'families' (*mišpāḥâh*), cf. Gen. 24:38; 1 Sam. 20: 29. When the tribe moved, each member went with his own house (1 Sam. 27:3; 2 Sam. 2:3). Unlike the Beduin tribe, the life of the Israelite tribe did not centre on the camel. Israelite tribes lived off their small cattle (Gen. 33:13). They needed water points (Gen. 21:25; 26:16–33). They might acquire fields (Gen. 26:12). The tribes travelled and moved their livestock among the cities and fields of the sedentary population, which

---

[3] For a discussion and bibliography, see H. Cazelles (ed.), *Introduction à la Bible, Introduction critique à l'Ancien Testament*, Paris, 1973, pp. 177–206.

[4] See R. de Vaux, *Ancient Israel: Its Life and Institutions*, London, 1961, pp. 3–13, 519 f., for a discussion and bibliography.

[5] J. R. Kupper, *Les Nomades en Mésopotamie au temps des rois de Mari*, Paris, 1957; A. Malamat, 'Mari and the Bible', *JAOS* lxxxii (1962), 143–60; 'Aspects of Tribal Society in Mari and Israel', *XVème rencontre assyriologique Internationale, Liège*, 1967, pp. 129–38.

they were tempted to plunder and capture, even if they did not settle there (Gen. 34).

The head of the family was the 'father', who might be the grandfather. As progenitor, he was in command. He led his people in war, negotiated the marriage of his sons or daughters, made vows, and gave his blessing. When he died he joined his *'am* in the tribal burial place. The same word *'am*, however, means a larger family group, or the one who represents it after the father, the uncle on the father's side. Otherwise the nearest relation exercised the right of *gô'ēl*, seeking blood revenge or acting as surety in a law suit. He had the right of priority over the sale of a piece of land and, as *yābām*, he received and wedded the wife of the deceased (levirate law). Normally, the young wife entered her husband's house, and the tendency was to choose a wife from the nearest families. Some find here a suggestion of exogamy. There was, however, no objection to marriage with a half-sister on the father's side (Gen. 20:12; 2 Sam. 13:13). As with the Arabs of Moab at the beginning of this century, the male cousin had a privileged right over his female cousin. In Israel, however, other forms existed, especially in Judah. Tribes are therefore family-groups (*šēbeṭ* or *maṭṭeh*). The image is that of a branch issuing from a common trunk.

Amongst the names of the ancestors of the ancient Israelite families, prominent is that of Abram, which (after his migration to the west) becomes Abraham. Ab(i)râm is a Mesopotamian name from the first half of the second millennium B.C. In the west, in the so-called Amorite area (Mari and later Ugarit), it means 'the Father is exalted'. The Mari texts contain toponyms where may be traced the names of relations of Abraham (Nahor, Serug), and as Harran is a site of the lunar cult, supposedly because of other names of Abraham's kindred (Terah, Laban), scholars agree that Abraham emigrated from Harran into Canaan. A first migration from Ur to Harran is possible but is still open to discussion. According to the Bible, Abra(ha)m goes to the sanctuaries of Shechem and Bethel, but settles in the region of Hebron and later of Beersheba. On the point, the traditions of Abram and Isaac are similar (cf. Gen. 26 with Gen. 12:9–20; 21:22–34).

Many arguments support the dating of Abraham and his migration and that of Jacob in the Amorite period: e.g. the names of these two patriarchs, the cultural expansion of Mesopotamian civilization in Syria-Palestine under the Amorite dynasty, and the discovery of the trade routes of the Bronze Age. Gen. 14 seemed to support this date, but its data and identifications are open to controversy and cannot support a secure chronology. N. Glueck, for example, on the basis of a surface exploration of the Negeb,[6] pushes back Abraham's date to the period of the 'caliciform' pottery (first half of the Middle Bronze Age or the intermediate period between the Early and Middle Bronze), others, on the basis of the small numbers of generations between Abraham and Moses in the Bible, would date the patriarch to the fourteenth–thirteenth centuries B.C.[7] They point to the later date of the Arameans' appearance, the analogies between patriarchal customs and Hurrian customs known from the Nuzi texts, the Hapiru in the El-Amarna period (fourteenth century B.C.), and the parallels with Ugarit. These data compel us to date some patriarchal scenes in a post-Amorite period, but they have more significance for Israel, the wandering Aramean of Deut. 26:5, than for Abraham.

Jacob (who will become Israel) is related to Abraham, but is not the only one. According to biblical tradition, the Ishmaelite Arabs of southern Judah are his descendants through Hagar, who, like Isaac (Gen. 24:62), visited Lahai Roi towards Kadesh (Gen. 16:14). The Midianites and other tribes of northern Arabia, like Dedan, are related to him through Keturah (Gen. 25:1–4). Near Hebron, Abraham is called a Hebrew (Gen. 14:13). Gen. 10:25–29, links Eber, ancestor of the Hebrews, to the southern Arabs (Hadramaut, Ophir, Saba), considering them the nephews of Peleg. Moreover, a tradition links the founding of Hebron to that of Tanis at the time of the Hyksos penetration at the end of the eighteenth century B.C. (Num. 13:22). It is therefore likely that Abraham was a powerful chieftain dominating a group of tribes in southern Palestine at about this time. It remains

---

[6] N. Glueck, *Rivers in the Desert*, London, 1959, 2nd edn., 1968, pp. 67–84.
[7] C. H. Gordon, 'Hebrew Origins in the Light of Recent Discovery', in A. Altmann (ed.), *Biblical and Other Studies*, Cambridge, Mass., 1963, pp. 3–14.

to be established how the later groups linked themselves to him, throughout the Hyskos period (1750–1580 B.C.), when Asiatic princes, mainly Semites, ruled over the Delta.

2. *Groups of Tribes*

If a tribe comprises 'houses' or 'families' issuing from a common ancestor through blood or legal fiction, this is even more true of groups of tribes. Two neighbouring tribes, nomadic or semi-nomadic, may solemnly unite in a bond of *Ben-'ameh*,[8] around the sword planted into the earth. The group considers itself as the 'son of the uncle' (*'am*) of the other group, this implying common ancestry. Genealogical schemes must thus be treated with caution; they always indicate a bond, but not necessarily a bond of kinship. Generally speaking, as Jaussen stresses, this fictional relationship establishes between the two tribes a real offensive and defensive alliance. It is very likely that certain Israelite tribes, like the neighbouring tribes of Dan and Naphtali or those of Manasseh and Ephraim, may have united in this way, either as a defence against the powerful kingdom of Hazor, or to penetrate into Canaan.

Some passages in Genesis, however, reveal another type of union by legal fiction, which is not really Israelite: adoption. It may be discerned in the reference to Manasseh in Gen. 50:23: 'The children of Machir the son of Manasseh were born on Joseph's knees', whereas the latter had seen the third generation of the children of Ephraim. To be born on someone's knees, is to be adopted by him; by this gesture Rachel adopts the children of Bilhah (Gen. 30:3) and Jacob adopts the two sons of Joseph (Gen. 48:12). If adoption is practically ignored by Mosaic Law, it is on the other hand widely practised by the Hurrians of Nuzu, where buyers must be 'adopted' by sellers.[9]

What position do the Israelite groups hold during the El-Amarna period? Must they be identified with the opponents

---

[8] See A. Jaussen, *Coutumes des Arabes au pays de Moab*, Paris, 1948 (new impression), pp. 149–62; A. Musil, *The Manners and Customs of the Rwala Bedouins*, New York, 1928, p. 47.

[9] E. Cassin, *L'Adoption à Nuzi*, Paris, 1938; R. Tournai, 'Nouzi', in *SDB* VI, cols. 646–74; C. J. Mullo Weir, 'Nuzi', in *AOTS*, pp. 73–9.

of Pharaoh, the Hapiru of the Jerusalem letters, corresponding
to the ideogram SA. GAZ of the other letters? The question
remains hotly debated. Some acts of the sons of Israel such as
the sack of Shechem by Simeon and Levi resemble the acts of
the Hapiru against the Canaanite cities. However, the Hapiru
cannot be identified with the Israelite tribes. Their area of
movement is much larger in time than in space. The nature
of these groups remains enigmatic. They may represent the
Indo-European aristocracy, which since the time of the
Mitanni had amalgamated with the Hurrians and gave kings
to Canaan in the El-Amarna period. These groups however
are nearer the Hurrians, though distinct. Under Sethos I (c.
1300 B.C.) they still threatened the Beisan area; they played
some role under Saul, then disappeared. There must have
been fusions and unions. It appears that it was chiefly through
Rachel's group that Hurrian customs influenced the Israelite
tribes.

Israel's penetration, however, seems more closely linked to
that of the Arameans.[10] Before Tiglath-Pileser I (c. 1100 B.C.)
the Arameans are known only by the name of a city, a
toponym in the Egyptian lists, and a few names of isolated
individuals. Thus around the thirteenth century B.C., before
the Aramean group entered political history, Aramean
pressure, akin to that of Israel, was brought to bear on Syria.
It put an end to the kingdom of Amurru, still very much alive
under Muwatallu and Ramesses II (1300–1235 B.C.)[11] who
coalesced instead of destroying each other, owing to the new
threats from Assyria and elsewhere. The Amorites were then
pushed back towards Moab (kingdom of Sihon) and Canaan
to the south of Hermon. The name 'Israel', which is still a
personal name in fourteenth- and thirteenth-century Ugarit,
appears in Gen. 32:29 as the name of a group located on the

[10] On the Arameans, see A. Malamat in *POTT*, pp. 134–55; A. Dupont-Sommer,
Les Araméens, Paris, 1949; J. R. Kupper, *Les Nomades en Mésopotamie*, Paris, pp.
111–41.

[11] Our knowledge of Syria in the fourteenth and thirteenth centuries B.C. has been
enriched by the translation of the Annals of the Hittite kings. Cf. A. Goetze in
ANET, pp. 318–20; E. Laroche, *Catalogue des textes hittites*, Paris, 1971, pp. 2–13, and
the archives of Ugarit discovered by C. A. Schaeffer and published by J. Nougayrol
in *PRU*, vols. iii, iv, vi; Summary in M. Liverani, *Storia di Ugarit*, Rome, 1962 (see
also M. S. Drower, *CAH*, rev. edn., ch. XXI (b), 1968); H. Klengel, *Geschichte
Syriens*, vols. ii, iii, 1969, 1970.

Jabbok, in Mahanaim, Penuel, Succoth, on the borders of
Gad and Manasseh (Machir), before advancing to Shechem
(Gen. 33:18), near which the Manassite clan of Abiezer (Num.
26:30) was to settle. Asriel, the name of a Manassite family,
seems to be derived from 'Israel'.[12] Possibly taking advantage
of the Aramean wave in Gilead (Gen. 31:47 f.) a tribe of
Rachel, having Israel as ancester, united with a tribe of Leah
or of Zilpah, having Jacob as ancestor; and the two ancestors
were then identified with each other.[13] In any case, the
Merenptah stele (c. 1230 B.C.) bears witness to the penetration
of Israel beyond the Jordan river. Israel was a group between
Yanoam and Gezer which had not adopted a settled way of
life.

The exact relationship between Abraham, Isaac, Jacob, and
Israel is disputed. Many consider the alleged kinship to be
fictitious. According to the well-known hypothesis of Alt,[14]
these different personages might originally have had different
paternal deities. It is, however, possible to maintain the family
relationship Abraham–Isaac–Jacob, if one admits that, taking
advantage of the Hyksos movement, of the Hurrian penetration and the Aramean pressure, some Israel groups linked up
with Jacob groups descended from Abraham.

Since the name Leah has been connected with the
Akkadian *littu* (cow), whereas Rachel (female sheep) recalls
the small cattle and the sheep-breeding tribes; a hypothesis
may be put forward. The tribes which according to biblical
tradition first constituted themselves (Gen. 29:32 ff.) were the
first to become sedentary like Isaac in the territory of Simeon
according to Gen. 26:12. These first tribes, Reuben, Simeon,
and Levi are found in the south and south-west after the
Shechem *coup*, in contact with Beersheba and Hebron the
centres of the traditions of Abraham and Isaac. The other

---

[12] A. Lemaire, 'Asriel, Sr'l, Israel et l'origine de la confédération israélite', *VT* xxiii
(1973), 239–45.

[13] So H. Cazelles, art. 'Patriarches', *SDB*, vii, cols. 136–41; Cf. H. Seebaass, *Der
Erzvater Israel*, BZAW xcviii, 1966.

[14] *Der Gott der Väter*, BWANT, iii, 12, 1929 (= *KS* i. 1–78); ETr in *Essays on Old
Testament History and Religion*, Oxford, 1966, pp. 3–77); cf. R. de Vaux, 'El et Baal,
le Dieu des Pères et Yahweh', *Ugaritica*, vi (1969), 501–17; H. Cazelles, art.
'Patriarches', cols. 142–5, and 'Essai sur le pouvoir de la divinité à Ugarit et en Israël',
Ugaritica vi (1969), 36–40. For a different view, see J. Hoftijzer, *Die Verheissungen an
die drei Erzväter*, Leiden, 1956.

Leah tribes, Issachar and Zebulun, appear in Gen. 30, only after Rachel's intervention and the appearance of Dan and Naphtali and even of the group Gad-Asher. Although linked together, the tribes continued to lead an autonomous life. Simeon settled near Beersheba, particularly open to Egyptian pressure. Levi was a warlike tribe near Edom; the tenth-century Annals of Sheshonk mention a Levi in the Negeb (Exod. 32:25–9). Asher was met by the Egyptian troops, probably near the coast, and is mentioned in Pap. Anastasi I between Megiddo and Sharon. It is also found near the coast in Josh. 13:2 and Num. 24:22, where there is manifestly an orthographical error;[15] it has left traces in the hill country of Ephraim (1 Chr. 7:30ff.), and its link with the Transjordanian Gad remains to be explained.

3. Independence

Ramesses II and Merenptah had maintained Egyptian supremacy over Canaan south of Lebanon. The armies of Ramesses III were still active in Palestine, after he had defeated the 'Sea Peoples' in the Nile Delta and settled the Philistines c. 1180 B.C. along the coast from Gaza to Ekron. After 1150 B.C., the Egyptian presence dwindled. First, from the Egyptian provinces emerged the kingdoms of Edom, Moab and Ammon, before the formation of a kingdom of Israel (Gen. 36:31). Between the Jordan river and the Mediterranean, the tribes preserved the memory of having fought against Egyptian troops before they attacked the Canaanite cities. The book of Judges, however, does not mention any Egyptian presence.

What Israel remembered most vividly was the deliverance from bondage to Pharaoh. The term 'Exodus'[16] has been applied to it because of the experience of the groups established in the Delta, who fled from Egypt. However, it must be remembered that the most ancient biblical expression is not 'to come out of the land of Egypt' but 'to go up from the

---

[15] The clue to the reading is found in 2 Sam. 2:9, where Asher is spelt Ashwr.

[16] De Vaux distinguishes between the 'flight-Exodus' and the 'expulsion-Exodus', on the basis of the biblical terminology. The reality must have been even more complex if, as he says, with some justification, 'there is no biblical tradition about the "sojourn" in Egypt' (*Histoire ancienne d'Israël* i (Paris, 1971), p. 278).

land of Egypt'.[17] Hosea retained precisely this expression
(12:13), which also occurs in the account of the call of Moses
on Horeb (Exod. 3:8, 17). Micah of Moresheth, who lived in
the hill country of Judah, states that three chieftains were sent
to lead Israel out of bondage: Moses, Aaron, and Miriam
(6:4). According to tradition, all three died outside the region
which was to be conquered: Miriam at Kadesh (Num. 20:1),
south of Beersheba and Lahai-roi (Gen. 16:14), Aaron on the
border of Edom (Num. 20:28), either on Mount Hor or at
Moserah, near a region of wells or streams (Deut. 10:6–7), and
finally Moses on Mount Nebo in Moab (Deut. 34). The
historical problem is to know why and how the recognized
pre-eminence of Moses[18] over these other chieftains, who also
had a religious aspect, was transmitted and accepted, and
why the Yahwist, whose synthesis is monarchical and
Judahite, attributed such importance to Moses, who was most
vividly remembered by the northern tribes (cf. Hos. 12:13).
The tradition of Miriam at Kadesh is the most westerly one.
Miriam is of the prophetic type but seems linked to a cult
with dancing (Exod. 15:20), healing (Exod. 15:26; Num.
12:11–16), and evocation of a victory of the deity over the sea,
similar to the cult of Baal Saphon (Exod. 15:21). Westphal[19]
had already noticed that Miriam was associated with Aaron
(Exod. 15:20; Num. 12:1) before being associated with Moses.

The name of Aaron the Levite (Exod. 4:14) is connected
with the tribe of the same name. This warlike tribe (Gen. 34;
Exod. 32:25–29) was dispersed, but an important settlement
is noticed in south-western Judah on the fringes of Edom
(Josh. 21:13–16) as far as Hebron. The problem is to determine
whether his descendants came to Jerusalem, where the priest
Zadok is found at the time of David (cf. 1 Chr. 5:25–38; cf.
Ezra 7:1–5) or whether they introduced the cult of the golden
calf in Bethel. In Dan, the family of Moses was in charge,
through Jonathan, son of Gershom (Judg. 18:30).

[17] Cf. J. Wijngaards in *VT* xv (1965), 91–102.

[18] For the discussion of the historicity of Moses, see R. Smend, *Das Mosebild von
Heinrich Ewald bis Martin Noth*, 1959; H. Schmid, 'Der Stand der Moseforschung',
Judaica xxi (1965), 194–211; id., *Mose, Überlieferung und Geschichte*, BZAW cx, 1968;
H. Cazelles, 'Moïse', *SDB* iv, cols. 1308–37; M. Greenberg, 'Moses .... Critical
Assessment', *EJ* xii, cols. 378–88.

[19] 'Aaron und die Aaroniden', *ZAW* xxvi (1906), 201–30, especially 208.

The Mosaic tradition was, however, borne particularly by the powerful tribe of Ephraim, to which belonged Joshua, who is called the servant of Moses (Exod. 24:13; 33:11; Num. 11:28) in the Elohist texts. According to Hosea, Moses was a prophet; but in Num. 12:7 he is a faithful warden of a sanctuary of Yahweh. His connections with Reuben in Moabite territory are also quite strong both because of the rebellion of the Reubenites, Dathan and Abiram (Num. 16) and also by his Midianite or Cushite marriage (Exod. 2:21; Num. 12:1), considering the close relations between Midianites and Moab at that time (Num. 22:4, 7). Lastly, although only the late texts place Aaron in Egypt, the name of Moses suggests Egyptian origin, and ancient traditions indicate that he was born in Egypt and left it with a Josephite group. In the biblical history of Joseph the precise indications of the tradition are blurred by the literary composition, whether it be simpler or complex;[20] but the presence of Semites in Egypt is clearly attested. They are there either as prisoners or as family groups requesting hospitality, or as a dominating mass under the Hyksos. The coming and going of the Josephite groups is better explained by a period of bondage in the Eighteenth and Nineteenth Dynasties, but with features associated with the Hyksos traditions.

The Bible certainly records at least two routes for the Exodus.[21] One goes through the Semitic sanctuary of Baal-Saphon between Sirbonis and the Mediterranean (Exod. 14:2, 9); this is the Philistine road along the coast. The other avoids the Philistine route (Exod. 13:17), follows the Red Sea to Marah and penetrates into the peninsula. To solve these discrepancies, the hypothesis of several Exoduses has been put forward. It is unnecessary if one accepts that what de Vaux calls the 'flight-Exodus' is the historical Exodus of a small group of Josephite families under the leadership of

---

[20] J. Vergote, *Joseph en Égypte*, Louvain, 1959, has collected important data. D. B. Redford, *A Study of the Biblical Story of Joseph*, SVT xx, 1970, has added some and questioned others (the dates he assigns to the biblical sources are difficult to accept on a critical view). See also S. Herrman, *Israel in Egypt*, SBT 2nd series, xxvii, 1973.

[21] H. Cazelles, 'Les localisations de l'Exode et la Critique littéraire', *RB* lxii (1955), 321–64; J. Botterweck, 'Israels Errettung im Wunder am Meer', *Bibel und Leben* viii (1967), 8–33; M. Haran, 'The Exodus Routes in the Pentateuchal Narratives', *Tarbiz* xl (1970/1), 113–43.

Moses and that the 'expulsion Exodus' recalls the expulsion of the Hyksos, as recorded by literary tradition. The flight-Exodus took place in the first years of the reign of Ramesses II when the Nineteenth Dynasty established its authority over the Delta and had to ensure its control of Canaan against the Hittite threat. Sethos I established a series of fortified posts between the Delta and Gaza. Ramesses II developed Pi-Ramesse and Pithom (cf. Exod. 1:11) as garrison towns by using a labour force unaccustomed to this type of work (Exod. 5).

The route is difficult to trace. The presence of Moses' group is best attested in Midian, east of Aqabah. From there, the group had peaceful or difficult contacts with the Levites in Edom, the Calebites of Kadesh, the Reubenites of Moab, and Sihon the Amorite of Heshbon. Finally, Moses settled on Nebo, near the 'forest of Ephraim' (2 Sam. 18:6).

This presupposes a struggle against the Amalekites 'the first of the nations' (Num. 24:20), an Edomite group according to Gen. 36:12, which had moved from southern Judah to the hills near Beisan (Judg. 6:33; 7:12). Machir, the firstborn of Manasseh, was not far away and it was probably then that the house of Joseph adopted Manasseh (Gen. 50:23). In touchy relations with the Moabites and the sanctuary of Baal-Peor (Num. 25), the Israelites probably assembled in the riverside sanctuary of Gilgal, starting-point of the Ephraimite campaigns of Joshua. An Israel was assembling against the populations west of the Jordan.

4. *The Establishment of the Tribes*[22]

Critical scholarship still gives preference to the description of the establishment of the tribes given by Judg. 1. The book of Joshua is a synthesis with some historical basis; but the

[22] A. Alt ('The Settlement of the Israelites in Palestine', *Essays on Old Testament History and Religion*, pp. 135–69) and M. Noth (*The History of Israel*, 2nd edn., pp. 68–84), prefer to speak of *Landnahme* rather than of conquest in the strict sense. Against the purely sociological theory of G. E. Mendenhall ('The Hebrew Conquest of Palestine', *BA* xxv (1962), 66–87), that there was a nomadic revolt against urban domination, M. Weippert has reviewed the entire question (*The Settlement of the Israelite Tribes in Palestine*, SBT, 2nd series, xxi, 1971). S. Yeivin has taken the debate further by an argument based on lists and genealogies. See also R. de Vaux, *Histoire*, pp. 443–620; R. Amiran, 'The Problem of the Settlement in Palestine', *IEJ* xiii (1953), 68–78, 250–7.

tribes settled separately. Various geographical groups must be distinguished.

A. The Transjordanian Tribes The current theory is that the settlement east of the Jordan was but a colonization from the west. Thus Gad broke away from Ephraim to settle in Gilead. Reuben went west (Josh. 15:6) before moving on to Moab. Machir went into the hill country of Ephraim (Judg. 5:14) before going to Gilead (Num. 32:39; Deut. 3:13; Josh. 17:1). This contradicts biblical tradition and is supported by little evidence.

(1) There are no traces of Gad in Cisjordan. At the time of Mesha, Gad had been established for a long time in Moab.

(2) The tradition of a son of Reuben in Cisjordan (1 Chr. 5:8) presupposes an incursion of Reuben from the east. The itineraries of Num. 21 fit tribes coming from Midian, whether Reuben or Gad, and settling east of the Jordan.

(3) Judg. 5:14 does not presuppose that Machir was in the hill country of Ephraim. Princes came down from Machir, which is explained if they came down from the north of Gilead in the Jordan valley to join Ephraim and Benjamin and fight alongside them in the plain of Esdraelon. The earliest settlement seems to have been that of Reuben, firstborn of twelve. Reuben was weakened, however, by the Moabite offensive, which reached Jericho and Benjamin (Judg. 3); and it was totally absorbed by Gad (Deut. 33:3) at the time of Mesha. Already in Num. 32, Gad has towns in the 'territory of Reuben'; and according to Deut. 33:20 f., it has taken the 'chieftain's share'. At the time of Deborah, it is identified with Gilead, of which it must have absorbed some elements, probably Aramean.

If, as has been maintained above, Machir was always Transjordanian, it settled in Bashan at the expense of the Amorites (Num. 32:39), of the Rephaim, of Og, and of a Hurrian element detected in the 'group (*hebel*) of Argob'.[23] With it, Jair settled in the townlets of Jair and Nobah at Kenath. Upon the establishment of the Aramean kingdom of Damascus, all that part of the Hauran was lost by the tribes

---

[23] H. Cazelles, 'Argob biblique, Ugarit et les mouvements hurrites', *Studi sull' Oriente e la Bibbia*, Genoa, 1967, pp. 21–7.

of Israel and the frontier was fixed near Mizpah in Gilead
(Judg. 11:29; cf. Gen. 31:49 ff.).

B. *The Central Cisjordanian Tribes*   Here the major factor is
the establishment of Ephraim. From the 'forest of Ephraim'
(2 Sam. 18:6), where the Ephraimites were only an element in
Gilead (Judg. 12:4), they moved to the hill country of Ephraim
under the direction of the Ephraimite Joshua, who was buried
at Timnath-heres in Ephraim, not far from Benjamin. Indeed,
it was in Benjamin that the memory of Joshua's victories was
preserved; Jericho and Ai, and almost as far as Aijalon, which
became Danite. Two treaties demonstrate the limits of the
Ephraimite conquest: the treaty with the Gibeonites in the
south (Josh. 9; cf. 2 Sam. 21:2) and the covenant at Shechem
with groups whose attitude to Yahwism was questionable
(Josh. 24:19). With the future territory of Benjamin as a
geographical base, Ephraim had been able to establish itself,
but found itself limited by the wooded region in the hill
country of Ephraim, which was difficult for occupation (Josh.
17:15). There was also an Ephraimite thrust towards the
south; for it is impossible to dissociate Ephrathah from
Ephraim, the adjectival form of which is *'ep̄rātî*. There was,
therefore, an Ephrathite presence at Bethlehem, with certain
connections southwards as far as Tekoa (1 Chr. 2:24).

The northern region of the hill country of Ephraim must
have belonged, with Shechem, not to Ephraim but to
Manasseh. Of the list of Manassite clans (Num. 26:29–34),
hardly any except Abiezer and Azriel are authentically
Josephite. The others, such as Shechem, Sepher, the daughters
of Zelopehad (Num. 27:1), and Tirzah were Canaanite cities
which were assimilated in the time of David.[24] In Num.
26:30, which is a relatively ancient list, Halek, (Ab)iezer,
Azriel, etc., are considered to be sons of Gilead, an indication
that the western territory of Manasseh was occupied by a
movement from Gilead and Machir, and not the reverse.

The tribe of Benjamin resulted from a fragmentation of

[24] A. Alt, 'Erwägungen über die Landnahme', pp. 10 f. = *KS* i. 128 f. Noah and
Hoglah, like Shemida and Abiezer are mentioned in the Samaria ostraca. See S.
Moscati, *L' epigrafia ebraica, antica*, Rome, 1951, pp. 30 f.; cf. T. T. Kaufman, 'The
Samaria Ostraca', Harvard thesis, 1966; A. Lemaire, 'Les Ostraca Hébreux de
l'époque royale israélite', Paris thesis, 1973.

Ephraim after the death of Joshua. It was the 'son of the south' in relation to Ephraim, established as a tribe after the death of Rachel (Gen. 35:16–21). The complex history of the tribe, wedged between Moab and the Canaanite cities, was to reach its climax in the kingship of Saul of the clan of Becher (Becorath in 1 Sam. 9:1), who, according to Num. 26:35, was an Ephraimite, but is a Benjaminite in Gen. 46:21 and 1 Chr. 7:6 f.

C. The Southern Tribes The Ephraimite conquest led to the occupation of a region abandoned by two tribes, Simeon and Levi, which had sacked Shechem and then retreated to Bethel (Gen. 34:30–35:1). At the time of the Judges, we find Simeon in the region of Ziklag, near Beersheba, where the Philistines settled David. Its independence is indicated by the capture of Hormah (Judg. 1:17), probably in association with the movements of the Kenites, who had been chased from their 'nest' and were settling in the Negeb of the Kenites (1 Sam. 27:10). Chronicles records the extension of their pasture grounds and their conflicts with the Amalekites (1 Chr. 4:24–43).

The other tribe which was dispersed after the Shechem incident was Levi. It is difficult to estimate what was originally Levite and what was leviticized by David and, later, by the Deuteronomic reform, which treated all the local clergy as Levites. There were Levites left in Ephraim (Judg. 17 f.); but a strong contingent of them survived in the south-west of Judah. The clan of Zerah was regarded as Edomite, or as Levite, or as Judahite. From the ancient list of five names in Num. 26:58, we may gather that they were at Libnah and at Hebron. From before the time of David, the Levites had a markedly sacerdotal character.[25] The kingdom of David at Hebron was to absorb the non-cultic elements among the Levites, as it was to assimilate the Simeonites, the Kenites, the Kenizzites, the Calebites, and the Jerahmeelites.

What was the tribe of Judah[26] before David reigned in

---

[25] On the nature of the Levites, see R. de Vaux, *Ancient Israel*, pp. 358–61; E. Nielsen, 'The Levites in Ancient Israel', *ASTI* iii (1964), 16–27.

[26] R. de Vaux, *Histoire*, 507–10; R. Smend, 'Gehörte Juda zum vorstaatlichen Israel?' *Proceedings of 4th Congress of Jewish Studies*, Jerusalem, 1967, pp. 57–62; E. Lipiński, 'L'étymologie de "Juda"', *VT* xxiii (1973), 380 f.

Hebron? Like Num. 26:20, the Yahwist (Gen. 38) knew of three basic groups, and two (Er and Onan) which were becoming extinct. Through Tamar, to the Canaanite group of Shelah near Adullam, were added two groups which were more 'Israelite': Zerah, which should have held primacy and which settled near Tamar, most probably the city of the 'palms' (*t^emārîm*) of Judg. 1:16, and Perez in the Jerusalem and Bethlehem area from which came David (Ruth 4:18–22). The name of Judah is most probably geographic,[27] denoting the region near Samson's territory (Judg. 15:11). The tribe may have been the product of Perizzite and Zerahite elements in Hebron. Amminadab and Nahshon appear in David's genealogy; but in Exod. 6:23; 1 Chr. 6:22 (MT, 7), they are Levites. Perhaps, by absorbing Levitic elements, Judah took Levi's place in the list of the twelve tribes.

D. *The Northern Tribes*[28]   After contact with Reuben (Bilhah), Dan had settled in Samson's territory. An important group broke away and settled in Laish (Leshem) under Sidonian influence. We have traced above the evolution of Asher, which settled on the coast under Egyptian control before coming under Philistine or Canaanite-Sidonian control (Judg. 1). Issachar and Zebulun were in the plain of Esdraelon but subject to forced labour; and Zebulun, before being a prince (*z^ebūl*), was probably subject to forced labour (*sābāl*; cf. Judg. 1.30), like Issachar (Gen. 49:14). Of the northern tribes in Galilee of the *gôyīm* (Isa. 9:1, MT, 8:23), only Naphtali seems to have become independent after the battle of the waters of Merom (Josh. 11.1–9; cf. Judg. 5:18).

5. *Israel at the Time of the Judges*

In the book of Judges, the history of the tribes between their establishment and the monarchy has been systematized, because of the notion of judge (*šôpēṭ*).[29] This title was borne by some chieftains before the monarchy and it indicates a

[27] M. Noth, *History*, p. 56.

[28] See Y. Aharoni, 'New Aspects of the Israelite Occupation of the North', *Essays in Honor of Nelson Glueck: Near Eastern Archeology in the Twentieth Century*, ed. J. A. Sanders, New York, 1970, pp. 254–67.

[29] The institution of *šôpēṭ* has been studied afresh recently, in the light of the Mari texts, by A. Marzal, in, 'The Provincial Governor at Mari', *JNES* xxx (1971), 188–204; see also W. Richter, 'Zu den Richtern Israels', *ZAW* lxxvii (1965), 40–71.

west-Semitic institution parallel to that of kingship but without the dynastic element and the religious aura. It appears that one edition of the book of Judges used this notion to trace a premonarchical history of the deliverance of the nation, but the historical figures which have been used for this picture do not correspond to a unique institution. Gideon and Jephthah are monarchs, Ehud and Othniel chieftains, Barak an officer, and the minor Judges are known only from their tombs, like the *welis* in the Arab world; finally, no political activity is attributed to Samson. Strikingly, the author has been able to connect nearly every Judge to a different tribe: Othniel to Judah, Ehud to Benjamin, Barak to Naphtali, Gideon to Manasseh, Tola to Issachar, Jair to Gilead (Machir), Jephthah to Gilead (Gad), Ibzan to Bethlehem in Zebulun (but for Asher), Elon to Zebulun, Hillel to Ephraim, and Samson to Dan. Reuben and Simeon, which disappeared early, are missing.

The vacuum left by the disappearance of Egyptian control after 1150 B.C. is striking. The Sea Peoples swept over Ugarit and the coast a little before 1200 B.C. With the help of Ramesses III, the Philistines held the south coast and the Tjekker the coast further north towards Dor. They did not, however, impose a Philistine peace replacing the Egyptian peace. Nevertheless they progressed inland for a century. If the presence of so-called Philistine pottery in the Jordan valley (Deir Alla) and in the hill country (Tell en-Nasbeh) may be explained by trade, it is certain that the Philistines occupied Bethshan and Gibeah in Benjamin.

This was not the only threat to the independence of the tribes. The Midianites penetrated as far as Ophrah of Abiezer; the Ammonites, who had been driven back by Jephthah, besieged Jabesh-gilead; the Moabites subjugated Reuben and penetrated into Benjamin. The tribes themselves were in accord only occasionally. Ephraim held a most important position and made its supremacy felt both by the Manassite Gideon (Judg. 8:1–3) and by Jephthah of Gilead (Judg. 12:1–6). After Joshua, however, there is no record of any outstanding chieftain in Ephraim.

On the contrary, a first monarchy, that of Gideon and Abimelech, established itself in the small Manassite territory.

This monarchy probably started in Ophrah with Gideon, whose harem was already royal, and whose sons 'resembled the sons of a king' (Judge. 8:18). His son Abimelech was accorded royal status in Shechem. The 'masters of Shechem' could not congratulate themselves on their choice, for it was a failure.

This was Iron Age I. The Anatolian technique, evolved in the fourteenth century B.C., had reached the coast with the Sea Peoples. The Israelites were compelled to obtain their metal tools, even for agriculture (1 Sam. 13:20 f.) from the Philistines. Iron Age I is marked by the destruction of some Canaanite towns: Tell Beit Mirsim/Debir (?) (mid-thirteenth century), Hazor (last quarter of the thirteenth century), Tirzah/Tell el-Far'ah (thirteenth century), Joppa (twice in the thirteenth century), Lachish (thirteenth or twelfth century), Beth-shemesh (thirteenth and eleventh centuries), Taanach (end of the twelfth century). Some were reoccupied: Laish-Dan at the end of the thirteenth century or the beginning of the twelfth, Hazor in the twelfth, Mizpah/Tell en-Nasbeh in the eleventh, Tirzah in the tenth. This presupposes battles between 1230 (Merenptah stele) and 1050 (Saul's accession). The book of Judges has preserved a memory of this, modified in the process of transmission.

(a) The attack of Cushan-Rishathaim, 'King of Aram-naharaim' (Judg. 3:8), is one of the most difficult to locate. It is tempting to read 'Edom' rather than 'Aram', since his opponent Othniel lived at Debir in Judah. Since, however, there are traces of Aramean penetration in southern Judah (the town Laban, Rebecca at Lahai-Roi, the name '*Bar*-Nea' given to the oasis of Kadesh), a writer may have linked the fourteenth–twelfth-century Aramean penetration to tensions between Othniel and Edom, in order to present Judah as the principal deliverer. The Cush may be the Midianite Cush of the execration texts (cf. Num. 12:1; Hab. 3:7). Malamat suggests that the episode may reflect the domination of the Asiatic Irsu over the Delta and neighbouring regions at the end of the thirteenth century.[30]

---

[30] 'Cushan-rishathaim and the Decline of the Near East around 1200 B.C.', *JNES* xiii (1954), 231 ff.; but see also S. Yeivin, *The Israelite Conquest of Canaan*, Istanbul, 1971, pp. 93 f.

(b) Ehud freed the Benjaminites from Moabite oppression. The Moabite expansion seems to have begun in the thirteenth century, when Ramesses II came into conflict with Moab. Its penetration beyond the Jordan river was earlier than the defeat of Moab by Ammon, to which Jephthah alludes (Judg. 11:24)

(c) The struggle of Shamgar with the Philistines (Judg. 3:31) is separate from the texts concerning the presence of the Philistines in the south (Judg. 13–16). It may refer to the penetration of the Sea Peoples in Canaan a little before the clash with Ramesses III (1180 B.C.)

(d) The campaign in which Barak was supported by Deborah is more complex. The narrative refers to Jabin of Hazor (cf. the Ibni-El of Hazor in the Mari tablets), which suggests a victory of Naphtali before the end of the thirteenth century. As with the Cushan-rishathaim incident, this important event was probably part of a larger action against Sisera whose capital Harosheth was near Acco. It was in this second action that Ephraim was involved, together with Deborah and the central and northern tribes. The name Sisera appears in the form Cush–Sisera in a list of Ramesses II and another, more suspect, of Ramesses III. The etymology may be Hurrian (Albright), or Illyrian and hence Philistine or the like (Alt), in which case the defeat of Sisera must have been later than the thirteenth century. Since the Song of Deborah speaks of 'waters' and not of a 'town' of Megiddo and of the town of Taanach, the battle would have taken place between layers VII and VI of Megiddo (end of the twelfth century according to Mazar and Yeivin) and before 1125, the approximate date of the destruction of Taanach.

(e) In the campaigns against Midian led by Gideon–Jerubbaal, Asher, and Naphtali (Judg. 7:23, and Zebulun in 6:35), are united to Manasseh, but not to Ephraim. The towns of Succoth (in Gad, Josh. 13:27) and of Penuel (in Gadite territory) have no feeling of solidarity towards Gideon the Abiezrite, and Ephraim is hostile. The union is far from being realized, but it is important to note Asher's role which was also a firm element in Saul's monarchy (Cf. 2 Sam. 2:9).

(f) The Jephthah narrative presupposes peace between Gad and Manasseh. Jephthah was from the northern Mizpah, and he sought refuge in the land of Tob which is perhaps the Aramean form of Zobah. The story ends with a victory over Ephraim, which lost its Transjordanian settlements. Yeivin considers that a date *c.* 1100 B.C. would fit the Aramean penetration into the land of Tob and the absence of Philistines from the Jordan valley.

(g) Gath, the most inland of the Philistine cities, faced Ephraim and Dan. In the Samson cycle, the Philistines controlled Danite territory (Beth-shemesh). About 1050 B.C. the battle of Aphek brought disaster on Ephraim (1 Sam. 4:1–11). The Philistines then organized a triple campaign to strengthen their control over the heart of the country (1 Sam. 4:17). A unit marched north towards Shiloh. In the centre, a second group took Michmash in Benjamin. A little further south, a third group skirted the desert by the vale of Zeboim and settled in Gibeah. Thus it was that between a new Ammonite threat to Jabesh-gilead and the Philistine pressure, a Benjaminite monarchy became a rallying point. The instability of Israelite society at that period is evident. What was its structure? Noth[31] has suggested an amphictyonic structure, which best explains the role of a sanctuary like Gilgal, perhaps also Shechem and Bethel, and even better the fact that there were twelve tribes. This number is fixed even when the tribes' names do not coincide in the lists; as in the amphictyonies, each tribe looks after the sanctuary one month out of twelve.

An over-systematized conception of this structure has brought about a reaction.[32] Some would rather speak of a league. The term 'league', however, fits but imperfectly the various group-mechanisms of the tribes, although it introduces the notion of alliance, which may have played some part in these groupings. In Hebrew the terms *ḳāhāl* and *'am* are used: the role of *'am* has already been examined. That of *ḳāhāl* deserves particular attention, for the term was taken up

---

[31] *Das System der zwölf Stämme Israels*, BWANT iv. 1, 1930.

[32] H. M. Orlinsky, 'The Tribal System of Israel and Related Groups in the Period of the Judges', *OA* i (1962), 11–20; G. W. Anderson 'Israel: Amphictyony: '*AM*, *ḲĀHĀL*, '*ĒDĀH*' in H. T. Frank and W. L. Reed (eds.), *Translating and Understanding the Old Testament*, 1970, pp. 135–51; R. de Vaux, 'La thèse de l' "amphictyonie israélite"', *HTR* lxiv (1917), 415–46; A. Soggin, *Das Königtum in Israel*, BZAW civ, 1967, p. 12, n. 1.

in Deuteronomic usage. Already in Gen. 49:6, it is the term used for a military grouping, that of Simeon and Levi against Shechem. If, as has been suggested, the term is derived from *ḳôl*, 'voice',[33] it would refer to a summons and particularly the sacred summons into the presence of the deity for the wars of Yahweh. The sanctuary at Gilgal, the base from which Joshua set out on several campaigns, was the privileged site for such a summons. Shechem with its temple of Baal-berith and Bethel (Judg. 20:26) may also have been sites of the summons to the army of Israel. Shiloh, with its sanctuary containing the Ark, may equally have been the meeting-point of a few tribes mobilizing for the holy war. But Gideon had rallied some groups on Tabor by the cry 'to Yahweh and to Gideon'. In the name of Yahweh a more durable dynasty was established, the 'first kingdom' (Mic. 4:8), whose hero was buried in Zela (2 Sam. 21:14) after his victories and his failure.

II. THE MONARCHY, FROM ITS ESTABLISHMENT TO ITS FALL

1. *The Monarchy and its Ideology*

What was meant by kingdom (*mamlāḵâh*) at that time? A kingdom was a state, however rudimentary its institutions and public services. The chief of state was still the head of a type of large patriarchal family or group of tribes. Oriental monarchy combines an ideology where the king is father of his people, called by God to rule it well, with a state organization requiring a technique, a culture, a 'wisdom'. According to 1 Sam. 8:5, 20, monarchy was introduced into Israel, in imitation of foreign nations. Oriental monarchies however did not conform to a single pattern. The Israelite monarchy had to find its own way: it was more Semitic with Saul, more Pharaonic with Solomon, but always priestly. This characteristic was spontaneously recognized by the population, as is evidenced by the words of the woman of Tekoa (2 Sam. 14:17–20).

The Israelite kings were first military leaders, like the

[33] L. Rost, *Die Vorstufen von Kirche und Synagoge im Alten Testament*, BWANT iv. 24, 1938; H. Vogt, *Studien zur nachexilischen Gemeinde in Ezra-Nehemia*, Werl, 1966, pp. 90 f.

Mesopotamian *šarru*. However, very soon, both in Mesopotamia and in Israel there came into being a professional army. The army was not the king's personal guard. It had its general-in-chief, its storehouses and strongholds in some towns. It consisted of archers, charioteers, infantry. Its drafting required a military administration and a census of the recruits.[34]

There is no Oriental monarchy without scribes capable of keeping the accounts in the towns, or without a central administration in the capital. To train these scribes, schools are necessary, where they learn to compute, and write reports, royal decrees, and diplomatic correspondence. The training of the scribe is a difficult art and the small courts learned from the amazing traditional experience of Egypt and Babylon. Besides arid name-lists, there were also documents which required literary skill for their composition.

Justice was also taught. It was the basis[35] of Oriental kingships although practised imperfectly. The Pharaoh received from his divine father the gift of *ma'at*: truth, rectitude, and justice. The Babylonian king received *kittu* and *mešaru* and the Phoenician king received *ṣdk* and *yšr* or *mšr*. All these terms are dangerous to translate. They are less norms than virtues by which the king gives the subjects of the national god a firm basis for their activities. This implies justice and also prosperity. Israelite orthodoxy kept the *ṣdk*, but linked justice to the judgements, (*mišpāṭîm*) of Moses (Gen. 18:19, 2 Sam. 8:15). The king must practise these virtues and solve difficult cases (1 Kgs. 3:16–28), a task often delegated to scribes.

Some of the scribes not only have to make sure that the traditional norms or the royal edicts are followed. They also have to give counsel to the king in complicated situations, negotiate abroad, appease the people at home in the midst of conflicts of different interests. More than by force and war, it is by this subtle art that the king has the understanding

---

[34] Light has been shed on David's census (2 Sam. 24) by the Mari texts. See J. R. Kupper, *Les Nomades en Mésopotamie*, pp. 23 ff.; E. A. Speiser, 'Census and Ritual Expiation in Mari and Israel', *BASOR* 149 (1958), 17–25; H. Cazelles, 'Mari et l'A.T.', *XVème rencontre assyriologique internationale, Liège*, 1967, p. 88.

[35] H. Cazelles, 'The Two Moral Foundations of the State in the Bible and the Ancient Near East', in D. Marcus (ed.), *The Gaster Festschrift*, New York, 1974.

(*bînâh*) and the wisdom (*ḥokmâh*) that help him to succeed (*hiskîl*).

The king receives from God his superior capacities of wisdom and intelligence, the 'wisdom' which was, for the Canaanites, the privilege of the supreme god El. Hence these curious and varied images through which is expressed the very special relationship of the king with the national god. The king is often called 'son'of the god and the interpretation of this formula varies according to the notion of divinity.

The king of Israel is called *nāgîd*,[36] a title which seems to have a religious value. He is one with his people, in accordance with the idea of corporate personality. As founder of a dynasty or as dynastic heir, he bears divine power; but he can lose it, as may be seen from the closing period of David's reign. Conflicts between rival dynasties (the houses of Saul and David) and the problem of legitimate succession within a dynasty reveal the weak points of the monarchical ideology.

2. *The Monarchy of Saul*

Of the three narratives which describe Saul's accession, the oldest seems to be 1 Sam. 11:1–5. On hearing in Gibea of the siege of Jabesh-gilead, Saul sent messages 'across the whole territory of Israel', though the tribes which were summoned are not named. After his victory, his kingship is inaugurated in Gilgal. The territorial basis of this monarchy is the central Jordan valley with Gilead to the east and the hill country of Ephraim to the west, including Benjamin. Even after Saul's death, this valley remained the axis of the kingdom (2 Sam. 2:9). However, the Benjaminite action exercised itself in the south-west in the region of Geba and Gibeah. The Philistines were present at Michmash and Gibeah. They are mentioned in the second narrative of the accession of Saul (1 Sam. 9:1–10:16) at Gibeah. The city where Saul met Samuel is not mentioned, but it is in the hill country of Ephraim, in the land of Zuph. In the third narrative, the most recent one, the city is Mizpah, a few kilometres north of Gibeah. As Gibeah

---

[36] J. J. Glück, 'Nagid-Shepherd', *VT* xiii (1963), 144–50; W. Richter, 'Die nagid-Formel', *BZ* ix (1965), 71–83; F. Langlamet, 'L'institution de la royauté', *RB* lxxvii (1970), 188–99; L. Schmidt, *Menschlicher Erfolg und Jahwes Initiative*, WMANT xxxviii, 1970, pp. 141–71.

became Gibeah of Saul, it is certain that Saul expelled the Philistines, probably after the victory of Michmash, 8 kilometres to the north-west. Having liberated Gibeah, the present Tell el-Ful, 5 kilometres to the north of Jerusalem, Saul clashed with several Canaanite cities. He did not bother with Jerusalem, but may have been concerned to support Kiriath-jearim, which was probably already occupied by Benjaminites (Josh. 18:15; cf. v. 14). Saul seized Beeroth and Gibeon, breaking the ancient pact between the Gibeonites and Joshua (Josh. 9). He penetrated even farther: reference is made twice to the presence of his forces in the wilderness of Judah (1 Sam. 15 and 24/26). 2 Sam. 21:2 speaks of Saul's zeal for the Israelites and for Judah. The Amalekites had temporarily dominated the Jordan valley. Saul struck at them in their southern lair, aiming to protect his own main base in this valley.

To the west, against Gath, from which had come the Philistine attacks against the region of Benjamin, Saul pushed into the valley of Elah opposite a Philistine army established at Ephes-dammim (1 Sam. 17:1–2).

One of the three Philistine thrusts was directed to the south of Benjamin and threatened the region of Lehi (2 Sam. 23:11; cf. Judg. 15:9 ff.). Saul's pressure became so strong that the Philistines concentrated a little further north at Aphek. Rather than attempting a frontal attack on the mountainous region, they preferred to lure Saul into the upper Jordan valley to the Gilboa mountains. Saul was defeated and killed together with Jonathan. The monarchy, however, was strong enough not to die. With the support of Abner, Saul's uncle and commander-in-chief, another son, Ishbaal (Ishbosheth) succeeded. His kingdom did not cover the whole of Israel, but Gilead (2 Sam. 2:9) with Mahanaim, Ephraim, Benjamin, Asher (spelt Ashurim), and Jezreel, a city of Issachar (Josh. 19:18). Thus Abner seems to have regained control over the plain of Esdraelon.

Born in victory, the Benjaminite dynasty spent its strength in foreign conflicts and internal feuds. It must have seemed that there was only a slight chance that the Judahite monarchy would survive. That it did so is a pointer to the greatness of David.

3. David

David was the son of Jesse, of the group ('*elep*) of Ephrathah (cf. Mic. 5:1). His genealogy appears in one of the short summaries by which the Bible indicates the complexity of origins (Ruth 4:18–22). Jesse's family is linked to the clan of Perez. The names of places near Jerusalem (Baal-perazim, Perez-uzzah, whose meaning has been reinterpreted) lead one to believe that the clan was originally settled between Jerusalem and Beth-shemesh. Through Ram, David was connected with Caleb of Hebron and with Jerahmeel farther south (1 Chr. 2:25, 42); through Amminadab and Nahshon, he may have had connections with the Kohathite Levites, and through Ruth, with Moab. He owed his Bethlehemite origin to his ancestor Boaz. The Northern Israelites considered him as one of their kin, being an Ephrathite (2 Sam. 5:2). The name 'David' is rare and remains enigmatic. Most probably it is a term of kinship, meaning 'uncle' (*dôḏ*) rather than 'ancestor'.

When Saul began his thrust to the south and west, David was one of the young men whom he enlisted (1 Sam. 14:52). However, the tension between Samuel the Ephrathite and Saul disturbed the relations between the king and Bethlehem–Ephrathah. Saul suspected that a plot was afoot; and David's incorporation into the royal family by marriage only made the king more worried and jealous. David was forced to flee and to send his own family to Moab, with which he had relations through Ruth (1 Sam. 22:3). A born chief, David was able to recruit 400 men, but had to retreat gradually under pressure from Saul. Finally he sought the protection of Achish, the Philistine king of Gath, which was the centre of Philistine attacks against Benjamin. Achish did not actually use David in the struggle against Saul. He gave him a post remote from the theatre of operations, that of Ziklag, where David had to control the unruly southern tribes.

The stay at Ziklag was of great importance. Ziklag was in the region of the tribe of Simeon, near the sanctuary of Beersheba where Abraham had stayed and worshipped El Olam (Gen. 21:33). This was not far from the Negeb and David's troop often had to reach the well of Lahai-roi. There Isaac had stayed; there Ishmael and Isaac had been in contact; and in that region David found clans (Simeon and Levi) which had previously been in the hill country of Ephraim (Gen. 34) and had broken up. David and his people were in contact with the cities and populations south of Hebron (1 Sam. 30:26–31) such as the Kenites, the Jerahmeelites, the Calebites of Hebron and of Carmel.[37] Farther west, in the 'Negeb of the Cherethites' (1 Sam. 30:14) he met the Cherethites and the Pelethites from whom he enlisted his personal guard, probably mixed racial elements of Mediterranean origin (Cretans?) like the Philistines. As the lieutenant of Achish, David had to lead several raids (1 Sam. 27:8). The most important raid was against the Amalekites in eastern Judah. To the west, he fought the Asherites (spelt here 'Geshur' as in Josh. 13:2) probably an element of Asher which had not gone north (cf. Num. 24:24). Lastly, he fought the Girzites, a more difficult group to identify.[38]

By his absence from the Philistine army which defeated Saul at Gilboa, David avoided the charge of being a traitor, and also was at hand in time to strike at the camp of the Amalekite raiders. He fixed the rules for the allocation of booty and returned to the Judahites what the Amalekites had taken. 1 Sam. 30:27–31 gives the list of the twelve cities (or groupings) to which he sent back part of the booty as a present (cf. Gen. 33:11). Upon Saul's death, the Judahites, whose protector David had become, anointed him as king of Judah, probably after a quick campaign against Hebron (2 Sam. 2:1–4).

Thus the 'house of Judah' was constituted as David announced to the inhabitants of Jabesh-gilead (2 Sam. 2:7). He did not set himself up as the rival of the dynasty of Saul 'your master'. The monarchy of Judah is an additional monarchy beside those of Israel, Moab, and Edom. It is certainly a monarchy in the name of Yahweh. The theophorous names with this element are numerous in the time and entourage of David;[39] and the letter to the Jabeshites emphasizes the name of Yahweh. The kingdom of Judah

---

[37] On these groups, see de Vaux, *Histoire ancienne*, pp. 496–500.

[38] Perhaps to be related to the Girgashites. In MT, the *kᵉrê* makes them inhabitants of Gezer; but they would have been near to the Philistines, and, in particular, to Gath. It would be difficult to understand Achish's ignorance (1 Sam. 27: 10).

[39] M. Noth, *Die israelitischen Personennamen*, BWANT iii 10, 1928, p. 107.

includes Israelite elements, both the colonizing elements from the north grouped in the clan of Perez and the Levitical elements from the south-east, the clan of Zerah in close relation with the city of Tamar, and finally the tribe of Simeon, now absorbed by Judah. Besides these Israelite elements, the three other clans of Gen. 38 have been assimilated, that of Shelah seemingly being the only one in existence. Lastly, the allies of David such as the Kenites, the Jerahmeelites, the Calebites of Hebron, the Kenizzites of Debir, and other mixed populations in contact with David at Ziklag were politically assimilated. The kingship of Saul was a national monarchy threatening minorities such as the Gibeonites and the Beerothites. David's kingship, on the contrary, assimilated and respected local religious traditions, whilst certainly aiming at a unification around the king and his god Yahweh.

Israel had no intention of forgiving the exiled David. On the other hand, David penetrated into Benjaminite territory. Abner decided to play David's game, for David, according to him, was the only one able to remove the Philistine danger (2 Sam. 3:18). Peace would have been concluded if Joab had not compromised everything by murdering Abner. Israel, however, felt cruelly the lack of an able chief and after Ishbaal's murder by the two Beerothites, the elders of Israel started negotiations anew. They made with David a type of treaty of vassalage 'before Yahweh' (2 Sam. 5:3) and anointed him king.

The Philistines' reaction to this news was to attack by the valley of Rephaim at the hinge of the two now united kingdoms. Perhaps they counted on the help of the Jebusites of Jerusalem which was encircled by the unified Israel. David broke their offensive at Baal-perazim, then, by a circular movement, coming this time from the Benjaminite territory north of Jerusalem, he pushed them back to Gezer. Jerusalem probably then fell to David. He made of it the 'city of David' and the capital of the unified kingdom.

The site was important strategically, neutral politically, well situated to control communication between both king-doms and east–west contacts. David established there his court with its administration and his wives. Although he intended to build a temple for the dynastic and national God, there was in his time only an embryonic cult just as there was only an embryonic civilian administration. The regular royal cult was limited to the presence of the Ark (2 Sam. 15:24).

Two lists of high-ranking officials (2 Sam. 8:15–18 and 20:23–26)[40] testify to some sort of administrative organization. David had in his entourage a *sōpēr* and a *mazkîr*: the titles (corresponding to Canaanite offices based on Egyptian usage) indicate something like a Secretary of State and a herald who proclaims the royal will. Near the ageing David were a friend (Hushai) and an adviser (Ahithophel); but there was not yet an official in charge of the crown property. Although one of the traditional aims of the monarchy was to establish 'justice and law' (*mišpāṭ* and *ṣᵉdākâh*), justice was not yet organized. This was one of the reasons behind Absalom's revolt (2 Sam. 15:2–3).

Military functions clearly predominate, Joab being commander of the army (for a time superseded by Amasa who was punished by death), and Benaiah commander of the guard.

The establishment of a unified monarchy forced David to take up Saul's inheritance and to protect Transjordan to both south and north. After the battles of the vale of the Rephaim, relations with the Philistines seem to have stabilized themselves. David had been on too good terms with Achish of Gath to push too far against him. At the beginning of Solomon's reign, Gath was still an independent kingdom (1 Kgs. 2:39 ff.) Difficulties were more acute to the east. The Aramean thrust was due to Hazadezer, king of Zobah. To contain it, David not only made an agreement with the king of Hamath, but also established his protectorate over Damascus (2 Sam. 8:6) and made Joab take Rabbah, the Ammonite capital. Further south, the Moabites were defeated and routed, and made to pay tribute. Finally, the Edomites became his 'servants' and were put under the rule of governors. David had created a real empire with a variety of vassal states.

Absalom's revolt broke out in Hebron as an episode in the tensions which brought gloom to the king's court in his old

---

[40] See T. N. D. Mettinger, *Solomonic State Officals, A Study of the Civil Government Officials of the Israelite Monarchy*, Lund, 1971.

age, tensions which came to be linked with oppositions between groups within the Empire. In the 'Succession Narrative' the political problems are not all clarified. Why did the rebellion start from Hebron before involving all of Israel? Had the Calebites not accepted David's conquest? Why did Gilead remain faithful? Is the fear of the Arameans sufficient to explain this fidelity? Obviously, neither Ephraim nor Benjamin had accepted this marginal southern monarchy. David's wishes ensured the succession; but there was no covenant with the elders of Israel and Judah as there had been for David and as there would be attempted upon Solomon's death. The monarchy emphasized its Pharaonic aspect and discarded ancient Semitic conceptions. Nevertheless, the achievement of Saul and David was so firmly rooted that it could survive in the north as well as in the south.

4. Solomon

David was first and foremost a warrior and even in his old age was dominated by a warrior, Joab. Solomon was less a *šarru* than a *malku* and with him diplomatic and administrative wisdom prevailed. Not for nothing does Israelite tradition show him as the paragon of wise men. His accession took place in the context of rivalries in the army, Benaiah against Joab, and among the priests, Zadok against Abiathar, but with the support of a man of strong character, Nathan, and two women, his mother and Abishag the Shunammite. He had to act with prudence, to consolidate his power, and he succeeded.

He first extended his capital and filled in by a *millô'* the depression which protected the ancient city of David on the north side. He built a palace larger than David's and better adapted to administrative needs. The latter had been surrounded by houses; but Solomon isolated his palace from the city. It was situated on the hill of a new Temple, palace and Temple being juxtaposed in accordance with ancient Near Eastern practice. The king was God's vice-gerent, his 'servant', and his palace was part of the house of Yahweh.

The seat of the royal administration was within this complex of buildings (1 Kgs. 4:1–6).[41] There were now two

---

[41] D. Ussishkin, 'King Solomon's Palace', *BA* xxxvi (1973), 78–105.

royal secretaries, a chief of the prefects, a majordomo who administered the crown property, a master of works for public works, in addition to the officials of David's time: priest, herald, commander of the army, commander of the guard.[42] The maintenance of this central administration, palace, and Temple was ensured by a prefectorial system (1 Kgs. 4:7–19).[43] The twelve prefectures paid their taxes in kind, on a twelve-monthly rota. They were territorial, each with an Israelite nucleus constituted by a tribe, but including many other racial elements and Canaanite cities newly conquered by David, like the capital itself. Prefects might be of royal blood, but more often they were eminent persons from the assimilated territories, succeeding each other from father to son, according to ancient custom.[44] Judah was separate. To train these administrators and teach them both to write and compute and also to express themselves, scribal schools were necessary, and that is how Solomon initiated wisdom in Israel. In his reign there flourished the great classical Hebrew literature, of which the Bible has preserved a few samples such as the Yahwistic document, the Succession Narrative, and the narratives about Joshua, Gideon, and Samson. Like the Canaanite princes before him, Solomon followed both the traditional procedures which had come from Babylon to Canaan under the Amorite dynasty, and also the Egyptian model. Some scribes appear to have had Egyptian names, hence there was at the court of Jerusalem a scribal tradition favourable towards Egypt, of which the Yahwist and, later, the prophets, told the faithful to beware.

The good relations between the new monarchy and the weakened Egypt of the Twenty-first Dynasty was crowned by a marriage, Gezer being the dowry (1 Kgs. 9:16). Like the Pharaohs, Solomon followed a policy of matrimonial alliances more involved than his father's, and the good relations were sanctified by the building on the Mount of Olives of temples in honour of the gods of his foreign wives.

If Solomon looked to Egypt for his scribes, he looked to the

[42] See Mettinger, op. cit.

[43] A. Caquot, 'Préfets', in *SDB* viii, cols. 273–86; D. B. Redford, 'The Taxation System of Solomon', in J. W. Wevers and D. B. Redford (eds.), *Studies in the Ancient Palestinian World*, London, 1972, pp. 141–56.

[44] A. Alt, 'Menschen ohne Namen', *KS* iii, 198–213.

Phoenicians for his buildings, especially the Temple, even perhaps for his fortifications at Hazor, Megiddo, and Gezer. This brought about exchanges and trade to the point of effective associations for Red Sea trading (1 Kgs. 9:26–28). Controlling part of the coast and access to the gulf of Aqabah, the country had some prosperous years owing to trade, particularly in horses, between Cilicia and Egypt (1 Kgs. 10:15, 27–29). This wealth paid for the enormous expenses of the Temple and the palace only in part. Solomon had to fall back on forced labour and the corvée imposed even on the Israelites. To meet his debt to Hiram of Tyre, Solomon had to cede villages in the region of Cabul, north-east of Acco.

The end of the reign was an anticlimax and the complex empire built up by David began to disintegrate. The Aramean pressure, which Saul and David had resisted, gained ground in the north-east. Rezon,[45] a former subject of Hadadezer of Zobah, replaced the Israelite governor and set up an independent kingdom. The weakening of Solomon's power was caused by the rise of the Egyptian Twenty-second Dynasty under Sheshonk I (c. 945 B.C.). The capital was moved from Tanis to Bubaste, further away from the border. Instead of pursuing a policy of *entente* and matrimonial alliances, the new Pharaoh welcomed an Edomite of royal blood, Hadad, a victim of Israelite annexation and of Joab's repression (1 Kgs. 11:14–15). He married a sister-in-law of Sheshonk,[46] but returned to his own country.

Sheshonk welcomed another fugitive, this time the Ephraimite, Jeroboam, who had been in charge of the corvée of 'the house of Joseph'. He rebelled only after the intervention of another Ephraimite, the prophet Ahijah of Shiloh, and then was obliged to flee to Egypt. He later returned and founded the third dynasty of Israel upon the death of David's son.

5. *The Kingdom of Israel and the Fate of Judah*

Rehoboam was forty-five years old at his accession and

---

[45] On Rezon, see B. Mazar, 'The Aramean Empire and its Relations with Israel', *BA* xxv (1962), 104, n. 12; A. Malamat, 'The Arameans', in *POTT*, p. 143.

[46] There is uncertainty about the identification; see A. Gardiner, *Egypt of the Pharaohs*, Oxford, 1961, p. 329; and cf. J. Gray *I & II Kings*, 2nd edn., 1970, p. 285.

therefore was perhaps the eldest son. It is however very probable that there were other claimants to the throne, born of other mothers. The best explanation of the assembly at Shechem lies in the need to secure widespread support by renewing David's pact with the elders of Israel (2 Sam. 5:3) in a place where Abraham, Israel, and Joshua had been. The text (1 Kgs. 12:2)[47] is not specific about the time of Jeroboam's return. Had he been recalled by the opposition, or did he return only after the disruption? It is certain that instead of being acclaimed as king, Rehoboam had to face a request for a diminution of the corvée, which he refused, with disastrous results.

When Jeroboam became king, Ephraim at last had its own dynasty. The idea that the northern monarchy was 'charismatic' (advocated with such force by Alt) should be treated with caution. It is acknowledged that the $ru^a\dot{h}$ was associated with the institution of monarchy before the editor of the book of Judges applied it to certain 'Judges' who had no dynastic successors. In fact, the principle of dynastic succession was well established in the Northern Kingdom. Jeroboam seems to have modelled his kingship on the Solomonic model which was based on the Egyptian model. He retained its ideology and built royal temples at Dan and Bethel (1 Kgs. 12:26–33) whose priests he appointed. He made Shechem his capital but later moved to Tirzah, probably to protect himself more easily from the Aramean pressure on Gilead.

During two centuries the true political heir of David's kingdom was the Northern Kingdom, comprising at least ten tribes with a part of Benjamin.

Sheshonk I waged a campaign against Israel in the fifth year of Rehoboam. According to the Karnak list,[48] he traversed Israel lengthwise and crosswise but spared Jerusalem and Judah, from which he was content to exact heavy tribute. The best explanation is that Rehoboam, threatened by Edom and Israel, had become his vassal and that Sheshonk had taken advantage of this to show Israel his strength.

[47] See J. A. Soggin, *Das Königtum in Israel*, pp. 90–5; J. Gray, *I & II Kings*, pp. 299–311.

[48] See B. Mazar, 'The Campaign of Pharaoh Shishak to Palestine', *Volume du Congrès, Strasbourg 1956*, SVT iv (1957), pp. 57–66.

Egypt's growing weakness under Libyan rule made this raid a success without any future. Three years separate the deaths of Jeroboam and Rehoboam.[49] Nadab, Jeroboam's son, was unable to keep the throne. *Circa* 909 B.C. he was assassinated whilst besieging the Philistine city of Gibbethon (1 Kgs. 15:27) while the war continued between Israel and Judah (1 Kgs. 15:7–16). This is a further pointer to an alliance in the south (Egypt, Philistia, Judah) against the north. The war continued in the reign of Nadab's murderer, Baasha. With him, the tribe of Issachar took power at Tirzah. To ensure his freedom of movement, he decided to fortify Ramah. Asa, who was then king of Judah, initiated a policy which reappeared later. To alleviate the pressure over his border with Israel, he staged (by paying a tribute) a diversion by the powerful kingdom of Damascus whose king was Benhadad I, son of Tab-Rimmon. This king seized the border cities in northern Israel: Ijon, Dan, and Abel-beth-maacah, then crossed the whole of Naphtali and reached the sea of Galilee (1 Kgs. 15:20). Baasha was probably able to push back the Aramean, but during this time Asa took advantage of the situation by fortifying Geba and Mizpah with the stones which had been prepared for Ramah.

The dynasty of Issachar did not last any longer than that of Ephraim. Zimri, chief of half of the charioteers, assassinated the son of Baasha during a drinking party at his majordomo's. New divisions appeared; first in the army, when the force campaigning against Gibbethon acclaimed Omri. They recaptured Tirzah and Zimri committed suicide there. Then the nation was divided. Omri gained the upper hand over Tibni, son of Ginath, of whom nothing but his name is known. Alt[50] may well be right in his contention that the Jezreel area was more Israelite, whereas the area around

---

[49] The chronology of the kings of Israel and Judah continues to present numerous problems, in spite of the many studies devoted to it. Note especially, E. Thiele, *The Mysterious Numbers of the Hebrew Kings*, Chicago, 1951, 2nd edn. 1966; id., *Synchronisms of the Hebrew Kings, a Re-evaluation*, AUSS ii (1964), 120–36; V. Pavlovsky and E. Vogt, 'Die Jahre der Könige von Juda und Israel', *Biblica* xlv (1964), 321–47; H. Tadmor in *Enziklopedia Mikraït*, iv, cols. 245–310. The dates given in the present essay are often approximate.

[50] A. Alt, 'Der Stadtstaat Samaria', *KS* iii. 258–302.

Samaria where Omri established a new capital after a reign of ten years in Tirzah, was more Canaanite.

Omri was undoubtedly a great king, founder of a dynasty respected abroad. Even after the fall of the dynasty, the country remained *Bit-Humri*, the house of Omri, for Assyrian scribes. With Omri and Ahab, Israel launched upon an active policy in Syria and Phoenicia. By Ahab's marriage with Jezebel, daughter of Ittobaal of Tyre, close relations with Tyre were established, developing the Phoenician influence over Israel in the religious and commercial fields. It thus seems strange that Tyre and Sidon are not mentioned in the Qarqar coalition whereas Ahab appears beside Irhuleni of Hamath, Matan-baal of Arvad and especially the king of Damascus, Hadadezer. Tyre and Sidon must be amongst the twelve kings of the coast whose names are not all indicated. Omri and 'his son' (Mesha stele) were also active in the south, occupying Madaba and rebuilding Jahaz, east of the Dead Sea. At that point, threatened from the north and east, Judah entered Israel's sphere of influence. Jehoshaphat (870–848 B.C.), son of Asa, married Athaliah, sister of Joram (852–841 B.C.), son of Ahab, and joined both him and Edom for a joint campaign against Mesha, king of Moab, who had revolted (2 Kgs. 3:4–27). The expedition failed, thus enabling Edom to free itself from the suzerainty of the king of Judah, Joram (848–841 B.C.), son of Jehoshaphat.

In the north, the situation became much more dangerous for Israel. A change of monarch in Damascus again disturbed international relations. Between the fourteenth and the eighteenth years of Shalmaneser (844–840 B.C.), Hadadezer or his son was assassinated by Hazael. This usurper alarmed Shalmaneser, who besieged Damascus and pressed on to both the Hauran and the sea, but without seizing the city. Shalmaneser did not get the upper hand over Hazael and if he pushed towards the Hauran, it was because Hazael had invaded Transjordan and taken Ramoth-gilead. Joram failed to recapture the city and was wounded.[51] The Israelite

---

[51] The king of Israel who appears in 1 Kgs. 22 must be Joram. (See S. Herrmann, *A History of Israel in Old Testament Times*, ETr, London, 1973, pp. 214 f.) It was Joram who was visited by Ahaziah of Judah when he was recovering from the wound received at the battle of Ramoth-gilead (2 Kgs. 8:28–30). His name has been eliminated from a number of narratives in the Elijah cycle.

positions in Transjordan were threatened. Taking advantage of the army's discontent, Jehu staged a *coup*. He rushed to Jezreel, killed Joram and his mother Jezebel as well as Ahaziah of Judah. The rest of the royal family were slaughtered in Samaria. In the eighteenth year of his reign (840 B.C.), Shalmaneser campaigned against Hazael, and it was then that he received tribute from Tyre, Sidon, and Jehu (referred to as 'the son of Omri'). Three years later (837 B.C.) Shalmaneser returned, again without success, and there was no further question of tribute from Jehu. The Assyrian never came back; he had to fight in the north and his reign ended in civil wars. Hazael was thus free to act. He devastated the whole territory east of the Jordan (2 Kgs. 10:33). The situation was no better in the reign of Jehoahaz (814–798 B.C.). Israel suffered a grievous defeat and its forces were limited to fifty horsemen, ten chariots, and 10,000 infantry (2 Kgs. 13:7). This treaty also included the gift of cities and of trade interests to Samaria itself (1 Kgs. 20:34). The situation was more favourable in the reign of Joash of Israel. Worried by the progress of Hazael and the ambitions of his son Ben-Hadad,[52] the king of Assyria, Adad-Nirari III (810–783 B.C.) revived the policy of intervention in Syria.[53] He may be the anonymous liberator mentioned in 2 Kgs. 13:5. An attack by Ben-Hadad was repulsed and the Aramean was defeated at Aphek (2 Kgs. 13:17; cf. 1 Kgs. 20:26). Adad-Nirari III's intervention forced the Aramean to let go and Joash of Israel paid tribute to him. Joash recovered the cities ceded by Jehoahaz and obtained trade advantages in Damascus equal to those that Jehoahaz had been obliged to grant Hazael in Samaria (2 Kgs. 14:25; cf. 1 Kgs. 20:34a).

[52] See the stele of Zakir, *KAI* ii. 204–11; M. Black in *DOTT*, p. 242–50; cf. J. F. Ross, 'Prophecy in Hamath, Israel and Mari', *HTR* lxiii (1970), 1–28; J. Greenfield in *Proceedings of the Fifth World Congress of Jewish Studies*, Jerusalem, 1969, pp. 174–191.

[53] A new stele of Adad-Nirari III was discovered in D. Oates's excavations at Tell Rimah, on which see S. Page in *Iraq* xxx (1968), 139–53, and Pls. XL–XLI. The historical circumstances have been re-examined in the light of it by H. Cazelles in *CRAIBL*, 1969, pp. 106–17, H. Donner in *Archäologie und Altes Testament, Festschrift Kurt Galling*, pp. 49–59, E. Lipiński in *Proceedings of Vth World Congress of Jewish Studies*, pp. 157–73, A. R. Millard, 'Adad-Nirari III, Aram, and Arpah', *PEQ* cv (1973), 161–4.

During the seven years of Athaliah's reign in Jerusalem, after the massacre of her family by Jehu, the relations between the two capitals had become disastrously frigid. It is possible, but not proved, that Israel played a role in the assassination of Athaliah by a plot between the army and the clergy of Jerusalem (2 Kgs. 11). When Hazael invaded Northern Israel and encamped at Gath (2 Kgs. 12:18), Joash opted for submission and paid tribute at the expense of the Temple. There may therefore be two reasons for the tension between him and the clergy of Jerusalem (2 Chr. 24:17–22) and for his assassination by his ministers (2 Kgs. 12:21 f.). His son Amaziah, having revenged himself on the Edomites for the defeat of his grandfather Joram (2 Kgs. 14:7; cf. 8:20), provoked Joash of Israel, perhaps in alliance with Ben-Hadad, in the same way that Asa had allied with Ben-Hadad I against Baasha of Israel. He was, however, crushed and made prisoner at Beth-shemesh (c. 780 B.C.). Jerusalem was taken and its walls pulled down (2 Kgs. 14:13, cf. Amos 9:11).

For nearly half a century, Samaria was once again supreme, at the end of the reign of Joash and under the long reign of Jeroboam II. The latter recovered territories from Lebo-hamath to the Dead Sea (2 Kgs. 14:25; cf. Amos. 6:14). Having made Judah his vassal, Jeroboam let it build Elath at the expense of Edom (2 Kgs. 14:22) and even, it seems, gave it some compensation in Syria at the expense of Damascus (2 Kgs. 14:28), hence the contacts between Judah (Azriyau) and the king of Assyria[54] after 745 B.C.

The influence of Tyre, its trade, and its methods of government burdened the administration. There was a great contrast between rich and poor (Amos 2:6–8; 6:4–7; 8:4–6; Hos. 4:2–6, 10–12; Mic. 3:1–4; Isa. 5:8), between the rulers and the ruled (Amos 6:12). Undermined from within, the kingdom was nearing its fall and the disciples of the prophets sought support from without.

---

[54] Other interpretations are possible, but since the publication of H. Tadmor's study, 'Azriyahu of Yaudi', *Scripta Hierosolymitana* vii (1961), 232–71, it has been increasingly widely held that this Azriyahu cannot be a prince of Yahudi, the Sam'al of the Zinjirli inscriptions (called Sam'al in these same inscriptions of Tiglath-pileser III, but spelled differently), but of Judah; cf. K. Galling, *Textbuch zur Geschichte Israels*, 2nd edn., Tübingen 1968, p. 54. But see O. Eissfeldt, '"Juda" und "Judäa" als Bezeichnung nordsyrischer bereiche', *KS* iv. pp. 121–31.

6. The Syro-Ephraimite War and the Fall of Samaria

This war was at first sight but one episode in the diplomatic game in the Near East. The personality of the king of Assyria, Tiglath-pileser III, produced unexpected consequences, a redrawing of the political map, and the end of the kingdom of Damascus. The ruin of the state of Israel, which followed, brought new theological problems to the religious consciousness of the Israelites and gave the Israelite community a new orientation. The Assyrian texts (Annals of Tiglath-pileser III and eponym list)[55] give a relatively precise framework enabling one to date events alluded to in Amos, Hosea, Micah, and Isaiah, and in the books of Kings and Chronicles.

In 743 B.C., Tiglath-pileser III appeared in Syria and moved against Arpad and in the region of Hamath (Amos 6:2; cf. Isa. 10:9). He captured 'cities which had been taken for Azriyahu of Yaudi'[56] who could be no other than Azariah of Judah (2 Kgs. 15:17) also called Uzziah. Jeroboam II and Uzziah/Azariah died c. 740 B.C. (cf. Isa. 6:1; 2 Kgs. 14:29; 15:7); Jeroboam's son was assassinated, and his murderer, Shallum, was killed a month later by Menahem who became king. He was still on the throne in 738 B.C., the date of the capture of Kullani (Calneh or Calnoh in Hebrew; cf. Amos 6:2; Isa. 10:9) according to the list of eponyms. His power was weak and he paid tribute to Tiglath-pileser (2 Kgs. 15:19) together with Damascus and Tyre. Having thus 'reinforced' his position, he was still king in 737 B.C.[57] He died not long after and his son Pekahiah was assassinated by Pekah, who replaced him and embarked upon a policy of close alliance with Rezin of Damascus to resist the Assyrian pressure. A great coalition was formed, with the support of the Phoenicians and the Philistines. The king of Judah, Jotham son of Uzziah, refused to join it (2 Kgs. 15:37).

[55] E. Vogt, 'Die Texte Tiglat-Pilesers III über die Eroberung Palästinas', Bibl. xlv (1964), 348–54; H. Tadmor, 'A New Edition of the Annals of Tiglath-Pileser III', Proceedings of the Israel Academy of Science and Humanities ii (1968), 168–87.

[56] The text is mutilated and difficult; see ANET, pp. 282 f.; D. J. Wiseman in DOTT, pp. 53–8; H. W. Saggs in POTT, pp. 160 f.

[57] See the new inscription published by B. D. Levine, 'Menahem and Tiglath-pileser: A New Synchronism', BASOR 206 (1972), 40–2; M. Weippert, 'Menahem von Israel und seine Zeitgenossen in einer Steleninschrift des assyrischen Königs Tiglathpileser III aus dem Iran', ZDPV lxxxix (1973), 26–53.

In 734 B.C. Tiglath-pileser was in Philistia. Northern Israel had already invaded Judah (Mic. 1:5–6, 10–15). Jerusalem was practically besieged (Isa. 7:1–2). The allies wanted to end the Davidic dynasty and to put on the throne a son of Tabeel, probably Tubail of Tyre.[58] The occupation of the Philistine coast by the Assyrian king changed the situation but did not solve the problem. In two campaigns, in 733 and 723 B.C., the power of Damascus was destroyed, Gaza was taken and the kingdom of Israel dismembered. Judah was no longer the attacked but the attacker and moved the frontier (i.e. the border with Samaria) to its own advantage (Hosea 5:10).[59] In 732 B.C., or possibly in 733, Israel lost to Assyria three provinces, Galilee, Gilead, and the coastal region south of the Carmel range (Isa. 8:23; cf. 2 Kgs. 15:29). A palace revolution took place in Samaria. Pekah was killed and superseded by Hoshea, who embarked upon a pro-Assyrian policy. Ahaz rendered allegiance to the Assyrian king in conquered Damascus (2 Kgs. 16:10).

Under Tefnakht, the So of 2 Kgs. 17:4, the Sibe of the Assyrian texts,[60] Egypt intervened diplomatically. Hoshea was pursued to default in the payment of tribute to Assyria, probably upon the death of Tiglath-pileser in 727 B.C. Unable to offer effective resistance, he was deported to Assyria by Shalmaneser V in 725. Kingless, Samaria held on till December 722,[61] without any help from Judah. Ahaz pursued the pro-Assyrian policy of Azariah and Jotham until his death c. 715.

7. Hezekiah of Judah and His Successors

According to 2 Kgs. 18:1 Hezekiah, son of Ahaz,[62] was

---

[58] See p. 308 above.

[59] A. Alt, 'Ein Krieg und seine Folgen in prophetischer Beleuchtung', KS ii. 163–187.

[60] R. Sayed, 'Tefnakht ou Horus SI'–IB', VT xx (1970), 116–18.

[61] H. Tadmor, who has re-examined the Annals of Sargon II and the relevant chronology (JCS xii (1958), 22–40, 77–100), concludes that the city fell to Shalmaneser V, shortly before his death, and that Sargon combined this capture with that of 720, when he subdued a subsequent rebellion in the city. There are references to the deported Israelites in the cuneiform texts; B. Parker, 'Administrative Tablets from the North-West Palace, Nimrud', Iraq xxiii (1961), 27 f.; W. F. Albright, 'An Ostrakon from Calah and the North-Israelite Diaspora', BASOR 149 (1958), 33–36.

[62] For the date of his birth, see J. McHugh, 'The Date of Hezekiah's Birth', VT xiv (1964), 446–53.

enthroned in the third year of Hoshea of Israel, i.e. c. 729 B.C. Ahaz wanted to associate his son with the throne at a difficult time for the dynasty. It was probably at this moment, that the Davidic dynasty was looked upon as the light of salvation, by the three annexed provinces (Isa. 8:23; 9:5–6), Ahaz, however, was still king. At the time of Samaria's rebellion against Sargon in 720 B.C. he made no move. Sargon secured his own position in Philistia, having repelled an attack of Shilkanni,[63] king of Egypt. Philistia was under heavy pressure from Assyria and its ally Ahaz. The death of Ahaz changed the situation (Isa. 14:28–32). Hezekiah embarked upon a new policy which was agreeable to Philistia. He welcomed refugees, most probably Northern Israelites (Isa. 14:32) who did not want to be subject to Assyria and its gods. A new quarter was founded on the slope of the Temple hill:[64] this was the 'daughter of Zion',[65] protected by a rampart, which, victorious, will join the Babylon of Merodach-baladan (Mic. 4:10). It is the Maktesh of Zeph. 1:11, the Mishneh of 2 Kgs. 22:14. Hezekiah started a reform (2 Kgs. 18:4), of which Micah of Moresheth (3:9–12) was the successful prophet (Jer. 26:19). Isaiah was more hesitant, knowing the weakness of a divided Egypt (Isa. 18 f.) which Piankhi[66] was on his way to conquer from the south, being allied to Assyria against Saïs. Concerned about the northern situation, Sargon did not react at once; but he was strong enough to control Ashdod in 713 B.C. and replace king Azuri by his brother Ahimitti. The people of Ashdod expelled Ahimitti and enthroned Yamani (a Greek?). Sargon sent his *tartan* to put an end to a great coalition including Judah, Edom, Moab, and a king of the Egyptian delta, 'incapable of saving them' according to the Assyrian chronicle.[67] Judah

[63] Text published by E. F. Weidner in *AfO* xiv (1941), 40 ff.; ETr in *ANET*, p. 286b.

[64] See N. Avigad, 'Excavations in the Jewish Quarter of the Old City of Jerusalem', *IEJ* xx (1970), 129–40; E. M. Laperrousaz, 'Quelques aperçus sur les dernières découvertes faites à Jérusalem', *REJ* cxxxi (1972), 257–61.

[65] L. Delekat in *VT* xiv (1964), 9–11; H. Cazelles, 'Histoire et géographie en Michée iv. 6–13', *Proceedings of the IVth World Congress of Jewish Studies*, pp. 87–9.

[66] He was probably the Pir'u (Pharaoh?) mentioned in the inscriptions who handed over Yamani of Ashdod to Sargon. From 716 B.C. he paid tribute to Assyria; cf. *ANET*, p. 286b.

[67] *ANET*, p. 287a.

suffered a humiliating defeat (Isa. 22:1-14). The Assyrian text which mentions the capture of Azekah may refer to this campaign.[68] Sargon recaptured Babylon from Merodach-baladan in 710 B.C., but went no farther.

In 705 B.C., after Sargon's death, there was a general insurrection against Assyria. Merodach-baladan reconquered Babylon for nine months and sent an embassy to Hezekiah to evaluate his resources (Isa. 39; cf. 2 Kgs. 20:12-19). The king fortified Jerusalem, and had the Siloam tunnel constructed. A great coalition was set up, at the instigation of Shabaka of Egypt. The members were Luli of Sidon, Sidkia of Ashkelon, who had replaced Sharruludari, the preceding king, and Hezekiah, who agreed to be the gaoler of Padi, king of Ekron. Isaiah was opposed to this policy (30:1-7; 31:1-3) which he considered to be doomed to failure. Sennacherib, Sargon's successor, recaptured Babylon in 703 B.C., crushed Phoenicia in 702 and defeated the Egyptians at Eltekeh on the Philistine coast. He restored his faithful vassals to their thrones, Padi at Ekron, Sharruludari at Ashkelon, Mitinti at Ashdod, and Sillibel in Gaza. The land of Judah was devastated; and Hezekiah was forced to accept a costly treaty which took away from him forty-six cities allotted by Sennacherib to his faithful Philistines (2 Kgs. 18:13-16).[69] Having established his camp in Lachish, Sennacherib seems to have demanded even more;[70] but Jerusalem was miraculously saved and Sennacherib returned to Assyria with an army decimated by the plague. There is no trace of a subsequent campaign.[71] Hezekiah ended his reign as a vassal of Assyria, but had led Judah towards a reconciliation with the North. Judah had much to ask forgiveness for.

Manasseh was as powerful as his father during his long reign. Under Esarhaddon and during the first decades of Ashurbanipal, Assyria was at its apogee. The Assyrian armies followed the coast road to attack Egypt, capture Memphis in

---

[68] See H. Tadmor in *JCS* xii (1958), 81.

[69] Cf. *ANET*, p. 288; *DOTT*, pp. 64-9.

[70] B. S. Childs, *Isaiah and the Assyrian Crisis*, SBT, 2nd Series, iii, 1967; E. Vogt, 'Sennacherib und die letzte Tätigkeit Jesajas', *Bibl.* xlvii (1966), 427-37; cf. Herodotus ii. 143.

[71] On the hypothesis of a later invasion, see W. F. Albright, *BASOR* cxxx (1953), 8-11.

671 B.C., then Thebes in 664 B.C. Assyrian fashions penetrated into Jerusalem (Zeph. 1:4–9). Esarhaddon tried to make his succession secure by treaties of vassalage[72] which include many curses on those who renounce their allegiance. He made a treaty with Baal of Tyre and exacted tribute from him as well as from Manasseh of Judah, Sillibel of Gaza, and other kinglets.[73] Perhaps, at a time when Ashurbanipal was dealing with the revolt in Babylon and Elam and Psammetichus I was becoming independent at Saïs, Manasseh tried to gain independence; but he had to submit.[74]

8. Josiah

Amon, son of Manasseh and father of Josiah, acceded to the throne c. 641 B.C. The glory of Ashurbanipal culminated in 640 B.C. with the sack of Susa. After 639/638 B.C. the Assyrian annals[75] are silent. Medes and Persians occupied ancient Elam. To the west, Psammetichus I had gained independence and entered into negotiations with Gyges (Gugu, Gog) of Lydia. Around 639 B.C., he sought to develop his advantages by occupying Philistia with Ashdod.[76] At this time Amon was assassinated by his officers (2 Kgs. 21:23); and it is likely that the pro-Egyptian party, powerful in Jerusalem, were hand in glove with Psammetichus. Assyria, however, was still strong enough to react, possibly not with fresh Assyrian forces but at least with Scythian contingents which remained faithful up to the very last month preceding the fall of Nineveh in 612 B.C. For this reason Herodotus, informed by the Egyptian priests and shocked by the burning of the temple of Ashkelon by the Scythians, speaks of a Scythian domination for twenty-eight years.[77] The 'people of the

---

[72] D. J. Wiseman, 'The Vassal Treaties of Esarhaddon', *Iraq* xx, part 1 (1958). Some of the curses in these treaties resemble those in Deut. 28.

[73] *ANET*, p. 290a.

[74] This is a possible interpretation of 2 Chr. 33:11ff.

[75] On the last years of Ashurbanipal, see J. Oates, 'Assyrian Chronology, 631–612 B.C.', *Iraq* xxvii (1965), 135–59; J. Reade, 'The Accession of Sin-shar-ishkun', *JCS* xxiii (1970), 1–10.

[76] A. Malamat, 'The Historical Background of the Assassination of Amon, King of Judah', *IEJ* iii (1953), 26–29; H. Cazelles, 'Sophonie, Jérémie et les Scythes en Palestine', *RB* lxxiv (1967), 24–44.

[77] There is not time for such a Scythian domination between the Assyrian and the Egyptian periods of supremacy in the region. But if the account in Jer. 4–6 of an

land',[78] always favourable to the dynasty, did not support the plotters and supported the accession to the throne of the eight-year-old Josiah (2 Kgs. 21:24; cf. Jer. 2:18). The date of Ashurbanipal's death cannot be precisely determined, but it was *c.* 629. His successors,[79] Ashur-etililani, Sin-shum-lishir, and Sin-shar-ishkun, faced an increasingly difficult situation. In 627–626 B.C. Nabopolassar the Chaldean regained independence for Babylon. According to 2 Chr. 34:3, Josiah had already (in 628–627 B.C., the twelfth year of his reign) initiated a religious reform. In 622 B.C. he judged that Assyria was weak enough for him to launch an active religious reform. The basis of his reform was the code of Deuteronomy, discovered during a restoration of the Temple. According to recent research,[80] this text is a compilation of laws brought by northern refugees, which is supported by the fact that a prophetess from the refugee quarter, the Mishneh, was consulted. The main aim of the laws was the centralization of the cult in a chosen sanctuary, under a king (an Israelite and not a foreigner) chosen by Yahweh (Deut. 17:15). This perfectly suited the views of Josiah and his government, who wished to take advantage of the Assyrian decline to reunite the twelve tribes around the dynasty of David, its capital, and its Temple.

This policy of reunification, although based on a code which had become the law of the state, inspired by northern customs, seems to have encountered serious opposition. The northern tribes had bad memories of the policy of the kings of Israel. The messengers sent to the north to destroy the high places and eliminate the local clergy soon realized that there was resistance. In some cases they found support among the

---

invasion from the north has been edited in terms of the Babylonian threat, these chapters appear to have originally described an earlier campaign which could have been waged by Scythian contingents acting for Assyria.

[78] On the force of this expression, see R. de Vaux, 'Le sens de l'expression "Peuple du pays" dans L'Ancien Testament et le Rôle politique du peuple en Israël', *RA* lviii (1964), 167–72, with bibliography; E. W. Nicholson, 'The Meaning of the Expression 'am hā'āreṣ in the OT', *JSS* x (1965), 59–66.

[79] On the vexed question of the succession, see H. W. Saggs in *POTT*, p. 166: and cf. D. J. Wiseman, *Chronicles of Chaldean Kings*, London, 1961, pp. 90–3.

[80] A. Alt, 'Die Heimat des Deuteronomiums', *KS* ii. 250–75; E. W. Nicholson, *Deuteronomy and Tradition*, Oxford, 1967; M. Weinfeld, *Deuteronomy and the Deuteronomic School*, Oxford, 1972, pp. 366–70.

local population. Thus, in Benjamin (already annexed to Judah), Jeremiah narrowly escaped death for having sided with those who were destroying the local sanctuary (Jer. 11:21; 12:6).

The decisive blow to Judah came from the outside, from Egypt, perhaps unintentionally. The Babylonian Chronicle states that already in 616 B.C. Egypt had changed its policy and was supporting on the battlefield a declining Assyria; the Scythian garrisons still held Ashdod and Gaza. Then the pace of events quickened. In 615 Nabopolassar was unable to seize Ashur; but in 614 Cyaxares the Mede captured the city, where he was joined by the Babylonians. In the following months, the Umman-Manda (including Herodotus' Scythians) abandoned the Assyrians and Nineveh fell in 612 after a siege of three months. King Sin-shar-ishkun was killed and Ashur-uballit, the last king of Assyria, retreated to Harran and continued the fight for four years. He seems to have expected help from Egypt, but the Babylonian Chronicle does not mention any help before 610 B.C. Harran fell and an Egypto-Assyrian army was unable to recapture it. The following year, a larger Egyptian army intervened; and no more is heard of Ashur-uballit. Necho II, who was now ruling in Egypt, captured Gaza; and it was on his northward march that he met Josiah and killed him (609 B.C.)[81]

9. The End of the Davidic Kingdom[82]

Necho could not spare any time then to deal with the problems of Judah. The reforming party was therefore free to attempt to carry on Josiah's policy. They set aside Eliakim the eldest son, who was suspect, and put on the throne Jehoahaz, son of another wife. However, once the front had been stabilized, Necho summoned Jehoahaz to Riblah, took him prisoner, and sent him to Egypt where he died (2 Kgs. 23:33f.; Jer. 22:11–12). He imposed a heavy tribute on the country and made Eliakim king, whose regnal name,

---

[81] It is uncertain whether there was a battle; see M. Noth, *History*, pp. 278 f.; S. Herrmann, *History*, pp. 271 f.; B. Couroyer, 'Le litige entre Josias et Néchao', *RB* lv (1948), 388–396; A. Malamat, 'Josiah's Bid for Armageddon', *Journal of the Ancient Near Eastern Society of Columbia University*, v (1973), 267–78.

[82] A. Malamat, 'The Last Kings of Judah and the Fall of Jerusalem', *IEJ* xviii (1968), 137–55.

Jehoiakim, indicated that the name of the national God was to be respected; but it was no longer the Yahweh of Deuteronomy.

Between 609 and 605 B.C. Necho and Nebuchadrezzar fought each other between Harran and the Euphrates near Carchemish, with alternating success. In the spring or early summer of 605, the Babylonian army crossed the Euphrates; and in a terrible battle the Egyptian army was routed and finally annihilated in the Hamath region. All of Syro-Palestine, the 'land of Hatti' according to the Assyro-Babylonian scribes,[83] fell to Nebuchadrezzar. He was unable to complete his conquest, for his father Nabopolassar died and the victor had to return in great haste to Babylon to secure the succession.

Such a collapse of Egyptian power in Asia could not but have far-reaching repercussions on the small capitals of Judah, Edom, Moab, and Philistia (cf. Jer. 45–9; 25; and 36). The opponents of Jehoiakim and of Egyptian influence regained power and prepared to eliminate all those who had yielded to Egyptian suzerainty. Nebuchadrezzar returned to 'Hatti' in the autumn and secured his positions. For unknown reasons, however, it was only in the following year that he secured control of the coast up to the wadi of Egypt (2 Kgs. 24:7), having sacked Ashkelon in November.[84]

Nebuchadrezzar came back in the spring of 603 and again in 602. He took tribute and besieged various cities, but there was no decisive battle. In the Saqqara papyrus, a Philistine prince appeals to Egypt for help.[85] The latter intervened in 601 and defeated Babylon—a fact which even the Chronicle admits.[86] Jehoiakim took advantage of this to free himself from bondage (2 Kgs. 24:1) and return to his old ally. In 599 the Babylonians, joined by contingents of Arameans, Moabites, and Ammonites (2 Kgs. 24:2), intervened. The country was laid waste (Jer. 10:17–25; 11:15f.; 12:7–13) and Jerusalem

[83] See Wiseman, op. cit., pp. 66–9.
[84] Ibid., pp. 68 f.
[85] Published by A. Dupont-Somer, *Semitica* i (1948), 43–68; *KAI* ii. 312; F. Vattioni, 'Il papiro di Saqqarah', *Studia Papyrologica* v (1966), 103–17; S. Horn, 'Where and When was the Aramaic Saqqara Papyrus Written?', *AUSS* vi (1968), 29–45.
[86] Wiseman, op. cit., pp. 70 f.

besieged. Jehoiachin, who had succeeded his father Jehoiakim, was forced to capitulate three months later.

On the fringes of a dangerous Egypt, Nebuchadrezzar was bent on having in Jerusalem a secure government. He deposed Jehoiachin and sent him as a prisoner to Babylon with the queen mother (Jer. 22:26; 2 Kgs. 24:12), his wives, eunuchs, and dignitaries (10,000, 7,000 or 3,023 according to the sources, 2 Kgs. 24:14-16 and Jer. 52: 28), as well as craftsmen. The king of Babylon knew that the Temple was the heart of nationalism. He deported members of the clergy, amongst them the priest-prophet Ezekiel. Nebuchadrezzar granted his favour to the opposing party. The 'king according to his heart'[87] was a third son of Josiah, Mattaniah, now renamed Zedekiah.

For reasons beyond his will, the new king rapidly changed his loyalty. The tribute was heavy, Babylon far away and unpopular. In and around the Temple a perfervid fanaticism was kindled by memories of the deliverance of 701 and by resentment at the spoliations of 597. Nebuchadrezzar came back to Syria and Palestine in 594 and 593, in spite of a revolt in Babylonia, and reimposed tribute.[88] Once again the Jerusalem court looked towards Egypt. Necho II had not come outside his borders after 601 B.C. Psammetichus, who succeeded him in 594, had first to deal with Nubia. He visited Phoenicia in the fourth year of his reign.[89] Egypt seems to have been renewing active policy in Asia. In 589 Psammetichus died and was succeeded by Hophra, who reigned for twenty years, an active but somewhat muddle-headed sovereign. A new coalition was afoot in Ammon (Jer. 27:3; Ezek. 21:23ff.). Nebuchadrezzar reacted quickly. Already in January 588,[90] he was able to lay siege to Jerusalem. Soon only Jerusalem, Lachish, Azekah (Jer. 34:7) were holding out. The siege was interrupted when Hophra's army threatened

[87] Wiseman, op. cit., pp. 72 f.

[88] Ibid., pp. 72-5.

[89] F. K. Kientz, *Die politische Geschichte Aegyptens vom 7 bis zum 4. Jahrhundert vor der Zeitwende*, 1953, p. 25.

[90] Or 587. On the vexed question of the chronology of the closing years of the kingdom of Judah, see W. F. Albright, 'The Nebuchadnezzar and Neriglissar Chronicles', *BASOR*, 143 (1956) 28-33; D. N. Freedman, 'Old Testament Chronology', in *The Bible and the Ancient Near East*, ed. by G. Ernest Wright, London, 1961, pp. 212 f.; E. R. Thiele, 'New Evidence on the Chronology of the Last

Nebuchadrezzar's lines of communication (Jer. 37:11; 32:1). The Egyptian army withdrew and the siege was resumed. When the Chaldeans succeeded in making a breach in the wall in July 587 B.C., Zedekiah attempted to escape. He was caught at Jericho, brought before Nebuchadrezzar at Riblah, and blinded after having to witness the execution of his sons (2 Kgs. 25:7).

According to Jer. 52:12, although the breach was made on the ninth day of the fourth month, it was only on the tenth day of the fifth month, that Nebuzaradan, the commander of the Babylonian guard, entered the city and set fire to it and to the Temple. Is this due to different reckonings? Did the city resist another month without its king, in the same way that Samaria had held out for nearly three years?[91]

Jerusalem was destroyed and the organs of government liquidated. Gedaliah, son of Ahikam, was made governor at Mizpah, a site which recalled Samuel and Saul, rather than David. The attempt to form a community failed, for at the instigation of the Ammonites, who were still at war, Gedaliah was assassinated and his followers forced Jeremiah to flee with them to Egypt (Jer. 42; 2 Kgs. 25:26). Judah was attached to Samaria as its administrative headquarters. The country remained troubled, for in 582, as the result of another revolt by Moabites and Ammonites, 745 Judaeans were deported (Jer. 52:30). The Edomites took the south as far as Hebron, the future Idumea, and the Arabs infiltrated from the east. Such was the situation that those who were repatriated after the Exile found unchanged.

BIBLIOGRAPHY

ALBRIGHT, W. F. *From the Stone Age to Christianity*, 2nd edn., New York, 1957.

BARON, S. W. *A Social and Religious History of the Jews*, i, New York, 1952.

Kings of Judah', *BASOR* 143 (1965), 22–27; H. Tadmor, 'Chronology of the Last Kings of Judah', *JNES* xv (1956), 226–30; E. Vogt, *Bibl.* xxxviii (1957), 229–33; A. Malamat, 'The Last Kings of Judah and the Fall of Jerusalem', *IEJ* xviii (1968), 137–156; id., 'The Twilight of Judah: in the Egyptian-Babylonian Maelstrom', *Congress Volume, Edinburgh 1974*, SVT xxviii, 1975, pp. 122–45.

[91] For a proposed solution, see G. Brunet, 'La Prise de Jérusalem sous Sédécias', *RHR* clxvii (1965), 157–65; id., *Les Lamentations contre Jérémie*, Paris, 1968.

BRIGHT, J. *A History of Israel*, 2nd edn., London, 1972.

Cambridge Ancient History, rev. edn., i, ii, Cambridge, 1970, 1971 (EDWARDS, I. E. S., GADD, C. J., and HAMMOND, N. G. L., eds.)

DEHAYES, J. *Les Civilisations de l'ancien Orient*, Paris, 1969.

DESNOYERS, L. *Histoire du peuple hébreu*, i–iii, Paris, 1922, 1930, 1930.

GALLING, K. *Textbuch zur Geschichte Israels*, 2nd edn., Tubingen, 1968.

GARELLI, P. *Le Proche Orient antique. Des origines aux invasions des Peuples de la Mer*, Paris, 1969.

HEICHELHEIM, F. M. *An Ancient Economic History*, i, ii, Leiden, 1964.

HERRMANN, S. *A History of Israel*, ETr, London, 1975.

KITTEL, R. *Geschichte des Volkes Israel*, i–iii, Stuttgart, 1923, 1925, 1927/9.

MAZAR, B. (ed.) *The World History of the Jewish People*, ii, iii, London, 1971.

MEULEAU, M. *Le Monde antique*, i, ii, Paris, 1971.

NOTH, M. *History of Israel*, E Tr, 2nd edn., London, 1960.

OESTERLEY, W. O. E., and ROBINSON, T. H. *A History of Israel*, i, ii, Oxford, 1932.

RICCIOTTI, G. *The History of Israel*, i, ii, ETr, Milwaukee, 1955.

SCHMÖKEL, H. *Geschichte des alten Vorderasiens (Handbuch der Orientalistik*, ii, 3), Leiden, 1957.

VAUX, R. DE *Histoire ancienne d'Israël: Des origines à l'installation en Canaan*, Paris, 1971. *La Période des Juges*, Paris, 1973.

Also *ANET, AOTS, DOTT, POTT* (see list of abbreviations).

XI

THE HISTORY OF ISRAEL IN THE EXILIC AND POST-EXILIC PERIODS

P. R. ACKROYD

IF strictly the exilic period of Israel's history must be said to begin from the first fall of the city in 597 B.C., with the exiling of the young king Jehoiachin and leading members of the community, it is more logical to see the total collapse of 587, with the loss of the separate existence of the kingdom and the first-magnitude disaster of the destruction of Temple and capital, as marking a more appropriate starting-point. Later thinkers such as the Chronicler, but also the eventual compilers of the books of Jeremiah and Ezekiel, and probably also the Deuteronomic historians,[1] could simplify the issue by supposing the true people to exist from 597 onwards in the Exile in Babylonia. That such a total movement of population as is envisaged in 2 Kgs. 25:26 and Jer. 43:5–7 is unlikely is just as evident as when it is suggested in even more radical terms in 2 Chr. 36:20 f.; in each case we are dealing with a theological interpretation of the exilic age. The judgement passed on the community is total, inescapable. But to others, nearer the events, whether in Palestine or in Babylonia, the focal point was in Jerusalem, as for example in the source underlying Jer. 40–1. The strong hope of a restoration of Jehoiachin (e.g. Jer. 28:4), detectable in the use of his regnal years as a dating system (e.g. Ezek. 1:2) and in the brief narrative of 2 Kgs. 25:27–30[2]; the fact that the Temple was still intact in the years of Zedekiah; the address to the Babylonian exiles of judgement oracles on Jerusalem and

---

[1] For literature, cf. e.g. E. W. Nicholson, *Preaching to the Exiles*, Oxford, 1970; W. Zimmerli, *Ezechiel*, BKAT xiii/1, 2, Neukirchen, 1969; E. Janssen, *Juda in der Exilszeit*, FRLANT lxix, 1956.

[2] Cf. K. S. Freedy and D. B. Redford, *JAOS* xc (1970), 462–85; E. Zenger, *BZ* xii (1968), 12–30.

Judah by Ezekiel, all underline this. Even later, in those circles in Babylonia to which we appear to owe so much of the reinterpretation of earlier material, there is the recognition that hope for the future is undergirded by the conviction that its focus can only be in Jerusalem, though the working out of such hopes in the realities of political and economic conditions was not to be so simply resolved.

The other end of the period is much more open. A coverage of the Old Testament period must involve a sufficient extension to include at least all those writings which eventually belong to the canon. This (to include Daniel) takes us to the mid-second century on a minimal canonical view; it takes us a great deal further if account is taken of that massive, closely related literary output of the last centuries B.C. and the first century A.D.

A division into 'exilic', 'Persian', and 'Greek (Roman)', appears both convenient and simple. The community which thought of itself as 'Israel' must have felt pressures from the changes in imperial control and from consequent invasions and conquests and rebellions. Of greater interest and importance is the consideration of how the community itself both lived and understood its life and nature. The external political events, known from actual experience or from resultant economic pressures, must for many have been of relatively little concern compared with the daily preoccupation with actually living. Yet the line should not be drawn too sharply between the few who endeavoured in speaking and writing or in political action to articulate the nature of this 'Israel' to which they belonged and its continuity with what they knew or believed about its prior existence in the earlier periods, and those others, 'the quiet in the land', for whom, even though less explicitly affirmed, the reality of that continuity was a matter of claim to family property, of ancestral links, of national tradition, of story and psalmody and prophetic pronouncement and sermon, of all that made them conscious of being this community and belonging to it and not to some other. There is a close interrelationship between conscious attempts at formulating the nature of the community and the actual feelings and beliefs of those who consider themselves to belong to it. Some attempt needs to be made at examining the nature of this experience and of its articulation, in relation to the past history, to the contemporary experiences of alien rule and of a short period of independence, and to the hopes for the future which differing members and groups within the community cherished.

The historical problems of this whole period are enormous, more even because of lack of information than because of what we do have. Its description as 'the nameless period' (D. Arenhoevel) is not inappropriate, though the same writer's supposition that it is largely 'without history' (*geschichtslos*) because the community was bound up in itself is less adequate.[3] The internal developments cannot in the last analysis be properly described without a satisfactory relating of them to wider events.

A. THE EXILIC AGE

Discussion of the historical problems of this period depends in the first instance on the understanding of the background of events in the whole Near Eastern area in which Israel was involved, as a surviving community in Palestine, and as exiled or refugee groups in other areas, particularly Babylonia and Egypt, but also at least in small measure in regions contiguous to Judah. Since the biblical record provides no account of the period between 587 B.C. and the return of the first group in the early years of Cyrus (shortly after 538), other than the brief Gedaliah passages (2 Kgs. 25:22–26; Jer. 40:1–43:7), we are dependent on minimal information and on inference for discussing the nature of the people's experience.[4] The continuing military campaigns of Nebuchadrezzar, particularly against Tyre and Egypt; the disruptions and brief reigns following his death; the problematic period of the last and usurping ruler, Nabonidus;[5] the emergence of Cyrus as new supreme ruler of the Medes and Persians, and his taking over

---

[3] 'Die nachexilische Zeit: Zeit ohne Namen' in *Wort und Botschaft*, ed. J. Schreiner, 2nd edn., Würzburg, 1969, pp. 265–74.

[4] Cf. S. Herrmann, *Prophetie und Wirklichkeit in der Epoche des babylonischen Exils*, ATh. I, 32, 1967.

[5] Cf. esp. K. Galling, *Studien zur Geschichte Israels im persischen Zeitalter*, Tübingen, 1964, pp. 1–60.

of the Babylonian empire, must all have had some influence on Israel. Certain of the campaigns find reflection in foreign nation oracles, particularly in Ezek. 25–32 and Jer. 46–51, in some elements to be found in Isa. 13–23 and even in Amos 1–2 (e.g. Tyre). The one recorded event of Jehoiachin's release from prison in 562 B.C. (2 Kgs. 25:27–30) must also have had some repercussions, though the identifying of these, for example in Second Isaiah, remains conjectural.[6] The clearest reflection to be found there concerns the rise of Cyrus himself, mentioned by name (Isa. 44:28; 45:1; cf. also 2 Chron. 36: 22 f. = Ezra 1:1 f.),[7] and probably alluded to in other passages. Nabonidus' policy, particularly in religious matters, has been thought to underlie both the hostile attitude to Babylon in Second Isaiah, with its possible hints of actual persecution (e.g. 50:4–9;53), and the picture of Babylon and its rulers presented by the much later book of Daniel (particularly in chs. 2–6, and cf. the Qumran 'Prayer of Nabonidus').[8] It is an understandable part of the developing tradition concerning the exilic age that Babylon the conqueror becomes Babylon the oppressor, and this hardly without some justification in the experiences of the community at the time. The exhortations of Jer. 29, the indications of Jewish settlements and their apparent continuing self-ordered life under their elders in Ezekiel, and the evidence of ration allocations to Jehoiachin in the Weidner tablets, may be held to suggest that conditions in Babylonia were tolerable enough. This may be supported by the existence of the writings which were taking more definitive shape there in this period; such opportunities for literary activity must argue for at least relative security and undisturbed life. Any assessment is a matter of balancing probabilities. The picture of the worship in the exilic situation, whether this includes synagogue-type assemblies or occasions for lament and reflection,[9] remains equally a matter of

[6] For other attempts at correlating history and prophecy here, cf. J. D. Smart, *History and Theology in Second Isaiah*, Philadelphia, 1965; M. Haran in *Congress Volume Bonn 1960*, SVT ix, 1963, pp. 127–55, esp. 141 ff.

[7] Cf. K. Koch, *ZAW* lxxxiv (1972), 352–6.

[8] Cf. J. M. Wilkie, *JTS* N.S. ii (1961), 34–44, and K. Galling (see above, p. 322, n. 5).

[9] H. E. von Waldow, *Anlass und Hintergrund der Verkündigung des Deutero-jesaja*, Diss. Bonn, 1953; *Der traditionsgeschichtliche Hintergrund der prophetischen Gerichtsreden*, BZAW lxxxv, 1963; cf. also *Interpretation*, xxii (1968), 259–87. More generally, K. Hruby, *Die Synagoge*, S. Jk. iii, 1971.

hypothesis, though a controlled imaginative approach does make possible a helpful understanding of the nature and function of the writings which emerge from the obscurity of the time.

Much the same has inevitably to be said about the situation in Palestine. The revival of life under Gedaliah which is indicated in the fuller account in Jer. 40–3, with its very evident awareness of a tradition that Jeremiah not only aligned himself with the new governor but that even after Gedaliah's assassination he saw the future lying in Judah and not in Egypt, suggests that, difficult as the situation must have been in a land devastated by war, there existed a continuing life for a community there.[10] If it is proper to see reflections of the contemporary situation in some detail in the poems of Lamentations[11] and to understand them as liturgical compositions belonging to a continuing or revived worship at the Jerusalem sanctuary, then something about what was going on there may be deduced from these as well as from the narratives.[12] In general, however, rather than seek precise information in such poetry, we may more usefully see how conventional forms may be applied, in some degree perhaps modified, but essentially simply read in the light of a new situation and hence become meaningful in a new way. To the generation of the Exile the words of such laments took on a precise historical and personal significance.

In such a situation of disaster, the need to maintain continuity is acute. This operates at both the political and the religious level. We therefore find concern about the royal succession, reflected in the position of Jehoiachin, exiled but still reckoned as king (cf. above)—and between 597 and 587 the status of Zedekiah, whose position may be said to be challenged by the belief in Jehoiachin's continuing status, or by the prophecy (cf. Jer 28:4) that he would be speedily restored. It is to be seen also in the problem of Gedaliah's status. He is given no official title in our sources; it is only stated that he was appointed (*pḳd*) over Judah. It is usual to

---

[10] Cf. esp. E. Janssen, (see p. 322, n. 1); S. Herrmann (see p. 322, n. 4).
[11] Cf. literature in D. R. Hiller, *Lamentations*, AncB, New York, 1972.
[12] Cf. D. R. Jones, *JTS*, N.S. xiv (1963), 12–31; E. Janssen (see p. 320, n. 1.).

term him 'governor', but this is only an inference; on the negative side we may observe that no term such as 'king' is employed. On the other hand the presence of the *beṇôṭ hammelek* (Jer. 41:10) could mean not simply that he had charge of them, but that he was given effective royal status; *beṇôṭ hammelek* could equally mean 'royal women' or 'royal daughters' and recognized by Babylon as the successor to the royal house.[13] The family of Shaphan is prominent in the period; the choice of a ruler, whether or not he was granted royal status, from such a family is intelligible. Gedaliah's murder and the capture of the 'royal women' by Ishmael of the Davidic house constitute a claim to kingship; the recovery of the captives undermines Ishmael's claim, but we have no clue to the sequel. The rehabilitation of Jehoiachin in 562 B.C. marks the next stage.[14] The appointment of Zerubbabel of the royal house under Darius is a further sequel (see below).

The problem of priestly succession is similarly obscure. The possibility that some part of the material incorporated in the Priestly writings represents a reordering of older forms of worship, sacrificial practice, and the like, both to meet the contemporary problems of the exilic age and to affirm the continuity of worship across the disaster, is suggestive of a real situation.[15] The hints of controversy in the post-exilic period over the priesthood and its validity, reflected in some measure in Zech. 3 and in Ezek. 40–8 and later in the writings of the Chronicler, argue for alternative types of claim to the true succession, on the one hand by those who remained in Jerusalem to attempt a continuation there, on the other hand by those in Babylonia who sought (as may be particularly seen in some aspects of the Chronicler's writings and in his portrayal of Ezra) to claim a more valid line.[16] The conflict between claims based on geographical and cultic continuity, with a revival of practice in a sanctuary destroyed but

---

[13] I owe this suggestion to a private comment made by Dr. N. Lohfink.

[14] E. Zenger (see p. 320, n. 2) firmly demonstrates the positive emphasis of this narrative.

[15] Cf. K. Koch, *Die Priesterschrift*, FRLANT lxxi, 1959; H. Jagersma, *Leviticus 19*, SSN xiv, 1972; and literature in K. Elliger, *Leviticus* HAT, 1966. For Ezek. 40–8, in this context, cf. W. Zimmerli, *VT* xviii (1968), 229–55, and G. C. Macholz, *VT* xix (1969), 322–52 who deals especially with the new interpretation of the land.

[16] Cf. below, p. 322, nn. 36, 37.

recoverable, and those based on a better priestly line (since it appears that the exiles included the leading priests) must in the end lead either to a reconciling or compromise solution or to breaks within the community. Both the writings of the Chronicler and the final form of the book of Ezekiel have been seen, and perhaps rightly, as attempting reconciliation. The separatist groups in the second century B.C., where the earliest stages of the Qumran community are detectable, and the emergence of the Samaritan community, allow the possibility that there were those who, like other religious reformers, saw the only way forward in an abandonment of the established order, in this case the Jerusalem set-up, and the acceptance of a new order either at a completely new centre (Qumran, Leontopolis) or one which could claim greater antiquity (Shechem, Gerizim). It is within the same logical position that we find the priest Mattathias withdrawing from an apostate situation in Jerusalem to Modein and the Christian community withdrawing under both political and religious pressure to Pella. It would be oversimple to attribute later movements and controversies simply to the problems of the exilic age. In some measure they may well go even further back into the political and religious disputes of the pre-exilic period; no doubt we must also look for factors in post-exilic history, perhaps in part tied in with the whole problem of the community's nature and existence, to discover immediate occasions for the extreme move of schism or secession.[17]

With such a lack of historical information, the most that we may hope is to reconstruct something of the nature of the experience and the outlook of the community during these years. In the collections attributed to earlier prophets, the evidence of reapplication to the exilic age provides one type of clue; words which originally referred to judgement at the hands of Assyria are now seen as fulfilled by Babylon.[18] The more immediate interpretation of the years leading up to the Exile in the prophecies of Jeremiah is given a fuller exposition,

[17] Cf. Morton Smith, *Palestinian Parties and Politics that shaped the Old Testament*, New York, 1971, for a controversial but stimulating examination of this whole theme, and more briefly his chapter on the Persian period in H. Bengtson *et al.*, *The Greeks and the Persians*, 1969, pp. 386–401.

[18] Cf. e.g. I. Willi-Plein, *Vorformen der Schriftexegese innerhalb des Alten Testaments*, BZAW cxxiii, 1971; J. Jeremias, *ZAW*, lxxxiii (1971), 330–55.

drawing out both the meaning of judgement and the possibilities of hope, in the sermonic passages which make up so large a part of the book.[19] A similar process may be detected in Ezekiel.[20] Alongside these, the writings of the Deuteronomic and Priestly groups provide other evidence both of explaining the past and hence clarifying the present and future and of reordering earlier material to meet the needs of the immediate situation.[21] What kind of context may we postulate for such interpretative activity? The use of liturgical material has suggested the existence of assemblies for worship, for the use of laments and the answer of lament in oracles of salvation (so e.g. von Waldow). The preaching techniques of Deuteronomy and of the Deuteronomic sermons in Jeremiah have similarly suggested meetings for exposition (so e.g. Nicholson). The appearance of the strongly homiletic tone in so much of the material of the seventh to sixth centuries B.C. and its continuance and development in the more formal style of the post-exilic period, with the use particularly in prophecy of the rhetorical question and the disputation, suggest circles in which older material was expounded, assemblies in which the words of older narrative or prophecy or psalm were given immediate application to the contemporary scene.

But to do more than generalise is to go beyond the evidence.[22] Even the localizing of the activity in Palestine or in Babylonia remains uncertain. The view that in the post-exilic period the impetus to renewal came from Babylonia alone belongs largely to the Chronicler. Ezekiel and the Holiness Code are so related as to suggest the same area of formation, but each may represent an independent reapplication of older priestly law; the latter or some other elements

[19] Cf. E. W. Nicholson (see p. 320, n. 1); G. Wanke, *Untersuchungen zur sogenannten Baruchschrift*, BZAW cxxii, 1971.

[20] Cf. W. Zimmerli, see *Ezechiel*; O. Kaiser, *Einleitung*, Gütersloh, 1969, 196 ff.; ETr, *Introduction to the Old Testament*, Oxford, 1975, pp. 251 ff.

[21] Cf. M. Weinfeld, *Deuteronomy and the Deuteronomic School*, Oxford, 1972, pp. 179 ff. for a sociological sketch; P. Diepold, *Israels Land*, BWANT xcv, 1972, for the development of Deuteronomic thought on judgement and restoration; M. Weippert, *VT* xxiii (1973), 415–42 on the Deuteronomic history. Cf. also works cited on p. 325, n. 15.

[22] For a stimulating but inadequately argued presentation, cf. Y. Kaufmann, *The Babylonian Captivity and Deutero-Isaiah*, New York, 1970.

now incorporated in the Priestly writings may reflect the needs of Jerusalem.

In the end conclusions about the exilic age and its activities inevitably involve the view taken of what followed. The events and movements of the Persian period must in part derive from the legacy of the exilic period, however much there are new impetuses to be detected in the historical events of the next centuries.

B. THE PERSIAN PERIOD

Evidence for the wider political history of the period from the rise of Cyrus to the collapse of Persian power brought about by Alexander the Great (c. 540–331 B.C.) is extensive.[23] Greek writers describe the repeated conflicts between Persia and Greece leading up to Alexander's conquests. These and other sources, particularly the Elephantine and other Egyptian papyri, point to the situation in Egypt and the relationship between Persia and Egypt.[24] Some independent documentary evidence such as the Samaria papyri,[25] indications from coinage and other artefacts, provide insight into contemporary conditions, and new light is gradually being added to these by archaeological work which has in recent years revealed more of the remains of this particular period, which has often been passed over too lightly.[26] But the internal history of the Jewish community remains obscure. In the early years the

[23] For an outline and refs. cf. G. Widengren, *POTT*, pp. 312–37; also H. Bengtson (see p. 326, n. 17), and esp. M. Meuleau on 'Persian Rule in Mesopotamia', pp. 354–85.

[24] Cf. F. K. Kienitz, *Die politische Geschichte Ägyptens vom 7. bis zum 4. Jahrhundert vor der Zeitwende*, Berlin, 1953; H. Bresciani, in H. Bengtson (see p. 326, n. 17), pp. 333–53.

[25] Strictly 'Dâliyeh papyri'; cf. F. M. Cross, *HTR* lix (1966), 201–11; *New Directions in Biblical Archaeology*, ed. D. N. Freedman and J. C. Greenfield, New York, 1969 (1971), pp. 45–69. F. M. Cross is preparing a full edition. For Palestine and Greece, cf. D. Auscher, *VT* xvii (1967), 8–30, for a survey and assessment of the evidence from the period before Alexander.

[26] Cf. reports in the archaeological journals, especially *IEJ*. Convenient summaries are provided in S. Yeivin, 'A Decade of Archaeology in Israel. 1948–58', *Nederlands Historisch-Archaeologisch Instituut te Istanbul*, viii (1960); E. Stern, *Qadmoniot* ii (1969), 110–24 (Heb.); E. Stern, *The Material Culture of Palestine in the Persian Period* (Heb.). Diss. Jerusalem, 1969, ETr forthcoming; S. S. Weinberg, 'Post-Exilic Palestine: An Archeological Report', *Proc. Israel Acad. Sc. Hum.* iv, v (1971), 78–97 (pre-print 1969); P. W. Lapp in *Archäologie und Altes Testament: Festschrift für Kurt Galling*, ed. A. Kuschke and E. Kutsch, Tübingen, 1970, pp. 179–97.

centre of interest lies in the restoration of the Temple described in the problematic text of Ezra 1–6 and reflected in Haggai, Zech. 1–8. There is documentation for the periods of Nehemiah and Ezra, but many uncertainties about dating, chronological order, and the exact nature of their intentions and achievements. The major international upheavals of the period find no unequivocal reflection in the writings which may with some probability be assigned to it. The attempt in recent years by J. Morgenstern at discovering precise reflections of a major crisis of 485 B.C. at the change of Persian ruler from Darius to Xerxes[27] cannot be regarded as successful; it becomes increasingly less convincing as more Old Testament writings are claimed to reflect it. A similar attempt, on a much smaller scale, has been made in relation to upheavals in the mid-fourth century, in the reign of Artaxerxes III Ochus.[28]

Similarly, endeavours at finding, particularly in Zech. 9–14, reflections of the period of Alexander the Great, remain unproved. We have no good reason to doubt that the major campaigns of the period, the major changes of ruler, the rebellions in Egypt and in the western part of the empire, all had some effect upon the Jewish community, both in its Palestinian centre and in its scattered groups in the Dispersion;[29] but at no point can we determine these effects with precision. We may usefully generalize about the status and attitudes of a small subject people. In some measure we may detect within this period the administrative problems more fully documented in the next centuries—the problems which face the controlling imperial power as it endeavours to

---

[27] In a series of articles in *HUCA* from 1956 onwards; similarly his speculative association of Isa. 61 with 440 B.C. in *HUCA* xl–xli (1969), 109–22.

[28] Cf. W. O. E. Oesterley and T. H. Robinson, *History of Israel* ii, Oxford, 1932, pp. 140 f.; cf. now D. Barag, *BASOR* clxxxiii (1966), 6–12; F. M. Cross, *JBL* xciv (1975), 4–18.

[29] For the Dispersion cf. e.g. S. W. Baron, *Social and Religious History of the Jews*, i, 2nd edn., 1952 New York and London. A full study of the Elephantine Jewish military colony is in B. Porten, *Archives from Elephantine*, Berkeley, 1968. For other aspects of this period, cf. G. R Driver, *Aramaic Documents of the Fifth Century B.C.*, Oxford, 1954; revised and abridged edn., 1957. The Murashu tablets (cf. *DOTT*, pp. 95 f., *ANET*, pp. 221 f.) provide only minimal information concerning Jewish residents in Babylonia. Reflections of Babylonian conditions may be detectable in the narrative materials of Esther and Daniel, but no secure picture can be reconstructed from these.

deal with a particular national community which is also a religious community and which exists both in a concentrated centre and also in scattered groups elsewhere, and those problems which face the community itself in determining the relationship between its political and its religious status. We may suggest too a degree of tension between Babylonia and Palestine, indicated both in hints of reluctance to return on the part of Jews in the former,[30] in hostility to such a leader as Nehemiah, and in the activity of such a reformer as Ezra with its implication that Palestinian Judaism was in need of modification.

The first significant period is that of the restoration of the Temple, beginning from such action as was taken by Cyrus towards the rehabilitation of national religious life, indicated in Ezra 1 and 6 and paralleled in the Cyrus cylinder.[31] The initial failure to bring about full restoration under Sheshbazzar remains unexplained; financial difficulties and external pressures within Palestine, perhaps combined with opposition from those who had remained there to those who now came armed with Persian authority, may have been involved. The precise administrative situation is not known, but the probability of control of Judah from Samaria remains the most likely,[32] and the revival of Jerusalem and Judah could well have been unacceptable there. Further activity waited for the advent of Darius I, reflected in the prophecies of Haggai and Zechariah,[33] as also in the differing narrative presentations of Ezra 3–6 where more than one source has been combined. Background to the events is to be seen in the period of uncertainty at the death of Cambyses, with Darius establishing himself amid considerable opposition. Claims to

[30] Cf. e.g. Zech. 2:10 (EVV. 6), which may point to a need for encouragement, and N. Lohfink in *Die Zeit Jesu (Festschrift H. Schlier)*, ed. G. Bornkamm and K. Rahner, Freiburg, 1970, 38–57, see pp. 52 ff. on the Priestly narrative's interpretation of Num. 13–14 and Num. 20 in terms of the exiles' 'belittling (*Verleumdung, dibbâh*) of the land' and of their leaders' lack of faith. On the relationship between the communities, cf. also M. D. Coogan, *JSJ* iv (1973), 183–91.

[31] Cf. e.g. L. Rost, in *Verbannung und Heimkehr (Festschrift W. Rudolph)*, ed. A. Kuschke, Tübingen, 1961, pp. 301–7.

[32] As argued by A. Alt in 1934, see *KS* ii, 1953, 316–37; but sharply criticized by Morton Smith (see p. 326, n.17).

[33] Cf. e.g. A. Petitjean, *Les Oracles du Proto-Zacharie. Un programme de restauration pour la communauté juive après l'exil*, Paris and Louvain, 1969; and *ETL* xlii (1966), 40–71.

Babylonian independence at this point make it likely that members of the Jewish community there found themselves involved. Jewish tradition, both in Ezra 5–6 and in 1 Esdras 3–4 attributes to Darius a favourable attitude to Jewish aspirations. The nature of the upsurge in Jerusalem under Zerubbabel and Joshua the High Priest, and the precise relationship between their activity and the warnings and encouragements of Haggai and Zechariah, and the degree to which these indicate political aspirations, hopes of independence, belief in Zerubbabel as a Davidic anointed leader, remain points of debate. This would appear to be a case where the often too narrowly defined categories of political and religious thought and action do not adequately describe a complex moment within which there may in fact be several strands or levels.[34]

A particular problem is that of legitimation. The final words of 2 Kgs. 25 concerning Jehoiachin make a claim for the re-establishment of his royal status. The presence of Zerubbabel in the early years of Persian rule would appear to mark a situation in which Persian authority was prepared to meet the needs of the Jewish community for an acceptable restoration and for a valid leadership; the choice of Zerubbabel of the Davidic line, to which Sheshbazzar evidently did not belong, may be seen as a conciliatory move.[35] It may well have seemed the beginning of a new Davidic era to some; but the Chronicler, writing perhaps two centuries later, plays down the Davidic element. Alongside Zerubbabel is a new High Priest, Joshua. In Haggai the two leaders appear side by side, and this is made more precise in Zechariah where, in addition, a description of the rehabilitation of the High Priest (Zech. 3), may be regarded, whatever its precise connotation, as concerned with legitimacy and continuity. What we do not know for certain is the relationship between this High Priest and what had preceded him. We do not know for certain

---

[34] Cf. G. Sauer, in *Das ferne und nahe Wort (Festschrift L. Rost)*, ed. F. Maass, Berlin, 1967, pp. 199–207; K.-M. Beyse, *Serubbabel und die Königserwartungen der Propheten Haggai und Sacharja*, Berlin, 1971.

[35] On Sheshbazzar, cf. P.-R. Berger, *ZAW* lxxxiii (1971), 98 ff., demonstrating that he is not to be identified with the Davidide Shenazzar; more broadly, the discussion by K. Baltzer in *Studien zur Theologie der alttestamentlichen Überlieferungen (Festschrift G. von Rad)*, ed. R. Rendtorff and K. Koch, Neukirchen 1961, pp. 33–43.

whether he had come from Babylonia—which appears very probable (so Neh. 12:1)—and so needed a legitimation which declared him free from the impurity of foreign contact; or whether he was of the continuing line in Jerusalem and needed legitimation for him to be acceptable to those who regarded the practices which had continued in the land as improperly ordered; or indeed whether the legitimation is concerned rather with a wider problem, that of the full re-establishment of the Temple and its worship after a period of desuetude or neglect which had itself issued from a moment of destruction, a radical break in continuity which needed to be bridged.[36] Again we may note how the Chronicler, looking back on this period, stresses both continuity of priestly line (cf. Ezra 2 and in particular the mention there of priests whose genealogy is in doubt, vv. 61–3) and the bringing back of the true temple vessels to their full number (Ezra 1).[37]

The obscurity of the years from the rededication of the Temple until the middle of the fifth century remains. The light supposedly shed by the book of Malachi on some moment within this period is very meagre: possible allusion to the beginnings of Nabataean encroachment[38] in the Edomite area is doubtful in material which is probably concerned rather with the theme of judgement on the typical enemy than with mere history; the problems of inadequacy in worship and of foreign marriages and their religious consequences are hardly secure pointers to this period. The evidence on which Malachi is dated is in fact very slender. Ezra 4:6–23 contains (v.6) an unstated charge against the Jewish community during Xerxes' reign; a second (v.7) similarly unstated, and a third (vv. 8–23) more fully described complaint. The latter two are from the period of Artaxerxes, presumably I (465–424). The reference here to the 'foundations and walls' (v.12) has suggested that the passage points to the situation just before the commission of Nehemiah (cf.

---

[36] Cf. F. Willesen, *VT* iv (1954), 289–306.

[37] Cf. P. R. Ackroyd in *Studies in the Religion of Ancient Israel*, SVT xxiii, 1972, pp. 166–81; and for a related theme M. F. Collins, *JSJ* iii (1972), 97–116, A. Zeron, *JSJ* iv (1973), 165–8.

[38] For refs. cf. J. R. Bartlett and A. K. Irvine in *POTT*, pp. 243 ff. and 296 ff. respectively.

Neh. 1:3); this may be so, though the Nehemiah material does not necessarily imply a recent event, as it may already indicate the developing of that view, fully expressed in 2 Macc. 1, that Nehemiah was the true restorer of the community after the disaster of Exile. What such material does provide is a realistic picture of a community struggling to rehabilitate itself, to re-establish its capital as a place of security, meeting with opposition from outside, and in all probability divided within itself over the right measures to be taken. This last may also be properly inferred from the opposition to Nehemiah.

The dating of Ezra and Nehemiah remains an unresolved issue. The dating of Nehemiah to 445 B.C., in the reign of Artaxerxes I, still appears to be sufficiently assured both by reference to Sanballat and in relation to the evidence of the Elephantine papyri. But it must be allowed that the Samaria papyri,[39] indicating that there were probably three officials named Sanballat (a possibility already apparent in Josephus), give a more complex picture: Sanballat (I), during the reign of Artaxerxes I and still alive, though less active than his sons Delaiah and Shelemiah in about 410 B.C. (Elephantine papyrus 30); Sanballat (II) whose son Hananiah is attested for about 350 B.C.; and Sanballat (III) in the time of Darius III (so Josephus, *Ant.* xi. 7–8). A dating for Nehemiah in the reign of Artaxerxes II (404–358) cannot be ruled out absolutely. The dating of Ezra remains controversial.[40] The traditional view which places him in 458 B.C. is still held by some, not only conservatives; the lack of real integration with Nehemiah would be no problem if Nehemiah in fact belonged to a much later date. U. Kellermann[41] has argued for a date of *c.* 448 B.C., taking a very radical view of the Ezra material and of the Chronicler's presentation of him.[42] The emendation of date in Ezra 7 to place him in 428 B.C. removes none of

---

[39] Cf. p. 328, n. 25.

[40] Cf. the careful discussion in S. Herrmann, *Geschichte*, pp. 378–91, ETr, pp. 307–18.

[41] *ZAW* lxxx (1968), 55–87; cf. also his important study *Nehemia. Quellen, Überlieferung und Geschichte*, BZAW clii, 1967. For Ezra, cf. W. T. In der Smitten, *Esra. Quellen, Überlieferung und Geschichte*, SSN xv, 1973, who offers a full and careful analysis of the Ezra tradition, though very different in its results.

[42] Cf. also K. Koch, *JSS* xix (1974), 173–97.

the other problems in the text and appears unconvincing.[43] The late date of 398 B.C. (Artaxerxes II) remains possible, even probable, but unproven.[44] Two further factors must be taken into account. The one is the literary question: is the now increasingly held view right that the Nehemiah material did not belong originally in the work of the Chronicler?[45] The other is the more general historical question: against what background may the commissioning of the two men be best understood? Again the arguments are of a general rather than a specific nature, but it must be allowed that we have clear evidence of difficulties in the province Beyond-the-River[46] just after 450 B.C. (rebellion of the satrap Megabyzos, linked to the rebellion of Egypt between 460 and 454); and some indications from the Elephantine papyri of the interest and perhaps involvement of the Jewish community with what was happening to the military colony in Elephantine during the last years of Persian rule before Egypt gained independence at the beginning of the fourth century B.C.[47] We cannot conclude that these were the only moments at which Persian policy might dictate the wisdom of sending such special commissioners, and indeed the relationship between their sending and wider aspects of Persian policy must be recognized as a supposition based on political probabilities, since no indication of the wider issues appears in our sources. It does, nevertheless, remain more probable that the Persian rulers concerned were serving their own interests in part than that their action was based purely upon the whims of favouritism or the like.

With the chronological uncertainties, the assessment of the nature and purpose of the two missions must also remain in some measure obscure. The purpose of Nehemiah's first visit,

[43] Still firmly maintained by J. Bright, *History*, 2nd edn., London, 1972, pp. 392–403; cf. the critical comments of J. A. Emerton, *JTS*, N.S. xvii (1966), 1–19.

[44] Cf. the valuable discussion by H. Cazelles, *VT* iv (1954), 113–40.

[45] For full discussion and refs. cf. K.-F. Pohlmann, *Studien zum dritten Esra*, FRLANT civ, 1970. The critical comments of W. T. In der Smitten, *BZ* xvi (1972), 207–21 provide no convincing counter-arguments; cf. also his *Ezra* (see p. 333, n. 41, above), especially for a critique of the evidence for the later datings.

[46] On the province, cf. E. E. Herzfeld, *The Persian Empire*, 1968, pp. 304–6.

[47] Cf. Galling, *Studien*, 149–84; and critical comments in U. Kellermann, *ZAW* lxxx (1968), 55–87. On the background, cf. In der Smitten, *Esra*, esp. pp. 110–23.

a twelve-year period according to Neh. 5:14, is described almost exclusively in terms of the repair of the walls[48] and gates of Jerusalem and of the repopulating of the city, but indications of social reforms in Neh. 5 suggest that the commission covered a normal range of government activities. The indications of opponents who had a substantial following (Neh. 6:17–19) show the sharpness of internal dissensions in Jerusalem, and the point is underlined both by what is said of Nehemiah's discovery of a more aggravated situation on his second visit (Neh. 13) and by the refrains which invite a divine remembering of his good deeds and his opponents' evil ones, refrains which, whatever other significance they have for the understanding of the nature of the Nehemiah narratives, point to a polemical intention. We may suppose a continuing body of opposition to what Nehemiah had done, existing alongside an equally strong favourable view which finds its expression in Ben Sira (Ecclus. 49:13) and in 2 Maccabees (1:10–2:18). One of Kellermann's notable contributions is to see a possible political context for the activity of Nehemiah, as last representative of the institution of the *nāsī*, to be replaced by the growing power of the High Priests.[49] It may well be too neat so to arrange such opposing parties in a probably more complex situation; but the awareness of political struggle is important to an assessment of the obscurities of the period. The second period of Nehemiah's activity as it is portrayed in Neh. 13 raises further literary questions and perhaps some suspicion that a primarily political figure, portrayed as having a high sense of divine calling and a due regard for the weight of the traditional Law, is being presented more in the guise of a religious reformer, an emphasis which appears to belong rather to his counterpart, Ezra.

The strongly political and indeed nationalistic aims of Nehemiah may be contrasted, though not artificially sharply, with the religious reformation aims of Ezra. If the late date is accepted, Ezra's work belongs in a period not only of

---

[48] The problems of the walls and of the extent of post-exilic Jerusalem remain unresolved. Cf. N. Avigad, *IEJ* xxi (1971), 168 f., for a summary in the light of recent work.

[49] *Nehemia*, esp. pp. 174 ff.

international upheaval but also of very sharp internal dissension in Judah, if we may judge from Josephus' account (*Ant.* xi. 7.1) of the High Priest's murder of his brother in the Temple.[50] This has been seen as an argument against the late dating, but it may equally be held that the Chronicler, in describing the work of Ezra, the climax of his writing, has concentrated on his understanding of Ezra the reformer and Ezra the conciliator, drawing together into one community all who accept the Law, and excluding from it only those who either refuse obedience or exclude themselves by virtue of religious contamination through alien marriage.[51]

Without imposing too rigid a scheme of interpretation upon the activity of these two leaders, we may see in them the epitomizing of the two major concerns of the community in the Persian period.[52] The first of these is the very nature of that community's existence. This involves its relation to the outside world, to Persian power, to the representatives of that power, particularly in Samaria but within the whole province of Beyond-the-River, to the surrounding areas with which an uneasy relationship prevailed. The names of Nehemiah's opponents point to a sharp degree of opposition to the redevelopment of Judah, and this is indicated also in such a passage as Ezra 4:6–23. Probably in the exilic age there had been encroachment on Judaean territory, and in the Persian period Lachish may have been the administrative centre of Edom.[53] The hostility to Edom found in many Old Testament passages may combine political motifs with the wider concern of preserving Judah's own national life against such encroachment; its aftermath is to be seen in the hostility to the Herod family. In part this is the further working out of the religiously based Deuteronomic hostility to the outside world[54] which is sharpened against Ammon and Moab but remarkably lenient towards Edom (Deut. 23:3–8), and in this it may be recognized that there was no single policy within the community. A different view of the attitude of Nehemiah might well be

---

[50] Cf. K. Galling, *Studien*, pp. 149–84.

[51] For comments on the transformation of the Ezra narrative by the Chronicler, cf. Koch, op. cit.

[52] Cf. the discussion and references in Bright, *History*, pp. 430 ff.

[53] So Noth, *History*, p. 345.

[54] Cf. O. Bächli, *Israel und die Völker*, ATANT xli, 1962.

taken by those who both for political reasons—'we have to
live with our neighbours'—and for religious reasons—'they
are descended from a common ancestor'—could consider that
relationships with the surrounding peoples should be on a
less narrow and exclusive basis—a foreshadowing of the
controversies of the second century B.C.[55]
Questions are raised about the relationship between the
community and its own past. In what sense may the
contemporary community be understood as identifiable with
that which formerly existed? What is the validity of the divine
promise and of the laws which the community has inherited?
The working out of this is to be seen in the arranging and
interpreting of the older narratives and laws. The assessment
of the purpose of the Priestly writers in their version of the
earliest traditions, and the judgement of the purpose of the
incorporation into that writing of the earlier forms of
the material is one aspect of this.[56] The integrating into the
Pentateuch of the Priestly work (the Tetrateuch) and the
book of Deuteronomy, is another aspect, for the drawing
together of such divergent views of the past, though sharing
a common basis in the main Exodus traditions, itself suggests
an endeavour at effecting within the community a reconciliation of differing approaches to the problem of identity and
meaning.[57] The prevalence of laments in the Psalter is itself
an indication of awareness of the unsatisfactory contemporary
situation, and this is particularly underlined in such liturgical
structures as appear in Ezra 9 and Neh. 9, with their differing
concerns about the land as Israel's inheritance. The work of
the Chronicler offers a presentation which both underlines
the authenticity of the earlier presentations and gives them a
new dimension, an interpretation of the relevance of the past
for the present and a setting of the present with its misfortunes
in a context of confidence and hope. The exposition of
prophecy, both by the amplification and arrangement of older
material and by the eventual gathering of the prophetic books
into an acknowledged corpus of writings to be set alongside

[55] Cf. E. Bickerman on the rich and diversified contacts under Persian rule (*The Jews*, ed. L. Finkelstein, i. 4th edn., New York, 1970, pp. 72–118).
[56] Cf. J. G. Vink, in *OTS* xv (1969), 1–144, and N. Lohfink (see p. 330, n. 30).
[57] For fuller discussion of this, see Chapter IV.

the Torah and the Former Prophets, serves equally to emphasize the reality of the relationship with the past.[58] Another aspect of this is the more precise defining of the community both in its continuity with the past and in its conception of its limits.[59] The establishment and maintenance of continuity involves questions of organization, and it is here that, over the years of Persian rule and on into the following period, the status of the High Priest, now the 'anointed' who in many ways replaces the king, becomes increasingly important. Direct indications of governors are very limited (see below on evidence from coins and seals). Those whom we know are more often special commissioners with limited appointment than controllers on a more permanent basis; this may better account for the unexplained disappearance of Sheshbazzar and Zerubbabel than more extravagant theories. The allusion in Mal. 1:8 may be to a Persian official ruling over a wider area. The non-mention of any governor in the Ezra material (apart from harmonizing allusions to Nehemiah) may depend on the Chronicler's view of Ezra's claims to status, for it would appear that in Ezra 7:1 ff. he is presenting Ezra as the true and virtually immediate successor to the High Priest who was carried into exile in 587 B.C.[60] Thus both continuity of office and status are claimed. Elephantine papyri (30, line 18) show an appeal c. 410 B.C. to 'the High Priest Johanan and his associates the priests in Jerusalem', and such a 'collegiate' ruling group is suggested by the similar expression in Zech. 3:8 (cf. Lev. 21:10);[61] but the appeal here concerns a religious matter and this does not preclude the existence of a contemporary governor. When the situation becomes clearer under Greek rule, there is no governor; the authority is vested in a High Priesthood which is in tension between the political claims of Greek rulers to appointment and the religious demands of the faithful for a proper

[58] Cf. most recently, T. Willi, *Die Chronik als Auslegung*, FRLANT cvi, 1972; R. Mosis, *Untersuchungen zur Theologie des chronistischen Werkes*, Freiburg, 1973; P. Welten, *Geschichte und Geschichtsdarstellung in den Chronikbüchern*, WMANT xlii, 1973.

[59] Cf. H. C. M. Vogt, *Studie zur nachexilischen Gemeinde in Esra-Nehemia*, Werl, 1966.

[60] Cf. K. Koch, op. cit. 2 Esdras presents a later form of the tradition in which Ezra becomes the direct restorer of the community after the Exile.

[61] Cf. A. Petitjean, *ETL* xlii (1966), 40–71; E. Bickerman, op. cit., p. 76.

succession, and here lies one of the sources of internal dissension and external conflict.

The status of Judah as a Persian district is clarified in the fourth century with the appearance of *yhd* coins, indicating the granting of a right to mint money and defining independence over against neighbouring districts. A coin from Gerar of the period may include the name of the Judaean governor, though its precise placing must for the moment remain uncertain.[62] Seal impressions on jar handles add a little further information.[63] The territorial limits of Judah are also as yet insufficiently defined, but recent excavations at least begin to illuminate what may in the end prove to be significant topographical information for this period, possibly finding some reflection in the Chronicler's and other lists and genealogies. Here Neh. 3 is of significance both for the city and for the Judaean territory.[64]

Identity for the community is also determined by questions of membership,[65] and it is here that we may observe how older laws are understood. There are marriage limitations imposed; there is an emphasis on purity, the defining of the community in terms of its acceptability to the deity—foreign marriages and hence alien religion represent a threat to community life. There is, particularly in Ezra, an emphasis on acceptance of the law which itself determines membership of the community and which can in theory make possible a wider understanding of membership—developing older legislation concerning the rights of the *gēr* and allowing the possibility of the admission of outsiders with their full acceptance of community obligations, though in practice the degree of such wider acceptance does not appear to have been very great.[66]

[62] L. Y. Rahmani, *IEJ* xxi (1971), 158–60. More generally, Y. Meshorer, *Jewish Coins of the Second Temple* (Heb.), 1967; A. Reifenberg, *Ancient Jewish Coins*, 2nd edn., London, 1947, 4th edn., 1965, but with no new material; M. Avi-Yonah, *Prolegomenon* to F. W. Madden, *History of Jewish Coinage*, reprint, New York, 1967.

[63] Cf. Y. Aharoni, *AOTS*, pp. 173–6, arguing that some of the seals refer to a governor, *phw'*.

[64] Cf. Aharoni, *The Land of the Bible. A Historical Geography*, London, 1966 (Heb. 1962), pp. 356–65 on Judaean territory in the Persian period.

[65] On social structure and continuity, cf. J. P. Weinberg, *VT* xxiii (1973), 400–14.

[66] Cf. on Ezra, Koch, op. cit. For a political sequel see the comments on John Hyrcanus and the Idumaeans, below, p. 348.

The second of the community's major concerns ties in very closely with the question of its identity. It is the problem of unity and of orthodoxy. It is only in the succeeding period that clear and precise evidence is available regarding differing groups within the community, groups which eventually come to be known by particular names—Pharisees, Sadducees, Essenes, and others. The origin of any one of these groups remains obscure and it is hardly surprising that the interpretation of the Qumran texts has raised questions about all the various separate elements.[67] But the point to which we can press the evidence back (the period of Antiochus IV Epiphanes and Maccabean uprising) is in fact one in which the existence of divergent groups may already be detected even if no particular titles appear other than that of the Hasidaeans (Hasidim). How far may we legitimately postulate that the existence of divergent approaches to the problem of the *Auseinandersetzung* with Hellenism itself stems from earlier differences of view regarding the defining of the nature of the community and its position *vis-à vis* the outside world? How far, knowing that eventually the Samaritan community was to appear as a sharply defined entity, may we look further back and detect its forerunners? How far may we, in the divergent presentations and interpretations of the tradition, detect differences of emphasis which, if pressed into the realm of political action, must lead to antagonism and even to conflict? And how far may we properly observe the endeavours at conciliation within the community? This last seems properly to be a term which may, within certain limits, be applied to the Chronicler, and through him may be seen to be relevant to Ezra; the combining of theological elements in the Chronicler's thought is no doubt one-sided and there must have been some for whom his particular brand of orthodoxy was unacceptable; its emphasis on the centrality of Jerusalem could not, either at the time or later, be acceptable to those who were to centre their faith and practice at Shechem/Gerizim. This is not to argue that the Chronicler was engaged in anti-Samaritan polemic,[68] but simply to

---

[67] For literature, see below, p. 346. n. 81.

[68] Rightly underlined by R. J. Coggins, *ASTI* iv (1968), 35–48, see pp. 45 f. and further his *Samaritans and Jews*, Oxford, 1974; and R. Mosis (see p. 338, n. 58.).

observe that such an orthodoxy, by whomsoever presented, could not include all who claimed a true succession of faith and organization from the past. Nor does it seem proper to make so sharp a division between the Priestly and Chronicler writings as 'theocratic' and the development of apocalyptic as 'eschatological' as has been maintained by Plöger,[69] for if it is true that one line of development from such thought is into a narrow ecclesiasticism, there is also in the critique of the religious tradition offered in such writings a basis for the development of what may with some propriety be termed the 'protest' literature of the last centuries B.C.

It has already been suggested that the difference between those who went to Babylonia and whose experience and understanding of their faith and life were so conditioned and those who remained in Palestine, and further between the descendants of both groups for whom the particular interpretation was less a matter of experience and more a matter of what had come to be regarded as normative, may be a contributory factor to the problems of the post-exilic period. When this is allied (as we may see it to be in the Nehemiah situation) with differences of political view and with personal antagonisms, the likelihood of 'party' divisions becomes very strong indeed. With the Samaritan community the origins of the division come to be sought even further back, in the settlement of non-Israelites after 722 in Samaria, in the division between north and south, and even beyond that in the period just before and at the beginning of the monarchy, though this is not to suggest that such tracing back by both parties to the division represents a proper understanding of history.[70] For such a separated community, Jerusalem becomes anathema. For others, the sense of allegiance to Jerusalem may be so strong that it necessitates a withdrawal when Jerusalem as it now is ceases to be possible or acceptable. This may be seen in the Onias (IV) who went to Egypt and built a temple at Leontopolis (Josephus, *Ant.* xiii. 3); perhaps in Mattathias' withdrawal to Modein. The same is true of the

---

[69] O. Plöger, *Theocracy and Eschatology*, Oxford, 1968 (German, 1959, 2nd edn., 1962); cf. also O. H. Steck, *EvTh* xxviii (1968), 445–58; W. E. Rast, *Journal of Religion* l (1970), 101–11.

[70] Cf. further below pp. 346 f. and n. 82.

Qumran community which appears to believe in a true continuity with the Jerusalem Temple and at the same time to find involvement in the contemporary Jerusalem set-up impossible. Here the detail of interpretation depends upon the vexed problems surrounding the figures of the wicked priest and the true teacher, and the degree to which precise events can be reconstructed from allusive statements.

These last points inevitably move across the chronological limit of the Persian period, but to that extent the subdividing of the history is artificial. For the people and for their leaders, the problems of relationship with their overlords and the problems of their internal life and organization remain, and we may, with due caution, draw some inferences from later developments about the earlier conditions from which these emerged.

C. UNDER GREECE (AND ROME)[71]

It is again a matter for regret that so great an event as Alexander the Great's conquests passes without clear reflection in Old Testament writings, except for Daniel (cf. below) and 1 Macc. 1:1–9 which provides a brief note as introduction to the book's main concern, the events of the reign of Antiochus IV Epiphanes. There have been many attempts, none entirely convincing, at finding allusions to Alexander's activities, in Ezekiel, Zech. 9–14, and other Old Testament writings. Similar uncertainty exists in regard to the period of Ptolemaic control in the third century and to the change to Seleucid control at the beginning of the second. The possibility of the updating of earlier material in the light of these events must be allowed. The absence of precise allusion may be explained in various ways. Earlier material, now read in the light of new experiences, may take on a new meaning but may already have acquired a sufficiently 'canonical' status not to be significantly modified. Allusions to contemporary

---

[71] For full bibliographical coverage and discussion of the many historical and other problems of this period, cf. now the new edition of E. Schürer, *The History of the Jewish People in the Age of Jesus Christ (175 B.C.–A.D. 135)*, revised and edited by G. Vermes and F. Millar, i, Edinburgh, 1973; Vols. ii and iii in preparation. The appearance of this work suggests the propriety of treating this later period relatively briefly.

events may be couched in terms fully clear to those involved while leaving us unable to know precisely to what reference is being made. (This is a problem very evident in the interpretation of the Qumran material.) But we must nevertheless note that the book of Daniel, in addition to statements in symbolic terms (2:40; 7:7; 8:5–8), provides a historical review (11:2–45) which describes, sometimes cryptically, the succession of rulers under Persia and the period of Alexander and his successors, so that more direct reference to historical events could be made. We must also consider how far events which undoubtedly had far-reaching consequences for the history of the Jewish community were so viewed at the time.

Josephus (*Ant.* xi. 8. 3–5) has detailed information for the period of Alexander, but it is difficult to know how much of real historical value can be extracted from what is evidently pious legend.[72] That Alexander called on the subjects of Persia to rebel would seen reasonable enough; that rulers of the Palestinian area used the occasion to manoeuvre for position is also likely. But more precise information, if indeed such was available, is concealed in the legendary presentation.

For the ordinary inhabitants of Palestine, such a change of political control may have meant little. Undoubtedly for the rulers it was a situation of some delicacy, involving judicious decision as to when to accept the new situation as sufficiently permanent. For religious leaders and teachers we might expect there to be a searching for signs of divine action in judgement and promise, but the degree to which such material has survived remains doubtful, and it does not necessarily follow that the events were viewed as momentous in the way in which we might expect. A century and a half later, when a much closer impact on the life of the Jewish community was felt, there appears an immediate upsurge of literary activity. While the argument from silence is never satisfactory, the lack of clearly assignable material for the preceding period must be given due weight.

The much fuller attestation of the second century B.C. in the literature does not by any means solve the problems of

---

[72] Cf. Schürer, op. cit., p. 138.

interpretation. It is a matter for active discussion how far the outbreak of open hostilities between the Jewish community and the Seleucid rulers resulted from the policy of the latter in following Alexander's own line of action towards greater control and Hellenization[73] and how far from the internal conflicts—over the control of the High Priesthood, as between rival groups such as the Tobiad and Oniad families,[74] and over the degree to which Judaism should conform itself to the contemporary cultural climate. The third century B.C. is obscure, illuminated only in so far as we may trace indications of the position of the Jewish community in Alexandria, facing pressure from those hostile to or suspicious of a separate religious group.[75] Of Babylonian Jewish life we know virtually nothing; inferences from such a writing as Esther may suggest that there too Jews faced moments of violent hostility. Indications of impetus to new movements of thought and life stemming from Babylonia (traceable in the Persian period as already indicated) have been thought, with some justice, to be detectable in the succeeding period too. The stories in the books of Daniel and Esther, with their Babylonian/Persian setting and their subsequent modification in Palestine (so Daniel) or acceptance there (so Esther, with the taking over of the earlier unattested festival of Purim) point clearly to this. Signs of such influence have also been claimed for Qumran, and this has had some impact on views of the textual history of the Hebrew Bible.[76] The meagre indications of the literature from Babylon suggest a community endeavouring to maintain its own way of life in an alien context; to such a community older laws and

[73] On the degree of Hellenization, see Schürer, op. cit., p. 144; M. Hengel, *Judaism and Hellenism*, 2 vols., London, 1974, ETr of *Judentum und Hellenismus*, Tübingen, 1969, 2nd edn., 1973; esp. Ch. II. V. Tcherikover, *Hellenistic Civilization and the Jews*, Philadelphia, 1961 (Part I on Palestine; Part II on the Dispersion); A. H. M. Jones, *Cities of the Eastern Roman Provinces*, 2nd edn., Oxford, 1971. A further intangible is the assessment of the character of Antiochus IV Epiphanes, cf. Schürer, op. cit., pp. 146 f. Cf. also M. Stern, 'The Hasmonean Revolt and its Place in the history of Jewish Society and Religion', *Journal of World History* (*Cahiers d'Histoire Mondiale*), xi, 1–2 (1968), 92–106.

[74] Cf. Hengel, op. cit, esp. Ch. IV.

[75] For Graeco-Roman Egypt, see Claire Préaux in *The Legacy of Egypt*, ed. J. R. Harris, 2nd edn., Oxford, 1971, pp. 323–54.

[76] Cf. summary and references in *CHB* i, 191–9, and Chapter I, above.

narratives, particularly those which stressed separation from the outside world, would be increasingly meaningful. Somewhere within these obscure years the political organization shifted. The power of the High Priest, already increasing in the Persian period,[77] appears in its full form when relationships between Greek rulers and the Jewish community emerge into clearer light in the second century B.C. The indications of internal conflicts and of the degree to which the Greek rulers themselves claimed authority to appoint the political head who was also the religious leader, reveal the change. Along with this go the now sharply recognizable conflicts between differing views of the relationship of the community to contemporary culture, the stress upon what may be claimed as legitimate cultural advance over against strict adherence to ancestral traditions of separate religious and hence political life.

It is in the nature of the case that the description of this situation remains problematic. It is easy enough for a relatively propagandist work like 1 Maccabees to present the contrast between apostates, Hellenizers, on the one hand, and the loyal Maccabean family and the Asidaeans on the other.[78] Even that account does not conceal that there were differences of view concerning the status of individual High Priests, though we may detect a certain criticism of the less politically minded for their *naïveté* in accepting as High Priest one who would betray them (Alcimus, cf. 1 Macc. 7). It is easy to picture the Maccabean family as a truly faithful religious group, subsequently declining into intrigue and the acceptance of alien practices. But it is salutary to recall that the contemporary book of Daniel makes only the barest allusion to the endeavours of the Maccabees (Dan. 11:34);[79] for the author, hope did not lie there. The secession of the Qumran community at some moment in the succeeding years points to strong dissatisfaction with the political and religious situation, but interpretations of the evidence diverge.[80] A

[77] Cf. above, p. 338; Schürer, op. cit., p. 139 and n. 3.

[78] For literature, cf. Schürer, op. cit., p. 157, n. 46.

[79] But cf. the argument of H. Sahlin, *StTh* xxiii, 1 (1969), 41–68, that Daniel presents Judas as Messiah.

[80] For literature, cf. Schürer, ibid., pp. 118–22; a convenient survey in R. de Vaux, *Archaeology and the Dead Sea Scrolls*, 2nd edn., London, 1973.

consideration of the sharp conflicts between those involved in the war of A.D. 66–74 may well suggest that the earlier period too cannot be understood except with an awareness of the delicacy of balance between political aspirations and the desire to remain within the tradition. It is from this period that there begin to emerge into a clearer light the main religious groups within Judaism known to us from both Jewish writings and the New Testament, though the precise origin of any one of them (Sadducees, Pharisees, Essenes) remains obscure.[81] But we may certainly recognize that simple categorizations of their life and thought do not do justice to men who believed that the best chance of the preservation of their community lay in just the right combination of political realism with faithfulness to the religious tradition, as they understood it. And the degree to which there may have to be compromise is typified by the decision that the community must defend itself from attack on the sabbath rather than adopt the stricter view of observance which led to a total massacre (1 Macc. 2:34–41).

It is in this area that we must understand both the internal life of the community, concerned with its survival in a period of threat and achieving for a short period independence from outside control; and also the policies of succeeding Greek and Roman rulers. There were other factors too. In the period of the Seleucid rulers, the complexity of the history derives in part from the degree to which rival claimants to the throne invited support and promised or gave concessions to such groups as the Jewish community. Independence in fact came in the end less from military action and more from political finesse. Negotiation with Rome and with Sparta (so e.g. 1 Macc. 8; 12), support for one claimant to the Seleucid throne or another, complex relationships with the Ptolemaic rulers of Egypt, all formed part of the pattern. But essentially, within the community, the problem remained that of adapting the older ways of life to the new situations, interpreting the older

---

[81] A full discussion will appear in Schürer, op. cit., ii. See also Hengel, op. cit., ch. III; J. Le Moyne, *Les Sadducéens*, Paris, 1972; L. Finkelstein, *The Pharisees*, 2 vols., 3rd edn., Philadelphia, 1972; J. Neusner, *The Rabbinic Traditions about the Pharisees before 70*, 3 vols., Leiden, 1971; K. Schubert, *Die jüdischen Religionsparteien in neutestamentlicher Zeit*, Stuttgart, 1970; W. R. Farmer, *Maccabees, Zealots, and Josephus*, New York, 1956.

laws, seeing the significance of the accepted authoritative writings of the past, and mediating these either by offering contemporary elucidation (so in the Qumran commentaries) or by elaborating on themes within them and incorporating new material, some of this no doubt also traditional, in the many works which belong to this so-called intertestamental period—particularly the writings which purport to bring to the contemporary world new revelations and warnings from the past, Enoch, the Testaments, and the many writings associated with other great figures. In such reactions and attempts, there is no uniformity of view, though the main groupings remain in some measure known to us. Alongside those within the narrower confines of Judaism, we may also see such a community as the Samaritans, equally claiming ancient authority for its particular religious position and equally involved in the political manoeuvres of the period.[82]

The other side to this is the policy of succeeding rulers, together with the concessions offered by particular claimants to power. The indications of special terms offered to the Jewish community under Ptolemaic and Seleucid rule suggest both that there were political motives (the earlier Persian rulers had adopted policies which could similarly be regarded as conciliatory, since consideration of the wishes and needs of particular groups may well pay dividends in loyalty and peace) and that there was some understanding of the particular problems which face such a community. We have no knowledge of another such community in the ancient world (one with such a politico-religious centre and scattered adherents), though it does not follow that such another did not exist, any more than it is proper to see Jewish resistance to Hellenistic political and cultural pressure as isolated.[83] The commission granted to Ezra is a forerunner of the actions

---

[82] See J. D. Purvis, *The Samaritan Pentateuch and the Origin of the Samaritan Sect*, Cambridge, Mass., and Oxford, 1968; H. G. Kippenberg, *Garizim und Synagoge*, Berlin, 1971; R. J. Coggins, *Samaritans and Jews*. Reference may also be made to the existence of temples at 'Araq el-Amir and at Lachish (cf. Y. Aharoni, *IEJ* xviii (1968), 157 ff.), and to the problems associated with these and other religious centres in the post-exilic period, whether claiming to be 'orthodox' in the narrower sense or not (cf. above, pp. 341 f.).

[83] Cf. S. K. Eddy, *The King is Dead*, Lincoln, Nebr., 1961, on resistance to Hellenism.

taken by Greek and Roman rulers; it envisages support for the religio-political organization in Jerusalem/Judah, typified in material aid for the Temple, and a mechanism by which the coherence of the community may be recognized by obedience to the Law being held to be a mark of membership, extending to all (Jews) within the province Beyond-the-River. We may compare Seleucid attempts at rationalizing the boundaries.[84] The policy of various Roman rulers, adapted with greater or less wisdom to the problems of the situation, may be seen at a high point in the recognition by Julius Caesar of the particular nature of the Jewish community, and this was to have its consequences in the claims of both Jews and Christians after A.D. 70 to be the true successors and therefore the lawful claimants to such protection and favour. Military and taxation concessions form one aspect of such policies. Adjusting the areas under the control of particular rulers, appointed or supported by Roman authority, forms another. The counterpart to this in the internal policy of Jewish rulers may be observed in military campaigns of the second century B.C., where, for example, the forcible incorporation of the Idumaeans into the community by John Hyrcanus may be seen as one method of extending political control so as to offer protection to Jewish residents in the area, and movement of Jews from Galilee to Judaea (cf. 1 Macc. 5) as an alternative method of resolving community problems.[85] The changing patterns of political organization after the death of Herod the Great reveal a series of not very successful endeavours to handle the 'Jewish problem'. It is proper to see in such situations the radical difficulties which are posed by such a political and religious organization and the genuineness of the endeavours made to resolve the problems, as well as the ineptitude or the ambitions of particular Roman officials. The reasons for attempting a solution were themselves not simple, for they combined a concern with security on the eastern frontier and for political advantage (for the Roman power) with an endeavour to bring about at least some degree of reconciliation between differing parties and groups. It is in such a context too that we must judge the endeavours of the

---

[84] Cf. Schürer, op. cit., p. 141.
[85] Cf. Schürer, op. cit., pp. 140 f., 207.

later Hasmonean rulers at working out a judicious balance between political power and the control of the High Priesthood, and the degree of success achieved by Herod the Great as a Roman-appointed ruler in maintaining a considerable degree of order for a period, even though his endeavours at drawing together conflicting interests (for example by his marriage with Mariamne) can be seen to have been frustrated.[86] The reflections of life and thought in the literature of these years reveals its complexities and uncertainties; with all the new light which has been shed upon it in recent years, the period remains one in which the currents and crosscurrents are capable of widely differing interpretations.

BIBLIOGRAPHY

(This list does not include (a) works mentioned in the above essay or (b) general histories of Israel mentioned in the Bibliography to Ch. X. Books marked * are more suitable for introductory study.)

(i) General histories of Israel

*ANDERSON, B. W. *The Living World of the Old Testament*, Englewood Cliffs, 1957, London, 1958; 2nd edn., 1966, 1967.
*ANDERSON, G. W. *The History and Religion of Israel*, New Clarendon Bible, Oxford, 1966.
BEN-SASSON, H. H. (ed.) *History of the Jewish People* (Hebrew), i (Tel Aviv, 1969), 154–63 (H. Tadmor), 177–230 (M. Stern).
*EHRLICH, E. L. *A Concise History of Israel*, London, 1962; ETr of *Geschichte Israels*, Berlin, 1958.
GUNNEWEG, A. H. J. *Geschichte Israels bis Bar Cochba*, Stuttgart, 1972.
MAZAR, B. (ed.) *World History of the Jewish People*, iv, London, 1974.
HAYES, J. H. and MILLER, J. M. (eds.) *Israelite and Judaean History*, London and Philadelphia, 1977.

(ii) Works on the post-exilic period or parts thereof

ABEL, F.-M. *Histoire de la Palestine depuis la conquête d'Alexandre jusqu' à l'invasion arabe*, 2 vols., Paris, 1952; see vol. i, part 1.

---

[86] Cf. A. Schalit, *König Herodes*, Berlin, 1969.

ACKROYD, P. R. *Exile and Restoration*, London, 1968; corrected edn., 1972.
—— *Israel under Babylon and Persia*, New Clarendon Bible, Oxford, 1970.
—— 'The Jewish Community in Palestine in the Persian Period', in *Cambridge History of Judaism* i, forthcoming.
ALLEGRO, J. M. *The Chosen People*, London, 1971.
AVI-YONAH, M. (ed.) *Sepher Yerushalayim* (Hebrew), i (Jerusalem, 1956), 221–418.
—— *Jerusalem of the Second Temple* (in preparation; see *IEJ* xxi (1971), 221).
BICKERMAN, E. *From Ezra to the Last of the Maccabees*, New York, 1947, 2nd edn., 1949, 3rd edn., 1962, ETr, revised, of *Der Gott der Makkabäer*, Berlin, 1937.
HANSON, P. D. *The Dawn of Apocalyptic*, Philadelphia, 1975.
HEICHELHEIM, F. M. 'Geschichte Syriens und Palästinas ... (547 v. Chr.-641/2 n. Chr.)' in *Handbuch der Orientalistik*, ed. B. Spuler, Berlin, 1952, I, ii, 4, 2, pp. 99–192 (to A.D. 135); bibliography, pp. 265 ff.
KLAUSNER, J. *History of the Second Temple* (Hebrew), 5 vols., Jerusalem, 1954; see vols. i–iii.
*MYERS, J. M. *The World of the Restoration*, Englewood Cliffs, 1968.
REICKE, B. *The New Testament Era. The World of the Bible from 500 B.C. to A.D. 100*, London, 1969; ETr of *Neutestamentliche Zeitgeschichte*, Berlin, 1965.
*RUSSELL, D. S. *The Jews from Alexander to Herod*, New Clarendon Bible, Oxford, 1967.
WHITLEY, C. F. *The Exilic Age*, London, 1957.
WILLIAMSON, H. G. M. *Israel in the Books of Chronicles*, Cambridge, 1977.

(iii) Chronology

BICKERMAN, E. *Chronology of the Ancient World*, New York, 1968.
FREEDMAN, D. N. and CAMPBELL, E. F. in *The Bible and the Ancient Near East*, ed. G. E. Wright, London, 1961, pp. 203–28.
HANHART, R. in *Untersuchungen zur israelitisch-jüdischen Chronologie*, ed. A. Jepsen and R. Hanhart, BZAW lxxxviii, 1964, pp. 49–96, for 1 and 2 Maccabees.
PARKER, R. A., and DUBBERSTEIN, W. H. *Babylonian Chronology 626 B.C.–A.D. 75*, Providence, R. I., revised edn., 1956.

XII

THE HISTORY OF ISRAELITE RELIGION

W. ZIMMERLI

1. In *The Old Testament and Modern Study*, research on the history of Israelite religion in the previous twelve to fifteen years was presented in its most important trends by G. W. Anderson. Here in what follows the attempt must be made to pursue the course of research in the same field through the period from 1951 to 1973.

There can be no question of a complete presentation of all the work. For one thing, the period of time requiring survey is longer; but it must be made clear that the stream of publications has grown incomparably stronger, like the Temple stream described in Ezek. 47:1–12. The *mê birkayim* (waters that reach the knees) have become *mê sāḥû* (waters which only a swimmer may cross). All that can be offered here then is a sketching in of a few of the principal directions taken in studies, and the elucidation of their methods. Also for the sake of illustration a few particularly important blocks of research will be singled out, but with no claim to completeness.

A second preliminary consideration will serve to clarify the demarcation of the field to be treated. In his contribution to *The Bible in Modern Scholarship*, 1965, R. de Vaux reflected by way of introduction on the three aspects under which the historical interpretation of the Old Testament can occur, and on their demarcation: (1) The historian regards Israel as one of the ancient peoples of the Near East and reconstructs its political and economic history. In so doing he pays attention *inter alia* to the religious institutions. (2) The historian of religion has regard for the faith of Israel which is founded on the conviction that God has directed the whole history of his chosen people Israel. He does this with the greatest possible objectivity, seeing as he does in Israel's religion one of the ancient religions. (3) The theologian, by contrast, starts from the presupposition that God has revealed himself in this history—the God with whom his own faith has to do. It is the second task sketched which is the business of this paper.

One thing more: *Tradition and Interpretation* has independent contributions treating of Prophecy and Wisdom. This contribution must therefore approach Israel's religion with due regard to the limitations thereby imposed.

2. The phase of research delineated in *The Old Testament and Modern Study* was essentially defined by the discussion of a few great projects on a grand scale (Yahweh's Enthronement Festival, Mowinckel; Divine Kingship, Engnell; Myth and Ritual, Hooke; Mosaic Monotheism, Albright). These stood in opposition to the views of Wellhausen and his school about the history of Israel's religion, and sought each in its own way to break the historical 'evolutionism' of these views. A continuation of this discussion into the period of time under review here has taken place; but for all that there has been a perceptible retreat in the face of more recent questions.

The thesis of Hooke and Engnell had reckoned with a fixed cultic 'pattern'. As in the religions of Israel's environment, so in her own too this could be shown to be the fundamental ideal of her faith. The protest against these generalizing views came on the one side from the orientalists. H. Frankfort had already shown in 1948 that in Egypt and Mesopotamia we meet two very different types of belief about God and King.[1] Moreover he had made clear in an epilogue, 'The Hebrews', which was only briefly sketched out, that we must reckon in Israel with a quite different type of kingship. 'The transcendentalism of Hebrew Religion prevented kingship from assuming the profound significance which it possessed in Egypt and Mesopotamia.'[2] What he had only indicated here, Frankfort took up again in his Frazer lecture, in a fundamental consideration of the reliability of analogies across a religion's boundaries.[3] From the history of Egypt's

---

[1] *Kingship and the Gods*, Chicago, 1948.
[2] Op. cit., p. 343.
[3] *The Problem of Similarity in Ancient Near Eastern Religions*, Oxford, 1951.

religion, G. Posener[4] has made clear that throughout the Egyptian accounts there is also revealed beside the divine king the picture of a figure that reaches into the human sphere and, as an earthly being, stands over against the deity. Doubtless that leads us closer to the everyday reality of Israelite kingship, too, as that is presented in many Old Testament texts (as in the Deuteronomist). For the Mesopotamian world in its turn, Falkenstein's scrupulous study of Tammuz,[5] with a strict textual orientation, has shown just how little it is permissible to reckon simply in all periods with one fixed pattern of belief in the god Tammuz who dies and rises again. W. von Soden has expressed a similar opinion. In an article on the seasons of the year in ancient Mesopotamia he has rejected the idea of rating the Babylonian New Year festival in March/April as a simple spring festival.

If we read without bias the sources available for this festival, then it appears as a festival of external and internal purification on the occasion of the year-change, which in Babylon was associated with the conception of the creative acts of Marduk. There is no sanction in the texts for the opinion that there was any associated thought of a god dying with nature and rising again—and it would be quite wrong to believe it permissible to view Marduk in particular as one such. Ideas attested for Syria and Asia Minor have been interpreted into the Babylonian texts without adequate reason.[6]

And so on the one side, that of the Egyptologists and Assyriologists, notice has been given of opposition to a presentation that suggests uniformity of belief in God and the divine king, and the demand made that there should be greater differentiation in the approach to the religious notions too.

3. On the other side, opposition has been expressed on the basis of considerations relating to Old Testament. At the memorable Third Congress of the International Organization for the Study of the Old Testament in Oxford (1959), Engnell on the one side spoke on 'Methodological Aspects of Old

---

[4] *De la divinité du Pharaon*, Paris, 1960.

[5] *Compte rendu de la IIIème rencontre assyriologique internationale, Liège*, 1954, pp. 41–67.

[6] 'Die Jahreszeiten im alten Zweistromland', *Studium generale*, ix (1956), 14–18. Cf. also 'Gibt es ein Zeugnis dafür, dass die Babylonier an die Wiederauferstehung Marduks geglaubt haben?', *ZA* li (NF xvii) (1955), 130–66.

Testament Studies'. Against the literary-critical method ('the anachronistic literary-critical method is out of date'), he postulated once again the 'traditio-critical' method, to be operated as a comparative method, more specifically as a patternist method. He thereby ratified the 'institution of sacral kingship' as the dominating institution.[7] By contrast at the same Congress, V. Maag indicated that Israel had brought from its nomadic past and still possessed an inherited understanding of God quite other than that which was inherent in the divine kingship beliefs of the great sedentary cultures of her environment. Alluding to the phenomenon of transmigration amongst the Bachtiari, he elaborated the belief in the god who leads on the way.

Nomadic religion is a religion of promise. The nomad's life is of course not in the cycle of sowing and harvest but in the world of migration . . . . . In the sphere of transmigration, event is experience as advance, as a leaving-behind. Existence is perceived there as history. This god leads to a future which is not a simple repetition and confirmation of the present, but is the goal for the incidents that are presently taking their course. The goal gives point to the wandering and its miseries; and today's decision for trust in the god who calls is pregnant with the future.

In its myths, dramatically realized in the annual ritual for the maintenance of the world, Israel's environment is familar with the deity as creator and maintainer of the world. Cosmostatic myth and cosmostatic magic are linked in the ritual of the New Year festival. In this context, the king too is understood by the Uppsala School to be a 'cosmostatically indispensable figure. He heads the social cosmos as the *summus deus* heads that of the divine world.' Maag indicates by contrast that Israel, in distinction to its whole environment, knows Yahweh as the one who is to be faced in the future on a 'day of Yahweh'. That leads to quite another root for eschatology than that asserted by Mowinckel and also by Gressmann. Eschatological expectation originates in Israel not from the experience of disappointment by those who had exalted Yahweh's royal authority in the cult yet experienced his powerlessness in the reality of life, nor from any mythical

[7] SVT vii, 1960, pp. 13–30.

cyclical thinking. Its roots are in the experiences of the period of Israel's nomadic origins. It is in the occurrence of transmigration, experienced first by the patriarchs in giving up their Mesopotamian homeland, and then a second time by those groups of the later people who subsequently detached themselves from Egypt, that Israel experiences decisively the 'shepherd of Israel', the God who in history leads towards the future. Transmigration is to be distinguished from the phenomenon of transhumance, by which Alt explained the settlement of the tribes. Whereas the latter refers to the annual change of pasture by semi-nomads who then eventually remain settled exclusively in the cultivated land, transmigration refers to the definitive breaking-away from established dwelling-places, and to the way into the unsecured 'new' in confidence in the divine leadership.[8]

With his demonstration of the historical 'way'-character of Israel's faith there is no doubt that Maag has introduced an important factor for the understanding of the fundamental structure of the religion of Israel. That is the case, however we may judge the weight of the analogy he cites of the Bachtiari and the linking of the 'way'-element directly to the monarchy, which at first appeared to Israel rather suspect according to the evidence of Jotham's fable.

4. Frankfort, Posener, and von Soden had pressed for a stricter differentiation in statements about the divine king on the basis of material from Israel's environment; and Maag had brought into play her nomadic prehistory. Similarly, the historian too registered his reservations about that fundamentally ahistorical patternism which mistakenly set the essential constituents of Myth and Ritual back into the tradition available to the original Israel. M. Noth had already posed the historical question in 1950 in his article 'God, King and Nation in the Old Testament',[9] which he expressly designated

---

[8] SVT vii, 1960, pp. 129–53. In his paper on 'Das Gottesverständnis des Alten Testaments', NedTT xxi, (1966/7), 161–207, Maag offered a further presentation in a wider context of Israel's faith as understood from this starting-point. H. D. Preuss took up this point of view in his monograph on *Jahweglaube und Zukunftserwartung*, BWANT v. 7, 1968, and in his explanation of the formula 'Ich will mit dir sein' in ZAW lxxx (1968), 139–73.

[9] 'Gott, König, Volk im Alten Testament', ZThK xlvii (1950), 157–91; ETr in *The Laws in the Pentateuch and Other Studies*, Edinburgh, 1966, pp. 147–78.

'a methodological discussion of a contemporary tendency in research': Is it possible to do as the Myth and Ritual ideology and the 'patternism' of the Uppsala School do and claim the divine king ritual as a leading element in Israelite religion, if the historian establishes that the monarchy in Israel is a late arrival and, what is more, appears subsequently in south and north in quite different structures? Is it not necessary to take into account more precisely that 'it is the monarchy of the Davidic line which is the first to come into question as a point at which ancient oriental divine king ideology in its customary Syro-Palestinian dress could have gained entry into Israel's domain?'[10]

De Fraine,[11] who limits himself to comparison with Mesopotamian kingship, and Bernhardt,[12] with reference to the historical reports of the origin of the monarchy, have criticized the method of patternism even more massively than Noth's article mentioned above. In so doing Bernhardt lays particular weight on the voices in the Old Testament that reject the monarchy. These in fact have no full analogue in the conception of kingship in Israel's environment and therefore represent an indication of the special position of Israel's belief about kingship. They compel a careful exegetical delineation of the area in which the high royal ideology was fostered; and in any case they forbid us to see in that ideology the central all-determining element in Israel's religion.

5. There clearly is no unanimity in the research into the problem area just sketched. A new volume of essays on Myth and Ritual, entitled *Myth, Ritual, and Kingship*, was edited by S. H. Hooke, who had been responsible for the two previous volumes, but with an altered team of contributors. As for Engnell's thesis about Divine Kingship in Israel and the assumption that belief in the deity's death and resurrection had a place in Israel's religion, that is approached most closely by Widengren in his contribution 'Early Hebrew Myths and their Interpretation'.[13] By contrast, the thesis of the suffering

---

[10] This is the present translator's own rendering of Noth's words; cf. *The Laws in the Pentateuch*, p. 171.

[11] *L'Aspect religieux de la royauté israélite*, AB iii, 1954.

[12] *Das Problem der altorientalischen Königsideologie im Alten Testament*, SVT viii, 1961.

[13] Op. cit., pp. 149–243. He had previously expounded his conception in the 1952

and dying god is very clearly rejected as far as Israel is concerned by Johnson in his contribution 'Hebrew Conceptions of Kingship'. He had previously carried out in 1955 a scrupulous analysis of the psalms which speak of Yahweh's kingship or are connected with the enthronement of the earthly king.[14] The king's sacral character and his representative function in the Jerusalem cult are maintained. However there is no talk here of divine kingship. And despite the opposition of, e.g., G. W. Ahlström[15] the caution of Johnson must be characterized as being more in accord with the statements of the Old Testament.

Ringgren, Engnell's successor in the Uppsala chair, presents the significance of the kingship in a similarly cautious way in his *Israelite Religion*.[16] He makes it incomparably more evident (and doubtless too with greater faithfulness to the text) that it is not just in the pre-Davidic period that Israel's religion is determined by traditions other than sacral kingship, but that this is still so in the period of the monarchy. That monarchy in Israel has the character of a late arrival is clearly established. The difference between an Old Testament presentation that affirms kingship and one that is critical of it (Psalms against certain parts of the narrative corpus) is taken candidly into account, and the difference in the conception of kingship in the southern and northern kingdoms is confirmed. 'Any talk of *an* Israelite royal ideology must be considered extremely questionable.'[17] It is only after carrying through these delimitations that Ringgren proceeds to collate the psalmodic assertions of the Jerusalem cult which speak of the king's high dignity, and which may bear the imprint of Egypt's royal ritual. That the king who can be described as son of God, as the anointed, as servant of Yahweh, and as the wise ruler of righteousness could also have acquired the predicate of divinity is a theory against which an emphatic question mark is set. 'It might be better

Franz Delitzsch Lectures: *Sakrales Königtum im Alten Testament und im Judentum*, Stuttgart, 1955.
[14] Op. cit., pp. 204–35, and *Sacral Kingship in Ancient Israel*, Cardiff, 1955, 2nd edn., 1967.
[15] *Psalm 89*, Lund, 1959, p. 167, n. 1.
[16] ETr, London, 1966, of *Israelitische Religion*, Stuttgart, 1963.
[17] Op. cit., p. 221.

... to avoid the term "divine kingship" and speak instead of "sacral kingship". The Israelite king is not divine, but he does have sacral duties and functions.'[18] In connection with these duties, Ringgren considers it possible that 'some kind of humiliation of the king ... followed by his restoration'[19] could have taken place. However, it is not in these elements that what is specifically Israelite consists, but in the linking of the Davidic monarchy to the covenant concept, which will be discussed later.

Over against these explanations from the Scandinavian area may be set the brief statements of Fohrer in his *History of Israelite Religion*[20] which proceeds on the basis of a reintensified literary criticism.[21] Here kingship is denied any sacral character. Perhaps the Jerusalem king is termed son of God and anointed of Yahweh. But to be 'son of God' gives him no sacral quality but only a 'portion in Yahweh's dominion, property and heritage'. The idea of divine adoption is quite inappropriate. In its presentation of the king as monarch of the world, the national-religious hope is preserving the memory of David's former empire. In addition to this, the king is further described as governor of the social order. Since for Fohrer the covenant too is not an important category for Israel's religion in the pre-Deuteronomic period,[22] he holds that there is no ground for Ringgren's assertion that in the 'Davidic covenant' there occurs in Israel's religious thinking an incorporation of the kingship into its own more ancient terminology. Nor is there any question for Fohrer in this connection of a messianic royal expectation in the pre-exilic period. However, this extremely negative estimate of the Old Testament's assertions about the king in the Psalms is incapable of doing them justice. Furthermore it does not allow sufficient recognition to the international religio-historical context in which they stand.

6. And so it must be asserted for the period under review that there has been a clear departure from the extreme theses

---

[18] Op. cit., p. 221.
[19] Ibid., p. 236.
[20] ETr, London, 1973, of *Geschichte der israelitischen Religion*, Berlin, 1969.
[21] See below, p. 377.
[22] See below, p. 378.

of kingship-patternism. However, this in no way implies for the broad sweep of religio-historical research into the Old Testament simply a return to the earlier methodology of the Wellhausen School. The beginning of the development of other forms of traditio-historical methodology had already been revealed in the review in *The Old Testament in Modern Study*. The first phase of this effort, which anticipated Mowinckel's effort, was represented in the German-speaking world by the names of Gunkel and Gressmann. In a second phase, it is the names of Alt, Noth, von Rad, Galling, Begrich, Jepsen, etc., which must be mentioned. The methodology of this other form of traditio-historical effort differs at three main points from the 'history of tradition' characterized as patternism by Engnell:

(a) This traditio-historical effort is without anti-literary-critical animus. It does not accept the dogma of Oral Tradition, against whose one-sidedness G. Widengren[23] had already expressed himself. In 1959 A. H. J. Gunneweg demonstrated for the prophetical books how oral and written tradition intermingle, and how written tradition in no way represents only a late fixation of what had at first been handed down only orally.[24] The way is thus made clear for a scrupulous literary-critical analysis of the written texts, on whose foundation traditio-historical questioning continues to build.[25]

(b) The traditio-historical question is closely linked to form-critical analysis. It often grows directly out of it. The specific contents of forms and traditions too have their specific *Sitz im Leben*. Thus in one very recent phase, redactio-historical inquiry is beginning to attain significance to an increasing extent alongside form-critical inquiry. It directs its attention to the 'post-history' of the prophetic tradition (to its achievement of literary form). It inquires after the intention of the final shape of, e.g., the prophetic book (a final shape produced ultimately by a 'redactor') and after its mental and

[23] *Literary and Psychological Aspects of the Hebrew Prophets*, UUÅ, 1948: 10.
[24] *Mündliche und schriftliche Tradition der vorexilischen Prophetenbücher als Problem der neueren Prophetenforschung*, FRLANT, N.F. lv, 1959.
[25] As early as 1932 J. Begrich had directed cautious methodical considerations to the delimitation of literary-critical and traditio-historical work in an article on 'Die Paradieserzählung', *ZAW* l (1932), 93–116 (=*GSAT*, Munich, 1964, pp. 11–38).

religio-historical *Sitz im Leben.*[26] Built into all of this is a sociological component. Specific forms, traditional matter, and literary patterns too have their roots in specific institutions and communal forms of social life whose content must be the object of inquiry.

(*c*) However, this cannot be asserted in a timeless and ahistorical manner; rather does it impel one to inquire into the historical situation and into the events which provide the background for fixation and alteration in the traditions and for their final literary formation.

Now this methodology of form-critical and traditio-historical inquiry has also been used in the approach to the phenomena of Israel's religious history, especially in the period before the establishment of the state. Alt's *Der Gott der Väter* already mentioned in *The Old Testament and Modern Study*, has had continuing significance as a classic example of such enquiry. Von Rad's clearly worked-out and influential monograph on the Holy War in ancient Israel (1951) falls in the period under review. From the frequently recurring, and in part stereo-typed, war-reports of the Old Testament there is clearly developed in this the picture of a 'cultic institution' of holy war which is presupposed in a downright pattern-like fashion in a fixed sequence. At set forms of call-up the 'people of Yahweh' gather to the war-camp which is organized in strict sacral fashion. Sacrifice is offered. A response bearing Yahweh's authority ensures that Yahweh has given the enemy into Israel's hands. The war is waged as a Yahweh War—and before it begins Israel's leader exhorts in a 'battle-address' not to fear but to trust. Courage deserts the enemy. At Israel's war-cry they are overcome by divine terror. Victory achieved, Israel dedicates the booty to Yahweh by means of the ban and is dismissed again to its tents. To the historical question posed here von Rad answers that there is no historically demonstrable case of a war waged on precisely this model with all the specified criteria. However the wars of the pre-monarchical period manifest each in a different manner individual characteristics of this kind of war. Von Rad leaves open the question too of this institution's historical

[26] Cf. e.g. J. Jeremias, *Kultprophetie und Gerichtsverkündigung in der späten Königszeit*, WMANT xxxv, 1970, or O. Kaiser, *Isaiah 13–39*, London, 1974, ETr of ATD xviii, 1973.

place of origin. It exists principally in the Israel of the period of the Judges with its 'primitive pansacrality' (Buber). The foundation on which it rests is the hypothesis of a Yahweh-amphictyony, the result of a similar traditio-historical inquiry carried out by Noth in 1930.[27] Von Rad goes on to follow up the later effects of this ancient institution on Israel's faith and literature: in the post-Solomonic composition of short stories, in the prophets' demand for faith, in Deuteronomy and in the Chronicler. In a later study, von Rad has sought to base on the Holy War too his understanding of the theologoumenon of the 'Day of Yahweh', derived by Gressman from mythology and by Mowinckel from Yahweh's Enthronement festival, as Yahweh's coming day of struggle and victory.[28] By an instance of polemical reversal, the 'Day of Yahweh' then becomes in the prophets a day of judgement. According to R. Bach, 'the summonses to flight and to fight in the Old Testament prophetic sayings'[29] are also to be interpreted by means of the elements of the Holy War.

Von Rad's thesis about the Holy War leaves in its trail all sorts of questions. Is it really a good thing to talk of a 'cultic institution' anchored to the amphictyony, when in fact the Old Testament itself nowhere vouches for the participation of all twelve tribal members, and when the connection with the sanctuary of Yahweh, the 'God of Israel', in Shechem is nowhere discernible? It is for this reason that R. Smend has demanded a sharper separation of the elements 'Yahweh War' and 'sacral tribal federation' in the tradition.[30] A distinction must accordingly be made between the tribal federation based on the central sanctuary of the amphictyony, whose life was determined by Yahweh's law (Sinai tradition) proclaimed there, and the faith of the Moses group which came out of Egypt and which for its part brought with it the element of the Yahweh War. Very recently, in an even more far-reaching attack involving Smend's thesis too, F. Stolz has sought to show that the elements portraying war that are to be found at

---

[27] Das System der zwölf Stämme Israels, BWANT iv. 1, 1930.

[28] 'The Origin of the Concept of the Day of Yahweh', JSS iv (1959), 97–108.

[29] Die Aufforderungen zur Flucht und zum Kampf im alttestamentlichen Prophetenspruch, WMANT ix, 1962.

[30] Jahwekrieg und Stämmebund, FRLANT lxxxiv, 1963; ETr, Yahweh War and Tribal Confederation, Nashville, 1970.

different places in the Old Testament in no way lead to an over-all picture of Yahweh War.[31] On the other hand, M. Weippert has collected material from Mari and from Hittite and neo-Assyrian texts which indicates the existence outside Israel of the related phenomenon of a war of the god.[32] However neither attempt is capable of disposing of the observation that in the 'Wars of Yahweh', which are referred to expressly by this name in one of the extremely infrequent quotations of the title of an early book (Num. 21:14), there comes to the surface a not unimportant element of the life of the people of Yahweh before the formation of the state. It may be the case that not every feature stressed by von Rad bears closer examination and that the characterization as 'sacral institution' fixes the whole too statically. However, one can hardly fail to perceive that in the Yahweh War we have lit upon an actual vital element of early Israelite religious history. From its further interpretation much is rendered comprehensible right down to the piety in Israel's psalmody.

As has been demonstrated here, by one example, it is fundamental to the traditio-historical method that when a 'tradition' springs up it is not just an intellectual ingredient that emerges, but also its supporting substratum in real life, Gunkel's *Sitz im Leben*. Even in his large-scale *Theologie des Alten Testaments*[33] von Rad seeks to hold to this estimate. His teacher Procksch's *Theologie des Alten Testaments*, which he published posthumously in 1950, had divided the material more or less equally between two main parts: A. The historical world, and B. The intellectual world. This divorce, influenced ultimately by idealistic thought, of an intellectual 'doctrine'[34] from its irrational historical 'substructure' von Rad would like to overcome. However much they subsequently develop their own life, the kerygmatic outlines formulated and

<hr/>

[31] *Jahweh und Israels Kriege*, ATANT lx, 1972.

[32] '"Heiliger Krieg" in Israel und Assyrien', *ZAW* lxxxiv (1972), 460–93.

[33] Vol. i, Munich, 1957; 6th edn., 1969; vol. ii, 1960; 5th edn. 1968; ETr, vol. i, Edinburgh, 1962; vol. ii, 1965.

[34] The three spheres: God and the world, God and the people, God and man, into which Procksch divided this 'intellectual world' reappear in the *Theology* of W. Eichrodt (who had also studied under Procksch), but without the introductory part on the 'historical world'. E. Sellin had characterized still more distinctly his own arrangement, related to Procksch's main parts, with his titles (1) 'History of Israelite-Jewish Religion', (2) 'Theology of the Old Testament'.

subsequently further interpreted by Israel should not be detached from their moorings in supporting 'institutions'. So it is that Procksch's 'historical part' has in von Rad's *Theology* turned into a brief introductory sketch of a 'history of faith in Yahweh and of the sacral institutions in Israel'. That is first and foremost a clearly religio-historical starting-point. What is subsequently developed in theological outlines, and what von Rad sees under the aspect of reinterpretation of historical traditions, should not be understood detached from the 'cultic institutions' which function as their original native soil. All the same, it cannot be said that in its further realization the bracketing of 'institution' and the 'tradition' deriving from it has been a completely convincing success.

The search for cultic institutions in which Mowinckel's formulation of the questions is perpetuated has remained characteristic of the investigation of particular tradition-complexes of Israel's religion. According to Kraus, the linkage of the traditions about David and Zion was fostered at a 'Royal Zion festival'. After the catastrophe of the exile in which the kingship came to an end, the royal celebration was sublimated into a celebration of the divine kingship. It finds expression in the *Yahweh-mālak*-psalms which H. J. Kraus assigns to this late phase of the history of Israel's religion.[35] H. Wildberger has followed up leads given by von Rad and Kraus and postulated the feast of Unleavened Bread, as celebrated in Gilgal in the period of the Judges with a festive procession down to the Jordan, as 'feast of Israel's Election'— its momentous festal pericope being found in Exod. 19:3–6.[36] J. N. M. Wijngaards, building further on these theses, has wanted to infer an earlier pilgrimage from Succoth to Shechem.[37] A. Weiser in turn advocated the thesis which became especially important for his exegesis of the Psalms, that behind many psalms we must recognize a covenant festival cult in which the essential core is constituted by the theophany of Yahweh. The question as to how the theophany occurred in the cult cannot receive a detailed certain answer.

[35] *Die Konigsherrschaft Gottes im Alten Testament*, Tübingen, 1951.
[36] *Jahwes Eigentumsvolk*, ATANT xxxvii, 1960.
[37] 'The Dramatization of Salvific History in the Deuteronomic Schools', *OTS* xvi, 1969.

... The theophany process was presumably accompanied by dramatic cultic actions'.[38] In this assumption he has been followed by his pupils, W. Beyerlin[39] and O. Kaiser.[40] J. Jeremias however arrives, by way of an inquiry into the theophany texts of the Old Testament which pays strict attention to the classification of types, at the assumption that the original setting of the 'theophany portrayal' type is to be looked for in victory celebrations as reflected for example in the Song of Deborah. It subsequently detached itself from this setting and penetrated into Zion hymns, into the prophetic preaching about judgement and salvation, and hymnody in a wider sense.[41] However it is above all H. Graf Reventlow who has taken up the thesis of the covenant festival cult. He has sought to make the living process of law proclamation and parenetic interpretation the basis of an understanding not just of the legal texts of the Holiness Code and the Decalogue, but similarly even of the 'prophetic office' which is supposedly apparent behind the sayings of Amos, Jeremiah, and Ezekiel.[42]

The methodical formulation of the question in all these endeavours is to be welcomed even if the capacity of the texts used seems frequently to have been unduly strained and the liveliness with which even set forms of speech may be linguistically developed often not sufficiently noted. It can, if handled with sober criticism, lead back here and there to living processes of Israel's religious life. Similarly the present author himself thought he could conjecture actual events in public worship behind Yahweh's characteristic self-introductory statements (*Selbstvorstellungsaussagen*) in the Decalogue and Holiness Code—actual events in which an officiating

---

[38] 'Zur Frage nach den Beziehungen der Psalmen zum Kult: Die Darstellung der Theophanie in den Psalmen und im Festkult', *Festschrift A. Bertholet*, Tübingen, 1950, pp. 513–31.

[39] *Herkunft und Geschichte der ältesten Sinaitraditionen*, Tübingen, 1961; ETr, *Origins and History of the Oldest Sinaitic Traditions*, Oxford, 1965.

[40] 'Traditionsgeschichtliche Untersuchung von Gen. 15', *ZAW* lxx, (1958), 107–26.

[41] *Theophanie, Die Geschichte einer alttestamentlichen Gattung*, WMANT x, 1965.

[42] *Das Heiligkeitsgesestz*, WMANT vi, 1961; *Gebot und Predigt im Dekalog*, Gütersloh, 1962; *Das Amt des Propheten bei Amos*, FRLANT lxxx, 1962; *Liturgie und prophetisches Ich bei Jeremia*, Gütersloh, 1963; *Wächter über Israel. Ezechiel und seine Tradition*, BZAW lxxxii, 1962.

spokesman spoke with full authority for Yahweh. The prophetic 'demonstration word' (*Erweiswort*) includes this statement by Yahweh of self-introduction in a fuller 'cognition formula' (*Erkenntnisformel*) to become the medium of the prophet's proclamation of law and salvation, a proclamation detached from the cult. So then, in this secondary utilization of the self-introduction by Yahweh, which had at first been bound to the cult, there is made plain the specific characteristic of Israel's religion, that Yahweh makes himself manifest to his people not only in the cult but amidst historical experience of judgement and deliverance.[43]

7. In the period under review there stands beside those studies of Israel's early traditions which direct their attention at one and the same time to their *Sitz im Leben* and the institutions that support them the profusion of further researches which deal exclusively with the contents of the traditions. The work by E. Rohland from the school of von Rad on the significance of Israel's election traditions for the eschatology of the Old Testament prophets[44] may be selected as an example of these. It examines the three great strands of tradition: the traditions about Exodus, Zion, and David. It maintains that Israel's eschatological expectation cannot be attributed to one single self-contained conceptual complex. It was just this that Gressmann (mythical change of epochs) and Mowinckel (experience of the Enthronement festival) had attempted to show each in his own particular way. Rather the individual prophets each lived in different circles of tradition: Isaiah in those of David and Zion, Hosea in that of the Exodus. However, their statements about the future *are* linked in this, that each in its own way announces 'that the election existing hitherto must be annulled, but then renewed and fulfilled'.[45] Von Rad has adopted the idea in his *Theology*

---

[43] W. Zimmerli, 'Ich bin Jahwe', *Geschichte und Altes Testament. Festschrift für A. Alt*, Leipzig, 1953, pp. 179–209; *Erkenntnis Gottes nach dem Buche Ezechiel*, ATANT xxvii, 1954; 'Das Wort des göttlichen Selbsterweises(Erweiswort), eine prophetische Gattung', *Mélanges bibliques rédigés en l'honneur de André Robert*, Paris, 1957, pp. 154–64 (= *Gottes Offenbarung*, Munich, 1963; 2nd edn., 1969, pp. 11–40; 41–119; 120–132).

[44] *Die Bedeutung der Erwählungstraditionen Israels für die Eschatologie der alttestamentlichen Propheten*, Diss., Heidelberg, 1956.

[45] Op. cit., p. 269.

and used it to produce a novel definition of prophetic eschatology. 'It was when Israel was expelled by her prophets from the sanctuary of the hitherto existing facts, and when the basis of her salvation was suddenly shifted to a future divine action and only then that the prophetic preaching became eschatological.'[46] Here, in a context of resolutely traditio-historical scrutiny, eschatology is defined wholly by the formal phenomenon of the break in the tradition. This break is established similarly for each of the three great strands of tradition dealt with by Rohland. It must be asked of this traditio-historical point of view whether it would not be more correct to start with what is fundamental to Israel's faith in Yahweh, Yahweh's personal relation with Israel. The specifically prophetic 'eschatology' is to be understood from the tension between Yahweh's jealous holiness and constancy as he leads Israel on the way to the future. Th. C. Vriezen has attempted to regulate the ambiguity of the concept 'eschatology' by a sharper differentiation of the different understandings of eschatology. He distinguishes between 1. a pre-eschatological phase before classical prophecy, which is most clearly evidenced by Am. 5:18; 2. a proto-eschatological phase discernible in Isaiah and his prophetic contemporaries; 3. a 'topically' eschatological (*aktuell-eschatologische*) phase in Deutero-Isaiah who believes that the definitive intervention of Yahweh is being realized in his own days; and 4. a transcendentalizing phase in apocalyptic which reckons in dualistic manner with the discontinuance of the present godless world, which perishes in a catastrophe, and the definitive breakthrough of the kingdom of God and a new world.[47]

The three strands of tradition examined by Rohland have each experienced their own independent revision. H. Lubscyk has studied the Exodus tradition in the prophets.[48] N. Poulssen has followed up the link between David and Temple

---

[46] Op. cit., cf. ETr ii. 118, where a slightly different rendering of von Rad's words is given.

[47] 'Prophecy and Eschatology', *Congress Volume, Copenhagen 1953*, SVT i. (1953), pp. 199–229.

[48] *Der Auszug Israels aus Aegypten. Seine theologische Bedeutung in prophetischer und priesterlicher Ueberlieferung*, Erfurt, 1963.

in a study which is certainly more than just traditio-historical.[49] The Exodus and the David traditions clearly take their departure from within the compass of events in Israel's history or in the early history of that part of the later Israel which came out of Egypt. By contrast, the Zion/Jerusalem tradition is of a distinct kind. It was only late that Jerusalem became an Israelite city. It imported with it, as is becoming ever clearer, pre-Israelite traditional material. To this pre-Israelite material belongs the recollection of its pre-Davidic kingship. In King Melchizedek of Salem, the 'priest of '*ēl* '*elyôn*' (Gen. 14:18, 20) there is unmistakably preserved the dual recollection of Jerusalem's pre-Israelite traditions of god and king. Its penetration is likely to have been via the originally Jebusite Zadok, raised by David to be priest of Yahweh, whose antecedents have also been further discussed in the period under review.

It is understandable that in the context of traditio-historical research a special interest was swiftly directed to this element of Israel's faith. Where kingship on Zion was under discussion bridges could be thrown over to the studies on sacral kingship, whose traditional material became linked to Zion together with that of the Davidic line.[50] Here discussion turned in particular on the elements contained in the Zion psalms of the assault by the nations on the mountain of God and of its invulnerability, which are apparently also reflected in Isaiah's preaching about Zion. H. M. Lutz has investigated these traditions on the basis of Zech. 12:1–8; 14:1–5;[51] while F. Stolz began by placing the material to be gained from the information in the Old Testament in a wide religio-historical context.[52]

8. It becomes particularly clear here that traditio-historical

---

[49] *König und Tempel im Glaubenszeugnis des Alten Testamentes*, Stuttgart, 1967.

[50] Schmid undertook a classification of Jerusalem's cult-traditions in *ZAW* lxvii (1955), 168–205. Vriezen wrote in 1962 on Yahweh and his city, and Schreiner in 1963 wrote on Zion–Jerusalem, Yahweh's royal seat.

[51] *Jahwe, Jerusalem und die Völker*, WMANT xxvii, 1968, rejecting G. Wanke's study, originating in Fohrer's school, *Die Zionstheologie der Korachiten*, BZAW xcvii, 1966, which pleads for a late origin for 'Zion Theology', in particular one subsequent to Ezekiel.

[52] *Strukturen und Figuren im Kult von Jerusalem, Studien zur altorientalischen vor- und frühisraelitischen Religion*, BZAW cxviii, 1970.

work cannot forgo a glance at the surrounding world. That had certainly been fully realized in the previous phase of research too. Jerusalem, as is made very obvious by Gen. 14:18–20, is an especially clearly recognizable entry point for the invasion of traditions from the Canaanite environment. It was certainly not the only one.

Thus the more recent traditio-historical work too has been intensively concerned with those traditions of Israel which (by contrast with these of Exodus, Sinai, and David) have to be understood against their environment. In the period in which this review was being produced there was again made available additional rich material. Gunkel's *Schöpfung und Chaos in Urzeit und Endzeit* had adduced the comparative material from the high cultures of Mesopotamia; and the Myth and Ritual and the Uppsala schools also made rich contributions in this area. Unless I am mistaken, there has been something of a retreat from this in subsequent traditio-historical research. It has certainly been recently shown by H. Gese how strongly Israel's idea of primal time is determined by the Mesopotamian idea of history.[53] Lambert and Millard in their *Atra-ḥasīs*, Oxford, 1969, have produced material, some of it previously unknown, about the earliest history of gods and men and about the great flood. Particularly in the realm of Sumerian-Babylonian wisdom, much new material has become known. None of this occupied the foreground of research into the history of Israel's religion.

More important for this was knowledge of the great royal archives of Mari.[54] Related forms of nomenclature, a special form of covenant-making (to which we must return in a later connection), etc., have forced open the question of their relationship to Israel's patriarchal traditions.[55] Most of all, the phenomenon of spontaneously delivered divine decisions has led to the question whether we are not confronted here with a 'prototype' (*Vorform*) of prophecy in Israel. Since

[53] 'Geschichtliches Denken im Alten Orient und im Alten Testament', *ZThK* lv, (1958), 127–45.
[54] In 1950 there appeared the first three volumes of the French translation of texts from the royal archives of Mari, which have been followed in the ensuing years by many others.
[55] Cf. e.g. M. Noth, *Die Ursprünge des alten Israel im Lichte neuer Quellen*, Cologne, 1961.

prophecy is dealt with in this volume by a special contribution, closer detail cannot be entered into here.

Where comparison has been made with Egyptian material, the phenomenon of wisdom too has been of moment in the period under review. This is also the subject of a special contribution in this volume. K. Koch has shown[56] by reference to the 'monument of Memphitic theology' that Egyptian influence could also be present in the account of creation in Gen. 1, even in its central assertion about creation by means of the word.

However, the phenomenon of Canaanite religion, with its more obvious relevance to Israel, has excited disproportionately greater interest in the period under review. Pope, Kapelrud, Gese, Gray, and others have published monographs investigating the individual figures of the Ugaritic pantheon with ever clearer results. Here, too, there has certainly been an ebbing of the first wave of enthusiasm in which the religion of Ugarit was summarily claimed as the religion of Canaan, and each epic text as a cultic text. It has been more soberly recognized that in Ugarit, Hurrian and Mediterranean influences have also to be reckoned with; and the texts have been more scrupulously investigated as to their cultic relevance. But even after these limitations there remains a broad area of comparison between Israel's religious traditions and those of Ugarit.

Significant are the shifts which resulted in the picture of belief in El. While Alt in his confrontation of the 'God of the Fathers' with Canaanite deity worship had still understood the different El-deities mentioned in Genesis to be local deities with a restricted sphere of influence, El now became ever more clearly recognizable as universal high god and lord of an extended pantheon. This specifically titled El of particular sanctuaries in Canaan turned out, when seen from this angle, to be a local manifestation of the one lofty, great god. There appeared alongside the examinations of El in the Ugaritic context the comparative studies which sought to evaluate from the newly established point of view the El-

---

predications of Yahweh.[57] The question posed here was the following: In statements such as, e.g., Deut. 32:8 or Ps. 82, is Yahweh (who must have been referred to in the latter passage instead of the *ᵉlōhîm* of the Elohistic Psalter) to be understood as a figure in the pantheon still distinct from El or the 'Highest'? Or have the deities of 'El's Assembly' been reduced to figures serving Yahweh? Given the knowledge of the 'jealousy of Yahweh', the second view enjoys the greater probability. It is from El that Yahweh assumes the royal title.[58] From him he comes to be regarded as 'creator of heaven and earth' (Gen. 14:22).[59] In him he becomes (transcending whatever may already have been stated of El in pre-Israelite Jerusalem as god of 'prime movement and chaos struggle'[60]) the God, at once distant and near, of creation and of history.

A radical shift would take place in the picture of the beginnings of the history of the religion of Israel were F. M. Cross's thesis correct that we should view even the early belief in Yahweh before Israel's settlement in Canaan as after all within the scope of belief in El. For him the chief argument for the understanding which is then necessary of the God of the Fathers as a manifestation of El lies in the observation that to the 'God of the Fathers' of the earlier tradition (Exod. 3) there corresponds the '*ēl šadday* in the Priestly Document (Exod. 6; cf. Gen. 17). Then Yahweh's dwelling place on Mount Sinai can be linked with El's dwelling on the divine mountain, and the phenomenon of Yahweh as the Divine Warrior with the warlike traits of Baal belief.[61] The thesis is presented with ingenuity; however, its argumentation does not as yet appear to me to be compelling, and without any doubt it still requires intensive discussion. Moreover, its

[57] O. Eissfeldt, 'El and Yahweh', *JSS* i (1956), 25–37; R. Rendtorff, 'El, Ba'al und Jahwe. Erwägungen zum Verhältnis von kanaanäischer und israelitischer Religion', *ZAW* lxxviii (1966), 277–92.

[58] A. Alt, 'Gedanken über das Königtum Jahwes', *KS* i (Munich, 1953), 345–57; W. Schmidt, *Königtum Gottes in Ugarit und Israel*, BZAW lxxxvi, 1961, 2nd edn., 1966.

[59] W. Zimmerli, 'Abraham und Melchisedek', *Das ferne und nahe Wort*, BZAW cv (1967), pp. 255–64.

[60] Stolz, op. cit., pp. 149–80.

[61] *Canaanite Myth and Hebrew Epic. Essays in the History of the Religion of Israel*, Cambridge, Mass., and Oxford, 1973.

evaluation rests largely on the literary-critical estimate of texts such as the Song of Moses, Exod. 15:1b–18, or the Priestly Document. Amongst the Ugaritic texts there is myth of Šaḥar and Šalim. This has prompted the question whether we are not to recognize in the name Jerusalem the tradition of a god Šalim. Albright wanted to understand the name as 'Šalim's foundation'.[62] Stolz explains it as 'Šalim gives instruction'.[63] Steck has raised the question whether the Old Testament conceptions of 'peace' (*šālôm*) do not direct religio-historical attention to 'Jebusite-Jerusalemite backgrounds'.[64] In Ps. 85:9 f. and Isa. 60:17 we also find linked with *šālôm* (and both of them almost personified) *ṣedeḳ*, 'the power of wholesomely righteous world-order' (Schmid). Given the evidence of the name *malkîṣedeḳ* (and *ʾadōnîṣedeḳ*, Josh.10:1, 3), a god (of ancient Jerusalem?) may also be detected in *ṣedeḳ*. This results in our asking whether the unusually strong emphasis given in Israel's faith to the concept *ṣedeḳ*/*ṣᵉdāḳâh* in both cultic (von Rad, Koch) and wisdom spheres is to be understood on this basis. In his comprehensive exposition of 'righteousness as world-order',[65] H. H. Schmid has sought to understand the Old Testament usage of 'righteousness' against a horizon of meaning available to the religion of Israel, some aspects being given particular prominence and others subordinated. As he does this, the problem posed to research in the history of religion by traditio-historical methodology appears with particular clarity. Research into the religion of Israel cannot just be a matter of establishing by diachronic observation the outside influences and the religio-historical material available to Israel. On the contrary, it is necessary to test synchronically just how what is exclusively Israelite is presented in any given contemporary manifestation, whether by adaptation or rejection of what it encounters. In El (Šalim, *ṣedeḳ*) Israel's faith encountered a deity whose attributes it could claim, with the name El itself, to effect a fuller description of its God, Yahweh, and in such a way that the independent deity El

---

[62] *JPOS* viii (1928), 248.
[63] Op. cit., p. 182.
[64] *Friedensvorstellungen im alten Jerusalem*, ThS cxi, 1972.
[65] *Gerechtigkeit als Weltordnung*, Tübingen, 1968.

with his mythical divine relationships in the Canaanite pantheon would be completely submerged. The challenge by the El faith led to the response in which Yahweh was able to articulate in a new context with universal comprehensiveness, his claim to be creator and king, with the aid of the attributes of El.

Quite different is the challenge of belief in Baal, whom Israel encountered in the Canaanite pantheon in just the same way. The final result here is an unequivocal polemical rejection of the name and basic characteristics of Baal. The same holds good for Anat, who was important in Ugarit as consort of Baal, and whose significance for pre-Israelite Canaan is unequivocally demonstrated by place names like Anathoth and Beth Anath. That the temptation of an association with Yahweh did exist here too can be verified from earlier proper names (Bealiah, Ishbaal, etc.), and in the later period from the circumstances in the Temple of Yahweh at Elephantine. All other female deities, too, with their symbols fell victim to this law of rejection. Being a deity of procreative male sexual power, linked with the seasons of growth and with fertility, and as such worshipped in its sexual specificity, Baal could enter no relationship with Israel's Yahweh. Nor could the cycles of dying and rising again that corresponded to nature's annual course, already discussed in the context of the patternism of the previous phase of research, find any lasting place in Israel's Yahweh-religion.

9. In the El and the Baal concept, which proved so lively in the discussion of the prehistory of Israel's religion through the discovery of texts from the surrounding world, we were dealing with elements whose antecedents in Canaanite religion were already quite familiar. By contrast Eichrodt in his *Theology*, for example, saw what was peculiar to the religion of Israel in the covenant concept which stood under an incomparably stronger influence from history.[66] Even in his presentation of the history of Israel's religion, Eichrodt

---

[66] J. Barr, *Old and New in Interpretation*, London, 1966, pp. 65–102, and B. Albrektson, *History and the Gods. An Essay on the Idea of Historical Events as Divine Manifestations in the Ancient Near East and in Israel*, Lund, 1967, had turned with different argumentation against an abrupt antithesis of historical religion (Israel) and nature religion (the religions of the surrounding world).

described Yahweh as the covenant God and Israel as the covenant people.[67] During the period under review, this notion of covenant, seemingly most exclusively Israelite, has been illuminated in a new way in traditio-historical discussion by phenomena from Israel's environment, and has been interpreted in terms of its intrinsic content.

While Pedersen in 1914 had described the covenant, comparing it with the Arabic 'ahd and ḥilf, 'as the bilateral relationship of solidarity with all rights and duties implied by this relationship'[68] Begrich in his last essay in 1944 advocated the thesis that Israel as she immigrated had understood the 'covenant' as a gift accorded unilaterally by a stronger party to a weaker. It was only when she had settled in the land that the idea of covenant then turned, under the influence of the Canaanite idea of treaty, into an idea of a partnership arranged subject to conditions.[69] Then in 1955 Noth made reference to a Mari-text in which an emissary of the king arranged a peace between two warring tribes by means of an obviously well-defined ritual of 'ass-killing'. In so doing he went beyond Begrich and substantiated a type of covenant-making in which a third party mediated the covenant between two partners; his aim accordingly is to understand Josh. 24:25, for example, as Joshua's covenant mediation between Yahweh and Israel.[70]

Then there has been inaugurated a wide-ranging discussion about the understanding of Yahweh's covenant with Israel and the light which it sheds on the Old Testament's religious assertions. Of primary importance here is the adducing of the suzerainty treaties of the Hittite kings with their vassals. The texts of these treaties were published as early as 1923 by Weidner, and 1926 by Friedrich, and they were analysed in 1931 by the lawyer Korošec; but at first, apart from a casual mention by Hempel, they found no echo amongst Old Testament scholars. The real discussion was inaugurated by Mendenhall,[71] and in German by Baltzer's form-critical

[67] *Religionsgeschichte Israels*, Berne and Munich, 1969.
[68] *Der Eid bei den Semiten*, Strassburg, 1914, pp. 33 f.; cf. p. 8.
[69] 'berit', *ZAW* lx (1944), 1–11 = *GSAT*, Munich, 1964, pp. 55–66.
[70] 'Old Testament Covenant-making in the Light of a Text from Mari', *The Laws in the Pentateuch*, pp. 108–17.
[71] 'Covenant Forms in Israelite Tradition', *BA* xvii (1954), 50–76.

monograph.[72] Mendenhall assigns far-reaching significance to the form of treaty-covenant which he elaborated. 'Innumerable incidents and ideas in the entire history of Israel can be adequately understood only from this complex of covenant patterns of thought.' This assumption has not proved false. It is no exaggeration to speak of a new wave of patternism which deluged Old Testament studies in the following decade. Just as in a previous phase the royal pattern, defined by the ancient oriental environment, was regarded as the key to the explanation of most phenomena in the history of Israel's religion, so now the attempt was being made to unlock the assertions of the Old Testament by means of the key of the pattern won from the Hittite vassal treaties. While in the case of the kingship ideology an ahistorical mythical pattern was involved, here what was in question was a complex closely related to history. 'Covenant' is fundamentally a historico-political phenomenon. However at the same time it is a key-word of Israelite faith. Here, too, historical questions are directly linked with religio-historical ones.

Mendenhall finds in the Old Testament two passages which correspond to the type of covenant recognizable in the Hittite treaties: the Decalogue, in which he sees the document of the Mosaic covenant-making; and elements of the report of Joshua's assembly at Shechem in Josh. 24. According to Korošec's analysis, the full covenant formulary comprises six elements: (1) a preamble in which the sovereign (suzerain) who is making the treaty with the semi-independent vassals gives his name; (2) the particularly characteristic element of a historical preamble which delineates the history prior to the treaty and in particular underlines the overlord's benevolence towards his vassal; (3) the stipulations, i.e. the actual duties imposed on the vassal; (4) the regulation that the covenant document should be deposited in the sanctuary and read out at regular intervals; (5) the list of gods who are witnesses to the treaty; and (6) curse and blessing formulations. In both Exod. 20 and Josh. 24, only some of these elements are to be found. Baltzer, whose work has a one-sidedly form-critical orientation, claims to be able to isolate a 'declaration of

[72] *Das Bundesformular*, WMANT iv, 1960; ETr, *The Covenant Formulary*, Oxford, 1971.

principle' too, after the historical prologue and before the stipulations, which maintains the exclusive relationship of the vassal to his overlord. He is silent about the Decalogue, but seeks to show how Josh. 24, the Sinai pericope, and Deuteronomy are influenced by the covenant formulary, which remains of consequence right down to the Qumran and early Christian texts.

The theses about the covenant formulary were advanced against a background of earlier postulates about the existence of a Covenant or Covenant-renewal festival. Mowinckel had incorporated these perspectives into his festival of Yahweh's Enthronement. In his examination of the origins of Israelite law, and on the basis of Deut. 31:9 ff., Alt had arrived at the assumption of a regular festival of Law-recital with a view to covenant-renewal; and von Rad had adopted this in his analysis of the Sinai traditions. Weiser's assumption about a representation of a theophany in the covenant-renewal festival was discussed above.

The studies of Mendenhall and Baltzer were followed by the broad debate whether the 'covenant formulary' did influence the ritual of the historical concluding of covenants and of the celebrations of covenant-renewal which had possibly been influenced by them.[73] Written prophecy, which in its curse-oracles is reminiscent of the formulations of covenant curses, poses a special problem here.[74] In its *rîb* pattern, in which heaven and earth are called as witnesses, it appears to carry out the procedural action for a covenant infringement.[75] Moran tried to go further and demonstrate that the demand in Hosea and Deuteronomy to love God, and also the talk about what is 'good' (*tôḇ*) is influenced by the

[73] D. J. McCarthy, who had studied the question independently in his dissertation *Treaty and Covenant*, AB xxi, 1963, recently reported on the course of the debate in *Old Testament Covenant. A Survey of Current Opinions*, Oxford, 1973.

[74] D. R. Hillers, *Treaty-Curses and the Old Testament Prophets*, Rome, 1964; F. C. Fensham, 'Common Trends in Curses of the Near Eastern Treaties and kudurru-Inscriptions compared with Maledictions of Amos and Isaiah', *ZAW* lxxv (1963), 155–75.

[75] J. Harvey, 'Le "rîb-Pattern", réquisitoire prophétique sur la rupture de l'alliance', *Bibl.* xliii (1962), 172–96; H. B. Huffmon, 'The Covenant Lawsuit and the Prophets', *JBL* lxxviii (1959), 286–95; G. E. Wright, 'The Lawsuit of God. A Formcritical Study of Deut. 32', in *Israel's Prophetic Heritage*, ed. B. W. Anderson and W. Harrelson, New York, 1962.

covenant formulary.[76] J. L'Hour has understood the whole ethic of the Old Testament from the covenant.[77] However in the earlier pre-exilic canonical prophets (with the exception of Hosea?) express mention of the *berît* is avoided to a remarkable degree.

The course of the lively debate about these theses has demonstrated three points with some clarity: (a) There is no question of linking directly to the covenant formulary each and every mention of a *berît* whose character is theological; and in addition to these there is a series of references to covenant conclusions between man and man which have no need to be mentioned in the context of this religio-historical inquiry. Alongside the type of the covenant that is linked with demands and which appears in the Sinai–Horeb reports there stands the type of covenant of pure bestowal linked with promises which we must assume for the patriarchal period and possibly for David. The distinction drawn by Begrich is coming into play again in a somewhat modified form. Of course Gerstenberger has made the attempt to separate completely covenant and command in the first instance too.[78] De Vaux, on the other hand, was of the opinion that David, as 'servant' of Yahweh, had to be seen in the position of the vassal in the 'treaty' relationship, and the Davidic covenant had to be understood as a conditional one.[79] (b) It is in Deuteronomy that the closest approximation to the covenant formulary can be unmistakably recognized. R. Smend's demonstration in a meticulous study of the 'covenant formula' (not to be confused with 'covenant formulary') must also be mentioned here: that the bilateral covenant formula 'I am your God and you are my people' is first to be found with certainty in the context of Deuteronomism (though possibly already in Hos. 1:9?). It is in Deut. 26:16–19 that he finds the reference to the actual proclamation of the covenant.[80] (c) G. M. Tucker in turn has shown that in Israel's

[76] W. L. Moran, 'The Ancient Near Eastern Background of the Love of God in Dt.', *CBQ* xxv (1963), 77–87.

[77] *La Morale de l'alliance*, Paris, 1966.

[78] 'Covenant and Commandment', *JBL* lxxiv (1965), 38–51.

[79] R. de Vaux, 'Le roi d'Israel, vassal de Yahwé', *Mélanges Eugène Tisserant*, Rome, 1964, pp. 119–33. ETr in *The Bible and the Ancient Near East*, London, 1972.

[80] *Die Bundesformel*, ThS lxviii, 1963.

environment too a clear distinction must be made between private contract and international treaty, it being only for the latter that the oath is constitutive.[81]

10. In the course of this discussion there have not been lacking energetic denials of the existence of a 'covenant formulary'. It was from different positions that this arose.

F. Nötscher in particular has objected in a vehement critique, provocatively entitled 'Covenant formulary and red tape'[82] that the thesis about the covenant formulary overestimates the power of the 'simile' and underestimates the possibility of the independent origin of a form because of analogous needs in different places. In several articles E. Kutsch has attacked the covenant thesis at its etymological base by the thesis that $b^e r \hat{\imath} \underline{t}$ does not mean 'covenant' at all but rather 'obligation'.[83]

It has already been mentioned that the thesis about the covenant formulary has an intrinsically close link with particular historical views. It was the view of history founded on literary criticism which was the main cause of its being queried. The period under review, that is to say, provides evidence of an undeniable new advance in work using the analyses of literary criticism, alongside the dominance of form-critical and type-historical and traditio-historical methodology. This was practised not only in the realm of Protestant but also to a not inconsiderable extent in the realm of Catholic Old Testament research. The renewed application to literary criticism was obviously influenced in part by a hypertrophy of formcritical and type-historical inquiry. This had disregarded the connection with literary-critical, literary-historical, and historical inquiry closely maintained in its beginnings by Alt and Noth. Studies of form, type, and tradition which came to concern themselves intensively with minute details (Noth once spoke with gentle scorn of 'formula-criticism'— *Formelgeschichte*) threatened in so doing to become completely ahistorical. The contrary demand was made more and more loudly heard that the careful literary-critical examination of

---

[81] 'Covenant Forms and Contract Forms', *VT* xv (1965), 487–503.

[82] 'Bundesformular und "'Amtsschimmel'"', *BZ* ix (1965), 182–214.

[83] *Verheissung und Gesetz*, BZAW cxxxi, 1973, offers something of a recapitulation of the different articles.

a text must be carried out to the last detail before traditio-historical work can be done. 'Exegesis as Study of Literature' is the title of a programmatic study published by W. Richter in 1971, bearing the sub-title 'Sketch of an Old Testament Theory of Literature and Methodology'.[84] This study, which is obviously closely allied to a structuralist methodology of textual analysis, presses most trenchantly for the primacy of the literary analysis of the written text. It seems to me that it is not as yet evident how far structuralist linguistics (which has only very recently found favour as a method) can produce results for the history of Israel's religion.

It was from Fohrer in 1966 that the protest came against the assumption that Israel's religion since its origins was based on a 'covenant' with Yahweh annually renewed in an annual covenant festival at the amphictyonic centre.[85] He rejects the assumption that an amphictyony held together at an amphictyonic centre by common worship of Yahweh was the form of tribal union in the period before the foundation of the state. According to him, the twelvefold grouping consists simply in a genealogical list already ossified in the period of the Judges. It served to establish relationships of descent and kinship, and has nothing to do with the religion of Israel. For all that, the pre-Yahwistic and early Yahwistic period is familiar with the *berît* concept. But the historical event that established the link between Yahweh and the people led by Moses must not be interpreted by means of a covenant formulary. What emerged was simply a connection 'in the sense of a continuing association of a nomadic kind', i.e. a kind of 'kin-relationship in which the people led by Moses counts as *ʿam Yahweh*'. The term *berît*, however, recedes subsequently, and becomes a theologoumenon of Israel only in the Deuteronomic period. It was in this period, too, that the Decalogue was produced.

Whereas Fohrer admits the maintenance of a *berît* concept in the period of Moses, though at first it had no influence on

---

[84] *Exegese als Literaturwissenschaft: Entwurf einer alttestamentliche Literaturtheorie und Methodologie*, Göttingen, 1971.

[85] G. Fohrer, 'Altes Testament—"Amphiktyonie" und "Bund"' *ThLZ* xci (1966), 801–16, 893–904 = *Studien zur alttestamentlichen Theologie und Geschichte (1949–1966)*, BZAW 115, 1969, pp. 84–119.

the subsequent religion of Israel, L. Perlitt raises objections to this too.[86] Every mention of a *bᵉrît* in the Sinai accounts of the earlier sources is eliminated by incisive literary-critical procedures. The account of Yahweh's *bᵉrît* with Abraham in Gen. 15 in its present form is an early Deuteronomic document and to be dated at the beginning of the seventh century. While the earlier tradition had spoken simply of the promise of the land to Abraham (Gen. 12, J), there is now talk (in view of the menacing possibility after the collapse of the Northern Kingdom that the land would be lost) of an oath reinforced by a solemn *bᵉrît* ritual.[87] Once Josiah, in the Deuteronomic reform according to 2 Kgs. 23:1–3, has made the code of Deuteronomy into a 'covenant code' for the community, the further component of obligation enters into the understanding of covenant, limiting its reality in a conditional way. It is by this route that we arrive at the 'Janus-concept, *bᵉrît*, which means both the dependability of Yahweh and the unique deliverance that depends on Yahweh.'[88]

The picture of Israelite religious history is brought back into close approximation to Wellhausen's view by Perlitt who, in 1965, had published an impressive dissertation on Vatke and Wellhausen. For Perlitt, what stands at the beginning is a Sinai event which, according to the tradition, grounds 'a relationship' between Yahweh and Israel on a theophany and a subsequent vision of God by the elders as representatives of Israel, a relationship in which God is the grantor and men are the grantees ... Whoever uses the word 'covenant', in whatever sense, in face of these scenes ruins them.[89] This initial relationship is experienced without any word and, more important, without any command. Then, in the period of Judah's crisis, and significantly not without prophetic influence, it becomes a *bᵉrît* relationship, in which command does begin to play a part alongside promise pledged under oath. The Decalogue, too, is a product of this Deuteronomic period.

[86] *Bundestheologie im Alten Testament*, WMANT xxxvi, 1969.
[87] N. Lohfink, *Die Landverheissung als Eid. Eine Studie zu Gen. 15*, Stuttgart, 1967. For the rest he maintains a distance from Perlitt's theses.
[88] Perlitt, op. cit., p. 280.
[89] Ibid., p. 186.

This examination operates with shrewd literary criticism and makes irrefutably clear the weight which the *bᵉrît* concept possesses in the context of Deuteronomic theology. At the same time it is a critical warning to the traditio-historical method of operation that it should not too readily evade by means of traditio-historical surmises questions posed by literary criticism. Yet on the other hand, its pan-Deuteronomic attitude (of which Perlitt is not the only exponent at present),⁹⁰ fails to carry conviction, in the analysis of important passages like Gen. 15; Exod. 24; 34; and Josh. 24. While the disavowal of a traditio-historical methodology no longer conscious of its limits is justified, the genuine force of enduring traditions, which may be able to retain their efficacy even in later linguistic and stylistic dress, is underrated. To shift all theological creativity regarding the assertion of a *bᵉrît* into the single century in which *bᵉrît* demonstrably played a large part represents an unmistakable shortening of the perspective. In this connection the urgent challenge is raised once again to develop criteria more keenly differentiated for the phenomenon of 'Deuteronomism', which certainly did not fall suddenly complete from heaven. A keener appreciation of this so dimly comprehended phenomenon and of its prehistory is an urgent necessity for a proper grasp of the religion of Israel in particular, in which this phenomenon occupies a position of the highest importance.

11. It is principally from the point of view of their methods of operation that this examination has been carried out, in the expositions offered, of the research on the religion of Israel from 1951 to 1973. As was demonstrated in the final exposition of *bᵉrît*, research has not achieved unanimous opinions about the course of the history of Israel's religion. There are yawning chasms between opinions on fundamental points.

It is clear that three principal streams concurred in the faith of early Israel after its settlement: The faith of the people led by Moses, who came out of Egypt and imported the exciting proclamation of Yahweh as the deliverer from

⁹⁰ In a rather different manner S. Herrmann, 'Die konstruktive Restauration. Das Deuteronomium als Mitte biblischer Theologie', *Festschrift G. von Rad*, 1971, pp. 155–70; and also *Die prophetischen Heilserwartungen im Alten Testament*, BWANT v. 5, 1965.

Egyptian bondage. Fohrer speaks here of the first impulse in Israel's religious history. In the land it encountered the Canaanite El-pantheon. However, in the faith of the related tribes which had made an earlier entry, this had already amalgamated at certain points with the belief in the God of the fathers. According to Cross, this had already occurred in the pre-settlement period.[91] In the challenge of encounter with this religious heritage, belief in Yahweh gained from belief in the God of the fathers knowledge of the anticipatory promise to the fathers and consolidated its knowledge about Yahweh's going with his people on their way. However, in the confrontation with the elements of the Canaanite belief in El, Yahweh laid claim to be universal Creator and King. Doubtless, even if in Josh. 24 a recollection has been preserved of situations of decision, it was not in one fell swoop that all this happened, but in a rather long process of religious confrontation. The monarchy, which Fohrer terms the second impulse, and all that that imported in terms of further Canaanite tradition, had a not insignificant share in this. The crisis over the ultimate rejection of the interpretation of Yahweh as Baal ensued only in the early prophetic period. In this it is true that Yahweh took over elements from the victory over the chaotic sea (the Baal–Yam struggle); but he also differentiated himself sharply from the belief in dying and reviving, and also in the cultic marriage of the vegetation god. Fohrer finds the third impulse in the emergence of the prophets, derivable from no traditionally available material, in the period of ultimate threat to the people's existence from the imperial power in the east. This made it possible for Israel to deduce that even its political collapse was the work of its God and in such knowledge to hope for new life in the future. The Deuteronomic theology, in which Fohrer finds the fourth impulse, contributed to this in its own way with its central assertion of the *berît*. It is not likely that the beginnings of eschatological expectation cannot be linked with anything earlier than exilic prophecy, as Fohrer, who sees here the fifth impulse, would have it. What is clear is that post-exilic prophecy leads on to the fully developed apocalyptic which

[91] Cf. above, p. 370, n. 61.

keeps knowledge of the way and of the future awake in the period when Israel/Judah, now without a king, is fashioning its new shape around the rebuilt Temple in a cultic community committed to Yahweh's command.

What the people led by Moses brought with them into the land over and above their confession of Yahweh (Tent, Ark, Sabbath, Yahweh-war, Commandments of Yahweh) has remained a matter of controversy in the period under review. There has been renewed strife about whether Israel amalgamated in the land in a sacral confederacy (amphictyony) and whether it was familiar with a regular proclamation of law at a sacral sanctuary. There is not even any unanimous answer to the question of what sacral significance the king had and how much traditional material was imported by Jerusalem–Zion into the faith of at least the Southern Kingdom (assault of the peoples, preservation of the city of God, mountain of God, region of paradise). There remain divergent views about the importance of the cult, and about how close the great canonical prophets are to the cult, about the range of so-called Deuteronomism, and about the influence of wisdom on the developing apocalyptic of the post-exilic period.

The phase of research now behind us has been determined in exceptional fashion in its study of the content of the religion of Israel by the interrogation of the traditions. Israel's environment, too, has been implicated in this interrogation to a large extent. This has involved a displacement of the themes which held a central position. The discussion of the sacral king has made a considerable retreat before the discussion of the covenant and the newly posed form of the 'Deuteronomic question'.[92] It may be that the traditio-historical method has reached certain limits beyond which profitable inquiry cannot be pursued. By contrast, redactio-historical inquiry ought to experience still further development. However in this phase of research there ought to have been renewed clarity that the

---

[92] On the important transition from the Exile to the post-exilic period which could not be touched on in the foregoing, see especially P. R. Ackroyd, *Exile and Restoration*, London, 1968. On the particular problem whether Chronicles should still be understood under the heading of 'Interpretation of Tradition' or that of 'Exposition of Holy Scripture', see T. Willi, *Der Chronik als Auslegung*, FRLANT cvi, 1972. P. R. Ackroyd, 'The Theology of the Chronicler', *Lexington Theological Quarterly*, viii (1973), 101–16.

absolutizing of one single method on its own does not lead to secure results. Only the circumspect employment of the different methods of inquiry and their rightful collaboration, soberly aware of the bounds of each method, can lead to new assured insights.

BIBLIOGRAPHY

ACKROYD, P. R. *Exile and Restoration*, London, 1968.
ALBRIGHT, W. F. *Yahweh and the Gods of Canaan*, London, 1968.
BALTZER, K. *The Covenant Formulary in Old Testament, Jewish and Early Christian Writings*, Oxford, 1971 (ETr).
BARR, J. *Old and New in Interpretation*, London, 1966.
BERNHARDT, K. H. *Das Problem der altorientalischen Königsideologie im Alten Testament*, SVT viii, 1961.
CODY, A. *A History of Old Testament Priesthood*, AB xxxv, 1969.
CROSS F. M. *Canaanite Myth and Hebrew Epic*, Cambridge, Mass. and Oxford, 1973.
EICHRODT, W. *Religionsgeschichte Israels*, Berne and Munich 1969.
EISSFELDT, O. 'Die israelitisch-jüdische Religion,' *Saeculum-Weltgeschichte* ii (1966), 217–60.
FOHRER, G. *History of Israelite Religion*, London, 1973 (ETr).
HEMPEL, J. 'Altes Testament und Religionsgeschichte', *TLZ* lxxxi (1956), Cols. 259–80.
—— 'Die alttestamentliche Religion', *Handbuch der Orientalistik*, (ed. B. Spuler), I 8, 1 (Leiden, 1964), 122–46.
HOOKE, S. H. (ed.) *Myth, Ritual, and Kingship*, Oxford, 1958.
KAUFMANN, Y. *The Religion of Israel, from its Beginnings to the Babylonian Exile*, Chicago and London, 1960 (ETr).
MCCARTHY, D. J. *Treaty and Covenant*, AB xxi, 1963.
—— *Old Testament Covenant. A Survey of Current Opinions*, Oxford, 1972; 2nd edn., 1973.
MAAG, V. 'Malkut Jhwh', *Congress Volume, Oxford 1959*, SVT vii (1960), pp. 129–53.
—— 'Das Gottesverständnis des Alten Testaments', *NedTT* xxi (1966/7), 161–207.
MENDENHALL, G. E. *Law and Covenant in Israel and the Ancient Near East*, 1955 = *BA* xvii, 1954, 26–46, 50–76.
MUILENBURG, J. 'The History of the Religion of Israel', *IB* i (1952), 292–348.
NIELSEN, E. 'Die Religion des Alten Israel', *Handbuch der Religionsgeschichte* ii (Göttingen, 1972), 61–148 (= *Illustreret Religionshistorie*, 1968).
PENNA, A. *La religione di Israele*, Brescia, 1958.
VON RAD, G. *Old Testament Theology*, 2 vols., Edinburgh, 1962, 1965 (ETr).
—— *Der Heilige Krieg im alten Israel*, ATANT xx, 1951.

RINGGREN, H. *Israelite Religion*, London, 1966 (ETr).
SCHMID, H. H. *Gerechtigkeit als Weltordnung*, Tübingen, 1968.
SCHMIDT, W. H. *Königtum Gottes in Ugarit und Israel*, BZAW lxxx, 1961;
    2nd edn., 1966.
VRIEZEN, TH. C. *The Religion of Ancient Israel*, London, 1967 (ETr).

XIII

THE THEOLOGY AND INTERPRETATION OF THE OLD TESTAMENT

F. F. BRUCE

I THEOLOGY AND HISTORY OF RELIGION

WHATEVER may be said about the interpretation of the Old Testament, the propriety of talking about its theology has been repeatedly questioned. Can one in fact speak of the theology of the Old Testament in anything approaching a unitary sense? We can readily speak about the theology of Jeremiah or the theology of the Chronicler, but when we think of the Old Testament as a whole, should we not speak rather of the variety of its *theologies*? What is there in common between the theology of Judges and the theology of Second Isaiah? We may reply at once: 'A recognition that Yahweh, the righteous God, is Lord of history'—but should we have thought of asking the question, let alone of offering a reply, did it not so happen that Judges and Isaiah 40-55 are included in the same corpus of 'sacred' literature?

In an article published in 1960 under the title 'Is there an Old Testament theology?' Preben Wernberg-Møller distinguished two senses which the word 'theology' might bear in that question. On the one hand it might mean 'systematic theology, and more particularly, Christian systematic theology (because the starting-point is then the New Testament)', while on the other hand it might be 'firmly based on a critical linguistic, philological and historical study', in which case it would be used 'in a purely descriptive, non-committal way of the religious contents which may be detected in the Old Testament writings themselves, either in the smaller units, or in the redaction of what appear originally to be isolated traditions into larger wholes'.[1]

As for the former of these two senses, it is true that many approaches to the problems of Old Testament theology are undertaken from a Christian perspective and are concerned with assessing the Old Testament contribution to an over-all biblical theology. Since the Old Testament is an integral part of the Christian canon, there can be no doubt of the historical relevance or validity of such an approach. But a symposium sponsored by the Society for Old Testament Study is not a suitable setting for the expression of this concern. In any case, the attempt to construct a systematic Old Testament theology need not be distinctively Christian; it may equally well be Jewish, and the norm could then be rabbinical tradition rather than New Testament fulfilment. But the attempt should be made to investigate Old Testament theology in its own right and on its own terms, without seeking an interpretative norm outside the Old Testament itself. In such an investigation Jews, Christians, and others may fruitfully co-operate.

There have, indeed, been Christian theologians like Marcion in the second century and his disciples ever since who have denied the relevance of the Old Testament to the Christian faith, holding (as Harnack did) that to maintain its canonicity at this time of day betokens 'a religious and ecclesiastical paralysis'.[2] Or we have Rudolf Bultmann declaring that 'Jesus is God's demonstration of grace in a manner which is fundamentally different from the demonstrations of divine grace attested in the Old Testament'.[3] But there is a curious ambivalence in Professor Bultmann's appraisal of the Old Testament, as appears from his insistence in the same essay that 'it is only in critical dialogue with the Old Testament ... that we can gain an understanding of existence with such clarity that it directs our own historical

---

[1] P. Wernberg-Møller, *HibJ* lix (1960–61), 22; cf. O. Eissfeldt, 'Israelitisch-jüdische Religionsgeschichte und alttestamentliche Theologie', *ZAW* xliv (1926), 1 ff. = *KS* i (Tübingen, 1962), 105 ff.

[2] A. Harnack, *Marcion: Das Evangelium vom fremden Gott*, Leipzig, 1921, p. 217.

[3] R. Bultmann, 'The Significance of the Old Testament for the Christian Faith', in B. W. Anderson (ed.), *The Old Testament and Christian Faith*, New York, 1963, p. 29.

will and action' and that 'only in such dialogue is it possible to clarify the question . . . as to what meaning Christianity has for the present; indeed, as to whether it can claim to have any meaning at all'.[4] This is almost as much as to say that the Old Testament provides a dimension without which the New Testament cannot be viewed in proper perspective—and this is true.

Moreover, the Old Testament retains its independent quality of divine revelation, over and above its preparatory and propaedeutic function. There are occasions even today when a word of God can be heard from the Old Testament more directly relevant than anything in the New. Gerhard Ebeling tells how, when news of Adolf Hitler's suicide began to circulate among units of the German army early in May, 1945, he asked his comrades if he might read them a passage of Holy Writ, and he read the celebration of the downfall of the king of Babylon in Isa. 14:3 ff. The text spoke so clearly to the situation that comment would have been worse than superfluous:

> Is this the man who made the earth tremble,
>   who shook kingdoms,
> who made the world like a desert
>   and overthrew its cities,
>   who did not let his prisoners go home?

'The silence that followed the reading impressively testified to how readily it was heard.'[5]

To object that this is a word of judgement, not of grace, is to presuppose a false dichotomy between the Testaments: there is judgement in the New Testament and no lack of grace in the Old, and judgement on an oppressor is an act of grace to those oppressed.

As for the latter sense mentioned by Dr. Wernberg-Møller, it has become common procedure to refer to this as the study of the religion of Israel. For example, Th. C. Vriezen has written two books respectively entitled (in their English translations) *An Outline of Old Testament Theology*, Oxford,

----

[4] Ibid., p. 21.

[5] G. Ebeling, *Die Geschichtlichkeit der Kirche und ihrer Verkündigung als theologisches Problem*, Tübingen, 1954, p. 4, quoted by Carl Michalson in B. W. Anderson (ed.), *The Old Testament and Christian Faith*, p. 57.

1958, 2nd edn., 1970, and *The Religion of Ancient Israel*, London, 1967. The former book is written self-confessedly from a Christian point of view: while the main part (two thirds of the whole) is devoted to the content of Old Testament theology, this is preceded by a substantial introduction (one-third of the whole) which deals largely with the place of the Old Testament in the Church. The latter book is more 'objective' and descriptive: it deals with Israel's religion against the background of the religions of the ancient east, religious life about the year 1000 B.C., the victory of Yahwism, the great prophets, reformation and downfall, regeneration and recovery, centralization and disintegration. Descriptive as the treatment is, however, there is no lack of value judgements: Israel's religion is seen as reaching its finest flowering in the great prophets, from Amos to Second Isaiah, in whom, moreover, serious attempts are made to resolve the tension between particularism and universalism which characterized Israel's religion (the product of Yahweh's struggle with the gods of Canaan). Even this work, moreover, reveals a Christian perspective:

Through its fidelity to the Law Judaism maintained itself, spiritually; but at the same time, because of this bondage to tradition it created, to begin with, no new forms of living. The renewal that came with Christianity was repulsed. After the destruction of the second temple Pharisaism was for centuries the undisputed guide and leader of Judaism.[6]

But usually it would be agreed that the history of Israel's religion in the Old Testament period could be recorded, on the basis of the available evidence, in purely descriptive and uncommitted terms. The historian's personal assessment of religious phenomena might be evident to the discerning reader, just as Gilbert Murray's personal attitude is not concealed in his *Five Stages of Greek Religion*, Oxford, 1925, but it would not impose itself on the material.

A more objective account than Professor Vriezen's is given by Helmer Ringgren in his *Israelite Religion*, ETr, London, 1966, which excludes points of view, like those based on *Heilsgeschichte*, which 'have their place, but only within a

---

[6] Th. C. Vriezen, *The Religion of Ancient Israel*, p. 273.

theological presentation'.[7] Professor Ringgren's approach is comparative, and he concentrates especially on religion during the Israelite monarchy, to which the pre-Davidic period serves as prologue and the exilic and post-exilic periods as epilogue. He does not attempt to conceal his conscious alliance with the so-called Uppsala school, but does not allow himself to treat his material from a partisan perspective. Still more recently Georg Fohrer's excellent *History of Israelite Religion*, ETr, London, 1973, does not hesitate to express its author's positive interpretation of the subject-matter, together with his sceptical appraisal of several popular views, but it gives an adequate account of rival assessments and constitutes a fine introduction for the student.

An account of Old Testament theology, however, if it is to be distinct from a history of Israel's religion, will treat the writings not simply as historical source-material but as confessional documents, which in due course were gathered together and treated as a confessional corpus, by Jews and Christians alike. Here theological judgements will be in place. The diversity of outlook will be recognized, but the question will be asked: Is there in the Old Testament one dominant witness to God and his interaction with man—dominant enough to be acknowledged as the essence of Old Testament theology? To this question the proper answer is 'Yes'. There is a mainstream theological interpretation of Israel's history which outlives all rival interpretations, persisting from the Exodus and wilderness wanderings through the period of the settlement and the early monarchy, becoming more articulate in the later monarchy, guaranteeing the survival of Israel's faith through the Babylonian Exile and re-establishing it on so firm a foundation after the return from Exile that it resisted assimilation to Hellenistic culture whether under the tolerant domination of the Ptolemies and earlier Seleucids or under the brutal compulsion of Antiochus Epiphanes.

This theological interpretation often runs counter to prevalent tendencies in the religion of Israel, especially (but not exclusively) in the pre-exilic age. The cult of the queen of heaven (Jer. 44:17 ff.) must be given its due place in any

---

[7] Op. cit., p. v.

history of Israelite religion, but the theology of the Old Testament has no room for it, any more than it has room for the sacral feasts arranged for Fortune and Destiny at a later date (Isa. 65:11).

II. COVENANT AND SALVATION HISTORY

But, if we may legitimately speak of the theology of the Old Testament, how should its exposition be arranged? Th. C. Vriezen, in the first edition of the *Outline* mentioned above, classifies the content of Old Testament theology under six main headings: (1) the knowledge of God; (2) God; (3) Man; (4) the intercourse between God and man; (5) the intercourse between man and man (ethics); (6) God, man, and the world in the present and the future. This arrangement emphasizes that in the Old Testament theology belongs to the realm of personal relationships: the knowledge of God has the nature of 'an intimate relationship between the holy God and man'.[8]

This organization of the subject marks an advance on the older and more formal treatment of it under the heads of (1) the doctrine of God, (2) the doctrine of man, (3) the doctrine of salvation. We may compare H. H. Rowley's arrangement in *The Faith of Israel*, London, 1956, where the successive topics are (1) revelation and its media, (2) the nature of God, (3) the nature and need of man, (4) individual and community, (5) the good life, (6) death and beyond, and (7) the day of the Lord. More recently H. W. Wolff, in his *Anthropologie des Alten Testaments*, Munich, 1973 (ETr, *Anthropology of the Old Testament*, London, 1974), organizes what is in essence a work on Old Testament theology around the Old Testament portrayal of man's existence in the world, leading up to the purpose of his existence in relation to God.

But of all the studies which have endeavoured to organize the elements of Old Testament theology around a dominant central theme, pride of place remains with Walther Eichrodt and Gerhard von Rad. Eichrodt chose the covenant principle as the central theme for the first part—'God and the People'— of his *Theology of the Old Testament*, 2 vols., ETr, London,

---

[8] Op. cit., p. 128.

1961–7; von Rad's *Old Testament Theology*, 2 vols., ETr, Edinburgh, 1962–5 found its central theme in salvation history—more precisely, in the proclamation of Yahweh's mighty works in Israel's cult. (This presents a sharp contrast with Ludwig Köhler's treatment, in which Israel's cult is subsumed under the doctrine of man, being described as 'man's expedient for his own redemption'.[9])

Eichrodt deals with 'God and the People' under the successive heads: (1) the covenant relationship; (2) the covenant statutes; (3) the name of the covenant God; (4) the nature of the covenant God; (5) the instruments of the covenant; (6) covenant-breaking and judgement; (7) fulfilling the covenant (the consummation of God's dominion). When, however, he comes to the second and third parts, 'God and the World' and 'God and Man', the covenant does not provide such a convenient principle of organization, and other patterns have had to be used. But Eichrodt never forgets that the subject matter of theology is the knowledge of God, and God remains the standard of reference throughout his whole work.

Perhaps, however, Eichrodt does less than justice to the diversity of the covenant principle in the Old Testament. The Abrahamic covenant, related to the land, and the Sinai covenant, related to the Law, differ from each other and from the Davidic covenant, related first to the royal dynasty and then, in the post-exilic period, to the restored people of Israel as a whole (Isa. 55:3–5). It was the last of these that gave classic form to the national hope, as we shall see below.

Von Rad was conscious of a gulf existing between Yahweh's mighty acts declared in the cult and the actual course of events reconstructed by historical research. It is the events as Israel remembered them, however, not the events as modern study has reconstructed them, that are of importance in the *theology* of the Old Testament. Some of his pupils have endeavoured to bridge the gulf by showing how history and proclamation mutually imply each other. In this regard Rolf Rendtorff has made important contributions, maintaining on the one hand that the actual course of events, established by

---

[9] L. Köhler, *Old Testament Theology*, ETr, London, 1957, pp. 181 ff.

critical evaluation of the evidence, is integral to Old Testament theology and on the other hand that the cultic interpretation of those events is part of Israel's history. The findings of historical research must be accepted, but so must Israel's confessional recital, which is a historical datum in its own right; it is part of the Old Testament theologian's task to explore more thoroughly the relation between the two. In this Professor Rendtorff is working on parallel lines to his New Testament associates in the Pannenberg group who refuse to be content with a dichotomy between the Jesus of history and the Christ of the apostolic kerygma. As the Jesus of history (the Jesus whose career can be established by historical research) is an integral element in New Testament theology, so the history of Israel as established by scholarly research (says Rendtorff, as against von Rad) belongs to the essence of Old Testament theology, as truly as does Israel's cultic and confessional rehearsal of her history. The historical events and the way in which later generations called them to mind alike have their place in the ongoing history of transmission (*Überlieferungsgeschichte*) in which Old Testament theology takes shape.[10] But this means that Old Testament theology is a living organism, which cannot be pinned down as an exhibit in the museum of dogmatics without ceasing to be what it is.

There is, in fact, no basic incompatibility between the central themes selected by Eichrodt and von Rad, between the covenant principle and salvation history. Throughout the Old Testament Yahweh's covenant is regularly formulated in association with the recital of his mighty acts. Yahweh is the living God, whose throne is established in righteousness and whose covenant-mercy endures for ever; his will is that his people, bound to him by covenant, should themselves practise righteousness and love mercy, and thus in humility walk in step with him (Micah 6:8). And it is the record of his dealings with his people, or of their experience of him (to put it the other way round) that provides the stage on which his righteousness and mercy are most clearly seen in action.

If Eichrodt takes issue with the idea that there can be a

---

[10] R. Rendtorff, 'Geschichte und Überlieferung', in R. Rendtorff and K. Koch (eds.), *Studien zur Theologie der alttestamentlichen Überlieferungen*, Neukirchen, 1961, pp. 81 ff.

history of Israelite religion but no theology of the Old Testament, von Rad tackles such problems as those of form criticism and the history of transmission, and does so in such a way as to contribute more than Eichrodt does to the elucidation of the Old Testament text. His own work in the exegetical field is outstanding, notably his Genesis commentary in Das Alte Testament Deutsch (1949; 9th edn., 1972; ETr, 1961). There we see how his studies in the history of transmission can illuminate the understanding of the biblical material, in its pre-literary and literary stages alike.[10a] Or we may consider his use of the Deuteronomistic theology, according to which the word of Yahweh directs salvation history to its fulfilment,[10b] as a hermeneutical scheme for the interpretation of the Old Testament as a whole. To this must be added some reference to his work on typological exegesis, especially the correspondence between *Urzeit* and *Endzeit*,[10c] which he recognizes not only as an interpretative principle in the Old Testament but also as a major factor in 'the actualisation of the Old Testament in the New',[10d] enabling 'the Old Testament traditions, and all the narratives, prayers and predictions, to be taken over by the New Testament'.[10e]

III. CONFESSION AND OBEDIENCE

While Yahweh's covenant with Israel was the bringing by a vastly superior party of a much inferior party into a bond with himself, the inferior party did not play a completely passive role. It undertook obligations—especially the obligation of obedience to the covenant-God. How this obligation was discharged forms a large part of the covenant history. Not only at the beginning of the history but throughout its course we find a pattern of revelation and response. Much of the history of Israel as presented in the Old Testament is the

---

[10a] Cf. H. W. Wolff, 'Gerhard von Rad als Exeget', in H. W. Wolff, R. Rendtorff, and W. Pannenberg, *Gerhard von Rad: seine Bedeutung für die Theologie*, Munich, 1973, pp. 16 f.

[10b] *Old Testament Theology*, i. 334 ff.

[10c] Cf. his 'Typological Interpretation of the Old Testament', in C. Westermann (ed.), *Essays on Old Testament Interpretation*, London, 1963, pp. 17–39.

[10d] *Old Testament Theology*, ii. 319 ff.

[10e] *Old Testament Theology*, ii. 333.

record of Israel's response to Yahweh's revelation—a response sometimes of obedience but all too often of disobedience; a response now in action and now in word. The record is concerned to emphasize that (as was made plain in the covenant stipulations) the response of obedience leads to blessing, while the response of disobedience incurs disaster. As for the response in word, this finds pre-eminent expression in the Psalter. Here men and women to whom the word of Yahweh had come voice their response to it by telling him or telling others about their experience of him: 'thou, O Yahweh, art a shield about me' (Ps. 3:3); 'Yahweh is my shepherd, I shall not want' (Ps. 23:1).

In his presidential address to the Society for Old Testament Study in 1963 (entitled 'Israel's Creed: Sung, not Signed'), G. W. Anderson quoted and expanded H. W. Robinson's observation that 'the Book of Psalms ... supplies the data for an epitome of Old Testament theology'.[11] The Old Testament canon, Professor Anderson pointed out, is 'a confessional document', and the Psalter 'is representative of practically the whole range of Old Testament literature' (Torah, recital of Yahweh's acts, prophecy, 'wisdom') comprising in concentrated form the insights and the problems which characterize the Old Testament as a whole, expressing its dominant themes 'in the prayers and praises in which, generation after generation, Israel confessed Yahweh, and in confessing Him encountered Him'. In short, he concludes, 'if all the copies of the Old Testament were lost or destroyed, any scholar who could remember the text of the Psalms would have at his disposal the essential materials for an Old Testament theology.'[12]

In recent years much study has been devoted to a comparison between Israel's 'apodictic' law and the treaty formulation of the ancient Near East.[13] Whereas the casuistic element in the Old Testament law-codes has its counterpart

[11] H. W. Robinson, *Inspiration and Revelation in the Old Testament*, Oxford, 1946, p. 269.

[12] *Scottish Journal of Theology* xvi (1963), 277 ff.

[13] A. Alt, *Die Ursprünge des israelitischen Rechts*, Leipzig, 1934, ETr in his *Essays on Old Testament History and Religion*, Oxford, 1966, pp. 79 ff.; G. E. Mendenhall, *Law and Covenant in Israel and the Ancient Near East*, Pittsburgh, 1955; *The Tenth Generation: The Origins of the Biblical Tradition*, Baltimore, 1973.

in several law-codes of Western Asia, those laws cast in the
form 'Thou shalt (not) . . .' or 'Whoever does such-and-such
shall be put to death' have their counterpart in the stipulations
of treaties. Moreover, the treaties which provide the closest
parallels here are the Hittite suzerainty treaties and (later) the
Assyrian vassal treaties, in which an inferior power is brought
into federal relationship with a superior ruler and swears
allegiance to him. Israel's apodictic laws are thus the
stipulations of the covenant into which the nation enters with
Yahweh as its king to whom it swears allegiance. It has,
indeed, been argued by Volker Wagner in *Rechtssätze in
gebundener Sprache und Rechtssatzreihen im israelitischen
Recht*, BZAW cxxvii, 1972 that the subject matter of the
apodictic laws was non-religious in origin; but in the Hebrew
codes these laws are given the character of Yahweh's covenant-
stipulations, as, to be sure, the case-laws also are.

   As the suzerainty and vassal-treaties of the ancient Near
East are introduced by a narrative preamble, so are the main
corpora of apodictic law in Israel. Of these the best known is
the Decalogue of Exod. 20:1–17 and Deut. 5:6–21. In the
latter passage it is made explicitly clear that the Decalogue
comprises the stipulations of Yahweh's covenant with Israel:
'Yahweh our God made a covenant with us in Horeb . . . He
said, "I am Yahweh your God . . ."' In the Decalogue, Exodus
and covenant are brought into close association.[14] The
preamble to the first of the ten 'words' identifies Yahweh in
terms of salvation-history. 'You shall have no other gods
before me' is meaningless unless the identity of the speaker is
known; his identity is accordingly disclosed in the preamble,
'I am Yahweh your God, who brought you out of the land of
Egypt, out of the house of bondage' (Exod. 20:2; Deut. 5:6).
He is identified in terms of his redemptive activity; the
covenant of Sinai-Horeb is based on the deliverance from
Egypt. The Decalogue, in its original form of ten simple
sentences, is best dated in the pre-settlement period;[15] this
may well have been 'the book of the covenant' which was read

---

[14] For the association between the Exodus and Sinai traditions see W. Beyerlin,
Origins and History of the Oldest Sinaitic Traditions, ETr, Oxford, 1965.
[15] Cf. H. H. Rowley, 'Moses and the Decalogue', in *Men of God*, London, 1963, pp.
1 ff.

by Moses and accepted by the people as the basis of their corporate life at the ceremony described in Exodus 24:3–8. What used to be called the 'Ritual Decalogue' of Exod. 34:17–26 similarly sets forth covenant stipulations. 'Behold, I make a covenant', says Yahweh in the preamble (Exod. 34:10a), and at the end he commands Moses: 'Write these words; in accordance with these words I have made a covenant with you and with Israel' (Exod. 34:27). But the narrative preamble here declares not what Yahweh has done in bringing his people out of Egypt but what he is going to do in settling them in Canaan (Exod. 34:10b, 11); the terms of their covenant with Yahweh preclude any thought of a covenant between them and the Canaanites (Exod. 34:12–16).

A much more elaborate instance of the treaty pattern is found in Deuteronomy. Not only is the Decalogue expressly associated with Yahweh's covenant; the covenant is renewed in Transjordan, at the end of the wilderness wanderings, and again it is preceded by a rehearsal of Yahweh's mighty works from the plagues of Egypt to the overthrow of Sihon and Og and the occupation of their lands (Deut. 29:1–30:20). Indeed, the Deuteronomic law-code itself (Deut. 12:1–26:19) is probably presented as a corpus of covenant stipulations (it is explicitly called 'the book of the covenant' in 2 Kgs. 23:2 in the account of Josiah's reformation), to which the historical retrospect in Moses' speeches (Deut. 1:6–4:50; 5:1–11:32) provides the preamble.[16]

IV. THE HOUSE OF DAVID

It is inevitable that the Israelite smallholder's annual confession at the harvest festival should be recalled in this connection:

A wandering Aramaean was my father, and he went down into Egypt and sojourned there, few in number; and there he became a nation ... And the Egyptians treated us harshly ... Then we cried to Yahweh the God of our fathers ... and Yahweh brought us out of Egypt ... and he brought us into this place and gave us this land, a land flowing with milk and honey (Deut. 26:5–9).

[16] Cf. D. J. McCarthy, *Treaty and Covenant*, Rome, 1963; M. G. Kline, *Treaty of the Great King*, Grand Rapids, 1963.

Here the settlement in Canaan is the climax of Yahweh's gracious guidance of his people, which is traced from the patriarchal period onwards. In later generations the perspective could be extended; the climax was recognized in the establishment of the Davidic dynasty and the Temple in Jerusalem:

> He rejected the tent of Joseph,
>   he did not choose the tribe of Ephraim;
> but he chose the tribe of Judah,
>   Mount Zion, which he loves.
> He built his sanctuary like the high heavens,
>   like the earth, which he has founded for ever.
> He chose David his servant,
>   and took him from the sheepfolds;
> from tending the ewes that had young he brought him
>   to be the shepherd of Jacob his people,
>   of Israel his inheritance.
> With upright heart he tended them,
>   and guided them with skilful hand. (Ps. 78:67–72)

The establishment of David's rule is the perspective from which the Yahwist's narrative is composed. After the primeval history (Genesis 1–11), which serves as a prologue, it follows the line of the confession in Deut. 26:5–9, but enters into vivid biographical detail, telling of Israel's forefathers and their wanderings in Canaan, of their descent into Egypt and multiplication there, of the oppression and divine deliverance, of the wilderness experiences and the initial conquest of Canaan. It does not carry the story down to David's time, but David's achievements completed the work of conquest and made possible the realization of the promises to the patriarchs that their offspring would be a great nation, numerous as the dust of the earth, occupying all the territory from the Egyptian frontier to the Euphrates (Gen. 13:14–17; 15:18; 18:18; 28:13f.; cf. 1 Kgs. 4:20f.).

The sequel to this narrative tells how Yahweh's covenants with Abraham and at Sinai were renewed in a special form with David and his descendants—'an everlasting covenant, ordered in all things and secure', according to the 'oracle of David' preserved in 2 Sam. 23:1–7. But it is scarcely true to say that in this renewal 'Yahweh's sovereignty was *limited* by the covenant, since he was no longer free to choose or reject Israel, as Amos maintained, but he was obliged to preserve her.'[17] Whatever David and his dynasty may have supposed, Yahweh retained his freedom as their suzerain; if they proved unfaithful to this special covenant, they too would be cast off. If even so, after the declaration that none of Jehoiachin's offspring would 'succeed in sitting on the throne of David, and ruling again in Judah' (Jer. 22:30), the promise is heard of a 'righteous Branch' to be raised up for David (Jer. 23:5; 33:15), this is the voice of Yahweh's free grace; it does not rise from any obligation on his side to maintain a covenant which the other party has broken.

In Psalm 78 we may see one ideology (the Jerusalem-Davidic) pitted against another (which maintained the prerogatives of the house of Joseph); perhaps that other ideology finds a singer to champion it in Psalm 80, where the Shepherd of Israel is entreated to shine forth on the Rachel tribes, 'before Ephraim and Benjamin and Manasseh' (Ps. 80:1 f.). But it was the Jerusalem-Davidic ideology that was to triumph. Repeatedly in the prophets the restoration of Israel's fortunes is associated with the repairing of David's fallen booth (Amos 9:11 f.; cf. Isa. 9:2-7; 11:1-5, 10).

After the power of Assyria had begun to diminish and her yoke was lifted from Judah, the religious revival and territorial expansion of Josiah's reign might have seemed to promise that David's fallen booth was indeed being repaired. But the sequel proved that expectation to be hollow, and presented serious thinkers with a problem in the theology of history.

The career of Josiah can be explained on one level by the simple fact that one great Near Eastern empire (Assyria) was on the point of collapse, while her powerful neighbours (Egypt, Media, Babylonia) were not quite ready to enter into the vacuum created by her recession and share out her possessions. In that brief interval the king of Judah was able to assert his independence, to extend his rule into the territory of the former kingdom of Israel, and to inaugurate a religious reformation which not only got rid of the installations of Assyrian worship but closed down the local sanctuaries or

[17] B. W. Anderson, *The Living World of the Old Testament*, London, 1958, p. 290, based on G. E. Mendenhall, *Law and Covenant*, Pittsburgh, 1955, pp. 44 ff.

hill-shrines throughout the land and centralized the national worship in the temple at Jerusalem. But when the surrounding powers moved in to seize the rich heritage left by the moribund Assyrian empire, the end of Judah's short-lived independence was inevitable, and Josiah's attempt to bar the Egyptian advance at Megiddo could have only one outcome. But Josiah's death, and the disasters which followed, culminating in the destruction of Jerusalem and its Temple, the fall of the house of David, and the deporting of a great part of the population, called for an explanation from the Deuteronomist writers. Josiah's reformation had been carried through in strictest conformity with the Deuteronomic law; why then was it not followed by the prosperity which that law held out to those who kept it? The answer was that the national apostasy under Manasseh, Josiah's grandfather, was so wholesale as to be irremediable save by the crucible of exile; Josiah's piety might avail for himself but could not atone for the sins of the nation. And indeed it seems clear that Josiah's reformation was largely his own policy, carried through with the backing of a small body of advisers. The people's heart was not in it, and when he was killed at Megiddo they saw no reason why they should not revert to their former ways. In fact, some of them put down the disasters which followed his death not (as the Deuteronomists did) to the apostasy under Manasseh but to Josiah's reformation. The last recorded scene in the life of Jeremiah depicts the Jews who had fled to Egypt after the assassination of Gedaliah refusing to listen to the prophet's warning, and asserting that before Josiah's reformation 'we had plenty of food, and prospered, and saw no evil; but since we left off burning incense to the queen of heaven and pouring out libations to her, we have lacked everything and have been consumed by the sword and by famine' (Jer. 44:17 f.).

Here, then, we have two opposed theological interpretations of the catastrophe: Jeremiah and the Deuteronomists put it down to the worship of the queen of heaven and associated cults in the days before these were abolished by Josiah; the others put it down to Josiah's abolition of those cults. With which side did the right interpretation lie? Or were both sides wrong in seeking a theological interpretation for events which the historian can explain in political terms? The mainstream message of the Old Testament gives an unambiguous answer. When Jeremiah was accused of causing alarm and despondency by his prophecies of disaster, he told his accusers that if they put him to death they would make the disaster all the more certain, 'for in truth Yahweh sent me to you to speak all these words in your ears' (Jer. 26:15). His claim was confirmed not only by the fact that his prophecies came true, but also, and more permanently, by the fact that Israel's religious identity was preserved by those who shared his interpretation of events and not by those who lamented the discontinuance of the cult of the queen of heaven.

V. EXILE AND AFTER

In Second Isaiah the renewal of the Davidic covenant takes its place within the renewal of the covenant with Israel. The renewal of the covenant with Israel is confirmed in the person of the Servant of Yahweh, but in him the covenant blessings reach out beyond Israel to her neighbours: 'I have given you as a covenant to the people, a light to the nations' (Isa. 42:6; cf. 49:6, 8). Outside of the Servant Songs, the meaning of this promise is spelt out as Israel is addressed:

Incline your ear, and come to me;
  hear, that your soul may live;
and I will make with you an everlasting covenant,
  my steadfast, sure love for David.
Behold, I made him a witness to the peoples,
  a leader and commander for the peoples.
Behold, you shall call nations that you know not,
  and nations that knew you not shall run to you,
because of Yahweh your God, and of the Holy One of Israel,
  for he has glorified you (Isaiah 55:3–5).

In David's day non-Israelite nations had been brought under Yahweh's sway, and history will repeat itself in the new order, but whereas then the methods used were those of military conquest, now they are those of missionary witness, procuring a willing submission instead of a forced obedience. This paves the way for the line of reinterpretation of earlier Davidic prophecies which we shall find in the Septuagint (see p. 409).

In a famous covenant renewal ceremony after the return from Exile the historical retrospect again plays a part, but now the period of retrospect is extended to take in the Exile and the return. After the conclusion of the feast of Booths in that month of Tishri which had been inaugurated by the public reading of the Torah under Ezra's direction, the people of Judah and Jerusalem held a day of national humiliation and entered into a 'firm covenant' to 'do all the commandments of Yahweh' from that day forth (Neh. 9:38 ff.). Their leaders' subscription to the covenant was preceded by a long prayer in which Ezra recalled Yahweh's faithfulness and the people's faithlessness from the call of Abraham on through their deliverance from Egypt's affliction, their wilderness wanderings and their occupation of Canaan.

Many years thou didst bear with them, and didst warn them by thy Spirit through thy prophets; yet they would not give ear. Therefore thou didst give them into the hand of the peoples of the lands. Nevertheless in thy great mercies thou didst not make an end of them or forsake them; for thou art a gracious and merciful God.
Now therefore, our God . . . let not all the hardship seem little to thee that has come upon us, upon our kings, our princes, our priests, our prophets, our fathers, and all thy people, since the time of the kings of Assyria until this day . . . Behold, we are slaves this day; in the land that thou gavest to our fathers to enjoy its fruit and its good gifts, behold, we are slaves. And its rich yield goes to the kings whom thou hast set over us because of our sins; they have power also over our bodies and over our cattle at their pleasure, and we are in great distress. (Neh. 9:30-7)

Even the relief from Exile could not obliterate from their minds the fact that they were still tributary to a Gentile monarch—how unlike their forefathers who as freeholders rejoiced before Yahweh their God in all the good which he had given them!

As for the detailed stipulations which the signatories to the renewed covenant took upon themselves (Neh. 10), I am indebted to D. J. A. Clines for the observation that all of them 'are really re-interpretations of conflicting or out-dated Pentateuchal laws'.[18]

---

[18] From a personal letter. I gather that Mr. Clines hopes to publish a study along these lines.

For the Chronicler the golden age has arrived—or nearly so.[19] Living at peace under their Persian and Macedonian overlords, the citizens of the Judaean temple-state are able to worship Yahweh and live as his people according to the Law of Moses and the liturgy of David. The reforms of Ezra and Nehemiah have cleansed them from ritual defilement; they have successfully resisted the compromising overtures of their fellow-Israelites in Samaria. The ideal situation has at length been almost realized: could the future bring anything better—unless indeed it be the restoration of the dynasty of David according to the promise of 1 Chr. 17? David's response to that promise concludes with the words: 'what thou, Yahweh, hast blessed is blessed for ever' (1 Chr. 17:27). The Chronicler knew the oracle of Jeremiah (33:17-22) affirming that Yahweh's covenant with the families of David and Levi was as indissoluble as his covenant with day and night; if the Levitical priests had been restored to this ministry, so surely would the descendants of David be restored to theirs. If the Chronicler prefers to imply this than to assert it, he may have had his reasons for doing so. But the words of Ezra's prayer (Neh. 9:36f.) would have awakened, however faintly, a sympathetic echo in his mind.

The Wisdom of Ben Sira reflects the relaxed and relatively prosperous way of life which the people of Judaea continued to enjoy in their temple-state early in the second century B.C., when their passing from Ptolemaic to Seleucid domination made little practical difference to most of them. No necessity was felt of finding a theological explanation of the way things were. But the punitive measures of Antiochus IV against Jerusalem after the frustration of his second Egyptian campaign (168 B.C.), the abolition of the temple-state constitution, the ban on the practice of their religion, the setting up of the abomination of desolation in Yahweh's Temple—all this demanded an answer from heaven, and it was not certain that any answer was to be had. 'We do not see our signs; there is no longer any prophet, and there is none among us who knows how long' (Ps. 74:9)—whether these words belong to

---

[19] Cf. W. Rudolph, *Chronikbücher*, HAT, Tübingen, 1955, pp. xiii ff.; P. R. Ackroyd, *Chronicles–Ezra–Nehemiah*, TC, London, 1973, pp. 19 ff.; R. Mosis, *Untersuchungen zur Theologie des chronistischen Geschichtswerkes*, Freiburg, 1973.

this critical period or not, they aptly express the bewildered anguish of many faithful souls in Israel. Once again, a modern historian would explain the events in terms of international rivalry, power politics, and the requirements of internal and external defence; but to the Israelites who had to live with the religious implications of the royal policy these explanations were inadequate. If the God of Israel was the Lord of history, why had he allowed all this to happen? The godly in Israel continued to strengthen their faith in Yahweh, who keeps 'covenant and steadfast love with those who love him and keep his commandments' (Dan. 9:4), and again their confidence was vindicated.

VI. UNCOVENANTED MERCIES

Even towards those outside the covenant, or those whose disloyalty to it has disqualified them from appealing to its protection, decent conduct is required by Yahweh. Thus Hosea announces the fall of the dynasty of Jehu because of the atrocities against the house of Ahab which attended its rise to power. True, the house of Ahab had flagrantly broken the covenant with Yahweh and incurred his judgement; true also that the execution of that judgement was entrusted to Jehu by one of the prophetic guilds, but the treachery and bloodthirstiness with which Jehu had carried it out were in themselves an affront to the ethics of the covenant, and his dynasty was in due course punished for 'the blood of Jezreel' (Hos. 1:4). Amos, for his part, denounces Israel's neighbours not only for genocide against Israelites in Transjordan but for conduct towards each other which violated accepted canons of decency, as when the Moabites burned the bones of the king of Edom into lime instead of granting them honourable burial; and it is Yahweh who will execute judgement upon them, just as he will execute severer judgement on the Israelites because their crimes were breaches of their covenant with him (Amos 1:13–3:2). For Yahweh is a God of uncovenanted mercies as well as of covenant-mercy; his character as displayed towards Israel does not radically change in his dealings with other nations. There is thus nothing inconsistent with the covenant principle in the inclusion among the canonical books of the wisdom literature, with its international flavour. Yahweh's covenant with Israel may be the implicit background of this literature, but it does not come to expression in it, as it does in the later wisdom books which did not establish their position in the Hebrew Bible. Ben Sira, in praising famous men, says that 'their descendants stand by the covenants' (Sir. 44:12), and in Wisdom the recital of Yahweh's mighty works reappears as a rehearsal of the achievements made possible by the guidance of divine wisdom (Wis. 10:1 ff.); but this is not the language of the earlier wisdom books. In the later books wisdom is identified with the Torah, so that a line of demarcation is drawn between Israel and her neighbours (Sir. 24:23; Baruch 3:24 ff.); but in the canonical books wisdom is the common heritage of both. It is not by chance that the hero of the book of Job is a non-Israelite, or that Arabian and possibly Egyptian wisdom-collections are incorporated in the book of Proverbs. Wisdom, in short, is a gift with which the Creator has endowed mankind. Walther Zimmerli has related Hebrew wisdom to the creation theme of the primeval narrative of Genesis.[20] The world is Yahweh's handiwork, and it is there for men to enjoy and explore. To study the creation and find delight in it is to appreciate increasingly the glory of the Creator. It is possible, indeed, to worship the creation rather than the Creator, but this is a perversion of his purpose. When Zophar asks, 'Can you find

[20] W. Zimmerli, 'The Place and Limit of the Wisdom in the Framework of the Old Testament Theology', *Scottish Journal of Theology* xvii (1964), 146 ff.; cf. D. A. Hubbard, 'The Wisdom Movement and Israel's Covenant Faith', *Tyndale Bulletin* xvii (1966), 3 ff. See G. von Rad, *Old Testament Theology*, i. 446, 450, on the difficulty which a 'salvation history' scheme finds in accommodating the Wisdom literature — and also apocalyptic which, he holds, originated from the Wisdom matrix (op. cit. ii. 306). In 1970 von Rad added to his earlier work a study in depth entitled *Wisdom in Israel*, ETr, London, 1972, in which he advanced substantially beyond the position stated in his *Old Testament Theology* and argued that the wisdom tradition presents an independent theological approach, based on the eternal order in things and not on the unique historical occurrence. Yet even wisdom theology discloses the salvation principle, arising out of man's encounter with creation. This helps to fill in an important area of Old Testament theology, which was given a minor place in his earlier writing; cf. 'The Theological Problem of the Old Testament Doctrine of Creation' (1936), in *The Problem of the Hexateuch and Other Essays*, Edinburgh, 1966, pp. 131–43, and the critique by J. Barr in *Old and New in Interpretation*, London, 1966, pp. 74 ff., 98.

out the deep things of God?' (Job 11:7), this must not be treated as an oracular question requiring the answer 'No' or as a warning not to go too far in investigating the mysteries of the universe, as it has sometimes been treated by preachers and others who have taken the text out of its context. Wisdom's highest function is to guide man in his arduous quest and lead him to the knowledge of God.

VII. INTERPRETATION IN THE OLD TESTAMENT

Old Testament interpretation can be considered at various levels. Many of the Old Testament books are themselves essays in interpretation. The prophets interpreted the course of events in terms of Yahweh's purpose, and his purpose, as they saw it, was always consistent with his character as a God whose righteousness manifested itself in acts of judgement and mercy. If the Babylonian Exile was interpreted as his judgement on his people because of their failure to keep his covenant, the restoration from Exile was interpreted as his delivering grace. In the Exile the other nations might see his impartiality in visiting on his own people all their iniquities, but lest they should conclude that (like the gods of Hamath and Arpad) he was powerless to help them in their distress, he ordered the process of history in such a way as to bring them home again, that the nations might know that he was the living God (Isa. 45:3-6; Ezek. 28:25 f.; etc.).

The historical books also interpret the course of events theologically, as appears pre-eminently in the works of the Deuteronomists and the Chronicler. Earlier interpretative principles are present in these writers' source-material, and in the very incidents which are recorded. The outbreak of famine or plague, for example, is repeatedly traced to sin of some kind, expecially to a covenant-violation. Thus the three years' famine in David's reign was explained by the oracular response, when David made inquiry, as due to the blood-guiltiness incurred by Saul and his house because he broke the national covenant with the Gibeonites; and the ensuing events were the sequel to this interpretation (2 Sam. 21:1-14).

As for the interpretation of the Old Testament text itself, the beginnings of this are also to be found within the Hebrew

Bible.[21] We have it, for example, in the reinterpretation of earlier laws in later codes, in the reworking of earlier historical material by later historians, in the reapplication of earlier prophecy by later prophets, and sometimes even by the same prophet. Thus Deuteronomy is interpreted by Jacob Weingreen[22] as what might be described as a proto-Mishnah, amplifying, adapting, and expounding the earlier laws of Exod. 20–3. The Chronicler reworks material in the books of Samuel and Kings, presenting it afresh in the light of his own post-exilic situation. According to E. W. Nicholson, Jeremiah's earlier prophetic message was reapplied by himself to the new situation brought about by the Babylonian victory at Carchemish in the fourth year of Jehoiakim's reign (Jer. 36:1 ff.) and his oracles formed the basis of sermons preached by others to the exiles in the next generation.[23] Habakkuk depicts the Chaldeans (Hab. 1:5 ff.) and Ezekiel depicts Gog (Ezek. 38:1 ff.) after Isaiah's picture of the Assyrian invader of an earlier day (Isa. 10:28 ff.; 28:17–21; 29:14; 31:8; 37:34): 'Are you he of whom I spoke in former days by my servants the prophets of Israel, who in those days prophesied for years that I would bring you against them?' (Ezek. 38:17). And we know how Daniel reinterprets the seventy years of Jer. 25:11, after which Jerusalem's desolations would be at an end, as seventy heptads of years (Dan. 9:24–27), sees Balaam's prophecy of 'ships ... from Kittim' (Num. 24:24) fulfilled in the career of Antiochus Epiphanes (Dan. 11:30),[24] and recasts Isaiah's Assyrian prophecies and Ezekiel's Gog oracles so as to portray Antiochus's last invasion of the land of Israel and his downfall there 'with none to help him' (Dan. 11:45).

[21] Cf. G. Vermes, 'Bible and Midrash: Early Old Testament Exegesis', in *CHB* i Cambridge, 1970, 199 ff.; F. F. Bruce, 'The Earliest Old Testament Interpretation', *OTS* xvii (1972), 37 ff.

[22] Cf. J. Weingreen, 'Rabbinic-Type Glosses in the Old Testament', *JSS* ii (1957), 149 ff.; 'Exposition in the Old Testament and in Rabbinical Literature', in *Promise and Fulfilment*, ed. F. F. Bruce, Edinburgh, 1963, pp. 187 ff.; 'Oral Torah and Written Records', in *Holy Book and Holy Tradition*, ed. F. F. Bruce and E. G. Rupp, Manchester, 1968, pp. 54 ff.; also E. Robertson, *The Old Testament Problem*, Manchester, 1950, pp. 80 ff., 183 ff.

[23] E. W. Nicholson, *Preaching to the Exiles: A Study of the Prose Tradition in the Book of Jeremiah*, Oxford, 1970.

[24] It is noteworthy that as Daniel's 'ships of Kittim' are paraphrased as 'Romans' in the earlier Greek (LXX) version of Daniel 11:30, so Balaam's 'Kittim' become 'Romans' in the Onkelos Targum of Num. 24:24.

The titles to the Psalms (apart from the musical and liturgical directions) represent attempts to relate the Psalms to historical life-settings, expecially to incidents in David's career, and should be recognized as early exercises in Old Testament interpretation.[25]

VIII. JEWISH INTERPRETATION

1. The Scribal Tradition

Some form of interpretation is implied in the account of the public reading of the Law which Ezra had brought from Babylon to Jerusalem (Ezra 7:14): Ezra and his assistants 'read from the book, from the law of God, with interpretation ($m^e p\bar{o}r\bar{a}\check{s}$); and they gave the sense, so that the people understood the reading' (Neh. 8:8). Whether this 'interpretation' involved an Aramaic targum is uncertain, but it is not at all improbable.

This at any rate marks the beginning of the scribal and rabbinical interpretation of the sacred scriptures which was developed during later centuries. In this interpretation two methods were early distinguished—$p^e \check{s}a\underline{t}$, 'plain (meaning)' and $d^e ra\check{s}$, 'exposition', by which religious or social ethics were derived from the text, often artificially. There was, however, no feeling of conflict between the two.

The most important form of interpretation in this period was the detailed application of the written Torah to the new circumstances of Jewish existence in the Graeco-Roman world. The fashioning of this new interpretation was a mark of the Pharisees as against the Sadducees (who, in theory at least, maintained the letter of the written Law); among the Pharisees there were rival schools of interpretation, the best known of which are the milder school of Hillel and the stricter school of Shammai (both these teachers flourished c. 10 B.C.). In the new situation which followed the downfall of the Second Commonwealth in A.D. 70, the school of Hillel was dominant. The Qumran community looked upon all schools of Pharisaic interpretation as deplorably lax; it is probably the Pharisees who are referred to in the Qumran texts as

[25] Cf. B. S. Childs, 'Psalm Titles and Midrashic Exegesis', *JSS* xvi (1971), 137 ff.

'expounders of smooth things' (dôrᵉšê haḥᵃlāḳôṯ—an echo of Isa. 30:10. The Qumran interpretation of the Law outdid that of the school of Shammai in strictness.

The name of Hillel is linked with seven interpretative *middôṯ* or canons: (1) inference from less important to more important and vice versa, (2) inference by analogy, (3) the grouping of related texts under an exegetical principle which primarily applies to one of them, (4) similar grouping where the principle primarily applies to two texts, (5) inference from particular to general and vice versa, (6) exposition by means of a similar text, (7) inference from the context. R. Ishmael (c. A.D. 100) expanded these canons to thirteen, while R. Eliezer ben Jose the Galilean (c. A.D. 150) formulated thirty-two canons, which embodied rational principles of exegesis and remained normative into the Middle Ages.[26]

2. Septuagint, Pseudepigrapha, and Philo

In the last two or three centuries B.C. the Greek version of the Hebrew scriptures, popularly called the Septuagint, includes some evidence for the line of Old Testament interpretation current in the Jewish community of Alexandria. In general, the Greek translators endeavoured to represent the Hebrew faithfully: where their rendering appears deliberately to deviate from the Hebrew, an interpretative motive may be sought for the deviation. Attention has been drawn to the anti-anthropomorphisms of the Septuagint (such as 'they saw the place where the God of Israel stood' for 'they saw the God of Israel' in Exod. 24:10), but these are not so numerous as might have been expected, and some renderings that have been explained thus should perhaps be given a different explanation.[27] The description of Yahweh as a 'man of war' in Exod. 15:3 and Isa. 42:13 is converted into the picture of a God who 'destroys (συντρίβων) war'.

Sometimes changes in the sequence of narrative sections set a situation or a character in a different light; it has, for example, been pointed out by D. W. Gooding that by this

[26] Cf. J. Weingreen, 'The Rabbinic Approach to the Study of the Old Testament', *BJRL* xxxiv (1951–52), 166 ff.; G. Vermes, *Scripture and Tradition in Judaism*, Leiden, 1961.

[27] Cf. C. T. Fritsch, *The Anti-Anthropomorphisms of the Greek Pentateuch*, Princeton, 1943.

means the Septuagint of 1 Kings (3 Reigns) presents a more sympathetic portrait of Solomon and Ahab than does the traditional Hebrew text.[28]

Israel's relation to the Gentiles undergoes a change here and there in the Septuagint. Thus the prophecy in Amos 9:11 f. concerning the restoration of David's fallen booth speaks not of the reoccupation of Edom by the Davidic dynasty but of the seeking of the Lord by the rest of mankind. This rendering may be based on two or three corruptions in the Hebrew *Vorlage*, but it spiritualizes the sense and universalizes it by envisaging the extension of true religion throughout the world, and thus provided a text for both Jewish and Christian missionary enterprise (cf. Acts 15:15-18).

The book of Proverbs in particular has been paraphrased along the lines of Greek ethical and metaphysical teaching. 'Know thyself' ($\gamma\nu\hat{\omega}\theta\iota$ $\sigma\epsilon\alpha\nu\tau\acute{o}\nu$) is as basic a principle of Greek wisdom as the knowledge of God is primary in Israelite thought; 'those who know themselves are wise' (Prov. 13:10, LXX) is a far cry from the sense of the Hebrew: 'with those who take counsel there is wisdom'.

Again, in keeping with the climate of opinion in which the translators lived, intimations of immortality find more frequent expression in the Septuagint than in the Hebrew Bible. For instance, 'the upright will dwell before thee' (Ps. 140:13) is rendered $\kappa\alpha\tau o\iota\kappa\acute{\eta}\sigma o\upsilon\sigma\iota\nu$ $\epsilon\mathring{\upsilon}\theta\epsilon\hat{\iota}s$ $\sigma\mathring{\upsilon}\nu$ $\tau\hat{\omega}$ $\pi\rho o\sigma\acute{\omega}\pi\omega$ $\sigma o\upsilon$, 'upright men will dwell with thy presence' (139:14), which, while a very literal rendering, would convey to a Greek reader a nuance absent from the Hebrew text.

Here and there, too, something can be gathered about interpretations of Old Testament prophecy current in the translators' environment. The appearance of Gog in place of Agag in Num. 24:7 and as the name of the locust king in Amos 7:1 suggests a unitive exegesis of these contexts with the Gog oracles of Ezek. 38-39; and other features in the vocabulary of Amos 7:1 suggest that Joel's description of the locust plague, understood as the figurative account of a

<hr />

[28] D. W. Gooding, 'The Septuagint's Version of Solomon's Misconduct', *VT* xv (1965), 323 ff.; 'Ahab according to the Septuagint', *ZAW* lxxvi (1964), 269 ff.; 'Problems of Text and Midrash in the Third Book of Reigns', *Textus* vii (1969), 1 ff.

coming invasion by human enemies, was brought into the same complex, and interpreted of Israel's last assailant, who will be overthrown by the Davidic Messiah.

The influence of the Graeco-Roman environment on Old Testament interpretation is more marked in the apocryphal and pseudepigraphic writings, where for the most part it was not kept in check by the call for a reasonably faithful translation. The brief account of Enoch in Gen. 5:21–4, with the enigmatic statement that he 'walked with God ... three hundred years' and then 'was not, for God took him', was expanded into an appraisal of him on the one hand as a paragon of righteousness and wisdom (Sir. 44:16; Wis. 4:11–14) and on the other hand as the recipient of exceptional revelations regarding outer space, the angelic world, and the ages to come (1 Enoch). The Greek Esther imports into the Hebrew book a religious element which was absent from the original story. The Fall narrative of Gen. 3 is related to the on-going human predicament in the later wisdom books (Sir. 25:24; Wis. 2:24) but particularly in the Apocalypses of Baruch and Ezra, which stress the involvement of all mankind in Adam's sin and death (2 Bar. 48:42 f.; 54:15–19; 4 Ezra 7:118 f.).

Apart from the Septuagint, the main contribution to Old Testament exegesis in Jewish Alexandria came from Philo (c. 20 B.C.–A.D. 50), who himself used the Greek Bible as his basic text. He was convinced by an immediate intellectual response to Plato's theory of ideas that ultimate truth lay here; at the same time, his Jewish upbringing taught him that ultimate truth lay in the law of Moses. Inevitably, therefore, both Moses and Plato must say the same thing in different language, and so Philo interpreted the Pentateuch in terms of Platonic idealism coupled with Stoic ethics and a dash of Neopythagorean mysticism. His interpretation, however, found but little echo in Judaism; it was more influential among the Christian Platonists of Alexandria.

3. *The Qumran Community*

Apart from its strict *halakhah*, the Qumran community interpreted the scriptures, expecially the prophetic scriptures, in the belief that they were concerned with the time of the end, which had set in with the foundation of the community. God had revealed his purpose to the prophets, but one thing he had withheld from them: knowledge of the time at which his purpose would be accomplished. This knowledge he revealed in due course to the Teacher of Righteousness and through him to his disciples. Thus in the Qumran commentary on Habakkuk, Hab 2:2 is interpreted thus:

God commanded Habakkuk to write the things that were coming upon the last generation, but the fulfilment of the epoch he did not make known to him. And as for the words, *so he may run who reads it*, their interpretation concerns the Teacher of Righteousness, to whom God made known all the mysteries of the words of his servants the prophets. (1 Qp Hab. 7:1–5)

We may compare what Josephus says about Daniel, that 'he was not only accustomed to prophesy future events, as the other prophets did, but he also specified the time at which they would come to pass' (*Ant.* x. 267). The men of Qumran regarded themselves as standing in the succession of Daniel and his *maśkīlîm*, but even Daniel's indications of time called for such more precise elucidation as the Teacher of Righteousness could supply.

Although the Qumran community believed that the last days of the current age had set in, nowhere in the Qumran literature, so far as it has been published, is the coming messianic era viewed as having been inaugurated. At best its conditions were partially anticipated in miniature in the life of the community. The great prophet, priest, and prince of the end-time are consistently spoken of in the future tense. But since the last days have set in, events in the experience of the community are viewed as the designed fulfilment of prophetic oracles. The persecuted righteous man of (e.g.) Ps. 34:15, 19, or Hab. 1:4 is the Teacher of Righteousness; his oppressor is the Wicked Priest (probably a Hasmonean ruler). The Romans, who occupied Judaea in 63 B.C., and who are regularly referred to as the 'Kittim', are the fulfilment not only of Balaam's Kittim (Num. 24:24; cf. Dan. 11:30) but also of Isaiah's Assyrian (Isa. 10:5; 31:8), Ezekiel's Gog (Ezek. 38:1 ff.) and Habakkuk's Chaldeans (Hab. 1:6). The 'lion' of Nahum 2:11 f., who 'filled his caves with prey and his dens with torn flesh' is no longer the Assyrian king in Nineveh but a later tyrant who 'hung men up alive, a thing never done in Israel before'—a reference, almost certainly, to Alexander Jannaeus's crucifixion of the captured leaders of the rebellion against him in 88 B.C.

All this exegesis involves the atomization of the biblical text, but it was not in the biblical text that the Qumran commentators looked for coherence, but in the situation to which the biblical text pointed forward.

IX. EARLY CHRISTIAN INTERPRETATION

The early Christian Church also adopted an eschatological interpretation of the Old Testament; but whereas the latest Qumran texts are still waiting for the messianic age to dawn, for the early Christians it has dawned with Jesus. In Jesus' own ministry the advent of the kingdom of God, to be bestowed (as in Daniel's visions) on 'the saints of the Most High', played a central part: the character of this kingdom was determined by the character of the God whose kingdom it was. In such an interesting mixture of metaphors as we find in his words in Luke 12:32—'Fear not, little flock, for it is your Father's good pleasure to give you the kingdom'—the King of the kingdom is the Father of his children and the Shepherd of his sheep.

Jesus' early followers recognized in him the fulfiller of many figures of Old Testament expectation—the prince of the house of David, the prophet like Moses of Deut. 18:15 ff., the priest after Melchizedek's order of Ps. 110:4, the afflicted saint of the Psalms who triumphs through suffering, the pierced one of Zech. 12:10 for whom the people mourn, the stone which the builders rejected (Ps. 118:22).

Not only so, but in his saving work they recognized the definitive exhibition of that pattern of divine action exemplified in Old Testament times by the deliverance from Egyptian bondage and the return from Babylonian exile. Both those occasions in Israel's history supplied a pictorial vocabulary for describing the new redemption. 'Christ, our paschal lamb, has been sacrificed; let us, therefore, celebrate the festival ... with the unleavened bread of sincerity and truth' (1 Cor.

5:7 f.). His followers' baptism is the counterpart to the earlier passage through the sea; their eucharistic bread and wine correspond to the manna and the water from the rock; their present period of probation on earth is their wilderness experience, and if they in their turn are guilty of unbelief and rebellion, it is the *heavenly* Canaan that they will forfeit (1 Cor. 10:1–12; Heb. 3:7–4:11; Jude 5).

Similarly, the whole context of Isa. 40–66 becomes a corpus of Gospel *testimonia*, from the 'voice' of Isa. 40:3 which is that of John the Baptist, preparing in the wilderness the way of the Lord, to the 'new heavens and new earth' of Isa. 65:17; 66:22, which will come into being with 'the day of God' as envisaged by Christians (2 Pet. 3:13; Rev. 21:1). The impetus to the Christian interpretation of these chapters may have been given by the identification of Jesus with the Servant of Yahweh, who is their central figure. In the Gospel tradition the Servant of Yahweh is merged with Daniel's 'one like a son of man' who receives world sovereignty from the Ancient of Days (Dan. 7:13 f.); such a question as 'how is it written of the Son of Man, that he should suffer many things and be treated with contempt?' (Mark 9:12), is best answered if 'the Son of Man' be equated with the Servant of Yahweh, who is explicitly described as enduring suffering and contempt.

In great areas of Old Testament interpretation in the New there is a coherence such as we do not find in Qumran exegesis. Atomizing exegesis like that of the Qumran texts is present in the New Testament too, but the distinctive feature of the New Testament use of the Old is the *contextual* exegesis that so often lies behind the citation of individual texts.[29]

In comparison with the Old Testament interpretation of the second-century Church, the christological application of the Old Testament in the New is positively restrained. Such a work as Justin Martyr's *Dialogue with Trypho* shows how a debate between a Jew and a Christian, with good will on both sides, was bound to be fruitless because, although both appealed to what was substantially the same Bible, their exegetical canons were so mutually incompatible that they might almost as well have been appealing to two different

---

[29] Cf. C. H. Dodd, *According to the Scriptures*, London, 1952; B. Lindars, *New Testament Apologetic*, London, 1961; F. F. Bruce, *This is That*, Exeter, 1968.

Bibles. When polemic and counter-polemic enter in, as in the
Cyprianic *Testimonia aduersus Iudaeos* (third century A.D.)
and the rabbinical care to exclude as inadmissible interpretations which, however time-honoured they might be, now
lent themselves to Christian arguments, a great gulf was fixed
which persisted until recent times and the adoption of the
historical method by Jewish and Christian scholars. The
adoption of the historical method does not exclude the validity
of a *sensus plenior*, an interpretative tradition growing up
generation by generation in communities for which the Old
Testament is not only a sacred book but a perennial wellspring
of spiritual life and refreshment. What Dorothy L. Sayers has
said about Dante may be said even more emphatically, *mutatis
mutandis*, about the Old Testament:

A phrase used by Dante not only contains and is illumined by the
meanings it derived from Virgil or the Vulgate: it, in its turn,
illuminates Virgil and the Vulgate and gives new meaning to them.
It not only passes on those meanings, supercharged with Dante's
own meaning, to Tennyson and Landor, to Rossetti and Yeats, to
Williams and Eliot and Pound, but it receives back from them the
reflected *splendore* of their own imaginative use of it.[30]

But to have real validity, any such *sensus plenior* must be
firmly rooted in the primary meaning of the text, established
by the historical method.

BIBLIOGRAPHY

1. Theology

ALBRIGHT, W. F. *From the Stone Age to Christianity*, 2nd edn., New York,
1957.
ALT, A. *Kleine Schriften zur Geschichte des Volkes Israel*, 3 vols., Munich,
1953, 1959, 1964; ETr of a selection, *Essays on Old Testament History and
Religion*, Oxford, 1966.

[30] D. L. Sayers, *The Poetry of Search and the Poetry of Statement*, London, 1963, p.
272. From what has been said above, it will be evident that the earliest instances of
sensus plenior are found within the Old Testament itself. To give another example:
when pre-exilic 'royal' psalms were incorporated in the hymn-book of the Second
Temple, they inevitably meant something different to worshippers then (and since)
from what they had meant under the monarchy.

ANDERSON, B. W. *The Living World of the Old Testament*, 2nd edn., London, 1967.

—— (ed.) *The Old Testament and Christian Faith*, New York, 1963, London, 1964.

BALTZER, K. *Das Bundesformular*, WMANT iv, 2nd edn., 1964; ETr, *The Covenant Formulary*, Oxford, 1971.

CHILDS, B. S. *Biblical Theology in Crisis*, Philadelphia, 1970.

EICHRODT, W. *Theologie des Alten Testaments*, Stuttgart, vol. i, 6th edn., 1959, vols. ii/iii, 5th edn., 1964; ETr, *Theology of the Old Testament*, 2 vols., London, 1961, 1967.

FOHRER, G. *Theologische Grundstrukturen des Alten Testaments*, Berlin, 1972.

KRAETZSCHMAR, R. *Die Bundesvorstellung im Alten Testament in ihrer geschichtlichen Entwicklung*, Marburg, 1896.

KUTSCH, E. *Verheissung und Gesetz*, BZAW cxxxi, 1973.

McCARTHY, D. J. *Treaty and Covenant*, AB xxi, 1963.

—— *Old Testament Covenant*, Oxford, 1972.

MENDENHALL, G. E. *Law and Covenant in Israel and the Ancient Near East*, Pittsburgh, 1955.

—— *The Tenth Generation*, Baltimore, 1973.

NOTH, M. *Gesammelte Studien zum Alten Testament*, Munich, 2nd edn., 1960; ETr, *The Laws in the Pentateuch and Other Studies*, Edinburgh, 1966.

PERLITT, L. *Bundestheologie im Alten Testament*, WMANT xxxvi, 1969.

VON RAD, G. *Theologie des Alten Testaments*, Munich, vol. i, 6th edn., 1969; vol. ii, 5th edn., 1968; ETr *Old Testament Theology*, 2 vols., Edinburgh and London, 1962, 1965.

—— *Gesammelte Studien zum Alten Testament*, Munich, 1958; ETr (amplified), *The Problem of the Hexateuch and Other Essays*, Edinburgh, 1966.

—— *Weisheit in Israel*, Neukirchen–Vluyn, 1970; ETr, *Wisdom in Israel*, London, 1972.

RENDTORFF, R., and KOCH, K. (eds.) *Studien zur Theologie der alttestamentlichen Überlieferungen*, Neukirchen, 1961.

ROBINSON, H. W. *Inspiration and Revelation in the Old Testament*, Oxford, 1946.

ROWLEY, H. H. *The Unity of the Bible*, London, 1953.

—— *The Faith of Israel*, London, 1956.

SMEND, R. *Die Mitte des Alten Testaments*, Zürich, 1970.

VRIEZEN, TH. C. *Hoofdlijnen der Theologie van het Oude Testament*, Wageningen, 2nd edn., 1954; ETr, *An Outline of Old Testament Theology*, Oxford, 2nd edn., 1970.

WESTERMANN, C. (ed.) *Probleme alttestamentlicher Hermeneutik*, Munich, 1960; ETr, *Essays in Old Testament Interpretation*, London, 1963.

WOLFF, H. W., RENDTORFF, R., and PANNENBERG, W. *Gerhard von Rad: seine Bedeutung für die Theologie*, Munich, 1973.

WRIGHT, G. E. *God Who Acts*, London, 1952.

ZIMMERLI, W. *Grundriss der alttestamentlichen Theologie*, Stuttgart, 1972.

2. Interpretation

BARR, J. *Old and New in Interpretation*, London, 1966.
—— *The Bible in the Modern World*, London, 1973.
BETZ, O. *Offenbarung und Schriftforschung in der Qumransekte*, Tübingen, 1960.
DODD, C. H. *According to the Scriptures*, London, 1952.
GOODING, D. W. *Relics of Ancient Exegesis*, Cambridge, 1976.
KOCH, K. *Was ist Formgeschichte?*, Neukirchen, 2nd edn. 1967; ETr, *The Growth of the Biblical Tradition*, London, 1969.
LINDARS, B. *New Testament Apologetic*, London, 1961.
SMALLEY, B. *The Study of the Bible in the Middle Ages*, Oxford, 2nd edn., 1952.
VERMES, G. *Scripture and Tradition in Judaism*, Leiden, 1961.
WEINGREEN, J. *From Bible to Mishna*, Manchester, 1976.

INDEX OF BIBLICAL REFERENCES

OLD TESTAMENT

NEW TESTAMENT

APOCRYPHA

SCROLLS AND PSEUDEPIGRAPHA

INDEX OF AUTHORS

GENERAL INDEX